JavaScript, Second Edition
Comprehensive

Don Gosselin

COURSE
TECHNOLOGY

THOMSON LEARNING

Australia • Canada • Mexico • Singapore • Spain • United Kingdom • United States

JavaScript, Second Edition—Comprehensive

by Don Gosselin

Senior Editor
Jennifer Muroff

Senior Product Manager
Margarita Donovan

Development Editor
Marilyn Freedman

Marketing Manager
Angie Laughlin

Editorial Assistant
Janet Aras

Production Editor
Aimee Poirier

Cover Designer
Christy Amlicke
Aaron Schneider
Black Fish Design

Compositor
GEX Publishing
Services

Disclaimer
Course Technology reserves the right to revise this publication and make changes from time to time in its content without notice.

ISBN 0-619-06334-3

Preface

JavaScript: Comprehensive is designed to provide a guide for the beginning programmer to develop Web applications using the JavaScript programming language. This textbook focuses on ECMAScript Edition 3, which is compatible with both Microsoft Internet Explorer 4.0 and later and Netscape 6.0 and later. It also discusses the Document Object Model (DOM) specification published by the World Wide Web Consortium (W3C). This textbook assumes that students have no programming language experience or knowledge of HTML.

Organization and Coverage

JavaScript: Comprehensive introduces users to basic JavaScript programming concepts along with the syntax to implement them. The World Wide Web, HTML, and JavaScript are introduced in Tutorial 1, along with programming logic and debugging. Variables, functions, objects, and events are discussed in Tutorial 2. This early introduction of variables, functions, objects, and events gives users a framework for better understanding more advanced concepts and techniques later in the text and allows them to work on more comprehensive projects from the start. Tutorials 3 and 4 teach users the fundamentals of data types and operators, and structured logic using control structures and statements. Tutorial 5 introduces window and frame concepts, and Tutorial 6 explains how to use JavaScript to create and manipulate forms. Tutorial 7 provides a thorough discussion of debugging programs and shows how to use two debugging tools, JavaScript Debugger for Netscape and Script Debugger for Internet Explorer. In Tutorial 8, users learn about dynamic HTML through animation.

JavaScript: Comprehensive combines text explanation with step-by-step exercises that illustrate the concepts being explained, reinforcing understanding and retention of the material presented. Throughout the book, HTML tags and syntax are introduced as necessary.

The individual using *JavaScript: Comprehensive* builds applications from the bottom up rather than using pre-written code. This technique facilitates a deeper understanding of the concepts used in Web programming with JavaScript. When individuals complete this book, they will know how to create and modify simple JavaScript language applications, and they will have the tools to create more complex applications. Users will also have a fundamental knowledge of programming concepts that will be useful whether they continue to learn more about the JavaScript language or go on to learn other scripting languages or object-oriented languages, such as C++ and Visual Basic.

JavaScript: Comprehensive distinguishes itself from other JavaScript language books in the following ways:

- It is written and designed specifically for individuals without previous programming experience or knowledge of HTML.
- The code examples are short; one concept is featured in each code example.
- Variables, functions, objects, and events are covered earlier than in many other texts, giving users a better understanding of the more advanced concepts and techniques that occur later in the text, and allowing them to work on significant projects from the start.
- Text explanations are interspersed with step-by-step exercises.
- HTML tags and syntax are introduced throughout the text, as necessary.
- JavaScript applications are built from the bottom up; the user gains a clear picture of how complex programs are built.
- Programming techniques are presented in easy-to-understand lessons.

Features

JavaScript: Comprehensive is a superior textbook because it also includes the following features:

- **"Read This Before You Begin" Page** This page is consistent with Course Technology's unequaled commitment to helping instructors introduce technology into the classroom. Technical considerations and assumptions about hardware, software, and default settings are listed in one place to help instructors save time and eliminate unnecessary aggravation.
- **Case Approach** Each chapter addresses programming-related problems that individuals could reasonably expect to encounter in business. All of the cases are followed by a demonstration of an application that could be used to solve the problem. Showing users the completed application before they learn how to create it is motivational and instructionally sound. By allowing users to see the type of application they will create after completing the chapter, users will be more motivated to learn because they can see how the programming concepts that they are about to learn can be used and, therefore, why the concepts are important.
- **Step-by-Step Methodology** The unique Course Technology methodology keeps users on track. They write program code always within the context of solving the problems posed in the tutorial. The text constantly guides users and lets them know where they are in the process of solving the problem. The numerous illustrations guide the individuals to create useful, working programs.
- **Tips** These notes provide additional information—for example, an alternate method of performing a procedure, background information on a technique, a commonly-made error to watch out for, debugging techniques, or the name of a Web site the user can visit to gather more information.

- **Summaries** Following each chapter is a Summary that recaps the programming concepts and commands covered in each section.
- **Review Questions** Each tutorial concludes with meaningful, conceptual Review Questions that test users' understanding of what they learned in the tutorial.
- **Exercises** Programming Exercises provide users with additional practice of the skills and concepts they learned in the lesson. These exercises increase in difficulty and are designed to allow the user to explore the language and programming environment independently.

What's New in this Edition?

One goal of any good JavaScript text should be to present JavaScript code that is compatible with the widest number of browsers possible. In order to teach cross-browser compatible JavaScript, the code and techniques presented in this second edition of *JavaScript: Comprehensive* have been written to conform to ECMAScript Edition 3, the most recent version of the international, standardized version of JavaScript.

Other enhancements include the addition of:

- Graduated and more comprehensive end-of-chapter exercises.
- Cross-browser DHTML techniques in the Document Object Model tutorial for W3C DOM-compatible browsers.
- A new Debugging chapter that introduces valuable debugging techniques and tools.

Unfortunately, the browser wars are not over. Major differences still exist in some of the coding techniques that are required for the two dominant browsers, Internet Explorer and Netscape, even though both browsers claim to conform to ECMAScript Edition 3 and the W3C DOM. For this reason, throughout the text the areas of JavaScript programming that continue to differ between the two browsers are pointed out.

Web Browser Environments

This textbook focuses on ECMAScript Edition 3. Individuals can user either Netscape 6 and higher or Internet Explorer 4 and higher to create solutions to the exercises in this text. To use Internet Explorer 4 with ECMAScript Edition 3, the user must install Windows Script 5.5, which can be downloaded from *www.microsoft.com/msdownload/vbscript/scripting.asp*.

Teaching Tools

All the teaching tools for this text are found in the Instructor's Resource Kit, which is available from the Course Technology Web site (*www.course.com*) and on CD-ROM.

- **Instructor's Manual**
  The Instructor's Manual has been quality assurance tested. It is available on CD-ROM and through Course Technology Faculty Online Companion on the World Wide Web. The Instructor's Manual contains the following items:

- Answers to all the review questions and solutions to all the programming exercises in the book.

- Technical Notes that include troubleshooting tips.

- **Solutions Files** Solution files contain possible solutions to all the problems users are asked to create or modify in the tutorials and cases. (Due to the nature of software development, user solutions might differ from these solutions and still be correct.)

- **Data Files** Data files, containing all data that readers will use for the tutorials and exercises in this textbook, are provided through Course Technology's Online Companion on the Instructor's Resource Kit CD-ROM. A Help file includes technical tips for lab management. See the "Read This Before You Begin" page preceding Tutorial 1 for more information on data files.

- **ExamView** This textbook is accompanied by ExamView, a powerful testing software package that allows instructors to create and administer printed, computer (LAN-based), and Internet exams. ExamView includes hundreds of questions that correspond to the topics covered in this text, enabling students to generate detailed study guides that include page references for further review. The computer-based and Internet testing components allow students to take exams at their computers, and also save the instructor time by grading each exam automatically.

- **PowerPoint Presentations** This book comes with Microsoft PowerPoint slides for each chapter. These are included as a teaching aid for classroom presentation, to make available to students on the network for chapter review, or to be printed for classroom distribution. Instructors can add their own slides for additional topics they introduce to the class.

- **MyCourse.com** MyCourse.com is an online syllabus builder and course enhancement tool. Hosted by Course Technology, MyCourse.com adds value to your course by providing additional content that reinforces what students are learning.

  More importantly, MyCourse.com is flexible. You can choose how you want to organize the material – by date, by class session, or by using the default organization, which organizes content by chapter. MyCourse.com allows you to add your own materials, including hyperlinks, school logos, assignments, announcements, and other course content. If you are using more than one textbook, you can even build a course that includes all of your Course Technology texts in one easy-to-use site!

  Start building your own course today! Just go to www.mycourse.com/instructor.

Acknowledgements

A text such as this represents the hard work of many people, not just the author. I would like to thank all of the people who helped make this book a reality. First and foremost, I would like to thank Marilyn Freedman, Developmental Editor, for her outstanding work and for making me a better writer. I would also like to thank Nan Fritz and her staff at nSight; Kristen Duerr, Senior Vice President and Publisher; Margarita Donovan, Senior Product Manager; Jennifer Muroff, Senior Editor; Aimee Poirier, Production Editor; and John Freitas, Brendan Taylor, Jonathan Greacen, and Nicole Ashton, Quality Assurance testers. Thanks also to Scott Davis of Old Dominion University for all his great work as Technical Editor. Thanks to Mary Ann O'Brien and Ellie Lottero of Harvard University and Peggy Beckley of RWD Technologies for giving me the time off to write. I owe a very special thanks to Peter Atkins and Jon Dillon of NextCard for helping me to understand the complexities of the browser wars.

Many, many thanks to the reviewers for their invaluable comments and suggestions, including Raymond Calvert, Manatee Community College; Jim Dunne, Arapahoe Community College; Ed Kaplan, Bentley College; Catherine Leach, Henderson State University; Le Nguyen, Parker Compumotor; Dave Reed, Dickinson College; Mildred Tassone, Chase Bank; and Rod Tosten, Gettysburg College.

As always, thanks to my friend and colleague, George T. Lynch, for getting me started. Most important, thanks to my wonderful wife, Kathy, for her eternal patience. Thanks also go to my cat, Mabeline, for keeping me company; to my dog, Noah, for taking me out for a walk on those rare occasions when I unchain myself from my computer; and to all of my friends and family for their understanding when I disappear for days and weeks on end.

Don Gosselin
Napa, California

Contents

t u t o r i a l   5

WINDOWS AND FRAMES *229*

t u t o r i a l   8

DYNAMIC HTML AND ANIMATION   423

t u t o r i a l   9

COOKIES AND SECURITY *501*

t u t o r i a l   1 0

SERVER-SIDE JAVASCRIPT *559*

tutorial   1 2

WORKING WITH JAVA APPLETS
AND EMBEDDED DATA *717*

appendix A

JAVASCRIPT REFERENCE　*A-1*

Read This Before You Begin

To the User

Data disks

To complete the tutorials and exercises in this book, you need Data disks. Your instructor will provide you with Data disks or ask you to make your own.

If you are asked to make your own Data disks, you will need four blank, formatted high-density disks. You will need to copy a set of folders from a file server or standalone computer onto your disks. Your instructor will tell you which computer, drive letter, and folders contain the files you need. The following table shows you which folders go on each of your disks, so that you will have enough disk space to complete all the tutorials and exercises:

Student Disk	Write this on the disk label	Put these folders on the disk
1	Tutorials 1, 2, and 3	Tutorial.01, Tutorial.02, and Tutorial.03
2	Tutorials 4, 5, and 6	Tutorial.04, Tutorial.05, and Tutorial.06
3	Tutorials 7, 8, and 9	Tutorial.07, Tutorial.08, and Tutorial.09
4	Tutorials 10, 11, and 12	Tutorial.10, Tutorial.11, and Tutorial.12

When you begin each tutorial, make sure you are using the correct Data disk. Ask your instructor for more information.

Using Your Own Computer

You can use your own computer to complete the Tutorials and exercises in this book. To use your own computer, you will need the following:

- Web Browser Software. You can download Netscape 6 or a later version from the Netscape Products home page at *home.netscape.com/download/index.html*. You can download a copy of the latest version of Internet Explorer from the Internet Explorer home page at *www.microsoft.com/windows/ie/.* You can upgrade Internet Explorer 4.0 and later to the most recent version of JavaScript by downloading the latest version of Windows Script from *www.microsoft.com/msdownload/vbscript/scripting.asp.*

- Text Editor or HTML Editor You will need a text editor or an HTML editor in order to create the exercises. You can use Notepad, WordPad, or any word processing program capable of creating simple text files. You can also use an HTML editor, such as Microsoft FrontPage or Adobe PageMill, with a graphical interface that allows you to create Web pages and immediately view the results.

- Data Files You can get the Data files from your instructor. You will not be able to complete all the tutorials and exercises in this book using your own computer until you have the Data files. The user files may also be obtained electronically through the World Wide Web.

Visit Our World Wide Web Site

Additional materials designed especially for you might be available for your course on the World Wide Web. Go to **www.course.com.** Search for this book title periodically on the Course Technology Web site for more details.

To the Instructor

To complete all the exercises and tutorials in this book, your users must use a set of user files, called a Data disk. These files are included in the Instructor's Resource Kit. They may also be obtained electronically through the Course Technology Web site at **www.course.com.** Follow the instructions in the Help file to copy the user files to your server or standalone computer. You can view the Help file using a text editor, such as WordPad or Notepad.

Once the files are copied, you can make Data disks for the users yourself, or tell them where to find the files so they can make their own Data disks. Make sure the files get copied correctly onto the Data disks by following the instructions in the Data disks section, which will ensure that users have enough disk space to complete all the tutorials and exercises in this book.

Course Technology Data Files

You are granted a license to copy the Data files to any computer or computer network used by individuals who have purchased this book.

Introduction to JavaScript

case ▶ WebAdventure, Inc., a Web site design firm, has recently hired you in an entry-level position. You are excited about working for a Web site design firm because, like many other people today, you spend a lot of time surfing the Internet. You know that Web pages consist of different types of information formatted in various ways. You have also noticed that some Web sites are more interactive than others and have different types of features that were not available several years ago. Games, order forms, animation, and various visual effects now seem to be part of almost every Web page you visit. You are excited about learning how to develop these types of Web pages. Your first challenge at WebAdventure is to gain an understanding of Web development and programming and find out where JavaScript fits in.

SECTION A
objectives

In this section you will learn:

- About the World Wide Web
- What JavaScript is used for
- About Hypertext Markup Language
- How to create an HTML document
- About the JavaScript programming language
- About logic and debugging

Programming, HTML, and JavaScript

The World Wide Web

JavaScript lives and works within Web pages on the World Wide Web. To understand how JavaScript functions, it helps to know a little about how the World Wide Web operates.

The **World Wide Web** (the "Web") was created in 1989 at the European Laboratory for Particle Physics in Geneva, Switzerland, as a way to easily access cross-referenced documents that exist on the Internet. Documents are located and opened using **hypertext links**, which contain a reference to a specific document. **Hypertext Markup Language (HTML)** is a simple language used to design the Web pages that appear on the World Wide Web. A **Web browser** is a program that displays HTML documents on your computer screen. Currently, the two most popular Web browsers are Netscape Navigator and Microsoft Internet Explorer.

tip

··
This textbook uses the terms HTML documents and Web pages interchangeably.
··

Every Web page or document has a unique address known as a **Uniform Resource Locator (URL)**. A URL is a type of **Uniform Resource Identifier (URI)**, which identifies names and addresses on the World Wide Web. You can think of a URL as a Web page's telephone number. Each URL consists of four parts: a protocol (usually HTTP), a service, either the domain name for a Web server or a Web server's Internet Protocol address, and a filename. **Hypertext Transfer Protocol (HTTP)** manages the hypertext links that are used to navigate the Web; you can think of HTTP as driving the Web. HTTP ensures that Web browsers correctly process and display the various types of information contained in Web pages (text, graphics, audio, and so on). The protocol portion of a URL is followed by a colon, two forward slashes, and the service, which is usually *www* for "World Wide Web." A **domain name** is a unique address used for identifying a computer, often a Web server, on the Internet and identifies one or more IP addresses. The domain name consists of two parts separated by a period. The first part of a domain name is usually composed of text that easily identifies a person or an organization, such as DonGosselin or Course. The last part of a domain name identifies the type of institution or organization. For instance, com (for *company*) represents private companies, gov (for *government*) represents government agencies, and edu (for *educational*) represents educational institutions. For example, course.com is the domain name for Course Technology. An entire URL would be *www.DonGosselin.com* or *www.course.com*.

An Internet Protocol, or IP address, is another way to uniquely identify computers or devices connected to the Internet, using a series of four groups of numbers separated by periods. All Internet domain names are associated with a unique IP address.

In a URL, a specific filename, or a combination of directories and a filename, can follow a domain name or IP address. If the URL does not specify a filename, the requesting Web server looks for a file with one of the following names located in the root or specified directory: index.html, index.shtml, index.htm, default.html, default.shtml, or default.htm. Figure 1-1 points out the parts of a sample URL that opens an HTML document named `index-f.html`.

Sample URL: http://home.netscape.com/webmail/index-f.html

Protocol

Domain name

Directory

Filename

Figure 1-1: Sample URL

JavaScript's Role on the Web

The original purpose of the World Wide Web was locating and displaying information. Once the Web grew beyond a small academic and scientific community, people began to recognize that greater interactivity would make the Web more useful. As commercial applications of the Web grew, the demand for more interactive and visually appealing Web sites also grew. Documents created using basic HTML, however, are static; the main purpose of HTML is to tell a browser how the document should appear. You can think of an HTML document as being approximately equivalent to a document created in a word-processing or desktop publishing program—the only thing you can do with it is view or print it. In response to the demand for greater interactivity, Netscape developed the JavaScript programming language for use in Navigator Web browsers.

JavaScript brings HTML to life and makes Web pages dynamic. Instead of HTML documents being static, JavaScript can turn them into applications, such as games or order forms. You can use JavaScript to change the contents of a Web page after it has been rendered by a browser, to interact with a user through forms and controls, to create visual effects such as animation, and to control the Web browser window itself. None of these things was possible before the creation of JavaScript.

Thanks in large part to JavaScript, the Web today is used for many different purposes, including advertising and entertainment. Many businesses today (and probably most in the future) have a Web site. To attract people to a Web site, and keep them there, a business's Web site must be exciting, interactive, and visually stimulating. Business Web sites use "flashing signs" that advertise specials, animation, interactivity, intuitive navigation controls, and many other types of effects to help sell their products. It is also easy to find games, animation, and other forms of entertainment on the Web. All of these types of applications and effects can be created with JavaScript.

To gain a better idea of what you can do with JavaScript, examine Figures 1-2, 1-3, and 1-4. You will be creating these programs in later tutorials. The map displayed in Figure 1-2 is an image map. Passing your mouse over a country on the map highlights the country and displays its name at the bottom of the Web page. You will create the image map in Tutorial 2. Figure 1-3 displays an online calculator you will create in Tutorial 3. The last program, in Figure 1-4, is an online product registration form that you will create in Tutorial 6. These examples are just some of the programs you will create with JavaScript in this textbook.

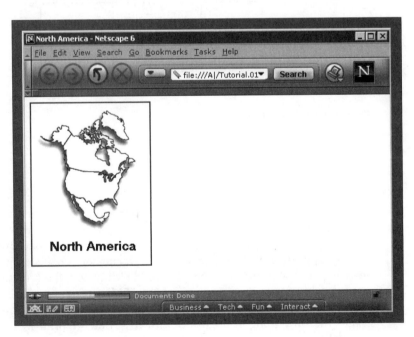

Figure 1-2: Image map

Figure 1-3: Online calculator

Figure 1-4: Product Registration form

Hypertext Markup Language

To work with JavaScript, you must understand Hypertext Markup Language and how to construct Web pages, because JavaScript exists within Web pages. This section explains the basic principles of HTML that you will need to know to work with JavaScript. Throughout this book, additional HTML will be introduced as necessary. You can skip this section if you are already familiar with HTML.

HTML documents must be text documents that contain formatting instructions, called **tags**, along with the text that is to be displayed on a Web page. HTML tags range from formatting commands that make text boldface and italic, to controls that allow user input, such as radio buttons and check boxes. Other HTML tags allow you to display graphic images and other objects in a document or Web page.

HTML documents must have a file extension of `.html` or `.htm`.

When you open an HTML document in a Web browser, the document is assembled and formatted according to the instructions contained in its tags. A Web browser's process of assembling and formatting an HTML document is called **parsing** or **rendering**. Tags are enclosed in brackets (< >), and most consist of a starting tag and an ending tag that surround the text or other items they are formatting or controlling. For example, the starting tag to make a line of text boldface is <B> and the ending tag is </B>. Any text contained between this pair of tags appears in boldface when you open the HTML document in a Web browser. The following line is an example of how to make text boldface in an HTML document:

```
<B>This text will appear in boldface in a Web browser.</B>
```

HTML is not case-sensitive, so you can use <b> in place of <B>. However, this book primarily uses uppercase letters for HTML tags.

All HTML documents begin with <HTML> and end with </HTML>. These tags tell a Web browser that the instructions between them are to be assembled into an HTML document. The opening and closing <HTML>...</HTML> tags are required and contain all the text and other tags that make up the HTML document. HTML contains many tags for creating HTML documents. Some of the more common tags are listed in Figure 1-5.

You use various parameters, called **attributes**, to configure many HTML tags. Attributes are placed before the closing bracket of the starting tag. For example, the <IMG> tag that embeds an image or video clip in an HTML document can be configured with a number of attributes, including the SRC attribute, which specifies the filename of the image file or video clip. To include the SRC attribute within the <IMG> tag, you type <IMG SRC="mygraphic.gif">. You must enclose the value of the attribute in double quotation marks.

HTML Tag	Description
<B></B>	Formats enclosed text in a bold typeface
<BODY></BODY>	Encloses the body of the HTML document
 	Inserts a line break
<DIV></DIV>	Divides a document into separate sections or divisions
<HEAD></HEAD>	Encloses the page header and contains information about the entire page
<H*n*></H*n*>	Heading level tags, where *n* represents a number from 1 to 6
<HR>	Inserts a horizontal rule
<HTML></HTML>	Required tags that start and end an HTML document
<I></I>	Formats enclosed text in an italic typeface
<IMG src="...">	Inserts an image file
<P></P>	Identifies enclosed text as a paragraph
<STRONG></STRONG>	Formats enclosed text in a strong typeface, similar to bold
<TABLE></TABLE>	Creates a table. Each table row is defined by <TR>, and each table cell is defined by <TD>
<U></U>	Underlines enclosed text

Figure 1-5: Common HTML tags

Two important HTML tags are the <HEAD> tag and the <BODY> tag. The <HEAD> tag contains information that is used by the Web browser and is placed at the start of an HTML document, after the opening <HTML> tag. Several tags are placed within the <HEAD>...</HEAD> tag pair to help manage a document's content. The <TITLE> tag contains text that is displayed in a browser's title bar and is the only required element for the <HEAD> tag. With the exception of the <TITLE> tag, elements contained in the <HEAD> tag do not affect the rendering of the HTML document. When JavaScript programs are included in an HTML document, they often appear within the <HEAD>...</HEAD> tag pair. Figure 1-6 lists some of the tags placed within the <HEAD>...</HEAD> tag pair.

HTML Tag	Description
<TITLE>…</TITLE>	Encloses the page title, which is the text that appears in the browser title bar
<STYLE>…</STYLE>	Identifies Cascading Style Sheet (CSS) properties
<LINK>	Specifies an external link between the HTML document and an external source
<SCRIPT>…</SCRIPT>	References embedded scripts
<BASE>	Identifies the document base URL
<META>	Contains document properties

Figure 1-6: HTML tags placed within the <HEAD>…</HEAD> tag pair

Following the <HEAD> tag is the <BODY> tag, which contains the body of the HTML page. The attributes of the <BODY> tag determine the appearance of an HTML document. Figure 1-7 lists some of the attributes of the <BODY> tag.

Attribute	Determines
ALINK	The color of an active link
BACKGROUND	The background image
BGCOLOR	The background color
LINK	The color of an unvisited link
TEXT	Text color
VLINK	The color of a visited link

Figure 1-7: <BODY> tag attributes

When a Web browser parses or renders an HTML document, it ignores non-printing characters such as spaces, tabs, and carriage returns in the code; only recognized HTML tags and text are included in the final document that appears in the Web browser. You cannot use carriage returns in the body of an HTML document to insert spaces before and after a paragraph; the browser recognizes only paragraph <P> and line break <BR> tags for this purpose. If you use paragraph <P> tags to create blank lines in an HTML document, be aware that certain Web browsers, such as Internet Explorer, ignore tags that do not contain content. If you use the tag <P> to create an empty line in an HTML document, the Web browser may completely ignore it. To prevent this from happening, include a **non-breaking space** code— —and an ending tag so that the paragraph tag reads <P> </P>. Figure 1-8 shows an HTML document, while Figure 1–9 shows how it appears in a Web browser.

```
<HTML>

<HEAD>

<TITLE>Hello World</TITLE>

</HEAD>

<BODY>

<H1>Hello World (this is the H1 tag)</H1>

<H2>This line is formatted with the H2 tag</H2>

<P>This body text line contains several character formatting
tags including <I>italics</I>, <B>bold</B>, <U>underline</U>,
and <STRIKE>strikethrough</STRIKE>. The following code line
creates a line break followed by a horizontal rule:<BR>

<HR>

<IMG src="Checkmrk.jpg">This line contains an image.

</BODY>

</HTML>
```

Figure 1-8: An HTML document

Figure 1-9: An HTML document in a Web browser

Some HTML tags, such as the paragraph tag <P>, do not necessarily require ending tags. In addition, different browsers have different requirements as to when an ending tag is necessary.

Creating an HTML Document

Because HTML documents are text files, you can create them in any text editor such as Notepad, WordPad, or any word-processing program capable of creating simple text files. (What is surprising to many new HTML designers is that you cannot use a Web browser to create an HTML document.) If you use a text editor to create an HTML document, you cannot view the final result until you open the document in a Web browser. However, many applications (called HTML editors) are designed specifically for creating HTML documents. Some popular HTML editors, such as Microsoft FrontPage and Adobe PageMill, have graphical interfaces that allow you to create Web pages and immediately view the results, similar to the WYSIWYG (what-you-see-is-what-you-get) feature in word-processing programs. In addition, many current word-processing applications, including Microsoft Word and WordPerfect, allow you to save files as HTML documents. All these HTML editors still create simple text files, but they automate the process of applying tags. For example, if you create a document in Word that contains boldface text, then save it as an HTML document, the bold <B> tag is automatically added to the text in the HTML text file that is created.

Be aware that different Web browsers render HTML documents in different ways. For example, an HTML document displayed in Internet Explorer can appear differently in Navigator.

Next, you will create an HTML document containing some of the tags you have seen in this section. You can use any text editor, such as Notepad or WordPad, or an HTML editor.

To create an HTML document:

1 Start your text editor or HTML editor and create a new document.

2 Type **<HTML>** to begin the HTML document. Remember that all HTML documents must begin and end with the <HTML>...</HTML> tag pair.

3 Press **Enter** and add the following <HEAD> and <TITLE> to the document. The title will appear in your Web browser's title bar. Remember that the <HEAD>...</HEAD> tag pair must include the <TITLE>...</TITLE> tag pair. The <TITLE>...</TITLE> tag pair cannot exist outside the <HEAD>...</HEAD> tag pair.

```
<HEAD>
<TITLE>Web Page Example</TITLE>
</HEAD>
```

4 Press **Enter** and type <BODY> to begin the body section of the HTML document.

5 Press **Enter** and type the following tags and text to create the body of the HTML document.

```
<H1>Hello World</H1>
<P>This is my first Web page.</P>
<HR>
<H2>This line is H2</H2>
<H3>This line is H3</H3>
<P>The following line is empty.</P>
<P> </P>
<P><B>bold</B>, <I>italic</I>, <U>underline</U></P>
```

6 Press **Enter**, then finish the document by typing the following tags to close the <BODY>...</BODY> and <HTML>...</HTML> tag pairs:

```
</BODY>
</HTML>
```

7 Save the file as **HelloWorld.html** in the **Tutorial.01** folder on your Data Disk.

> Some Web servers do not correctly interpret spaces within the name of HTML files. For example, a filename of *Hello World.html* (with a space between *Hello* and *World*) may not be interpreted correctly on some servers. For this reason, filenames in this book do not include spaces.

8 Start Navigator, Internet Explorer, or another Web browser. Then open the **HelloWorld.html** file in your Web browser. Figure 1-10 displays the HelloWorld.html file as it appears in Navigator 6.0.

9 Close your Web browser by clicking the **Close** button.

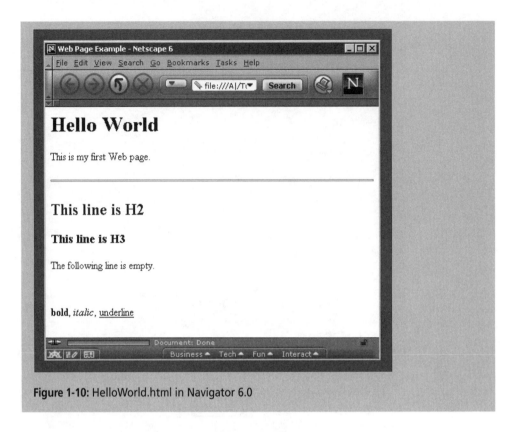

Figure 1-10: HelloWorld.html in Navigator 6.0

The JavaScript Programming Language

JavaScript is a scripting language. The term **scripting language** refers to programming languages that are executed by an interpreter from within a Web browser. An **interpreter** translates programming code into an executable format *each time* the program runs, one line at a time. Programs written in scripting languages, such as JavaScript, are interpreted when a scripting engine loads an HTML page. A **scripting engine** is an interpreter that is part of the Web browser. A Web browser that contains a scripting engine to translate scripts is called a **scripting host**. Navigator and Internet Explorer are both examples of scripting hosts for JavaScript programs.

JavaScript was first introduced in Navigator and was originally called LiveScript. With the release of Navigator 2.0, the name was changed to JavaScript 1.0. Subsequently, Microsoft released its own version of JavaScript in Internet Explorer 4.0 and named it JScript. The most current versions of each implementation are JavaScript 1.5 in Navigator and JScript 5.5, which is available for Internet Explorer versions 4.0 and later.

If you are using Internet Explorer 4.0 or higher, you can upgrade the version of JavaScript by installing the most recent version of Windows Script from *www.microsoft.com/msdownload/vbscript/scripting.asp*.

When Microsoft released JScript, a number of major problems occurred. For example, the Netscape and Microsoft versions of the JavaScript language differed so greatly that programmers were required to write almost completely different JavaScript programs for Navigator and Internet Explorer. This divergence led to the creation of an international, standardized version of JavaScript called **ECMAScript**. The most recent version of ECMAScript is Edition 3. Both Netscape JavaScript 1.5 and Microsoft JScript 5.5 conform to ECMAScript Edition 3. Although they both conform to ECMAScript Edition 3, Netscape JavaScript and Microsoft JScript each include their own unique programming features that are not supported by the other language.

In spite of the differences between JavaScript and JScript, the goal of this book is to create JavaScript programs that run on either Navigator or Internet Explorer. To achieve compatibility with both browsers, this tutorial focuses on ECMAScript Edition 3 code that is supported by Navigator 6 and higher and Internet Explorer 4 and higher. At the time of this writing, older versions of Navigator and Internet Explorer that are not 100% compatible with ECMAScript Edition 3 are widely used, particularly Netscape browsers. With Internet Explorer 4.0 and higher, you can upgrade the version of JScript that is used by the browser. However, with Navigator, the JavaScript version you use is built directly into the browser. In order to update the version of JavaScript you use in Navigator, you must update the browser itself. To provide backward-compatibility with older versions of Navigator, this book will list the necessary code changes, where appropriate.

Many people think that JavaScript is related to or is a simplified version of the Java programming language. However, the languages are entirely different. Java is a compiled, object-oriented programming language that was created by Sun Microsystems and is considerably more difficult to master than JavaScript. JavaScript is an interpreted scripting language that was created by Netscape. Although Java is often used to create programs that can run from a Web page, Java programs are external programs that execute independently of a browser. In contrast, JavaScript programs run within a Web page and control the browser.

JavaScript is available in two formats: client-side JavaScript and server-side JavaScript. Netscape JavaScript version 1.5 and Microsoft JScript 5.5 are client-side versions of JavaScript. **Client-side execution** refers to a program running on a local browser (the client) instead of on a server. In comparison, **server-side execution** refers to a program running on a server instead of on a client. JavaScript version 1.2 in Navigator 4.0 and ECMAScript are also client-side versions of JavaScript. Server-side JavaScript is used with Web servers to access file systems, communicate with other applications, access databases, and perform other tasks. Currently, server-side JavaScript is proprietary and vendor-specific. You must know a slightly different version of the language for each vendor's Web server; there is no server-side standard similar to ECMAScript. Client-side and server-side JavaScript share the same basic programming features. Figure 1-11 illustrates how client-side and server-side JavaScript are related.

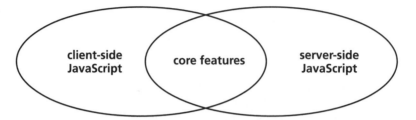

Figure 1-11: Relationship of client-side and server-side JavaScript

Logic and Debugging

All programming languages, including JavaScript, have their own **syntax,** or rules of the language. To write a program, you must understand a given programming language's syntax. You must also understand computer programming logic. The **logic** underlying any program involves executing the various parts of the program in the correct order to produce the desired results. For example, although you know how to drive a car well, you may not reach your destination if you do not follow the correct route. Similarly, you might be able to use a programming language's syntax correctly, but be unable to execute a logically constructed, workable program. Examples of logical errors include multiplying two values when you meant to divide them, or producing output prior to obtaining the appropriate input. The following JavaScript code contains another example of a logic error:

```
var count = 1;
while (count <= 10) {
     alert("The number is " + count);
}
```

The code in the example uses a `while` statement, which is used to repeat a command or series of commands based on the evaluation of certain criteria. The criterion in the example is the value of a variable named count (you will learn about variables in Tutorial 2). The `while` statement is supposed to execute until the count variable is less than or equal to 10. However, there is no code within the `while` statement body that changes the count variable value. The count variable will continue to have a value of 1 through each iteration of the loop. In this case, an alert dialog box containing the text string *The number is 1* will be displayed over and over again, no matter how many times you press the OK button. This type of logical error is called an **infinite loop.**

Do not worry about how the JavaScript code in the example is constructed. The example is only meant to give you a better understanding of a logical error.

Any error in a program that causes it to function incorrectly, whether due to incorrect syntax or flaws in logic, is called a bug. **Debugging** describes the act of tracing and resolving errors in a program. Legend has it that Grace Murray Hopper, a mathematician who was instrumental in developing the COBOL programming language, first coined the term *debugging*. As the story from the 1940s goes, a moth short-circuited a primitive computer that Hopper was using. Removing the moth from the computer *debugged* the system and resolved the problem. Today, a bug refers to any sort of problem in the design and operation of a program.

Do not confuse bugs with computer viruses. Bugs are problems within a program that occur because of syntax errors, design flaws, or run-time errors. Viruses are self-contained programs designed to "infect" a computer system and cause mischievous or malicious damage. Actually, virus programs themselves can contain bugs if they contain syntax errors or do not perform (or do damage) as their creators envisioned.

As you read the debugging tips, keep in mind that debugging is not an exact science—every program you write is different and requires different methods of debugging. Your own logical and analytical skills are the best debugging resources you have.

In the next section, you will start learning how to create JavaScript programs.

S U M M A R Y

- Hypertext Markup Language (HTML) is a simple protocol used to design Web pages that appear on the World Wide Web.

- The World Wide Web is driven by Hypertext Transfer Protocol (HTTP), which manages the hypertext links that are used to navigate the Web.

- Every Web document has a unique address known as a Uniform Resource Locator (URL).

- A Uniform Resource Identifier (URI) identifies names and addresses on the World Wide Web.

- A domain name is a unique address used for identifying a computer, often a Web server, on the Internet and identifies one or more IP addresses.

- JavaScript brings HTML to life and makes Web pages dynamic, turning them into applications, such as games or order forms.

- HTML documents must be text documents that contain formatting instructions, called tags, along with the text that is to be displayed on a Web page.

- HTML tags range from formatting commands to controls that allow user input, to tags that allow the display of graphic images and other objects.

- A Web browser's process of assembling and formatting an HTML document is called parsing or rendering.

- An interpreter translates programming code into an executable format each time the program is run—one line at a time.

- JavaScript is an interpreted programming language.

- A scripting engine is an interpreter that is part of the Web browser. A Web browser that contains a scripting engine to translate scripts is called a scripting host.

- The international, standardized version of JavaScript is called ECMAScript; the most recent version of ECMAScript is Edition 3.

- Both Netscape JavaScript 1.5 and Microsoft JScript 5.5 conform to ECMAScript Edition 3. Although both conform to ECMAScript Edition 3, each includes its own unique programming features that are not supported by the other language.

- Client-side execution refers to a program running on a local browser (the client) instead of on a server.

- Server-side execution refers to a program running on a server instead of on a client.

- Standardized client-side JavaScript is the JavaScript format available to HTML pages displayed in Web browsers.

- All programming languages, including JavaScript, have their own syntax, or rules of the language.

- The logic behind any program involves executing the various parts of the program in the correct order to produce the desired results.

- Debugging describes the act of tracing and resolving errors in a program.

QUESTIONS

1. _____ manages the hypertext links that are used to navigate the Web.
   a. Netscape Navigator
   b. The European Laboratory for Particle Physics
   c. Hypertext Transfer Protocol
   d. Internet Explorer

2. Every Web document has a unique address known as _____.
   a. its IP address
   b. a hyperlink
   c. a Uniform Resource Locator
   d. its domain name

3. A _____ identifies one or more IP addresses.
   a. protocol
   b. URI
   c. URL
   d. domain name

4. HTML elements _____.

    a. must include a starting tag and an ending tag

    b. only include a starting tag

    c. may contain an ending tag, depending on the HTML element

    d. do not contain starting or ending tags

5. The Web browser process of assembling and formatting an HTML document is called parsing or _____.

    a. compiling

    b. refreshing

    c. rendering

    d. browsing

6. HTML _____.

    a. is case-sensitive

    b. is not case-sensitive

    c. must be created using initial caps

    d. must be created using uppercase letters

7. HTML attributes are placed within the _____.

    a. opening bracket of the starting tag

    b. opening bracket of the ending tag

    c. closing bracket of the starting tag

    d. closing bracket of the ending tag

8. HTML documents start and end with the _____ tag pairs.

    a. <BODY>...</BODY>

    b. <HEAD>...</HEAD>

    c. <HTML>...</HTML>

    d. <WEB>...</WEB>

9. What is the correct syntax for a non-breaking space code?

    a. #NOBREAK

    b.

    c. $space

    d. @break

10. Which of the following can be used for creating HTML documents?

    a. A text editor

    b. A word-processing program capable of creating simple text files

    c. An HTML editing program

    d. A Web browser

11. The rules of a programming language are known as its _____.

    a. procedures

    b. assembly

    c. syntax

    d. logic

12. The term _____ language refers to programming languages that are executed by an interpreter from within a Web browser.
   a. scripting
   b. compiled
   c. browser
   d. host

13. The most recent version of ECMAScript is _____.
   a. Edition 1
   b. Edition 2
   c. Edition 3
   d. Edition 4

14. Executing the various statements and procedures of a program in the correct order to produce the desired results is called _____.
   a. reasoning
   b. directional assembly
   c. syntax
   d. logic

15. The term _____ language is used to refer to interpreted languages that run from within a Web browser.
   a. Internet programming
   b. machine
   c. assembly
   d. scripting

16. The version of JavaScript that is the format available to HTML pages in a Web browser is called _____ JavaScript.
   a. precompiled
   b. server-side
   c. embedded
   d. client-side

EXERCISES

The World Wide Web Consortium (W3C) is responsible for developing the technology guidelines, including HTML standards, that govern the Web. The W3C's main Web site is located at *www.w3.org*. The W3C Web site includes an outstanding online HTML tutorial at *www.w3schools.com/html/default.asp*. For the following HTML exercises, refer to the W3C's HTML tutorial for any topics that you do not understand. Save all files you create in the Tutorial.01 folder on your Data Disk.

1. Create a simple HTML document that lists the names of five technology companies. Place each company name on its own line. Save the HTML document as LineBreaks.html.

2. Save the LineBreaks.html document you created in exercise 1 as HorizontalRules.html. Leave each company name on its own line, but separate each line with a horizontal rule. Do you still need separate line break tags to place each company name on its own line?

3. Create an HTML document that displays six lines, with each line formatted using one of the six heading level tags. Start with the largest tag and end with the smallest. Save the HTML document as HeadingTags.html.

4. Create an HTML document that contains two body paragraphs (make up whatever text you like). Above each body paragraph, place a centered <H1> heading tag, and left justify each body paragraph. Save the HTML document as Alignment.html.

5. Create an HTML document with a gray background. Place a single line of text on the page that reads *The background of this Web page is gray*. Format the line of text with the <STRONG> tag . Save the HTML document as Background.html.

6. Create an HTML document that uses the following text formatting styles: bold, italic, big, small, strong, emphasized, superscript, and subscript. Save the HTML document as TextFormats.html.

7. Create an HTML document that contains three tables. Create the first table with one column and three rows; create the second table with one row and three columns; and create the third table with three rows and three columns. Place a simple border around each table. Save the HTML document as Tables.html.

8. Create a personal Web page. Find a digital image that you can use as a background image using the BACKGROUND attribute of the <BODY> tag. Place your name as the first line on the page and format it with the <H1> tag. If you have a digital picture of yourself, place it directly beneath the <H1> tag. Next, add the following categories to your Web page using <H2> tags:

- Contact Information
- Work Information
- Current Projects
- Biographical Information
- Hobbies and Interests

Separate each <H2> section with a horizontal rule. When necessary, use <H3> tags within an <H2> section to emphasize a subcategory. For example, in Work Information, you may place <H3> tags describing your Job Title, Department, and Responsibilities. Save the HTML document as PersonalPage.html.

9. Design an HTML document that will be used as the home page for a company that sells sporting goods. If you have access to clip art, include pictures of sports equipment that the company sells, such as basketballs, baseball gloves, and tennis rackets. For each item, include information such as the manufacturer and sales price. Include <HEAD> and <BODY> sections in your document. In the <HEAD> section, include a <TITLE>. Use at least five different HTML elements to format the <BODY> section. Save the HTML document as SportsCompany.html. Although you are only using static HTML elements to create the Web page (that is, you cannot yet include any dynamic JavaScript elements such as order forms), make a list of dynamic elements you would like to add to your Web page, such as a catalog request form.

10. Before the early 1990s, the Web was used almost exclusively as a communication tool for scientists and members of the academic community. Search the Internet using Yahoo! or another search engine for more information on the evolution of the World Wide Web. How and why do you think the Web evolved from its humble roots as a communication mechanism to the powerful business role it plays today?

11. Visit the Web site of the World Wide Web Consortium (W3C) at *www.w3.org*, and read about the latest HTML specifications. What are some of the improvements being made to the HTML language, and how do you think those improvements will affect Web page design?

12. One very important step in the evolution of the HTML language is the creation of Extensible Markup Language, or XML. Some proponents believe that XML will eventually replace the HTML language. Will you still be able to use the JavaScript programming language in Web pages that use XML?

13. Many different types of Web sites, ranging from personal sites to large corporate Web sites, incorporate JavaScript into their Web pages. Search the Web for personal and professional examples of JavaScript programs or effects. Describe the programs or effects and state whether you think they were effective and how you would improve them.

14. Jakob Nielsen writes a popular Internet column called Alertbox at *www.useit.com/alertbox/*. Read the following three columns from Alertbox and write a brief description of what you learned: "The Top Ten New Mistakes of Web Design" (May 30, 1999), "Who commits the Top Ten Mistakes in Web design?" (May 16, 1999), and "'Top Ten Mistakes' revisited three years later" (May 2, 1999).

15. Visit your local library or bookstore, or search the Internet for information on programming logic and debugging. How can you incorporate what you learned into the JavaScript programs you will write in this book?

16. Search the Internet for information on Internet protocols, domain names, and IP addresses. How do these items interact?

A First JavaScript Program

In this section you will learn:

■ About the <Script> tag

■ How to create a JavaScript source file

■ How to add comments to a JavaScript Program

■ How to hide JavaScript from incompatible browsers

■ About placing JavaScript in HEAD or BODY sections of HTML documents

The <SCRIPT> Tag

JavaScript programs run from within an HTML document. The statements that make up a JavaScript program in an HTML document are contained between the <SCRIPT>...</SCRIPT> tag pairs. The **<SCRIPT>** tag is used to notify the Web Browser that the commands that follow it need to be interpreted by a scripting engine. The **LANGUAGE** attribute of the <SCRIPT> tag tells the browser which scripting language and which version of the scripting language are being used. To tell the Web browser that the statements which follow need to be interpreted by the JavaScript scripting engine, you include the following code in your HTML document:

```
<SCRIPT LANGUAGE="JavaScript">
JavaScript statements;
</SCRIPT>
```

tip

Although this book covers JavaScript, you can use other types of scripting languages with Web pages. Microsoft's VBScript is another type of scripting language, and is based on the Visual Basic programming language. To use VBScript in your HTML document, you would use the code `<SCRIPT LANGUAGE="VBScript">VBScript statements</SCRIPT>`**. Do not confuse JScript with VBScript. JScript is Microsoft's version of the JavaScript scripting language. To specify the JScript language, you specify** *JavaScript* **as the LANGUAGE attribute.**

JavaScript is the default scripting language for most Web browsers. If you omit the LANGUAGE attribute from the <SCRIPT> tag, your JavaScript program should still run. However, the Internet is always changing. New technologies, including new scripting languages, are being introduced constantly. It is difficult to determine whether competing scripting languages, such as VBScript, will become dominant. Therefore, it is advisable that you always use the LANGUAGE attribute of the <SCRIPT> tag to tell the browser which scripting language you are using.

You also use the LANGUAGE attribute to specify which version of JavaScript you are using. Certain Web browsers support only certain versions of JavaScript.

For example, Navigator 3.0 supports only JavaScript versions 1.1 and lower. When you specify a JavaScript version number using the LANGUAGE attribute of the <SCRIPT> tag, you remove the space between the word *JavaScript* and the appropriate version number. If you include a space between the scripting language name and the version number, the browser will not interpret your code. A Web browser cannot interpret *JavaScript 1.1* because there is a space between JavaScript and the version number. The following code specifies that the JavaScript code to follow is compatible with JavaScript versions 1.1 and lower:

```
<SCRIPT LANGUAGE="JavaScript1.1">
JavaScript statements
</SCRIPT>
```

Figure 1-12 lists the versions of Navigator, along with the versions of JavaScript they support and the appropriate code to include in the <SCRIPT> tag.

Netscape Version	JavaScript Compatibility	Code
Navigator earlier than 2.0	not supported	—
Navigator 2.0	JavaScript 1.0	<SCRIPT LANGUAGE="JavaScript">...</SCRIPT>
Navigator 3.0	JavaScript 1.1 and lower	<SCRIPT LANGUAGE="JavaScript1.1">...</SCRIPT>
Navigator 4.0 – 4.05	JavaScript 1.2 and lower	<SCRIPT LANGUAGE="JavaScript1.2">...</SCRIPT>
Navigator 4.06 – 4.5	JavaScript 1.3 and lower	<SCRIPT LANGUAGE="JavaScript1.3">...</SCRIPT>

Figure 1-12: JavaScript versions supported in Navigator

When an HTML document is being loaded, the Web browser checks the JavaScript version number that is specified by the LANGUAGE attribute of the <SCRIPT> tag. If the Web browser you are using does not support the specified JavaScript version, it ignores all statements between the <SCRIPT>...</SCRIPT> tag pairs. If you want your Web page to be compatible with older versions of Web browsers, then you should specify the JavaScript version number that is supported by those older browsers. For example, if you want your Web page to be displayed in Navigator version 3.0, then the <SCRIPT> tag in your HTML code should read <SCRIPT LANGUAGE="JavaScript1.1">...</SCRIPT> because Navigator 3.0 only supports JavaScript versions 1.1 and earlier. Later in this section, you will learn how to completely hide JavaScript statements from incompatible browsers.

Specifying the JavaScript version number in the LANGUAGE attribute is only necessary if you anticipate your program will run in an earlier version of Navigator. To write JavaScript programs for browsers that are compatible with ECMAScript Edition 3, you should exclude the version number and simply specify JavaScript as the script language using the statement `<SCRIPT LANGUAGE="JavaScript">`.

▶ **tip**

If you anticipate that your JavaScript programs will run only in Internet Explorer, then you can specify "JScript" as your scripting language using the statement `<SCRIPT LANGUAGE="JScript">`**. However, few browsers other than Internet Explorer will recognize "JScript" as a valid language attribute for the `<SCRIPT>` tag, so it is safer to always use "JavaScript."**

In addition to being an interpreted scripting language, JavaScript is an object-based programming language. An **object** is programming code and data that can be treated as an individual unit or component. Individual lines in a programming language are called **statements**. Groups of related statements associated with an object are called **methods**. JavaScript treats many things as objects. One of the most commonly used objects in JavaScript programming is the Document object. The **Document object** represents the content of a browser's window. Any text, graphics, or other information displayed in a Web page is part of the Document object. One of the most common uses of the Document object is to add new text to a Web page. You create new text on a Web page with the **write() method** or the **writeln() method** of the Document object.

To execute, or call, an object's method, you append the method to the object with a period, and include any required arguments between the method's parentheses. An **argument** is any type of information that can be passed to a method. The write() and writeln() methods of the Document object require a text string as an argument. A **text string**, or **literal string**, is text that is contained within double quotation marks. The text string that is passed as an argument to the write() and writeln() methods of the Document object is the text that the Document object uses to create new text on a Web page. For example, `document.write("this is a text string");` writes the text *this is a text string* to the HTML document. When you want to include a quoted string within a literal string, you surround the quoted text with single quotation marks. For example, `document.write("this is a 'text' string");` writes the text *this is a 'text' string* to the HTML document. Note that literal strings must be on a single line. If you include a line break within a literal string you will receive an error message.

The write() and writeln() methods perform essentially the same function that you perform when you manually add text to the body of a standard HTML document. Whether you add text to an HTML document using standard HTML tags or using the write() or writeln() methods, the text is added according to the order in which the statement is encountered in the HTML file. Unlike standard HTML text, the write() and writeln() methods can add new text to an HTML document after a browser has rendered the document.

The only difference between the write() and writeln() methods is that the writeln() method adds a carriage return after the line of text. Carriage returns, however, are only recognized inside the HTML `<PRE>...</PRE>` tag pair.

The <PRE>...</PRE> tag pair is short for preformatted text. This tag pair tells a Web browser that any text and line breaks contained between the opening and closing tag are to be rendered exactly as they appear. The <PRE>...</PRE> tag pair is known as a **container element** because it contains text and other HTML tags. For a Web browser to recognize the line break following the writeln() method, you must enclose the <SCRIPT>...</SCRIPT> tag pairs within the <PRE>...</PRE> tag pairs.

Figure 1-13 contains a script that prints *Hello World* to a Web browser using the writeln() method of the Document object. Notice that the <SCRIPT>...</SCRIPT> tag pairs are enclosed in the <PRE>...</PRE> tag pairs. Figure 1-14 shows the output.

```
<PRE>

<SCRIPT LANGUAGE="JavaScript">

document.writeln("Hello World");

document.writeln(
"This line is printed below the 'Hello World' line.");

</SCRIPT>

</PRE>
```

Figure 1-13: Hello World script using the writeln() method of the Document object

For simple JavaScript files such as the Hello World script, you can omit the <HTML>, <HEAD>, and <BODY> tags.

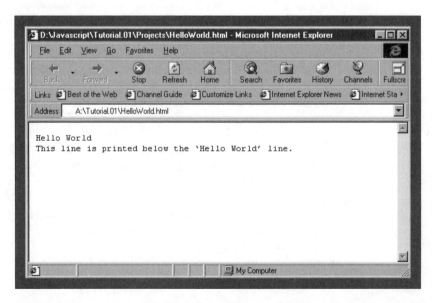

Figure 1-14: Output of the Hello World script using the writeln() method of the Document object

Objects that are part of the JavaScript programming language itself, such as the Document object, are commonly referred to with an initial cap to distinguish them as "top-level" objects. However, unlike HTML, JavaScript is case-sensitive. Although we refer to the Document object in the course of this book with an uppercase D, you must use a lowercase d when referring to the Document object in a script. The statement `Document.write("Hello World");` will cause an error message since the JavaScript interpreter does not recognize an object named Document with an uppercase D. Similarly, the following misspelled statements will cause an error:

```
DOCUMENT.write("Hello World");
Document.Write("Hello World");
document.WRITE("Hello World");
```

Figure 1-15 shows the error message that appears when you attempt to execute an invalid statement in Navigator, and Figure 1-16 shows the error message that appears when you attempt to execute this statement in Internet Explorer.

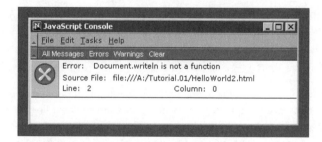

Figure 1-15: Error message in Navigator

If you are using a version of Internet Explorer higher than 4, you need to turn on error notification by selecting Internet Options from the Tools menu and clicking the Advanced tab. In the Browsing category on the Advanced tab, make sure the Display a notification about every script error check box is selected, and click the OK button to close the dialog box. In versions of Navigator that support JavaScript 1.3 and higher, to view error messages you must point to Tools on the Tasks menu and select JavaScript Console. Depending on your browser version, the error messages you see may appear differently from the error messages you see in the figures in this book.

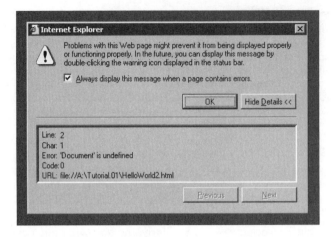

Figure 1-16: Error message in Internet Explorer

Next, you will create a simple JavaScript document.

To create a JavaScript document:

1 Create a new document in your text editor or HTML editor.

2 Type **<PRE>** to start a preformatted text container.

3 Press **Enter** and type **<SCRIPT LANGUAGE="JavaScript">** to begin the JavaScript document.

4 Press **Enter** and type **document.writeln("This is the first line in my JavaScript file.");**.

> The string in Step 4 is broken due to space limitations in this book. Space limitations in this book often require that text strings wrap to the next line. However, remember that strings cannot be broken, or you will receive an error message. Wherever you see a broken string, be sure to type the entire string on a single line.

help

5 Press **Enter** again and type **document.writeln("This is the second line in my JavaScript file.");**.

6 Press **Enter** one more time and type **</SCRIPT>** to close the <SCRIPT>...</SCRIPT> tag pair.

7 Type **</PRE>** to close the preformatted text container.

8 Save the file as **MyFirstJavaScript.html** in the **Tutorial.01** folder on your Data Disk.

9 Open the **MyFirstJavaScript.html** file in your Web browser. If you receive one of the error messages displayed in Figure 1-15 or 1-16, check the case of the object and the writeln() method in the document.writeln() statements. Figure 1-17 displays the MyFirstJavaScript.html file as it appears in Internet Explorer.

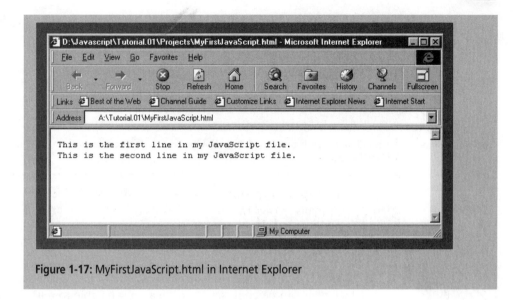

Figure 1-17: MyFirstJavaScript.html in Internet Explorer

Creating a JavaScript Source File

JavaScript is often incorporated directly into an HTML document. However, you can also save JavaScript code in an external file called a source file. A JavaScript source file is usually designated with the file extension .js and contains only JavaScript statements; it does not contain the HTML <SCRIPT>...</SCRIPT> tag pair. Instead, the <SCRIPT>...</SCRIPT> tag pair is located within the HTML document that calls the source file. To access JavaScript code that is saved in an external file, you use the SRC attribute of the <SCRIPT> tag. The **SRC attribute** accepts a text string that specifies the URL or directory location of a JavaScript source file. For example, to load a JavaScript source file named SampleSourceFile.js located in the C:\javafiles directory, you include the following code in an HTML document:

```
<SCRIPT LANGUAGE="JavaScript"
SRC="c:\javafiles\samplesourcefile.js">
</SCRIPT>
```

JavaScript source files cannot include HTML tags. If you include HTML tags in a JavaScript source file, you will receive an error message. Also, when you specify a source file in your HTML document using the SRC attribute, the browser will ignore any other JavaScript code located between the <SCRIPT>...</SCRIPT> tag pairs. For example, consider the following JavaScript code. The JavaScript source file specified by the SRC attribute of the <SCRIPT> tag executes properly, but the document.write() statement is ignored.

```
<SCRIPT LANGUAGE="JavaScript"
SRC="c:\javafiles\samplesourcefile.js">
document.write("this JavaScript statement will be ignored");
</SCRIPT>
```

tip

···

Certain older Web browsers, such as Navigator 2.0, do not recognize the SRC attribute of the <SCRIPT> tag.

···

If the JavaScript code you intend to use in an HTML document is fairly short, then it is usually easier to include JavaScript code in an HTML document. However, for longer JavaScript code it is easier to include the code in a .js source file. There are several reasons you may want to use .js source files instead of adding the code to an HTML document:

■ Your HTML document will be neater. Lengthy JavaScript code in an HTML document can be confusing—you may not be able to tell at a glance where the HTML code ends and the JavaScript code begins.

■ The JavaScript code can be shared among multiple HTML documents. For example, your Web site may contain pages that allow users to order an item. Each Web page displays a different item, but uses the same JavaScript code to gather order information. Instead of re-creating the JavaScript order information code within each HTML document, the Web pages can share a central JavaScript source file. Sharing a single source file among multiple HTML documents reduces disk space. In addition, when you share a source file among multiple HTML documents, a Web browser only needs to keep one copy of the file in memory, which reduces system overhead.

■ JavaScript source files hide JavaScript code from incompatible browsers. If your HTML document contains JavaScript code, instead of calling an external JavaScript source file, an incompatible browser will display the code as if it were standard text.

You can use a combination of embedded JavaScript code and JavaScript source files in your HTML documents. The ability to combine embedded JavaScript code and JavaScript source files in a single HTML document is advantageous if you have multiple HTML documents, each of which requires individual JavaScript code statements, but all of which also share a single JavaScript source file. Suppose you have a Web site with multiple Web pages. Each page displays a product that your company sells. You may have a JavaScript source file that collects order information, such as a person's name and address, that is shared by all the products you sell. Each product may also require other types of order information that you need to collect using JavaScript code. For example, one of your products may be a shirt, for which you need to collect size and color information. On another Web page, you may sell jellybeans, for which you need to collect quantity and flavor information. Each of these products can share a central JavaScript source file to collect standard information, but can also include embedded JavaScript code to collect product-specific information.

When you include multiple JavaScript sections in an HTML document, you must include the <SCRIPT>...</SCRIPT> tag pair for each section. Each JavaScript section in an HTML document is executed in the order in which it appears. Figure 1-18 displays an HTML document that calls an external source file and includes embedded JavaScript.

```
<HTML>

<HEAD>

<TITLE>HTML Document with Two JavaScript Sections</TITLE>

</HEAD>

<BODY>

The following two lines call an external
JavaScript source file.<BR>

<SCRIPT LANGUAGE="JavaScript"
SRC="c:\javafiles\samplesourcefile.js">

</SCRIPT>

<PRE>

<SCRIPT LANGUAGE="JavaScript">

document.writeln("Your order has been confirmed.");

document.writeln("Thank you for your business.");

</SCRIPT>

</PRE>

</BODY>

</HTML>
```

Figure 1-18: HTML document that calls an external source file and includes embedded JavaScript

Next, you will create an HTML document that calls an external JavaScript source file and that includes embedded JavaScript. First you will create the main HTML document.

To create the main HTML document:

1   Create a new document in your text editor or HTML editor.

2   Type the opening <HTML> and <HEAD> tags:

```
<HTML>
<HEAD>
```

3   Press **Enter** and add the title: `<TITLE>Multiple JavaScript Calls</TITLE>`.

4   Press **Enter** and type `</HEAD>` to close the <HEAD>...</HEAD> tag pair.

5   Press **Enter** and add the following code to begin the body of the HTML document and to call an external JavaScript source file:

```
<BODY>
<SCRIPT LANGUAGE="JavaScript" SRC="javascriptsource.js">
</SCRIPT>
```

6   Press **Enter** and type the following code that executes embedded JavaScript code in a preformatted text container:

```
<PRE>
<SCRIPT LANGUAGE="JavaScript" >
document.writeln(
"This line was created with embedded JavaScript code.");
document.writeln(
"This line was also created with embedded JavaScript code.");
</SCRIPT>
</PRE>
```

7   Press **Enter** and add the following code to close the <HTML> and <BODY> tags:

```
</BODY>
</HTML>
```

8   Save the file as **MultipleJavaScriptCalls.html** in the **Tutorial.01** folder on your Data Disk.

Next you will create the JavaScript source file, and then open MultipleJavaScript Calls.html.

To create the JavaScript source file and open MultipleJavaScriptCalls.html:

1   Create a new document in your text editor or HTML editor.

2   Type `document.write("This line was printed from the JavaScript source file.")`. This will be the only line in the document. Remember that you do not include the <SCRIPT> tag within a source file.

3 Save the file as **javascriptsource.js** in the **Tutorial.01** folder on your Data Disk.

4 Open the **MultipleJavaScriptCalls.html** file in your Web browser. Figure 1-19 displays the MultipleJavaScriptCalls.html file as it appears in Navigator 6.0.

> **Multiple JavaScript Calls - Netscape 6**
>
> File Edit View Search Go Bookmarks Tasks Help
>
> file:///A|/Tutorial.01/MultipleJavaScriptCall   Search
>
> This line was printed from the JavaScript source file.
>
> This line was created with embedded JavaScript code.
> This line was also created with embedded JavaScript code.
>
> Document: Done
>
> Business ▲   Tech ▲   Fun ▲   Interact ▲

Figure 1-19: MultipleJavaScriptCalls.html in Navigator 6.0

Adding Comments to a JavaScript Program

When you create a program, whether it is with JavaScript or any other programming language, it is considered good programming practice to add comments to your code. **Comments** are nonprinting lines that you place in your code to contain various types of remarks, including the name of the program, your name and the date you created the program, notes to yourself, or instructions to future programmers who may need to modify your work. When you are working with long scripts, comments make it easier to decipher how a program is structured.

JavaScript supports two types of comments: line comments and block comments. **Line comments** are created by adding two slashes // before the text you want to use as a comment. The // characters instruct the JavaScript interpreter to ignore all text to the end of the line. Line comments can appear at the end of a line of code, or they can exist on an entire line by themselves. **Block comments** span multiple lines and are created by adding /* to the first line that is to be included in the block. You close a comment block by typing */ after the last text to be included in the block. Any text or lines between the opening /* characters and the closing */ characters is ignored by the JavaScript interpreter. Figure 1-20 displays a JavaScript file containing line and block comments.

 tip

• •

Comments in JavaScript use the same syntax as comments created in C++ and Java.

• •

```
<SCRIPT LANGUAGE="JavaScript">

/*

This line is part of the block comment.

This line is also part of the block comment.

*/

document.writeln("Comments Example");   // Line comments can
follow code statements

// This line comment takes up an entire line.

/* This is another way of creating a block comment. */

</SCRIPT>
```

Figure 1-20: JavaScript file with line and block comments

Next you will add comments to the MyFirstJavaScript.html file.

To add comments to the MyFirstJavaScript.html file:

1   Open the **MyFirstJavaScript.html** file in your text editor or HTML editor.

2   Place the insertion point at the end of the line containing the opening <SCRIPT> tag, press **Enter,** and add the following comment block:

```
/*
JavaScript code for MyFirstJavaScript.html
your name
today's date
*/
```

> **help**
>
> When you create comments in your JavaScript programs, be sure to use a forward slash (/) and not a backward slash (\). People often confuse these two characters. If you include a backward slash instead of a forward slash when creating a comment, you will receive an error when you attempt to open the file in a Web browser.

3   Place the insertion point at the end of the line that reads **document.writeln ("This is the first line in my JavaScript file.");**, press **Tab,** then type **// Line 1.**

4 Place the insertion point at the end of the line that reads `document.writeln` `("This is the second line in my JavaScript file.");`, press **Tab,** and type `// Line 2`.

5 Save the **MyFirstJavaScript.html** file, then open it in your Web browser to confirm that the comments are not displayed.

Hiding JavaScript from Incompatible Browsers

Creating JavaScript source files hides JavaScript code from incompatible browsers. However, if your HTML document contains embedded JavaScript codes instead of calling an external .js source file, then an incompatible browser will display the codes as if they were standard text. To hide embedded JavaScript code from incompatible browsers, you enclose the code between the <SCRIPT>...</SCRIPT> tag pair in an HTML comment block. HTML comments are different from JavaScript comments. HTML comment blocks begin with `<!--` and end with `-->`. The browser does not render any text located between the opening and closing comment tags. For example, Figure 1-21 displays an HTML document containing comments. Figure 1-22 shows the output. The browser does not render text located between the comment tags.

```
<HTML>

<HEAD>

<TITLE>HTML Comments</TITLE>

</HEAD>

<BODY>

The browser renders this line normally since it is located before
the opening comment tag.<BR>

<!--Text on this line does not appear

Text on this line does not appear

This line does not appear either -->

The browser renders this line normally since it is located after
the closing comment tag. <BR>

</BODY>

</HTML>
```

Figure 1-21: HTML document with comments

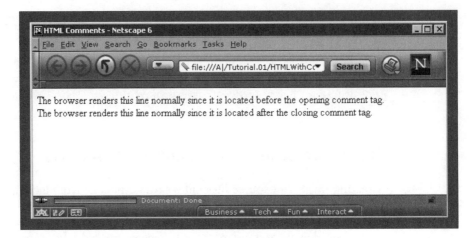

Figure 1-22: Output of HTML document with comments

Most Web browsers do not display lines that are set off with an HTML comment tag. However, browsers compatible with JavaScript ignore the HTML comment tags and execute the JavaScript code normally. Remember that JavaScript-compatible browsers never display JavaScript code. Instead, the code is interpreted by the browser's scripting engine. Only JavaScript comment tags can be used to hide JavaScript code from the interpreter. Figure 1-23 shows an example of JavaScript code that is hidden from incompatible browsers, using HTML comments, but that would be executed by compatible browsers.

```
<SCRIPT LANGUAGE="JavaScript">

<!--  This line starts the HTML comment block

document.writeln("Your order has been confirmed.");

document.writeln("Thank you for your business.");

// This line ends the HTML comment block -->

</SCRIPT>
```

Figure 1-23: JavaScript code hidden from incompatible browsers, using HTML comments

Notice in Figure 1-23 that the line containing the closing HTML comment (-->) begins with a JavaScript line comment (//). The line comment instructs the JavaScript compiler to ignore the closing HTML comment and gives you an opportunity to leave a text comment that identifies the end of the HTML comment block.

Incompatible browsers, however, will ignore the line comment and recognize the closing HTML comment as the end of the HTML comment block. Internet Explorer recognizes a closing HTML comment on a line by itself within a <SCRIPT>...</SCRIPT> tag pair, although Navigator does not. Therefore, in order to make your code compatible with both browsers, you should always begin the statement that contains a closing HTML comment with a line comment. Note that instead of using a JavaScript line comment to close an HTML comment block, you can add a second opening HTML comment to the statement containing the closing HTML comment as follows: <!-- comment -->.

When your HTML document is displayed by a browser that is incompatible with JavaScript, or by a browser with JavaScript disabled, you usually want to display some sort of message to tell users that their browser is not compatible with your program. You can display an alternate message to users of incompatible browsers by using the <NOSCRIPT>...</NOSCRIPT> tag pair. The <NOSCRIPT>...</NOSCRIPT> tag pair usually follows the <SCRIPT>...</SCRIPT> tag pair. Figure 1-24 illustrates how to use the <NOSCRIPT> tag.

```
<SCRIPT LANGUAGE="JavaScript">

<!--  This line starts the HTML comment block

document.writeln("Your order has been confirmed.");

document.writeln("Thank you for your business.");

// This line ends the HTML comment block -->

</SCRIPT>

<NOSCRIPT>

Your browser does not support JavaScript or JavaScript is
disabled.<BR>

</NOSCRIPT>
```

Figure 1-24: JavaScript code with <NOSCRIPT> tag

tip

Alternate text in the <NOSCRIPT> tag is also displayed if a user has disabled JavaScript support in their Web browser.

Next you will modify the MyFirstJavaScript.html file so that it is hidden from incompatible browsers and displays an alternate message using the <NOSCRIPT> tag.

To modify the MyFirstJavaScript.html file so that it is hidden from incompatible browsers and displays an alternate message using the <NOSCRIPT> tag:

1   Open the **MyFirstJavaScript.html** file in your text editor or HTML editor.

2   Place the insertion point at the end of the line containing the opening <SCRIPT> tag, press **Enter**, and then type `<!-- This line starts the HTML comment block` to start the HTML comment block that hides the JavaScript code from incompatible browsers.

3   Place the insertion point at the end of the line that reads `document.writeln("This is the second line in myJavaScript file."); // Line 2`, press **Enter**, and then type `// This line ends the HTML comment block -->` to close the HTML comment block.

4   Place the insertion point at the end of the line that reads </PRE>, press **Enter** to insert a new line, and type the following code to display a message to browsers that do not support JavaScript:

```
<NOSCRIPT>
Your browser does not support JavaScript or JavaScript
is disabled.<BR>
</NOSCRIPT>
```

5   Save the **MyFirstJavaScript.html** file and open it in your Web browser. If you are using a recent version of Navigator or Internet Explorer, the JavaScript section should execute normally. However, if you are using a browser that does not support JavaScript, you will see the message *Your browser does not support JavaScript.*

Placing JavaScript in HEAD or BODY sections

A Web browser renders tags in an HTML document in the order in which they are encountered. When you have multiple JavaScript code sections in an HTML document, each section is also executed in the order in which it appears. For example, in the following code, the embedded JavaScript code executes before the call to the JavaScript source file since the embedded code appears first.

```
The following embedded JavaScript code executes first. <BR>
<SCRIPT LANGUAGE="JavaScript">
document.writeln(
"First JavaScript code section in document");
</SCRIPT> <BR>
The following JavaScript source file executes after the
embedded JavaScript code. <BR>
<SCRIPT LANGUAGE="JavaScript" SRC="javascriptsource.js">
</SCRIPT>
```

The order in which a browser executes JavaScript code also depends on which section of the HTML document the JavaScript code is placed in. HTML documents usually consist of a <HEAD> section and a <BODY> section. The <HEAD> section contains information that is used by the Web browser and is rendered before the <BODY> section. The <BODY> section usually contains the content of a Web page that will be displayed. JavaScript code can be placed in either section or between the two sections. Where you place your JavaScript code will vary, depending on the program you are writing.

It is a good idea to place as much of your JavaScript code as possible in the <HEAD> section, since the <HEAD> section of an HTML document is rendered before the <BODY> section. When placed in the <HEAD> section, JavaScript code will be processed before the main body of the HTML document is displayed. You may want to place JavaScript code in the <HEAD> section when your code performs behind-the-scenes tasks that are required by JavaScript code sections located in the <BODY> section.

S U M M A R Y

- The statements that make up a JavaScript program in an HTML document are contained between the <SCRIPT>...</SCRIPT> tag pairs.

- The LANGUAGE attribute of the <SCRIPT> tag specifies which scripting language is being used and the scripting language's version.

- JavaScript is the default scripting language for most Web browsers.

- If the Web browser you are using does not support the specified JavaScript version, all statements between the <SCRIPT>...</SCRIPT> tag pairs are ignored.

- If you anticipate that your Web page will be displayed on older versions of Web browsers, then you should use the LANGUAGE attribute to specify the JavaScript version number for the version of JavaScript that is supported by that browser.

- The Document object represents the content of a browser's window.

- You can create new text on a Web page using the write() method or the writeln() method of the Document object.

- An argument is any type of information that can be passed to a method.

- A text string, or literal string, is text that is contained within quotation marks.

- The write() and writeln() methods perform essentially the same function as adding text directly to the body of a standard HTML document. The only difference between the write() and writeln() methods is that the writeln() method adds a carriage return after the line.

- Unlike HTML, JavaScript is case-sensitive.

- You can save JavaScript code in an external file called a source file. A JavaScript source file is usually designated with the file extension .js and contains only JavaScript statements; it does not contain the <SCRIPT>...</SCRIPT> tag pair.

- You use the SRC attribute of the <SCRIPT> tag to access JavaScript code that is saved in an external file. The SRC attribute accepts a text string that specifies the URL or directory location of a JavaScript source file.

- JavaScript source files cannot include HTML tags.

- HTML documents can use a combination of embedded JavaScript code and JavaScript source files.

- When you include multiple JavaScript sections in an HTML document, you must include the <SCRIPT>...</SCRIPT> tag pair for each section.

- Comments are nonprinting lines that you place in your code to contain various types of remarks.

- You create line comments by adding two slashes // before the text you want to use as a comment.

- Block comments span multiple lines. You create a block comment by adding /* to the first line that is to be included in the block. You close a comment block by typing */ after the last text to be included in the block.

- To hide embedded JavaScript code from incompatible browsers, you enclose the code between the <SCRIPT>...</SCRIPT> tag pair in an HTML comment block (<!-- ... -->).

- Most Web browsers do not display lines that appear between HTML comment tags (<!--...-->). However, browsers compatible with JavaScript ignore the HTML comment tags and execute the JavaScript code normally.

- You display an alternate message to users of incompatible browsers with the <NOSCRIPT>...</NOSCRIPT> tag pair. The <NOSCRIPT>...</NOSCRIPT> tag pair usually follows the <SCRIPT>...</SCRIPT> tag pair.

- When you have multiple JavaScript code sections in an HTML document, each section is executed in the order in which it appears.

- It is a good idea to place as much of your JavaScript code as possible in the <HEAD> section, since the <HEAD> section of an HTML document is rendered before the <BODY> section.

 # QUESTIONS

1. Scripting code in an HTML document is located _____.
   a. inside the closing bracket of the <SCRIPT> tag
   b. between the <SCRIPT>...</SCRIPT> tag pairs
   c. before the opening <SCRIPT> tag
   d. after the closing <SCRIPT> tag

2. The <SCRIPT> tag _____.
   a. is used only with JavaScript
   b. is used only with VBScript
   c. can be used with both JavaScript and VBScript
   d. is not used with either JavaScript or VBScript

3. Which of the following is not valid with the LANGUAGE attribute of the <SCRIPT> tag?
   a. JavaScript1.2
   b. JAVASCRIPT1.2
   c. javascript1.2
   d. JavaScript 1.2

4. When should you specify the JavaScript version number with the LANGUAGE attribute of the <SCRIPT> tag?
   a. When your program will run in earlier versions of Navigator
   b. When your program will run in earlier versions of Internet Explorer
   c. For earlier versions of both Navigator and Internet Explorer
   d. When your program will run in any ECMAScript-compatible browser

5. If a Web browser does not support the version of JavaScript specified by the LANGUAGE attribute, then the JavaScript statements contained in the <SCRIPT>...</SCRIPT tag pairs _____.
   a. are converted to a supported version
   b. close the Web browser
   c. are ignored
   d. are displayed as text

6. A(n) _____ refers to programming code and data that can be treated as an individual unit or component.
   a. icon
   b. procedure
   c. concealed unit
   d. object

7. The JavaScript object that represents the contents of a browser's window is called the _____ object.
   a. Document
   b. HTML
   c. Browser
   d. Contents

8. With JavaScript, new text is created on a Web page using the write() method or the _____ method.
   a. output()
   b. writeln()
   c. print()
   d. println()

9. Which of the following is the correct syntax for including a quoted string within a literal string?
    a. "this is a " "quoted" " string"
    b. 'this is a 'quoted' string'
    c. "this is a "quoted" string"
    d. "this is a 'quoted' string"

10. The _____ tag pair tells a Web browser that any text and line breaks it contains are to be rendered as is.
    a. <FORMAT>...</FORMAT>
    b. <CONTAINER>...</CONTAINER>
    c. <COMPOSE>...</COMPOSE>
    d. <PRE>...</PRE>

11. Which of the following statements is correct?
    a. DOCUMENT.write("Hello World")
    b. Document.Write("Hello World")
    c. document.write("Hello World")
    d. document.WRITE("Hello World")

12. A JavaScript source file is called using the _____ attribute of the <SCRIPT> tag.
    a. LANGUAGE
    b. FILE
    c. SOURCE
    d. SRC

13. JavaScript source files _____.
    a. can include HTML tags
    b. cannot include HTML tags
    c. can include certain types of HTML tags
    d. cannot include JavaScript statements

14. When an HTML document calls a JavaScript source file, the <SCRIPT>...</SCRIPT> tag pairs are _____.
    a. located in the HTML document
    b. located in the JavaScript source file
    c. located in both the HTML document and the JavaScript source file
    d. not necessary

15. When would you *not* use a JavaScript source file?
    a. when you will use the JavaScript code with incompatible browsers
    b. when the JavaScript source file is shared by multiple HTML documents
    c. when the JavaScript code is fairly short and is not shared
    d. when you do not want to share your code with other programmers

16. HTML documents can contain _____.
    a. embedded JavaScript code but not JavaScript source files
    b. JavaScript source files but not embedded JavaScript code
    c. either JavaScript code or JavaScript source files
    d. both embedded JavaScript code and JavaScript source files

17. You create line comments in JavaScript code by adding _____ to a line you want to use as a comment.

    a. ||

    b. **

    c. //

    d. \\

18. Block comments begin with /* and end with _____.

    a. */

    b. /*

    c. //

    d. **

19. You hide JavaScript code from incompatible browsers by using _____.

    a. an HTML filter

    b. the <MASK> tag

    c. JavaScript comment tags

    d. HTML comment tags

20. You display alternate text to users of incompatible browsers by using the _____ tag pair.

    a. <NOSCRIPT>...</NOSCRIPT>

    b. <SUBMESSAGE>...</SUBMESSAGE>

    c. <MESSAGEBOX>...</MESSAGEBOX>

    d. <NOJAVASCRIPT>...</NOJAVASCRIPT>

21. How are JavaScript code sections executed in an HTML document?

    a. All embedded JavaScript code is executed first.

    b. All JavaScript source files are executed first.

    c. Each JavaScript code section is executed according to the sequence in which you added it to the HTML document.

    d. Each JavaScript code section is executed in the order in which it appears.

22. JavaScript _____ of an HTML document.

    a. cannot be placed in either the <HEAD> or <BODY> sections

    b. can be placed in either the <HEAD> or <BODY> sections

    c. can be placed only in the <HEAD> section

    d. can be placed only in the <BODY> section

EXERCISES

1. Explain when you should use embedded JavaScript and when you should use a JavaScript source file.

2. Create a simple JavaScript program that prints the statement *Printed from a JavaScript Program* to the screen. Save the HTML document as SimpleOutput.html in the Tutorial.01 folder on your Data Disk.

3. Correct the syntax errors in the following JavaScript code. Also, modify the LAN-GUAGE attribute of the <SCRIPT> tag so the JavaScript code is compatible with ECMAScript. Save the program as SyntaxErrors.html in the Tutorial.01 folder on your Data Disk. Be sure the program runs successfully in a browser.

```
<SCRIPT LANGUAGE="JavaScript1.2"
Document.Write("Hello World"<BR>);
document.writeLn("Hello World");
<SCRIPT>
```

4. Create an HTML document named MarkTwain.html that uses JavaScript to create the same output as the following HTML statements. Save the file in the Tutorial.01 folder on your Data Disk.

```
<STRONG>Mark Twain said <STRONG><BR>
<I>Everybody talks about the weather,<BR>
but nobody does anything about it.</I>
```

5. Add appropriate comments to the following program that hide JavaScript from incompatible browsers. Save the program as HideJavaScript.html in the Tutorial.01 folder on your Data Disk.

```
<SCRIPT LANGUAGE="JavaScript">
document.writeln("These statements should be ignored ");
document.writeln("by incompatible browsers.");
</SCRIPT>
```

6. Save the HideJavaScript.html document you created in exercise 5 as NoJavaScript.html. Add the appropriate HTML tags to display an alternate message to browsers that do not support JavaScript or that have disabled JavaScript.

7. Create an HTML document, using the following instructions. Create the document header using an HTML tag. Add the first text line using embedded JavaScript code and add the second line using a JavaScript source file. Be sure to include the LANGUAGE attribute in the <SCRIPT> tags. Include a <HEAD> section with a <TITLE>; use *Tutorial 1 Exercise 7* for the title text. Add an HTML comment with your name and the date. Add the same comment information to the embedded JavaScript and the JavaScript source file, using JavaScript comments. Hide the JavaScript code from incompatible browsers by using HTML comment tags, and create a <NOSCRIPT> section that says *Your browser does not support JavaScript or JavaScript is disabled.* Save the file as TwoScripts.html in the Tutorial.01 folder on your Data Disk. An example of how your document should look appears in Figure 1-25.

Figure 1-25: Tutorial 1 Exercise 7

8. Create an HTML document that prints the names of the continents. Create the document header using an HTML tag. Create the numbers in each line using standard HTML tags, but create the continent names using embedded JavaScript. (You will need to use multiple JavaScript sections.) Be sure to include the LANGUAGE attribute in the <SCRIPT> tags. Include a <HEAD> section with a <TITLE>; use *Tutorial 1 Exercise 8* for the title text. Add an HTML comment with your name and the date. Add the same information to the first embedded JavaScript section, using JavaScript comments. Hide the JavaScript code from incompatible browsers by using HTML comment tags, and create a <NOSCRIPT> section that says *Your browser does not support JavaScript or JavaScript is disabled*. Save the file as Continents.html in the Tutorial.01 folder on your Data Disk. Your HTML document should look similar to Figure 1-26.

The Continents

1. Africa
2. Antarctica
3. Asia
4. Australia
5. Europe
6. North America
7. South America

Figure 1-26: Tutorial 1 Exercise 8

9. Create an HTML document that prints the preamble to the Constitution. Build the paragraph and its formatting using a combination of JavaScript code and HTML tags. Be sure to include the LANGUAGE attribute in the <SCRIPT> tags. Include a <HEAD> section with a <TITLE>; use *Tutorial 1 Exercise 9* for the title text. Add an HTML comment with your name and the date. Add the same information to the first JavaScript section, using JavaScript comments. Hide the JavaScript code from incompatible browsers by using HTML comment tags, and create a <NOSCRIPT> section that says *Your browser does not support JavaScript or JavaScript is disabled*. Save the file as Preamble.html in the Tutorial.01 folder on your Data Disk. Your HTML document should resemble the sample document in Figure 1-27.

The Preamble of the Constitution

*We, **the people of the United States**, in order to form a more perfect **Union**, establish justice, insure <u>domestic tranquility</u>, provide for the <u>common defense</u>, promote the <u>general welfare</u>, and secure the blessings of liberty to ourselves and our posterity, do ordain and establish this **Constitution** for the **United States of America.***

Figure 1-27: Tutorial 1 Exercise 9

TUTORIAL 2

Variables, Functions, Objects, and Events

case▶ Image maps are very popular features on Web sites. They consist of an image that is divided into regions, and each region is associated with a URL. You can open the URL associated with each region by clicking the region. You can use JavaScript code to perform various tasks when a user's mouse passes over or moves off a region in an image map.

One of WebAdventure's clients, a car rental agency, wants an image map to be the centerpiece of its home page. They want to let their customers know that they can use the Web site to find the closest location for car pick-up and drop-off anywhere in North America. Your task is to create an image map that displays the name of a country and changes the color of the country when the mouse passes over it.

Previewing the NorthAmericaImageMap.html File

In this tutorial, you will create an HTML document named NorthAmericaImage Map.html that uses JavaScript to display the name of each North American country and change the country's color when a mouse passes over it.

To preview the NorthAmericaImageMap.html file:

1 In your Web browser, open the **NorthAmericaImageMap.html** file from the Tutorial.02 folder on your Data Disk. An image of North America appears. Figure 2-1 shows an example of the program in a Web browser.

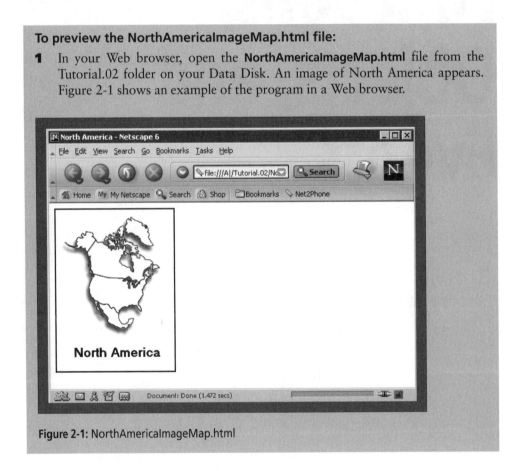

Figure 2-1: NorthAmericaImageMap.html

2 Move your mouse over each of the countries on the map. As your mouse enters a country, the country is highlighted and the text at the bottom of the map changes to display the country name. When you move your mouse off a highlighted country, the original image of North America reappears.

3 When you are finished, close your browser window.

4 Next, open the **NorthAmericaImageMap.html** file in your text editor or HTML editor and examine the code. Notice the statements that start with "function". The functions contain the code that changes the highlighted country on the image map. The image map itself is created with the <IMG>, <MAP>, and <AREA> tags in the body section.

5 Close your text editor or HTML editor when you are finished examining the code.

In this lesson you will learn:

■ How to declare and use variables

■ How to define and call functions

■ About built-in JavaScript functions

■ How to use JavaScript objects

■ How to use object inheritance and prototypes

■ How to use object methods

■ About built-in JavaScript objects

■ About variable scope

Working with Variables, Functions, and Objects

Variables

One of the most important aspects of programming is the ability to store and manipulate values in computer memory locations. The values stored in computer memory locations are called **variables**. Data contained in a specific variable often change. For example, you may have a program that creates a variable with the current time. Each time the program runs, the time is different, so the value *varies*. Another example is a payroll program that assigns employee names to a variable named **employeeName**. The memory location referenced by the variable **employeeName** might contain different values (a different value for every employee of the company) at different times.

In JavaScript, you use the reserved keyword var to create variables. **Reserved words**, or **keywords**, are part of the JavaScript language syntax. Reserved words cannot be used for variable names. Figure 2-2 lists the JavaScript reserved words.

abstract	char	delete	extends
boolean	class	do	false
break	const	double	final
byte	continue	else	finally
case	debugger	enum	float
catch	default	export	for

Figure 2-2: JavaScript reserved words

function	long	short	true
goto	native	static	try
if	new	super	typeof
implements	null	switch	var
import	package	synchronized	void
in	private	this	volatile
instanceof	protected	throw	while
int	public	throws	with
interface	return	transient	

Figure 2-2: JavaScript reserved words (continued)

Some reserved words in Figure 2-2 are not currently used, but are reserved for future use.

When you use the reserved word **var** to create a variable, you **declare** the variable. You can assign a value to a variable at declaration using the syntax **var** *variable_name* = **value;**. The equal sign in a variable declaration assigns a value to the variable. This use is different from the standard use of the equal sign in an algebraic formula.

The value you assign a variable can be a literal string or a numeric value. For example, the statement **var myVariable = "Hello";** assigns the literal string Hello to the variable myVariable. The statement **var myVariable = 100;** assigns the numeric value 100 to the variable myVariable.

You are not required to use the var keyword to declare a variable. However, omission of the var keyword can change where a variable can be used in a program. Regardless of where in your program you intend to use a variable, it is good programming practice to use the var keyword when declaring a variable.

You can declare multiple variables in the same statement using a single **var** keyword followed by a series of variable names and assigned values separated by commas. For example, the following statement creates several variables using a single **var** keyword:

```
var firstVar = "text", secondVar = 100, thirdVar = 2.5;
```

Notice in the preceding example that each variable is assigned a value. Although you can assign a value when a variable is declared, you are not required to do so. Your program may assign the value later, or you may use a variable to store user input. When you declare a variable without assigning it a value, you must use the **var** keyword.

Regardless of whether you assign a value to a variable when it is declared, you change the variable's value at any point in a program by using a statement that includes the variable's name, followed by an equal sign, followed by the value you want to assign to the variable. The following code declares a variable named myDog, assigns it an initial value of *Golden Retriever*, and prints it using the document.writeln() function. The third statement changes the value of the myDog variable to *Irish Setter*, and the fourth statement prints the new value. The myDog variable is declared with the **var** keyword only once.

```
var myDog = "Golden Retriever";
document.writeln(myDog);
myDog = "Irish Setter";
document.writeln(myDog);
```

The name you assign to a variable is an identifier. Identifiers must begin with an uppercase or lowercase ASCII letter, dollar sign ($), or underscore (_). You can use numbers in an identifier, but not as the first character.

There are some rules and conventions you need to follow when naming a variable. Reserved words cannot be used for variable names, and you cannot use spaces within a variable name. Common practice is to use an underscore (_) character to separate individual words within a variable name, as in my_variable_name. Another common practice is to use a lowercase letter for the first letter of the first word in a variable name, with subsequent words starting with an initial cap, as in myVariableName. Figure 2-3 lists examples of some legal variable names, and Figure 2-4 lists examples of some illegal variable names.

```
my_variable

$my_variable

_my_variable

my_variable_example

myVariableExample
```

Figure 2-3: Examples of legal variable names

```
%my_variable

1my_variable

#my_variable

@my_variable

~my_variable

+my_variable
```

Figure 2-4: Examples of illegal variable names

 tip

Some versions of Web browsers, including Navigator 2.02 and Internet Explorer 3.02, do not recognize the dollar sign in variable names. If you want your JavaScript programs to operate with older Web browsers, avoid using the dollar sign in variable names.

Variable names, like other JavaScript code, are case-sensitive. Therefore, the variable name myVariable contains different values than variables named myvariable, MyVariable, or MYVARIABLE. If you receive an error when running a JavaScript program, be sure that you are using the correct case when referring to any variables you have declared.

Defining Custom Functions

Individual statements used in a computer program are often grouped into logical units called procedures. In JavaScript programming, procedures are called functions. A **function** allows you to treat a related group of JavaScript statements as a single unit. Functions, like all JavaScript code, must exist within the <SCRIPT>...</SCRIPT> tag pair. Before you can use a function in a JavaScript program, you must first create, or define, it. The lines that compose a function within an HTML document are called the **function definition**. The syntax for defining a function is:

```
function name_of_function(parameters) {
statements;
}
```

A function definition consists of three parts:

- The reserved word `function` followed by the function name. The reserved word `function` notifies the JavaScript interpreter that the code that follows is a function. As with variables, the name you assign to a function is called an identifier. The same rules and conventions that apply to variable names apply to function names.
- Any parameters required by the function, contained within parentheses following the function name
- The function statements, enclosed in curly braces { }

Parameters are placed within the parentheses that follow a function name. A **parameter** is a variable that will be used within a function. For example, you may write a function named calculate_square_root() that calculates the square root of a number contained in a variable named number. The function name would be written as calculate_square_root(number). Functions can contain multiple parameters separated by commas. To add three separate number arguments to the calculate_square_root() function, you write the function name as calculate_square_root(number1, number2, number3).

••

Functions are not required to contain parameters. Many functions only perform a task and do not require external data. For example, you may have a function that displays the same message each time a user visits your Web site; this type of function only needs to be executed and does not require any other information.

••

Following the parentheses containing function parameters is a set of curly braces containing the function statements. Function statements must be contained within the function braces. Figure 2-5 displays an example of a function that prints the names of multiple companies.

```
function print_company_name(company1, company2, company3) {

    document.writeln(company1);

    document.writeln(company2);

    document.writeln(company3);

}
```

Figure 2-5: Function that prints the name of multiple companies

Notice how the function in Figure 2-5 is structured. The opening curly brace is on the same line as the function name, and the closing curly brace is on its own line following the function statements. Each statement between the curly braces is indented one-half inch. This structure is the preferred format among many JavaScript programmers. However, for simple functions it is sometimes easier to include the function name, curly braces, and statements on the same line. Recall that JavaScript ignores line breaks, spaces, and tabs. The only syntax requirement for spacing in JavaScript is that a semicolon separate statements on the same line.

Calling Functions

A function definition does not execute automatically. Creating a function definition only names the function, specifies its parameters, and organizes the statements it will execute. To execute a function, you must invoke, or **call**, it from elsewhere in your program. To call a function, you create a statement that includes the function name followed by parentheses containing any variables or values to be assigned to the function arguments. Sending arguments (variables or values) to the parameters of a called function is called **passing arguments**. The parameter takes on the value of the arguments that are passed.

Always create functions within the <HEAD> section, and place calls to a function within the <BODY> section. The <HEAD> section of an HTML document is always rendered before the <BODY> section. Placing functions in the <HEAD> section and function calls in the <BODY> section ensures that functions will be created before they are actually called. If your program does attempt to call a function before it has been created, you will receive an error. Figure 2-6 shows a JavaScript program that prints the name of a company. Figure 2-7 shows the output. Notice that the function is defined in the <HEAD> section of the HTML document and is called from the <BODY> section.

```
<HTML>

<HEAD>

<TITLE>Print Company Name Function</TITLE>

<SCRIPT LANGUAGE="JavaScript">

<!-- HIDE FROM INCOMPATIBLE BROWSERS

function print_company_name(company_name) {

      document.writeln(company_name);

}

// STOP HIDING FROM INCOMPATIBLE BROWSERS -->

</SCRIPT>

</HEAD>

<BODY>

<SCRIPT LANGUAGE="JavaScript">

<!-- HIDE FROM INCOMPATIBLE BROWSERS

print_company_name("My Company");

// STOP HIDING FROM INCOMPATIBLE BROWSERS -->

</SCRIPT>

</BODY>

</HTML>
```

Figure 2-6: JavaScript function being called from the <BODY> section

Figure 2-7: Output of the JavaScript function being called from the <BODY> section

In the program in Figure 2-6, the statement that calls the function passes the literal string *My Company* to the function. When the print_company_name() function receives the literal string, it assigns it to the company_name variable.

A JavaScript program is composed of all the <SCRIPT> sections within an HTML document; each individual <SCRIPT> section is not necessarily its own individual JavaScript program (although it could be if there are no other <SCRIPT> sections in the HTML document).

In many instances, you may want one function to receive a value from another function that you can then use in other code. For instance, if you have a function that performs a calculation on a number that is passed to it, you would want to receive the result of the calculation. Consider a function that calculates the average of a series of numbers that you pass to it—the function would be useless if you never saw the result. To return a value to a calling statement, you assign the calling statement to a variable. The following statement calls a function named average_numbers() and assigns any return value to a variable named returnValue. The statement also passes three literal values to the function.

```
var returnValue = average_numbers(1, 2, 3);
```

To actually return a value to a returnValue variable, you must include the return statement within the average_numbers() function. The following code contains the average_numbers() function, which calculates the average of three numbers and returns the value contained in the result variable to the calling statement using the return statement:

```
function average_numbers(a, b, c) {
    var sum_of_numbers = a + b + c;
    var result = sum_of_numbers / 3;
    return result;
}
```

You are not required to return a value from a function.

You will learn more about performing calculations in Tutorial 3.

The variable name that is returned from a function and the variable name that receives the returned value can be the same. For instance, in the preceding examples, the variable name in the `return` statement in the function and the variable name in the calling statement could both be returnValue. Also, when you pass variables as arguments to a function, the passed variables and the parameter names within the function itself can also be the same. If you pass variables to the average_numbers() function, instead of literal values you can use the statement `average_numbers(a, b, c);`, even though the argument names within the function itself are *a*, *b*, and *c*. However, most programmers usually use unique names to identify specific variables in their code.

Using unique names to identify specific variables makes it easier to understand a program's logic and assists in the debugging process.

You do not need to receive return values from all functions. For example, you would not need to receive a return value from a function that changes the background color of an HTML document or performs some other task that does not create or return a useful value. If you do not need to receive a return value from a function, then you are not required to assign the calling statement to a variable. For instance, if you want to call the average_numbers() function to calculate the average of the three literal values 2, 3, and 4, but do not require a return value, you type `average_numbers(2, 3, 4);` without assigning the statement to the returnValue variable.

▶ **tip**

When a function performs a calculation such as an average, you normally want to receive a return value.

Next you will create a JavaScript program that contains two functions. The first function will print a message when it is called, and the second function will return a value that is printed after the calling statement.

To create a JavaScript program that contains two functions:

1   Create a new document in your text editor or HTML editor.

2   Type the opening <HTML> and <HEAD> tags, and also type the <TITLE>...</TITLE> tag pair, as follows:

```
<HTML>
<HEAD>
<TITLE>Two Functions Program</TITLE>
```

3 Type the opening <SCRIPT> tag and HTML comments to hide the code from incompatible browsers:

```
<SCRIPT LANGUAGE="JavaScript">
<!-- HIDE FROM INCOMPATIBLE BROWSERS
```

4 Type the first function, which writes a message to the screen using an argument that is passed from the calling statement:

```
function print_message(first_message) {
    document.writeln(first_message);
}
```

5 Type the second function that displays the second message. The only purpose of this function is to return the literal string *This message was returned from a function* to the calling statement.

```
function return_message(second_message) {
    return "This message was returned from a function";
}
```

6 Type the following lines to close the <SCRIPT> section:

```
// STOP HIDING FROM INCOMPATIBLE BROWSERS -->
</SCRIPT>
```

7 Add </HEAD> to close the <HEAD>...</HEAD> tag pair.

8 Add the following code to begin the body of the HTML document and to create a preformatted text container:

```
<BODY>
<PRE>
```

9 Add the opening statements for the JavaScript section that calls the functions in the <HEAD> section:

```
<SCRIPT LANGUAGE="JavaScript">
<!-- HIDE FROM INCOMPATIBLE BROWSERS
```

10 Type the following two statements to call the functions in the <HEAD> section. The first statement sends the text string *This text was printed from a function* and does not receive a return value. The second statement assigns the function call to a variable named return_value, but does not send any arguments to the function.

```
print_message("This text was printed from a function");
var return_value = return_message();
```

11 Write the value of the return_value variable to the screen by adding `document.writeln(return_value);`.

12 Add the following code to end the HTML comments and close the <SCRIPT> tag pair:

```
// STOP HIDING FROM INCOMPATIBLE BROWSERS -->
</SCRIPT>
```

13 Close the <PRE>, <BODY>, and <HTML> tags:

```
</PRE>
</BODY>
</HTML>
```

14 Save the file as **TwoFunctionsProgram.html** in the **Tutorial.02** folder on your Data Disk. Open the **TwoFunctionsProgram.html** file in your Web browser. Figure 2-8 shows how the TwoFunctionsProgram.html file looks in a Web browser.

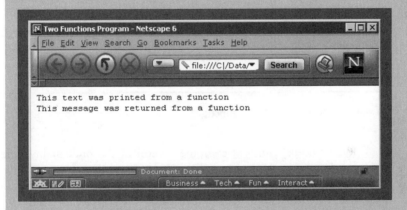

Figure 2-8: TwoFunctionsProgram.html

help

If you receive error messages, make sure that all of your JavaScript code is in the correct case—remember that JavaScript is case-sensitive. Also check to see that you have entered all of the opening and closing HTML tags.

15 Close the Web browser window and the text editor.

Built-In JavaScript Functions

JavaScript includes the built-in functions listed in Figure 2-9.

Function	Description
eval()	Evaluates expressions contained within strings
isFinite()	Determines whether a number is finite
isNaN()	Determines whether a value is the special value NaN (Not a Number)
parseInt()	Converts string literals to integers
parseFloat()	Converts string literals to floating-point numbers
encodeURI()	Encodes a text string into a valid URI
encodeURIComponent()	Encodes a text string into a valid URI component
decodeURI()	Decodes text strings encoded with encodeURI()
decodeURIComponent()	Decodes text strings encoded with encodeURIComponent()

Figure 2-9: **Built-in JavaScript functions**

In this book, you will examine several of the built-in JavaScript functions as you need them, so they will not be discussed now. For now, the only thing you need to understand about built-in JavaScript functions is that you call them in the exact same way as you call a custom method. For example, the following code calls the isNaN() function to determine whether the socialSecurityNumber variable is not a number. Because the Social Security number assigned to the socialSecurityNumber variable contains dashes, it is not a true number. Therefore, the isNaN() function returns a value of true to the checkVar variable.

```
var socialSecurityNumber = "054-74-7984";
var checkVar = isNaN(socialSecurityNumber);
document.write(checkVar);
```

Understanding JavaScript Objects

Traditional object-oriented programming languages, such as C++ and Java, create objects through which you access variables and functions. Objects are based on classes. In object-oriented programming, variables, functions, and statements are contained in a structure known as a **class. Objects** are instances of classes and inherit all the class's variables, functions, and statements; you do not access a class directly. Objects can also be based on other objects. Objects based on another class or object are said to *descend* from the object. Similarly, a class or object from which an object descends is called an ancestor class or object. When you base an object on, or declare and object from, a class or other object, you are said to be **instantiating** an object.

JavaScript is not truly object-oriented because you cannot create real classes. Instead, you base new JavaScript objects on custom functions called constructor functions. You can also base objects in your programs on several built-in JavaScript objects. For these reasons, JavaScript is said to be an object-based programming language. First, you will examine how you can build your own custom JavaScript objects, and then you will learn about JavaScript built-in objects.

Custom JavaScript Objects

Custom JavaScript objects are based on functions called constructor functions. A function that is used as the basis for an object is called an object definition, or a **constructor function.** When you create a new object from a constructor function, you are said to be instantiating a new object or extending the old object. As with the inheritance found in traditional class-based objects, JavaScript objects inherit all the variables and statements of the constructor function on which they are based. Any JavaScript function can serve as a constructor.

A constructor function is more like a template on which an object is based than a class from which an object is instantiated.

Constructor functions have two types of elements: properties and methods. A **property** is a variable within a constructor function. These variables, or properties, are considered to be the data of any objects that are created from the constructor function. A **method** is a function—whether a built-in JavaScript function or a function you create—that is called from within an object.

Properties are also called fields.

The following code is a constructor function named Animal and contains three properties: animal_type, animal_sound, and animal_transport_mode:

```
function Animal(type, sound, transport_mode) {
    this.animal_type = type; // dog, cat, etc.
    this.animal_sound = sound;    // woof, meow, etc.
    this.animal_transport_mode = transport_mode;
        // walk/run, fly, swim
}
```

Class names in traditional object-oriented programming languages usually begin with an uppercase letter. Since constructor functions are the equivalent of classes, it is customary to begin the name of constructor functions with an uppercase letter to differentiate constructor functions in your code from regular functions.

Notice the `this` keyword in the preceding example. The **this** keyword refers to the current object that called the constructor function. The three statements assign the three arguments, type, sound, and transport_mode, to the animal_type, animal_sound, and animal_transport_mode properties (which are variables) of whichever object (`this`) is instantiated from the constructor function. The use of the `this` reference is one of the primary differences between standard functions and constructor functions. Standard functions do not include a `this` reference, because they are not used as the basis of objects.

The `this` reference is also used with the <FORM> tag to refer to a form that contains an object. You will learn about forms in Tutorial 6.

Objects are created from constructor functions using the **new** keyword. The following code creates a new object named pet from the animal constructor function and passes the appropriate arguments, which are assigned to the object properties:

```
pet = new Animal("dog", "woof", "walk/run");
```

The pet object now has three properties: type, sound, and transport_mode. To access an object property, you add a period and the property name to the object. For example, to access the sound property of the pet object you type pet.sound. Unlike methods, such as document.write(), a property is not followed by parentheses. If you add parentheses to a property, JavaScript will attempt to locate a method (or function) by that name. For example, if you wrote pet.sound() instead of pet.sound, JavaScript assumes you are running the sound() method of the pet object instead of accessing the sound property of the pet object.

Built-In JavaScript Objects

The JavaScript language includes the 11 built-in objects listed in Figure 2-10. Each object contains various methods and properties for performing a particular type of task. The Math object, for instance, contains methods and properties for performing mathematical calculations in your programs. In comparison, the String object contains methods and properties for manipulating text strings.

Object	Description
Array	Creates new array objects
Boolean	Creates new Boolean objects
Date	Retrieves and manipulates dates and times
Error	Returns run-time error information
Function	Creates new function objects
Global	Represents the JavaScript built-in methods
Math	Contains methods and properties for performing mathematical calculations
Number	Contains methods and properties for manipulating numbers
Object	Provides common functionality to all built-in JavaScript objects
RegExp	Contains properties for finding and replacing in text strings
String	Contains methods and properties for manipulating text strings

Figure 2-10: Built-in JavaScript objects

Several of the built-in JavaScript objects will be discussed when they are used during the course of this book, so they will not be examined in detail right now. You can use some of the built-in JavaScript objects directly in your code, while other objects require you to instantiate a new object. For example, you use the Math object directly in your programs without instantiating a new object. The following example shows how you can use the Math object PI property and sqrt() method (for calculating a square root) in a JavaScript program:

```
<SCRIPT LANGUAGE="JAVASCRIPT">
// The following statement prints 3.141592653589793
document.write("The value of PI is " + Math.PI);
// The following statement prints 12
document.write(
"The square root of 144 is " + Math.sqrt(144));
</SCRIPT>
```

In comparison with the Math object, the Array object creates a special type of variable called an **array** that contains a set of data instead of a single piece of information. Arrays are represented in JavaScript by the Array object, which contains a constructor function named Array(). You create new arrays in your code using the new keyword and the Array() constructor function, in the same manner that you instantiate objects from your own custom constructor functions. The syntax for instantiating a new array using the Array() constructor function is as follows:

```
variableName = new Array(number of elements);
```

For now, do not worry about what an array is or how it is used since you will study them in Tutorial 3. Simply understand that some built-in JavaScript objects can be used directly in your code, while others require that you instantiate a new object.

Custom Object Inheritance and Prototypes

Objects inherit the properties and methods of the constructor functions from which they are instantiated. When you instantiate a new object named cat based on the Animal constructor function, the new object includes the animal_type, animal_sound, and animal_transport_mode properties. After instantiating a new object, you can assign additional properties to the object, using a period. The following code creates a new object named cat based on the Animal constructor function, then assigns to the cat object a new property named size.

```
cat = new Animal("feline", "meow", "walk/run");
cat.size = "fat";
```

Constructor functions do not require parameters, such as the type, sound, and transport_mode parameters in the Animal constructor function. You are also not required to pass arguments to a constructor function when you instantiate an object. For instance, you can instantiate the cat object using the statement cat = new Animal();, then assign the property values later. However, if you attempt to use a property that does not have an assigned value, you will receive a special value of *undefined*. If you add the size property to the cat object, then attempt to print the property using the statement document.write(cat.size); without assigning the size property a value, the value *undefined* will print instead.

When you add a new property to an object that has been extended from a constructor function, the new property is only available to that specific object; the property is not available to the constructor function or to any other objects that were extended from the same constructor function. However, if you use the prototype property, any new properties you create will also be available to the constructor function and any objects that extend it. The **prototype property** is a built-in property that specifies the constructor from which an object was extended. The following code adds the size property, which is a prototype of the cat object, to the

Animal constructor function. By using a prototype property, all objects that extend the Animal constructor function will also have access to the size property.

```
cat = new Animal("feline", "meow", "walk/run");
Animal.prototype.size = "fat";
```

In this case, all Animal objects would have a size of *fat*. Because not all animals can be described as fat, you can assign an empty value to the size property using the statement `Animal.prototype.size = "";`. You can then assign the size property to each individual object. The statement to assign a size property to the cat object would be `cat.size = "fat";`.

Object definitions can extend other object definitions. Consider the Animal constructor function that contains three generic properties that can be applied to all animals. You may need to create additional object definitions that extend Animal and that contain properties specific to certain types of animals. To extend one object definition from another object definition, you use the prototype property, followed by the **new** keyword and the name of the constructor function for the object definition to extend. Figure 2-11 shows two additional object definitions, WildAnimal and FarmAnimal, both of which extend Animal, and that include properties specific to each animal type.

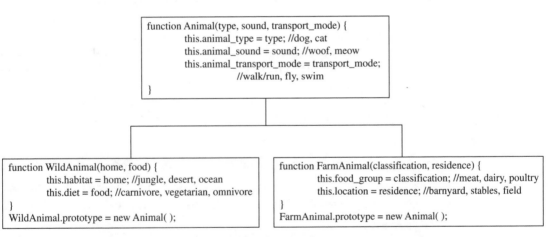

Figure 2-11: Two object definitions extending another object definition

Objects instantiated from either WildAnimal or FarmAnimal will include the three properties from the Animal constructor function, along with the properties specific to each individual object. For example, the following code instantiates an object from FarmAnimal and assigns properties to the object:

```
chicken = new FarmAnimal();
// Animal object definition
chicken.animal_type = "chicken";
// Animal object definition
chicken.animal_sound = "cluck";
// Animal object definition
chicken.animal_transport_mode = "walk/fly";
// FarmAnimal object definition
chicken.location = "barnyard";
// FarmAnimal object definition
chicken.food_group = "poultry"
// FarmAnimal object definition
```

▶ **tip**

••

Some object-oriented programming languages allow objects to inherit from more than one object definition. JavaScript, however, allows objects to inherit from only a single object definition.

••

Next you will create a JavaScript program that demonstrates objects and inheritance. The program will contain a Company object definition. The Company object definition contains several properties that apply to all departments within the company. You will also create two object definitions, Sales and Production, which extend Company. The Sales and Production object definitions include properties unique to each department. After you create the object definitions, you will create instances of each object and print the associated properties.

To create a JavaScript program that demonstrates objects and inheritance:

1 Start your text editor or HTML editor, if necessary, and create a new document.

2 Type the opening <HTML>, <HEAD>, and <TITLE> tags:

```
<HTML>
<HEAD>
<TITLE>Company Objects Program</TITLE>
```

3 Type the opening <SCRIPT> tag and HTML comments to hide the code from incompatible browsers:

```
<SCRIPT LANGUAGE="JavaScript">
<!-- HIDE FROM INCOMPATIBLE BROWSERS
```

4 Type the first constructor function, which creates the properties that apply to all departments within the company:

```
function Company() {
    this.company_name = "WebAdventure, Inc.";
    this.company_products = "Internet services";
}
```

5 Next create the constructor function for the Sales department, which extends the Company object definition:

```
function Sales() {
    this.territory = "North America";
    this.sales_reps = "50";
}
Sales.prototype = new Company();
```

6 Now create the constructor function for the Production department, which also extends the Company object definition:

```
function Production() {
this.facilities =
"New York, Chicago, and Los Angeles";
this.personnel = "100";
}
Production.prototype = new Company();
```

7 Type the following lines to close the <SCRIPT> and <HEAD> sections.

```
// STOP HIDING FROM INCOMPATIBLE BROWSERS -->
</SCRIPT>
</HEAD>
```

8 Add the following code to begin the body of the HTML document and to create a preformatted text container.

```
<BODY>
<PRE>
```

9 Add the opening statements for the JavaScript section that calls the constructor functions in the <HEAD> section:

```
<SCRIPT LANGUAGE="JavaScript">
<!-- HIDE FROM INCOMPATIBLE BROWSERS
```

10 Add the following code to instantiate a new Sales object and write its properties to the screen. Notice that the document.write() and document.writeln() methods use a plus sign (+) to combine literal strings with properties.

```
sales_object = new Sales();
document.writeln(sales_object.company_name);
document.writeln("Producer of " +
     sales_object.company_products);
document.write(sales_object.sales_reps + " sales reps");
document.writeln(" in " + sales_object.territory);
```

 tip

••

In Tutorial 3, you will learn more about operations that you can perform in JavaScript.

••

11 Next add the following code to instantiate a new Production object and write its properties to the screen.

```
production_object = new Production();
document.write(production_object.company_name);
document.writeln(" has " + production_object.personnel +
     " production personnel");
document.write("with facilities in " +
     production_object.facilities);
```

12 Add the following lines to close the HTML comments and <SCRIPT> tag:

```
// STOP HIDING FROM INCOMPATIBLE BROWSERS -->
</SCRIPT>
```

13 Close the <PRE>, <BODY>, and <HTML> tags:

```
</PRE>
</BODY>
</HTML>
```

14 Save the file as **CompanyObjects.html** in the **Tutorial.02** folder on your Data Disk, then open it in your Web browser. Figure 2-12 shows the CompanyObjects.html file as it appears in a Web browser.

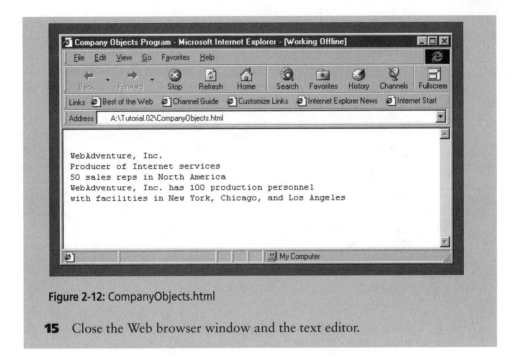

Figure 2-12: CompanyObjects.html

15 Close the Web browser window and the text editor.

Custom Object Methods

Object methods are functions associated with a particular object. When you create a function that will be used as an object method, you use the `this` reference in the same manner as you do when creating a constructor function. Consider the Animal object definition. To create a method that prints the three object properties (animal_type, animal_sound, animal_transport_mode), you write a function as follows:

```
function displayAnimalProperties() {
    document.write(this.animal_type + "<BR>");
    document.write(this.animal_sound + "<BR>");
    document.write(this.animal_transport_mode + "<BR>");
}
```

....

Because the displayAnimalProperties() method is not a constructor function, the first letter of the method name is not capitalized.

....

Recall that you must place the writeln() method within a <PRE>...</PRE> tag pair for it to work. There may be times, however, when it is easier not to include the <PRE>...</PRE> tag pair. Notice that the code in the preceding example does not use a <PRE>...</PRE> tag pair. Instead, each document.write() method contains a literal string that includes a <BR> tag. Using the <BR> tag as a literal value inside the <SCRIPT>...</SCRIPT> tag pair is an alternative to using the <PRE>...</PRE> tag pairs required for document.writeln() methods.

After a method is created, it must be added to the constructor function, using the syntax `this.methodName = functionName;`. The *methodName* following the `this` reference is the name that is being assigned to the function within the object. Be sure not to include the parentheses following the function name, as you would when calling a function in JavaScript. The statement `this.methodName = functionName();` is incorrect, because it includes parentheses. To add the displayAnimalProperties() method to the Animal function definition, you include the statement `this.displayAnimalProperties = displayAnimalProperties;` within the function definition braces.

After you instantiate an object based on an object definition, you call the object methods by adding a period and the method name to the object name, followed by parentheses containing any arguments that need to be passed to the method. The syntax for calling an object method is `objectNAME.METHODname(arguments);`. The following statements instantiate a new object based on the Animal object definition and call the object's displayAnimalProperties() method.

```
guppy = new Animal("fish", "blub", "swim");
guppy.displayAnimalProperties();
```

Next you will modify the CompanyObjects program so that the document.write() and document.writeln() functions for the Sales and Production objects are contained within their own methods.

To modify the CompanyObjects program so that the document.write() and document.writeln() functions for the Sales and Production objects are contained within their own methods:

1 Open the **CompanyObjects.html** file in your text editor or HTML editor, then immediately save it as **CompanyObjectsWithMethods.html**.

2 Just before the statement that reads // STOP HIDING FROM INCOMPATIBLE BROWSERS --> in the <SCRIPT> section between the <HEAD>...</HEAD> tag pair, add the following function that will be used as a method of the Sales object. Notice that the function uses <BR> tags to add line breaks, instead of using document.writeln() functions.

```
function displaySalesInfo() {
    document.write(this.company_name + "<BR>");
    document.write(
        "Producer of " + this.company_products + "<BR>");
    document.write(
        "with" + this.sales_reps + "sales reps");
    document.write(" in " + this.territory + "<BR>");
}
```

3 Immediately after the displaySalesInfo() function, add the following displayProductionInfo() function:

```
function displayProductionInfo() {
    document.write(this.company_name);
    document.write(" has " + this.personnel + "
        production personnel"+ "<BR>");
    document.write("with facilities in " +
        this.facilities);
}
```

4 Add the statement `this.displaySalesInfo = displaySalesInfo;` just before the closing brace for the Sales() function definition.

5 Add the statement `this.displayProductionInfo = display ProductionInfo;` just before the closing brace for the Production() function definition.

6 Delete the seven document.write() and document.writeln() methods located in the <SCRIPT> section within the <BODY>...</BODY> tag pair. The <SCRIPT> section should now contain only the two lines that instantiate the sales_object and production_object.

7 Insert a line after the statement that instantiates the sales_object and add the statement `sales_object.displaySalesInfo();`.

8 Insert a line after the statement that instantiates the production_object and add the statement `production_object.displayProductionInfo();`.

9 Save the **CompanyObjectsWithMethods.html** file, then open it in your Web browser. The file should appear the same as Figure 2-12.

10 Close the Web browser window and your text or HTML editor.

Variable Scope

When you use a variable in a Java Script program, particularly a complex JavaScript program, you need to be aware of the variable's scope. **Variable scope** refers to where in your program a declared variable can be used. A variable's scope can be either global or local. A **global variable** is one that is declared outside a function and is available to all parts of your program. A **local variable** is declared inside a function and is only available within the function in which it is declared. Local variables cease to exist when the function ends. If you attempt to use a local variable outside the function in which it is declared, you will receive an error message.

tip

· ·

The parameters within the parentheses of a function declaration are considered to be local variables.

· ·

You must use the var keyword when you declare a local variable. However, when you declare a global variable, the var keyword is optional. For example, you can write the statement var myVariable = "This is a variable."; as myVariable = "This is a variable.";. However, it is considered good programming technique to always use the var keyword when declaring variables.

The following code includes a global variable and a function containing a local variable. Both the global variable and the function are contained in the <SCRIPT>...</SCRIPT> tag pair in the <HEAD> section. When the function is called from the <BODY> section, the global variable and the local variable print successfully from within the function. After the call to the function, the global variable again prints successfully from the <BODY> section. However, when the program tries to print the local variable from the <BODY> section, an error message is generated because the local variable ceases to exist when the function ends.

```
<HTML>
<HEAD>
<TITLE>Variable Scope</TITLE>
<SCRIPT LANGUAGE="JavaScript">
<!--HIDE FROM INCOMPATIBLE BROWSERS
var firstGlobalVariable = "First global variable";
function scopeExample() {
    secondGlobalVariable = "Second global variable";
    var localVariable = "Local variable";
    document.writeln(firstGlobalVariable);
// prints successfully
    document.writeln(secondGlobalVariable);
// prints successfully
    document.writeln(localVariable);
// prints successfully
}
// STOP HIDING FROM INCOMPATIBLE BROWSERS -->
</SCRIPT>
</HEAD>
<BODY>
<PRE>
<SCRIPT LANGUAGE="JavaScript">
<!--HIDE FROM INCOMPATIBLE BROWSERS
scopeExample();
document.writeln(firstGlobalVariable);
// prints successfully
document.writeln(secondGlobalVariable);
// prints successfully
document.writeln(localVariable);
```

```
// error message
// STOP HIDING FROM INCOMPATIBLE BROWSERS -->
</SCRIPT>
</PRE>
</BODY>
</HTML>
```

When a program contains a global variable and a local variable with the same name, the local variable takes precedence when its function is called. However, the value assigned to a local variable of the same name is not assigned to a global variable of the same name. In the following code, the global variable showDog is assigned a value of Golden Retriever before the function that contains a local variable of the same name is called. Once the function is called, the local showDog variable is assigned a value of Irish Setter. After the function ends, Golden Retriever is still the value of the global showDog variable.

```
var showDog = "Golden Retriever";
function duplicateVariableNames() {
     var showDog = "Irish Setter";
}
duplicateVariableNames();
document.writeln(showDog);
// value printed is Golden Retriever
```

 # SUMMARY

- The values stored in computer memory locations are called variables.

- You use the reserved word var to declare a variable.

- Words that are part of the JavaScript language syntax are called reserved words, or keywords. Reserved words cannot be used for function names or variable names in a JavaScript program.

- When you declare a variable without assigning it a value, the variable will initially contain the value undefined.

- A function allows you to treat a related group of JavaScript statements as a single unit. Functions, like all JavaScript code, must exist between the <SCRIPT>...</SCRIPT> tag pair.

- Before you can use a function in a JavaScript program, you must first create, or define, the function. The statements that compose a function are called the function definition.

- A parameter is a variable that will be used within a function. Arguments are contained in parentheses following the function name.

- To execute a function, you must invoke, or call, it from elsewhere in your program.

- Sending arguments (variables or values) to the parameters of a called function is called passing arguments.

- To return a value to the calling statement, you include the return statement within the called function.

- JavaScript includes various built-in functions that you execute in the same manner that you execute custom functions.

- In object-oriented programming, data, procedures, and other attributes are contained in a structure known as a class.

- Objects are instances of classes and inherit all the class's procedures and data.

- When you base an object on, or declare an object from, a class, you are said to be instantiating an object.

- JavaScript is an object-based programming language.

- A function that is used as the basis for an object is called an object definition, or a constructor function.

- Two types of elements are found within constructor functions: properties and methods. A property is a variable within a constructor function that is considered to be the data of any objects that are created from the constructor function. A method is a function—whether a built-in JavaScript function or a function you create—that is called from within an object.

- The `this` keyword refers to the current object that called the constructor function. Standard functions do not include a `this` reference, since they are not used as the basis of objects.

- The JavaScript language includes 11 built-in objects. Each object contains various methods and properties for performing a particular type of task.

- The prototype property is a built-in property that specifies the constructor from which an object was extended.

- Object definitions can extend other object definitions.

- Object methods are essentially functions associated with a particular object.

- Variable scope refers to where in your program a declared variable can be used. A variable's scope can be either global or local. Global variables are declared outside funtions and are available to all parts of your program. Local variables are declared inside functions and are available only within the functions in which they are declared.

QUESTIONS

1. Reserved words, or _____, are part of the JavaScript language syntax.
   a. variables
   b. functions
   c. keywords
   d. interpreted symbols

2. Which is the correct syntax for declaring a variable and assigning it a string?
   a. `var myVariable = "Hello";`
   b. `var myVariable = Hello;`
   c. `"Hello" = var myVariable;`
   d. `var "Hello" = myVariable;`

3. What is the correct syntax for declaring multiple variables in the same statement?
   a. `multivar intVar = 100, decimalVar = 2.5, textVar = "Hello";`
   b. `var intVar = 100 : decimalVar = 2.5 : textVar = "Hello";`
   c. `var intVar = 100 + decimalVar = 2.5 + textVar = "Hello";`
   d. `var intVar = 100, decimalVar = 2.5, textVar = "Hello";`

4. Which of the following is a legal name for a variable?
   a. %variable_name
   b. 1variable_name
   c. variable_name
   d. +variable_name

5. Identifiers in JavaScript cannot begin with _____.
   a. an uppercase or lowercase ASCII letter
   b. the dollar sign ($)
   c. an underscore character (_)
   d. a number

6. A(n) _____ allows you to treat a related group of JavaScript commands as a single unit.
   a. statement
   b. variable
   c. function
   d. event

7. The lines that compose a function within an HTML document are called the function

   _____.
   a. section
   b. unit
   c. container
   d. definition

8. Which item is *not* part of a function definition?
   a. the reserved word `function` followed by the function name
   b. the opening <SCRIPT>...</SCRIPT> tag pair
   c. any parameters required by the function, contained within parentheses following the function name
   d. the function statements enclosed in braces { }

9. JavaScript reserved words can be used as _____.
   a. function names
   b. variables
   c. both of the above
   d. none of the above

10. A variable that is contained within a function's parentheses is called a _____.
    a. field
    b. routine
    c. method
    d. parameter

11. Function statements are located between which characters?
    a. { }
    b. [ ]
    c. < >
    d. ( )

12. Sending arguments to a called function is called _____ arguments.
    a. generating
    b. passing
    c. routing
    d. submitting

13. You use a _____ statement to return a value to the statement that called a function.
    a. return
    b. result
    c. reply
    d. send

14. Why should JavaScript functions be placed within an HTML document <HEAD> section?
    a. You are not allowed to create functions within the <BODY> section.
    b. Doing so ensures that each function will be created before it is called.
    c. They are not used as often as other types of JavaScript code.
    d. You are less likely to forget to create each function.

15. A function that is used as the basis for an object is called an object definition or a(n) _____.
    a. method
    b. class
    c. constructor function
    d. object variable

16. When you base an object on, or declare an object from, a class or other object, you are said to be _____ an object.
    a. instantiating
    b. developing
    c. summoning
    d. expounding

17. Variables found within a constructor function that are considered to be the data of any objects that are created from the constructor function are called _____.
   a. properties
   b. methods
   c. object files
   d. bits

18. Any functions, whether built-in JavaScript functions or functions you create, are called _____ when they are called from within an object.
   a. procedures
   b. methods
   c. constructors
   d. statements

19. The this keyword refers to _____.
   a. the HTML document
   b. the Web browser window
   c. the currently executing JavaScript statement
   d. the current object that called the constructor function

20. What is the correct syntax for creating an object named my_car from a constructor function named Chevrolet that requires two arguments: color and engine?
   a. `my_car() = new Chevrolet "red", "V8";`
   b. `my_car = new Chevrolet("red", "V8");`
   c. `new Chevrolet("red", "V8") = my_car;`
   d. `my_car("red", "V8") = new Chevrolet;`

21. When you create an object from a constructor function that includes two arguments in the function definition, you _____.
   a. must pass both arguments to the constructor function
   b. must pass at least one of the arguments to the constructor function
   c. are not required to pass the arguments to the constructor function
   d. pass the arguments to the constructor function prior to creating the object

22. The built-in property that specifies the constructor from which an object was extended is called the _____ property.
   a. origination
   b. default
   c. source
   d. prototype

23. What is the correct syntax for adding a new property named sales to a constructor function named company?
   a. `Company.prototype.sales = "";`
   b. `prototype.Company.sales = "";`
   c. `sales.Company.prototype = "";`
   d. `Company.prototype = sales("");`

24. What is the correct syntax for adding an object method named myMethod to a constructor function named myConstructorFunction?
    a. `myConstructorFunction = new myMethod();`
    b. `myMethod = this.myMethod;`
    c. `this.myMethod = myMethod();`
    d. `this.myMethod = myMethod;`

25. A variable that is declared outside a function is called a(n) _____ variable.
    a. local
    b. class
    c. program
    d. global

26. A local variable must be declared _____.
    a. before a function
    b. after a function
    c. within the braces of a function definition
    d. with the local keyword

 # EXERCISES

Save all files you create in the Tutorial.02 folder on your Data Disk.

1. Create an HTML document named StockVariables.html. Create a script section in the document body and declare five variables for holding the names of stocks. Declare each variable on its own line. Following the variable declarations, add statements that assign a value to each of the stock variables. Finally, print each of the variables using writeln() methods, starting with your most preferred stock choice. Also, combine write() methods with the writeln() methods to add descriptive text before the stock name. For example, if your most preferred stock choice is Microsoft, you should print *My first stock choice is Microsoft*.

2. Modify the following code so that the variables are declared and assigned values on a single line using a single **var** keyword. Add output statements to the modified program to be sure that the variables are being declared and assigned values correctly. Save the program as ClassVariables.html.

```
<SCRIPT LANGUAGE="JavaScript">
<!-- HIDE FROM INCOMPATIBLE BROWSERS
var firstClass;
var secondClass;
var thirdClass;
firstClass = "Chemistry";
secondClass = "Algebra";
thirdClass = "Spanish";
// STOP HIDING FROM INCOMPATIBLE BROWSERS -->
</SCRIPT>
```

3. Modify the statements in the following script section so that the variable statements are contained within a function named payrollTaxes(). The function should contain two parameters: federal and state. Instead of assigning literal values to the federalRate and stateRate variables, assign the values that are passed to the federal and state parameters. Print the value of the federalRate and stateRate variables using write() and writeln() methods. Following the payrollTaxes() function definition, call the payrollTaxes() function and pass to it a value of .28 for federal taxes and .05 for state taxes. Save the program as Payroll.html.

```
<HTML>
<HEAD>
<TITLE>Payroll</TITLE>
<SCRIPT LANGUAGE="JavaScript">
<!-- HIDE FROM INCOMPATIBLE BROWSERS
var federalRate = .28;
var stateRate = .05;
// STOP HIDING FROM INCOMPATIBLE BROWSERS -->
</SCRIPT>
</HEAD>
<BODY>
</BODY>
</HTML>
```

4. Modify the getCompanyName() function in the following code so that it returns the company name to another calling function. Also, add statements after the getCompanyName() function definition that call the getCompanyName() function and assign the return value to a variable named retValue. Finally, print the contents of the retValue variable. Save the program as CompanyName.html.

```
<HTML>
<HEAD>
<TITLE>Company Name</TITLE>
<PRE>
<SCRIPT LANGUAGE="JavaScript">
<!-- HIDE FROM INCOMPATIBLE BROWSERS
function getCompanyName() {
   var companyName = "Course Technology";
}
// STOP HIDING FROM INCOMPATIBLE BROWSERS -->
</SCRIPT>
</PRE>
</HEAD>
<BODY>
</BODY>
</HTML>
```

5. The following code includes a RealEstate object definition. A more specific type of real estate object that can descend from the RealEstate object is commercial real estate. Therefore, add a new object definition named Commercial to the program. Include two properties in the Commercial object definition named property_zoning and property_use. Following the Commercial object definition, add a statement that extends the Commercial object from the RealEstate object. Then add statements that instantiate a new Commercial object and assign values to its properties. Finally, print the values assigned to each of the properties of the Commercial object using write() and writeln() methods. Save the program as RealEstate.html.

```
<HTML>
<HEAD>
<TITLE>Real Estate</TITLE>
<PRE>
<SCRIPT LANGUAGE="JavaScript">
<!-- HIDE FROM INCOMPATIBLE BROWSERS
function RealEstate(location, value) {
   this.property_location = location;
   this.property_value = value;
}
// STOP HIDING FROM INCOMPATIBLE BROWSERS -->
</SCRIPT>
</PRE>
</HEAD>
<BODY>
</BODY>
</HTML>
```

6. Save the RealEstate.html file as RealEstate2.html. Add an object method named printCommercialProperties() to the Commercial object you created in the previous exercise. The new object method should print the values assigned to the properties of the Commercial object. Replace the write() and writeln() methods with a single call to the printCommercialProperties() method.

7. Each of the functions in the following program declares a companyName variable and assigns the same value to it. Rewrite the program so that the companyName variable is declared only once, but do *not* use an object definition. Save the modified program as SingleCompanyName.html.

```
<HTML>
<HEAD>
<TITLE>Company Name</TITLE>
<PRE>
<SCRIPT LANGUAGE="JavaScript">
<!-- HIDE FROM INCOMPATIBLE BROWSERS
function printCompanyLogo() {
    var companyName = "Course Technology";
    var companyLogo = "Leading the way in IT publishing";
    document.write ("The ");
    document.write(companyName);
    document.write(" company logo is ");
    document.writeln(companyLogo);
}
function printCompanyCity() {
    var companyName = "Course Technology";
    var companyCity = "Boston";
    document.write(companyName);
    document.write(" is located in ");
    document.writeln(companyCity);
}
function printCompanyWebAddress() {
    var companyName = "Course Technology";
    var companyWebSite = "www.course.com";
    document.write ("The ");
    document.write(companyName);
    document.write(" Web site is ");
    document.writeln(companyWebSite);
}
printCompanyLogo();
printCompanyCity();
printCompanyWebAddress();
// STOP HIDING FROM INCOMPATIBLE BROWSERS -->
</SCRIPT>
</PRE>
</HEAD>
<BODY>
</BODY>
</HTML>
```

8. Create an HTML document named PersonalInfo.html with a function in the <HEAD> section named printPersonalInfo(). Within the printPersonalInfo() function, use the document.write() and document.writeln() methods to print your name, address, date of birth, and Social Security number to the screen. Call the function from the <BODY> section of the document.

9. Create an HTML document named CarObject.html that includes a constructor function in the <HEAD> section named Automobile. Include four properties in the Automobile object definition: make, model, color, and engine. Instantiate a new Automobile object in the <BODY> of the HTML document, then assign the values of your car to each of the Automobile properties. Print each of the properties to the screen.

10. Create an HTML document named CompanyInfo.html that includes a constructor function in the <HEAD> section named Company. Include four properties in the Company object definition: name, products, motto, and employees. Also create a method named Employees() that prints the number of employees. Instantiate a new Company object in the <BODY> of the HTML document, then assign values to each of the properties. Print the name, products, and motto properties to the screen using writeln() methods. Print the number of employees using the Employees() method. Combine each printed property with a descriptive string. For example, when you print the company name, it should read something like *The company name is MyCompany.*

11. The following program should print a single statement that reads *This line is returned from the sampleScript() function.* However, the following code contains a design error that generates error messages when you attempt to open the program in a Web browser. Correct the error and make sure the program runs successfully in a browser. Save the program as DesignError.html. (*Hint*: the problem has to do with where the script sections are placed in the HTML document.)

```
<HTML>
<HEAD>
<TITLE>Design Error</TITLE>
<SCRIPT LANGUAGE="JavaScript">
document.write(sampleScript());
</SCRIPT>
</HEAD>
<BODY>
<SCRIPT LANGUAGE="JavaScript">
function sampleScript() {
    return "This line returned from the sampleScript() function."
}
</SCRIPT>
</BODY>
</HTML>
```

SECTION B

objectives

In this section you will learn:
- About events
- About HTML tags and events
- How to use event handlers
- About links
- How to use link events
- How to create an image map

Using Events

Understanding Events

One of the primary ways in which JavaScript makes HTML documents dynamic is through events. You can use JavaScript events to add interactivity between your Web pages and users. An **event** is a specific circumstance that is monitored by JavaScript. The most common events are actions that users take. For example, when a user clicks a button, a *click* event is generated. You can think of an event as a trigger that fires specific JavaScript code in response to a given situation.

One common use of events is to run some sort of code in response to a user request. For example, one type of JavaScript program found on the Web today is a calculator program, such as a mortgage calculator. After users enter the required information for a mortgage, such as the interest rate, number of years, and amount of the loan, they may click a Calculate button that calculates the amount of a monthly mortgage payment. Calculation of the monthly mortgage payment is executed by the event that occurs when a user clicks the Calculate button. The image map you will create in this tutorial relies on an event that occurs when a user passes a mouse over a portion of the map. This type of event is called a *mouseover* event; it executes code that changes the highlighted portion of the map.

User-generated events, however, are not the only types of events monitored by JavaScript. Events that are not direct results of user actions, such as the *load* event, are also monitored. The load event, which is triggered automatically by a Web browser, occurs only when an HTML document finishes loading in a Web browser. The load event is often used to execute code that performs some type of visual effect, such as animation, that should not occur until a Web page is completely loaded. In the case of animation, the JavaScript program that executes the animation knows not to begin until it receives a signal in the form of the load event from the Web browser. Figure 2-13 displays a list of JavaScript events and when they occur.

Event	Triggered When
abort	The loading of an image is interrupted
blur	An element, such as a radio button, becomes inactive
click	An element is clicked once
change	The value of an element changes
error	There is an error when loading a document or image
focus	An element becomes active
load	A document or image loads
mouseOut	The mouse moves off an element
mouseOver	The mouse moves over an element
reset	A form resets
select	A user selects a field in a form
submit	A user submits a form
unload	A document unloads

Figure 2-13: JavaScript events

HTML Tags and Events

One of the most commonly used HTML tags that allows users to generate events is the <INPUT> tag. The **<INPUT> tag** creates input fields that interact with users. The <INPUT> tag has a number of attributes, including the TYPE attribute. The basic syntax for the <INPUT> tag is <INPUT TYPE="*input type*">. The TYPE attribute is a required field and determines the type of input field that the <INPUT> tag generates. For example, the statement <INPUT TYPE="radio"> creates a radio button, and the statement <INPUT TYPE="text"> creates a text field. You will use the <INPUT> tag throughout this text. The <INPUT> tag is most often used with forms and is placed within the <FORM>...</FORM> tag pair.

•••

You will learn about forms and how <INPUT> tags are used in forms in Tutorial 6.

•••

The following code shows an example of an <INPUT> tag that includes an onBlur event handler and is placed between a <FORM>...</FORM> tag pair. The blur event occurs when the focus leaves a control. In the example, the onBlur event handler displays the <INPUT> tag value when it loses focus.

```
<FORM NAME="myForm">
    <INPUT TYPE="text" VALUE="default text"
        NAME="textButton" onBlur="alert(this.value);">
</FORM>
```

Notice that both the <FORM> and the <INPUT> tag in the example have NAME attributes. The NAME attribute allows you to assign to an HTML tag a unique name that can be referenced in JavaScript code. In order to reference an HTML tag in a function or from another tag, you append its name to any of its ancestor objects, starting with the Document object. This allows you to retrieve information about a tag or change its properties. The statement `document.myForm.textButton.value = "new value";` could be used in a JavaScript function to change the value of the textButton to *new value*.

 tip

••

Unlike most HTML code, the NAME attribute is case-sensitive.

••

Figure 2-14 lists various types of HTML tags and their associated events.

Element	Description	Event
<A>...</A>	Link	click mouseOver mouseOut
<IMG>	Image	abort error load
<AREA>	Area	mouseOver mouseOut
<BODY>...</BODY>	Document body	blur error focus load unload
<FRAMESET>...</FRAMESET>	Frame set	blur error focus load unload

Figure 2-14: HTML elements and associated events

Element	Description	Event
\<FRAME>...\</FRAME>	Frame	blur focus
\<FORM>...\</FORM>	Form	submit reset
\<INPUT TYPE="text">	Text field	blur focus change select
\<TEXTAREA>...\</TEXTAREA>	Text area	blur focus change select
\<INPUT TYPE="submit">	Submit	click
\<INPUT TYPE="reset">	Reset	click
\<INPUT TYPE="radio">	Radio button	click
\<INPUT TYPE="checkbox">	Check box	click
\<SELECT>...\</SELECT>	Selection	blur focus change

Figure 2-14: HTML elements and associated events (continued)

Event Handlers

When an event occurs, a program executes JavaScript code that responds to the event. Code that executes in response to a specific event is called an **event handler**. An event itself, such as a click event, only informs JavaScript that it is okay to execute an event handler. You include event handler code as an attribute of the HTML tag that initiates the event. The syntax of an event handler within an HTML tag is:

```
<HTMLtag eventHandler="JavaScript Code">
```

Event handler names are the same as the name of the event itself, but with a prefix of *on*. For example, the event handler for the Click event is onClick, and the event handler for the Load event is onLoad. Recall that HTML tags are not case-sensitive, whereas JavaScript code is. Since event handlers are part of an HTML tag, they are not case-sensitive. Therefore, you could write the name of the onClickEvent event handler as ONCLICK, onclick, or ONclick. However, capitalizing only the first letter of the event name itself is a standard convention.

The JavaScript code for an event handler is contained within the quotation marks following the name of the JavaScript event handler. The following code uses the <INPUT> tag to create a command button, which is similar to an OK or Cancel button. The tag also includes an onClick event handler that executes the built-in JavaScript alert() method, in response to a click event (which occurs when the button is clicked). Notice that the code executed by the onClick event handler (the alert() method) is contained within double quotation marks.

```
<INPUT TYPE="button" onClick="alert('You clicked a
button!')">
```

The **alert() method** displays a pop-up dialog box with an OK button. You pass a single literal string or variable as an argument to the alert() method. Notice in the example that the literal string being passed is contained in single quotation marks, since the alert() method itself is already enclosed in double quotation marks.

The alert() method is the only statement being executed in the example. You can include multiple JavaScript statements if semicolons separate them. For example, to include two statements in the event handler example, a statement that creates a variable and another statement that uses the alert() method to display the variable, you would type the following:

```
<INPUT TYPE="button" onClick="var message='You clicked a
button'; alert(message)">
```

Another built-in JavaScript function that responds to events is prompt(), which is similar to alert(). The **prompt() method** displays a dialog box with a message, a text box, an OK button, and a Cancel button. Any text that is entered into a prompt() method text box by a user can be assigned to a variable. The syntax for the prompt() method is variable_name = prompt(message, default_text);.

The following code shows an example of a prompt() function that displays the text *How old are you?*. The second argument in the prompt() method is the default text *Your Age* that appears in the prompt dialog box text box. If the user presses the OK button, any text entered into the text box is assigned to the yourAge variable, which then appears in an alert dialog box. If the user presses the OK button without changing the default text, then the default text, *Your Age*, is assigned to the yourAge variable. No value is assigned to the yourAge variable if the user presses the Cancel button.

```
yourAge = prompt("How old are you?", "Your Age");
alert("Your age is " + yourAge);
```

Next you will create an HTML document that demonstrates JavaScript onLoad, onUnload, onClick, and onChange events and uses both the alert() and the prompt() functions.

To create an HTML document that demonstrates JavaScript events:

1   Start your text editor or HTML editor and create a new document.

2   Type the opening <HTML> and <HEAD> tags along with the title, opening <SCRIPT> tag, and HTML comments to hide the code from incompatible browsers:

```
<HTML>
<HEAD>
<TITLE>JavaScript Events</TITLE>
<SCRIPT LANGUAGE="JavaScript">
<!-- HIDE FROM INCOMPATIBLE BROWSERS
```

3   Type `var visitor_name = "";` on the next line to create a variable that will store the name of a visitor to the Web page.

4   Type `function greet_visitor(){` on the next line to begin the greet_visitor() function. You will call the greet_visitor() function with the onLoad event in the <BODY> tag.

5   Add the following statement, which prompts the user for his or her name and assigns the name to the visitor_name variable.

```
visitor_name = prompt("Please enter your name",
      "Enter your name here");
```

6   Type an alert() method, which displays a personalized greeting to the visitor, followed by a closing brace for the function.

```
alert("Welcome, " + visitor_name + "!");
}
```

7   Next add the following farewell_visitor() function, which will be called by the onUnload event in the <BODY> tag. The farewell_visitor() function also uses the visitor_name variable.

```
function farewell_visitor() {
    alert("Thanks, " + visitor_name +
          ", for visiting this Web page!");
}
```

8   Type the following lines to close the <SCRIPT> and <HEAD> sections.

```
// STOP HIDING FROM INCOMPATIBLE BROWSERS -->
</SCRIPT>
</HEAD>
```

9   Type the following <BODY> tag, which uses the onLoad and onUnload events to call the greet_visitor() and farewell_visitor() functions.

```
<BODY onLoad="greet_visitor();"
onUnload="farewell_visitor();">
```

10 Type **<FORM>** to start a form section.

11 Create the following two <INPUT> tags. The first <INPUT> tag creates a text field that includes an onChange event handler. The onChange event handler displays an alert() dialog box whenever a user leaves the text field after changing its contents. The second <INPUT> tag creates a button that displays the contents of the text field using its NAME attribute.

```
<INPUT TYPE="text" NAME="text_field" SIZE="25"
    onChange="alert(
         'The value of the text_field has changed.');">
<BR>
<INPUT TYPE="button" VALUE="Display Text Field Contents"
    onClick="alert(text_field.value);">
```

12 Add **</FORM>** to close the form.

13 Add the following tags to close the <BODY> and <HTML> tags:

```
</BODY>
</HTML>
```

14 Save the file as **GreetVisitor.html** in the **Tutorial.02** folder on your Data Disk, then open it in your Web browser. The onLoad event handler is called, and the greet_visitor() function executes, displaying the prompt dialog box. Figure 2-15 displays an example of the prompt.

Figure 2-15: The prompt() method

15 Enter your name into the dialog box and click the **OK** button. An alert dialog box displays the personalized greeting. Click the **OK** button on the alert dialog box. Click in the text field and type **Sample Text**, then press the **Tab** key to exit the field. Since you made a change in the text field, the onChange event handler is called, and another alert dialog box appears. Click the **OK** button on the alert dialog box. Now click the Display Text Field Contents button to call the onClick event handler, which displays an alert dialog box with the contents of the text field (*Sample Text*). Click the **OK** button on the alert dialog box.

16 To demonstrate the onUnload event handler, open the **CompanyObjects.html** file you created in Section A. Before your Web browser displays the CompanyObjects.html file, the onUnload event handler executes and the farewell_visitor() function executes, displaying the last alert dialog box, which thanks the visitor. Click **OK** to close the alert dialog box.

17 Close the Web browser window.

Links

Recall that HTML documents contain hypertext links, which are used to open files or to navigate to other documents on the Web. You activate a hypertext link by clicking it with your mouse button. A hypertext link in an HTML document is underlined and often a vivid color. Blue is the default color for unvisited links, while red is the default color of previously visited links. The hypertext link can display the actual name and location of a file or HTML document or some sort of descriptive text. Other types of elements, such as images, can also be hypertext links to other HTML documents, images, or files. The text or image used to represent a link in an HTML document is called an **anchor**. Figure 2-16 displays an HTML document containing several anchors.

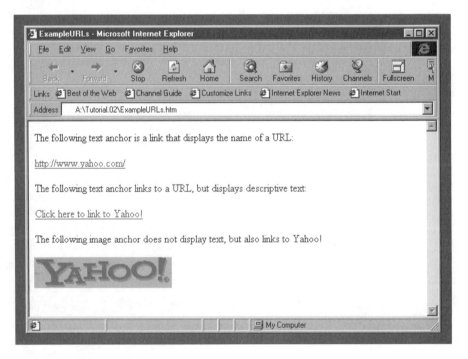

Figure 2-16: HTML document with anchors

You use the <A>...</A> tag pair (the A stands for *anchor*) to create a link in an HTML document. The syntax for the <A> tag is <A *attributes*>anchor text or image</A>. Figure 2-17 displays some of the attributes for the <A> tag.

Attribute	Description
NAME	The name of the anchor
HREF	The URL of the file, HTML document, or image to be loaded
TITLE	The title of the file, HTML document, or image to be loaded

Figure 2-17: Common <A> tag attributes

An anchor uses the Uniform Resource Locator (URL) to specify the name and location of an HTML document. There are two types of URLs in an HTML document: absolute and relative. An **absolute URL** refers to a specific drive and directory or to the full Web address of an HTML document. The following tag displays an anchor of *My Web Site* and contains an absolute reference to an HTML document named index.htm located at a Web site named www.MyWebSite.com.

```
<A HREF="http://www.MyWebSite.com/index.html">
My Web Site</A>
```

An absolute URL can also refer to a file on a local computer, as in the following code.

```
<A HREF="c:\MyWebPages\HomePage.html">My Web Site</A>
```

A **relative URL** specifies the location of a file according to the location of the currently loaded HTML document. Relative URLs are used to load HTML documents located on the same computer as the currently displayed HTML document. If the currently displayed HTML document is located at http://www.MyWebSite.com/WebPages, then the following relative URL looks in the WebPages folder for the AnotherWebPage.html file:

```
<A HREF="AnotherWebPage.html">Another Web Page</A>
```

You can also use a URL that locates subfolders that are *relative* to the location of the current Web page folder, as follows:

```
<A HREF="/MoreWebPages/YetAnotherWebPage.html">Yet Another
Web Page</A>
```

When all of your HTML documents reside within the same folder, relative URLs are convenient, since you do not have to type the entire location of each file. In addition, you do not have to update the location of relative URLs if you rename the folder containing the primary HTML document and linked documents, or move the folder to a different computer. For example, if you have a primary HTML document that contains 10 links to HTML documents located within the same folder, then you do not have to update the relative links if you move the primary document and the 10 linked documents to a new location. However, if you created each of the 10 links as absolute URLs, then you would need to update each URL before the links would function properly.

tip

If you specify a URL in an HTML document using the <BASE> tag (which establishes a universal URL for the document), then relative URLs are relative to the URL in the <BASE> tag, not to the URL of the HTML document itself. The <BASE> tag is used most often with frames.

Link Events

The primary event used with links is the click event. Clicking a link automatically executes the click event, and the URL associated with the link opens. When a user clicks a link, execution of the click event is handled automatically by the Web browser—you do not need to add an onClick event handler to the <A> tag.

There may be cases, however, when you want to override the automatic click event with your own code. For instance, you may want to warn the user about the content of the HTML document that a particular link will open. When you want to override the automatic click event with your own code, you add to the <A> tag an onClick event handler that executes custom code. When you override an internal event handler with your own code, you must return a value of true or false, using the return statement. With the <A> tag, a value of true indicates that you want the Web browser to perform its default event handling operation of opening the URL referenced in the link. A value of false indicates that you do *not* want the <A> tag to perform its default event handling operation. For example, the <A> tag in Figure 2-18 includes a custom onClick event handler. The warn_user() function that is called by the onClick event handler returns a value generated by the confirm() method. The **confirm() method** displays a dialog box that contains a Cancel button as well as an OK button. When a user clicks the OK button in the confirm dialog box, a value of true is returned. When a user clicks the Cancel button, a value of false is returned.

```
<HTML>

<HEAD>

<TITLE>Custom onClick Event Example</TITLE>

<SCRIPT LANGUAGE="JavaScript">

<!-- HIDE FROM INCOMPATIBLE BROWSERS

function warnUser() {

     return confirm(
"This link is only for people who love golden retrievers!");

}

// STOP HIDING FROM INCOMPATIBLE BROWSERS -->

</SCRIPT>

</HEAD>

<BODY>

<A HREF="GoldenRetrievers.html" onClick=
"return warnUser();">Golden Retriever Club Home Page</A>

</BODY>

</HTML>
```

Figure 2-18: Link with a custom onClick event handler

Notice that there are two return statements in Figure 2-18. The return statement in the warnUser() function returns a value to the onClick event handler. The return statement in the onClick event handler returns the same value to the Web browser.

Two other events that are used with links are the MouseOver and MouseOut events. The **MouseOver event** occurs when the mouse is moved over a link. The MouseOut event occurs when the mouse is moved off a link. One of the most common uses of the MouseOver and MouseOut events is to change the text that appears in a Web browser status bar. By default, a link's URL appears in the status bar when the mouse passes over a link. Instead, you can use the onMouseOver event handler to display your own custom message for a link in the status bar. To make your custom message appear in the status bar, use the JavaScript **status** property.

The onMouseOut event handler is used to reset the text displayed in the status bar after the mouse is moved off a link. Most often, any text that is displayed in the status bar is cleared using the statement onMouseOut="status = ' ';" to set the status property to an empty string. The two single quotation marks specify an empty string. You use single quotation marks instead of double quotation marks because the statement is already contained within a pair of double quotation marks. (Remember that you cannot use double quotation marks inside another set of double quotation marks.) The semicolon marks the end of the JavaScript statement. Instead of an empty string, you can also display another custom message in the status bar.

The following code uses the onMouseOver event handler to display the text *Golden Retriever Club Home Page* in the status bar instead of the link's URL, *GoldenRetrievers.html*. The onMouseOut event handler displays the text *You almost visited the Golden Retriever Home Page!* after the mouse moves off the link:

```
<A HREF = "GoldenRetrievers.html" onMouseOver =
"status = 'Golden Retriever Club Home Page'; return true;"
onMouseOut = "status = 'You almost visited the Golden
Retriever Club Home Page'; return false;" >Golden Retriever
Club Home Page</A>
```

 tip

You can also use the defaultStatus property within a <SCRIPT>...</SCRIPT> tag pair to specify the default text that appears in the status bar whenever the mouse is not positioned over a link. The syntax for the defaultStatus property is defaultStatus = "Enter default status text here.";. Note that the defaultStatus property overrides any text specified by an onMouseOut event handler.

Notice that the immediately preceding onMouseOver event handler includes a return statement that returns a value of true. Unlike the return value for the onClick event handler, a return value of true from the onMouseOver event handler tells the Web browser *not* to perform its own event handling routine of displaying the name of the link's URL in the status bar. In contrast, the onMouseOut event handler returns a value of false to prevent the Web browser from performing its default event handling routine of displaying the value assigned to the defaultStatus property (if any) in the status bar. It is important to remember that there is little consistency in the return values for event handlers; some event handlers require a value of true and others require a value of false.

Next you will create two HTML documents that demonstrate the Click, MouseOver, and MouseOut events of a link.

To create an HTML document that demonstrates the Click, MouseOver, and MouseOut events of a link:

1 Return to your text editor or HTML editor, and create a new document.

2 Type the opening <HTML> and <HEAD> tags along with the title, opening <SCRIPT> tag, and HTML comments to hide the code from incompatible browsers:

```
<HTML>
<HEAD>
<TITLE>Red Page</TITLE>
<SCRIPT LANGUAGE="JavaScript">
<!-- HIDE FROM INCOMPATIBLE BROWSERS
```

3 Add the following function, which will be called from the onClick event handler of a link. The function confirms that a user wants to open the URL specified by a link.

```
function confirmPageChange() {
    return confirm
("Are you sure you want to display the green page?");
}
```

4 Type the following lines to close the <SCRIPT> and <HEAD> sections:

```
// STOP HIDING FROM INCOMPATIBLE BROWSERS -->
</SCRIPT>
</HEAD>
```

5 Type the opening <BODY> tag, which also includes the BGCOLOR attribute, which determines the document background color:

```
<BODY BGCOLOR="red">
```

6 Create the following link that contains onClick, onMouseOver, and onMouseOut event handlers:

```
<A HREF="GreenPage.html"
onClick="return confirmPageChange();"
onMouseOver=
"status = 'This link opens the green page';
return false;"
onMouseOut=
"status = 'You did not open the green page!!';
return true;">
Click here to open the green page</A>
```

7   Add the following tags to close the <BODY> and <HTML> tags:

```
</BODY>
</HTML>
```

8   Save the file as **RedPage.html** in the **Tutorial.02** folder on your Data Disk, then immediately save it as **GreenPage.html**.

9   Within the new GreenPage.html file, change the text in the <TITLE> tag to **Green Page**.

10   In the confirmPageChange() function, change the word green to **red** within the text string.

11   Change the BGCOLOR attribute in the <BODY> tag to **green**.

12   Within the <A> tag, change the HREF from GreenPage.html to **RedPage.html**. Also change the word green to **red** within the two event handlers in which it appears. Notice that you are using relative URLs since the GreenPage.html and RedPage.html files are located within the same folder. Finally, change the descriptive text between the <A>...</A> tag pair from *Click here to open the green page* to **Click here to open the red page**.

13   Save the file, then open either RedPage.html or GreenPage.html in your Web browser. Clicking the link in either file should display the Confirm dialog box, which in turn should open the other file when you click OK. Also check to see that the status bar text is being updated during the MouseOver and MouseOut events for each file. An example of GreenPage.html and the Confirm dialog box appears in Figure 2-19.

14   Close the Web browser window.

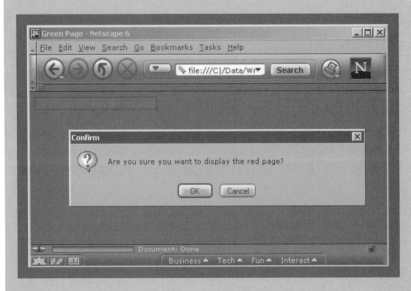

Figure 2-19: GreenPage.html and the Confirm dialog box

Creating an Image Map

An image map consists of an image that is divided into regions. Each region is then associated with a URL by means of the <A> tag; these regions are called hot zones. You can open the URL associated with each region by clicking the **hot zone** with your mouse. You use the <IMG>, <MAP>, and <AREA> tags to create an image map on a Web page. To create an image map, you must include the following tags on your Web page:

- An <IMG> tag that contains an SRC attribute specifying the name of the image file and a USEMAP attribute specifying the value assigned to the NAME attribute of the <MAP>...</MAP> tag pair that contains the mapping coordinates
- A <MAP>...</MAP> tag pair that includes a NAME attribute that has been assigned the same value used by the <IMG> tag USEMAP attribute
- <AREA> tags within the <MAP>...</MAP> tag pair that identify the coordinates within the image that will be recognized as hot zones.

▶ **tip**

There are two types of image maps: server-side image maps and client-side image maps. With server-side image maps, the code that *maps* each region of an image is located on a server. A client-side image map is part of an HTML document. This tutorial covers client-side image maps.

When an image specified by the <IMG> tag is rendered in an HTML document, the Web browser creates the image within a rectangle corresponding to the height and width of the image. The size of an image's rectangle is measured in pixels. A **pixel** (short for **pic**ture **el**ement) represents a single point on a computer screen. You can think of pixels as thousands or millions of tiny dots arranged in columns and rows on your monitor. The number of pixels available depends on a computer monitor's resolution. For example, a VGA monitor contains 640 columns by 480 rows of pixels, or about 300,000 pixels; a Super VGA monitor contains 1024 columns by 768 rows of pixels, or approximately 800,000 pixels.

You reference image pixels with x-axis and y-axis coordinates, starting at the upper-left corner of the image rectangle and ending at the lower-right corner. Figure 2-20 shows how pixels are referenced in an image that is 200 pixels wide by 200 pixels high.

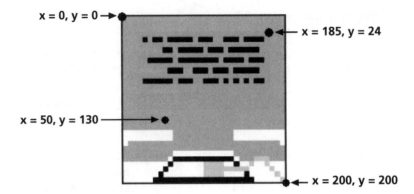

Figure 2-20: Pixel references

The <MAP> tag has only one attribute, NAME, which is used to specify the name of the map. To create a <MAP> tag with a name of imageMap, you use the statement <MAP NAME="imageMap">.

The <AREA> tag is placed between <MAP>...</MAP> tag pairs and contains several attributes, as shown in Figure 2-21.

Attribute	Description
COORDS	The coordinates of the shape in pixels. The coordinates you enter depend on the shape you specify with the SHAPE attribute.
HREF	The URL associated with the area
NAME	The name of the area
NOHREF	A placeholder for areas that are not to be associated with a URL
SHAPE	The shape of the defined region

Figure 2-21: Common <AREA> tag attributes

When you use the <AREA> tag to define a region as a hot zone on an image map, you use the SHAPE attribute to specify the shape of the region and the COORDS attribute to specify the coordinates of the shape's pixels. The SHAPE attribute can be set to circle, rect (for rectangle), or poly (for polygon). The syntax for each type of shape is as follows:

```
SHAPE=RECT COORDS="upper-left x, upper-left y,
     lower-right x, lower-right y"
SHAPE=CIRCLE COORDS="center-x, center-y, radius"
SHAPE=POLY COORDS="x1,y1, x2,y2, x3,y3,..."
```

To use an image map with an image rendered by the <IMG> tag, you include the USEMAP attribute. The name of the image map must be preceded by the number sign (#) and must be placed within double quotation marks. The syntax for an <IMG> tag that loads an image named sports.gif and that uses an image map named sports_map is as follows:

```
<IMG SRC="sports.gif" USEMAP="#sports_map">
```

As with the <A> tag, <AREA> tags can include onMouseOver and onMouseOut event handlers. Figure 2-22 shows an example of an HTML document that creates an image map with four hot zones, one for each quadrant of a rectangle. The total size of the rectangle is 250 pixels in height and 300 pixels in width. Clicking a hot zone opens the URL corresponding to the HREF attribute in the region's <AREA> tag. The onMouseOver event handler for each region displays custom text in the status bar, and the onMouseOut event handler resets the status bar text to an empty string. Figure 2-23 shows the output.

```
<HTML>
<HEAD>
<TITLE>Sports Map</TITLE>
</HEAD>
<BODY>
<IMG SRC="sports.gif" USEMAP="#sports_map">
<MAP NAME="sports_map">
<AREA HREF="baseball.html" SHAPE="rect" COORDS="0,0,150,125"
    onMouseOver="status='Baseball Web Page.';
    return true;" onMouseOut="status=''; return true;">
<AREA HREF="football.html" SHAPE="rect" COORDS="150,0,300,125"
    onMouseOver="status='Football Web Page.'; return true"
    onMouseOut="status=''; return true;">
<AREA HREF="soccer.html" SHAPE="rect" COORDS="0,125,150,250"
    onMouseOver="status='Soccer Web Page.'; return true"
    onMouseOut="status=''; return true;">
<AREA HREF="tennis.html" SHAPE="rect" COORDS="150,125,300,250"
    onMouseOver="status='Tennis Web Page.'; return true"
    onMouseOut="status=''; return true;">
</MAP>
</BODY>
</HTML>
```

Figure 2-22: HTML document with an image map

Figure 2-23: Output of an HTML document with an image map

Next you will create the image map of North America that you first previewed at the beginning of this tutorial. The image that is loaded when the Web page is first rendered is a map of North America without any highlighted countries. Passing your mouse over the image highlights each country and displays its name. This is accomplished using a series of maps, one for each North American country. When the mouse passes over a country, a JavaScript function temporarily changes the image being displayed. The maps you will need are in the Tutorial.02 folder on your Data Disk.

To create the image map of North America:

1   In the Tutorial.02 folder on your Data Disk, create a new folder named **ImageMap**. Copy the six image files **alaska.gif**, **canada.gif**, **greenland.gif**, **continential_us.gif**, **mexico.gif**, and **north_america.gif** from the Tutorial.02 folder to the new ImageMap folder.

2   Start your text editor or HTML editor, if necessary, and create a new document.

3   Type the opening <HTML> and <HEAD> tags along with the title, opening <SCRIPT> tag, and HTML comments to hide the code from incompatible browsers:

```
<HTML>
<HEAD>
<TITLE>North America</TITLE>
<SCRIPT LANGUAGE="JavaScript">
<!-- HIDE FROM INCOMPATIBLE BROWSERS
```

4   Type the following change_image() function. Each of the onMouseOver event handlers will call this function to display the image associated with each North American country. Each onMouseOver event handler passes the name of the required image file to the argument named image_name. The statement **document.northAmerica.src = image_name;** is used to change the image displayed by the <IMG> tag named northAmerica. You will create the north_america <IMG> tag in the next few steps.

```
function change_image(image_name) {
    document.northAmerica.src = image_name;
}
```

5   Add the following function that is called by the onMouseOver event handlers to reset the image to north_america.gif once the mouse is moved off a specific country:

```
function reset_image() {
    document.northAmerica.src = "north_america.gif";
}
```

6   Type the following lines to close the <SCRIPT> and <HEAD> sections:

```
// STOP HIDING FROM INCOMPATIBLE BROWSERS -->
</SCRIPT>
</HEAD>
```

7   Type the opening <BODY> tag.

8   Type the following code that creates the image and builds the image map. You should recognize that the onMouseOver and onMouseOut event handlers are passing the names of the necessary image files to the functions. Notice that each <AREA> tag includes the NOHREF attribute. This prevents users from directly opening each region's associated image file. Also notice that the <AREA> tags use circle and poly shapes rather than rect.

```
<IMG SRC="north_america.gif"
  USEMAP="#northAmerica_map" NAME="northAmerica">
<MAP NAME="northAmerica_map">
  <AREA SHAPE="circle" COORDS="44,46,20" NOHREF
        onMouseOver="change_image('alaska.gif');
        return false"
        onMouseOut="reset_image(); return false">
  <AREA SHAPE="poly"
        COORDS="110,10,144,22,152,60,107,31"
        NOHREF
        onMouseOver="change_image('greenland.gif');
        return false"
        onMouseOut="reset_image(); return false">
  <AREA SHAPE="poly"
        COORDS=
        "62,45,107,23,162,86,125,111,106,100,55,96,49,64"
        NOHREF
        onMouseOver="change_image('canada.gif');
        return false"
        onMouseOut="reset_image(); return false">
  <AREA SHAPE="poly"
        COORDS=
        "60,96,125,105,142,98,134,153,97,155,50,123"
        NOHREF
        onMouseOver="change_image('continental_us.gif');
        return false"
        onMouseOut="reset_image(); return false">
  <AREA SHAPE="poly"
        COORDS=
        "61,135,122,165,109,181,65,159,60,136"
        NOHREF
        onMouseOver="change_image('mexico.gif');
        return false"
        onMouseOut = "reset_image(); return false">
</MAP>
```

9   Add the following tags to close the <BODY> and <HTML> tags:

```
</BODY>
</HTML>
```

10 Save the file as **ShowCountry.html** in the ImageMap folder in the **Tutorial.02 folder** on your Data Disk, then open it in your Web browser. Test the program and be sure each image file loads correctly. If you receive errors or the program does not function correctly, check whether you have included all the necessary opening and closing tags. Also make sure you have used the correct case for JavaScript code.

11 Close the browser window.

S U M M A R Y

- An event is a specific circumstance that is monitored by JavaScript.

- Various HTML tags generate various types of events.

- The <INPUT> tag is used for creating input fields with which users interact.

- Code that executes in response to a specific event is called an event handler.

- Event handler code is included as an attribute of the HTML tag from which the event is initiated.

- An event handler name is the same as the name of the event itself, but with a prefix of *on*.

- The alert() method displays a pop-up dialog box with an OK button. The prompt() method displays a dialog box with a message, a text box, a Cancel button, and an OK button.

- The text or image used to represent a link in an HTML document is called an anchor.

- There are two types of URLs in an HTML document: absolute and relative. An absolute URL refers to a specific drive and directory or to the full Web address and location of an HTML document. A relative URL specifies the location of a file according to the location of the currently loaded HTML document.

- The confirm() method displays a dialog box with a message, a Cancel button, and an OK button.

- The MouseOver event occurs when the mouse is moved over a link. The MouseOut event occurs when the mouse is moved off a link.

- You can use the JavaScript status property to display custom messages in the status bar.

- An image map consists of an image that is divided into regions. You use the <A>, <IMG>, <MAP>, and <AREA> tags to create an image map.

- Image pixels are referenced using x-axis and y-axis coordinates, starting at the upper-left corner of the image's rectangle and ending at the lower-right corner.

- You include the USEMAP attribute to use an image map with an image rendered by the <IMG> tag.

- The <AREA> tag can include onMouseOver and onMouseOut event handlers.

QUESTIONS

1. A(n) _____, or trigger, is a specific circumstance that is monitored by JavaScript.
    a. notification
    b. event
    c. alert
    d. prompt

2. The _____ event occurs when an HTML document finishes loading in a Web browser.
    a. load
    b. complete
    c. display
    d. click

3. The _____ tag is used for creating input fields that interact with users.
    a. <INTERFACE>
    b. <USERRESPONSE>
    c. <BUTTON>
    d. <INPUT>

4. What is the correct case of the Click event handler?
    a. OnClick
    b. onCLICK
    c. onClick
    d. Event handlers are not case-sensitive.

5. Which of the following is the correct syntax?
    a. `onClick="alert('You clicked a button!');"`
    b. `onClick="alert("You clicked a button!");"`
    c. `onClick="alert(You clicked a button!);"`
    d. `onClick=alert('You clicked a button!');`

6. Multiple JavaScript statements in an event handler _____.
    a. are contained within separate sets of parentheses
    b. must be separated with the <BR> tag
    c. must be separated by semicolon
    d. You cannot include multiple JavaScript statements in an event handler.

7. What is the second argument that you pass to the prompt() method used for?
    a. Default text in the prompt dialog text box
    b. As title bar text for the prompt dialog box
    c. As a variable to which the value passed as the first argument to the prompt() method is assigned
    d. You cannot pass a second argument to the prompt() method.

8. Which of the following is *not* a valid JavaScript dialog box function?
    a. confirm()
    b. alert()
    c. prompt()
    d. message()

9. The text or image used to represent a link in an HTML document is known as a(n) _____.
   a. placeholder
   b. anchor
   c. hookup
   d. chain

10. You use the _____ tag pair to create a link in an HTML document.
    a. <URL>...</URL>
    b. <ANCHOR>...</ANCHOR>
    c. <LINK>...</LINK>
    d. <A>...</A>

11. There are two types of URLs: absolute and _____.
    a. static
    b. nonabsolute
    c. permanent
    d. relative

12. You have multiple HTML documents within the same folder that are linked to each other with absolute URLs. If you move the documents to a different Web site, _____.
    a. you must manually update each of the URLs
    b. it is not necessary to update the URLs
    c. the URLs will function correctly provided that they are placed in a folder with the same name as the original
    d. the URLs will automatically update themselves to reflect the new Web site location

13. Which of the following is the correct syntax for canceling a link's default Click event?
    a. `<A HREF="HomePage.html" onClick="return true;">`
    b. `<A HREF="HomePage.html" onClick="return false;">`
    c. `<A HREF="HomePage.html" onClick="return cancel;">`
    d. `<A HREF="HomePage.html" onClick="return override;">`

14. Which of the following is the correct syntax for printing *Welcome to My Home Page* in the status bar, using the MouseOver event?
    a. `<A HREF="HomePage.html"`
       `onMouseOver="status = 'Welcome to My Home Page; return true;">`
       `Welcome to My Home Page</A>`
    b. `<A HREF="HomePage.html"`
       `onMouseOver="status = true;">`
       `Welcome to My Home Page</A>`
    c. `<A HREF="HomePage.html"`
       `onMouseOver="status = 'Welcome to My Home Page'; return true;">`
       `My Home Page</A>`
    d. `<A HREF="HomePage.html"`
       `onMouseOver="status = 'Welcome to My Home Page'; return true;">`
       `My Home Page</A>`

15. The default text that appears in the status bar whenever the mouse is not positioned over a link is set using the _____ property.
    a. originalStatus
    b. onMouseOutDefault
    c. defaultText
    d. defaultStatus

16. Which of the following tags is not required for an image map?
    a. <IMG>
    b. <MAP>
    c. <AREA>
    d. <IMAGEMAP>

17. A(n) _____ represents a single point on a computer screen.
    a. pixel
    b. bit
    c. cell
    d. element

18. Which attribute of the <AREA> tag designates the tag as a placeholder for areas that are not to be associated with a URL?
    a. NOURL
    b. NOLINK
    c. NOHREF
    d. NOURI

19. Which of the following shapes is not a valid option of the SHAPE attribute of the <AREA> tag?
    a. circle
    b. rectangle
    c. triangle
    d. polygon

EXERCISES

Save all files you create in the Tutorial.02 folder on your Data Disk.

1. Add an event handler to the following form that displays an alert dialog box whenever the value in the salesAmount text box changes. Display the new value of the text box in the alert dialog box. Save the file as ChangedValue.html.

```
<FORM NAME="salesForm">
  <INPUT TYPE="text" NAME="salesAmount">
</FORM>
```

2. The following event handlers in a <FORM> section should display *Yahoo!* when your mouse passes over the link, and *You did not select Yahoo!* when your mouse moves off the link. However, only the onMouseOut event handler is working properly. Fix the error and save the correct file as CorrectStatus.html.

```
<A HREF = "Yahoo.html"
  onMouseOver = "status = 'Yahoo!'"
  onMouseOut = "status = 'You did not select Yahoo!'">
Yahoo!</A>
```

3. Create an HTML document containing a list of links to your favorite Web sites. Create a unique function for each link. Call the functions using each link's onClick event handler. Each function should display a confirm dialog box asking if the user really wants to visit the associated Web page. Save the file as ConfirmLinks.html.

4. Create a political survey as an HTML document. Create the survey using text fields in a form. Use fields that ask users for their political party affiliation, what state they live in, and which politician got their vote for president, governor, senator, and so on. Include an onLoad event handler that writes *This is an online political survey* to the status bar. As the user enters each field, use an onFocus event handler to display helpful information in the status bar. As the user leaves a text field, use an onBlur event handler to display an alert dialog box containing the information they typed in that text field. Also include an onUnload event handler that displays an alert dialog box containing the text *Thank you for filling out the survey.* Save the file as PoliticalSurvey.html.

5. Use a graphics program, such as Paint, to create an image of a stick figure (or a more developed figure, if you have artistic skills). Create an HTML file named BodyParts.html that includes an image map of the stick figure. Create hot spots over each of the figure's body parts. When a mouse passes over each body part, display the part's name in the status bar. Change the status bar to an empty string when the mouse passes off the image. Also create alert dialog boxes that display each body part's name when you click it.

6. Create an image map using a scanned photograph of your family and name it FamilyImageMap.html. (If you do not have access to a scanner or digital camera, search the Internet for any public domain family photograph that you can use for practice.) Include an onLoad event handler that writes your family name to the status bar using the defaultStatus property. Over each individual in the photo, create a hotspot that writes his or her name and relationship to you in the status bar. Create a personal Web page for each family member that opens when you click on his or her image. Include information about each family member on his or her personal Web page. Also include a link back to the FamilyImageMap Web page.

7. Use a graphics program, such as Paint, to create an image containing the names of animals, then search the Internet for public domain clip art images that represent each animal. Create an HTML document named ShowAnimal.html. In the ShowAnimal.html file, create an image map that contains the names of the animals for the graphic you created. Use each animal's name as a hot spot that displays a picture of the animal when your mouse passes over its name. Create a temporary image that displays the text *Click an animal's name to display its picture here.* when your mouse is not positioned over an animal's name.

Data Types and Operators

case ▶ One of WebAdventure's long-term clients is a large bank, GlobalBank, with an elaborate Web site. The bank likes to add interactive features to its Web site on a regular basis to entice customers to use its online banking services. So far, WebAdventure has added a mortgage calculator and a car loan calculator to GlobalBank's Web site. Recently, GlobalBank's marketing department requested that a simple calculator, which customers can use when conducting online transactions or balancing their accounts, be added to the Web site. Your boss, impressed by how quickly you are picking up JavaScript, has put you in charge of developing this calculator program.

Previewing the Calculator Program

In this tutorial, you will create a JavaScript program that displays an online calculator. To create the calculator, you must learn how to work with data types and operators.

To preview the calculator program:

1   In your Web browser, open the **Tutorial3Calculator.html** file from the Tutorial.03 folder on your Data Disk. An online calculator appears, as shown in Figure 3-1.

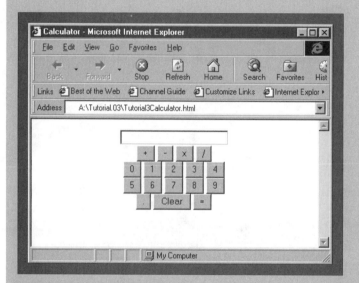

Figure 3-1: Tutorial3Calculator.html

2   Use your mouse to perform various types of calculations with the calculator to see how it works.

3   Next, open the **Tutorial3Calculator.html** file in your text editor or HTML editor and examine the code. In the head of the document, notice the <INPUT> tags and the updateString() function, which work together to perform calculations.

4   Close your text editor or HTML editor when you are finished examining the code.

In this section you will learn:
- How to use data types
- About numeric data types
- About Boolean values
- How to use strings
- How to use arrays

Using Data Types

Data Types

Variables can contain many different kinds of values—for example the time of day, a dollar amount, or a person's name. The values or data contained in JavaScript variables can be classified by categories known as data types. A **data type** is the specific category of information that a variable contains. Data types that can be assigned only a single value are called **primitive types**. JavaScript supports five primitive data types: integer numbers, floating-point numbers, Boolean values, strings, and the null value, all of which are described in Figure 3-2.

Data Type	Description
Integer numbers	Positive or negative numbers with no decimal places
Floating-point numbers	Positive or negative numbers with decimal places or numbers written using exponential notation
Boolean	A logical value of true or false
String	Text such as "Hello World"
Undefined	A variable that has never had a value assigned to it, has not been declared, or does not exist
Null	An empty value

Figure 3-2: Primitive types

The null value is a data type as well as a value that can be assigned to a variable. Assigning the value null to a variable indicates the variable does not contain a value. A variable with a value of null has a value assigned to it—null is really the value "no value." In contrast, an undefined variable (which you learned about in Tutorial 2) has never had a value assigned to it, has not been declared, or does not exist.

The JavaScript language also supports **reference**, or **composite**, data types, which are collections of data represented by a single variable name. The three reference data types supported by the JavaScript language are functions, objects, and arrays. You are already familiar with functions and the data (variables and statements) they contain. In Tutorial 2, you learned how to instantiate an object using a statement similar to `pet = new Animal("dog", "woof", "walk/run");`. The collections of data in an object are its methods and properties. You can work with an object, such as the pet object, in much the same way you work with a variable. In fact, programmers often use the terms variable and object interchangeably. Arrays, which you will learn about later in this tutorial, are sets of data represented by a single variable name. The variable name that represents an array is often referred to as an object, or array object. For now, do not worry about how you create and use arrays because they will be discussed in detail later in this tutorial. Simply understand that reference data types contain multiple pieces of information, whereas primitive data types contain a single piece of information.

Many programming languages require that you declare the type of data that a variable contains. Programming languages that require you to declare the data types of variables are called **strongly typed programming languages**. Strong typing is also known as **static typing**, since data types do not change after they have been declared. Programming languages that do not require you to declare the data types of variables are called **loosely typed programming languages**. Loose typing is also known as **dynamic typing** since data types can change after they have been declared. JavaScript is a loosely typed programming language. Not only are you not required to declare the data type of variables in JavaScript, you are not allowed to do so. Instead, the JavaScript interpreter automatically determines what type of data is stored in a variable and assigns the variable's data type accordingly. The following code demonstrates how a variable's data type changes automatically each time the variable is assigned a new literal value.

```
changingVariable = "Hello World";  // String
changingVariable = 8;              // Integer number
changingVariable = 5.367;          // Floating-point number
changingVariable = true;           // Boolean
changingVariable = null;           // null
```

The data type of variables can change during the course of program execution. This can cause problems if you attempt to perform an arithmetic operation and one of the variables is a string or the null value. JavaScript includes a typeof() operator that you can use to determine the data type of a variable. An operator is used for manipulating different parts of a statement. (You will learn about operators in Section B.) The syntax for the typeof() operator is typeof(*variablename*);. The values that can be returned by the typeof() operator are listed in Figure 3-3.

Return Value	Returned For
Number	Integers and floating-point numbers
String	Text strings
Boolean	True or false
Object	Objects, arrays, and null variables
Function	Functions
Undefined	Undefined variables

Figure 3-3: Values returned by typeof() operator

Next you will create a program that assigns different data types to a variable and prints the variable's data type. You will use the typeof() operator to determine the data type of each variable.

To create a program that assigns different data types to a variable and prints the variable data type:

1 Create a new document in your text editor or HTML editor.

2 Type the <HTML> and <HEAD> sections of the document:

```
<HTML>
<HEAD>
<TITLE>Print Data Types</TITLE>
</HEAD>
```

As you recall from Tutorial 1, JavaScript code can be placed in either the <HEAD> or <BODY> section. Where you place your JavaScript code will vary, depending on the program you are writing.

3 Add the following code to begin the body of the HTML document and create a preformatted text container:

```
<BODY>
<PRE>
```

4 Add the opening statements for a JavaScript section:

```
<SCRIPT LANGUAGE="JavaScript">
<!-- HIDE FROM INCOMPATIBLE BROWSERS
```

5 Declare a variable named differentType by typing the statement **var differentType;**.

6 Type the following line, which prints the data type contained in the differentType variable. The data type is currently undefined, since differentType has not yet been assigned a value.

```
document.writeln("The differentType variable is "
    + typeof(differentType));
```

7 Add the following two lines, which assign a string to the differentType variable and repeat the statement that prints the data type.

```
differentType = "This is a text string.";
document.writeln("The differentType variable is "
    + typeof(differentType));
```

8 Now add the following lines, which change the differentType variable to the integer, floating-point, Boolean, and null data types. The statement that prints each data type repeats each time the variable's data type changes.

```
differentType = 100;
document.writeln("The differentType variable is "
    + typeof(differentType));
differentType = 3.679;
document.writeln("The differentType variable is "
    + typeof(differentType));
differentType = false;
document.writeln("The differentType variable is "
    + typeof(differentType));
differentType = null;
document.writeln("The differentType variable is "
    + typeof(differentType));
```

9 Add the following code to close the <SCRIPT>, <PRE>, <BODY>, and <HTML> tags:

```
// STOP HIDING FROM INCOMPATIBLE BROWSERS -->
</SCRIPT>
</PRE>
</BODY>
</HTML>
```

10 Save the file as PrintDataTypes.html in the Tutorial.03 folder on your Data Disk. Open the PrintDataTypes.html file in your Web browser. You should see the same lines as shown in Figure 3-4.

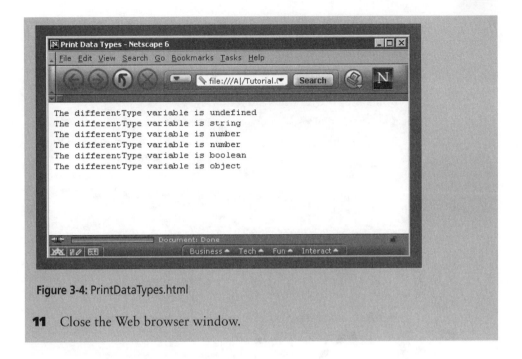

Figure 3-4: PrintDataTypes.html

11 Close the Web browser window.

Numeric Data Types

Numeric data types are an important part of any programming language, and are particularly useful when doing arithmetic calculations. JavaScript supports two numeric data types: integers and floating-point numbers. An **integer** is a positive or negative number with no decimal places. Integer values in JavaScript can range from -9007199254740990 (-2^{53}) to 9007199254740990 (2^{53}). The numbers -250, -13, 0, 2, 6, 10, 100, and 10000 are examples of integers. The numbers -6.16, -4.4, 3.17, .52, 10.5, and 2.7541 are not integers; they are floating-point numbers, since they contain decimal places. A **floating-point number** contains decimal places or is written using exponential notation. **Exponential notation**, or **scientific notation**, is a way of writing very large numbers or numbers with many decimal places, using a shortened format. Numbers written in exponential notation are represented by a value between 1 and 10 multiplied by 10 raised to some power. The value of 10 is written with an uppercase or lowercase *E*. For example, the number 200,000,000,000 can be written in exponential notation as 2.0e11, which means "two times ten to the eleventh power." Floating-point values in JavaScript range from approximately $\pm 1.7976931348623157 \times 10^{308}$ to $\pm 5 \times 10^{-324}$.

Floating-point values that exceed the largest positive value of $\pm 1.7976931348623157 \times 10^{308}$ result in a special value of Infinity. Floating-point values that exceed the smallest negative value of $\pm 5 \times 10^{-324}$ result in a value of –Infinity.

Next you will create a program that assigns integers and exponential numbers to variables and prints the values.

To create a program that assigns integers and exponential numbers to variables and prints the values:

1   Create a new document in your text editor or HTML editor.

2   Type the <HTML> and <HEAD> sections of the document:

```
<HTML>
<HEAD>
<TITLE>Print Numbers</TITLE>
</HEAD>
```

3   Add the following code to begin the body of the HTML document and to create a preformatted text container:

```
<BODY>
<PRE>
```

4   Add the opening statements for a JavaScript section.

```
<SCRIPT LANGUAGE="JavaScript">
<!-- HIDE FROM INCOMPATIBLE BROWSERS
```

5   Add the following lines that declare an integer variable and a floating-point variable:

```
var integerVar = 150;
var floatingPointVar = 3.0e7;
// floating-point number 30000000
```

6   Now add the following statements to print the variables:

```
document.writeln(integerVar);
document.writeln(floatingPointVar);
```

7   Add the following code to close the <SCRIPT>, <PRE>, <BODY>, and <HTML> tags:

```
// STOP HIDING FROM INCOMPATIBLE BROWSERS -->
</SCRIPT>
</PRE>
</BODY>
</HTML>
```

8   Save the file as **PrintNumbers.html** in the Tutorial.03 folder on your Data Disk. Open the **PrintNumbers.html** file in your Web browser. The integer 150 and the number 30,000,000 (for the exponential expression 3.0e7) should appear in your Web browser window.

9   Close the Web browser window.

Boolean Values

A **Boolean value** is a logical value of true or false. You can also think of a Boolean value as being *yes* or *no*, or *on* or *off*. Boolean values are most often used for decision making and comparing data. You used Boolean values in Tutorial 2 when you overrode an internal event handler with your own code. When you override an internal event handler with your own code, you are required to return a value of true or false, using the return statement. You also used the confirm dialog box to return a value of true or false to an event handler. When a user clicks the OK button in the confirm dialog box, a value of true is returned, while clicking the Cancel button returns a value of false. Figure 3-5 displays the program you first saw in Tutorial 2 that demonstrates how a Boolean value is returned to an event handler.

```
<HTML>

<HEAD>

<TITLE>Custom onClick Event Example</TITLE>

<SCRIPT LANGUAGE="JavaScript">

<!-- HIDE FROM INCOMPATIBLE BROWSERS

function warnUser() {

        // The following line generates a Boolean value of true or
        // false and returns it to the event handler

        return confirm(
"This link is only for people who love golden retrievers!");

}
// STOP HIDING FROM INCOMPATIBLE BROWSERS -->

</SCRIPT>

</HEAD>

<BODY>

<A HREF = "GoldenRetrievers.html" onClick =
      "return warnUser();">
      Golden Retriever Club Home Page</A>

</BODY>

</HTML>
```

Figure 3-5: Program that returns a Boolean value to an event handler

In JavaScript programming, you can only use the words true and false to indicate Boolean values. In other programming languages, you can use the integer values of 1 and 0 to indicate Boolean values of true and false—1 indicates true and 0 indicates false. JavaScript converts the values true and false to the integers 1 and 0 when necessary. For example, when you attempt to use a Boolean variable of true in a mathematical operation, JavaScript converts the variable to an integer value of 1.

Boolean values get their name from the 19th century mathematician George Boole, who is credited with developing the theories of mathematical logic.

Strings

A text string contains zero or more characters surrounded by double or single quotation marks. Examples of strings you may use in a program are company names, user names, comments, and other types of text. You can use text strings as literal values or assign them to a variable. You first used literal strings with the document.write() and document.writeln() functions in Tutorial 1. Literal strings can be assigned a zero-length string value called an empty string. For example, `emptyVariable = "";` assigns an empty string to the variable emptyVariable. Empty strings are valid values for string literals and are not considered to be null or undefined. Why would you want to assign an empty string to a string literal? Think for a moment about the prompt() method, which displays a dialog box with a message, a text box, an OK button, and a Cancel button. You can pass two string arguments to the prompt() method: The first argument displays an instruction to the user, while the second argument is the default text that appears in the prompt dialog box text box. If you do not include the second argument, then the value *undefined* appears as the default text of the prompt dialog box. To prevent *undefined* from displaying as the default text in the prompt dialog text box, you pass an empty string as the second argument of the prompt() method.

When you want to include a quoted string within a literal string surrounded by double quotation marks, you surround the quoted string with single quotation marks. When you want to include a quoted string within a literal string surrounded by single quotation marks, you surround the quoted string with double quotation marks. Whichever method you use, a string must begin and end with the same type of quotation marks. For example, document.write("This is a text string."); is valid, since it starts and ends with double quotation marks. The statement document.write("This is a text string.'); is invalid, since it starts with a double quotation mark and ends with a single quotation mark. In this case you would receive an error message, since the Web browser cannot tell where the literal strings begin and end. Figure 3-6 shows an example of a program that prints literal strings. Figure 3-7 displays the output.

```
<HTML>

<HEAD>

<TITLE>Literal Strings</TITLE>

</HEAD>

<BODY>

<PRE>

<SCRIPT LANGUAGE="JavaScript">

document.writeln(
    "This is a literal string.");

document.writeln(
    "This string contains a 'quoted' string.");

document.writeln(
    'This is another example of a "quoted" string.');

var firstString =
    "This literal string was assigned to a variable.";

var secondString =
    'This literal string was also assigned to a variable.';

document.writeln(firstString);

document.writeln(secondString);

</SCRIPT>

</PRE>

</BODY>

</HTML>
```

Figure 3-6: LiteralStrings program

tip

Unlike other programming languages, there is no special data type in JavaScript for a single character, such as the *char* data type in the C, C++, and Java programming languages.

You need to use extra care when using single quotation marks with possessives and contractions in strings, since the JavaScript interpreter always looks for the first closing single or double quotation mark to match an opening single or double quotation mark. For example, consider the following statement:

```
document.writeln('My city's zip code is 01562.');
```

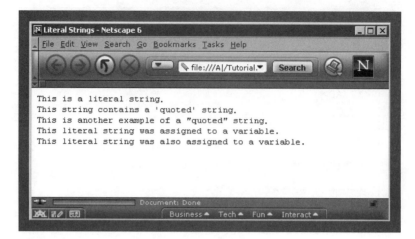

Figure 3-7: Output of LiteralStrings program in a Web browser

This statement causes an error. The JavaScript interpreter assumes that the literal string ends with the apostrophe following *city* and looks for the closing parentheses for the document.writeln() function immediately following *city's*. To get around this problem, you include an escape character before the apostrophe in *city's*. An **escape character** tells the compiler or interpreter that the character that follows it has a special purpose. In JavaScript, the escape character is the backslash (\). Placing a backslash in front of an apostrophe tells the JavaScript interpreter that the apostrophe is to be treated as a regular keyboard character, such as a, b, 1, or 2, and not as part of a single quotation mark pair that encloses a text string. The backslash in the following statement tells the JavaScript interpreter to print the apostrophe following the word *city* as an apostrophe.

```
document.writeln('My city\'s zip code is 01562.');
```

You can also use the escape character in combination with other characters to insert a special character into a string. When you combine the escape character with other characters, the combination is called an **escape sequence**. The backslash followed by an apostrophe (\') and the backslash followed by a double quotation mark (\") are both examples of escape sequences. Most escape sequences carry out special functions. For example, the escape sequence \t inserts a tab into a string. Figure 3-8 describes some of the escape sequences that can be added to a string in JavaScript.

Escape Sequence	Character
\b	Backspace
\f	Form feed
\n	New line

Figure 3-8: JavaScript escape sequences

Escape Sequence	Character
\r	Carriage return
\t	Horizontal tab
\'	Single quotation mark
\"	Double quotation mark
\\	Backslash

Figure 3-8: JavaScript escape sequences (continued)

Notice that one of the characters generated by an escape sequence is the backslash. Since the escape character itself is a backslash, you must use the escape sequence "\\" to include a backslash as a character in a string. For example, to include the path "C:\WebPages\JavaScript_Files\" in a string, you must include two backslashes for every single backslash you want to appear in the string, as in the following statement:

```
document.writeln("My JavaScript files are located in
C:\\WebPages\\JavaScript_Files\\");
```

Figure 3-9 shows an example of a program containing strings with several escape sequences. Figure 3-10 shows the output.

```
<HTML>

<HEAD>

<TITLE>Escape Sequences</TITLE>

</HEAD>

<BODY>

<PRE>

<SCRIPT LANGUAGE="JavaScript">

document.writeln("This line is printed \non two lines.");
    // New line

document.writeln("\tThis line includes a horizontal tab.");
    // Horizontal tab

document.writeln("My personal files are in c:\\personal.");
    // Backslash
```

Figure 3-9: Program containing strings with escape sequences

```
document.writeln("My dog's name is \"Noah.\"");
    // Double quotation mark

document.writeln('Massachusetts\' capital is Boston.');
    // Single quotation mark

</SCRIPT>

</PRE>

</BODY>

</HTML>
```

Figure 3-9: Program containing strings with escape sequences (continued)

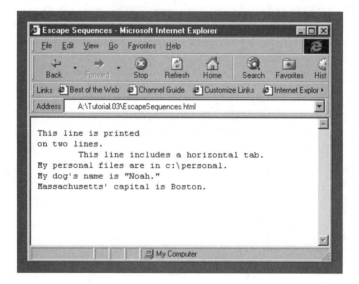

Figure 3-10: Output of program containing strings with escape sequences

•••

The new line and carriage return escape sequences are only recognized inside a container element such as the <PRE>...</PRE> tag pair.

•••

In addition to including escape sequences in strings, you can include HTML tags. If you include HTML tags within JavaScript strings, they must be located within a string's opening and closing quotation marks. For example, to include the line break tag <BR> in a string printed with the document.write() function, the statement should read document.write("There is a line break following this sentence.
");. HTML tags cannot be used directly within JavaScript code. Therefore, the statement document.write("There is a line break following this sentence."
); causes an error, since the <BR> tag is located outside the literal string. Figure 3-11 shows an example of a program containing strings with HTML tags. Figure 3-12 shows the output.

```
<HTML>

<HEAD>

<TITLE>Strings with HTML Tags</TITLE>

</HEAD>

<BODY>

<PRE>

<SCRIPT LANGUAGE="JavaScript">

heading1_string = "<H1>Hello World (this is the H1 tag)</H1>";

document.writeln(heading1_string);

heading2_string =
    "<H2>This line is formatted with the H2 tag </H2>";

document.writeln(heading2_string);

italic_string = "<I>This line is italicized.</I>";

document.writeln(italic_string);

bold_string = "<B>This line is bolded.</B>";

document.writeln(bold_string);

underlined_string = "<U>This line is underlined.</U>";

document.writeln(underlined_string);

formatted_string =
    This line includes <B>bolded</B> and <U> underlined</U> text.";

document.writeln(formatted_string);

hr_string = "Following this line is a horizontal rule.<HR>";

document.writeln(hr_string);

</SCRIPT>

</PRE>

</BODY>

</HTML>
```

Figure 3-11: Program containing strings with HTML tags

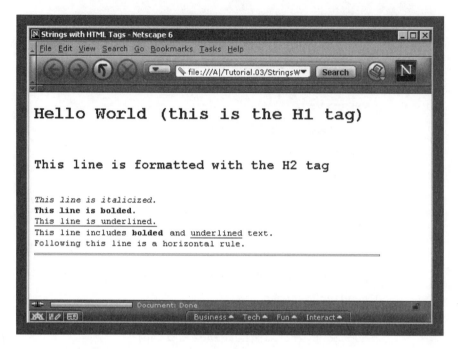

Figure 3-12: Output of program containing strings with HTML tags

Next you will create a file that displays a restaurant's daily menu, by combining strings with escape characters and HTML tags. Note that you can create the same document more easily using only HTML tags. The purpose of this exercise is to demonstrate how text strings can be combined with HTML tags and escape characters.

To create a file that combines strings with escape characters and HTML tags:

1 Create a new document in your text editor or HTML editor.

2 Type the <HTML> and <HEAD> sections of the document, along with the opening <BODY> tag:

```
<HTML>
<HEAD>
<TITLE>Daily Specials</TITLE>
</HEAD>
<BODY>
```

3 Add the opening statements for a JavaScript section:

```
<SCRIPT LANGUAGE="JavaScript">
<!-- HIDE FROM INCOMPATIBLE BROWSERS
```

4 Declare the following variables and assign to them strings containing combinations of text, HTML tags, and escape characters.

```
var restaurant = "<H1>Small Town Restaurant</H1><BR>";
var specials = "<H2>Daily Specials for Wednesday</H2>";
var prixfixe =
    "<I>Prix fixe price:</I> <B>$9.95</B><HR>";
var appetizer = "<H3>Caesar Salad</H3>";
var entree = "<H3>Chef\'s \"Surprise\"</H3>";
var dessert = "<H3>Chocolate Cheesecake</H3><HR>";
```

5 Next add the following statements to print the variables:

```
document.write(restaurant);
document.write(specials);
document.write(prixfixe);
document.write(appetizer);
document.write(entree);
document.write(dessert);
```

 tip

> The preceding statements include the write() method instead of the writeln() method, since the heading level styles contained in the string variables automatically force line breaks.

6 Add the following code to close the <SCRIPT>, <BODY>, and <HTML> tags:

```
// STOP HIDING FROM INCOMPATIBLE BROWSERS -->
</SCRIPT>
</BODY>
</HTML>
```

7 Save the file as **DailySpecials.html** in the **Tutorial.03** folder on your Data Disk. Open the **DailySpecials.html** file in your Web browser. Figure 3-13 shows the output.

8 Close the Web browser window.

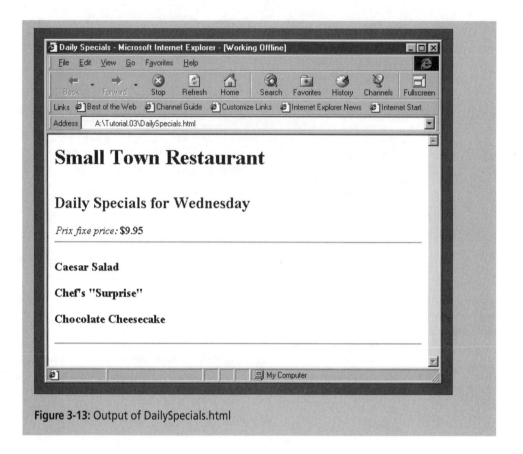

Figure 3-13: Output of DailySpecials.html

Arrays

An **array** contains a set of data represented by a single variable name. You can think of an array as a collection of variables contained within a single variable. You use arrays when you want to store groups or lists of related information in a single, easily managed location. Lists of names, course listings, test scores, and price lists are all typical examples of the information you store in arrays. For example, Figure 3-14 shows that you can manage the lengthy and difficult-to-spell names of a hospital's departments using a single array named *hospitalDepartments*. You can use the array to refer to each department without having to retype the names and possibly introduce syntax errors through misspellings.

Arrays are represented in JavaScript by the Array object, which contains a constructor function named Array(). You create new arrays by using the new keyword and the Array() constructor function, in the same manner that you instantiate objects from your own custom constructor functions. The syntax for instantiating a new array using the Array() constructor function is as follows:

```
hospitalDepartments = new Array(number of elements);
```

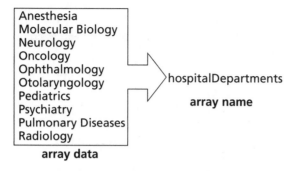

Figure 3-14: Conceptual example of an array

Notice that the Array() constructor function receives a single argument representing the number of elements to be contained in the array. Each piece of data contained in an array is called an **element**. The following code creates an array named hospitalDepartments that has 10 elements:

```
hospitalDepartments = new Array(10);
```

The numbering of elements within an array starts with an index number of zero (0). You refer to a specific element by enclosing its index number in brackets at the end of the array name. For example, the first element in the hospitalDepartments array is hospitalDepartments[0], the second element is hospitalDepartments[1], the third element is hospitalDepartments[2], and so on. You assign values to individual array elements in the same fashion as you assign values to a standard variable, except that you include the index for an individual element of the array. The following code assigns values to the ten elements within the hospitalDepartments array:

```
hospitalDepartments[0] =
    "Anesthesia";    // first element
hospitalDepartments[1] =
    "Molecular Biology";    // second element
hospitalDepartments[2] =
    "Neurology";    // third element
hospitalDepartments[3] =
    "Oncology";    // fourth element
hospitalDepartments[4] =
    "Ophthalmology";    // fifth element
hospitalDepartments[5] =
    "Otolaryngology";    // sixth element
hospitalDepartments[6] =
    "Pediatrics";    // seventh element
hospitalDepartments[7] =
    "Psychiatry";    // eighth element
hospitalDepartments[8] =
    "Pulmonary Diseases";    // ninth element
hospitalDepartments[9] =
    "Radiology";    // tenth element
```

You use an element in an array in the same manner that you use other types of variables. For example, the following code prints the values contained in the ten elements of the hospitalDepartments array:

```
document.writeln(hospitalDepartments[0]);
     // prints "Anesthesia"
document.writeln(hospitalDepartments[1]);
     // prints "Molecular Biology"
document.writeln(hospitalDepartments[2]);
     // prints "Neurology"
document.writeln(hospitalDepartments[3]);
     // prints "Oncology"
document.writeln(hospitalDepartments[4]);
     // prints "Ophthalmology"
document.writeln(hospitalDepartments[5]);
     // prints "Otolaryngology"
document.writeln(hospitalDepartments[6]);
     // prints "Pediatrics"
document.writeln(hospitalDepartments[7]);
     // prints "Psychiatry"
document.writeln(hospitalDepartments[8]);
     // prints "Pulmonary Diseases"
document.writeln(hospitalDepartments[9]);
     // prints "Radiology"
```

Once you have assigned a value to an array element, you can change it later, just as you can change other variables in a program. To change the first array element in the hospitalDepartments array from *Anesthesia* to *Anesthesiology*, you include the statement hospitalDepartments[0] = "Anesthesiology"; in your code.

Most programming languages require that all of the elements in an array be of the exact same data type. However, since JavaScript is a loosely typed language, the values assigned to array elements can be of different data types. For example, the following code creates an array and stores values with different data types in the array elements:

```
multiple_types = new Array(5);
multiple_types[0] = "Hello World"; // string
multiple_types[1] = 10;            // integer
multiple_types[2] = 3.156;         // floating-point
multiple_types[3] = true;          // Boolean
multiple_types[4] = null;          // null
```

When you create a new array with the Array() constructor function, declaring the number of array elements is optional. You can create the array without any elements and add new elements to the array as necessary. The size of an array can change dynamically. If you assign a value to an element that has not yet been created, the element is created automatically, along with any elements that might precede it. For example, the first statement in the following code creates the hospitalDepartments array without any elements. The second statement then assigns *Anesthesia* to the third element, which also creates the first two elements (hospitalDepartments[0] and hospitalDepartments[1]) in the process. However, note that until you assign values to them, hospitalDepartments[0] and hospitalDepartments[1] will both contain *undefined* values.

```
hospitalDepartments = new Array();
hospitalDepartments[2] = "Anesthesia";
```

You can assign values to array elements when you first create the array. The following code assigns some values to the hospitalDepartments array when it is created, then prints each of the values, using the array element numbers:

```
hospitalDepartments =
    new Array("Anesthesia", "Molecular Biology",
    "Neurology");
document.writeln(hospitalDepartments[0]);
    // prints "Anesthesia"
document.writeln(hospitalDepartments[1]);
    // prints "Molecular Biology"
document.writeln(hospitalDepartments[2]);
    // prints "Neurology"
```

The Array object contains various methods for working with arrays, and also contains a single property, called length. The Array object methods are somewhat advanced, so they will not be discussed in this book. You can find a list of the Array object methods in the appendix. However, the Array object **length** property, which returns the number of elements in an array, is quite useful. You append the length property to an array name using the syntax `arrayName.length`. The following code prints the value *10* by using the length property to return the number of elements in the hospitalDepartments array.

```
hospitalDepartments = new Array();
hospitalDepartments[0] = "Anesthesia";
hospitalDepartments[1] = "Molecular Biology";
hospitalDepartments[2] = "Neurology";
hospitalDepartments[3] = "Oncology";
hospitalDepartments[4] = "Ophthalmology";
hospitalDepartments[5] = "Otolaryngology";
hospitalDepartments[6] = "Pediatrics";
hospitalDepartments[7] = "Psychiatry";
hospitalDepartments[8] = "Pulmonary Diseases";
hospitalDepartments[9] = "Radiology";
document.write(hospitalDepartments.length);
    // prints '10'
```

Next you will create an array containing the months of the year and use the length property to print the number of array elements.

To create an array containing the months of the year:

1 Create a new document in your text editor or HTML editor.

2 Type the <HTML> and <HEAD> sections of the document:

```
<HTML>
<HEAD>
<TITLE>Months of the Year</TITLE>
</HEAD>
```

3 Add the following code to begin the body of the HTML document and create a preformatted text container:

```
<BODY>
<PRE>
```

4 Add the opening statements for a JavaScript section:

```
<SCRIPT LANGUAGE="JavaScript">
<!-- HIDE FROM INCOMPATIBLE BROWSERS
```

5 Type this statement to declare a new array containing 12 elements: **var monthsOfYear = new Array(12);**.

6 Assign the 12 months of the year to the 12 elements of the array. Remember that the first element in an array starts with 0. Therefore, the element in the array that will hold January is monthsOfYear[0].

```
monthsOfYear[0] = "January";
monthsOfYear[1] = "February";
monthsOfYear[2] = "March";
monthsOfYear[3] = "April";
monthsOfYear[4] = "May";
monthsOfYear[5] = "June";monthsOfYear[6] = "July";
monthsOfYear[7] = "August";
monthsOfYear[8] = "September";
monthsOfYear[9] = "October";
monthsOfYear[10] = "November";
monthsOfYear[11] = "December";
```

7 Next, add the following statements to print each element of the array:

```
document.writeln(monthsOfYear[0]);
document.writeln(monthsOfYear[1]);
document.writeln(monthsOfYear[2]);
document.writeln(monthsOfYear[3]);
document.writeln(monthsOfYear[4]);
document.writeln(monthsOfYear[5]);
document.writeln(monthsOfYear[6]);
document.writeln(monthsOfYear[7]);
document.writeln(monthsOfYear[8]);
```

```
document.writeln(monthsOfYear[9]);
document.writeln(monthsOfYear[10]);
document.writeln(monthsOfYear[11]);
```

▶ **tip**

A looping statement provides a more efficient method for printing all the elements of an array. You will learn about looping statements in Tutorial 4.

8 Add the following statement that uses the length property to return the number of elements in the array:

```
document.writeln("There are " + monthsOfYear.length
     + " months in a year.");
```

9 Add the following code to close the <SCRIPT>, <PRE>, <BODY>, and <HTML> tags:

```
// STOP HIDING FROM INCOMPATIBLE BROWSERS -->
</SCRIPT>
</PRE>
</BODY>
</HTML>
```

10 Save the file as **MonthsOfYear.html** in the **Tutorial.03** folder on your Data Disk. Then open the **MonthsOfYear.html** file in your Web browser. Figure 3-15 shows the output.

Figure 3-15: Output of MonthsOfYear.html

11 Close the Web browser window.

SUMMARY

- A data type is the specific category of information that a variable contains.

- Data types that can only be assigned a single value are called primitive types.

- Reference, or composite, data types, are collections of data represented by a single variable name.

- The null value is a data type as well as a value that can be assigned to a variable. Assigning the value null to a variable indicates the variable does not contain a value.

- Programming languages that require you to declare the data types of variables are called strongly typed programming languages.

- Programming languages that do not require you to declare the data types of variables are called loosely typed programming languages.

- JavaScript uses loose typing or dynamic typing and does not require data types of variables to be declared. In JavaScript, data types can change after they have been declared.

- An integer is a positive or negative number with no decimal point.

- A floating-point number contains decimal places or is written using exponential notation. Exponential notation, or scientific notation, is a way of writing very large numbers or numbers with many decimal places, using a shortened format.

- A Boolean value is a logical value of true or false.

- Literal strings and string variables contain zero or more characters. A string consisting of zero characters is called an empty string.

- An escape character is used to tell the compiler or interpreter that the character that follows it has a special purpose. When the escape character is combined with other characters, it is called an escape sequence.

- If you include HTML tags within JavaScript strings, they must be located within a string's opening and closing quotation marks.

- An array contains a set of data represented by a single variable name. Each piece of data contained in an array is called an element.

- You create an array with the Array() constructor object. The Array() constructor object receives a single argument representing the number of elements to be contained in the array. Specifying the number of array elements is optional.

- The numbering of elements within an array starts with an index number of zero (0).

- You can create an array without any elements and then add new elements to the array as needed.

- The size of an array can change dynamically.

- You can assign values to an array's elements when you first create the array.

- The Array object length property returns the number of elements in an array.

QUESTIONS

1. Data types that can be assigned only a single value are called _____ types.
   a. simple
   b. rudimentary
   c. primitive
   d. single-value

2. Which of the following is not a primitive data type?
   a. string
   b. number
   c. Boolean
   d. object

3. Which of the following is not a reference data type?
   a. function
   b. array
   c. Boolean
   d. object

4. Text that is enclosed within quotation marks is _____.
   a. a literal string
   b. quoted text
   c. a comment
   d. an element

5. A loosely typed programming language _____.
   a. does not require data types of variables to be declared
   b. requires data types of variables to be declared
   c. does not have different data types
   d. does not have variables

6. Which type of programming language is JavaScript?
   a. loosely typed
   b. untyped
   c. strongly typed
   d. static typed

7. You can determine the data type of a variable using the _____.
   a. returnValue function
   b. typeof() operator
   c. parseFloat() function
   d. toString operator

8. How many decimal places does an integer store?
   a. 0
   b. 1
   c. 2
   d. as many as necessary

9. Which of the following is not a floating-point number?
   a. -439.35
   b. 3.17
   c. 10
   d. -7e11

10. Boolean values in JavaScript are the logical values _____.
    a. minimum and maximum
    b. positive and negative
    c. 1 and 2
    d. true and false

11. Which of the following is the correct syntax for including double quotation marks within a string that is already surrounded by double quotation marks?
    a. "Some computers have \"artificial\" intelligence."
    b. "Some computers have "artificial" intelligence."
    c. "Some computers have /"artificial/" intelligence."
    d. "Some computers have ""artificial"" intelligence."

12. A(n) _____ tells the compiler or interpreter that the character that follows it has a special purpose.
    a. integer
    b. floating-point number
    c. array object
    d. escape character

13. Which of the following character combinations inserts a carriage return into a text string?
    a. \b
    b. \f
    c. \n
    d. \r

14. The numbering of elements within an array starts with an index number of _____.
    a. -1
    b. 0
    c. 1
    d. 2

15. What is the correct syntax for creating an array?
    a. `variable_name = new Array;`
    b. `variable_name = Array(number of elements);`
    c. `variable_name = new Array(number of elements);`
    d. `new Array(number of elements);`

16. Which of the following refers to the first element in an array named employees[]?
    a. employees[0]
    b. employees[1]
    c. employees[first]
    d. employees[a]

17. You return the number of elements in an array using the _____ property of the Array object.

a. size

b. length

c. elements

d. dimension

 EXERCISES

Save all files you create in the Tutorial.03 folder on your Data Disk.

1. Identify the data types assigned to the result variable in each of the following statements:

a. `var result;` _____

b. `var result = 3e10;` _____

c. `var result = 10;` _____

d. `var result = null;` _____

e. `var result = 874.0;` _____

f. `var result = new Array();` _____

g. `var result = true;` _____

2. Create a program that declares and assigns three integer variables: one for your house number or apartment number (*not* your street name), one for your zip code, and another for your area code. Use document.write() and document.writeln() statements to print each variable, along with the typeof() operator to make sure each variable is of the number data type. Save the document as IntVariables.html.

3. Create a program that declares and assigns floating-point variables for the interest rate you are paying on your car, credit card, mortgage, student loan, or some other type of loan. If you do not have any type of loan with an interest rate, then look in your local newspaper or on the Internet for current interest rates for mortgages and autos. Use document.write() and document.writeln() statements to print each variable, along with a description of the loan, and the typeof() operator to make sure each variable is of the number data type. Save the document as DecimalVariables.html.

4. Create a program that declares and assigns three Boolean variables: one that declares whether you are a student, one that declares whether you invest in the stock market, and another that declares whether you own your own home. Use document.write() and document.writeln() statements to print each variable, along with the typeof() operator to make sure each variable is of the Boolean data type. Save the document as BooleanVariables.html.

5. Create a program that declares and assigns three string variables: one for your street name, one for your city, and another for your state. Use document.write() and document.writeln() statements to print each variable, along with the typeof() operator to make sure each variable is of the string data type. Save the document as StringVariables.html.

6. Modify the following program so that it uses escape sequences instead of document.writeln() statements to print each line of text on its own line. Save the document as EscapeSequences.html.

```
<HTML>
<HEAD>
<TITLE>Escape Sequences</TITLE>
</HEAD>
<BODY>
<PRE>
<SCRIPT LANGUAGE="JavaScript">
<!-- HIDE FROM INCOMPATIBLE BROWSERS
document.writeln("Line 1");
document.writeln("Line 2");
document.writeln("Line 3");
document.writeln("Line 4");
document.writeln("Line 5");
// STOP HIDING FROM INCOMPATIBLE BROWSERS -->
</SCRIPT>
</PRE>
</BODY>
</HTML>
```

7. In Tutorial 1 you created an HTML document that used various types of HTML formatting and JavaScript to print the preamble to the United States Constitution. Re-create the document, including HTML formatting, using only JavaScript. Save the document as PreambleJavaScript.html.

8. Modify the following JavaScript program so that the variables are saved in an array named ratesArray. Assign the number of array elements in the array declaration. Also, add statements to the program that print the contents of each array element. Save the document as InterestArray.html.

```
<HTML>
<HEAD>
<TITLE>Interest Array</TITLE>
</HEAD>
<BODY>
<PRE>
<SCRIPT LANGUAGE="JavaScript">
<!-- HIDE FROM INCOMPATIBLE BROWSERS
interestRate1 = .0725;
interestRate2 = .0750;
interestRate3 = .0775;
interestRate4 = .0800;
interestRate5 = .0825;
interestRate6 = .0850;
interestRate7 = .0875;
// STOP HIDING FROM INCOMPATIBLE BROWSERS -->
```

```
</SCRIPT>
</PRE>
</BODY>
</HTML>
```

9. Create an HTML document that displays a simplified version of your work history, including the names of your former employers, position within each company, and dates of employment. When you create the document, include all HTML commands inside string literals. Also, use the document.write() method instead of the document.writeln() method. To create line breaks, use either an escape character or an HTML tag within the string literals. Save the document as WorkHistory.html.

10. Create an HTML document containing your resume. Use the write() method to build heading sections such as your name, address, former employer names, and dates of employment. Format the heading sections using HTML tags and escape sequences within the text strings that build each line. Create the main paragraphs of the resume in the body section of the document. You will need to use multiple script sections. Save the document as Resume.html.

11. Create an HTML document that creates and prints an array of all the family members you can think of. The array should be contained in a <SCRIPT> section in the document <BODY>. Save the document as FamilyArray.html.

12. Create an HTML document that uses arrays to print your favorite songs from the 1990s, along with the year each song was released. Use two arrays in the document and place them in a <SCRIPT> section in the document <BODY>. Name the first array songs[ ], and fill it with a list of your favorite songs from the 1990s. Create another array containing 10 elements, one for each year in the 1990's decade (1990, 1991, 1992, and so on). Name this second array nineties[ ]. Using the arrays, print each song, along with the year it was released. Save the document as SongYears.html.

In this section you will learn:

- How to use expressions
- How to use arithmetic, assignment, comparison, and logical operators
- How to work with strings
- How to create the calculator program

Expressions and Operators

Expressions

Variables and data become most useful when you use them in an expression. An **expression** is a combination of literal values, variables, operators, and other expressions that can be evaluated by the JavaScript interpreter to produce a result. The JavaScript interpreter recognizes the literal values and variables in Figure 3-16 as expressions.

```
"this is a string variable"
     // string literal expression

10   // integer literal expression

3.156  // floating-point literal expression

true   // Boolean literal expression

null   // null literal expression

employee_number   // variable expression
```

Figure 3-16: Literal and variable expressions

You can use operands and operators to create more complex expressions. **Operands** are variables and literals contained in an expression. **Operators** are symbols used in expressions to manipulate operands. You have worked with several simple expressions so far that combine operators and operands. Consider the following statement:

```
myNumber = 100;
```

This statement is an expression that results in the value 100 being assigned to myNumber. The operands in the expression are the *myNumber* variable name and the integer value *100*. The operator is the equal sign (=) assignment operator. The equal sign operator is an assignment operator, because it *assigns* the value (100) on the right side of the expression to the variable (myNumber) on the left side of the expression. Figure 3-17 lists the main types of JavaScript operators.

Operator Type	Description
Arithmetic	Used for performing mathematical calculations
Assignment	Assigns values to variables
Comparison	Compares operands and returns a Boolean value
Logical	Used for performing Boolean operations on Boolean operands
String	Performs operations on strings
Special	Used for various purposes, and includes the conditional, instance of, in, delete, void, new, this, typeof, and comma operators

Figure 3-17: JavaScript operator types

Other types of JavaScript operators include bitwise operators, which operate on integer values and are a complex topic.

Although special operators are not specifically discussed in this tutorial, they are introduced throughout the book when necessary.

JavaScript operators are binary or unary. A **binary operator** requires an operand before the operator and an operand after the operator. The equal sign in the statement myNumber = 100; is an example of a binary operator. A **unary operator** requires a single operand either before or after the operator. For example, the increment operator (++), an arithmetic operator, is used for increasing an operand by a value of one. The statement myNumber++; changes the value of the myNumber variable to 101.

The operand to the left of an operator is known as the left operand, and the operand to the right of an operator is known as the right operand.

Next you will learn about the different types of JavaScript operators.

Arithmetic Operators

Arithmetic operators are used to perform mathematical calculations, such as addition, subtraction, multiplication, and division, in JavaScript. You can also return the modulus of a calculation, which is the remainder left when you divide one number by another number. JavaScript binary arithmetic operators and their descriptions are listed in Figure 3-18. Code examples using the arithmetic binary operators are shown in Figure 3-19.

Operator	Description
+ (addition)	Adds two operands
- (subtraction)	Subtracts one operand from another operand
* (multiplication)	Multiplies one operand by another operand
/ (division)	Divides one operand by another operand
% (modulus)	Divides two operands and returns the remainder

Figure 3-18: Arithmetic binary operators

```
var x, y, returnValue;


// ADDITION
x = 100;
y = 200;
returnValue = x + y;          // returnValue changes to 300


// SUBTRACTION
x = 10;
y = 7;
returnValue = x - y;          // returnValue changes to 3


// MULTIPLICATION
x = 2;
y = 6;
returnValue = x * y;          // returnValue changes to 12


// DIVISION
x = 24;
y = 3;
```

Figure 3-19: Examples of arithmetic binary operators

```
returnValue = x / y;            // returnValue changes to 8


// MODULUS

x = 3;

y = 2;

returnValue = x % y;            // returnValue changes to 1
```

Figure 3-19: Examples of arithmetic binary operators (continued)

Notice in Figure 3-19 that when JavaScript performs an arithmetic calculation, it performs the operation on the right side of the assignment operator, and then assigns the value to a variable on the left side of the assignment operator. For example, in the statement `returnValue = x + y;`, the operands x and y are added, then the result is assigned to the returnValue variable on the left side of the assignment operator.

You can include a combination of variables and literal values on the right side of an assignment statement. For example, the addition statement could be written `returnValue = 100 + y;`, `returnValue = x + 200;`, or `returnValue = 100 + 200;`. However, you cannot include a literal value as the left operand, since the JavaScript interpreter must have a variable to which to assign the returned value. Therefore, the statement `100 = x + y;` will cause an error.

When performing arithmetic operations on string values, the JavaScript interpreter will attempt to convert the string values to numbers. The variables in the following example are assigned as string values instead of numbers, since they are contained within quotation marks. Nevertheless, the JavaScript interpreter will correctly perform the multiplication operation and return a value of 6.

```
x = "2";
y = "3";
returnValue = x * y;     // the value returned is 6
```

The JavaScript interpreter will not convert strings to numbers when you use the addition operator. When you use the addition operator with strings, the strings are combined instead of being added together. In the following example, the operation returns a value of 23 since the x and y variables contain strings instead of numbers:

```
x = "2";
y = "3";
returnValue = x + y;     // a string value of 23 is returned
```

Arithmetic operations can also be performed on a single variable using unary operators. Figure 3-20 lists the unary arithmetic operators available in JavaScript.

Operator	Description
++ (increment)	Increases an operand by a value of one
-- (decrement)	Decreases an operand by a value of one
- (negation)	Returns the opposite value (negative or positive) of an operand

Figure 3-20: Arithmetic unary operators

The increment (++) and decrement (--) unary operators can be used as prefix or postfix operators. A **prefix operator** is placed before a variable. A **postfix operator** is placed after a variable. The statements ++myVariable; and myVariable++; both increase myVariable by one. However, the two statements return different values. When you use the increment operator as a prefix operator, the value of the operand is returned *after* it is increased by a value of one. When you use the increment operator as a postfix operator, the value of the operand is returned *before* it is increased by a value of one. Similarly, when you use the decrement operator as a prefix operator, the value of the operand is returned *after* it is decreased by a value of one, and when you use the decrement operator as a postfix operator, the value of the operand is returned *before* it is decreased by a value of one. If you intend to assign the incremented or decremented value to another variable, then whether you use the prefix or postfix operator makes a difference. For example, in the following code the count variable is increased by a value of one, using the prefix increment operator, then assigned to the newValue variable:

```
var count = 10;
var newValue = ++count;   // newValue is assigned '11'
```

In this example, the prefix operator returns a value after adding one to the operand, the count variable is increased to 11, and the newValue variable is assigned a value of 11. In contrast, in the next example, the count variable is increased by a value of one, using the postfix increment operator, then assigned to the newValue variable. The postfix increment operator returns a value before adding one to the operand, and the newValue variable is assigned a value of 10.

```
var count = 10;
var newValue = count++;   // newValue is assigned '10', and
count is assigned '11'
```

Unlike the increment and decrement unary operators, the negation (-) unary operator cannot be used as a postfix operator. The negation (-) unary operator must be placed as a prefix in front of the operand that will be changed to a negative value. In the following code, the variable x is initially assigned a value of positive 10; then x is changed to -10 using the negation unary operator.

```
var x = 10;
x = -x;           // x is changed to -10
```

Next you will create a program that performs arithmetic calculations.

To create a program that performs arithmetic calculations:

1 Create a new document in your text editor or HTML editor.

2 Type the <HTML> and <HEAD> sections of the document:

```
<HTML>
<HEAD>
<TITLE>Arithmetic Examples</TITLE>
</HEAD>
```

3 Add the following code to begin the body of the HTML document and to create a preformatted text container:

```
<BODY>
<PRE>
```

4 Add the opening statements for a JavaScript section:

```
<SCRIPT LANGUAGE="JavaScript">
<!-- HIDE FROM INCOMPATIBLE BROWSERS
```

5 Type the following statements to declare two variables: a number variable to contain a number, which you will use in several arithmetic operations, and a result variable to contain the value of each arithmetic operation.

```
var number = 100;
var result;
```

6 Now add the following statements that perform addition, subtraction, multiplication, and division operations on the number variable and assign each value to the result variable. The result variable is printed each time it changes.

```
result = number + 50;
document.writeln(
    "Result after addition = " + result);
result = number / 4;
document.writeln(
    "Result after division = " + result);
result = number - 25;
document.writeln(
    "Result after subtraction = " + result);
result = number * 2;
document.writeln(
    "Result after multiplication = " + result);
```

7 Next add the following two statements. The first statement uses the increment operator to increase the value of the number variable by one and assigns the new value to the result variable. The second statement prints the result variable. Notice that the increment operator is used as a prefix, so the new value is assigned to the result variable. If you used the postfix increment operator, you would assign the old value of the number variable to the result variable, before the number variable is incremented by one.

```
result = ++number;
document.writeln("Result after increment = " + result);
```

8   Add the following code to close the <SCRIPT>, <PRE>, <BODY>, and <HTML> tags:

```
// STOP HIDING FROM INCOMPATIBLE BROWSERS -->
</SCRIPT>
</PRE>
</BODY>
</HTML>
```

9   Save the file as **ArithmeticExamples.html** in the **Tutorial.03** folder on your Data Disk. Open the **ArithmeticExamples.html** file in your Web browser. Figure 3-21 shows the output.

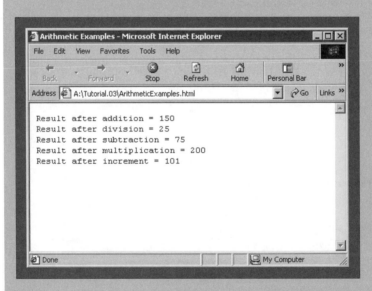

Figure 3-21: Output of ArithmeticExamples.html

10   Close the Web browser window.

Assignment Operators

Assignment operators are used for assigning a value to a variable. You have already used the most common assignment operator, the equal sign (=), to assign values to variables you declared using the **var** statement. The equal sign assigns an initial value to a new variable or assigns a new value to an existing variable. For example, the following code creates a variable named myCar, uses the equal sign to assign it an initial value, then uses the equal sign again to assign it a new value.

```
var myCar = "Ford";
myCar = "Corvette";
```

JavaScript includes other assignment operators in addition to the equal sign. These additional assignment operators perform mathematical calculations on variables and literal values in an expression, and then assign a new value to the left operand. Figure 3-22 displays a list of the common JavaScript assignment operators.

Operator	Description
=	Assigns the value of the right operand to the left operand
+=	Combines the value of the right operand with the value of the left operand or adds the value of the right operand to the value of the left operand and assigns the new value to the left operand
-=	Subtracts the value of the right operand from the value of the left operand and assigns the new value to the left operand
*=	Multiplies the value of the right operand by the value of the left operand and assigns the new value to the left operand
/=	Divides the value of the left operand by the value of the right operand and assigns the new value to the left operand
%=	Divides the value of the left operand by the value of the right operand and assigns the remainder to the left operand (modulus)

Figure 3-22: Assignment operators

You can use the += assignment operator to combine two strings as well as to add numbers. In the case of strings, the string on the left side of the operator is combined with the string on the right side of the operator, and the new value is assigned to the left operator. Before combining operands, the JavaScript interpreter will attempt to convert a non-numeric operand, such as a string, to a number. If a non-numeric operand cannot be converted to a number, you will receive a value of NaN. The value **NaN** stands for Not a Number and is returned when a mathematical operation does not result in a numerical value. Figure 3-23 shows code examples of the different assignment operators.

```
var x, y;


x = "Hello ";

x += "World";    // x changes to "Hello World"
```

Figure 3-23: Examples of assignment operators

```
x = 100;
y = 200;
x += y;          // x changes to 300


x = 10;
y = 7;
x -= y;          // x changes to 3


x = 2;
y = 6;
x *= y;          // x changes to 12


x = 24;
y = 3;
x /= y;          // x changes to 8


x = 3;
y = 2;
x %= y;          // x changes to 1


x = "100";
y = 5;
x *= y;          // x changes to 500


x = "one hundred";
y = 5;
x *= y;          // x changes to NaN
```

Figure 3-23: Examples of assignment operators (continued)

Next you will create an HTML document that uses assignment operators.

To create an HTML document that uses assignment operators:

1 Create a new document in your text editor or HTML editor.

2 Type the <HTML> and <HEAD> sections of the document:

```
<HTML>
<HEAD>
<TITLE>Assignment Examples</TITLE>
</HEAD>
```

3 Add the following code to begin the body of the HTML document and to create a preformatted text container:

```
<BODY>
<PRE>
```

4 Add the opening statements for a JavaScript section:

```
<SCRIPT LANGUAGE="JavaScript">
<!-- HIDE FROM INCOMPATIBLE BROWSERS
```

5 Type the following statements that perform several assignment operations on a variable named changingVar. After each assignment operation, the result is printed.

```
var changingVar = "text string 1";
changingVar += " & text string 2";
document.writeln(
     "Variable after addition assignment = "
     + changingVar);
changingVar = 100;
changingVar += 50;
document.writeln(
     "Variable after addition assignment = "
     + changingVar);
changingVar -= 30;
document.writeln(
     "Variable after subtraction assignment = "
     + changingVar);
changingVar /= 3;
document.writeln(
     "Variable after division assignment = "
     + changingVar);
changingVar *= 8;
document.writeln(
     "Variable after multiplication assignment = "
     + changingVar);
```

```
changingVar %= 300;
document.writeln(
    "Variable after modulus assignment = "
    + changingVar);
```

6 Add the following code to close the <SCRIPT>, <PRE>, <BODY>, and <HTML> tags:

```
// STOP HIDING FROM INCOMPATIBLE BROWSERS -->
</SCRIPT>
</PRE>
</BODY>
</HTML>
```

7 Save the file as **AssignmentExamples.html** in the **Tutorial.03** folder on your Data Disk. Open the **AssignmentExamples.html** file in your Web browser. Figure 3-24 shows the output.

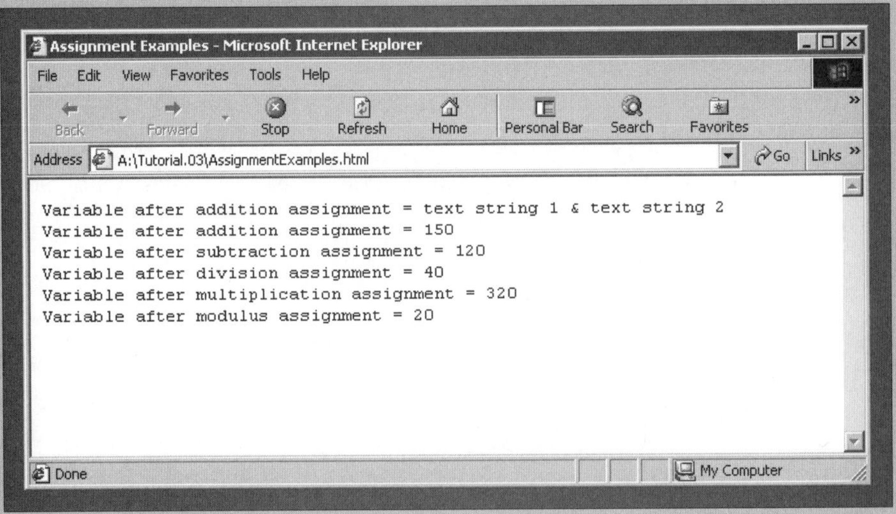

Figure 3-24: Output of AssignmentExamples.html

8 Close the Web browser window.

Comparison Operators

Comparison operators are used to compare two operands for equality and to determine if one numeric value is greater than another. A Boolean value of true or false is returned after two operands are compared. Figure 3-25 lists the JavaScript comparison operators.

Operator	Description
== (equal)	Returns true if the operands are equal
=== (strict equal)	Returns true if the operands are equal and of the same type
!= (not equal)	Returns true if the operands are not equal
!== (strict not equal)	Returns true if the operands are not equal or not of the same type
> (greater than)	Returns true if the left operand is greater than the right operand
< (less than)	Returns true if the left operand is less than the right operand
>= (greater than or equal)	Returns true if the left operand is greater than or equal to the right operand
<= (less than or equal)	Returns true if the left operand is less than or equal to the right operand

Figure 3-25: Comparison operators

tip

The comparison operator (==) consists of two equal signs and performs a function different from the assignment operator consisting of a single equal sign (=). The comparison operator *compares* values, while the assignment operator *assigns* values.

You can use number or string values as operands with comparison operators. When two numeric values are used as operands, the JavaScript interpreter compares them numerically. For example, the statement `returnValue = 5 > 4;` results in true, since the number *5* is numerically greater than the number *4*. When two non-numeric values are used as operands, the JavaScript interpreter compares them in alphabetical order. The statement `returnValue = "b" > "a";` returns true, since the letter *b* is alphabetically greater than the letter *a*. When one operand is a number and the other is a string, the JavaScript interpreter attempts to convert the string value to a number. If the string value cannot be converted to a number, a value of false is returned. For example, the statement `returnValue = 10 == "ten";` returns a value of false, since the JavaScript interpreter cannot convert the string "ten" to a number. Figure 3-26 shows additional code examples using comparison operators.

```
var x = 5, y = 6;

x == y;                              // false

x != y;                              // true

x > y;                               // false

x < y;                               // true

x >= y;                              // false

x <= y;                              // true

x = "text string";

y = "different string";

x != y;                              // true

"abc" == "abc";                      // true

"abc" == "xyz";                      // false

x = 5;

y = "5";

x === y;                             // false

x !== y;                             // true
```

Figure 3-26: Examples of comparison operators

Comparison operators are often used within conditional and looping statements such as the if...else, for, and while statements. In addition, you can use the comparison operators with the conditional operator. Although you will not learn about conditional and looping statements until Tutorial 4, learning about the conditional operator now will help you better understand how to work with comparison operators. The **conditional operator** executes one of two expressions, based on the results of a conditional expression. The syntax for the conditional operator is *conditional expression ? expression1: expression2;*. If the conditional expression evaluates to true, then *expression1* executes. If the conditional expression evaluates to false, then *expression2* executes. The following code shows an example of the conditional operator. In the example, the conditional expression checks to see if the intVariable variable is greater than 100. If intVariable is greater than 100, then the text *intVariable is greater than 100* is assigned to the result variable. If intVariable is not greater than 100, then the text *intVariable is less than or equal to 100* is assigned to the result variable. Since intVariable is equal to 150, the conditional statement returns a value of true and *expression1* executes, and *intVariable is greater than 100* prints to the screen.

```
var intVariable = 150;
var result;
(intVariable > 100) ? result =
    "intVariable is greater than 100" : result =
    "intVariable is less than or equal to 100";
```

```
document.write(result);
```

Next you will create an HTML document that uses comparison operators.

To create an HTML document that uses comparison operators:

1 Create a new document in your text editor or HTML editor.

2 Type the <HTML> and <HEAD> sections of the document:

```
<HTML>
<HEAD>
<TITLE>Comparison Examples</TITLE>
</HEAD>
```

3 Add the following code to begin the body of the HTML document and to create a preformatted text container:

```
<BODY>
<PRE>
```

4 Add the opening statements for a JavaScript section:

```
<SCRIPT LANGUAGE="JavaScript">
<!-- HIDE FROM INCOMPATIBLE BROWSERS
```

5 Type the following statements that perform various comparison operations on two variables. The result is assigned to the returnValue variable and printed. Notice that the first comparison is performed using the conditional operator.

```
var returnValue;
var value1 = "first text string";
var value2 = "second text string";
value1 == value2 ?  document.writeln(
    "value1 equal to value2: true")
    : document.writeln("
    value1 equal to value2: false");
value1 = 50;
value2 = 75;
returnValue = value1 == value2;
document.writeln("value1 equal to value2: "
    + returnValue);
returnValue = value1 != value2;
```

```
document.writeln("value1 not equal to value2: "
    + returnValue);
returnValue = value1 > value2;
document.writeln("value1 greater than value2: "
    + returnValue);
returnValue = value1 < value2;
document.writeln("value1 less than value2: "
    + returnValue);
returnValue = value1 >= value2;
document.writeln(
    "value1 greater than or equal to value2: "
    + returnValue);
returnValue = value1 <= value2;
document.writeln(
    "value1 less than or equal to value2: "
    + returnValue);
value1 = 25;
value2 = 25;
returnValue = value1 === value2;
document.writeln(
    "value1 equal to value2 AND the same data type: "
    + returnValue);
returnValue = value1 !== value2;
document.writeln(
    "value1 not equal to value2 AND not the same data type: "
    + returnValue);
```

6 Add the following code to close the <SCRIPT>, <PRE>, <BODY>, and <HTML> tags:

```
// STOP HIDING FROM INCOMPATIBLE BROWSERS -->
</SCRIPT>
</PRE>
</BODY>
</HTML>
```

7 Save the file as **ComparisonExamples.html** in the **Tutorial.03** folder on your Data Disk. Open the **ComparisonExamples.html** file in your Web browser. Figure 3-27 shows the output.

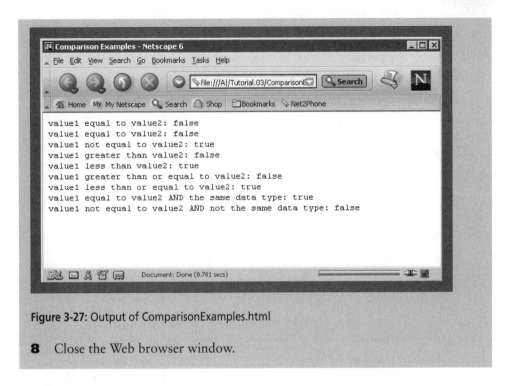

Figure 3-27: Output of ComparisonExamples.html

8 Close the Web browser window.

Logical Operators

Logical operators are used for comparing two Boolean operands for equality. As with comparison operators, a Boolean value of true or false is returned after two operands are compared. Figure 3-28 lists the JavaScript logical operators.

Operator	Description
&& (and)	Returns true if both the left operand and right operand return a value of true, otherwise it returns a value of false.
|| (or)	Returns true if either the left operand or right operand returns a value of true. If neither operand returns a value of true, then the expression containing the || (or) operator returns a value of false.
! (not)	Returns true if an expression is false and returns false if an expression is true.

Figure 3-28: Logical operators

The && (and) and || (or) operators are binary operators (requiring two operands), while the ! (not) operator is a unary operator (requiring a single operand). Logical operators are often used with comparison operators to evaluate expressions, allowing you to combine the results of several expressions into a single statement. For example, the && (and) operator is used for determining whether two operands return an equivalent value. The operands themselves are often expressions. The following code uses the && operator to compare two separate expressions:

```
var a = 2; var b = 3;
var returnValue = a==2 && b==3;      // returns true
```

In the above example, the left operand evaluates to true since "a" is equal to 2, and the right operand also evaluates to true since "b" is equal to 3. Because both expressions are true, returnValue is assigned a value of true. The statement containing the && operator essentially says "if variable a is equal to 2 AND variable b is equal to 3, then assign a value of true to returnValue. Otherwise, assign a value of false to returnValue." In the following code, however, returnValue is assigned a value of false, since the right operand does *not* evaluate to true:

```
var a = 2; var b = 3;
var returnValue = a==2 && b==4;      // returns false
```

The logical || (or) operator checks to see if either expression evaluates to true. For example, the statement in the following code says "if a is equal to 2 OR b is equal to 3, assign a value of true to returnValue. Otherwise, assign a value of false."

```
var a = 2; var b = 3;
var returnValue = a==2 ||  b==4;     // returns true
```

The returnValue variable in the above example is assigned a value of true, since the left operand evaluates to true, even though the right operand evaluates to false. This result occurs because the || (or) statement returns true if *either* the left *or* right operand evaluates to true.

The following code is an example of the ! (not) operator, which returns true if an operand evaluates to false and returns false if an operand evaluates to true. Notice that since the ! (not) operator is unary, it requires only a single operand.

```
var x = true;
var returnValue = !x;     // returns false
```

 tip

··

Logical operators are often used within conditional and looping statements such as the `if else`, `for`, and `while` statements. You will learn about conditional and looping statements in Tutorial 4.

··

Next you will create an HTML document that uses logical operators.

To create an HTML document that uses logical operators:

1 Create a new document in your text editor or HTML editor.

2 Type the <HTML> and <HEAD> sections of the document:

```
<HTML>
<HEAD>
<TITLE>Logical Examples</TITLE>
</HEAD>
```

3 Add the following code to begin the body of the HTML document and to create a preformatted text container:

```
<BODY>
<PRE>
```

4 Add the opening statements for a JavaScript section:

```
<SCRIPT LANGUAGE="JavaScript">
<!-- HIDE FROM INCOMPATIBLE BROWSERS
```

5 Type the following statements that use logical operators on two variables:

```
var trueValue = true;
var falseValue = false;
var returnValue;
document.writeln(!trueValue);
document.writeln(!falseValue);
document.writeln(trueValue || falseValue);
document.writeln(trueValue && falseValue);
```

6 Add the following code to close the <SCRIPT>, <PRE>, <BODY>, and <HTML> tags:

```
// STOP HIDING FROM INCOMPATIBLE BROWSERS -->
</SCRIPT>
</PRE>
</BODY>
</HTML>
```

7 Save the file as **LogicalExamples.html** in the **Tutorial.03** folder on your Data Disk. Open the **LogicalExamples.html** file in your Web browser. Figure 3-29 shows the output.

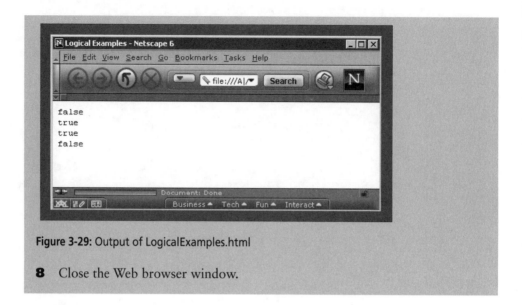

Figure 3-29: Output of LogicalExamples.html

8   Close the Web browser window.

Working with Strings

JavaScript has two operators that can be used with strings: + and +=. When used with strings, the plus sign is known as the concatenation operator. The **concatenation operator** (+) is used to combine two strings. The following code combines a string variable and a literal string, and assigns the new value to another variable:

```
var firstString = "Ernest Hemingway wrote ";
var newString;
newString = firstString + "<I>For Whom the Bell Tolls</I>";
```

The combined value of the firstString variable and the string literal that is assigned to the newString variable is Ernest Hemingway wrote *For Whom the Bell Tolls*.

You can also use the += assignment operator to combine two strings. The following code combines the two text strings, but without using the newString variable:

```
var firstString = "Ernest Hemingway wrote ";
firstString += "<I>For Whom the Bell Tolls</I>";
```

Note that the same symbol—a plus sign—serves as the concatenation operator and the addition operator. When used with numbers or variables containing numbers, expressions using the concatenation operator will return the sum of the two numbers. However, if you use the concatenation operator with a string value and a number value, the string value and the number value will be combined into a new string value, as in the following example:

```
var textString = "The legal voting age is ";
var votingAge = 18;
newString = textString + votingAge;
```

The String Object

All literal strings and string variables in JavaScript are represented by a String object. The **String object** contains methods for manipulating text strings. Figure 3-30 lists commonly used methods of the String object.

Method	Description
anchor(*anchor name*)	Adds an <ANCHOR>...</ANCHOR> tag pair to a text string
big()	Adds a <BIG>...</BIG> tag pair to a text string
blink()	Adds a <BLINK>...</BLINK> tag pair to a text string
bold()	Adds a <B>...</B> tag pair to a text string
charAt(*index*)	Returns the character at the specified position in a text string. Returns nothing if the specified position is greater than the length of the string
fixed()	Adds a <TT>...</TT> tag pair to a text string
fontcolor(*color*)	Adds a <FONT COLOR=*color*>...</FONT> tag pair to a text string
fontsize(*size*)	Adds a <FONT SIZE=*size*>...</FONT> tag pair to a text string
indexOf(*text, index*)	Returns the position number in a string of the first character in the *text* argument. If the *index* argument is included, then the indexOf() method starts searching at that position within the string. Returns -1 if the text is not found
italics()	Adds a <I>...</I> tag pair to a text string
lastIndexOf(*text, index*)	Returns the position number in a string of the last instance of the first character in the *text* argument. If the *index* argument is included, then the lastIndexOf() method starts searching at that position within the string. Returns -1 if the character or string is not found
link(*href*)	Adds a <A HREF=*URL*>...</A> tag pair to a text string
small()	Adds a <SMALL>...</SMALL> tag pair to a text string
split(*separator*)	Divides a text string into an array of substrings, based on the specified separator
strike()	Adds a <STRIKE>...</STRIKE> tag pair to a text string

Figure 3-30: Commonly used methods of the String object

sub()	Adds a _{...} tag pair to a text string
substring(*starting index, ending index*)	Extracts text from a string starting with the position number in the string of the *starting index* argument and ending with the position number of the *ending index* argument
sup()	Adds a ^{...} tag pair to a text string
toLowerCase()	Converts the specified text string to lowercase
toUpperCase()	Converts the specified text string to uppercase

Figure 3-30: Commonly used methods of the String object (continued)

The String object also contains a single property, the **length property**, which returns the number of characters in a string. You manipulate a string by appending a period to a string variable or a literal string, followed by a String method or the length property. Note that you use an index number of zero to refer to the first character in text strings. For instance, you refer to the first character, *J*, in the string *JavaScript* with an index number of 0. The second character, *a*, has an index number of 1, and so on. To use the charAt() method to return the first character (*J*) in the literal string JavaScript, you use the statement `"JavaScript".charAt(0);`.

The following code shows some examples of how to use several methods of the String object along with the length property. Comments at the end of each statement show the results of each method or property.

```
var newString;
newString = "JavaScript".bold();
     // <B>JavaScript</B>
newString = "JavaScript".charAt(5);          // c
newString = "JavaScript".indexOf("S");       // 4
newString = "JavaScript".lastIndexOf("a");   // 3
newString = "JavaScript".substring(4,10);    // Script
newString = "JavaScript".toUpperCase();      // JAVASCRIPT
newString = newString.length;                // 10
```

Recall that you can manipulate text strings with simple + and += assignment operators. For example, you can combine text strings using the statement `myName = "Don " + "Gosselin";`. This statement combines the strings *Don* and *Gosselin* and assigns the new string to the variable myName. You can use the + and += assignment operators and methods of the String object to create strings of text that store various kinds of information. To make information stored in long strings of text usable, the long strings usually must be parsed. When applied to text strings, the term **parsing** is the act of extracting characters or substrings from a larger string. This is essentially the same concept as the parsing that occurs in a Web browser when the Web browser extracts the necessary formatting information from an HTML document before displaying it on-screen. In the case of an HTML document, the document itself is one large text string from which formatting and other information needs to be extracted. However, when working on a programming level, parsing usually refers to the extraction of information from string literals and variables.

You use several String object methods and the length property to parse strings. For instance, the statement `newString  =  "JavaScript".substring(4,10);` from the preceding example uses the substring() method to parse the newString variable and extract the text *Script* from the *JavaScript* text string.

Figure 3-31 contains examples of several String methods, examples of the + assignment operator, and an example of the length property. Figure 3-32 displays the program in a Web browser.

```
<HTML>

<HEAD>

<TITLE>String Object Examples</TITLE>

</HEAD>

<BODY>

<PRE>

<SCRIPT LANGUAGE="JavaScript1.2">

<!-- HIDE FROM INCOMPATIBLE BROWSERS

var myCity = "Boston";

document.writeln("Length: " + myCity.length);

// The following line converts the variable

// to <B>Boston</B>

document.writeln("Bolded variable: " + myCity.bold());

document.writeln("Character at 3: " + myCity.charAt(3));

document.writeln("Index of 's': " + myCity.indexOf('s'));

document.writeln("Substring 3, 6: " +

    myCity.substring(3,6));

document.writeln("San Francisco".toLowerCase());

document.writeln("San Francisco".toUpperCase());

// STOP HIDING FROM INCOMPATIBLE BROWSERS -->
```

Figure 3-31: String object examples

```
</SCRIPT>
</PRE>
</BODY>
</HTML>
```

Figure 3-31: String object examples (continued)

Figure 3-32: String object examples in a Web browser

tip

The methods and the length property of the String object can be used whenever you need to manipulate text strings.

Next you will create an HTML document that uses string operators and String object methods.

To create an HTML document that uses string operators:

1 Create a new document in your text editor or HTML editor.

2 Type the <HTML> and <HEAD> sections of the document:

```
<HTML>
<HEAD>
<TITLE>String Examples</TITLE>
</HEAD>
```

3 Add the following code to begin the body of the HTML document and to create a preformatted text container:

```
<BODY>
<PRE>
```

4 Add the opening statements for a JavaScript section:

```
<SCRIPT LANGUAGE="JavaScript">
<!-- HIDE FROM INCOMPATIBLE BROWSERS
```

5 Type the following statements containing examples of string operators. Use your own name and place of birth where indicated.

```
var name;
firstName = "your first name";
lastName = "your last name";
var placeOfBirth;
name = firstName + " ";
name += lastName;
placeOfBirth = "city where you were born";
placeOfBirth += ", state where you were born";
```

6 Type the following print and String method statements:

```
nameArray = name.split(" ");
document.writeln("My first name is: " + nameArray[0]);
document.writeln("My last name is: " + nameArray[1]);
document.writeln("There are " + firstName.length + "
characters in my first name");
document.writeln("I was born in " + placeOfBirth);
document.writeln("My initials are: " + firstName.charAt
(0) + lastName.charAt(0));
```

7 Add the following code to close the <SCRIPT>, <PRE>, <BODY>, and <HTML> tags:

```
// STOP HIDING FROM INCOMPATIBLE BROWSERS -->
</SCRIPT>
</PRE>
</BODY>
</HTML>
```

8 Save the file as **StringExamples.html** in the **Tutorial.03** folder on your Data Disk. Open the **StringExamples.html** file in your Web browser. The output should appear similar to Figure 3-33.

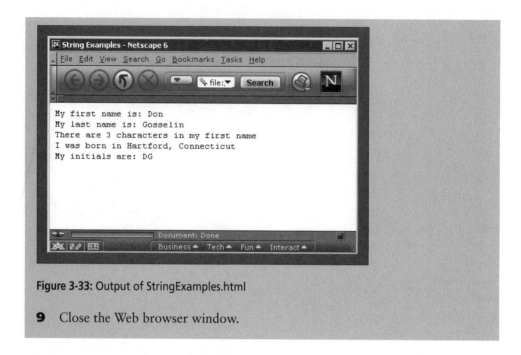

Figure 3-33: Output of StringExamples.html

9   Close the Web browser window.

Operator Precedence

When using operators to create expressions in JavaScript, you need to be aware of the precedence of an operator. **Operator precedence** is the order of priority in which operations in an expression are evaluated. Expressions are evaluated on a left-to-right basis with the highest priority precedence evaluated first. The order of precedence for JavaScript operators is as follows:

- Parentheses/brackets/dot (() [] .) — *highest precedence*
- Negation/increment (! - ++ -- typeof void)
- Multiplication/division/modulus (* / %)
- Addition/subtraction (+ -)
- Comparison (< <= > >=)
- Equality (== !=)
- Logical and (&&)
- Logical or (||)
- Assignment operators (= += -= *= /= %=)
- Comma (,) — *lowest precedence*

tip

The preceding list does not include all the operators that JavaScript evaluates in the order of precedence. Only operators discussed in this book are listed.

The statement 5 + 2 * 8 evaluates to 21 because the multiplication operator (*) has a higher precedence than the addition operator (+). The numbers 2 and 8 are multiplied first, for a total of 16, and then the number 5 is added. If the addition operator had a higher precedence than the multiplication operator, then the statement would evaluate to 56, since 5 would added to 2, for a total of 7, which would then be multiplied by 8.

As you can see from the list, parentheses have the highest precedence. Parentheses are used with expressions to change the order in which individual operations in an expression are evaluated. For example, the statement 5 + 2 * 8, which evaluates to 21, can be rewritten to (5 + 2) * 8, which evaluates to 56. The parentheses tell the JavaScript interpreter to add the numbers 5 and 2 before multiplying by the number 8. Using parentheses forces the statement to evaluate to 56 instead of 21.

Creating the Calculator Program

The calculator program performs calculations using a special type of conversion function, the built-in eval() function. The **eval()** function evaluates expressions contained within strings. You can include a string literal or string variable as the argument for the eval() function. If the string literal or string variable you pass to the eval() function does not contain an expression that can be evaluated, you will receive an error. The statement `var returnValue = eval("5 + 3");` returns the value 8 and assigns it to the returnValue variable. The statement `var returnValue = eval("10");` also evaluates correctly and returns a value of 10, even though the string within the eval() function did not contain operators. The eval() function has one restriction: You cannot send it a text string that does not contain operators or numbers. If you send the eval() function a text string that does not contain operators or numbers, an empty value is returned. For example, the statement `var returnValue = eval("this is a text string");` assigns an empty value to the returnValue variable since it does not contain numbers or operators. However, the statement `var returnValue = eval("'this is a text string' + ' and this is another text string'");` evaluates correctly, since the string sent to the eval() function contains the concatenation operator.

Next you will create the Calculator.html program. You will use the inputString variable to contain the operands and operators of a calculation. After a calculation is added to the inputString, the calculation is performed using the eval() function. The updateString function accepts a single value representing a number or operator. The value is then added to the inputString function using the += assignment operator. After the inputString is updated, it is assigned as the value of a text box named Input that will be created with the <INPUT> tag. The Input text box is part of a form named Calculator. The Calculator form and Input text box are called as part of the Document object.

You will learn more about forms in Tutorial 6.

To create the calculator program:

1 Create a new document in your text editor or HTML editor.

2 Type the <HTML> and <HEAD> sections of the document:

```
<HTML>
<HEAD>
<TITLE>Calculator</TITLE>
```

3 Add the opening statements for a JavaScript section:

```
<SCRIPT LANGUAGE="JavaScript">
<!-- HIDE FROM INCOMPATIBLE BROWSERS
```

4 Type the statement `var inputString = "";` to declare a variable named inputString with an initial value of an empty string.

5 Next type the following updateString() function, which will be used to update the inputString variable.

```
function updateString(value) {
    inputString += value;
    document.Calculator.Input.value = inputString;
}
```

6 Type the closing </SCRIPT> and </HEAD> tags as follows:

```
// STOP HIDING FROM INCOMPATIBLE BROWSERS -->
</SCRIPT>
</HEAD>
```

7 Add the opening **<BODY>** tag to begin the body of the HTML document.

8 Add the **<DIV ALIGN="center">** tag to align the calculator in the middle of the page.

9 Type **<FORM NAME="Calculator">** to start the Calculator form.

10 Create the Input text box by typing **<INPUT TYPE="text" NAME="Input" Size="22">**.

11 Type the following Input tags that create buttons representing the calculator operators. Each tag, along with the other tags that you will create, sends a value to the updateString() function, using an onClick method:

```
<BR>
<INPUT TYPE="button" NAME="plus"  VALUE=" + "
     onClick="updateString(' + ')">
<INPUT TYPE="button" NAME="minus" VALUE=" - "
     onClick="updateString(' - ')">
<INPUT TYPE="button" NAME="times" VALUE="  x "
     onClick="updateString(' * ')">
<INPUT TYPE="button" NAME="div"   VALUE="  /  "
     onClick="updateString(' / ')">
<INPUT TYPE="button" NAME="mod" VALUE=" MOD "
     onClick="updateString(' % ')"><BR>
```

help

When you create an <INPUT> tag with a button type of "button," you adjust the width of the button using spaces and characters within the label defined by the VALUE attribute. To adjust each button's spacing, the labels for each of the buttons you create for the calculator program with the VALUE attribute contain additional spaces.

12 Type the following <INPUT> tags for the calculator numbers:

```
<BR>
<INPUT TYPE="button" NAME="zero"    VALUE="  0  "
     onClick="updateString('0')">
<INPUT TYPE="button" NAME="one"     VALUE="  1  "
     onClick="updateString('1')">
<INPUT TYPE="button" NAME="two"     VALUE="  2  "
     onClick="updateString('2')">
<INPUT TYPE="button" NAME="three"   VALUE="  3  "
     onClick="updateString('3')">
<INPUT TYPE="button" NAME="four"    VALUE="  4  "
     onClick="updateString('4')">
<BR>
<INPUT TYPE="button" NAME="five"    VALUE="  5  "
     onClick="updateString('5')">
<INPUT TYPE="button" NAME="six"     VALUE="  6  "
     onClick="updateString('6')">
<INPUT TYPE="button" NAME="seven"   VALUE="  7  "
     onClick="updateString('7')">
<INPUT TYPE="button" NAME="eight"   VALUE="  8  "
     onClick="updateString('8')">
<INPUT TYPE="button" NAME="nine"    VALUE="  9  "
     onClick="updateString('9')">
```

13 Add the following <INPUT> tags for the decimal point, clear, and Calc buttons. Notice that the onClick event for the Calc button performs the calculation by using the eval() function with the inputString variable. The calculated value is then assigned as the value of the Input text box.

```
<BR>
<INPUT TYPE="button" NAME="point"  VALUE="  .  "
     onClick="updateString('.')">
<INPUT TYPE="button" NAME="clear"  VALUE=" Clear "
     onClick="Input.value=''; inputString=''">
<INPUT TYPE="button" NAME="Calc"   VALUE="  =  "
     onClick="Input.value=eval(inputString);
     inputString=''">
```

14 Add the following code to close the <FORM>, <DIV>, <BODY>, and <HTML> tags:

```
</FORM>
</DIV>
</BODY>
</HTML>
```

15 Save the file as Calculator.html in the Tutorial.03 folder on your Data Disk. Open the Calculator.html file in your Web browser. Figure 3-34 shows the output. Test the program to make sure all the functions work properly.

Figure 3-34: Output of Calculator.html

16 Close the Web browser window and your text or HTML editor.

 S U M M A R Y

- An expression is a single literal or variable or a combination of literal values, variables, operators, and other expressions that can be evaluated by the JavaScript interpreter to produce a result.

- Operands are variables and literals contained in an expression.

- Operators are symbols used in expressions to manipulate operands.

- A binary operator requires an operand before the operator and an operand after the operator.

- A unary operator requires a single operand either before or after the operator.

- Arithmetic operators are used for performing addition, subtraction, multiplication, and division in JavaScript.

- When performing arithmetic operations on string values, the JavaScript interpreter attempts to convert the string values to numbers. The JavaScript interpreter will not convert strings to numbers when you use the addition operator.

- The increment (++) and decrement (--) unary operators can be used as prefix or postfix operators. A prefix operator is placed before a variable, and a postfix operator is placed after a variable.

- You use assignment operators to assign a value to a variable.

- The value NaN stands for Not a Number and is returned when a mathematical operation does not result in a numerical value.

- You use comparison operators to compare two operands for equality and to determine if one numeric value is greater than another.

- The conditional operator executes one of two expressions, based on the results of a conditional expression.

- You use logical operators to compare two Boolean operands for equality.

- Logical operators are often used with comparison operators to evaluate expressions, allowing you to combine the results of several expressions into a single statement.

- When used with strings, the plus sign, or addition operator, is known as the concatenation operator.

- The String object contains methods and properties used for manipulating text strings.

- When applied to text strings, parsing refers to the act of extracting characters or substrings from a larger string.

- Operator precedence is the order of priority in which operations in an expression are evaluated.

- Parentheses are used with expressions to change the order in which individual operations in an expression are evaluated.

- You use the built-in eval() function to evaluate expressions contained within strings.

QUESTIONS

1. Operators that require an operand before the operator and an operand after the operator are called _____ operators.
   a. unary
   b. binary
   c. double
   d. multiplicity

2. The modulus operator (%) ———————.
   a. converts an operand to base 16 (hexadecimal) format
   b. returns the absolute value of an operand
   c. calculates the percentage of one operand compared to another
   d. divides two operands and returns the remainder

3. What value is assigned to the returnValue variable in the statement `returnValue = count++;`, assuming that the count variable contains the value 10?
   a. 10
   b. 11
   c. 12
   d. 20

4. What value is assigned to the returnValue variable in the statement `returnValue += "100";`, assuming that the returnValue variable contains the string value "50 Main Street"?
   a. 150
   b. 50 Main Street 100
   c. 100
   d. 100 Main Street 50

5. What value is returned when a mathematical operation does not result in a numerical value?
   a. null
   b. NaN
   c. undefined
   d. 0

6. What value is assigned to the returnValue variable in the statement `returnValue = "First String" == "Second String";`?
   a. First String
   b. Second String
   c. true
   d. false

7. What value is assigned to the returnValue variable in the statement `returnValue = 100 != 200;`?
   a. First String
   b. Second String
   c. true
   d. false

8. What value is assigned to the returnValue variable in the statement `returnValue = 50 == "fifty";`?
   a. true
   b. false
   c. 50
   d. "fifty"

9. The && (and) operator returns true if _____.
   a. the left operand returns a value of true
   b. the right operand returns a value of true
   c. the left operand and right operand both return a value of true
   d. the left operand and right operand both return a value of false

10. The operator that returns true if either its left or right operand returns a value of true is the _____ operand.
    a. ||
    b. ==
    c. %%
    d. &&

11. What value is assigned to the returnValue variable in the statement `returnValue = !x;`, assuming that x has a value of true?
    a. true
    b. false
    c. null
    d. undefined

12. The _____ operator is used for combining two strings.
    a. association
    b. junction
    c. combination
    d. concatenation

13. Methods and properties used for manipulating text strings are stored in the _____ object.
    a. String
    b. Text
    c. TextString
    d. StringText

14. _____ refers to the act of extracting characters or substrings from a larger string.
    a. Extrapolating
    b. Parsing
    c. Excerpting
    d. Concatenation

15. What is the correct syntax for returning the number of characters in a string?
    a. `text_string.length;`
    b. `text_string.characters();`
    c. `text_string.numChars();`
    d. `text_string.lastIndex;`

16. What is the correct syntax for converting a string to lowercase?
    a. `text_string.down();`
    b. `text_string.lower();`
    c. `text_string.LowerCase();`
    d. `text_string.toLowerCase();`

17. The order of priority in which operations in an expression are evaluated is known as
_____.
a. prerogative precedence
b. operator precedence
c. expression evaluation
d. priority evaluation

18. The operators with the highest order of precedence in JavaScript are _____.
a. assignment operators
b. addition/subtraction operators
c. comparison operators
d. parentheses ()

19. What is the value of the expression 4 * (2 + 3)?
a. 11
b. -11
c. 20
d. 14

20. What value is assigned to the returnValue variable in the statement `returnValue = eval(x + "2 * 2");`, assuming that x has a value of 1?
a. "1 + 2 * 2"
b. "12 * 2"
c. 6
d. 24

 # E X E R C I S E S

Save all files you create in the Tutorial.03 folder on your Data Disk.

1. Add code to the following program that assigns the areaCode, exchange, and number variables to the phoneNumber variable, separated by dashes. Display the phone number using a document.write() statement. Save the document as PhoneNumber.html.

```
<HTML>
<HEAD>
<TITLE>Phone Number</TITLE>
</HEAD>
<BODY>
<PRE>
<SCRIPT LANGUAGE="JavaScript">
<!-- HIDE FROM INCOMPATIBLE BROWSERS
var areaCode, exchange, number, phoneNumber;
areaCode = 212;
exchange = 555;
number = 1212;
// STOP HIDING FROM INCOMPATIBLE BROWSERS -->
</SCRIPT>
</PRE>
</BODY>
</HTML>
```

2. Create an HTML document that calculates the square feet of carpet required to carpet a room. Include three text boxes. Create one text box for the width of the room in linear feet and another for the length of the room in linear feet. Also create a text box for the cost per square foot of carpeting. When you calculate the cost, add 25% to the total number of square feet to account for closets and other features of the room. Display the total cost in an alert dialog box. Save the document as CarpetCost.html.

3. What value is assigned to returnValue for each of the following expressions?

   a. `returnValue = 2 == 3;`
   b. `returnValue = "2" + "3";`
   c. `returnValue = 2 >= 3;`
   d. `returnValue = 2 <= 3;`
   e. `returnValue = 2 + 3;`
   f. `returnValue = (2 >= 3) && (2 > 3);`
   g. `returnValue = (2 >= 3) || (2 > 3);`

4. Create an HTML document that declares these five global variables in a <SCRIPT> section contained in the document's <HEAD> section: name, age, monthOfBirth, dateOfBirth, and yearOfBirth. In another <SCRIPT> section, contained in the document's <BODY> section, declare another variable, named birthInfo. Combine all five global variables into the birthInfo variable using the += assignment operator, then print the birthInfo variable, using the document.write() method. Save the document as BirthInfo.html. Next, open the HTML document and see how it looks. Are you satisfied with the output? How can you improve the formatting and the way the strings were concatenated?

5. Create a temperature conversion calculator that converts Fahrenheit to Celsius and Celsius to Fahrenheit. To convert Fahrenheit to Celsius, subtract 32 from the Fahrenheit temperature, and then multiply the remainder by .55. To convert Celsius to Fahrenheit, multiply the Celsius temperature by 1.8, and then add 32. Save the document as ConvertTemperature.html.

6. Use parentheses to modify the order of precedence of the following code so that the final result of x is 581.25. (The result of x using the current syntax is 637.5.) Save the document as ImprovedProgram.html.

```
var  x  =  75;
x =   x + 30 * x / 4;
```

7. The JavaScript Math object contains advanced mathematical methods and constants. You can find a complete listing of Math object methods in the appendix. Using some of the Math object methods, create a calculator that performs advanced calculations, including the exp() (exponential value) function and the sqrt() (square root function). Instead of using the eval() method to evaluate the contents of a text field, allow users to type a number into a text field and then calculate the number directly using individual buttons for each advanced math function. Save the program as AdvancedCalculator.html.

Decision Making with Control Structures and Statements

case ▶ Cartoon and Animation Warehouse sells cartoon and animated film videos through their Web site. The company came to WebAdventure looking for a way to attract new business to their Web site. The creative staff at WebAdventure suggested running a promotional contest. Visitors to the Web site would take a simple quiz testing their knowledge of cartoons and animated films. People who got all the questions right would get a free T-shirt displaying their favorite cartoon character. Your boss at WebAdventure has asked you to create a quiz prototype to show to the client.

Previewing the CartoonQuiz.html File

In this tutorial, you will create a JavaScript quiz that tests a user's knowledge of cartoons and animated films. You will create several versions of the Cartoon Quiz program, using different control structures and statements.

To preview the CartoonQuiz.html file:

1 Open the **CartoonQuiz.html** file from the **Tutorial.04** folder on your Data Disk in your browser. Figure 4-1 displays an example of the program in a Web browser.

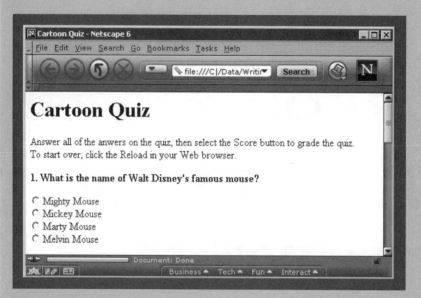

Figure 4-1: Cartoon Quiz

2 Answer the questions on the quiz, then click the **Score** button at the bottom of the page to see how you did.

3 When you are finished, close your browser window.

4 Next open the **CartoonQuiz.html** file in your text editor or HTML editor and examine the code. Notice the statements that begin with `for` and `if`. These statements are examples of some of the control structures you will work with in this tutorial. The multiple choice alternatives for each question are created using <INPUT> tags within a <FORM>...</FORM> tag pair.

5 Close your text editor or HTML editor when you are finished examining the code.

SECTION A
objectives

In this section you will learn how to use:

■ if statements

■ if...else statements

■ nested if statements

■ switch statements

Decision Making

if Statements

When you write a computer program, regardless of the programming language, you often need to execute different sets of statements, depending on some predetermined criteria. For example, you may need to execute different sets of code, depending on the time of day or what type of Web browser is running your program. Additionally, you may need to execute different sets of code, depending on user input. For instance, you may have a Web page through which users place online orders. If a user clicks an Add to Shopping Cart button, a set of statements that builds a list of items to be purchased must execute. However, if the user clicks a Checkout button, an entirely different set of statements, which complete the transaction, must execute. The process of determining the order in which statements execute in a program is called **decision making** or **flow control**. The special types of JavaScript statements used for making decisions are called decision-making structures.

One of the more common ways to control program flow is a technique that uses the if statement. The **if statement** is used to execute specific programming code if the evaluation of a conditional expression returns a value of true. The syntax for the if statement is as follows:

```
if (conditional expression) {
     statement(s);
}
```

The if statement contains three parts: the keyword if, a conditional expression enclosed within parentheses, and executable statements. Note that the conditional expression must be enclosed within parentheses.

If the condition being evaluated in an if statement returns a value of true, then the statement (or statements) immediately following the if keyword and its condition executes. After the if statement executes, any subsequent code executes normally. Consider the example in Figure 4-2. The if statement uses the equal (==) comparison operator to determine whether exampleVar is equal to 5. Since the condition returns a value of true, two alert dialog boxes appear. The first alert dialog box is generated by the `if` statement when the condition returns a value of `true`, and the second alert dialog box executes after the `if` statement is completed.

```
var exampleVar = 5;

if (exampleVar == 5)      // CONDITION EVALUATES TO 'TRUE'

    alert("The variable is equal to '5'.");

alert("This dialog box is generated after the if statement.");
```

Figure 4-2: An `if` statement that evaluates to `true`

The statement immediately following the `if` statement in Figure 4-2 can be written on the same line as the `if` statement itself. However, using a line break and indentation makes the code easier to read.

In contrast, the code in Figure 4-3 displays only the second alert dialog box. The condition evaluates to `false`, since exampleVar is assigned the value 4 instead of 5.

```
var exampleVar = 4;

if (exampleVar == 5)      // CONDITION EVALUATES TO 'FALSE'

    alert("This dialog box will not appear.");

alert("This is the only dialog box that appears.");
```

Figure 4-3: An `if` statement that evaluates to `false`

You can use a command block to construct a decision-making structure using multiple `if` statements. A **command block** refers to multiple statements contained within a set of braces, similar to the way function statements are contained within a set of braces. Each command block must have an opening brace ({) and a closing brace (}). If a command block is missing either the opening or closing brace, an error will occur. Figure 4-4 shows a program that runs a command block if the conditional expression within the `if` statement evaluates to `true`.

When an `if` statement contains a command block, the statements in the command block execute when the `if` statement condition evaluates to `true`. After the command block executes, the code that follows executes normally. When an `if` statement condition evaluates to `false`, the command block is skipped, and the statements that follow execute. If the conditional expression within the `if` statement in Figure 4-4 evaluates to `false`, then only the document.writeln() statement following the command block executes.

```
var exampleVar = 5;

if (exampleVar == 5) {      // CONDITION EVALUATES TO 'TRUE'

      document.writeln("The condition evaluates to true.");

      document.writeln("exampleVar is equal to 5.");

      document.writeln("Each of these lines will be printed.");

}

document.writeln(
      "This statement always executes after the if statement.");
```

Figure 4-4: An if statement with a command block

When you build an if statement, remember that after the if statement condition evaluates, either the first statement following the condition executes or the command block following the condition executes. Any statements following the if statement command or command block execute whether or not the if statement condition evaluates to true or false.

It is easy to forget to include inside a command block all the statements that are to execute when an if statement evaluates to true. For example, consider the following code:

```
if (exampleVar == true)
    var conditionTrue = "condition is true";
    alert(conditionTrue);
```

At first glance, the code looks correct. In fact, when the condition evaluates to true, the code runs correctly. However, when the condition evaluates to false, the alert dialog box displays *undefined,* since the declaration for the conditionTrue variable is skipped. To fix this problem, enclose the two statements within a command block, as follows:

```
if (exampleVar == true) {
    var conditionTrue = "condition is true";
    alert(conditionTrue);
}
```

Now if the condition evaluates to false, both statements will be bypassed, since they are contained within a command block.

The equal operator is only one of several comparison operators that you can use with an if statement. You can perform Boolean comparisons using any of the comparison operators you learned about in Tutorial 3. You can also use logical operators in combination with comparison operators. Figure 4-5 displays examples of comparison and logical operators with the if statement.

```
        var exampleVar1 = 5;
if (exampleVar1 != 3)      // not equal

    document.writeln("This line prints.");
if (exampleVar1 > 3)       // greater than

    document.writeln("This line prints.");
if (exampleVar1 < 3)       // less than

    document.writeln("This line does not print.");
if (exampleVar1 >= 3)      // greater than or equal

    document.writeln("This line prints.");
if (exampleVar1 <= 3)      // less than or equal

    document.writeln("This line does not print.");
var exampleVar2 = false;
if (exampleVar1 > 3 && exampleVar2 == true)   // logical and

    document.writeln("This line does not print.");
if (exampleVar1 == 5 || exampleVar2 == true) // logical or

    document.writeln("This line prints.");
if (!exampleVar2)  // logical 'not'

    document.writeln("This line prints.");
```

Figure 4-5: Comparison and logical operators with the `if` statement

Next you will start creating the Cartoon Quiz program you saw at the beginning of this tutorial. The program is set up so that users select answer alternatives by means of radio buttons created with the <INPUT> tag. When unselected, a radio button appears as a small empty circle; when selected, it appears to be filled with a black dot. A radio button is usually contained within a group of other radio buttons, and you can select only one of the grouped radio buttons at a time. The term *radio button* comes from car radios that have a group of push buttons, each of which is set to a radio station. In the same manner that you can select only one car radio button at a time, you can select only one radio <INPUT> button contained within a group of other radio buttons. All radio buttons in a group must have the same NAME attribute.

In this version of the quiz, each question is scored immediately. You will create the form containing the radio buttons, then use a series of `if` statements to score each question. First you will create the HTML document and the form section, then you will add the JavaScript code to score each of the questions.

To create the Cartoon Quiz program and its form section:

1 Create a new document in your text editor or HTML editor.

2 Type the <HTML> and <HEAD> sections of the document. This section also includes a <SCRIPT>...</SCRIPT> tag pair. You will use the <SCRIPT>...</SCRIPT> tag pair later to create code that scores the quiz:

```
<HTML>
<HEAD>
<TITLE>Cartoon Quiz</TITLE>
<SCRIPT LANGUAGE="JavaScript">
<!-- HIDE FROM INCOMPATIBLE BROWSERS
// ADD CODE HERE
// STOP HIDING FROM INCOMPATIBLE BROWSERS-->
</SCRIPT>
</HEAD>
```

3 Add the following lines, which contain the opening <BODY> tag, the text that will appear at the top of the quiz, and the opening <FORM> tag for the radio buttons:

```
<BODY>
<H1>Cartoon Quiz</H1>
<P>Answer all of the questions on the quiz, then select
the Score button to grade the quiz. </P>
<FORM>
```

4 Next add the following lines for the first question. The four radio buttons represent the answers. Since each button within a radio button group requires the same NAME attribute, these four radio buttons have the same name of "question1." Each radio button is also assigned a value corresponding to its answer number: *a*, *b*, *c*, or *d*. For each radio button group, the onClick event sends the button value to an individual function that scores the answer. Notice that the value for each button is sent to the function by using the this reference in the form of this.value. The this.value statement essentially says "send *this* button *value* to the function."

```
<P><B>1. What is the name of Walt Disney's famous mouse?</B></P>
<P><INPUT TYPE=radio NAME=question1 VALUE="a"
    onClick="scoreQuestion1(this.value)">Mighty Mouse<BR>
<INPUT TYPE=radio NAME=question1 VALUE="b"
    onClick="scoreQuestion1(this.value)">Mickey Mouse<BR>
<INPUT TYPE=radio NAME=question1 VALUE="c"
    onClick="scoreQuestion1(this.value)">Marty Mouse<BR>
<INPUT TYPE=radio NAME=question1 VALUE="d"
    onClick="scoreQuestion1(this.value)">Melvin Mouse</P>
```

help

> You can build the program quickly by copying the input button code for the first question and pasting it for questions two through five. If you use copy and paste to create the input buttons, make sure you change the question number for each input button name and the function it calls.

5 Add the lines for the second question:

```
<P><B>2. The character Buzz Lightyear was featured in
which animated film?</B></P>
<P><INPUT TYPE=radio NAME=question2 VALUE="a"
    onClick="scoreQuestion2(this.value)">Fantasia<BR>
<INPUT TYPE=radio NAME=question2 VALUE="b"
    onClick="scoreQuestion2(this.value)">Hercules<BR>
<INPUT TYPE=radio NAME=question2 VALUE="c"
    onClick="scoreQuestion2(this.value)">Toy Story<BR>
<INPUT TYPE=radio NAME=question2 VALUE="d"
    onClick="scoreQuestion2(this.value)">Mulan</P>
```

6 Add the lines for the third question:

```
<P><B>3. Pluto is a dog. What is Goofy?</B></P>
<P><INPUT TYPE=radio NAME=question3 VALUE="a"
    onClick="scoreQuestion3(this.value)">A bear<BR>
<INPUT TYPE=radio NAME=question3 VALUE="b"
    onClick="scoreQuestion3(this.value)">A mule<BR>
<INPUT TYPE=radio NAME=question3 VALUE="c"
    onClick="scoreQuestion3(this.value)">A horse<BR>
<INPUT TYPE=radio NAME=question3 VALUE="d"
    onClick="scoreQuestion3(this.value)">Also a dog</P>
```

7 Add the lines for the fourth question:

```
<P><B>4. Who was always trying to eat Tweety Bird?</B></P>
<P><INPUT TYPE=radio NAME=question4 VALUE="a"
    onClick="scoreQuestion4(this.value)">Porky Pig<BR>
<INPUT TYPE=radio NAME=question4 VALUE="b"
    onClick="scoreQuestion4(this.value)">Yosemite Sam<BR>
<INPUT TYPE=radio NAME=question4 VALUE="c"
    onClick="scoreQuestion4(this.value)">Sylvester<BR>
<INPUT TYPE=radio NAME=question4 VALUE="d"
    onClick="scoreQuestion4(this.value)">
    Foghorn Leghorn</P>
```

8 Add the lines for the fifth question:

```
<P><B>5. What is Winnie the Pooh's favorite food?</B></P>
<P><INPUT TYPE=radio NAME=question5 VALUE="a"
   onClick="scoreQuestion5(this.value)">Honey<BR>
<INPUT TYPE=radio NAME=question5 VALUE="b"
   onClick="scoreQuestion5(this.value)">Molasses<BR>
<INPUT TYPE=radio NAME=question5 VALUE="c"
   onClick="scoreQuestion5(this.value)">Peanut Butter<BR>
<INPUT TYPE=radio NAME=question5 VALUE="d"
   onClick="scoreQuestion5(this.value)">Yogurt</P>
```

9 Add the following code to close the <FORM>, <BODY>, and <HTML> tags:

```
</FORM>
</BODY>
</HTML>
```

10 Save the file as **CartoonQuiz1.html** in the **Tutorial.04** folder on your Data Disk.

Next you will add the functions to score each of the questions. The functions contain `if` statements that evaluate each answer.

To add JavaScript code to score each of the questions:

1 Replace the line `// ADD CODE HERE` with the following function that scores the first question. A response of *Correct Answer* appears if the user provides the correct answer. A response of *Incorrect Answer* appears if the user provides an incorrect answer.

```
function scoreQuestion1(answer) {
    if (answer == "a")
        alert("Incorrect Answer");
    if (answer == "b")
        alert("Correct Answer");
    if (answer == "c")
        alert("Incorrect Answer");
    if (answer == "d")
        alert("Incorrect Answer");
}
```

2 Add the scoreQuestion2() function:

```
function scoreQuestion2(answer) {
    if (answer == "a")
        alert("Incorrect Answer");
    if (answer == "b")
```

```
            alert("Incorrect Answer");
    if (answer == "c")
        alert("Correct Answer");
    if (answer == "d")
        alert("Incorrect Answer");
}
```

3   Add the scoreQuestion3() function:

```
function scoreQuestion3(answer) {
    if (answer == "a")
        alert("Incorrect Answer");
    if (answer == "b")
        alert("Incorrect Answer");
    if (answer == "c")
        alert("Incorrect Answer");
    if (answer == "d")
        alert("Correct Answer");
}
```

4   Add the scoreQuestion4() function:

```
function scoreQuestion4(answer) {
    if (answer == "a")
        alert("Incorrect Answer");
    if (answer == "b")
        alert("Incorrect Answer");
    if (answer == "c")
        alert("Correct Answer");
    if (answer == "d")
        alert("Incorrect Answer");
}
```

5   Add the scoreQuestion5() function:

```
function scoreQuestion5(answer) {
    if (answer == "a")
        alert("Correct Answer");
    if (answer == "b")
        alert("Incorrect Answer");
    if (answer == "c")
        alert("Incorrect Answer");
    if (answer == "d")
        alert("Incorrect Answer");
}
```

6 Save the file, and then open the **CartoonQuiz1.html** file in your Web browser. As you select a response for each question, you will immediately learn whether the answer is correct. Figure 4-6 shows the output if you select a wrong answer for question 1.

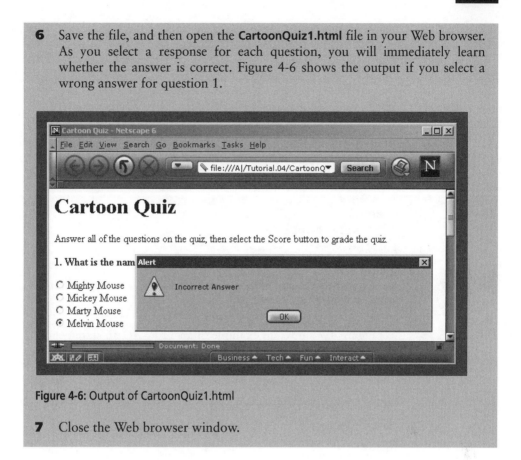

Figure 4-6: Output of CartoonQuiz1.html

7 Close the Web browser window.

if...else Statements

When using an `if` statement, you can include an `else` clause to run an alternate set of code if the conditional expression evaluated by the `if` statement returns a value of `false`. For instance, you may have a program that uses an `if` statement whose conditional expression evaluates the value returned from a confirm dialog box that asks users if they invest in the stock market. If the condition evaluates to `true` (the user pressed the OK button), then the `if` statement displays a Web page on recommended stocks. If the condition evaluates to `false` (the user pressed Cancel), then the statements in an `else` clause display a Web page on other types of investment opportunities. An `if` statement that includes an `else` clause is called an `if...else` statement. You can think of an `else` clause as being a back-up plan for when the `if` statement condition returns a value of `false`. The syntax for an `if...else` statement is as follows:

```
if (conditional expression)
     statement;
else
     statement;
```

You can use command blocks to construct an `if...else` statement as follows:

```
if (condition) {
     statements;
}
else {
     statements;
}
```

An **if** statement can be constructed without the `else` clause. However, the `else` clause can only be used with an **if** statement.

Figure 4-7 shows an example of an `if...else` statement.

```
var today = "Tuesday"

if (today == "Monday")

     document.writeln("Today is Monday");

else

     document.writeln("Today is not Monday");
```

Figure 4-7: Example of an `if...else` statement

In Figure 4-7, the today variable is assigned a value of *Tuesday*. Since `if (today == "Monday")` evaluates to `false`, control of the program passes to the `else` clause, the statement `document.writeln("Today is not Monday");` executes, and the string *Today is not Monday* prints. If the today variable had been assigned a value of *Monday*, the statement `if (today == "Monday")` would have evaluated to `true`, and the statement `document.writeln("Today is Monday");` would have executed. Only one set of statements executes: either the statements following the `if` statement or the statements following the `else` clause. Once either set of statements executes, any code following the `if...else` statements executes normally.

The JavaScript code for the CartoonQuiz1.html file you created earlier uses multiple `if` statements to evaluate the results of the quiz. Although the multiple `if` statements function properly, they can be simplified using an `if...else` statement. Next you will simplify the CartoonQuiz1.html program so that it contains an `if...else` statement instead of multiple `if` statements.

To add `if...else` statements to CartoonQuiz1.html:

1 Return to the **CartoonQuiz1.html** file and immediately save it as **CartoonQuiz2.html**.

2 Since you only need the `if` statement to test for the correct answer, you can group all the incorrect answers in the `else` clause. Modify each of the functions that scores a question so that the multiple `if` statements are replaced with an `if...else` statement. The following code shows how the statements for the scoreQuestion1() function should appear:

```
if (answer == 'b')
     alert("Correct Answer");
else
     alert("Incorrect Answer");
```

3 Save the **CartoonQuiz2.html** document and open it in your Web browser. The program should function the same as when it contained only `if` statements.

4 Close the Web browser window.

Nested `if` and `if...else` Statements

When you make a decision with a control structure such as an `if` or `if...else` statement, you may want the statements executed by the control structure to make other decisions. For instance, you may have a program that uses an `if` statement to ask users if they like sports. If users answer yes, you may want to run another `if` statement that asks users whether they like team sports or individual sports. Since you can include any code you like within the `if` statement or the `else` clause, you can include other `if` or `if...else` statements. An `if` statement contained within an `if` or `if...else` statement is called a **nested if statement**. Similarly, an `if...else` statement contained within an `if` or `if...else` statement is called a **nested if...else statement**. You use nested `if` and `if...else` statements to perform conditional evaluations in addition to the original conditional evaluation. For example, the following code performs two conditional evaluations before the `document.writeln()` statement executes:

```
var number = 7;
if (number > 5)
        if (number < 10)
            document.writeln(
                "The number is between 5 and 10.");
```

If either of the conditions in this example evaluates to `false`, then the JavaScript interpreter skips the rest of the `if` statement.

When you use `else` clauses with nested `if` statements, you need to be aware of which `if` statement an `else` clause is associated with. An `else` clause is part of the nearest `if` statement. Consider the following code:

```
var number = 7;
var numberRange;
if (number > 5)
    if (number > 10)
        numberRange = "The number is greater than 10.";
else
    numberRange = "The number is less than 5.";
document.writeln(numberRange);
```

Since an `else` clause is part of the nearest `if` statement, the `else` clause in the above example is part of the second `if` statement. In this case, since the number variable is not greater than 10, the statement in the `else` clause, which assigns *The number is less than 5* to the numberRange variable, executes. This result is incorrect, since the first `if` statement already determined that the number variable was greater than 5. It is easy to mistakenly think that the `else` clause is part of the first `if` statement, since that is how the indentation is aligned. Remember, however, that the JavaScript interpreter does not recognize indentations or white space; you use them only to make code easier to read. The following code shows a modified version of the program with an additional `else` clause that makes the program run correctly:

```
var number = 7;
var numberRange;
if (number > 5)
    if (number > 10)
        numberRange = "The number is greater than 10.";
    else
        numberRange = "The number is less than 10.";
else
    numberRange = "The number is less than 5.";
document.writeln(numberRange);
```

You can nest `if` statements as deeply as you like. However, `if` statements can become difficult to understand if they are nested too deeply. In Figure 4-8, each `if` statement evaluates the country variable, then program control moves to the next `if` statement, which is contained in an `else` clause.

```
var country = "France";
if (country == "Spain")

    document.writeln("Buenos Dias");

else

    if (country == "Germany")

        document.writeln("Guten Tag");

    else

        if (country == "Italy")

            document.writeln("Buon Giorno");

        else

            if (country == "France")

                document.writeln("Bonjour");

            else

                document.writeln(
                    "I don't speak your language!");
```

Figure 4-8: Greeting program with nested `if` statements

A more efficient way to design the program in Figure 4-8 is to include each `if` statement on the same line as the previous `else` clause. Again, remember that the JavaScript interpreter does not recognize white space. Therefore the statement `else if (country == "Germany")` will function the same, as if it were broken into two separate lines. Figure 4-9 shows a modified version of the program shown in Figure 4-8.

```
var country = "France";

if (country == "Spain")

    document.writeln("Buenos Dias");

else if (country == "Germany")

    document.writeln("Guten Tag");

else if (country == "Italy")

    document.writeln("Buon Giorno");

else if (country == "France")

    document.writeln("Bonjour");

else

    document.writeln("I don't speak your language!");
```

Figure 4-9: Modified Greeting program with nested `if` statements

The JavaScript code in the CartoonQuiz2.html file is somewhat inefficient, since it contains multiple functions that perform essentially the same task of scoring the quiz. A more efficient method of scoring the quiz is to include nested decision-making structures within a single function. Next you will modify the JavaScript code in the CartoonQuiz2.html file so that it contains a single function that checks the correct answer for all the questions, using nested `if...else` statements.

To add nested `if...else` statements to the Cartoon Quiz program:

1 Return to the **CartoonQuiz2.html** file and immediately save it as **CartoonQuiz3.html**.

2 Delete the five functions within the <SCRIPT>...</SCRIPT> tag pair.

3 Add the first line for the single function that will check all the answers: `function scoreQuestions(number, answer) {`. You will send an answer argument to the scoreQuestions() function, just as you did with the functions that scored each individual question. You will also send a new argument, *number*, which represents the question number, to the scoreQuestions() function.

4 Press **Enter** and add the opening `if` statement that checks to see if the question is equal to 1. If it is, a nested `if...else` statement evaluates the response.

```
if (number == 1) {
    if (answer == 'b')
        alert("Correct Answer");
    else
        alert("Incorrect Answer");
}
```

5 Add an `if...else` statement for question number 2:

```
else if (number == 2) {
    if (answer == 'c')
        alert("Correct Answer");
    else
        alert("Incorrect Answer");
}
```

6 Add an `if...else` statement for question number 3:

```
else if (number == 3) {
    if (answer == 'd')
        alert("Correct Answer");
    else
        alert("Incorrect Answer");

}
```

7 Add an `if...else` statement for question number 4:

```
else if (number == 4) {
    if (answer == 'c')
        alert("Correct Answer");
    else
        alert("Incorrect Answer");
}
```

8 Add an `if...else` statement for question number 5:

```
else if (number == 5) {
    if (answer == 'a')
        alert("Correct Answer");
    else
        alert("Incorrect Answer");
}
```

9 Add a closing brace (**}**) for the scoreQuestions() function.

10 Within each of the five <INPUT> tags, change the function called within the onClick() event handler to **scoreQuestions(*number*, this.value)**, changing the ***number*** argument to the appropriate question number. For example, the event handler for question 1 should read: **scoreQuestions(1, this.value)**.

11 Save the HTML document and open it in your Web browser. The program should still function the same way it did with the multiple `if` statements and the multiple functions.

12 Close the Web browser window.

`switch` **Statements**

Another JavaScript statement that is used for controlling program flow is the `switch` statement. The **switch statement** controls program flow by executing a specific set of statements, depending on the value of an expression. The `switch` statement compares the value of an expression to a label contained within a `switch` construct. If the value matches a particular label, then the statements associated with the label execute. For example, you may have a variable in your program named favoriteMusic. A `switch` statement can evaluate the variable (which is an expression) and compare it to a label within the `switch` construct. The `switch` statement may contain several labels, such as Jazz, Rock, or Gospel. If the favoriteMusic variable is equal to Rock, then the statements that are part of the Rock label execute. Although you could accomplish the same functionality using `if` or `if...else` statements, a `switch` statement makes it easier to organize different branches of code that can be executed.

A `switch` construct consists of the following components: the keyword `switch`, an expression, an opening brace, a `case` label, executable statements, the keyword `break`, a `default` label, and a closing brace. The syntax for the `switch` statement is as follows:

```
switch (expression) {
    case label:
        statement(s);
        break;
    case label:
        statement(s);
        break;

    ...
    default:
        statement(s);
}
```

The labels within a `switch` statement are called **case labels** and they identify specific code segments. A `case` label consists of the keyword `case`, followed by a literal value or variable name, followed by a colon. JavaScript compares the value returned from the `switch` statement expression to the literal value or variable name following the `case` keyword. If a match is found, the `case` label statements execute. For example, the `case` label `case 3.17:` represents a floating-point integer value of 3.17. If the value of a `switch` statement expression equals 3.17, then the `case 3.17:` label statements execute. You can use a variety of data types as `case` labels within the same `switch` statement. Figure 4-10 shows examples of different `case` labels.

tip

A `case` label can be followed by a single statement or multiple statements. However, unlike `if` statements, multiple statements for a `case` label do not need to be enclosed within a command block.

```
case exampleVar:                          // variable name

      statement(s)

case "text string":                       // string literal

      statement(s)

case 75:                                  // integer literal

      statement(s)

case -273.4:                              // floating-point literal

      statement(s)
```

Figure 4-10: Examples of case labels

Other programming languages, such as Java and C++, require all case labels within a switch statement to be of the same data type.

Another type of label used within `switch` statements is the `default` label. The **default label** contains statements that execute when the value returned by the `switch` statement conditional expression does not match a `case` label. A `default` label consists of the keyword `default` followed by a colon.

When a `switch` statement executes, the value returned by the conditional expression is compared to each `case` label in the order in which it is encountered. Once a matching label is found, its statements execute. Unlike the `if...else` statement, program execution does not automatically exit the `switch` construct after particular `case` label statements execute. Instead, the `switch` statement continues evaluating the rest of the `case` labels in the list. Once a matching `case` label is found, evaluation of additional `case` labels is unnecessary. If you are working with a large `switch` statement with many `case` labels, evaluation of additional `case` labels can potentially slow down your program.

It is good programming design to end a `switch` statement once it performs its required task. A `switch` statement ends automatically after the JavaScript interpreter encounters its closing brace (}) or when a `break` statement is found. A **break statement** is used to exit `switch` statements and other program control statements such as `while`, `do...while`, `for`, and `for...in` looping statements. To end a `switch` statement once it performs its required task, you should include a `break` statement within each `case` label.

You will learn more about looping statements in Section B.

Figure 4-11 displays an example of a `switch` statement contained within a function. When the function is called, it is passed an argument named americanCity. The `switch` statement compares the contents of the americanCity argument to the `case` labels. If a match is found, the city's state is returned and a `break` statement ends the `switch` statement. If a match is not found, the value *United States* is returned from the `default` label.

```
function city_location(americanCity) {

    switch (americanCity) {

        case "Boston":

            return "Massachusetts";

            break;

        case "Chicago":

            return "Illinois";

            break;

        case "Los Angeles":

            return "California";

            break;

        case "Miami":

            return "Florida";

            break;

        case "New York":

            return "New York";

            break;

        default:

            return "United States";

    }

}
document.writeln(city_location("Boston"));
```

Figure 4-11: Function containing a `switch` statement

You can use either the `if` statement or the `switch` statement to handle the same flow control procedures. It is more efficient, however, to use the `switch` statement if you need to evaluate only a single expression. For example, review the

Greeting program in Figure 4-9, which was created using a series of `if...else` statements. The program works, but it is not the most efficient program, because the conditional evaluation that compares the country variable to a specific country name repeats several times. You can write a more efficient version of the same program using a `switch` statement, as shown in Figure 4-12.

```
var country = "Germany";
switch (country) {
    case "Spain":
        document.writeln("Buenos Dias");
        break;
    case "Germany":
        document.writeln("Guten Tag");
        break;
    case "Italy":
        document.writeln("Buon Giorno");
        break;
    case "France":
        document.writeln("Bonjour");
        break;
    default:
        document.writeln("I don't speak your language");
}
```

Figure 4-12: Greeting program using a `switch` statement

Next you will modify the Cartoon Quiz program so that the scoreAnswers() function contains a `switch` statement instead of nested `if...else` statements. Each `case` statement in the modified program checks for the question number from the function number argument. The `switch` statement makes better programming sense, because it eliminates the need to check the question number multiple times, as is necessary with an `if...else` structure.

To add a `switch` statement to the Cartoon Quiz program:

1 Return to the **CartoonQuiz3.html** file and immediately save it as **CartoonQuiz4.html**.

2 Change the `if...else` statements within the scoreQuestions() function to the following `switch` statement.

```
switch (number) {
  case 1:
      if (answer == 'b')
              alert("Correct Answer");
      else
              alert("Incorrect Answer");
      break;
  case 2:
      if (answer == 'c')
              alert("Correct Answer");
      else
              alert("Incorrect Answer");
      break;
  case 3:
      if (answer == 'd')
              alert("Correct Answer");
      else
              alert("Incorrect Answer");
      break;
  case 4:
      if (answer == 'c')
              alert("Correct Answer");
      else
              alert("Incorrect Answer");
      break;
  case 5:
      if (answer == 'a')
              alert("Correct Answer");
      else
              alert("Incorrect Answer");
      break;
}
```

3 Save the HTML document and open it in your Web browser. The program should still function the same as it did with the nested `if...else` statements.

4 Close the Web browser window, and close your text or HTML editor.

S U M M A R Y

- Flow control is the process of determining the order in which statements execute in a program.

- The `if` statement is used to execute specific programming code if the evaluation of a conditional expression returns `true`.

- A command block refers to multiple statements contained within a set of braces, similar to the way function statements are contained within a set of braces.

- After an `if` statement condition evaluates as `true`, either the first statement following the condition executes or the command block following the condition executes.

- Statements following an `if` statement command or command block execute regardless of whether the `if` statement conditional expression evaluates to `true` or `false`.

- The `else` clause runs an alternate set of code if the conditional expression evaluated by an `if` statement returns a value of `false`.

- In an `if...else` construct, only one set of statements executes: either the statements following the `if` statement or the statements following the `else` clause. Once either set of statements executes, any code following the `if...else` construct executes normally.

- An `if` statement contained within another `if` statement is called a nested `if` statement. Similarly, an `if...else` statement contained within an `if` or `if...else` statement is called a nested `if...else` statement.

- The `switch` statement controls program flow by executing a specific set of statements, depending on the value returned by an expression.

- `Case` labels within a `switch` statement mark specific code segments.

- The `default` label contains statements that execute when the value returned by the `switch` statement conditional expression does not match a `case` label. A `default` label consists of only the keyword `default` followed by a colon.

- When a `switch` statement executes, the value returned by the conditional expression is compared to each `case` label in the order in which it is encountered. Once a matching label is found, its statements execute.

- A `break` statement is used to exit a `switch` statement.

QUESTIONS

1. The process of determining the order in which statements execute in a program is called _____.
   a. process manipulation
   b. flow control
   c. programmatic configuration
   d. architectural structuring

2. Which of the following is the correct syntax for an `if` statement?
   a. `if (myVariable == 10);`
      `alert("Your variable is equal to 10.");`
   b. `if myVariable == 10`
      `alert("Your variable is equal to 10.");`
   c. `if (myVariable == 10)`
      `alert("Your variable is equal to 10.");`
   d. `if (myVariable == 10),`
      `alert("Your variable is equal to 10.");`

3. An `if` statement can include multiple statements provided that they _____.
   a. execute after the `if` statement closing semicolon
   b. are not contained within a command block
   c. do not include other `if` statements
   d. are contained within a command block

4. What happens after you execute an `if` statement?
   a. The statement immediately following the `if` statement executes.
   b. The program ends.
   c. The `if` statement continues looping.
   d. The first matching `case` label in the `if` statement repeats.

5. Which operators can you use with an `if` statement?
   a. only comparison operators
   b. only logical operators
   c. both comparison and logical operators
   d. You cannot use operators with an `if` statement.

6. Which is the correct syntax for an `else` clause?
   a. `else(document.write("Printed from an else clause.");`
   b. `else document.write("Printed from an else clause.");`
   c. `else "document.write('Printed from an else clause.')";`
   d. `else; document.write("Printed from an else clause.");`

7. Which of the following statements is true?
   a. An `if` statement must be constructed with an `else` clause.
   b. An `else` clause can be constructed without an `if` statement.
   c. An `if` statement can be constructed without an `else` clause.
   d. An `else` clause cannot be constructed with an `if` statement.

8. How many if statements can be nested in another if statement?

a. 0

b. 1

c. 5

d. as many as necessary

9. The switch statement controls program flow by executing a specific set of statements, depending on _____.

a. the result of an if...else statement

b. the version of JavaScript being executed

c. whether an if statement executes from within a function

d. the value returned by a conditional expression

10. The case labels within a switch statement are used to _____.

a. mark specific code segments

b. evaluate a conditional expression

c. designate code that is to be ignored by the JavaScript interpreter

d. leave comments for other programmers

11. Which of the following is an incorrect syntax for a case label within a switch statement?

a. case "text string":

b. case 5.48 :

c. case myVariable

d. case 10 :

12. When the value returned by a switch statement conditional expression does not match a case label, then the statements within the _____ label execute.

a. exception

b. else

c. error

d. default

13 You can exit a switch statement using a(n) _____ statement.

a. break

b. end

c. quit

d. complete

EXERCISES

Save all files you create in the Tutorial.04 folder on your Data Disk.

1. Modify the following if statement so that it can contain multiple statements. Add a second statement that prints the value of the boolValue variable. Save the HTML document as MultipleStatements.html.

```
if (boolValue == true)
   document.writeln("The condition is equal to 'true'");
```

2. Rewrite the following conditional expression as an `if...else` statement. Save the HTML document as SimpleIfElse.html.

```
var intVariable = 75;
var result;
(intVariable > 100) ? result = "intVariable is greater than 100"
    : result =  "intVariable is less than or equal to 100";
document.write(result);
```

3. Identify and fix the logic flaws in the following `if` statement. Save the document as NumberCheck.html.

```
var num = 100;
if (num >= 100);
    document.write("The variable is greater than ");
    document.write("or equal to '100.'");
```

4. Add an `else` statement to the `if` statement in Exercise 3 that prints *The variable is less than '100'* to the screen if the num variable is less than 100.

5. Modify the code you used in Exercises 3 and 4 so that it includes a nested `if...else` statement that checks if the variable is greater than or equal to 50 or less than 50. Print the appropriate text to the screen describing the range of the num variable. For example, if the num variable is less than 100, but greater than 50, you should print two lines to the screen: *The variable is less than '100'.* and *The variable is greater than '50'.*

6. Create a Web page with an `if...else` statement that asks users whether they want to see a personalized greeting. If they select yes, display a prompt dialog box asking for their name, then display the name in an alert dialog box. If they select no, display a generic greeting in an alert dialog box. Save the HTML document as PersonalGreeting.html.

7. Add statements to the following `switch` statement so that after the statements in a case label execute, the `switch` statement ends. Save the HTML document as AreaCodes.html.

```
switch (areaCode) {
  case 617:
        document.write("Boston's area code is ");
        document.write(areaCode);
  case 212:
        document.write("Manhattan's area code is ");
        document.write(areaCode);
  case 415:
        document.write("San Francisco's area code is ");
        document.write(areaCode);
  case 813:
        document.write("Tampa's area code is ");
        document.write(areaCode);
}
```

8. Modify the switch statement from Exercise 7 so that a default value of *You did not enter a valid area code* prints to the screen if none of the case labels match the areaCode variable.

9. Rewrite the following statement using a `switch` statement. Save the document as SportsLocation.html.

```
if (sport == "golf")
    alert("Golf is played on a golf course.");
else if (sport == "tennis")
    alert("Tennis is played on a tennis court.");
else if (sport == "baseball")
    alert("Baseball is played on a baseball diamond.");
else if (sport == "basketball")
    alert("Basketball is played on a basketball court.");
else
   alert("You did not enter one of the four sports.");
```

10. Rewrite the following statement using an `if...else` statement. Save the document as Authors.html.

```
switch (writer) {
    case "Ernest Hemingway":
        document.write(writer +
        " wrote Islands in the Stream");
        break;
    case "William Faulkner":
        document.write(writer +
        " wrote The Sound and the Fury");
        break;
    case "Toni Morrison":
        document.write(writer +
        " wrote Song of Solomon");
        break;
    case "F. Scott Fitzgerald":
        document.write(writer +
        " wrote Tender is the Night");
        break;
    case "Henry Miller":
        document.write(writer +
        " wrote Tropic of Capricorn");
        break;
  default:
        document.write(
        "You did not correctly enter one of the four writers.");
        break;
    }
```

11. Create a program that prompts users for the name of the state where they live. Create a decision-making structure that evaluates the name of the state and displays an alert dialog box containing the name of the region where the state is located: North, South, East, West, Midwest, Southwest, and so on. Use the appropriate decision structure to create the program. Save the HTML document as Regions.html.

12. Create a program that calculates an employee's weekly gross salary, based on the number of hours worked and hourly wage. Compute any hours over 40 as time-and-a-half. Use the appropriate decision structure to create the program. Save the HTML document as Wages.html.

SECTION B

objectives

In this section you will learn
how to use:

- while **statements**
- do...while **statements**
- for **statements**
- for...in **statements**
- with **statements**
- continue **statements**

Repetition

while **Statements**

The statements you have worked with so far execute one after the other in a linear fashion. The if, if...else, and switch statements select only a single branch of code to execute, then continue to the statement that follows. But what if you want to repeat the same statement, function, or code section 5 times, 10 times, or 100 times? For example, you might want to perform the same calculation until a specific number is found. A **loop statement** repeatedly executes a statement or a series of statements while a specific condition is true or until a specific condition becomes true.

One of the simplest types of loop statements is the while statement. The **while statement** is used for repeating a statement or series of statements as long as a given conditional expression evaluates to true. The syntax for the while statement is as follows:

```
while (conditional expression) {
    statement(s);
}
```

Like the if...else and switch statements, the conditional expression that the while statement tests for is enclosed within parentheses following the keyword while. As long as the conditional expression evaluates to true, the statement or command block that follows will execute repeatedly. Each repetition of a looping statement is called an **iteration**. Once the conditional expression evaluates to false, the loop ends and the next statement following the while statement executes.

A while statement will keep repeating until its conditional expression evaluates to false. To end the while statement once the desired tasks have been performed, you must include code that tracks the progress of the loop and changes the value produced by the conditional expression. You track the progress of a while statement, or any other loop, with a counter. A **counter** is a variable that increments or decrements with each iteration of a loop statement.

tip

Many programmers often name counter variables *count*, *counter*, or something similar. The letters *i, j, k*, and *l* are also commonly used as counter names. Using a name such as *count*, or the letter *i* (for *increment*) or a higher letter, helps you remember (and lets other programmers know) that the variable is being used as a counter.

The following code shows an example of a simple program that uses a `while` statement. The program declares a variable named count and assigns it an initial value of one. The count variable is then used in the `while` statement conditional expression (`count <= 5`). As long as the count variable is less than or equal to five, the `while` statement will loop. Within the body of the `while` statement, the `document.writeln()` statement prints the value of the count variable, then the count variable increments by a value of one. The `while` statement loops until the count variable increments to a value of six.

```
var count = 1;
while (count <= 5) {
    document.writeln(count);
    ++count;
}
document.writeln("You have printed 5 numbers.");
```

The preceding code prints the numbers 1 to 5, which represent each iteration of the loop. Once the counter reaches 6, the message *You have printed 5 numbers.* prints to demonstrate when the loop ends. Figure 4-13 shows the output.

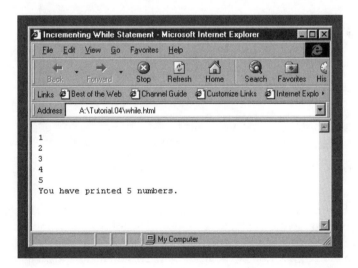

Figure 4-13: Output of a `while` statement using an increment operator

You can also control the repetitions in a `while` loop by decrementing counter variables. Consider the following program code:

```
var count = 10;
while (count > 0) {
    document.writeln(count);
    --count;
}
document.writeln("We have liftoff.");
```

In this example, the initial value of the count variable is 10, and the decrement operator (--) is used to decrease count by one. While the count variable is greater than zero, the statement within the `while` loop prints the value of the count variable. When the value of count is equal to zero, the `while` loop ends, and the statement immediately following it prints. Figure 4-14 shows the program output.

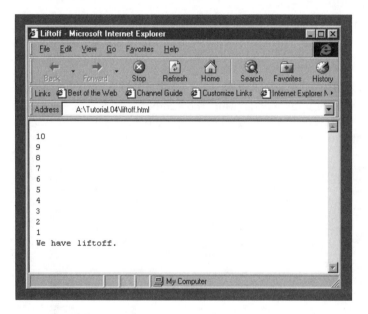

Figure 4-14: Output of a `while` statement using a decrement operator

There are many ways to change the value of a count variable and use count to control the repetitions of a `while` loop. The following example uses the `*=` assignment operator to multiply the value of the count variable by two. Once the count variable reaches a value of 128, the `while` statement ends. Figure 4-15 shows the program output.

```
var count = 1;
while (count <= 100) {
    document.writeln (count);
    count *= 2;
}
```

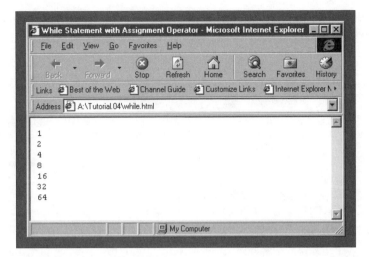

Figure 4-15: Output of a while statement using the while statement using the *= assignment operator

It is important to include code that monitors a while statement conditional expression. You also need to include code within the body of the while statement that changes *some* part of the conditional expression. If you do not include code that changes the value used by the conditional expression, your program will be caught in an infinite loop. An **infinite loop** is a situation in which a loop statement never ends because its conditional expression is never updated or is never false. Consider the following while statement:

```
var count = 1;
while (count <= 10) {
    alert("The number is " + count);
}
```

Although the while statement in the above example includes a conditional expression that checks the value of a count variable, there is no code within the while statement body that changes the count variable value. The count variable will continue to have a value of 1 through each iteration of the loop. In this case, an alert dialog box containing the text string *The number is 1* appears over and over again, no matter how many times you press the OK button.

tip

In most cases, you must force a Web browser that is caught in an infinite loop to close. The method for forcing the close of an application varies with the computer system. For Windows operating systems, you can force an application to close by pressing Ctrl+Alt+Delete to access Task List or Task Manager. When the Close Program dialog box appears, click the End Task button.

Next you will create a program that demonstrates the use of the while statement. The program uses a while statement to check the "speed" you enter into a prompt dialog box. The speed is then used as a counter by a while statement. As long as you enter a speed that is under 65 mph, you continue receiving prompt dialog boxes asking for new speeds. If you enter a speed over 65, or less than or equal to 0, then the `while` loop ends.

To create the speed limit program:

1 Create a new document in your text editor or HTML editor.

2 Type the opening <HTML> tag, the opening lines of a <HEAD> section, and a new <SCRIPT> section:

```
<HTML>
<HEAD>
<TITLE>Speed Limit</TITLE>
<SCRIPT LANGUAGE="JavaScript">
<!-- HIDE FROM INCOMPATIBLE BROWSERS
```

3 Type the opening constructor for a function that accepts a single *speed* argument: `function speedLimit(speed) {`, then press **Enter**.

4 Add the opening constructor for a `while` statement that keeps looping as long as the speed variable is less than or equal to 65: `while(speed <= 65){`, then press **Enter**.

5 Add the following line within the `while` statement that assigns the input from a prompt dialog box to a variable named newSpeed:

```
var newSpeed = prompt("Your speed is " + speed
     + ". Please enter a new speed", "");
```

6 Press **Enter** and add an `if...else` statement to check if the speed is over 65. If the speed is greater than 65, an alert dialog box appears, and the break statement is called.

```
if (newSpeed > 65) {
     alert("You are speeding!");
     break;
}
```

7 Press **Enter** again and add an `if...else` statement to check if the speed is less than or equal to 0. If the speed is less than or equal to 0, an alert dialog box appears, and the break statement is called.

```
else if (newSpeed <= 0) {
     alert("You are stopped!");
     break;
}
```

8   Next, add a final `else` clause that continues the `while` statement:

```
else {
        speed = newSpeed;
}
```

9   Add the following code to close the `while` statement, function, <SCRIPT> section, and <HEAD> section.

```
    }
}
// STOP HIDING FROM INCOMPATIBLE BROWSERS -->
</SCRIPT>
</HEAD>
```

10 Type the following lines for the opening <BODY> tag along with an <H1> tag. The <BODY> tag uses an onLoad event to call the speedLimit() function in the <HEAD>. The speedLimit() function is sent a starting speed of 55.

```
<BODY onLoad= "speedLimit(55);">
<H1>Select Reload or Refresh to restart the SpeedLimit
program.</H1>
```

11 Add the following code to close the <BODY> and <HTML> tags:

```
</BODY>
</HTML>
```

12 Save the file as **SpeedLimit.html** in the **Tutorial.04** folder on your Data Disk. Open the **SpeedLimit.html** file in your Web browser and test the program. Figure 4-16 shows an example of the output of SpeedLimit.html.

13 Close the Web browser window.

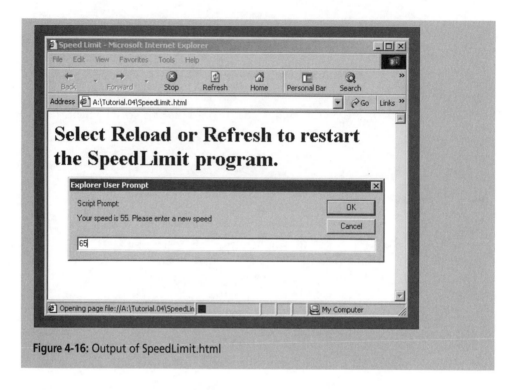

Figure 4-16: Output of SpeedLimit.html

do...while **Statements**

Another JavaScript looping statement that is similar to the `while` statement is the `do...while` statement. The **do...while statement** executes a statement or statements once, then repeats the execution as long as a given conditional expression evaluates to `true`. The syntax for the `do...while` statement is as follows:

```
do {
    statement(s);
} while (conditional expression);
```

As you can see in the syntax description, the statements execute *before* a conditional expression is evaluated. Unlike the simpler `while` statement, the statements in a `do...while` statement always execute once, before a conditional expression is evaluated.

The following `do...while` statement executes once before the conditional expression evaluates the count variable. Therefore, a single line that reads *The count is equal to 2* prints. Once the conditional expression (count < 2) executes, the `do...while` statement ends, since the count variable is equal to 2 and causes the conditional expression to return a value of `false`.

```
var count = 2;
do {
```

```
    document.writeln("The count is equal to " + count);
    ++count;
} while (count < 2);
```

Note that this do...while example includes a counter within the body of the do...while statement. As with the while statement, you need to include code that changes some part of the conditional expression in order to prevent an infinite loop from occurring.

In the following example, the while statement never executes, since the count variable does not fall within the range of the conditional expression:

```
var count = 2;
while (count > 2) {
    document.writeln("The count is equal to " + count);
    ++count;
}
```

Figure 4-17 shows an example of a do...while statement that prints the days of the week, using an array.

```
<PRE>

<SCRIPT>

var daysOfWeek = new Array();

daysOfWeek[0] = "Monday";

daysOfWeek[1] = "Tuesday";

daysOfWeek[2] = "Wednesday";

daysOfWeek[3] = "Thursday";

daysOfWeek[4] = "Friday";

daysOfWeek[5] = "Saturday";

daysOfWeek[6] = "Sunday";

var count = 0;

do {

    document.writeln(daysOfWeek[count]);

    ++count;

} while (count < daysOfWeek.length);

</SCRIPT>

</PRE>
```

Figure 4-17: Example of a do...while statement

In the example in Figure 4-17, an array is created containing the days of the week. A count variable is declared and initialized to zero. Remember, the first subscript or index in an array is zero. Therefore, in the example, the statement `daysOfWeek[0];` refers to Monday. The first iteration of the `do...while` statement prints *Monday*, then increments the count variable by one. The conditional expression in the `while` statement then checks the Array object length property to determine when the last element of the array has been printed. As long as the count is less than the Array object length property (which is one number higher than the largest element in the daysOfWeek[] array), the loop continues. Figure 4-18 shows the output of the Days of Week program in a Web browser:

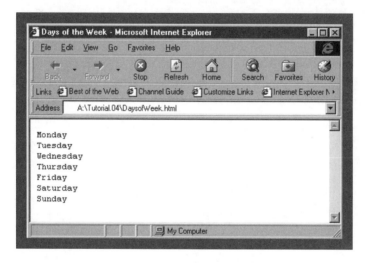

Figure 4-18: Days of Week program in a Web browser

Next you will modify the SpeedLimit program so that it uses a `do...while` statement instead of a `while` statement. Using a `do...while` statement eliminates the need to send an initial speed argument to the speedLimit() function. Instead, the speed variable is initialized during the first pass of the `do` statement, then the `while` statement checks the speed variable to see if the loop should continue.

To add a `do...while` statement to the SpeedLimit program:

1 Return to the **SpeedLimit.html** file and immediately save it as **SpeedLimit2.html**.

2 Delete the speed argument in the speedLimit() function.

3 Modify the `while` statement to create a `do...while` statement as follows. Notice that you no longer need the newSpeed variable. Also notice that you no longer need the final `else` clause to assign the value of the newSpeed variable to the speed variable.

```
do {
    var speed = prompt("Your speed is " + speed
        + ". Please enter a new speed", "");
    if (speed > 65) {
        alert("You are speeding!");
        break;
    }
    else if (speed <= 0) {
        alert("You are stopped!");
        break;
    }
} while(speed <= 65)
```

4 Delete the **55** in the statement that calls the speedLimit() function.

5 Save the file, then open it in your Web browser. When you first open it, the message in the dialog box reads *Your speed is undefined*. Remember that when a variable is declared, it contains an initial value of *undefined* until you explicitly assign a value to it. Since you removed the speed argument from the speedLimit() function, the speed variable contains a value of *undefined* until you enter a speed limit into the dialog box and press Enter.

6 Close the Web browser window.

`for` Statements

You can also use the `for` statement to loop through code. The `for` statement is used for repeating a statement or series of statements as long as a given conditional expression evaluates to `true`. The `for` statement performs essentially the same function as the `while` statement: if a conditional expression within the `for` statement constructor evaluates to `true`, then the `for` statement executes and will continue to execute repeatedly until the conditional expression evaluates to `false`. One of the primary differences between the `while` statement and the `for` statement is that in addition to a conditional expression, you can also include code in the `for` statement constructor to initialize a counter and change its value with each iteration. The syntax of the `for` statement is as follows:

```
for (initialization expression; condition; update statement) {
    statement(s);
}
```

When the JavaScript interpreter encounters a for loop, the following steps occur:

1. The initialization expression is started. For example, if the initialization expression in a for loop is var count = 1;, then a variable named count is declared and assigned an initial value of 1. The initialization expression is only started once when the for loop is first encountered.
2. The for loop condition is evaluated.
3. If the condition evaluation in Step 2 returns a value of true, then the for loop statements execute, Step 4 occurs, and the process starts over again with Step 2. If the condition evaluation in Step 2 returns a value of false, then the for statement ends and the next statement following the for statement executes.
4. The update statement in the for statement constructor is executed. For example, the count variable may increment by one.

tip

You can omit any of the three parts of the for statement constructor, but you must include the semicolons that separate each section. If you omit a section of the constructor, be sure you include code within the body that will end the for statement or your program may get caught in an infinite loop.

Figure 4-19 displays an example of a for statement that prints the contents of an array.

```
var fastFoods = new Array();

fastFoods[0] = "pizza";

fastFoods[1] = "burgers";

fastFoods[2] = "french fries";

fastFoods[3] = "tacos";

fastFoods[4] = "fried chicken";

for (var count = 0; count < fastFoods.length; ++count) {

        document.writeln(fastFoods[count]);

}
```

Figure 4-19: A for statement that displays the contents of an array

As you can see in the example, the counter is initialized, evaluated, and incremented within the constructor. You do not need to include a declaration for the count variable before the for statement, nor do you need to increment the count variable within the body of the for statement. Figure 4-20 shows the output of the Fast Foods program.

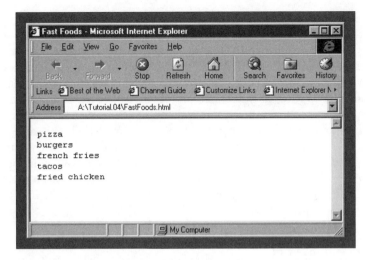

Figure 4-20: Output of Fast Foods program

Looping statements that are controlled by counters using `for` statements work more efficiently than `while` statements. Using a `for` statement is more efficient because you do not need as many lines of code. Consider the following `while` statement:

```
var count = 1;
while (count <= 5) {
     document.writeln(count);
     ++count;
}
```

You could achieve the same flow control more efficiently by using a `for` statement as follows:

```
for (var count = 1; count <= 5; ++count) {
     document.writeln(count);
}
```

There are times, however, when using a `while` statement is preferable to using a `for` statement. If you do not use a counter to update the conditional expression or if the counter must be updated from the body of the loop statement, a `while` construction works better than a `for` construction. The following code relies on a Boolean value returned from a confirm dialog box, rather than a counter, for program control.

```
var i = true;
while (i == true)
        i = confirm(
               "Do you want to redisplay this dialog box?");
```

You could accomplish the same task using a `for` statement, but in this case, the third part of the `for` statement constructor, which updates the counter, is unnecessary. Therefore, this code is better written using a `while` statement. If you use a `for` statement instead of a `while` statement in the preceding example, you must leave the update section out of the `for` statement constructor. You must also remember to leave in the semicolon that separates the conditional section from the update section. If you leave the update section in the constructor, you could create an infinite loop. The following code performs essentially the same task as the above `while` example, but causes an infinite loop, since the constructor always changes the i variable to `true` with each iteration. No matter how many times you press the confirm dialog box cancel button, which assigns a value of `false` to the i variable, the `for` constructor reassigns the variable to `true` each time the code repeats, causing an infinite loop.

```
for (var i = true; i == true; i = true) {
   i = confirm(
        "Do you want to redisplay this dialog box?");
}
```

To make the preceding `for` loop function correctly without causing an infinite loop, you must remove the update section from the constructor, as follows:

```
for (var i = true; i == true;) {
   i = confirm(
        "Do you want to redisplay this dialog box?");
}
```

Figure 4-21 shows an example of the Days of Week program you saw in Figure 4-17 that prints the contents of an array, but this time using a `for` statement instead of a `do...while` statement. Notice that the declaration of the count variable, the conditional expression, and the statement that increments the count variable are now all contained within the `for` statement constructor. Using a `for` statement instead of a `do...while` statement simplifies the program somewhat, since you do not need as many lines of code.

```
<PRE>
<SCRIPT>
var daysOfWeek = new Array();
daysOfWeek[0] = "Monday";
daysOfWeek[1] = "Tuesday";
daysOfWeek[2] = "Wednesday";
daysOfWeek[3] = "Thursday";
daysOfWeek[4] = "Friday";
daysOfWeek[5] = "Saturday";
daysOfWeek[6] = "Sunday";
for (var count = 0; count < daysOfWeek.length; ++count) {
     document.writeln(daysOfWeek[count]);
}
</SCRIPT>
</PRE>
```

Figure 4-21: Example of a for statement

Next you will create a final version of the Cartoon Quiz program that uses a single for statement containing a nested if statement to score the quiz. Although this for statement is somewhat more complicated than the if, if...else, and switch statements, it takes up considerably fewer lines of code. You will also include a Score button that grades the entire quiz after a user is finished, instead of grading the quiz answer by answer.

To create the final version of the Cartoon Quiz program:

1 Open the **CartoonQuiz4.html** file from the **Tutorial.04** folder on your Student Disk and immediately save it as **CartoonQuizFinal.html**.

2 Delete the entire scoreQuestions() function from the <HEAD> section, then add the following lines to create two arrays: answers[] and correctAnswers[]. The answers[] array holds the answers selected each time the quiz runs, and the correctAnswers[] array holds the correct response for each of the questions. The code also assigns the correct responses to each element of the correctAnswers[] array.

```
var answers = new Array(5);
var correctAnswers = new Array(5);
correctAnswers[0] = "b";
correctAnswers[1] = "c";
correctAnswers[2] = "d";
correctAnswers[3] = "c";
correctAnswers[4] = "a";
```

3 Press **Enter** and type the following function, which assigns the response from each question to the appropriate element in the answers[] array. The program sends the actual question number (1–5) to the function using the onClick event of each radio button. To assign question responses to the correct element, 1 must be subtracted from the question variable, because the elements in an array start with 0.

```
function recordAnswer(question, answer) {
    answers[question-1] = answer;
}
```

4 Type the opening constructor for the function that scores the quiz: **function scoreQuiz() {**. You call this function from a new Score button.

5 Press **Enter** and type **var totalCorrect = 0;** to declare a new variable and assign to it an initial value of 0. The totalCorrect variable holds the number of correct answers.

6 Press **Enter** and type the opening constructor for a for loop that scores the quiz: **for(var count = 0; count < correctAnswers.length; ++count) {**. A counter named count is initialized to a value of 0, since 0 is the starting index of an array. The conditional expression checks to see if count is less than or equal to the number of elements in the answers[] array. Finally, the count variable increments by one with each iteration of the loop.

7 Press **Enter** and add the following if statement within the for loop. The if statement compares each element within the answers[] array to each corresponding element within the correctAnswers[] array. If the elements match, the totalCorrect variable increments by one.

```
if (answers[count] == correctAnswers[count])
    ++totalCorrect;
```

8 Add the closing brace for the for loop. Then add the code for an alert dialog box that shows how many questions were answered correctly:

```
}
alert("You scored " + totalCorrect
    + " out of 5 answers correctly!");
```

9 Add a closing brace (**}**) for the scoreQuiz() function.

10 In the onClick event handlers for each radio button, change the name of the called function from scoreQuestions() to **recordAnswer()**, but use the same arguments that you used for the scoreQuestions() function. For example, the onClick event handlers for the Question 1 radio buttons should now read onClick="recordAnswer(1, this.value)".

11 Finally, add the following <INPUT> tag immediately after the last radio button for question 5. The <INPUT> tag creates a command button whose onClick event handler calls the scoreQuiz() function.

```
<INPUT TYPE=button VALUE="Score" onClick =
"scoreQuiz();"><P>
```

12 Save the file, then open it in your Web browser window. Test the program by answering all five questions and pressing the Score button. The result in your Web browser should appear similarly to Figure 4-22, depending on how many questions you answered correctly.

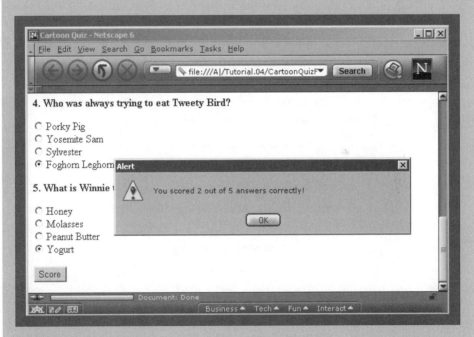

Figure 4-22: Output of CartoonQuizFinal.html

13 Close the Web browser window.

for...in Statements

In Tutorial 2 you worked with objects and properties. As you recall, you use special types of functions called constructor functions to create objects. The variables within a constructor function are the data of any objects created from the constructor function and are referred to as properties. The **for...in statement** is a looping statement that executes the same statement or command block for all the properties within an object. This is useful, for instance, if you want to print the names of all the properties in an object. The syntax of the for...in statement is as follows:

```
for (variable in object) {
    statement(s);
}
```

The variable name in the for...in statement constructor holds an individual object property. The object name in the constructor represents the name of an object that has been instantiated in a program. Unlike the other loop statements, the for...in statement does not require a counter or any other type of code to control how the loop functions. Instead, the for...in statement automatically assigns each property in an object to the variable name, performs the necessary statements on the property, then moves to the next property and starts over. The for...in statement ends automatically once it reaches the last property in an object. A typical use of the for...in statement is to retrieve the names of properties within an object, as shown in Figure 4-23.

```
function Animal(type, sound, transport_mode) {

    this.animal_type = type; // object property

    this.animal_sound = sound; // object property

    this.animal_transport_mode = transport_mode;
        // object property

}

livestock = new Animal("cow", "moo", "walk");
        // instantiate object

for (prop in livestock) {     // this for loop prints

    document.writeln(prop); // the names of the properties

}
```

Figure 4-23: A for...in statement printing the names of properties within an object

In the for...in statement in Figure 4-23, the variable name prop holds the names of each property in the livestock object, which was instantiated from the

Animal constructor function. The document.writeln() statement then writes the name of each property to the Web browser window as follows:

```
animal_type
animal_sound
animal_transport_mode
```

There is no set order or way to control how the properties in an object are assigned to the for...in **statement variable.**

One of the benefits of the for...in statement is that it **enumerates**, or assigns an index to, each property in an object, which is similar to the way elements in an array are indexed. You can use an enumerated object property to access the values contained within object properties. The code in Figure 4-24 is similar to the code in Figure 4-23, except that the document.writeln() statement within the body of the for...in statement has been changed to document.writeln(livestock[prop]);.

```
function Animal(type, sound, transport_mode) {

    this.animal_type = type;

    this.animal_sound = sound;

    this.animal_transport_mode = transport_mode;

}

livestock = new Animal("cow", "moo", "walk");

for (prop in livestock) {

    document.writeln(livestock[prop]);

}
```

Figure 4-24: A for...in statement printing the properties within an object

Each iteration of the for...in statement in Figure 4-24 now prints the contents of each property ("cow," "moo," and "walk") rather than just the property names. The code passes the livestock object to the document.writeln() method, along with the prop variable enclosed in brackets (livestock[prop]. You would use this same technique to print the contents of an array. Unlike the elements in an array, however, you cannot refer to the enumerated properties of an object outside a for...in loop; doing so generates an error. The statement document.writeln (livestock[prop]); causes an error outside a for...in loop.

Next you will create a program that uses the for...in statement to print the properties in an object.

To create a program that uses the `for...in` **statement to print the properties in an object:**

1 Create a new document in your text editor or HTML editor.

2 Type the opening <HTML> and <HEAD> sections of the document:

```
<HTML>
<HEAD>
<TITLE>Car Properties</TITLE>
```

3 Type the opening lines for a <SCRIPT> section:

```
<SCRIPT LANGUAGE="JavaScript">
<!-- HIDE FROM INCOMPATIBLE BROWSERS
```

4 Type the following class constructor that creates a Car constructor function:

```
function Car(make, model, color, doors) {
    this.car_make = make;
    this.car_model = model;
    this.car_color = color;
    this.car_doors = doors;
}
```

5 Type the following code to close the <SCRIPT> and <HEAD> sections.

```
// STOP HIDING FROM INCOMPATIBLE BROWSERS -->
</SCRIPT>
</HEAD>
```

6 Add the following code to begin the body of the HTML document and to create a preformatted text container:

```
<BODY>
<PRE>
```

7 Add the opening statements for the JavaScript section, which calls the function in the <HEAD> section:

```
<SCRIPT LANGUAGE="JavaScript">
<!-- HIDE FROM INCOMPATIBLE BROWSERS
```

8 Type `sports_car = new Car();` to instantiate a new sports_car object based on the Car constructor function.

9 Add the following lines to assign values to each of the sports_car properties:

```
sports_car.car_make = "Triumph";
sports_car.car_model = "Spitfire";
sports_car.car_color = "Yellow";
sports_car.car_doors = 2;
```

10 Press **Enter** and create the following `for...in` statement to print the properties of the sports_car object:

```
for (prop in sports_car) {
   document.writeln(sports_car[prop]);
}
```

11 Add the following code to close the <SCRIPT>, <PRE>, <BODY>, and <HTML> tags:

```
// STOP HIDING FROM INCOMPATIBLE BROWSERS -->
</SCRIPT>
</PRE>
</BODY>
</HTML>
```

12 Save the file as **SportsCar.html** in the **Tutorial.04** folder on your Data Disk. Open the **SportsCar.html** file in your Web browser. Figure 4-25 shows the output.

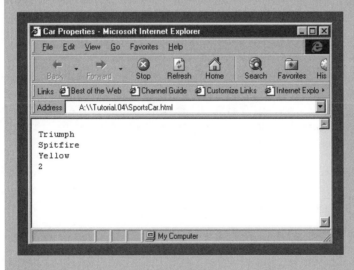

Figure 4-25: Output of SportsCar.html

13 Close the Web browser window.

`with` **Statements**

Another statement that is used for working with object properties is the `with` statement. The **`with` statement** eliminates the need to retype the name of an object when properties of the same object are being referenced in a series. Placing the statements within a `with` statement eliminates the need to retype the name of the object for each property; you can simply use the name of the property within a statement without referencing the property source object. The syntax for the `with` statement is as follows:

```
with (object) {
    statement(s);
}
```

In a `with` statement, the name of the object you want to reference is placed within the parentheses following the `with` keyword. The statements that will use properties of the object are then placed within braces. The following code repeats the document.writeln() method three times:

```
document.writeln("Mark Twain wrote: ");
document.writeln("Everybody talks about the weather, ");
document.writeln("but nobody does anything about it.");
```

You can eliminate the multiple references to the document object in the above code by placing the statements within a `with` statement, as follows:

```
with (document) {
    writeln("Mark Twain wrote: ");
    writeln("Everybody talks about the weather, ");
    writeln("but nobody does anything about it.");
}
```

The `with` statement is often used to eliminate the need to retype long object names. Figure 4-26 shows an example of a `with` statement that assigns values to properties of an unusually long object name.

```
function Animal(type, sound, transport_mode) {

    this.animal_type = type;

    this.animal_sound = sound;

    this.animal_transport_mode = transport_mode;

}

animal_that_lives_in_the_forest = new Animal();

with (animal_that_lives_in_the_forest) {

    animal_type = "wolf";

    animal_sound = "growl";

    animal_transport_mode = "run";

}
```

Figure 4-26: Example of a `with` statement assigning values to object properties

Without the `with` statement in Figure 4-26, the lines that assign values to the object properties would need to be written as follows:

```
animal_that_lives_in_the_forest.animal_type
    = "wolf";
animal_that_lives_in_the_forest.animal_sound
    = "growl";
animal_that_lives_in_the_forest.animal_transport_mode
    = "run";
```

Next you will add a `with` statement to the SportsCar.html file.

To add a `with` statement to the SportsCar.html file:

1 Return to the **SportsCar.html** file and immediately save it as **SportsCar2.html.**

2 Locate the following lines, which assign values to the sports_car object properties:

```
sports_car.car_make = "Triumph";
sports_car.car_model = "Spitfire";
sports_car.car_color = "Yellow";
sports_car.car_doors = 2;
```

3 Add a `with` statement to simplify the four lines as follows:

```
with (sports_car) {
   car_make = "Triumph";
   car_model = "Spitfire";
   car_color = "Yellow";
   car_doors = 2;
}
```

4 Save the file and reopen it in your Web browser. The output should be the same as in Figure 4-25.

5 Close the Web browser window.

`continue` Statements

In Section A, you learned that `break` statements are used for exiting `switch`, `while`, `do...while`, `for`, and `for...in` statements. The `break` statement halts the `switch` or looping statement and executes the next statement that follows the `switch` or loop construct. A similar statement, used only with looping statements, is the `continue` statement. The **continue statement** halts a looping statement and restarts the loop with a new iteration. You use the `continue` statement when you want to stop the loop for the current iteration, but want the loop to continue with a new iteration. For example, you may have a program that uses a `for` statement to loop through the elements of an array containing a list of stocks. For stocks worth more than $10, you print information to the screen such as purchase price, number of shares, and so on. However, you use the `continue` statement to skip stocks worth less than $10 and move on to a new iteration. Figure 4-27 displays a `for` loop containing a `break` statement. Figure 4-28 displays the same `for` loop, but with a `continue` statement.

```
for(var count = 1; count <=5; ++count) {

    if(count == 3)

        break;

    document.writeln(count);

}
```

Figure 4-27: A for loop with a break statement

```
for(var count = 1; count <=5; ++count) {

    if(count == 3)

        continue;

    document.writeln(count);

}
```

Figure 4-28: A for loop with a continue statement

The `for` loop in Figures 4-27 and 4-28 contains an `if` statement that checks whether the current value of count equals 3. In Figure 4-27, when count equals 3, the `break` statement immediately ends the `for` loop. The output of Figure 4-27 is:

1
2

In Figure 4-28, when count equals 3, the `continue` statement also stops the current iteration of the `for` loop, and the program skips printing the number 3. However, the loop will continue to iterate until the conditional expression `count <= 5` is `false`. The output of Figure 4-28 is:

1
2
4
5

Next you will add a `continue` statement to the SportsCar.html file so that the car_model property does not print.

To add a `continue` statement to the SportsCar.html file so that the car_model property does not print:

1 Save the SportsCar2.html file as **SportsCar3.html**.

2 Add the following lines just before `document.writeln (sports_car[prop]);`:

```
if (prop == "car_model")
     continue;
```

When the `for` statement encounters the car_model property, the `if` statement executes the `continue` statement, which immediately starts a new iteration of the `for` loop, preventing the car_model property from printing.

3 Save the **SportsCar3.html file** and open it in your Web browser. The output should appear similarly to Figure 4-29.

Figure 4-29: Output of SportsCar3.html

4 Close the Web browser window and your text or HTML editor.

 # S U M M A R Y

- A loop statement repeatedly executes a statement or a series of statements as long as a specific condition is `true` or until a specific condition becomes `true`.

- The `while` statement is used for repeating a statement or series of statements as long as a given conditional expression evaluates to `true`.

- Each repetition of a looping statement is called an iteration.

- You must include code that tracks the progress of the `while` statement and changes the value produced by the conditional expression once the desired tasks have been performed.

- A counter is a variable that increments with each iteration of a loop statement.

- If a counter variable is beyond the range of a `while` statement conditional expression, then the `while` statement will be bypassed completely.

- In an infinite loop, a loop statement never ends because its conditional expression is never updated.

- The `do...while` statement executes a statement or statements once, then repeats the execution as long as a given conditional expression evaluates to `true`.

- The `for` statement is used for repeating a statement or series of statements as long as a given conditional expression evaluates to `true`.

- You can omit any of the three parts of the `for` statement constructor, but you must include the semicolons that separate each section. If you omit a section of the constructor, be sure you include code within the body that will end the `for` statement, or your program may get caught in an infinite loop.

- The `for...in` statement executes the same statement or command block for all the properties within an object.

- The variable name in the `for...in` statement constructor holds an individual object property. The object name in the constructor represents the name of an object that has been instantiated in a program. Unlike the other loop statements, the `for...in` statement does not require a counter or any other type of code to control how the loop functions.

- The `for...in` statement enumerates, or assigns an index to, each property in an object.

- The `with` statement eliminates the need to retype the name of an object when properties of the same object are being referenced in a series.

- The `continue` statement halts a looping statement and restarts the loop with a new iteration.

 # QUESTIONS

1. Each repetition of a looping statement is called a(n) _____.
   a. recurrence
   b. iteration
   c. duplication
   d. re-execution

2. Counter variables _____.
   a. are used to count the number of times that a looping statement has repeated
   b. count the number of times that the Web browser has been opened and closed
   c. are used to count how many times a JavaScript program has been executed
   d. are only used within if or if...else statements

3. Which of the following is the correct syntax for a while statement?
   a.
   ```
   while (i <= 5, ++i) {
           document.writeln(i);
   }
   ```
   b.
   ```
   [begin code]while (i <= 5) {
           document.writeln(i);
           ++i;
   }
   ```
   c.
   ```
   while (i <= 5);
           document.writeln(i);
           ++i;
   ```
   d.
   ```
   while (i <= 5; document.writeln(i)) {
           ++i;
   }
   ```

4. Counter variables _____.
   a. can only be incremented
   b. can only be decremented
   c. can be changed using any conditional expression
   d. do not change

5. An infinite loop is caused _____.
   a. when you omit the closing brace for a decision-making structure
   b. when a conditional expression never evaluates to false
   c. when a conditional expression never evaluates to true
   d. whenever you execute a while statement

6. In most cases, what must you do if you are caught in an infinite loop in JavaScript?
   a. Add a break statement to the JavaScript code.
   b. Reload the HTML document in a Web browser window.
   c. Nothing—the program will end normally.
   d. Force the close of the Web browser window.

7. If a do...while statement conditional expression evaluates to false, how many times will the do...while statement execute?
   a. never
   b. once
   c. twice
   d. Repeatedly—this conditional expression causes an infinite loop.

8. Which of the following is the correct syntax for a do...while statement?
    ```
    a. do while (i < 10) {
            alert("Printed from a do...while loop.");
       }
    b. do { while (i < 10)
            alert("Printed from a do...while loop.");
       }
    c. do {
            alert("Printed from a do...while loop.");
            while (i < 10)
       }
    d. do {
            alert("Printed from a do...while loop.");
       } while (i < 10);
    ```

9. Which of the following is the correct syntax for a for statement?
    ```
    a. for (var i = 0; i < 10; ++i)
            alert("Printed from a for statement.");
    b. for (var i = 0, i < 10, ++i)
            alert("Printed from a for statement.");
    c. for {
            alert("Printed from a for statement.");
       } while  (var i = 0; i < 10; ++i)
    d. for (var i = 0; i < 10);
            alert("Printed from a for statement.");
            ++i;
    ```

10. When is a for statement initialization expression executed?
    a. when the for statement begins executing
    b. with each repetition of the for statement
    c. when the counter variable increments
    d. when the for statement ends

11. What type of counter should you use with a for...in statement?
    a. a Boolean variable
    b. an incremental or decremental variable
    c. an array length property
    d. You do not need to use a counter with the for...in statement.

12. What does a for...in statement property variable hold?
    a. an object name
    b. the name of an object property
    c. a counter variable
    d. the name of a class constructor

13. When does a for...in loop end?
    a. after you close the JavaScript program
    b. when you press Ctrl+Break
    c. when its conditional expression evaluates to false
    d. when the last property has been read

14. The _____ statement eliminates the need to retype the name of an object when properties of the same object are being referenced in a series.

    a. having
    b. include
    c. with
    d. contains

15. The _____ statement halts a looping statement, but instead of exiting the loop construct entirely, it restarts the loop with a new iteration.

    a. proceed
    b. reiterate
    c. restart
    d. continue

EXERCISES

Save all files you create in the Tutorial.04 folder on your Data Disk.

1. Write a `while` statement that prints all odd numbers between 1 and 100 to the screen. Save the HTML document as OddNumbers.html.

2. Rewrite the following `while` statement using a `for` loop. Save the HTML document as SimpleForLoop.html.

```
var count = 25;
while (count >= 0) {
    document.writeln("The current number is " + count);
    —count;
   }
```

3. The following code should print the numbers 1 through 100 to the screen. The code contains several logic flaws, however, that prevent it from running correctly. Identify and fix the logic flaws. Save the program as ForLogic.html.

```
var count = 0;
var numbers = new Array(100);
while (count > 100) {
  numbers[count] = count;
  ++count;
}
while (count > 100) {
  document.writeln(numbers[count]);
  ++count;
}
```

4. Rewrite the following `for` statement using a `while` loop. Save the HTML document as SimpleWhileLoop.html.

```
for(var i=1; i <= 15; ++i) {
    if (i == 10)
        break;
    else
        document.writeln("The current number is " + i);
}
```

5. Simplify the following program using `with` statements. Save the HTML document as SimpleWithProgram.html.

```
function Employee(name, number, position, department) {
    this.employee_name = name;
    this.employee_social_security = number;
    this.employee_position = position;
    this.employee_department = department;
}
new_entry_level_employee
    = new Employee();
new_entry_level_employee.employee_name
    = "John Doe";
new_entry_level_employee.employee_social_security
    = "000-12-3456";
new_entry_level_employee.employee_position
    = "Intern";
new_entry_level_employee.employee_department
    = "Accounting";
document.writeln(
    new_entry_level_employee.employee_name);
document.writeln(
    new_entry_level_employee.employee_social_security);
document.writeln(
    new_entry_level_employee.employee_position);
document.writeln(
    new_entry_level_employee.employee_department);
```

6. Change the program you created in Exercise 5 so that each of the Employee properties is printed with a `for...in` statement. Save the HTML document as SimpleForIn.html.

7. Create a questionnaire that prompts visitors to your Web site for personal information such as name, address, occupation, and so on. Assign each piece of information to an array, then use a `for` loop to print the information to the screen. Save the HTML document as Questionnaire.html.

8. In Tutorial 1, you created an HTML document that displayed six lines, with each line formatted using one of the six heading level tags, starting with the largest tag and ending with the smallest. Create a new version of the document that uses a `for` loop to print a line for each of the six heading level tags. Save the HTML document as HeadingTagsLoop.html.

9. Write a program that calculates a 15% return on an investment of $10,000. Calculate how many years it will take for a single $10,000 investment to reach $1,000,000 at an average annual return of 15%. Use a looping statement and assume that each iteration is equivalent to one year. Save the HTML document as Millionaire.html.

10. Use an appropriate looping statement to write a program that prints a list of the Celsius equivalents of zero degrees Fahrenheit through 100 degrees Fahrenheit. To convert Fahrenheit to Celsius, subtract 32 from the Fahrenheit temperature, and then multiply the remainder by .55. To convert Celsius to Fahrenheit, multiply the Celsius temperature by 1.8, and then add 32. Save the HTML document as TemperatureChart.html.

Windows and Frames

case ▶ WebAdventure is creating a Web site for a large popular zoo. The zoo hopes the Web site will help attract new visitors and help in its fundraising efforts. Part of the Web site will be a virtual zoo for children that includes pictures of animals, educational information, and games. You have been asked to create an HTML document that displays the picture of an animal when a user clicks a hyperlink of the animal's name. In simple Web pages, when users click a hyperlink, a new Web page replaces the original page. However, you do not want the animal's picture to completely replace the original virtual zoo page. Your solution is to create an HTML document using frames, which are independent, scrollable portions of a Web browser window, with each frame capable of containing its own unique HTML document or image file.

Previewing the VirtualZoo Program

In this tutorial you will create a "Virtual Zoo" Web page that displays a picture of an animal after a user clicks an animal's name. The list of animals is in one frame of the HTML document and each animal's picture appears in another frame.

To preview the Tutorial5_VirtualZoo.html program:

1 Open the **Tutorial5_VirtualZoo.html** file from the Tutorial.05 folder on your Data Disk in your Web browser. Figure 5-1 displays an example of the program in a Web browser.

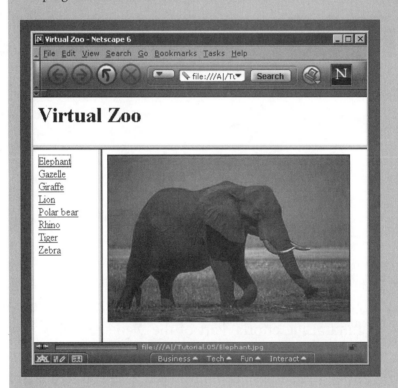

Figure 5-1: Tutorial5_VirtualZoo.html in a Web browser

2 Click the different animal names in the left frame to display each animal's picture in the right frame.

3 When you finish, close the Web browser window.

4 Next open the **Tutorial5_VirtualZoo.html** file in your text editor or HTML editor and examine the code. Notice the <FRAMESET> and <FRAME> tags. These tags create the three panels that compose the Tutorial5_VirtualZoo program. Each panel has a unique URL, as specified by the SRC attribute of each <FRAME> tag.

5 Close your text editor or HTML editor when you are finished examining the code.

Working with Windows

The JavaScript Object Model

There may be situations in which you want use JavaScript to control the Web browser. For example, you may want to change the Web page being displayed or write information to the Web browser's status bar. Or, you may want to control elements of the HTML document itself. To control the Web browser window or the HTML document, you use the browser object model. The **browser object model** is a hierarchy of objects, each of which provides programmatic access to a different aspect of an HTML page or the Web browser window. You can use methods and properties of objects in the browser object model to manipulate the window, frames, and HTML elements displayed in a Web browser. You do not have to explicitly create any of the objects or arrays in the browser object model; they are created automatically when a Web browser opens an HTML document. The most common objects in the browser object model are displayed in Figure 5-2.

The browser object model is also called the JavaScript object model or Navigator object model. However, other scripting technologies, such as VBScript, can also control aspects of an HTML page or Web browser window. Therefore, the terms browser object model or client-side object model are more accurate.

As you can see from Figure 5-2, the Window object is the top-level object in the browser object model. The **Window object** represents a Web browser window or an individual frame within a window. The Web browser automatically creates the Window object, and you use its properties and methods to control the Web browser window. For example, the focus() method of the Window object allows you to programmatically select which window to display as the topmost window.

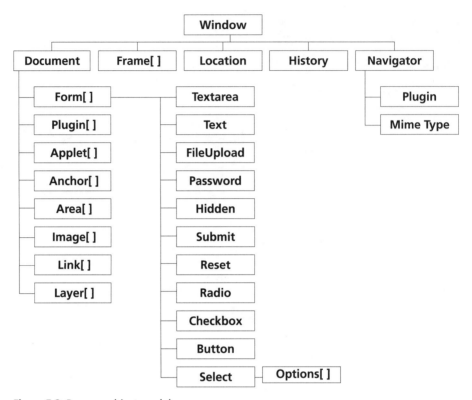

Figure 5-2: Browser object model

Another important object in the browser object model is the Document object that represents the HTML document displayed in a window. The Document object descends from a Window object. The write() and writeln() methods, with which you are familiar, refer to the Document object. The statement document.write("This is an example"); adds the text *This is an example* to an HTML document when it is rendered by a Web browser. All HTML elements exist within an HTML document represented by the Document object, and each element is represented in JavaScript by its own object. Therefore, the Document object is the parent or ancestor object for all the elements you create on an HTML page. The Form object, which is used by JavaScript to represent forms created with the <FORM>...</FORM> tag pair, descends from the Document object, which descends from the Window object. The Radio object, which is used by JavaScript to represent a radio button created with an <INPUT> tag, descends from the Form object, which descends from the Document object, which descends from the Window object.

You will learn more about the Document object in Tutorial 7.

In this text, objects in the browser object model are referred to with an uppercase letter (Document object). However, when you use the object name in code, you must always use a lowercase letter because you are actually referring to a property of the object. For example, in the statement `document.writeln("text string");`, the word *document* (with a lowercase d) represents the document property of the Document object.

Some of the JavaScript objects listed in Figure 5-2 represent arrays that contain other objects. In the figure, those objects that are arrays are followed by brackets, such as Form[] or Image[]. The contents of these array objects are created from the elements in an HTML document. For example, the Image object contains an images[] array that lists all the <IMG> tags in an HTML document.

To refer to a JavaScript object in code, you must refer to all of its ancestors as a series of properties separated by periods. Consider an <IMG> tag named myImage. To refer to the SRC property of the myImage object, you must include the myImage object's ancestor, the Document object. The syntax is `document.myImage.src`. Consider the following code that creates a simple form containing a single text field created with the <INPUT> tag:

```
<FORM NAME="myForm">
<INPUT TYPE="text" NAME="myTextBox">
</FORM>
```

To display the value of the text box in an alert dialog box, you must use the statement `alert(document.myForm.myTextBox.value);`. The myForm object (which is part of the Form object array) is appended to the document object as a property, while the myTextBox object (which is part of the Text object array) is appended to the myForm object as a property. Finally, the value property of the Text object returns the text contained in the text box.

When listing an object's ancestors, it is not necessary to include the Window object. The Web browser automatically assumes that you are always referring to the currently displayed window, which is the top-level object in the browser object model. You *could* list the Window object as part of an object's ancestors. For example, the statement `alert(window.document.myForm.myTextBox.value);` will work just as well as the statement `alert(document.myForm.myTextBox.value);`. However, since Web browsers automatically assume you are referring to the current window, listing the Window object is usually unnecessary.

It is also not necessary to include the Document object when listing an object's ancestors for Internet Explorer 4 and later and Netscape 6 and later. For example, you could eliminate the Document object in the preceding example, using the statement `alert(myForm.myTextBox.value);`, and the code would function correctly. However, it is considered good programming practice to always include the Document object when working with the browser object model in order to clearly identify that you are manipulating the current document. In addition, you *must* include the Document object for Netscape versions prior to version 6. Using a statement such as `alert(myForm.myTextBox.value);` with earlier versions of Netscape will generate errors, since it does not refer to all the text box's ancestor objects. Therefore, you should include the Document object in order to provide backward-compatibility with earlier versions of Netscape.

tip

In some cases, it is necessary to include the Window object when you need to clearly distinguish between the Window object and the Document object. For example, event-handling
code automatically assumes you are referring to the Document object instead of the Window
object. Therefore, in event-handling code you should include the Window object when you
are explicitly referring to the Web browser window.

Since a Web browser assumes you are referring to the current Window object, you also do not need to explicitly refer to the Window object when using one of its properties or methods. For example, the alert() dialog box is a method of the Window object. The full syntax for the alert() method is `window.alert(text);`, although, as you have seen throughout this text, the syntax alert(*text*); (without the Window object) works equally well. If you were required to include the Window object, your code could become quite lengthy. For example, if you needed to use the Window object to refer to the value of the myTextBox element on myForm, you would need to write:

```
window.alert(window.document.myForm.myTextBox.value);
```

Removing the references to the Window object shortens the statement some-what, as in the following example:

```
alert(document.myForm.myTextBox.value);
```

Another way of referring to the Window object is by using the self property. The **self property** refers to the current Window object. Using the self property is identical to using the window property to refer to the Window object. For example, the following lines are identical:

```
window.alert("text string");
self.alert("text string");
```

Some JavaScript programmers prefer to use the window property, while other JavaScript programmers prefer to use the self property. Whichever property you choose is up to you. However, if you attempt to decipher JavaScript code created by other programmers, it is important to be aware that both of these properties refer to the current Window object.

The Window Object

The Window object includes several properties that contain information about the Web browser window. For instance, the status property contains information displayed in a Web browser's status bar. Also contained in the Window object are various methods that allow you to manipulate the Web browser window itself. Methods of the Window object you have already used include the alert(), confirm(), and prompt() methods used for displaying dialog boxes. Figure 5-3 lists common Window object properties, and Figure 5-4 lists common Window object methods.

Property	Description
defaultStatus	Default text that is written to the status bar
document	A reference to the Document object
frames[]	An array listing the frame objects in a window
history	A reference to the History object
location	A reference to the Location object
navigator	A reference to the Navigator object
opener	The Window object that opens another window
parent	The parent frame that contains the current frame
self	A self-reference to the Window object; identical to the window property
status	Temporary text that is written to the status bar
top	The topmost Window object that contains the current frame
window	A self-reference to the Window object; identical to the self property
name	The name of a window

Figure 5-3: Window object properties

Method	Description
alert()	Displays a simple message dialog box with an OK button
blur()	Removes focus from a window
clearInterval()	Cancels an interval that was set with setInterval()
clearTimeout()	Cancels a timeout that was set with setTimeout()
close()	Closes a window
confirm()	Displays a confirmation dialog box with OK and Cancel buttons
focus()	Makes a Window object the active window
open()	Opens a new window
prompt()	Displays a dialog box prompting a user to enter information
setInterval()	Repeatedly executes a function after a specified number of milliseconds have elapsed
setTimeout()	Executes a function once after a specified number of milliseconds have elapsed

Figure 5-4: Window object methods

Opening and Closing Windows

Netscape and Internet Explorer both allow you to open new Web browser windows in addition to the Web browser window or windows that may already be open. There are several reasons why you may need to open a new Web browser window. You may want to launch a new Web page in a separate window, allowing users to continue viewing the current page in the current window. Or, you may want to use an additional window to display information such as a picture or an order form.

Whenever a new Web browser window is opened, a new Window object is created to represent the new window. You can have as many Web browser windows open as your system will support, each displaying a different Web page. For example, you can have one Web browser window display Microsoft's Web site, another Web browser window display Netscape's Web site, and so on. You can manually open a new Web browser window in Netscape by selecting New Window from the File menu. In Internet Explorer, you select Window from the New submenu on the File menu. When you manually open a new Web browser window in Netscape, the new window displays the default home page. However, when you manually open a new Web browser window in Internet Explorer, the new window opens the same URL or file that appears in the first Web browser window. If Internet Explorer is opened to the Course Technology Web site (*www.course.com*) and you open a new window, the new window also displays the Course Technology Web site.

With JavaScript you can open a new Web browser window using the open() method of the Window object. The syntax for the open() method is `window.open("URL", "name", options);`. The *URL* argument represents the Web address or filename to be opened. The *name* argument is used to assign a value to the name property of the new Window object. Note that quotation marks enclose both the URL and name arguments. The *options* argument represents a string that allows you to customize the new Web browser window's appearance. You can include all or none of the open() method arguments. The statement `window.open("http://www.course.com");` opens the Course Technology Web site in a new Web browser window, as shown in Figure 5-5. If you exclude the URL argument, then a blank Web page opens. For example, the statement `window.open();` opens the Web browser window displayed in Figure 5-6.

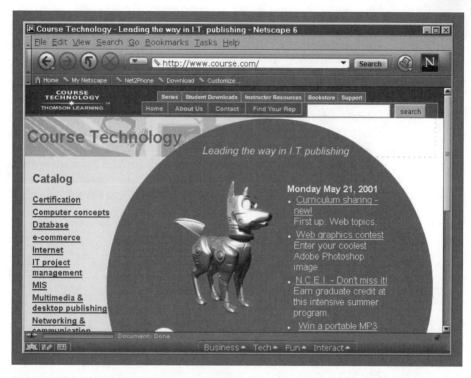

Figure 5-5: Web browser window opened with a URL argument of the open() method

Figure 5-6: Web browser window opened with the `window.open();` statement

••
When you open a blank window in Internet Explorer, the window title bar and Address box
will read about:blank.
••

You can use the name property of a Window object to specify a window as the target in which a hypertext link's URL opens or the results of a form submission appear. The program in Figure 5-7 creates a new, empty Web browser window named *targetWindow*. The original window includes a hypertext link that opens the Course Technology home page in the new targetWindow Web browser window. Notice that the URL for the open() method is a blank string (""), since we want to open the new Web browser window to a blank page. After the open() method executes, the statement self.focus returns focus to the original Web browser window.

```
<HTML>

<HEAD>

<SCRIPT LANGUAGE="JavaScript">

<!-- HIDE FROM INCOMPATIBLE BROWSERS

window.open("", "targetWindow");

self.focus();

// STOP HIDING FROM INCOMPATIBLE BROWSERS -->

</SCRIPT>

</HEAD>

<BODY>

<A HREF="http://www.course.com" TARGET="targetWindow">

Visit the Course Technology home page.</A>

</BODY>

</HTML>
```

Figure 5-7: A JavaScript program that includes a name argument

••
If the name argument of the open() method is already in use by another Web browser window, then JavaScript changes focus to the existing Web browser window instead of creating
a new window.
••

When you open a new Web browser window, you can customize its appearance using the options argument of the open() method. Figure 5-8 lists some common options that you can use with the open() method.

All the options listed in Figure 5-8, with the exception of the width and height options, are set using values of *yes* or *no*, or *1* for yes and *0* for no. To include the status bar, the options string should read "status=yes". You set the width and height options using integers representing pixels. For example, to create a new window that is 200 pixels high by 300 pixels wide, the string should read "height=200,width=300". When including multiple items in the options string, you must separate the items by commas.

Name	Description
directories	Includes directory buttons
height	Sets the window's height
location	Includes the URL Location text box
menubar	Includes the menu bar
resizable	Determines if the new window can be resized
scrollbars	Includes scroll bars
status	Includes the status bar
toolbar	Includes the Standard toolbar
width	Sets the window's width

Figure 5-8: Common open() method options

If you exclude the options string of the open() method, then all the standard options will be included in the new Web browser window. However, if you include the options string, you must include all the components you want to create for the new window; that is, the new window is created with only the components you explicitly specify. The following open() method creates the Web browser window displayed in Figure 5-9. The new Web browser window contains no interface elements, since the only items included in the options string were height and width properties. Interface elements include the menu bar, toolbars, scroll bars, and other items with which users interact.

```
window.open("http://www.course.com", "Course",
    "height=300,width=600 ");
```

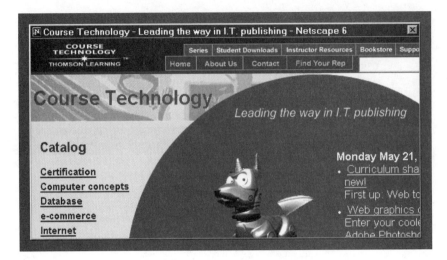

Figure 5-9: Web browser window with no interface elements

In comparison, the options string in the following open() method includes the toolbar and scroll bars. Figure 5-10 displays the window that is generated.

```
window.open("http://www.course.com", "Course",
    "height=300,width=600,toolbar=yes,scrollbars=yes");
```

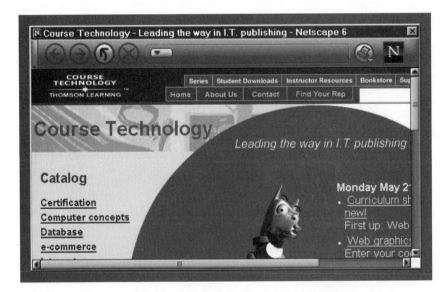

Figure 5-10: Web browser window with toolbar and scroll bars

If you include spaces in the options string of an open() method, the options may not display properly in Netscape. For an open() method to work properly with both Netscape and Internet Explorer, do not include any spaces in an options string.

A Window object's name property can be used only to specify a target window with hypertext links or forms, and cannot be used in JavaScript code. If you want to control the new window using JavaScript code located within the Web browser in which it was *created*, then you must assign the new Window object created with the open() method to a variable. The statement `var newWindow = window.open("http://www.course.com");` assigns an object representing the new Web browser window to a variable named newWindow. You can then use any of the properties and methods of the Window object with the newWindow variable. For example, if you want to set the focus to the newWindow variable using the focus method of the Window object, use the statement `newWindow.focus();`. The close() method is the Window object method you will probably use the most with variables representing other Window objects. For example, to close the Web browser window represented by the newWindow variable, use the statement `newWindow.close();`.

It is not necessary to include the Window object when listing an object's ancestors. However, the Document object also contains methods named open() and close(), which are used for opening and closing HTML documents. Therefore, the Window object is usually included with the open() and close() methods, in order to distinguish between the Window object and the Document object.

Next you will create a program that displays an HTML document containing a picture of a polar bear in a new, separate window. First you will create a source document from which you will be able to open a new window.

To create the source document:

1 Start your text editor or HTML editor and create a new document.

2 Type the opening <HTML>, <HEAD>, and <SCRIPT> sections of the document:

```
<HTML>
<HEAD>
<TITLE>See the Polar Bear</TITLE>
<SCRIPT LANGUAGE="JavaScript">
<!-- HIDE FROM INCOMPATIBLE BROWSERS
```

3 Create the following function that opens the PolarBear.html file. The new window containing the PolarBear.html file is created without any interface elements so that it appears as a simple "image window." Only the height and width items are included in the options string in the window.open() method.

```
function openPolarBear() {
window.open("PolarBear.html", "PolarBear",
       "height=350,width=320");
}
```

4 Add the following code to close the <HEAD> and <SCRIPT> sections:

```
// STOP HIDING FROM INCOMPATIBLE BROWSERS -->
</SCRIPT>
</HEAD>
```

5 Add **<BODY>** to begin the body of the HTML document and press **Enter**.

6 Type **<H1>See the Polar Bear</H1>** to create a heading 1 tag for the HTML document and press **Enter**.

7 Next add the following lines to create a hyperlink to the PolarBear.html document. The link to the PolarBear.html file is formatted with the <H2> tag. Note that instead of allowing the hyperlink to open the PolarBear.html document in the current window, an onClick event calls the openPolarBear() function, which uses the window.open() method to open the document in a new window. The onClick event then returns a value of false. If the onClick() event did not return a value of false, the PolarBear.html document would open in the current window as well as the new window.

```
<H2><A HREF="PolarBear.html"
onClick="openPolarBear(); return false;">
Click here to see the polar bear.</A></H2>
```

8 Add the following lines to close the <BODY> and <HTML> tags:

```
</BODY>
</HTML>
```

9 Save the file as **PolarBearMain.html** in the **Tutorial.05** folder on your Data Disk.

Next you will create the PolarBear.html document.

To create the PolarBear.html document:

1 Create a new document in your text editor or HTML editor.

2 Type the <HTML> and <HEAD> sections of the document:

```
<HTML>
<HEAD>
<TITLE>Polar Bear</TITLE>
</HEAD>
```

3 Add **<BODY>** to begin the body of the HTML document and press **Enter**.

4 Add the following heading tag and press **Enter**.

```
<H1>This is a Polar Bear</H1>
```

5 Add an <IMG> tag that displays an image named PolarBear.jpg. A copy of the PolarBear.jpg file is located in the Tutorial.05 folder on your Data Disk.

```
<IMG SRC="PolarBear.jpg">
```

6 Next add the following <FORM> and <INPUT> tags to create a button. When you click the button, the self.close() method is called to close the PolarBear.html document. Note that you can also use window.close() to perform the same task.

```
<FORM>
<INPUT TYPE=button NAME="quit"
VALUE=" Click here to close this window "
onClick="self.close();">
</FORM>
```

7 Add the following lines to close the <BODY> and <HTML> tags:

```
</BODY>
</HTML>
```

8 Save the file as **PolarBear.html** in the **Tutorial.05** folder on your Data Disk.

9 Open the **PolarBearMain.html** file in your Web browser, then click the **Click here to see the polar bear link**. Your screen should appear similar to Figure 5-11.

10 Close the **PolarBear.html** file by clicking the **Click here to close this window** button, then close the Web browser window containing the PolarBearMain.html file.

▶ **tip**

> Some monitor settings may cause the *Click here to close this window* button in the window containing PolarBear.html to be cut off. If you do not see the *Click here to close this window* button, try changing the height and width parameters of the window.open() method in PolarBearMain.html.

Figure 5-11: PolarBearMain.html and PolarBear.html windows

Working with Timeouts and Intervals

As you develop Web pages, you may need to have some JavaScript code execute repeatedly, without user intervention. Alternately, you may want to create animation or some other type of repetitive task that needs to execute automatically. You use the timeout and interval methods of the Window object to create code that performs functions that execute automatically. The **setTimeout() method** of the Window object is used in JavaScript to execute code after a specific amount of time has elapsed. Code executed with the setTimeout() method executes only once. The syntax for the setTimeout() method is var *variable* = setTimeout("*code*", *milliseconds*);. This variable declaration assigns a reference to the setTimeout() method to a variable. The code argument must be enclosed in double or single quotation marks and can be a single JavaScript statement, a series of JavaScript statements, or a function call. The amount of time the Web browser should wait before executing the code argument of the setTimeout() method is expressed in milliseconds. A millisecond is one thousandth of a second; there are 1000 milliseconds in a second. For example, five seconds is equal to 5000 milliseconds. The **clearTimeout() method** of the Window object is used to cancel a setTimeout() method before its code executes. The clearTimeout() method receives a single argument, which is the variable that represents a setTimeout() method call.

Figure 5-12 shows a program that contains a setTimeout() method call and a clearTimeout() method call. The setTimeout() method is contained in the <HEAD> section of the HTML document and is set to execute after 10000 milliseconds (10 seconds) have elapsed. If a user clicks the OK button, a buttonPressed() function calls the clearTimeout() method.

```
<HTML>

<HEAD>

<TITLE>Timeouts</TITLE>

<SCRIPT LANGUAGE="JavaScript">

<!-- HIDE FROM INCOMPATIBLE BROWSERS

var buttonNotPressed = setTimeout(
    "alert('You must press the OK button to continue!')",
    10000);

function buttonPressed() {

    clearTimeout(buttonNotPressed);

    alert("The setTimeout() method was canceled!");

}

// STOP HIDING FROM INCOMPATIBLE BROWSERS -->

</SCRIPT>

</HEAD>

<BODY>

<FORM>

<INPUT TYPE=button NAME="OK" VALUE=" OK "
    onClick="buttonPressed();">

</FORM>

</BODY>

</HTML>
```

Figure 5-12: Program using setTimeout() and clearTimeout() methods

Two other methods of the Window object are the setInterval() method and the clearInterval() method. The **setInterval() method** is similar to the setTimeout() method, except that it repeatedly executes the same code after being called only once. The **clearInterval()** method is used to clear a setInterval() method call in the same fashion that the clearTimeout() method clears a setTimeout() method. The setInterval() and clearInterval() methods are most often used for starting animation code that executes repeatedly. The syntax for the setInterval() method is the same as the syntax for the setTimeout() method: `var variable = setInterval("code", milliseconds);`. As with the clearTimeout() method, the clearInterval() method receives a single argument, which is the variable that represents a setInterval() method call. You will use the setInterval() method and the clearInterval() method extensively when creating animation in Tutorial 7.

Next you will add a setTimeout() method to the PolarBearMain.html file. The setTimeout() method automatically calls the confirmPolarBear() method if a user does not click the polar bear link within 10 seconds.

To add a setTimeout() method to the PolarBearMain.html file:

1   Return to the **PolarBearMain.html** file in your text editor or HTML editor.

2   Declare a global variable that reads **var polarBearOpened;** before the openPolarBear() function. A setTimeout() method will be assigned to the polarBearOpened variable. As you learned in Tutorial 2, global variables are available to all parts of a JavaScript program, not just to an individual function, as are local variables.

3   Add the following confirmPolarBear() function after the openPolarBear() function. The confirmPolarBear() function will be called when the timeout expires. The confirm() statement prompts the user to open the PolarBear.html file.

```
function confirmPolarBear() {
    var confirmation =
        confirm("Do you want to see the polar bear?");
    if (confirmation == true)
    window.open('PolarBear.html', 'PolarBear',
    'height=350,width=320');
}
```

4   Position the insertion point just before the closing bracket of the <BODY> tag, add a space, and add a timeout statement that reads **onLoad="polarBear Opened= setTimeout('confirmPolarBear()', 10000);".** If the timeout is not cleared within 10 seconds, the statement calls the confirmPolarBear message.

5   Finally, to cancel the timeout if the user clicks the polar bear link, add the statement **clearTimeout(polarBearOpened);** just before the window.open() statement in the openPolarBear() function.

6   Save the file, then open it in your Web browser. Wait 10 seconds and see if the confirm dialog box appears, prompting you to open the PolarBear.html file. When you see the confirm dialog box, click **OK** to make sure the code works properly.

7   Close both Web browser windows, and close your text editor or HTML editor.

S U M M A R Y

- The Window object represents a Web browser window or an individual frame within a window.

- The hierarchy of JavaScript objects is called the browser object model. It is important to understand the hierarchy of the browser object model because an object's descendants are properties of the object.

- You can use methods and properties of objects in the browser object model to manipulate the window, frames, and HTML elements displayed in a Web browser.

- An important object in the browser object model is the Document object, which represents the HTML document displayed in a window.

- Although objects in the browser object model are referred to in this book with an uppercase letter (Document object), you must always use a lowercase letter when using the object name in code, since you are actually referring to a property of the object.

- It is usually not necessary to include the Window object when listing an object's ancestors in a statement, because the Web browser automatically assumes that you are always referring to the currently displayed window, which is the top-level object in the browser object model. In some cases, it is necessary to include the Window object when you need to clearly distinguish between the Window object and the Document object.

- You can use the open() method of the Window object to open a new Web browser window.

- You can use the name property of a Window object to specify a target window in which a hypertext link's URL opens or the results of a form submission appear.

- In the open() method, the URL argument represents the Web address or filename to be opened. The name argument assigns a value to the name property of the new Window object. The options argument represents a string that controls how the new Web browser window will appear.

- If you exclude the options string of the open() method, then all the normal options will be created in the new Web browser window. If you include the options string, then you must include all the components you want to be created with the new window—the new window is created with only the components you explicitly specify.

- A Window object's name property can be used only to specify a target window with hypertext links or forms, and cannot be used in JavaScript code. If you want to use JavaScript code to control the new window located within the Web browser where it was created, then you must assign the new Window object that was created with the open() method to a variable.

- The Window object is usually included with the open() and close() methods to clearly distinguish between the Window object and the Document object.

- The setTimeout() method of the Window object is used in JavaScript to execute code after a specific amount of time has elapsed.

- The clearTimeout() method of the Window object is used to cancel a setTimeout() method call before its code executes.

- The setInterval() method of the Window object repeatedly executes the same code after being called only once.

- The clearInterval() method of the Window object is used to cancel a setInterval() method call.

QUESTIONS

1. The Window object represents a(n) _____.
   a. <SCRIPT>...</SCRIPT> tag pair
   b. HTML document
   c. Web browser window
   d. <HEAD>...</HEAD> tag pair

2. Which of the following terms does *not* refer to the browser object model?
   a. JavaScript object model
   b. client-side object model
   c. Navigator object model
   d. Internet Explorer object model

3. The Document object represents _____.
   a. the objects in a form
   b. the HTML document displayed in a window
   c. all JavaScript functions and methods within an HTML document
   d. the Web browser window

4. Which is the proper syntax for referring to the Document object in JavaScript code?
   a. `document.writeln("text string");`
   b. `Document.writeln("text string");`
   c. `DOCUMENT.writeln("text string");`
   d. `doc.writeln("text string");`

5. What is the correct syntax for referring to the value of a text box named inputField located on a form named application?
   a. `inputField.value`
   b. `application.inputField.value`
   c. `document.application.inputField.value`
   d. `application.value.inputField`

6. The self property refers to _____.
   a. a control that has the focus
   b. the currently executing function
   c. the current Document object
   d. the current Window object

7. Which of the following is *not* a correct way to code the alert() method?
   a. `alert("Hello World");`
   b. `window.alert("Hello World");`
   c. `self.alert("Hello World");`
   d. `document.alert("Hello World");`

8. Which method makes a Window object active?

    a. display()

    b. focus()

    c. select()

    d. self()

9. What happens when you include an empty string as the first argument in the window.open() method?

    a. An empty window opens.

    b. You receive an error message.

    c. A duplicate copy of the current window opens.

    d. Nothing. The JavaScript interpreter ignores the statement.

10. Which of the following arguments are used for including both horizontal and vertical scroll bars in a new Web browser window created with the window.open() method?

    a. `verticalscroll=1,horizontalscroll=1`

    b. `showScrollbars=on`

    c. `scrollbars=true`

    d. `scrollbars=yes`

11. How do you control a new window that you created with JavaScript code?

    a. By assigning the new Window object created with the open() method to a variable

    b. By using the NAME argument of the open() method

    c. By using the appropriate element in the windows[] array of the Windows object

    d. You cannot control a new window with JavaScript code.

12. If you exclude the options string in the window.open() method, _____.

    a. the new Web browser window will be created with just a menu bar and a toolbar

    b. a blank Web browser window opens without any user interface items

    c. all the normal options will be included in the new Web browser window

    d. you will receive an error message

13. Which method of the Window object do you use when you want to repeatedly execute the same code?

    a. setTimeout()

    b. clearTimeout()

    c. setInterval()

    d. clearInterval()

14. The amount of time in the setTimeout() method is expressed in _____.

    a. milliseconds

    b. seconds

    c. minutes

    d. 10-second intervals

15. A setTimeout() method is canceled using the _____ method.

    a. cancelTimeout()

    b. clearTimeout()

    c. endTimeout()

    d. You cannot cancel the setTimeout() method.

16. How many times does code executed with a setInterval() method automatically repeat?

a. once

b. twice

c. continually

d. never

17. A setInterval() method is canceled using the _____ method.

a. cancelInterval()

b. clearInterval()

c. endInterval()

d. You cannot cancel the setInterval() method.

 # E X E R C I S E S

Save all files you create in the Tutorial.05 folder on your Data Disk.

1. Add a command button to the following code that uses an onClick event handler to display the value entered in the salary field in an alert dialog box. Save the file as Exercise1A.html.

```
<FORM NAME="jobInfo">
<INPUT TYPE="text" NAME="" "salary">
</FORM>
```

2. Modify the preceding code so that the salary field value appears in a new window instead of in an alert dialog box. Save the file as Exercise2A.html.

a. Modify the event handler in the command button so it calls a function named showSalary (), instead of executing an alert dialog box.

b. In the showSalary () function, open a new window and assign the Window object to a variable named salaryWindow. Also, write the value of the salary field to the new window using a document.write() statement. (*Hint*: you will need to use the new Window object variable.)

c. Add a second command button to the parent window that closes the new window when you are through viewing its contents.

3. Most Windows applications include an About dialog box that displays copyright and other information about the application. In this exercise, you will create an HTML document with a command button that opens a new window that is similar to an About dialog box. You will use the onClick event in the new window's <BODY> tag so that the user can close the window by clicking anywhere in the document area.

a. Create an HTML document that contains a command button that opens a document named About.html in a new browser window. Make the new window 100 pixels high by 300 pixels wide, and do not use any other display options. Use *About this JavaScript Program* for the command button label. Save the file as AboutExercise.html.

b. Create an HTML document that includes an onClick event in the <BODY> tag that closes the current browser window. Add text to the document that reads *This program was created by <your name>. Click anywhere to close this window.* Save the file as About.html.

4. Create a program that calculates an employee's weekly gross salary, tax withholding (which is 15% of gross pay), and net pay, based on the number of hours worked and hourly wage. Compute any hours over 40 as time-and-a-half. Use the appropriate decision structures to create the program. Display the weekly gross pay, tax withholding, and net pay in text boxes, not in alert boxes. Save the file as GrossPay.html.

5. Create an HTML document that contains a list of hyperlinks to your favorite recipes. Clicking each hyperlink opens a document in a separate window to display the selected recipe. Include a close button within each recipe's window. Name the main HTML document Recipes.html, and name each recipe document according to the recipe name. For example, if you have a recipe for apple pie, name its associated HTML document ApplePie.html.

6. Create an HTML document that repeatedly turns a defaultStatus message on and off in the status bar, similar to a blinking neon sign. You will need to use a decision structure such as an `if...then` statement to create the document. Save the document as FlashGreeting.html.

7. Create an html document that allows users to play a guessing game. Think of a number and assign it to a variable. Use the <INPUT> tag in a form to create a text box that a user can use to guess the number. Use another <INPUT> tag to create a button named Guess. Write a timeout that asks users if they want to stop the game if they do not press the Guess button within 10 seconds. If the user selects OK, close the Web browser window. If the user decides to continue (by pressing the Cancel button), then restart the game and the timeout. Save the file as GuessNumber.html.

Working with Frames and Other Objects

Creating Frames

The HTML documents you have created so far have consisted of a single Window object that can hold only one URL at a time. Using frames, you can split a single Web browser window into multiple windows, each of which can open a different URL. **Frames** are independent, scrollable portions of a Web browser window, with each frame capable of containing its own URL. JavaScript treats each frame in an HTML document as an individual window. Each frame has its own Window object, separate from other frames in the document. In addition, each frame is part of a top-level HTML document that defines the frames in a window. The top-level HTML document contains a Window object from which each frame's Window object is descended. Although frames are HTML elements and are not actually created using JavaScript, JavaScript is frequently used to programmatically access and control individual frames.

An HTML document is divided into frames using the **<FRAMESET>...</FRAMESET>** tag pair. <FRAME> tags and other <FRAMESET>...</FRAMESET> tag pairs are the only items that can be placed inside a <FRAMESET>...</FRAMESET> tag pair. The Web browser ignores any other text or tags. The <FRAMESET>...</FRAMESET> tag pair replaces the <BODY>...</BODY> tag pair that is used in nonframe HTML documents. Be sure not to place <BODY> tags at the beginning of an HTML document containing <FRAMESET> tags. If you do, the <FRAMESET> tag is ignored and only the information contained within the <BODY> tags appears.

Frames in an HTML document can be created in horizontal rows, vertical columns, or both. Two attributes of the <FRAMESET> tag, ROWS and COLS, determine whether frames are created as rows or columns. The **ROWS attribute** determines the number of horizontal frames to create. The **COLS attribute** determines the number of vertical frames to create. To set the dimensions of the frame, you assign a string to the ROWS or COLS attribute containing the percentage of space or number of pixels each row or column should take up on the screen, separated by commas. For example,

<FRAMESET ROWS="50%, 50%" COLS="50%, 50%"> creates two rows, which each take up 50 percent of the height of the screen, and two columns, which each take up 50 percent of the width of the screen. Figure 5-13 shows an example of the frames created using <FRAMESET ROWS="50%, 50%" COLS="50%, 50%">.

Figure 5-13: Frames created with <FRAMESET ROWS="50%, 50%" COLS="50%, 50%">

 tip

You must define more than one row or more than one column or your frames will be completely ignored by the Web browser.

You can create frames using just rows or just columns. For example, Figure 5-14 shows the frames created with <FRAMESET ROWS="50%, 50%">, and Figure 5-15 shows the frames created with <FRAMESET COLS="50%, 50%">.

Figure 5-14: Frames created with <FRAMESET ROWS="50%, 50%">

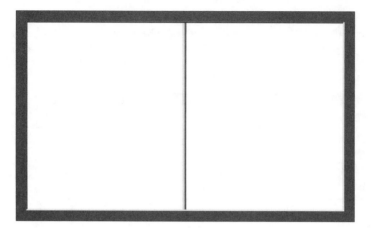

Figure 5-15: Frames created with <FRAMESET COLS="50%, 50%">

When you use percentages to specify the dimensions of a frame, the percentages are relative to the size of the window; that is, percentages adjust for the size of the window. In contrast, pixels represent exact or absolute sizes. They do not adjust for the size of the window. Users can set different default dimensions for their Web browser windows or resize their Web browser windows. Relative percentages can take these variations into account, whereas exact pixels cannot. For example, if you create two frames, each 100 pixels wide, they will not adjust for the actual dimensions of users' Web browser windows. If a user's screen is too small, your frames may be cut off. If a user's screen is a larger size, your frames might look strangely small. These size problems do not occur when you use percentages, because with percentages the dimensions of the frame are calculated on the basis of the visible window.

It is helpful to use an asterisk (*) to represent the size of frames in your document that do not require an exact number of pixels or exact window percentage. The asterisk allocates any remaining screen space to an individual frame. If more than one frame is sized using an asterisk, then the remaining screen space is divided evenly. For example, <FRAMESET COLS="100, *"> creates two frames in a column, using pixels to represent one column and an asterisk to represent the other column. The left column will always remain 100 pixels wide, but the right column will resize according to the visible screen space.

You can use combinations of pixels, percentages, and the asterisk to create frames. For example, the tag <FRAMESET ROWS="100, 50%, *" creates three rows: the first row is 100 pixels high, the second row takes up 50% of the visible window, and the asterisk allocates the remainder of the visible window to the third row.

The <FRAMESET> tag creates the initial frames within an HTML document. The **<FRAME> tag** is used to specify options for individual frames, including a frame's URL. The SRC attribute of the <FRAME> tag specifies the URL to be opened in an individual frame. Frame tags are placed within the <FRAMESET>...</FRAMESET> tag pair. Frames can be assigned a name using the NAME attribute; this name can then be used as a target for a hyperlink. You need a separate frame tag for each frame in your window.

The URLs of frames are opened in the order in which each <FRAME> tag is encountered, on a left-to-right, top-to-bottom basis. For example, the following code creates four frames, in two columns and two rows. Figure 5-16 shows the order in which the URL specified by a <FRAME> tag loads into each frame. The text displayed in each frame is contained within each file specified by the SRC attribute of each frame.

```
<HTML>
<TITLE>
<HEAD>Frames Example</HEAD>
</TITLE>
<FRAMESET ROWS="50%, 50%" COLS="50%, 50%">
     <FRAME SRC="FirstURL.html">
     <FRAME SRC="SecondURL.html">
     <FRAME SRC="ThirdURL.html">
     <FRAME SRC="FourthURL.html">
</FRAMESET>
</HTML>
```

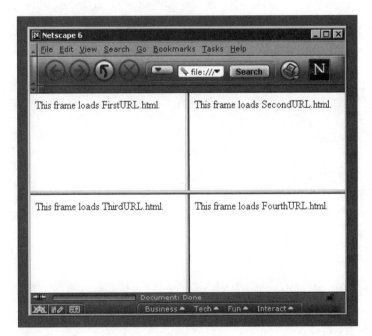

Figure 5-16: URL load order

Next you will start creating the Virtual Zoo program that you saw in the tutorial preview. First you will create the main HTML document containing the program's <FRAMESET> and <FRAME> tags. This program creates a narrow column, the left frame that contains the list of animal names. The right frame, which displays an animal's picture, is a larger column that takes up the remainder of the screen width.

To create the main HTML document for the Virtual Zoo program:

1   Start your text editor or HTML editor and create a new document.

2   Type the <HTML> and <HEAD> sections of the document:

```
<HTML>
<HEAD>
<TITLE>Virtual Zoo</TITLE>
</HEAD>
```

3   On the next line, add **<FRAMESET COLS="20%, *">** to start the frame set. The 20% in the code creates the narrow column on the left; the asterisk creates the wide column on the right.

4   Add the following two <FRAME> tags. The first <FRAME> tag opens an HTML file named list.html, which contains a list of animal names. The second frame opens an HTML file named welcome.html, which contains an opening message to display in the right frame. The window containing list.html is named *list*, and the window containing welcome.html is named *display*.

```
<FRAME SRC="list.html" NAME="list">
<FRAME SRC="welcome.html" NAME="display">
```

5   Type the following lines to close the <FRAMESET> and <HTML> tags:

```
</FRAMESET>
</HTML>
```

6   Save the file as **VirtualZoo.html** in the **Tutorial.05** folder on your Data Disk. Before you can open the VirtualZoo.html file, you need to create the welcome.html and list.html files.

Next you will create the welcome.html file. You will create the list.html file later.

To create the welcome.html file:

1   Create a new document in your text editor or HTML editor.

2   Type the opening <HTML> and <BODY> tags:

```
<HTML>
<BODY>
```

3   Add the following line to instruct the user to click an animal name in the list, and press **Enter**:

```
<P>Click an animal in the list to display its picture.</P>
```

4 Type the closing <HTML> and <BODY> tags:

```
</BODY>
</HTML>
```

5 Save the file as **welcome.html** in the **Tutorial.05** folder on your Data Disk.

Using the TARGET Attribute

One popular use of frames creates a table of contents frame on the left side of a Web browser window with a display frame on the right side of the window to show the contents of a URL selected from a link in the table of contents frame. This type of design eliminates the need to open a separate Web browser window when you want to display the contents of another URL, as you did with the PolarBear.html file in Section A. Figure 5-17 shows an HTML document that is split into two frames. Each frame displays a different HTML document associated with a different URL. The left frame contains an HTML document that lists musical instruments, and the right frame contains an HTML document instructing the user to select an instrument. When you click the name of a musical instrument, a new document containing its picture and description opens in the right frame, as shown in Figure 5-18.

Figure 5-17: Musical Instruments document

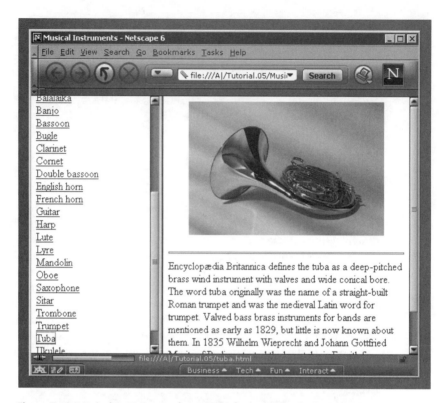

Figure 5-18: Musical Instruments document after selecting an instrument

The following code shows the <FRAMESET> and <FRAME> tags used to create the Musical Instruments document.

```
<FRAMESET COLS="200,*">

    <FRAME SRC="InstrumentsList.html" NAME="list">

    <FRAME SRC="Welcome.html" NAME="display">

</FRAMESET>

</HTML>
```

The Musical Instruments document creates two column frames. The first column is 200 pixels wide, and the second column takes up the remainder of the window. Two <FRAME> tags open HTML documents in each frame. The left frame of the Musical Instruments document contains hyperlinks for each instrument name. To cause the HTML document for each hyperlink to open in the right frame, you use the TARGET attribute of the <A> tag. The **TARGET attribute** determines in which frame or Web browser window a URL opens. For example, the name assigned to the right frame in the Musical Instruments document is *display*.

When you click the tuba hyperlink in the left frame (named *list*), the tuba.html file opens in the display frame. The syntax for the <A> tag to open the tuba.html file in the display frame is `<A HREF="tuba.html" TARGET="display">`. The following code uses the TARGET attribute repeatedly:

```
<A HREF="altooboe.html" TARGET="display">alto oboe</A><BR>
<A HREF="balalaika.html" TARGET="display">balalaika</A><BR>
<A HREF="banjo.html" TARGET="display">banjo</A><BR>
<A HREF="bassoon.html" TARGET="display">bassoon</A><BR>
<A HREF="bugle.html" TARGET="display">bugle</A><BR>
...additional instruments
```

When you are using the same target window or frame for a long list of hyperlinks, it is easier to use the <BASE> tag instead of repeating the TARGET attribute within each hyperlink. The **<BASE> tag** is used to specify a default target for all links in an HTML document, using the assigned name of a window or frame. Note that the <BASE> tag must be placed within the document head, not within its <BODY> section. The following code shows how you can write the preceding statements more efficiently using the <BASE> tag:

```
<HTML>
<HEAD>
<TITLE>Base Tag Example</TITLE>
<BASE TARGET="display">
</HEAD>
<BODY>
<A HREF="altooboe.html">alto oboe</A><BR>
<A HREF="balalaika.html">balalaika</A><BR>
<A HREF="banjo.html">banjo</A><BR>
<A HREF="bassoon.html">bassoon</A><BR>
<A HREF="bugle.html">bugle</A><BR>
...additional instruments
```

Next you will create the list.html file, which contains a list of the animals in the Virtual Zoo program.

To create the list.html file:

1 Create a new document in your text editor or HTML editor.

2 Type the opening <HTML> and <HEAD> sections:

```
<HTML>
<HEAD>
<TITLE>Animal List</TITLE>
```

3 Since each animal's picture will always open in the right frame, add **<BASE TARGET="display">** to specify the right frame (named *display*) as the default target.

4 Press **Enter**, then add the closing <HEAD> tag, the opening <BODY> tag, and the list of links for each animal. Note that instead of opening an HTML file in the display window, you are opening each .jpg graphic file. (The .jpg files for the animals are located in the Tutorial.05 folder on your Data Disk.)

```
</HEAD>
<BODY>
<A HREF="Elephant.jpg">Elephant</A><BR>
<A HREF="Gazelle.jpg">Gazelle</A><BR>
<A HREF="Giraffe.jpg">Giraffe</A><BR>
<A HREF="Lion.jpg">Lion</A><BR>
<A HREF="PolarBear.jpg">Polar bear</A><BR>
<A HREF="Rhino.jpg">Rhino</A><BR>
<A HREF="Tiger.jpg">Tiger</A><BR>
<A HREF="Zebra.jpg">Zebra</A><BR>
```

5   Type the closing <HTML> and <BODY> tags:

```
</BODY>
</HTML>
```

6   Save the file as **list.html** in the **Tutorial.05** folder on your Data Disk.

7   Now that you have created the list.html file and the welcome.html file, you can open the **VirtualZoo.html** file in your Web browser. Click each animal's name to see if the program works correctly. Figure 5-19 shows an example of the file displaying the giraffe in a Web browser.

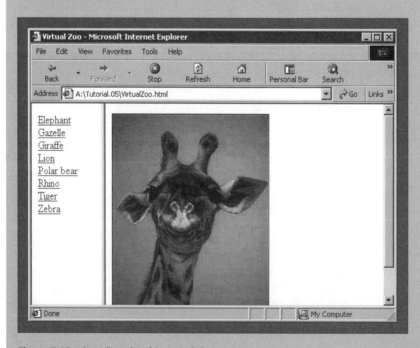

Figure 5-19: VirtualZoo.html in a Web browser

8   Close the Web browser window.

Nesting Frames

JavaScript treats each frame in an HTML document as an individual window. Therefore, each individual frame (which is also a window) within a window can contain its own set of frames. You accomplish this nesting by including a <FRAME-SET>...</FRAMESET> tag pair *inside* another <FRAMESET>...</FRAMESET> tag pair. Frames that are contained within other frames are called **nested frames**.

As a Web browser starts creating frames, the URLs of frames are loaded in the order in which each <FRAME> tag is encountered. The following code creates a parent frame set consisting of two rows and two columns. A nested frame set that also consists of two rows and two columns is created within the second frame. The text displayed in each frame is contained within each file specified by the SRC attribute of each frame. Figure 5-20 shows how the frames would appear.

```
<!-- The following line creates the main frame set -->
<FRAMESET ROWS="50%, 50%" COLS="50%, 50%">
    <!-- The following line assigns FirstURL.html as the
    URL of the first frame in the main frame set -->
    <FRAME SRC="FirstURL.html">
    <!-- The following line creates a nested frame set
    inside the second frame in the main frame set -->
    <FRAMESET ROWS="50%, 50%" COLS="50%, 50%">
        <!-- The following lines assign URLs
    to the nested frames -->
        <FRAME SRC="FirstURL.html">
        <FRAME SRC="SecondURL.html">
        <FRAME SRC="ThirdURL.html">
        <FRAME SRC="FourthURL.html">
    </FRAMESET>
    <!-- The following lines assign URLs to the
    third and fourth frames in the main frame set -->
    <FRAME SRC="ThirdURL.html">
    <FRAME SRC="FourthURL.html">
</FRAMESET>
```

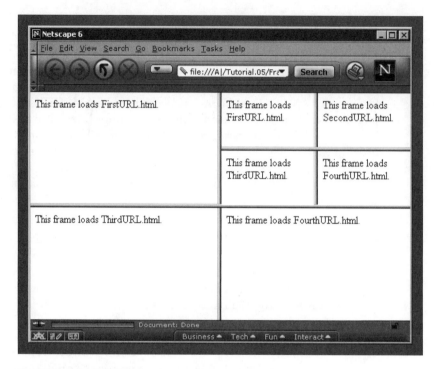

Figure 5-20: Nested frames

In Figure 5-20, the first <FRAMESET> tag creates the four parent frames in the window. The first <FRAME> tag assigns the URL frame1.html to the first frame in the parent frame set. The second <FRAMESET> tag is nested inside the second frame in the parent frame set. Each nested frame is then assigned a URL. The nested frames appearing in Figure 5-20 are more complicated than frames you would normally find on the Web.

The following code shows a more typical example, using the Musical Instrument program. The right column of the parent frame contains a nested frame set consisting of two rows. The first row displays a picture of the musical instrument and the second row displays the description. Figure 5-21 shows how the Musical Instrument program with a nested frame appears in a Web browser.

```
<FRAMESET COLS="200,*">
    <FRAME SRC="InstrumentsList.html" NAME="list">
    <FRAMESET ROWS="75%,*">
        <FRAME SRC="Instruments.jpg" NAME="picture">
        <FRAME SRC="Welcome.html" NAME="description">
    </FRAMESET>
</FRAMESET>
```

Figure 5-21: Musical Instruments document with nested frames

Next you will modify the Virtual Zoo program so that it includes a nested frame. The parent frame set will consist of two rows: the first row will display a title for the Virtual Zoo, and the second row will contain a nested frame set, consisting of the animal list and the frame that displays the animal's picture.

To add a nested frame to the Virtual Zoo program:

1 Open the **VirtualZoo.html** file in your text editor or HTML editor.

2 Add **<FRAMESET ROWS="20%,*">** above the existing <FRAMESET> tag. The existing frame set will be nested inside a new frame set.

3 After the opening tag for the new frame set, add **<FRAME SRC="title.html" NAME="title">** to specify that a document named title.html will be opened in the first frame.

4 Create a closing **</FRAMESET>** tag before the document's closing </HTML> tag to end the new frame set.

5 Save and close the file.

Next you need to create the title.html file that will be opened in the first frame of the Virtual Zoo program.

To create the title.html file:

1   Create a new document in your text editor or HTML editor.

2   Type the opening <HTML> and <BODY> tags:

```
<HTML>
<BODY>
```

3   Add **<H1>Virtual Zoo</H1>** to create a title line formatted with the <H1> tag.

4   Type the closing <HTML> and <BODY> tags:

```
</BODY>
</HTML>
```

5   Save the file as **title.html** in the **Tutorial.05** folder on your Data Disk, and then reopen the VirtualZoo.html file in your Web browser. Figure 5-22 shows an example of the file with the gazelle selected.

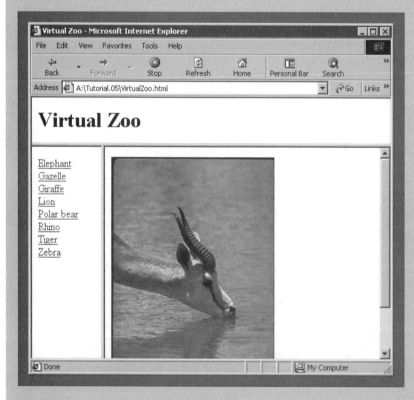

Figure 5-22: VirtualZoo.html with nested frames

6   Close the Web browser window.

Frame Formatting

The <FRAME> tag contains several attributes that change a frame's appearance and behavior. Figure 5-23 lists some of the attributes of the <FRAME> tag.

Attribute	Description
SRC	Specifies the URL to be opened in a frame
NAME	Assigns a name to an individual frame
NORESIZE	Disables the user's ability to resize an individual frame
SCROLLING	Determines whether a frame should include scroll bars
MARGINHEIGHT	Specifies the top and bottom margins of the frame in pixels
MARGINWIDTH	Specifies the left and right margins of the frame in pixels

Figure 5-23: <FRAME> tag attributes

You have already used the SRC attribute to specify a URL for a frame. You have also used the NAME attribute to specify a frame as a target for a hypertext link. The **NORESIZE attribute** disables the user's ability to resize an individual frame. Normally, users can adjust the size of frames to suit their own purposes. You use the NORESIZE attribute when, for example, you want to add a title that should always be visible in a frame or on a Web page. Or, you may want to create a list of hyperlinks at the bottom of a Web page to help users navigate through your site. To disable resizing of a frame, add the NORESIZE attribute to the <FRAME> tag.

By default, a Web browser will automatically add scroll bars to a frame when the contents of the frame are larger than the visible area. You can disable a frame's scroll bars using the **SCROLLING attribute**. Three values can be assigned to the SCROLLING attribute: yes, no, and auto. A value of *yes* always turns on the scroll bars, even when the contents of a frame fit within the visible area. A value of *no* completely disables a frame's scroll bars, even when the contents of a frame do not fit within the visible area. *Auto* turns the scroll bars on and off, depending on the visibility of the contents within a frame. Selecting a value of *auto* is equivalent to not including the SCROLLING attribute in the <FRAME> tag.

The following code shows an example of a program that includes both the NORESIZE and SCROLLING attributes. Figure 5-24 shows the output. The program contains three frames. The top frame provides a title for the Web page, and the bottom frame contains navigation buttons and hyperlinks. The middle frame contains the main content of the Web page. Since we do not want the user to resize the top and bottom frames, the NORESIZE attribute is included in the <FRAME> tags for the top and bottom frames. The SCROLLING attribute has also been set to *no* for the top and bottom frames, since the user does not need to scroll through them.

```
<FRAMESET ROWS="20%, *, 20%">
    <FRAME SRC="header.html" NORESIZE SCROLLING=no>
    <FRAME SRC="body.html">
    <FRAME SRC="navigationbar.html" NORESIZE SCROLLING=no>
</FRAMESET>
```

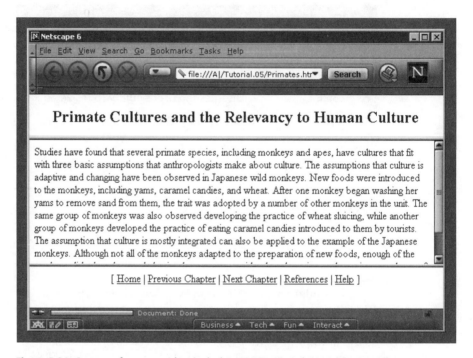

Figure 5-24: Output of program that includes NORESIZE and SCROLLING attributes

In the program output in Figure 5-24, the NORESIZE attribute in the top and bottom frames essentially eliminates resizing in the middle frame as well.

The **MARGINHEIGHT** and **MARGINWIDTH** attributes determine the margins of the frame in pixels. Figure 5-25 shows the output of the program in Figure 5-24 after the attributes MARGINHEIGHT=50 and MARGINWIDTH=50 have been added to the <FRAME> tag for the middle frame. The new tag for the middle frame reads <FRAME SRC="body.html" MARGINHEIGHT=50 MARGINWIDTH=50>.

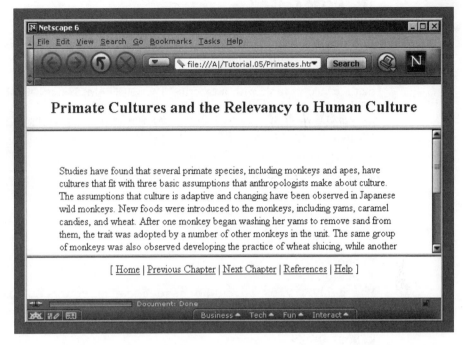

Figure 5-25: Middle frame changed to <FRAME SRC="body.html" MARGINHEIGHT=50 MARGINWIDTH=50>

Next you will add NORESIZE and SCROLLING attributes to the title frame of the Virtual Zoo program.

To add NORESIZE and SCROLLING attributes to the title frame of the Virtual Zoo program:

1 Open the **VirtualZoo.html** file in your text editor or HTML editor.

2 Add **NORESIZE** and **SCROLLING=no** just before the closing bracket for the <FRAME SRC="title.html" NAME="title"> line.

3 Save and close the file, then open the **VirtualZoo.html** file in your Web browser. You should no longer be able to resize the title frame. Since the title frame consists of only a single line, you should not have been able to see a scroll bar in the previous exercises. You would have seen a scroll bar in the title frame if you had resized the title frame so that it was smaller than the line of text it contains. However, even if you could still resize the title frame you would not see a scroll bar since it has been disabled.

The NOFRAMES Tag

Just as some older Web browsers are incompatible with JavaScript, they are also incompatible with frames. In Tutorial 1, you learned how to use the <NOSCRIPT>...</NOSCRIPT> tag pair to display a message to users of Web browsers that are incompatible with JavaScript. The **<NOFRAMES>...</NOFRAMES>** tag pair is a similar type of tag; it displays an alternate message to users of Web browsers that are not capable of displaying frames. The <NOFRAMES>...</NOFRAMES> tag pair usually follows the <FRAMESET>...</FRAMESET> tag pair. The following code shows an example of the <NOFRAMES> tag:

```
<FRAMESET ROWS="20%, *, 20%">
    <FRAME SRC="header.html" NORESIZE SCROLLING=no>
    <FRAME SRC="body.html">
    <FRAME SRC="navigationbar.html"
        NORESIZE SCROLLING=no>
</FRAMESET>
<NOFRAMES>
You cannot view this Web page because your Web browser
does not support frames. To view a no frames version of this
Web page, click <A HREF="no_frames.html">here</A>
</NOFRAMES>
```

 tip

Web browsers that are capable of displaying frames ignore the <NOFRAMES> tag.

Next you will add a <NOFRAMES> tag to the Virtual Zoo program.

To add a <NOFRAMES> tag to the Virtual Zoo program:

1 Return to the **VirtualZoo.html** file in your text editor or HTML editor.

2 After the last closing </FRAMESET> tag, add the following <NOFRAMES>...</NOFRAMES> tag pair to warn users of frame-incompatible browsers that they cannot use this Web page.

```
<NOFRAMES>
You cannot view this Web page because your Web browser
does not support frames.
</NOFRAMES>
```

3 Save and close the file. Now, if someone opens the VirtualZoo.html file in a frames-incompatible browser, he or she will see the NOFRAMES message.

The Location Object

When you want to allow users to open one Web page from within another Web page, you usually create a hypertext link with the <A> tag. You can also use JavaScript code and the Location object to open Web pages. The **Location object** allows you to change to a new Web page from within JavaScript code. One reason you may want to change Web pages with JavaScript code is to redirect your Web site visitors to a different or updated URL. The Location object contains several properties and methods for working with the URL of the document currently open in a Web browser window. When you use a method or property of the Location object, you must include a reference to the Location object itself. For example, to use the href property, you must write location.href = *URL*;. Figure 5-26 lists the Location object's properties, and Figure 5-27 lists the Location object's methods.

Name	Description
hash	A URL's anchor
host	The host and domain name (or IP address) of a network host
hostname	A combination of the URL's host name and port sections
href	The full URL address
pathname	The URL's path
port	The URL's port
protocol	The URL's protocol
search	A URL's search or query portion

Figure 5-26: Location object properties

Name	Description
assign()	Loads a new HTML document
reload()	Causes the page that currently appears in the Web browser to open again
replace()	Replaces the currently loaded URL with a different one

Figure 5-27: Location object methods

The properties of the Location object allow you to modify individual portions of a URL. When you modify any properties of the Location object, you generate a new URL, and the Web browser automatically attempts to open that new URL. Instead of modifying individual portions of a URL, it is usually easier to change the href property, which represents the entire URL. For example, the statement location.href = "http://www.netscape.com"; opens the Netscape home page.

The assign() method of the Location object performs the same action as changing the href property: It loads a new HTML document. The statement `location.assign("http://www.netscape.com");` is equivalent to the statement `location.href = "http://www.netscape.com";`.

The reload() method of the Location object is equivalent to the Reload button in Netscape or the Refresh button in Internet Explorer. It causes the page that currently appears in the Web browser to open again. You can use the reload() button without any arguments, as in `location.reload();`, or you can include a Boolean argument of true or false. Including an argument of true forces the current Web page to reload from the server where it is located, even if no changes have been made to it. For example, the statement `location.reload(true);` forces the current page to reload. If you include an argument of false, or do not include any argument at all, then the Web page reloads only if it has changed.

The replace() method of the Location object is used to replace the currently loaded URL with a different one. This method works somewhat differently from loading a new document by changing the href property. The replace() method actually *overwrites* one document with another and replaces the old URL entry in the Web browser's **history list**, a list of all the documents that have been opened during the current browser session, with the new URL. In contrast, the href property opens a different document and *adds* it to the history list. You will learn about the history list next.

The History Object

The **History object** maintains a history list of all the documents that have been opened during the current Web browser session. Each Web browser window and frame, regardless of how many windows and frames you have open, contains its own internal History object. You can write a JavaScript program that uses the history list to navigate to Web pages that have been opened during a Web browser session.

Two important security features are associated with the History object. First, the History object will not actually display the URLs contained in the history list. It only allows navigation to a particular URL according to that URL's position in the history list. You must understand that individual client information in a Web browser is private information. Preventing others from viewing the URLs in a History list is an important security aspect because it keeps people's likes and interests (as evidenced by the types of Web sites a person visits) confidential. This security feature is available in both Netscape and Internet Explorer.

A second important security feature of the History object is specific to Internet Explorer and has to do with the domain in which a Web page exists. You can use JavaScript code to navigate through a history list only if the currently displayed Web page exists within the same domain as the Web page containing the JavaScript code that is attempting to move through the list. If JavaScript code attempts to access the History object of a Web browser that contains a URL located in a different domain, the Web browser will ignore the JavaScript code. This security feature helps prevents malicious programmers and unscrupulous Web sites from seizing control of your browser or even your computer. Therefore, keep in mind that you should use the History object to help visitors navigate only through your particular Web site.

The History object includes three methods, listed in Figure 5-28. When you use a method or property of the History object, you must include a reference to the History object itself. For example, to use the back() method, you must write history.back().

Method	Description
back()	The equivalent of clicking a Web browser's Back button
forward()	The equivalent of clicking a Web browser's Forward button
go()	Opens a specific document in the history list

Figure 5-28: Methods of the History object

The back() and forward() methods allow a program to move backward or forward in a Web browser's history list. The code in Figure 5-29 shows a program named Site Navigator that consists of two files: SiteNavigator.html and Controls.html. The SiteNavigator.html file sets up a frame document consisting of two frames. The top frame, named *main*, is blank and the bottom frame, named *controls*, opens a file named Controls.html. The controls frame contains a URL text box and a Go To button that uses the location.href statement to change the URL displayed in the main frame. The controls frame also contains two buttons that simulate a Web browser's forward and back buttons. Clicking the back or forward buttons navigates through the history list of the pages that have been displayed in the main frame. Figure 5-30 shows an example of the program in Netscape before any Web pages have been opened in the main frame.

```
<!-- SiteNavigator.html -->

<HEAD>

<TITLE>Site Navigator</TITLE>

</HEAD>

<FRAMESET ROWS="75%,25%">

      <FRAME SRC="" NAME="main">

      <FRAME SRC="Controls.html" NAME="controls">

</FRAMESET>

</BODY>

<!-- Controls.html -->

<HTML>

<BODY>

<FORM NAME="controls">

URL Address:

<INPUT TYPE="text" NAME="newURL">

<INPUT TYPE="button" NAME="goto" VALUE=" Go To "
onClick="parent.main.location.href=document.controls.newURL.value;">

<INPUT TYPE="button" NAME="next" VALUE=" Next URL "
onClick="parent.main.history.forward();">

<INPUT TYPE="button" NAME="previous" VALUE=" Previous URL "
onClick="parent.main.history.back();">

</FORM>

</BODY>

</HTML>
```

Figure 5-29: Site Navigator program

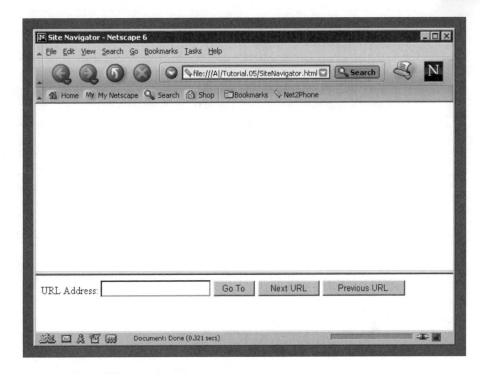

Figure 5-30: Site Navigator program in Netscape

To open a specific Web page in the Site Navigator program, you must type the full URL, including the HTTP protocol or the path on your local computer. Once you have visited a few Web pages in the main frame, you can use the buttons in the controls frame to navigate through the history list of the main frame. You can find a copy of the program files in the Tutorial.05 folder on your Data Disk. Remember, however, that in Internet Explorer you can only navigate through Web pages that exist in the same domain as the JavaScript code that you are using to move through the list. If you open a URL, such as microsoft.com, in the main frame and then click one of the buttons in the controls frame, you will receive an *Access denied* error message as shown in Figure 5-31.

Figure 5-31: Access denied error message

The go() method is used for navigating to a specific Web page that has been previously visited. The argument of the go() method is an integer that indicates how many pages in the history list, forward or backward, you want to navigate. For example, `history.go(-2);` opens the Web page that is two pages back in the history list; the statement `history.go(3);` opens the Web page that is three pages forward in the history list. The statement `history.go(-1);` is equivalent to using the back() method, and the statement `history.go(1);` is equivalent to using the forward() method.

The History object contains a single property, the length property, which contains the specific number of documents that have been opened during the current browser session. To use the length property, you use the syntax `history.length;`. The length property does not contain the URLs of the documents themselves, only an integer representing how many documents have been opened. The following code uses an alert dialog box to display the number of Web pages that have been visited during a Web browser session:

```
alert("You have visited " + history.length
      + " Web pages.");
```

The Navigator Object

The **Navigator object** is used to obtain information about the current Web browser. The Navigator object gets its name from Netscape Navigator, but is also supported by Internet Explorer. Figure 5-32 lists properties of the Navigator object that are supported by both Netscape and Internet Explorer.

Property	Returns
appCodeName	The Web browser code name
appName	The Web browser name
appVersion	The Web browser version
platform	The operating system in use
userAgent	The string stored in the HTTP user-agent request header, which contains information about the browser, the platform name, and compatibility

Figure 5-32: Navigator object properties

Netscape and Internet Explorer each contain unique methods and properties that cannot be used with the other browser. One useful method of the Navigator object that is supported by both Netscape and Internet Explorer is the javaEnabled()method. The javaEnabled() method returns a Boolean value indicating whether Java is enabled in the browser. You will work with Java at the end of this book.

The Navigator object is most commonly used to determine which type of Web browser is running. Due to the incompatibilities between Internet Explorer and Netscape, it is important to be able to distinguish which browser is running in order to execute the correct code for a specific browser. (Cross-browser compatibility issues will be discussed in detail in Tutorial 8.) The statement `browserType = navigator.appName;` returns the name of the Web browser in which the code is running to the browserType variable. You can then use the browserType variable to determine which code to run for the specific browser type. The following `with` statement prints the five properties of the Navigator object for Internet Explorer. Figure 5-33 shows the output.

```
with (navigator) {
     document.writeln("Browser code name: " + appCodeName);
     document.writeln("Web browser name: " + appName);
     document.writeln("Web browser version: " + appVersion);
     document.writeln("Operating platform: " + platform);
     document.writeln("User agent: " + userAgent);
}
```

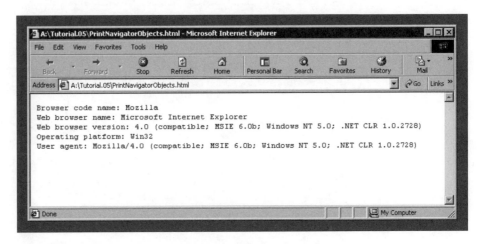

Figure 5-33: Output of Navigator object properties program

Next you will print the properties of the Navigator object for the Web browser you are using. Since Netscape and Internet Explorer contain different property names in their Navigator objects, you will use the `for...in` statement to loop through the properties in your specific type of Web browser.

tip

You learned about the `for...in` statement in Tutorial 4.

To print the properties of the Navigator object for the Web browser you are using:

1 Create a new document in your text editor or HTML editor.

2 Type the <HTML> and <HEAD> sections of the document:

```
<HTML>
<HEAD>
<TITLE>Navigator Properties</TITLE>
</HEAD>
```

3 Add **<BODY>** to begin the body of the HTML document and press **Enter**.

4 Add an opening <PRE> tag and the opening statements for a JavaScript section:

```
<PRE>
<SCRIPT LANGUAGE="JavaScript">
<!-- HIDE FROM INCOMPATIBLE BROWSERS
```

5 Type the following `for...in` statement to print the name and value for all the properties in the Navigator object:

```
for (prop in navigator) {
     document.writeln(prop + ": " + navigator[prop]);
}
```

6 Add the following code to close the <SCRIPT>, <PRE>, <BODY>, and <HTML> tags:

```
// STOP HIDING FROM INCOMPATIBLE BROWSERS -->
</SCRIPT>
</PRE>
</BODY>
</HTML>
```

7 Save the file as **NavigatorObjects.html** in the **Tutorial.05** folder on your Data Disk. Open the **NavigatorObjects.html** file in your Web browser. Figure 5-34 shows the output as it appears in Netscape. Figure 5-35 shows the output as it appears in Internet Explorer. Note that each figure shows properties that are unique to each browser. For example, Figure 5-35, which shows Internet Explorer, includes properties that are not available in Netscape, such as the systemLanguage and userLanguage properties.

Figure 5-34: Output of NavigatorObjects.html in Netscape

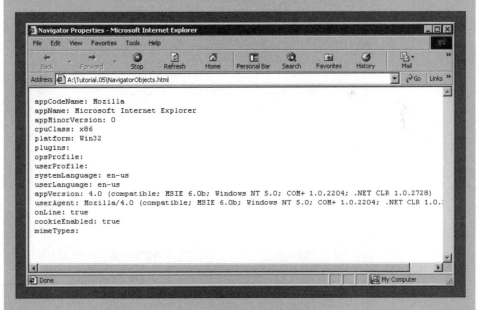

Figure 5-35: Output of NavigatorObjects.html in Internet Explorer

8 Close the Web browser window.

Referring to Frames and Windows

When working with multiple frames and windows, you need to be able to refer to individual frames and windows in JavaScript code. When you create a new window, for instance, you may want to change the content displayed in that window. Or, if you have multiple frames in a window, you may need to change the content displayed in one frame, depending on a link selected in another frame. Recall from Section A that some of the objects in the browser object model, including the Frame object, are arrays of objects. The Frame object includes a frames[] array that contains all the frames in a window. The first frame in a window is referred to as frames[0], the second frame is referred to as frames[1], and so on. If a window contains no frames, then the frames[] array is empty. To refer to a frame within the same frame set, you use the **parent property** of the Window object combined with the frame's index number from the frames[] array. For example, if you have an HTML document that creates four frames, the frames can be referred to as parent.frames[0], parent.frames[1], parent.frames[2], and parent.frames[3], respectively.

To better understand how to use the parent property and frames[] array, consider the HTML document shown in Figure 5-36.

Figure 5-36: Parent property and frames[] array example

The two frames in Figure 5-36 were created using the following code:

```
<FRAMESET ROWS="50%, 50%">
    <FRAME SRC="frame1.html" NAME="FirstFrame">
    <FRAME SRC="frame2.html" NAME="SecondFrame">
</FRAMESET>
```

The first frame refers to the second frame's URL by using an onClick event in an <INPUT> tag, as follows:

```
<INPUT TYPE="button"
    VALUE="Click here to display the 2nd frame's URL "
    onClick="alert(parent.frames[1].location.href);">
```

As you can see in the preceding code, the statement `parent.frames[1].location.href` returns the URL of the second frame. If the button were returning the first frame's URL, you would use the statement `self.location.href` or `parent.frames[0].location.href`, since it is the first frame in the frames[] array. Note that to display the href property of the Location object, you must include location in the statement, since it is necessary to refer to all of an object's ancestors (with the exception of the Window object).

tip

Remember that each frame contains its own Window object, as well as its own Location, History, and Navigator objects.

With nested frames, you can also use the parent property along with the name you assigned to a frame with the <FRAME> tag. Nested frames are also assigned to the window frames[] array in the order in which they are encountered. Figure 5-37 shows a variation of the program in Figure 5-36. In this figure, the column frame on the left is the first frame in the parent frame set. The two frames on the right are nested within the second frame of the parent frame set. For the column frame containing the button to obtain the URL of the last nested frame on the right, you use either `parent.frames[2].location.href` or `parent.thirdFrame.location.href` (assuming the last frame has been assigned a name of thirdFrame with the <FRAME> tag).

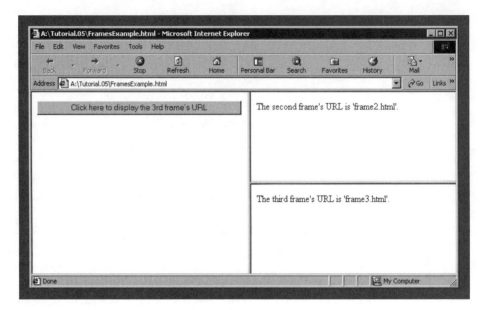

Figure 5-37: Referencing a nested frame

Another property that is used to refer to a window is the top property of the Window object. The top property refers to the topmost window in an HTML document. When working with frames, the top property refers to the window that constructed the frames. For example, if the code to create a parent frame set is located in a file named FramesExample.html, then the statement `top.location.href` would return the full URL for the FramesExample.html document, no matter which frame it was used in. When the top property is used in an HTML document that does not contain frames, then it refers to the window itself.

SUMMARY

- Frames are independent, scrollable portions of a Web browser window, with each frame capable of containing its own URL.

- Each frame has its own Window object, separate from other frames in the document.

- An HTML document is divided into frames using the <FRAMESET>...</FRAMESET> tag pair.

- The ROWS attribute of the <FRAMESET> tag determines the number of rows to create in a frame set. The COLS attribute of the <FRAMESET> tag determines the number of columns to create in a frame set.

- The <FRAME> tag is used for specifying options for individual frames, including a frame's URL. The SRC attribute of the <FRAME> tag specifies the URL to be opened in an individual frame.

- The URLs of frames are opened in the order in which each <FRAME> tag is encountered, from left to right and top to bottom.

- The TARGET attribute determines in which frame or window a URL opens.

- The <BASE> tag uses an assigned name of a window or frame to specify a default target for all links in an HTML document.

- Frames that are contained within other frames are called nested frames.

- The NORESIZE attribute disables the ability to resize an individual frame.

- You can disable a frame's scroll bars with the SCROLLING attribute.

- The <NOFRAMES>...</NOFRAMES> tag pair displays an alternate message to users of Web browsers that are unable to display frames.

- The Location object contains several properties and methods for working with the URL of the document currently open in a Web browser window.

- The History object maintains a history list of all the documents that have been opened during the current Web browser session.

- The Navigator object is used to obtain information about the current Web browser.

- The Navigator object is most frequently used to determine which type of Web browser is running.

- The Frame object includes a frames[ ] array that contains all the frames in a window.

- To refer to a frame within the same frame set, you use the parent property of the Window object combined with the frame's array index number. You can also use the name you assigned with the <FRAME> tag to refer to a frame within the same frame set.

- The top property refers to the topmost window in an HTML document.

QUESTIONS

1. Which of the following tag pairs is used to create frames?
   a. <BEGIN FRAME>...</END FRAME>
   b. <FRAMESET>...</FRAMESET>
   c. <NEW FRAME>...</NEW FRAME>
   d. <FRAMEBUILD>...</FRAMEBUILD>

2. The size of rows and columns in a frame can be set using a percentage of the screen size or by using _____.
   a. inches
   b. picas
   c. pixels
   d. a Web browser's internal sizing capability

3. Which symbol can be used to allocate any remaining screen space to an individual frame?
   a. *
   b. &
   c. %
   d. #

4. The URLs of frames are loaded in the order in which each <FRAME> tag is encountered _____.
   a. alphabetically
   b. top to bottom and left to right
   c. left to right and top to bottom
   d. according to each <FRAME> tag's ORDER attribute

5. Which is the correct syntax for a <FRAME> tag that loads a URL of MyHomePage.html?
   a. <FRAME HREF="MyHomePage.html">
   b. <FRAME URL="MyHomePage.html">
   c. <FRAME HTML="MyHomePage.html">
   d. <FRAME SRC="MyHomePage.html">

6. The attribute _____ of the <A> tag determines into which frame or window a URL opens.
   a. OPENINWIN
   b. SELECT
   c. GOAL
   d. TARGET

7. The tag _____ is used for specifying a default target for all links in an HTML document using the assigned name of a window or frame.
   a. <BASE>
   b. <SOURCE>
   c. <TARGET>
   d. <DEFAULT>

8. A frame set contained within another frame set is called a(n) _____ frame.
   a. controlling
   b. relative
   c. nested
   d. integral

9. To prevent a user from resizing a frame, you include the attribute within the _____ <FRAME> tag.
   a. NORESIZE
   b. RESIZE=NO
   c. FIXED
   d. LOCKED

10. Which of the following attributes of the <FRAME> tag turns off scroll bars for an individual frame?
    a. verticalscroll=0, horizontalscroll=0
    b. showScrollbars=off
    c. scrolling=no
    d. scrollbars=no

11. Which attribute(s) of the <FRAME> tag is/are used to determine a frame's left and right margins?
    a. SIDEMARGINS
    b. INSIDE and OUTSIDE
    c. MARGINLEFT and MARGINRIGHT
    d. MARGINWIDTH

12. Which tag pair is used to display an alternate message to users of Web browsers that are unable to display frames?
    a. <NOFRAMES>...</NOFRAMES>
    b. <NOSCRIPT>...</NOSCRIPT>
    c. <ALTERNATE>...</ALTERNATE>
    d. <MISSINGFRAMES>...</MISSINGFRAMES>

13. The History object is used for _____.
    a. determining when changes have been made to either an individual HTML document or to the Web site where it is contained
    b. tracking which users have accessed a particular Web site
    c. tracking which users have accessed a particular HTML document
    d. maintaining a list of the documents that have been opened for the current session of a Web browser window

14. Which of the following is *not* a method of the History object?
    a. back()
    b. forward()
    c. go()
    d. next()

15. The full URL of a Web page is located in the property of the History object
_____.

   a. src
   b. href
   c. hash
   d. url

16. To overwrite one HTML document with another, and replace the old URL entry in the Web browser's list of previously visited Web sites, you use the method of the History object _____.
   a. reload()
   b. refresh()
   c. replace()
   d. open()

17. The object is used to obtain information about the current Web browser
_____.

   a. Window
   b. Browser
   c. Explorer
   d. Navigator

18. To refer to a frame within the same frame set, you use the _____ property.
   a. parent
   b. frame
   c. frames
   d. frameset

 # E X E R C I S E S

Save all files you create in the Tutorial.05 folder on your Data Disk.

1. Create an HTML document with two vertical frames and two horizontal frames. Save the document as Quadrants.html. Format each quadrant's size with an asterisk. Also, create a document for each of the frames in Quadrant.html. Name the four frames Quadrant1.html, Quadrant2.html, Quadrant3.html, and Quadrant4.html, respectively. Within each of the quadrant files, add a single line formatted with the <STRONG> tag that displays the name of the document.

2. Format the main frame document you created in Exercise 1 so that each of the four frames cannot be resized and do not include scroll bars. Also, add a NOFRAMES section to display a message to users of Web browsers that are not capable of displaying frames.

3. Create an HTML document with three vertical frames. Save the document as ColoredFrames.html. Use an asterisk for the frame sizes so that each frame takes up the same amount of space as the other frames. The first frame should open a file named RedFrame.html, the second frame should open a file named BlueFrame.html, and the third frame should open a file named YellowFrame.html. Next, create the RedFrame.html, BlueFrame.html, and YellowFrame.html files. Change each document background color to the color used in its filename. Include a single <STRONG> tag that describes which file is being displayed.

4. Create a frame document named CollegeFrame.html with two vertical frames. Name the left frame CollegeList and the right frame CollegeFrame. Create a file named CollegeList.html to display in the CollegeList frame. Use the following links in CollegeList.html. Also, modify the following code so that the default target is specified with a <BASE> tag.

```
<A HREF="http://www.harvard.edu" TARGET="CollegeFrame">
   Harvard</A></BR>
<A HREF="http://www.yale.edu" TARGET="CollegeFrame">
   Yale</A></BR>
<A HREF="http://www.stanford.edu" TARGET="CollegeFrame">
   Stanford</A></BR>
<A HREF="http://www.brown.edu" TARGET="CollegeFrame">
   Brown</A></BR>
<A HREF="http://www.psu.edu" TARGET="CollegeFrame">
   Penn State</A></BR>
```

5. Although most Web browsers will let you get away with the following HTML code, it contains HTML code that is technically incorrect. Correct the problem and save the HTML document as AnchorTargets.html.

```
<HTML>
<HEAD>
<TITLE>Anchor Targets</TITLE>
<SCRIPT LANGUAGE="JavaScript">
var links = window.open("", "JavaScriptLinks");
</SCRIPT>
</HEAD>
<BODY>
<BASE TARGET=."JavaScriptLinks">
<A HREF="http://www.webreference.com/js/">Doc
JavaScript</A><BR>
<A HREF="http://wsabstract.com/">Website Abstraction</A><BR>
<A HREF="http://www.javascripts.com">JavaScripts.com</A><BR>
<A HREF="http://javascript.internet.com/">JavaScript
Source</A><BR>
</BODY>
</HTML>
```

6. The following nested frame tags should create the frames shown in Figure 5-38. However, when you open the document in a browser, only the four rows in the first frame set are showing. Fix the problem and save the document as FixedNestedFrames.html

```
<FRAMESET ROWS="50%, 50%">
    <FRAMESET ROWS="*, *, *, *">
        <FRAME SRC="">
        <FRAME SRC="">
        <FRAME SRC="">
        <FRAME SRC="">
    <FRAMESET COLS="*, *, *, *">
        <FRAME SRC="">
        <FRAME SRC="">
        <FRAME SRC="">
        <FRAME SRC="">
    </FRAMESET>
    <FRAME SRC="">
    <FRAME SRC="">
</FRAMESET>
```

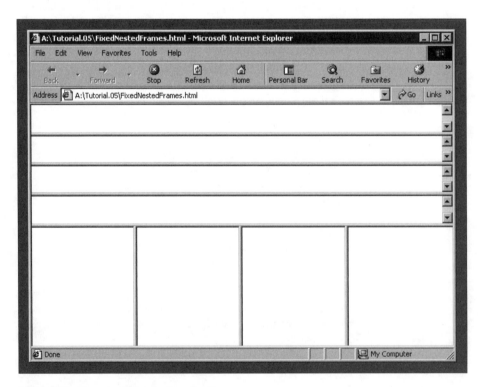

Figure 5-38: Correct output for Exercise 6

7. Create an HTML document with two frames. One frame takes up 200 pixels on the left side of the screen, and the other frame takes up the remainder of the right portion of the screen. Use hyperlinks to create a list of your favorite Web sites in the left frame. When a user clicks a favorite Web site in the left frame, it should open in the right frame. Use the <BASE> tag to specify the default target window. Format the frames so they cannot be resized. Save the file as Favorites.html.

8. Create an HTML document that displays all the properties of the Navigator object for your Web browser in an alert dialog box. Insert a line break between each property name. Save the HTML document as BrowserProperties.html.

9. Create an HTML document that redirects users to a different page. Automatically redirect users after 10 seconds, or allow them to click a hyperlink. Name the main redirection document Redirect.html and the target document as CorrectURL.html.

10. Create the necessary documents for the frames shown in Figure 5-39. Name the main frame document FrameReferences.html. Use whatever names you like for the documents displayed in each frame. Write JavaScript code so that each of the buttons retrieves the correct URL, as specified in Figure 5-39.

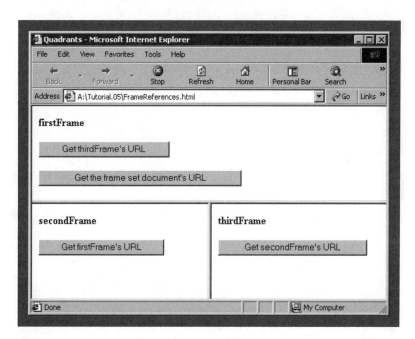

Figure 5-39: Correct output for Exercise 10

11. Some Web sites use frames that display someone else's Web page inside a frame at the originating Web site. For an example of this, visit AskJeeves.com, search for a topic, and then click the topic's URL. You will notice that the URL you clicked will open within a frame in the AskJeeves.com site. This is not necessarily a bad thing, since sites like Ask Jeeves can be enormously helpful in locating information and controlling where other Web sites may redirect you. However, there may be cases when you do not want your Web page displayed within someone else's frame, no matter what the circumstance. Think of a way you can prevent this from happening using the Location object and the top property. Write a simple HTML document named Breakout.html that displays the text *This document cannot be displayed in a frame*. Include a JavaScript section in the document head that prevents the document from being displayed in a frame. Then write a simple two-column frame document named BreakoutCheck.html to test your code. In the left column, include a link that attempts to open the Breakout.html document in the right frame column. Try to solve this exercise by yourself. But if you are stuck, refer to one of the JavaScript Web sites listed at the end of Tutorial 7.

TUTORIAL

6

Forms

case ▶ Many of WebAdventure's clients want to include guest books, comment forms, surveys, shopping carts for placing orders online, and games as part of their Web sites. Web sites use forms to create these applications. One of WebAdventure's clients, a new software company, wants to create an online product registration form to gather information from customers. WebAdventure has asked you to learn how to develop this product registration form.

Previewing the Product Registration Form

The form you will create in this tutorial is a product registration form. In Section A, you will learn how to put the different form tags together to create the product registration form. In Section B, you will learn how to use JavaScript to validate and check the form's data, as well as submit the form's data to a Web server or to an e-mail address.

To preview the Product Registration form:

1   In your Web browser, open the **Tutorial6_ProductRegistration.html** file from the Tutorial.06 folder on your Student Disk. The Tutorial6_ProductRegistration.html file creates two frames. The bottom frame displays the first page of the Product Registration form, Tutorial6_CustomerInfo.html. After a user clicks the Next button at the bottom of Tutorial6_CustomerInfo.html, the second page, Tutorial6_ProductInfo.html, appears. The frame at the top of the page contains hidden form fields that store the values of each field when a user switches from the Tutorial6_CustomerInfo.html file to the Tutorial6_ProductInfo.html file. Figure 6-1 displays an example of the customer information form in Netscape.

Figure 6-1: Tutorial6_CustomerInfo.html in a Web browser

2   Before entering data into the form fields, scroll to the bottom of the **Tutorial6_CustomerInfo.html** form and click the **Next** button. You will see an alert dialog box warning you that several fields on the form are required. Fill in the required fields. If you make a mistake, click the **Reset** button to start the form over. When you are finished, click the **Next** button.

3   The second form, shown in Figure 6-2, collects product information. Fill in the product information fields and click the **Submit Query** button. To submit the forms, you must fill in the serial number and date fields, or an alert dialog box will appear. The Submit Query button on the Tutorial6_ProductInfo.html form is used to send the form data to a Web server. Since you do not have a server to work with, clicking the Submit Query button does nothing. At the end of this tutorial, you will learn how to submit the form data to an e-mail address.

Figure 6-2: Tutorial6_ProductInfo.html

4   When you are finished, close the Web browser window.

5 Next examine the code for the Tutorial6_CustomerInfo.html and the Tutorial6_ProductInfo.html files in your text editor or HTML editor. The form tags in the <BODY> section of each file create the controls that appear on each form. The <SCRIPT>...</SCRIPT> tag pair in the <HEAD> section of each file copies the values from each field to hidden fields in the Tutorial6_TopFrame.html file, which appears in the frame at the top of the product registration page. The hidden fields keep track of each field value when a user navigates between the Tutorial6_CustomerInfo.html and the Tutorial6_ProductInfo.html files. It is the contents of these hidden fields that are sent to a Web server—not the contents of the fields on the Tutorial6_CustomerInfo.html and the Tutorial6_ProductInfo.html files.

6 Close your text editor or HTML editor when you are finished examining the code.

In this section you will learn:

- How to use HTML forms
- About the Common Gateway Interface
- How to use the <FORM> tag
- About form elements
- How to create and use input fields
- How to create selection lists
- How to create multiline text fields

Working with Forms in JavaScript

Overview of Forms

Forms are one of the most common HTML elements used with JavaScript. Many Web sites use forms to collect information from users and transmit that information to a server for processing. Typical forms you may encounter on the Web include order forms, surveys, and applications. Another type of form frequently found on Web pages gathers search criteria from a user. After the search criteria are entered, the information is sent to a database on a server. The server then queries the database, using the data gathered in the search form, and returns the results to a Web browser. You use JavaScript to make sure form fields were entered properly and to perform other types of preprocessing before the data is sent to the server. Without JavaScript, the only action that HTML can take on form data is to send it to a server for processing.

To process the data submitted from a Web browser to a server, you use a special protocol named Common Gateway Interface (CGI). Although there are now other ways of dealing with data transmitted to a server, including ASP, ISPI, and NSAPI, CGI is one of the oldest and most popular methods. Although it is not directly related to JavaScript programming, you will learn about CGI in this tutorial, since the processing of data on a server (for example, running a query against a database) is an important aspect of Web programming. You will also learn how to use forms and JavaScript to create programs and Web pages that do not require data to be processed on a server.

Since the focus of this book is on JavaScript programming, this tutorial does not cover the formatting and design aspects of forms. If you would like information on formatting and designing forms, refer to *Creating Web Pages with HTML*, written by Patrick Carey and published by Course Technology in their New Perspectives series.

You can also use HTML forms to create many types of programs that are driven by JavaScript and do not involve transmitting data to a server for processing. For example, the calculator program in Tutorial 2 is created with a form, and its functionality is created with JavaScript commands. In addition, forms provide a way of adding user interface controls, such as buttons and text boxes, to an HTML document. Without forms, few HTML elements other than hyperlinks can be used for interacting with users. A form within an HTML document can consist of a single button or control or can be composed of multiple elements. Figure 6-3 shows an example of a form containing custom navigation buttons.

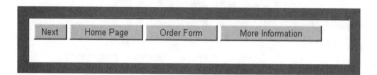

Figure 6-3: Custom navigation buttons created with a form

In earlier tutorials, you have seen a common form element, the <INPUT> tag, in action in several examples and have used it in various exercises. You have also used the <FORM> tag itself in several exercises. In Tutorial 2, you learned about JavaScript events; events associated with the <INPUT> tag are among the most commonly used types of JavaScript events. Although you have used the <FORM> and <INPUT> tags in simple applications, there are many other important aspects of forms that you should know about.

The Common Gateway Interface

The **Common Gateway Interface**, or **CGI**, is a simple protocol that allows Web pages to communicate with Web-server-based programs. CGI's function is to start a Web server-based program, then pass environment variables to it and receive environment variables from it. An **environment variable** is part of an operating system, not just part of a function or a program, as are JavaScript variables. An example of a CGI environment variable is server_name, which contains the domain name or IP address of a Web server. A Web server-based application that processes CGI environment variables is called a **CGI script** or **CGI program** and can be designed to perform a multitude of functions. Do not confuse the CGI protocol itself with a CGI script. The CGI protocol's primary purpose is to send the data received from a Web page to a program on a server, then to send any response from the program back to the Web page. The program that runs on the server can be a database program or some type of custom application. You can write server programs in a scripting language such as AppleScript, PERL, and TLC, or in a programming language such as Visual C++ or Visual Basic.

tip

∙∙∙

CGI scripts are often placed within a *bin* (for binary) or *cgi-bin* directory on a Web server. CGI script files usually have an extension of .cgi. If you see a URL similar to *http://www.ExampleWebPage/cgi-bin/example_script.cgi*, then you can safely assume that a CGI script is executing.

∙∙∙

CGI scripts are used to process information entered into HTML forms. HTML form elements are used to pass information that is entered into a form to CGI environment variables. These CGI environment variables are then sent to a CGI script on a Web server. The CGI script performs some sort of action, such as a query, and either sends a response back to the requesting Web page or generates a new HTML document. Figure 6-4 shows an example of a CGI script written in PERL that generates a new Web page as a response to the requesting Web page.

```perl
# !/usr/local/bin/perl

#

# formdata.pl— "Form Data Received" program

#

# The following line prints the CGI response header that
# is required for HTML output. Each \n sends
# a blank line (response headers must be followed
# by a blank line).

print "Content-type: text/html\n\n" ;


# The following lines print the HTML response
# page to STDOUT:

print <<EOF ;

<HTML>

<HEAD><TITLE>Form Data Received</TITLE></HEAD>

<BODY>

<H1>Your form data has been received.</H1>

</BODY>

</HTML>

EOF


exit ;
```

Figure 6-4: CGI script written in PERL

Do not worry about understanding how the PERL code in the CGI script functions. The example only demonstrates that CGI allows an HTML page to interact with a Web server application or programming language *other* than JavaScript.

The purpose of this book is to teach JavaScript. It does not explain the structure or syntax of other programming languages used to create CGI scripts. When a CGI script is included in an example, this book explains only the CGI script's functionality and not how the script or program works.

The <FORM> Tag

All forms begin with the <FORM> tag and end with the </FORM> tag. The **<FORM>...</FORM> tag pair** designates a form within an HTML document and contains all text and tags that make up a form. You can include as many forms as you like within an HTML document. However, you cannot nest one form inside another form. Be sure to close each form with a closing </FORM> tag. If the JavaScript interpreter encounters a new <FORM> tag before a closing </FORM> tag, then all the form elements following the second form tag will be included as part of the first form. Figure 6-5 shows an HTML document containing two forms. Figure 6-6 shows the document as it appears in a Web browser.

```
<HTML>

<HEAD>

<TITLE>Two Forms</TITLE>

</HEAD>

<BODY>

<H1>This document contains two forms.</H1>

<H2>This is the first form.</H2>

<FORM>

<INPUT TYPE="text">

<INPUT TYPE="button", VALUE="Click Me">

</FORM>

<HR>
```

Figure 6-5: HTML document with two forms

```
<H2>This is the second form.</H2>

<FORM>

<INPUT TYPE="text">

<INPUT TYPE="button", VALUE="Click Me"

</FORM>

</BODY>

</HTML>
```

Figure 6-5: HTML document with two forms (continued)

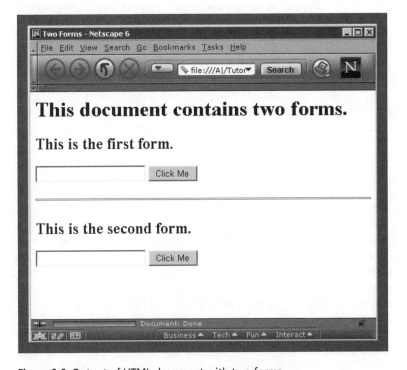

Figure 6-6: Output of HTML document with two forms

Figure 6-7 lists common attributes of the <FORM> tag.

Attribute	Description
ACTION	Specifies a URL to which form data will be submitted. If this attribute is excluded, the data is sent to the URL that contains the form. Typically you would specify the URL of a program on a server or an e-mail address.
METHOD	Determines how form data will be submitted. The two options for this attribute are GET and POST. The default option, GET, appends form data as one long string to the URL specified by the ACTION attribute. The POST option sends form data as a transmission separate from the URL specified by the ACTION attribute. Although GET is the default, POST is considered the preferred option, since it allows the server to receive the data separately from the URL.
ENCTYPE	Specifies the format of the data being submitted. The default value is *application/x-www-form-urlencoded*.
TARGET	Specifies a window in which any results returned from the server appear.
NAME	Designates a name for the form.

Figure 6-7: Attributes of the <FORM> tag

The ENCTYPE attribute specifies an encoding protocol known as Multipurpose Internet Mail Extension, or MIME. Encoding with MIME ensures that data does not become corrupt when transmitted across the Internet. The MIME protocol was originally developed to allow different file types to be transmitted as attachments to e-mail messages. Now MIME has become a standard method of exchanging files over the Internet, although the technology is still evolving. MIME types are specified using two-part codes separated by a forward slash (/). The first part specifies the MIME type, and the second part specifies the MIME subtype. The default MIME type of *application/x-www-form-urlencoded* specifies that form data should be encoded as one long string. The only other MIME types allowed with the ENCTYPE attribute are multipart/form-data, which encodes each field as a separate section, and text/plain, which is used to submit form data to an e-mail address.

Consider the code in Figures 6-8 and 6-9, which shows how to use attributes of the <FORM> tag. The code in Figure 6-8 contains HTML tags that set up a document with three frames; one of the frames includes a form. The code in Figure 6-9 displays the HTML tags for the simple form contained in the frame named *subscription*. Figure 6-10 shows how the program appears in a Web browser.

```
<HTML>

<HEAD>

<TITLE>Emily the Orangutan</TITLE>

</HEAD>

<FRAMESET ROWS="85%,*">

    <FRAMESET COLS="52%,*">

            <FRAME SRC="Emily.jpg" NAME="Emily">

            <FRAME SRC="dialog.html" NAME="dialog">

    </FRAMESET>

    <FRAME SRC="subscription.html" NAME="subscription">

</FRAMESET>

</HTML>
```

Figure 6-8: Three frames document

```
<HTML>

<BODY>

<FORM ACTION="http://www.Emily-the-Orangutan.org/
cgi-bin/process_subscription.cgi"

    METHOD="post" NAME="subscriptionForm" TARGET="dialog">

<INPUT TYPE="text" SIZE=50>

<INPUT TYPE="submit" VALUE="Subscribe">

</FORM>

</BODY>

</HTML>
```

Figure 6-9: Subscription frame

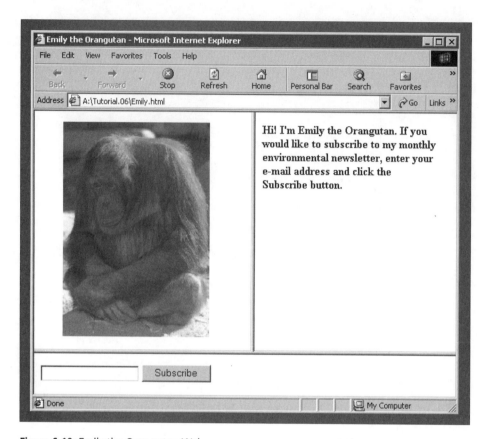

Figure 6-10: Emily the Orangutan Web page

The <FORM> tag in Figure 6-9 contains an ACTION attribute that sends the form data to the URL *http://www.Emily-the-Orangutan/cgi-bin/process_subscription.cgi*. The METHOD attribute of the <FORM> tag specifies that the form data will be sent using the POST method instead of the default GET method. Since the ENCTYPE attribute is omitted, the form data will be encoded with the default *application/x-www-form-urlencoded* format. The form is also assigned a name of *subscriptionForm*. The last attribute in the <FORM> tag, TARGET, is set to *dialog*. The TARGET attribute specifies the window in which text and HTML tags returned from the server are to be rendered. In this case, TARGET is set to the *dialog* frame created by the code shown in Figure 6-8. Let's assume that a user submits the form using the Subscribe button. After the data is received by the server, the imaginary *process_subscription* CGI script adds the e-mail address to a database, then returns a message to the *dialog* frame, as shown in Figure 6-11.

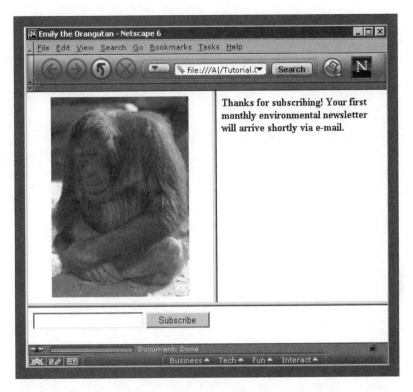

Figure 6-11: Emily the Orangutan Web page after form submission

Next you will start creating the Product Registration document that you saw in the preview of this tutorial. You use frames to create the Product Registration document. First you will create the main HTML document that loads the frame set tags. Then you will create the HTML documents for each frame.

To create the main HTML document that loads the frame set tags for the Product Registration form:

1   Start your text editor or HTML editor and create a new document.

2   Type the <HTML> and <HEAD> sections of the document:

```
<HTML>
<HEAD>
<TITLE>Product Registration</TITLE>
</HEAD>
```

3   Add **<FRAMESET ROWS="60, *">** to start the frame set. The top frame, which is set to 60 pixels, contains the title of the Product Registration form. The bottom frame takes up the remainder of the screen and contains the form itself.

4 Add the following two <FRAME> tags. The first <FRAME> tag opens an HTML file named TopFrame.html, which contains the form title. The second frame opens an HTML file named CustomerInfo.html, which contains the first form. The window containing TopFrame.html is named *topframe*, and the bottom window containing CustomerInfo.html is named *bottomframe*.

```
<FRAME SRC="TopFrame.html" NAME="topframe" SCROLLING=no>
<FRAME SRC="CustomerInfo.html" NAME="bottomframe">
```

5 Type the following lines to close the <FRAMESET> and <HTML> tags:

```
</FRAMESET>
</HTML>
```

6 Save the file as **ProductRegistration.html** in the **Tutorial.06** folder on your Data Disk.

7 Close **ProductRegistration.html**.

Next you will create the TopFrame.html file, which will appear in the frame named *topframe*.

To create the TopFrame.html file:

1 Create a new document in your text editor or HTML editor.

2 Add the following tags to create the simple HTML file containing the heading for the form:

```
<HTML>
<BODY>
<H1>Product Registration</H1>
</BODY>
</HTML>
```

3 Save the file as **TopFrame.html** in the **Tutorial.06** folder on your Data Disk.

4 Close **TopFrame.html**.

Finally, you will create the CustomerInfo.html file that contains the form tags for the Product Registration document.

To create the CustomerInfo.html file:

1 Create a new document in your text editor or HTML editor.

2 Type the <HTML>, Head, and <BODY> tags of the document:

```
<HTML>
<HEAD>
<TITLE>Customer Information</TITLE>
</HEAD>
<BODY>
```

3 Type **<H3>Customer Information</H3>** as a subtitle for the Product Registration document.

4 Add the following two tags to create the form section. Throughout the following sections of this tutorial, you will add form elements between these tags.

```
<FORM NAME="customerInfo">
</FORM>
```

> Since you will not actually be submitting this form to a CGI script, the <FORM> tag does not include the ACTION, METHOD, and ENCTYPE attributes.

5 Add the following code to close the <BODY> and <HTML> tags:

```
</BODY>
</HTML>
```

6 Save the file as **CustomerInfo.html** in the **Tutorial.06** folder on your Data Disk. Do not open the CustomerInfo.html file in a Web browser, since it does not yet contain any form elements.

Form Elements: An Overview

There are three tags used within the <FORM>...</FORM> tag pair to create form elements: <INPUT>, <SELECT>, and <TEXTAREA>. The <INPUT> tag, as you know, is used to create input fields that users interact with. The <SELECT> tag displays choices in a drop-down menu or scrolling list known as a selection list. The <TEXTAREA> tag is used to create a text field in which users can enter multiple lines of information. Any form element into which a user can enter data, such as a text box, or that a user can select or change, such as a radio button, is called a **field**.

The <INPUT>, <TEXTAREA>, and <SELECT> tags can include NAME and VALUE attributes. The NAME attribute defines a name for a tag, and the VALUE attribute defines a default value. When you submit a form to a CGI script, the form data is submitted in name=value tag pairs, based on the NAME and VALUE attributes of each tag. For example, if you have a text <INPUT> field created with the statement <INPUT TYPE="text" NAME="company_info" VALUE="ABC Corp.">, a name=value tag pair of *company_info=ABC Corp.* will be sent to a CGI script (unless the default value is changed to something else). If you intend to submit your form to a CGI script, you must include a NAME attribute for each <INPUT>, <TEXTAREA>, and <SELECT> tag. You are not required to include a VALUE attribute or enter a value into a field before the form data is submitted, since a value of null or empty is legal. However, it is a good idea to validate form data using JavaScript before the data is submitted to a CGI script. To validate the data using JavaScript, you need to specify a value for the VALUE attribute.

 tip

You will learn how to validate form data using JavaScript in Section B.

Input Fields

The <INPUT> tag is used to create **input fields** that use different types of interface elements to gather information. Attributes of the <INPUT> tag include ALIGN, CHECKED, MAXLENGTH, NAME, SIZE, TYPE, VALUE, and SRC. The TYPE attribute determines the type of element to be rendered and is a required attribute. Valid values for the TYPE attribute are text, password, radio, checkbox, reset, button, submit, image, and hidden. Figure 6-12 lists common attributes of the <INPUT> tag.

Attribute	Description
ALIGN	Specifies the alignment of an image created with the TYPE attribute. Valid values are ABSBOTTOM, ABSMIDDLE, BASELINE, BOTTOM, LEFT, MIDDLE, RIGHT, TEXTTOP, and TOP
CHECKED	Determines whether or not a radio button or a check box is selected
MAXLENGTH	Sets the maximum number of characters that can be entered into a field
NAME	Designates a name for the element; part of the name=value tag pair that is used to submit data to a CGI script
SIZE	Accepts an integer value that determines how many characters wide a text field is
SRC	Specifies the URL of an image
TYPE	Specifies the type of element to be rendered; TYPE is a required attribute. Valid values are text, password, radio, checkbox, reset, button, submit, image, and hidden
VALUE	Sets an initial value in a field or a label for buttons; part of the name=value tag pair that is used to submit data to a CGI script

Figure 6-12: Common attributes of the <INPUT> tag

Text Boxes

An <INPUT> tag with a type of *text* (<INPUT TYPE="text">) creates a simple text box that accepts a single line of text. You can include the NAME, VALUE, MAXLENGTH, and SIZE attributes with the <INPUT TYPE="text"> tag. The following tags create the text boxes shown in Figure 6-13:

```
<FORM ACTION="http://example_url/cgi-bin/cgi_program"
    METHOD="post" NAME="exampleForm">
Name<BR>
<INPUT TYPE="text" NAME="name"
    VALUE="The White House" SIZE=50><BR>
Address<BR>
<INPUT TYPE="text" NAME="address"
    VALUE="1600 Pennsylvania Ave." SIZE=50><BR>
City, State, Zip<BR>
<INPUT TYPE="text" NAME="city"
    VALUE="Washington" SIZE=38>
<INPUT TYPE="text" NAME="state"
    VALUE="DC" SIZE=2 MAXLENGTH=2>
<INPUT TYPE="text" NAME="zip"
    VALUE="20500" SIZE=5 MAXLENGTH=5>
</FORM>
```

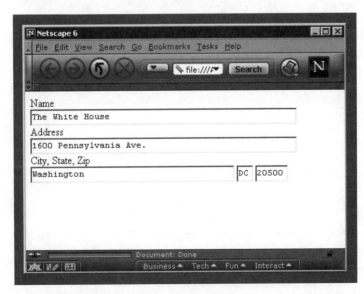

Figure 6-13: Output of several text <INPUT> tags

When you include the VALUE attribute in a text <INPUT> tag, the specified text is used as the default value when the form first loads, as shown in Figure 6-13.

Next you will add the first few text <INPUT> tags to the CustomerInfo.html file.

To add text <INPUT> tags to the CustomerInfo.html file:

1 Return to the **CustomerInfo.html file** in your text editor or HTML editor.

2 Within the <FORM>...</FORM> tag pair, add the following text <INPUT> tags, which gather a customer's name, address, city, state, zip, and e-mail address.

```
<P>Name<BR>
<INPUT TYPE="text" NAME="name" SIZE=50></P>
<P>Address<BR>
<INPUT TYPE="text" NAME="address" SIZE=50></P>
<P>City, State, Zip<BR>
<INPUT TYPE="text" NAME="city" SIZE=38>
<INPUT TYPE="text" NAME="state" SIZE=2 MAXLENGTH=2>
<INPUT TYPE="text" NAME="zip" SIZE=5 MAXLENGTH=5></P>
<P>E-Mail<BR>
<INPUT TYPE="text" NAME="email" SIZE=50></P>
```

3 Save and close the **CustomerInfo.html** document, then open **ProductRegistration.html** in your Web browser. The text <INPUT> fields in your file should resemble Figure 6-14.

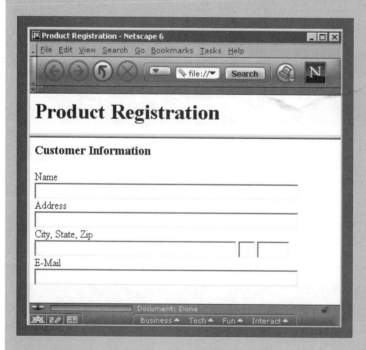

Figure 6-14: Product Registration program after adding text <INPUT> fields

4   Close the Web browser window.

Password Boxes

An <INPUT> tag with a type of *password* (<INPUT TYPE="password">) is similar to an <INPUT> tag with a type of text. However, each character that a user types in a password box appears as an asterisk to hide it from anyone who may be looking over the user's shoulder. You can include the NAME, VALUE, MAXLENGTH, and SIZE attributes with the <INPUT TYPE="password"> tag. The following code creates a password box with a maximum length of eight characters:

```
<FORM ACTION="http://exampleurl/cgi-bin/cgi_program"
     METHOD="post" NAME="exampleForm">
Please enter a password of 8 characters or less:<BR>
<INPUT TYPE="password" NAME="password" MAXLENGTH=8>
</FORM>
```

Next you will add a password <INPUT> tag to the CustomerInfo.html file that prompts users to enter a password that they will use when they call technical support.

To add a password <INPUT> tag to the CustomerInfo.html file:

1   Return to the **CustomerInfo.html file** in your text editor or HTML editor.

2   After the last text <INPUT> tag, add the following lines for the password <INPUT> tag, which prompts users for a password:

```
<P>Enter a password, which you will need when you call
technical support<BR>
<INPUT TYPE="password" NAME="password" SIZE=50></P>
```

3   Save and close the **CustomerInfo.html** document, then open **ProductRegistration.html** in your Web browser. Test the password field to see if the password you enter appears as asterisks. The password <INPUT> field in your file should resemble Figure 6-15.

4   Close the Web browser window.

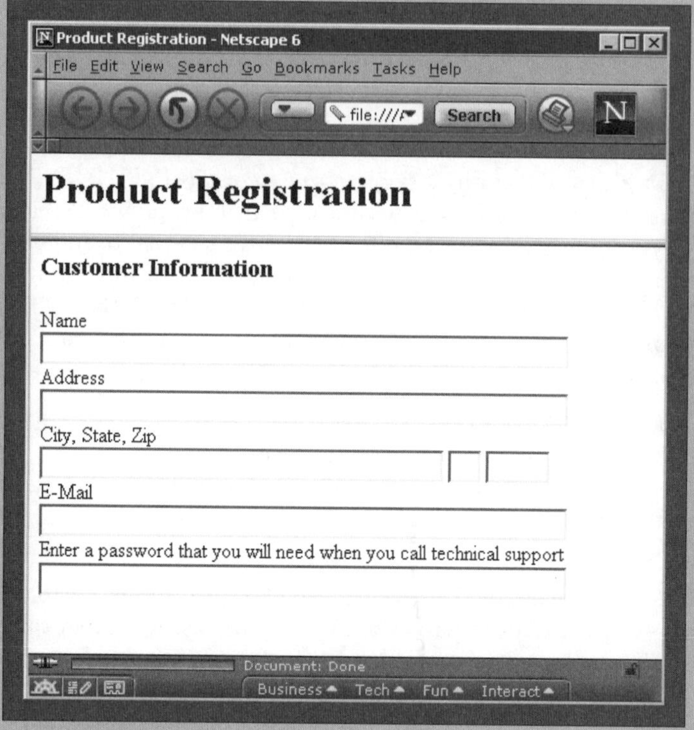

Figure 6-15: Product Registration program after adding a password <INPUT> field

Radio Buttons

An <INPUT> tag with a type of radio (<INPUT TYPE="radio">) is used to create a group of radio buttons from which you can select only one value. To create a group of radio buttons, all radio buttons in the group must have the same NAME attribute. Each radio button requires a VALUE attribute. Only one checked radio button in a group creates a name=value pair when a form is submitted to a CGI script. You can also include the CHECKED attribute in a radio <INPUT> tag to select an initial value for a group of radio buttons. If the CHECKED attribute is not included in any of the <INPUT TYPE="radio"> tags in a radio button group, then none of the buttons in the group are selected when the form loads. The following code creates a group of five radio buttons. Since the Rock radio button includes the CHECKED ATTRIBUTE, it will be selected when the form first loads.

```
<FORM ACTION="http://exampleurl/cgi-bin/cgi_program"
    METHOD="post" NAME="exampleForm">
```

```
Please select your favorite type of music:<BR>
<INPUT TYPE="radio" NAME="music"
     VALUE="jazz">Jazz<BR>
<INPUT TYPE="radio" NAME="music"
     VALUE="classical">Classical<BR>
<INPUT TYPE="radio" NAME="music"
     VALUE="country">Country<BR>
<INPUT TYPE="radio" NAME="music"
     VALUE="rock" CHECKED>Rock<BR>
<INPUT TYPE="radio" NAME="music"
     VALUE="r&b">Rhythm and Blues<BR>
</FORM>
```

Next you will add to the CustomerInfo.html file radio button <INPUT> tags that prompt users for the type of computer platform they are using.

To add radio <INPUT> tags to the CustomerInfo.html file:

1 Return to the **CustomerInfo.html file** in your text editor or HTML editor.

2 After the password <INPUT> field, add the following radio <INPUT> tags. Users select one radio button to indicate the type of computer platform they use. Notice that each radio button is given the same NAME attribute of *platform*.

```
<P>What platform do you use?<BR>
<INPUT TYPE="radio" NAME="platform"
     VALUE="win2K">Windows 2000
<INPUT TYPE="radio" NAME="platform"
     VALUE="win95-98">Windows 95/98
<INPUT TYPE="radio" NAME="platform"
     VALUE="winnt">Windows NT
<INPUT TYPE="radio" NAME="platform"
     VALUE="winme">Windows ME
<INPUT TYPE="radio" NAME="platform"
     VALUE="unix">UNIX
<INPUT TYPE="radio" NAME="platform"
     VALUE="mac">Macintosh</P>
```

3 Save and close the **CustomerInfo.html** document, then open **ProductRegistration.html** in your Web browser. The radio button <INPUT> fields in your file should resemble Figure 6-16.

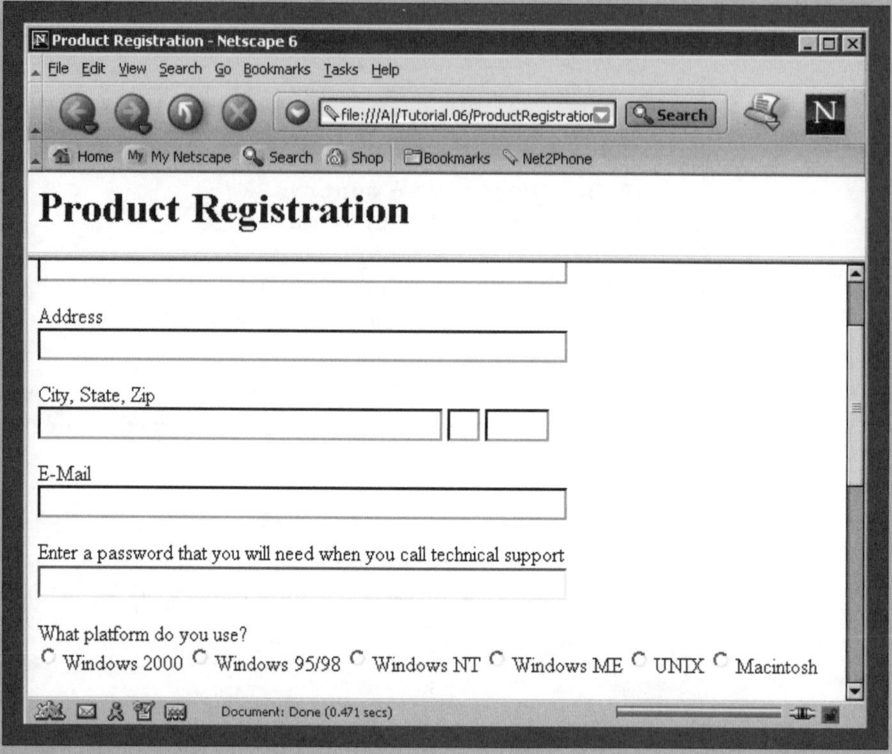

Figure 6-16: Product Registration program after adding radio <INPUT> fields

4   Close the Web browser window.

Check Boxes

An <INPUT> tag with a type of *checkbox* (<INPUT TYPE="checkbox">) creates a box that can be set to yes (checked) or no (unchecked). You use check boxes when you want users to select whether or not to include a certain item or to allow users to select multiple values from a list of items. Include the CHECKED attribute in a checkbox <INPUT> tag to set the initial value of a check box to *yes*. You can also include the NAME and VALUE attributes with the checkbox <INPUT> tag. If a check box is selected (checked) when a form is submitted, then the check box name=value pair is included in the form data. If a check box is not selected, a name=value pair will not be included in the data submitted from the form.

The following code creates several check boxes. Note that the JavaScript check box will be checked when the form first loads since it includes the CHECKED attribute.

```
<FORM ACTION="http://example_url/cgi-bin/cgi_program"
      METHOD="post" NAME="exampleForm">
<H3>Which programming languages do you know?</H3>
<INPUT TYPE="checkbox" NAME="prog_languages"
      VALUE="JavaScript"
      CHECKED>JavaScript<BR>
<INPUT TYPE="checkbox" NAME="prog_languages"
      VALUE="Java">Java<BR>
<INPUT TYPE="checkbox" NAME="prog_languages"
      VALUE="Visual Basic">
Visual Basic<BR>
<INPUT TYPE="checkbox" NAME="prog_languages"
      VALUE="Visual C++">
Visual C++<BR>
</FORM>
```

Like radio buttons, you can group check boxes by giving each check box the same NAME value, although each check box can have a different value. Unlike radio buttons, users can select as many check boxes in a group as they like. When multiple check boxes on a form share the same name, then multiple name=value pairs, each using the same name, are submitted to the CGI script. In the preceding example, if the JavaScript and Java check boxes are selected, then two name=value pairs, prog_languages=JavaScript and prog_languages=Java, are submitted. Note that you are not required to group check boxes with the same NAME attribute. Although a common group name helps to identify and manage groups of check boxes, it is often easier to keep track of individual values when each check box has a unique NAME attribute.

Next you will add to the CustomerInfo.html file checkbox <INPUT> tags that prompt users for the types of software they use. Later in this tutorial, you will copy each check box (and all other form fields) to corresponding hidden fields on another form. In order to make it easier to keep track of individual check box values as they are copied to the hidden form fields, each checkbox will include a unique NAME value.

To add checkbox <INPUT> tags to the CustomerInfo.html file:

1 Return to the **CustomerInfo.html file** in your text editor or HTML editor.

2 After the last radio <INPUT> field, add the following checkbox <INPUT> tags that prompt users for the types of software they use.

```
<P>What types of software do you use? (check all
    that apply)<BR>
<INPUT TYPE="checkbox" NAME="wp" VALUE="wp">
    Word Processing<BR>
<INPUT TYPE="checkbox" NAME="ss" VALUE="ss">
    Spreadsheets<BR>
<INPUT TYPE="checkbox" NAME="db" VALUE="db">
    Database<BR>
<INPUT TYPE="checkbox" NAME="gr" VALUE="gr">
    Graphics/CAD<BR>
<INPUT TYPE="checkbox" NAME="pr" VALUE="pr">
    Programming</P>
```

3 Save and close the **CustomerInfo.html** document, then open the **ProductRegistration.html** file in your Web browser. The checkbox <INPUT> fields in your file should resemble those in Figure 6-17.

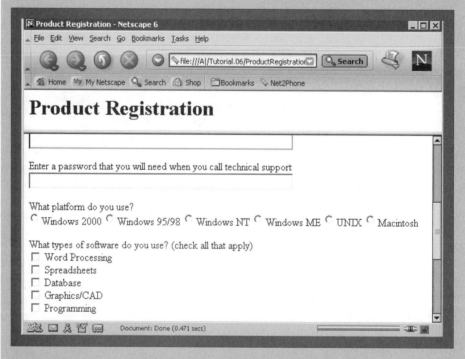

Figure 6-17: Product Registration program after adding checkbox <INPUT> fields

4 Close the Web browser window.

Reset Buttons

An <INPUT> tag with a type of *reset* (<INPUT TYPE="reset">) clears all form entries and resets each form element to its initial value specified by the VALUE attribute. Although you can include the NAME attribute for a reset button if you want to refer to it in JavaScript code, it is not required since reset buttons are never submitted to a CGI script as part of the form data. If you do not include a VALUE attribute, then the default label of the reset button, *Reset*, appears.

The following code creates a form with a reset button. Figure 6-18 shows the resulting Web page after entering some data.

```
<H3>Billing Information</H3>
<FORM ACTION="http://exampleurl/cgi-bin/cgi_program"
     METHOD="post" NAME="exampleForm">
<B>Name</B><BR>
<INPUT TYPE="text" NAME="name" SIZE=50><BR>
<B>Address</B><BR>
<INPUT TYPE="text" NAME="address" SIZE=50><BR>
<B>City, State, Zip</B><BR>
<INPUT TYPE="text" NAME="city" SIZE=38>
<INPUT TYPE="text" NAME="state" SIZE=2>
<INPUT TYPE="text" NAME="zip" SIZE=5 MAXLENGTH=5><BR>
<B>Credit Card</B><BR>
<INPUT TYPE="radio" NAME="creditcard" CHECKED>VISA
<INPUT TYPE="radio" NAME="creditcard">MasterCard
<INPUT TYPE="radio" NAME="creditcard">
     American Express<BR>
<INPUT TYPE="radio" NAME="creditcard">Discover
<INPUT TYPE="radio" NAME="creditcard">
     Diners Club<BR>
<B>Credit Card Number</B><BR>
<INPUT TYPE="text" NAME="cc#"
     VALUE="xxxx xxxxxx xxxxx" SIZE=50><BR>
<B>Expiration Date</B><BR>
<P><INPUT TYPE="text" NAME="expdate"
     VALUE="5/1/03" SIZE=50></P>
<INPUT TYPE="reset">
</FORM>
```

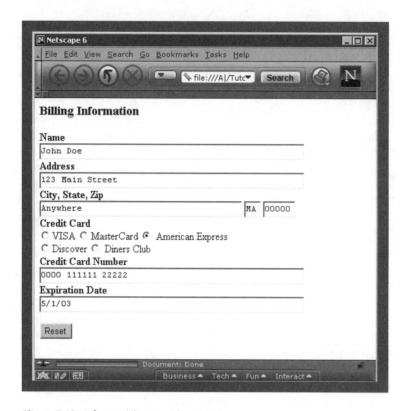

Figure 6-18: A form with a reset button

If you click the reset button in the form shown in Figure 6-18, then the contents of each field clear or reset to their default values, as shown in Figure 6-19.

The width of a button created with the reset <INPUT> tag depends on the number of characters in its VALUE attribute.

Next you will add a reset <INPUT> tag to the CustomerInfo.html file.

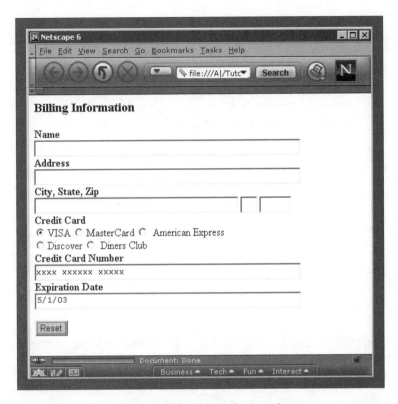

Figure 6-19: Output of a form after clicking the Reset button

---

To add a reset <INPUT> tag to the CustomerInfo.html file:

1 Return to the **CustomerInfo.html file** in your text editor or HTML editor.

2 After the last checkbox <INPUT> field, add **<P><INPUT TYPE="reset"></P>**.

3 Save and close the **CustomerInfo.html** document, then open the **ProductRegistration.html** file in your Web browser. The reset <INPUT> field in your document should resemble that in Figure 6-20.

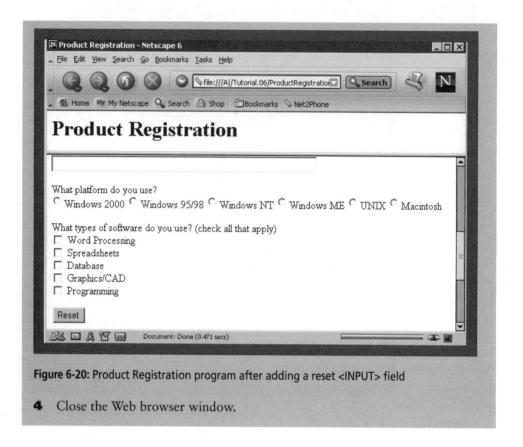

Figure 6-20: Product Registration program after adding a reset <INPUT> field

4   Close the Web browser window.

Command Buttons

An <INPUT> tag with a type of *button* (<INPUT TYPE="button">) creates a command button similar to the OK and Cancel buttons you see in dialog boxes. Command buttons are also similar to submit and reset buttons. However, command buttons do not submit form data to a CGI script as submit buttons do, nor do they clear the data entered into form fields as do reset buttons. Instead, command buttons use an onClick event handler to execute JavaScript code that performs some type of function, such as a calculation. Although a command button does not require an event handler, it is essentially useless without one, since its main purpose is to execute JavaScript code. You are not required to include the NAME and VALUE attributes, since a user cannot change the value of a command button. If you include the NAME and VALUE attributes, then the default value set with the VALUE attribute is transmitted to a CGI script along with the rest of the form data. The following code creates a simple command button:

```
<INPUT TYPE="button" NAME="command_button"
    VALUE="Click Here"
    onClick="alert('You Clicked a Command Button');">
```

The code for the <INPUT> tag creates a button with a value of *Click Here* and a name of *command_button*. The <INPUT> tag onClick event handler in the preceding example displays an alert dialog box containing the text *You Clicked a Command Button.*

tip

••

The width of a button created with the <INPUT TYPE="button"> tag is based on the number of characters in its VALUE attribute.

••

Next you will add a command button to the CustomerInfo.html file. The button will contain an onClick event handler that calls a function that opens a second page of the Product Registration form. The second page is another HTML document named ProductInfo.html.

To add a command button <INPUT> tag to the CustomerInfo.html file that opens a second page of the Product Registration form:

1 Open the **CustomerInfo.html file** in your text editor or HTML editor.

2 Just before the closing </HEAD> tag, create the following <SCRIPT>... </SCRIPT> tag pair, along with a function that uses the HREF property of the Location object to replace the CustomerInfo.html file with an HTML document named ProductInfo.html.

```
<SCRIPT LANGUAGE="JavaScript">
<!-- HIDE FROM INCOMPATIBLE BROWSERS
function nextForm() {
     location.href="ProductInfo.html";
}
// STOP HIDING FROM INCOMPATIBLE BROWSERS -->
</SCRIPT>
```

3 Before the closing </P> tag following the reset <INPUT> field in the body of the HTML document, add the following code to create a button <INPUT> tag named *Next*. The button onClick event calls the nextForm() function you added in Step 2.

```
<INPUT TYPE="button" NAME="next" VALUE=" Next "
     onClick="nextForm()">
```

4 Save and close the **CustomerInfo.html** document.

Next you will create the ProductInfo.html file that opens when a user clicks the Next button.

To create the ProductInfo.html file:

1   Create a new document in your text editor or HTML editor.

2   Type the following <HTML>, <HEAD>, and <BODY> tags to start the ProductInfo.html file:

```
<HTML>
<HEAD>
<TITLE>Product Information</TITLE>
</HEAD>
<BODY>
```

3   Create a heading for the document, using an <H3>...</H3> tag pair:

```
<H3>Product Information</H3>
```

4   Type the following form section, which contains a text box for the product serial number, a text box for the date of purchase, a radio button group to select how the product was purchased, and a reset button.

```
<FORM NAME="productInfo">
<P><B>Serial Number</B><BR>
<INPUT TYPE="text" NAME="serial" SIZE=50></P>
<P><B>Date Purchased</B><BR>
<INPUT TYPE="text" NAME="date" SIZE=50></P>
<P><B>Where did you purchase this product?</B><BR>
<INPUT TYPE="radio" NAME="where"
     VALUE="retail">Retail Store<BR>
<INPUT TYPE="radio" NAME="where"
     VALUE="catalog_mail">Catalog/Mail Order<BR>
<INPUT TYPE="radio" NAME="where"
     VALUE="internet">Internet Transaction<BR>
<INPUT TYPE="radio" NAME="where"
     VALUE="other">Other</P>
<P><INPUT TYPE="reset"></P>
```

5   Type the closing </FORM>, </BODY>, and </HTML> tags:

```
</FORM>
</BODY>
</HTML>
```

6   Save the file as **ProductInfo.html** in the **Tutorial.06** folder on your Data Disk. Close the **ProductInfo.html** file. Now open the **ProductRegistration.html** file in your Web browser and click the **Next** button. The bottom frame of the document should open the ProductInfo.html file, as shown in Figure 6-21.

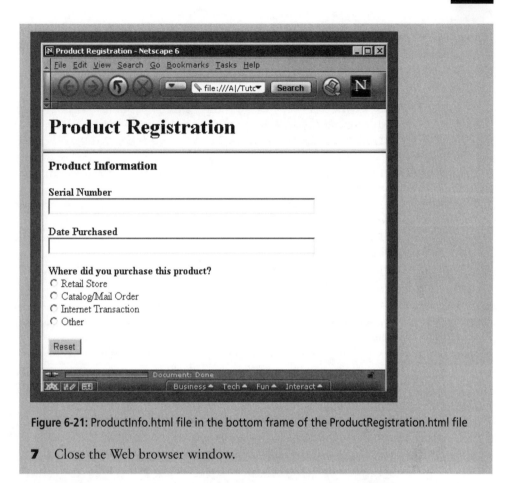

Figure 6-21: ProductInfo.html file in the bottom frame of the ProductRegistration.html file

7   Close the Web browser window.

Submit Buttons

An <INPUT> tag with a type of *submit* (<INPUT TYPE="submit">) creates a button that submits the form to a CGI script on a server. The ACTION attribute of the <FORM> tag that creates the form determines to what URL the form is submitted. You can include the NAME and VALUE attributes with the submit <INPUT> tag. If you do not include a VALUE attribute, then the default label of the submit button, *Submit Query*, appears.

The following code creates a Web page with a submit button:

```
<H1>Video of the Month Club</H1>
<H3>Select the types of movies you like to see and
click the Join button.<BR>
```

```
A new movie will be sent to you every month.<H3>
<FORM ACTION="http://exampleurl/cgi-bin/cgi_program"
     METHOD="post" NAME="exampleForm">
<INPUT TYPE="checkbox" NAME="genre" VALUE="action">
Action
<P><INPUT TYPE="checkbox" NAME="genre" VALUE="adventure">
Adventure<BR>
<INPUT TYPE="checkbox" NAME="genre" VALUE="comedy">
Comedy
<INPUT TYPE="checkbox" NAME="genre" VALUE="drama">
Drama<BR>
<INPUT TYPE="checkbox" NAME="genre" VALUE="sci_fi">
Science Fiction
<INPUT TYPE="checkbox" NAME="genre" VALUE="western">
Westerns</P>
<INPUT TYPE="submit" NAME="submit_button" VALUE="Join">
</FORM>
```

 tip

• •

The width of a button created with the submit <INPUT> tag is based on the number of characters in its VALUE attribute.

• •

Next you will add a submit <INPUT> tag to the ProductInfo.html file.

To add a submit <INPUT> tag to the ProductInfo.html file:

1   Open the **ProductInfo.html file** in your text editor or HTML editor.

2   Before the closing </P> tag following the reset <INPUT> field, add **<INPUT TYPE="submit">**. Do not add a VALUE attribute because the default value of *Submit Query* will work fine in this case.

3   Save and close the **ProductInfo.html** document, then open the **ProductRegistration.html** file in your Web browser. Click the **Next** button to display the ProductInfo.html file in the bottom frame of the Web page. The submit button in your file should resemble the submit button shown in Figure 6-22. Nothing will actually happen if you click the submit button, since the <FORM> tag in the ProductInfo.html file does not include an ACTION attribute.

4   Close the Web browser window.

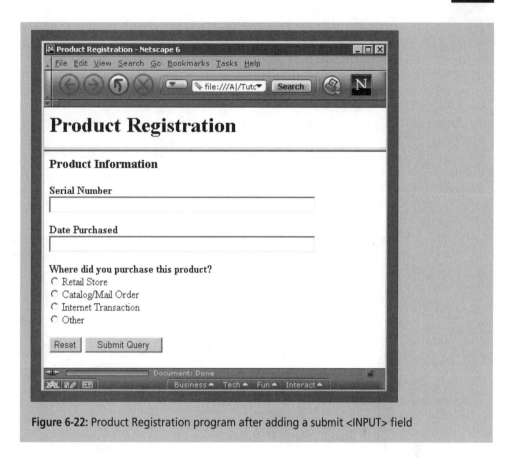

Figure 6-22: Product Registration program after adding a submit <INPUT> field

Image Submit Buttons

An <INPUT> tag with a type of *image* (<INPUT TYPE="image">) creates a button that displays a graphical image and submits a form to a CGI script on a server. The image <INPUT> tag performs exactly the same function as the submit <INPUT> tag. You include the SRC attribute to specify the image to display on the button. You can also include the NAME, VALUE, and ALIGN attributes with the image <INPUT> tag. The following code creates the Web page with an image <INPUT> tag, as shown in Figure 6-23:

```
<H1>Video of the Month Club</H1>
<H3>Select the types of movies you like to see and
click the videocassette image.<BR>
A new movie will be sent to you every month.</H3>
<FORM ACTION="http://exampleurl/cgi-bin/cgi_program"
    METHOD="post" NAME="exampleForm">
<P><INPUT TYPE="checkbox" NAME="genre" VALUE="action">
Action
```

```
<INPUT TYPE="checkbox" NAME="genre" VALUE="adventure">
Adventure<BR>
<INPUT TYPE="checkbox" NAME="genre" VALUE="comedy">
Comedy
<INPUT TYPE="checkbox" NAME="genre" VALUE="drama">
Drama<BR>
<INPUT TYPE="checkbox" NAME="genre" VALUE="sci_fi">
Science Fiction
<INPUT TYPE="checkbox" NAME="genre" VALUE="western">
Westerns</P>
<INPUT TYPE="image" SRC="videocassette.jpg">
</FORM>
```

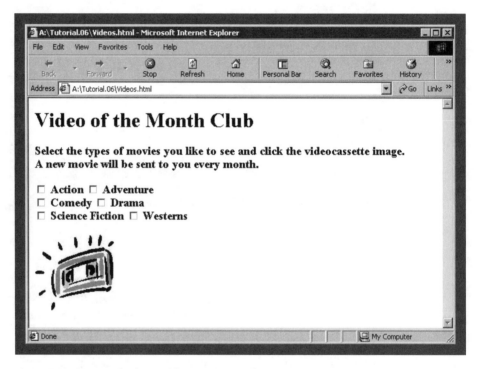

Figure 6-23: Output of a form with an image <INPUT> tag

Image <INPUT> tags are also used to create server-side image maps, which are similar to the client-side North America image map you created in Tutorial 2. The primary difference between server-side and client-side image maps is that with server-side image maps, most of the work is done on the server; for client-side image maps, most of the work is done in a Web browser.

Selection Lists

The **<SELECT>...</SELECT> tag pair** creates a **selection list** that presents users with fixed lists of values from which to choose. The selection list can appear as an actual list of choices or as a drop-down menu. Depending on the number of items in the list, a selection list can also include a scroll bar. Figure 6-24 lists frequently used attributes of the <SELECT> tag.

Attribute	Description
MULTIPLE	Specifies whether a user can select more than one item from the list
NAME	Designates a name for the selection list
SIZE	Determines how many lines of the selection list appear. If this attribute is excluded or set to one, then the selection list is a drop-down style menu

Figure 6-24: Attributes of the <SELECT> tag

<OPTION> tags, placed between the selection list's <SELECT>...</SELECT> tag pair, specify the items that appear in a selection list. Figure 6-25 lists frequently used attributes of the <OPTION> tag.

Attribute	Description
LABEL	Designates alternate text to display in the selection list for an individual option
SELECTED	An optional attribute that determines if an item is initially selected in the selection list when the form first loads
VALUE	The value submitted to a CGI script

Figure 6-25: Attributes of the <OPTION> tag

The following code creates two selection lists:

```
<FORM ACTION="http://exampleurl/cgi-bin/cgi_program"
    METHOD="post" NAME="exampleForm">
```

```
<P>This selection list displays a drop-down-style menu:<BR>
<SELECT NAME="music">
<OPTION VALUE="jazz">Jazz
<OPTION VALUE="classical">Classical
<OPTION VALUE="country">Country
<OPTION VALUE="rock" SELECTED>Rock
<OPTION VALUE="r&b">Rhythm and Blues
</SELECT></P>
<P>This selection list includes 5 items:<BR>
<SELECT NAME="music" SIZE=5>
<OPTION VALUE="jazz">Jazz
<OPTION VALUE="classical" SELECTED>Classical
<OPTION VALUE="country">Country
<OPTION VALUE="rock">Rock
<OPTION VALUE="r&b">Rhythm and Blues
</SELECT></P>
</FORM>
```

Next you will add to the CustomerInfo.html file a selection list that determines if the product is used at work, at school, at home, or in a home office.

To add a selection list to the CustomerInfo.html file:

1 Open the **CustomerInfo.html file** in your text editor or HTML editor.

2 Just above the <INPUT> tag for the reset button, add the following tags to create the selection list that determines if the product is used at work, at school, at home, or in a home office:

```
<P>Where will you use this product?
<SELECT NAME="location">
    <OPTION VALUE="work">Work
    <OPTION VALUE="school">School
    <OPTION VALUE="home">Home
    <OPTION VALUE="home_office">Home Office
</SELECT></P>
```

3 Save and close the **CustomerInfo.html** document, then open the **ProductRegistration.html** file in your Web browser. The selection list in your browser window should resemble that in Figure 6-26.

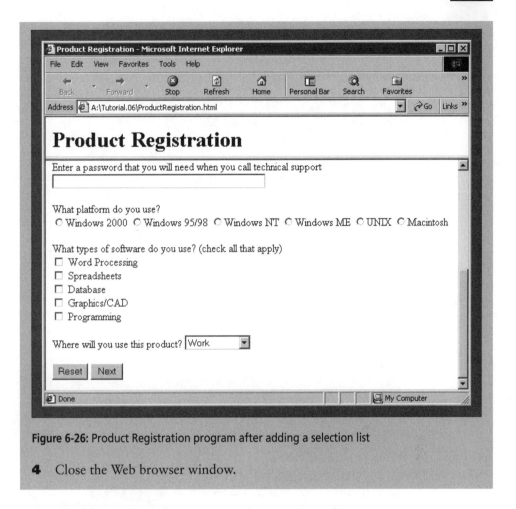

Figure 6-26: Product Registration program after adding a selection list

4   Close the Web browser window.

Multiline Text Fields

The <TEXTAREA> tag is used to create a field in which users can enter multiple lines of information. Fields created with the <TEXTAREA>...</TEXTAREA> tag pair are known as **multiline text fields** or **text areas**. Figure 6-27 lists frequently used attributes of the <TEXTAREA> tag:

Attribute	Description
NAME	Designates a name for the text area
COL	Specifies the number of columns to be displayed in the text area
ROWS	Specifies the number of rows to be displayed in the text area

Figure 6-27: Attributes of the <TEXTAREA> tag

The only items you place between the <TEXTAREA>...</TEXTAREA> tags are default text and characters you want to display in the text area when the form loads. Any characters placed between the <TEXTAREA>...</TEXTAREA> tags, including tab marks and paragraph returns, will be included in a text area. For example, a line of text that is indented with two tabs and placed between the <TEXTAREA>...</TEXTAREA> tags will be indented with two tabs when it appears in the text area on the Web page.

The following tags create a text area consisting of 50 columns and 10 rows, with the default text of *Enter additional information here.*

```
<FORM ACTION="http://exampleurl/cgi-bin/cgi_program"
    METHOD="post" NAME="exampleForm">
Comments<BR>
<TEXTAREA COLS=50 ROWS=10>
Enter additional information here
</TEXTAREA>
</FORM>
```

Next you will add to the CustomerInfo.html file a multiline text area in which users can type additional comments.

To add a multiline text area to the CustomerInfo.html file:

1 Open the **CustomerInfo.html file** in your text editor or HTML editor.

2 Just above the <INPUT> tag for the reset button, press **Enter** to start a new line. Then add the following tags to create the multiline text area for additional comments:

```
<P>Comments<BR>
<TEXTAREA NAME="comments" COLS=40 ROWS=5>
Enter any additional comments here
</TEXTAREA></P>
```

3 Save the **CustomerInfo.html** document, then open the **ProductRegistration.html** file in your Web browser. The multiline text area in your Product Registration document should resemble that in Figure 6-28.

4 Close the Web browser window, and then close your text editor or HTML editor.

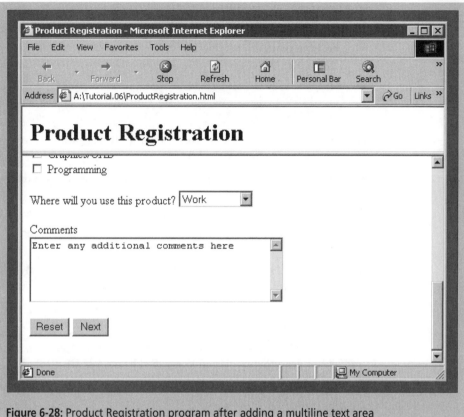

Figure 6-28: Product Registration program after adding a multiline text area

SUMMARY

- Common Gateway Interface, or CGI, is a simple protocol used to communicate between Web pages and Web server-based applications.

- An environment variable is part of an operating system, not just part of a function or a program, as are JavaScript variables.

- A Web server-based application that processes CGI environment variables is called a CGI script (or CGI program) and can be designed to perform many different functions.

- CGI scripts are often placed within a bin or cgi-bin directory on a Web server and have an extension of .cgi.

- The <FORM>...</FORM> tag pair designates a form within an HTML document and contains all text and tags that make up a form.

- Three tags used within the <FORM>...</FORM> tag pair are <INPUT>, <SELECT>, and <TEXTAREA>.

- Any form element into which a user can enter data, such as a text box, or that a user can select or change, such as a radio button, is called a field.

- When you submit a form to a CGI script, the form data is submitted in name=value tag pairs, based on the NAME and VALUE attributes of the <INPUT>, <TEXTAREA>, and <SELECT> tags.

- The <INPUT> tag is used to create input fields that gather information, using different types of user interface elements.

- An <INPUT> tag with a type of text creates a simple text box that accepts a single line of text.

- An <INPUT> tag with a type of password displays each character a user types as an asterisk, to hide the password from anyone who may be looking over the user's shoulder.

- An <INPUT> tag with a type of radio creates a group of radio buttons from which a user can select only one value.

- An <INPUT> tag with a type of checkbox creates a box that can be set to yes (checked) or no (unchecked).

- An <INPUT> tag with a type of reset clears all of the entries on a form and resets each form element to its initial value specified by the VALUE attribute.

- An <INPUT> tag with a type of button creates a command button similar to the OK and Cancel buttons you see in dialog boxes.

- An <INPUT> tag with a type of submit creates a button that displays text, such as Submit Query, and submits the form to a CGI script on the server.

- An <INPUT> tag with a type of image creates a button that displays a graphical image and submits the form to a CGI script on the server.

- The <SELECT>...</SELECT> tag pair creates a selection list that presents users with fixed lists of values from which to choose.

- The <TEXTAREA> tag is used to create a field in which users can enter multiple lines of information. Fields created with the <TEXTAREA>...</TEXTAREA> tag pair are known as multiline text fields or text areas.

 # Q U E S T I O N S

1. Which of the following items are not created with forms?
   a. guest books
   b. questionnaires
   c. online order systems
   d. They are all created with forms.

2. CGI is _____.
 a. a high-level programming language similar to Visual C++
 b. a low-level programming language similar to JavaScript
 c. a simple protocol that allows Web pages to communicate with Web server-based programs
 d. a machine language

3. CGI scripts are usually placed _____.
 a. within a *bin* or *cgi-bin* directory on a Web server
 b. in the local operating system utility folder
 c. in the folder where Netscape or Internet Explorer is installed
 d. within a <SCRIPT>...</SCRIPT> tag pair

4. How many forms can be created in an HTML document?
 a. 1
 b. 2
 c. as many as necessary
 d. None. Forms are not created in HTML documents.

5. The ACTION attribute of the <FORM> tag _____.
 a. designates a function to execute
 b. creates a button used for starting a program
 c. closes the Web browser window
 d. specifies a URL to which form data will be submitted

6. What is the default submission option for the METHOD attribute of the <FORM> tag?
 a. GET
 b. POST
 c. SEND
 d. SUBMIT

7. What is the default data format for the ENCTYPE attribute of the <FORM> tag?
 a. *application/jpeg/gif*
 b. *cgi.bin*
 c. *application/x-www-form-urlencoded*
 d. *text/plain*

8. How is form data submitted to a CGI script?
 a. in value,name tag pairs
 b. in name=value tag pairs
 c. as values separated by commas
 d. as values separated by paragraph marks

9. The text <INPUT> tag _____.
 a. displays a static label
 b. creates input fields that use different types of interface elements to gather information
 c. creates a simple text box that accepts a single line of text
 d. is a type of scrolling banner used for displaying messages in a Web browser window

10. The SIZE attribute is used with the <INPUT> tag _____.
   a. button
   b. image
   c. text
   d. submit

11. Each character entered into a text box created with a password <INPUT> tag appears _____.
   a. with the ampersand (&) symbol
   b. with the number (#) symbol
   c. as a percentage (%)
   d. as an asterisk (*)

12. Which attribute is used to designate a single button in a radio group as the default?
   a. CHECKED
   b. CHECK
   c. SELECTED
   d. DEFAULT

13. Which of the following statements about check boxes is true?
   a. You can select only one check box in a group at a time.
   b. You can select as many check boxes as necessary.
   c. When you select one check box, all other check boxes in the same group are also selected.
   d. Check boxes are not used for user input.

14. What is the purpose of the reset <INPUT> tag?
   a. to reload the current Web page
   b. to reset the contents of a single form element to its default value
   c. to reset all form elements in the current form to their default values
   d. to close and restart the Web browser

15. What type of <INPUT> tag creates a command button similar to the OK and Cancel buttons found in dialog boxes?
   a. radio
   b. ok_cancel
   c. dialog
   d. button

16. What is the default value of a submit button label?
   a. Submit
   b. Query
   c. Submit Query
   d. Execute

17. Which type of <INPUT> tag can be used to submit form data to a CGI script?
   a. image
   b. radio
   c. checkbox
   d. button

18. The contents of a selection list are determined by which HTML tags?

    a. <SELECT>

    b. <CONTENTS>

    c. <ITEMS>

    d. <OPTION>

19. Which is the correct syntax for creating a text area?

    a. `<TEXT COLS=50 ROWS=10></TEXT>`

    b. `<TEXTAREA COLS=50 ROWS=10></TEXTAREA>`

    c. `<TEXT SIZE=50></TEXT>`

    d. `<TEXTAREA SIZE=50></TEXTAREA>`

E X E R C I S E S

Save all files you create in the Tutorial.06 folder on your Data Disk.

1. Modify the <FORM> tag in the following document so that the form is submitted to a CGI script at the following address: http://www.webadventure.com/register.cgi. Be sure to add the METHOD attribute. (This is a fictitious Web address, so do not try to actually submit the form after you complete the exercise.) Save the HTML document as SendCGI.html.

```
<HTML>
<HEAD>
<TITLE>Send CGI</TITLE>
</HEAD>
<BODY>
<FORM>
<P>First name: <INPUT TYPE="text"
      NAME="first" SIZE=50></P>
<P>Last name: <INPUT TYPE="text"
      NAME="last" SIZE=50></P>
<P>Address: <INPUT TYPE="text"
      NAME="address" SIZE=50></P>
<P>City: <INPUT TYPE="text"
      NAME="city" SIZE=15>
State: <INPUT TYPE="text"
      NAME="state" SIZE=2>
Zip: <INPUT TYPE="text"
      NAME="zip" SIZE=10></P>
<P>E-mail: <INPUT TYPE="text"
      NAME="email" SIZE=50></P>
<P><INPUT TYPE="submit" VALUE="Enroll">
<INPUT TYPE="reset"></P>
</FORM>
</BODY>
</HTML>
```

2. Create the text boxes and password box displayed in Figure 6-29. Save the HTML document as SimpleForm.html.

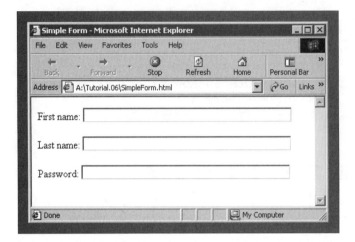

Figure 6-29: SimpleForm.html

3. Some types of surveys or applications ask you for your highest level of education. Using the following choices, create the HTML documents in Exercises 3a through 3d.

- High School
- Associates Degree
- Bachelors Degree
- Graduate Degree

a. Create an HTML document named EducationCheckboxes.html that includes each education level as a check box. Select *Graduate Degree* as the default selection.

b. Create an HTML document named EducationRadio.html that includes each education level as a radio button. Select *High School* as the default selection.

c. Create an HTML document named EducationCommand.html that includes each education level as a command button.

d. Create an HTML document named EducationSelect.html that includes each education level in a selection list. Select *Associates Degree* as the default selection.

4. Create the airline survey shown in Figure 6-30. Save the HTML document as AirlineSurvey.html.

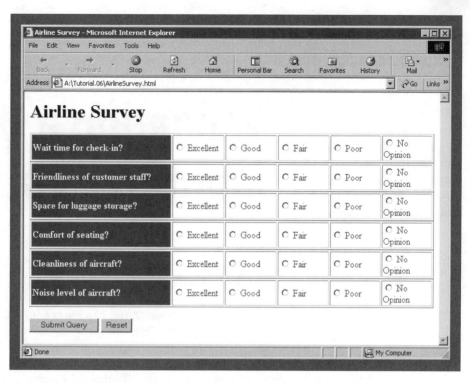

Figure 6-30: AirlineSurvey.html

5. Create a form to be used as a software development bug report. Include fields such as product name and version, type of hardware, operating system, frequency of occurrence, and proposed solutions. Save the HTML document as BugReport.html.

6. Create a form to be used for tracking, documenting, and managing the process of interviewing candidates for professional positions. Include fields such as candidate's name, communication abilities, professional appearance, computer skills, business knowledge, and the interviewer's comments. Save the HTML document as Interview.html.

7. Create a consent form for a school trip. Include fields such as child's name, parent or guardian's signature, and name, address, and telephone number of child's physician. Save the HTML document as ConsentForm.html.

8. Create an online employment application. Include sections such as Personal Information, Education History, and Employment History. Save the HTML document as EmploymentApp.html.

SECTION B
o b j e c t i v e s

In this section you will learn:

■ About hidden form fields

■ About the Form object

■ How to reference forms and form
  elements

■ About form event handlers,
  methods, and properties

■ How to e-mail form data

Validating a User's Input to a Form

Hidden Form Fields

A special type of form element, called a **hidden form field,** allows you to hide information from users. Hidden form fields are created with the <INPUT> tag. A Web browser cannot display hidden form fields, nor can users edit hidden form fields in any way from a Web browser window. Hidden form fields temporarily store information that needs to be sent to a server along with the rest of a form but that a user does not need to see. Examples of information stored in hidden fields include the result of a calculation or some other type of information that your program needs later. You create hidden form fields using the same syntax used for other fields created with the <INPUT> tag: <INPUT TYPE="hidden">. NAME and VALUE are the only attributes that you can include with a hidden form field.

Figure 6-31 contains the form section of the Calculator program you created in Tutorial 3. The program has been modified to store and recall numbers. Figure 6-32 shows the modified calculator in a Web browser. The four new form elements used to add storage functionality to the program are as follows:

```
<INPUT TYPE="button" NAME="mem" VALUE=" M+ "
   onClick="document.Calculator.storedValue.value
      = parseInt(document.Calculator.storedValue.value)
      + parseInt(document.Calculator.Input.value)">
<INPUT TYPE="button" NAME="recall" VALUE=" MRC "
   onClick="update String(
      document.Calculator.stored Value.value)">
<INPUT TYPE="button" NAME="memClear" VALUE=" MC "
   onClick="document.Calculator.storedValue.value=0">
<INPUT TYPE="hidden" NAME="storedValue" VALUE=0>
```

The first new button, named mem, stores the value of the Input text box in the hidden form field named storedValue. Notice that the mem button onClick event uses two calls to the parseInt() function. Form text fields only store data in the form of text strings. For this reason, you must use the built-in parseInt() function to convert text field contents to an integer before you can use it in a JavaScript calculation. (The built-in parseFloat() function performs a similar duty in that it forces text strings to floating-point values that can be used in JavaScript calculations.) If you did not use the parseInt() function in the mem button onClick event, then when you attempted to assign another number to the hidden storedValue field, the new number would be concatenated with the storedValue field current contents, the same as when you combine two text fields. The second new button, named recall, retrieves the information stored in the hidden storedValue field and passes it to the updateString() function. The third new button, named memClear, clears the contents of the hidden storedValue field.

```
<HTML>
<HEAD>
<TITLE>Calculator</TITLE>
<SCRIPT LANGUAGE="JavaScript">
<!-- HIDE FROM INCOMPATIBLE BROWSERS
var inputString = "";
var count = 0;
function updateString(value) {
    inputString += value;
    document.Calculator.Input.value = inputString;
}
// STOP HIDING FROM INCOMPATIBLE BROWSERS -->
</SCRIPT>
</HEAD>
<BODY>
<DIV ALIGN="center">
<FORM NAME="Calculator">
<INPUT TYPE="text" NAME="Input" Size="22"><BR>
<INPUT TYPE="button" NAME="plus" VALUE=" + "
    onClick="updateString(' + ')">
<INPUT TYPE="button" NAME="minus" VALUE=" - "
    onClick="updateString(' - ')">
<INPUT TYPE="button" NAME="times" VALUE=" x "
    onClick="updateString(' * ')">
```

Figure 6-31: Calculator.html with memory functions

```
<INPUT TYPE="button" NAME="div" VALUE=" / "
    onClick="updateString(' / ')">
<INPUT TYPE="button" NAME="mod" VALUE=" MOD "
    onClick="updateString(' % ')"><BR>
<INPUT TYPE="button" NAME="zero" VALUE=" 0 "
    onClick="updateString('0')">
<INPUT TYPE="button" NAME="one" VALUE=" 1 "
    onCLick="updateString('1')">
<INPUT TYPE="button" NAME="two" VALUE=" 2 "
    onCLick="updateString('2')">
<INPUT TYPE="button" NAME="three" VALUE=" 3 "
    onClick="updateString('3')">
<INPUT TYPE="button" NAME="four" VALUE=" 4 "
    onClick="updateString('4')"><BR>
<INPUT TYPE="button" NAME="five" VALUE=" 5 "
    onCLick="updateString('5')">
<INPUT TYPE="button" NAME="six" VALUE=" 6 "
    onClick="updateString('6')">
<INPUT TYPE="button" NAME="seven" VALUE=" 7 "
    onClick="updateString('6')">
<INPUT TYPE="button" NAME="eight" VALUE=" 8 "
    onCLick="updateString('8')">
<INPUT TYPE="button" NAME="nine" VALUE=" 9 "
    onClick="updateString('9')"><BR>
<INPUT TYPE="button" NAME="point" VALUE=" . "
    onClick="updateString('.')">
<INPUT TYPE="button" NAME="clear" VALUE=" Clear "
    onClick="document.Calculator.Input.value=''; inputString=''">
<INPUT TYPE="button" NAME="Calc" VALUE=" = "
    onClick=" document.Calculator.Input.value=eval(inputString)"><BR>
```

Figure 6-31: Calculator.html with memory functions (continued)

```
<INPUT TYPE="button" NAME="mem" VALUE=" M+ "

    onClick="document.Calculator.storedValue.value =
          parseInt(document.Calculator.storedValue.value)

        + parseInt(document.Calculator.Input.value)">
<INPUT TYPE="button" NAME="recall" VALUE=" MRC "

    onClick="updateString(document.Calculator.storedValue.value)">
<INPUT TYPE="button" NAME="memClear" VALUE=" MC "

    onClick="document.Calculator.storedValue.value=0">
<INPUT TYPE="hidden" NAME="storedValue" VALUE=0>
</FORM>
</DIV>
</BODY>
</HTML>
```

Figure 6-31: Calculator.html with memory functions (continued)

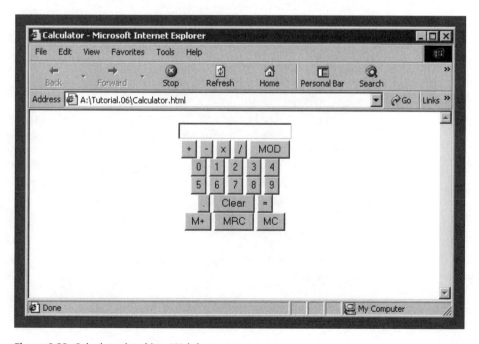

Figure 6-32: Calculator.html in a Web browser

Next, you will add hidden form fields to the ProductRegistration.html document you created in Section A. The ProductRegistration.html document has a serious problem: when you click the Next button to move from the Customer Information form to the Product Information form, the information entered into the Customer Information form disappears because the ProductInfo.html document replaces the CustomerInfo.html document. To solve this problem, you need to add hidden form fields to the TopFrame.html file, which appears in the frame at the top of the window. The fields in the Customer Information form and the Product Information form will be copied to and stored in the hidden form fields in a "master form" in the TopFrame.html file. First you will add the hidden form fields to the TopFrame.html file.

To add hidden form fields to TopFrame.html:

1 Start your text editor or HTML editor, and open the **TopFrame.html** file.

2 Add the following form and form elements before the </BODY> tag. The name of each form element corresponds to the name of a form element in CustomerInfo.html and ProductInfo.html. The hidden fields that correspond to the check boxes in CustomerInfo.html are assigned a default value of false to indicate that the check boxes are not selected.

```
<FORM NAME="hiddenElements">
<INPUT TYPE="hidden" NAME="name">
<INPUT TYPE="hidden" NAME="address">
<INPUT TYPE="hidden" NAME="city">
<INPUT TYPE="hidden" NAME="state">
<INPUT TYPE="hidden" NAME="zip">
<INPUT TYPE="hidden" NAME="email">
<INPUT TYPE="hidden" NAME="password">
<INPUT TYPE="hidden" NAME="platform">
<INPUT TYPE="hidden" NAME="wp" VALUE=false>
<INPUT TYPE="hidden" NAME="ss" VALUE=false>
<INPUT TYPE="hidden" NAME="db" VALUE=false>
<INPUT TYPE="hidden" NAME="gr" VALUE=false >
<INPUT TYPE="hidden" NAME="pr" VALUE=false >
<INPUT TYPE="hidden" NAME="comments">
<INPUT TYPE="hidden" NAME="location">
<INPUT TYPE="hidden" NAME="serial">
<INPUT TYPE="hidden" NAME="date">
<INPUT TYPE="hidden" NAME="where">
</FORM>
```

3 Save and close the **TopFrame.html** file.

Before you can write the code that copies the contents of each field in the CustomerInfo.html and ProductInfo.html files to the corresponding hidden form fields in TopFrame.html, you need to learn how to work with the Form object.

The Form Object

JavaScript is often used with forms to validate or process form data before the data is submitted to a CGI script on a server. For example, customers may use an online order form to order merchandise from your Web site. When a customer clicks the form Submit button, you need to make sure that information, such as the shipping address and credit card information, is entered correctly. To use JavaScript to verify form information, you use the properties, methods, and events of the **Form object.**

 tip

If a form requires advanced or complex validation or processing, it is a good idea to have a CGI script on a server do the work, since servers are usually much more powerful than an end user's desktop computer or workstation.

Referencing Forms and Form Elements

Tutorial 5 introduced the browser object model. Recall that some of the objects in the browser object model are arrays of other objects. For instance, the Window object includes a frames[] array that contains all the frames in a window. Similarly, the Document object includes a **forms[] array** that contains all of an HTML document's forms. If a window does not contain any forms, then the forms[] array is empty. The first form in a document is referred to as document.forms[0], the second form is referred to as document.forms[1], and so on.

Just as the Document object has a forms[] array, the Form object has an elements[] array. You can reference each element on a form, using the Form object **elements[] array.** Each element on a form is assigned to the elements[] array in the order in which it is encountered by the JavaScript interpreter. To refer to an element on a form, you reference the index number of the form in the forms[] array, followed by the appropriate element index number from the elements[] array. For example, if you want to refer to the first element in the first form of an HTML document, use the statement docu-ment.forms[0].elements[0];. The third element in the second form is referenced using the statement document.forms[1].elements[2];. The following code shows an example of how each element on a form is assigned to the elements[] array:

```
<FORM NAME="exampleForm">
The following element is assigned to elements[0]<BR>
<INPUT TYPE="text" NAME="field1"><BR>
The following element is assigned to elements[1]<BR>
<INPUT TYPE="text" NAME="field2"><BR>
The following element is assigned to elements[2]<BR>
<INPUT TYPE="text" NAME="field3"><BR>
The following element is assigned to elements[3]<BR>
<INPUT TYPE="text" NAME="field4"><BR>
The following element is assigned to elements[4]<BR>
<INPUT TYPE="text" NAME="field5">
</FORM>
```

When you create a form with the <FORM> tag, you can use the NAME attribute to assign a name to it. To reference a form by name, you append the form name to the Document object. For example, you reference a form created with a NAME attribute of orderForm by using the statement `document.orderForm`.

Similarly, you can assign a name to each form element with the NAME attribute. Why is it important to name form elements? If you intend to submit a form to a CGI script, you must include a NAME attribute for each form element. Naming an element also gives you an alternative to referencing the element by its position in the elements[] array. For example, if you have an element named textField1 on a form named orderForm, then you can refer to it using the statement `document.orderForm.textField1;`.

 tip

You are not required to include a NAME attribute for a <FORM> tag that will be submitted to a CGI script. The NAME attribute of the <FORM> tag is only used to make it easier to refer to the form in JavaScript.

When multiple form elements share the same name, JavaScript creates an array out of the elements using the shared name. Radio buttons, for instance, share the same name so that a single name=value pair can be submitted to a CGI script. For example, assume you have a group of radio buttons named ageGroup in a form named demographics. You can use the statement `document.demographics.ageGroup[1].value;` to return the value of the second radio button in the group. When you have an array that is created from a group of radio buttons or check boxes that share the same name, you can use the check property to determine which element in a group is selected. The **checked property** corresponds to the HTML CHECKED attribute and returns a value of true if a check box or radio button is selected, and a value of false if it is not. For example, if you have a group of radio buttons named maritalStatus on a form named personalInfo, then you can use a statement similar to `document.personalInfo.maritalStatus[0].checked;` to determine if the first radio button in the group is selected.

Next you will add to the CustomerInfo.html and ProductInfo.html files code that copies form field values to the corresponding hidden fields in the TopFrame.html file. First you will add code to the CustomerInfo.html file.

> **To add to the CustomerInfo.html file code that copies form field values to the corresponding hidden fields in the TopFrame.html file:**
>
> **1**   Open the **CustomerInfo.html** file in your text editor or HTML editor.
>
> **2**   In the function named nextForm(), above the line that reads `location.href="ProductInfo.html";`, insert a new line and add the following code, which copies the values from the first few fields in the CustomerInfo.html file to the hidden form fields in TopFrame.html. The statements use the parent property of the Window object to refer to the name of each frame. The code appears complicated at first, but remember that you

have already learned how each of the statements is constructed. If you break down the parts of each statement, they will begin to make sense. For example, on the left side of the first statement, *parent* refers to the ProductRegistration.html document that defined the frame set, *topframe* refers to the frame at the top of the window that contains the TopFrame.html document, and *document* refers to the TopFrame.html file Document object. The next item in the statement is the form name in the TopFrame.html file, *hiddenElements*, followed by *name,* which refers to the name field on the hiddenElements form. The last portion of the left side of the statement is *value,* which returns the information entered into the *name* field. The right side of the statement is similar to the left side, except that it does not require the parent property or the name of the frame, since you are referring to the current frame.

```
parent.topframe.document.hiddenElements.name.value
    = document.customerInfo.name.value;
parent.topframe.document.hiddenElements.address.value
    = document.customerInfo.address.value;
parent.topframe.document.hiddenElements.city.value
    = document.customerInfo.city.value;
parent.topframe.document.hiddenElements.state.value
    = document.customerInfo.state.value;
parent.topframe.document.hiddenElements.zip.value
    = document.customerInfo.zip.value;
parent.topframe.document.hiddenElements.email.value
    = document.customerInfo.email.value;
parent.topframe.document.hiddenElements.password.value
    = document.customerInfo.password.value;
```

3 Add the following statements, which copy the selected value from the platform radio group to the hidden platform field in TopFrame.html. The `if` statements use the check property to determine which radio button is selected, and then copy the radio button's value to the hidden platform field in TopFrame.html.

```
if (document.customerInfo.platform[0].checked == true)
  parent.topframe.document.hiddenElements.platform.value
    = document.customerInfo.platform[0].value;
if (document.customerInfo.platform[1].checked == true)
  parent.topframe.document.hiddenElements.platform.value
    = document.customerInfo.platform[1].value;
if (document.customerInfo.platform[2].checked == true)
  parent.topframe.document.hiddenElements.platform.value
    = document.customerInfo.platform[2].value;
if (document.customerInfo.platform[3].checked == true)
  parent.topframe.document.hiddenElements.platform.value
    = document.customerInfo.platform[3].value;
```

```
if (document.customerInfo.platform[4].checked == true)
  parent.topframe.document.hiddenElements.platform.value
    = document.customerInfo.platform[4].value;
if (document.customerInfo.platform[5].checked == true)
  parent.topframe.document.hiddenElements.platform.value
    = document.customerInfo.platform[5].value;
```

4 Next add the following statements for the software check boxes. The code also uses the checked property to see which check boxes are selected. Instead of assigning the value of each selected check box to its corresponding hidden field in TopFrame.html, a value of *true* is assigned to indicate that the check box is selected. Otherwise, the default value of *false* (indicating the field is not selected) will continue to be the value of the corresponding hidden field of each check box.

```
if (document.customerInfo.wp.checked == true)
  parent.topframe.document.hiddenElements.wp.value = true;
if (document.customerInfo.ss.checked == true)
  parent.topframe.document.hiddenElements.ss.value = true;
if (document.customerInfo.db.checked == true)
  parent.topframe.document.hiddenElements.db.value = true;
if (document.customerInfo.gr.checked == true)
  parent.topframe.document.hiddenElements.gr.value = true;
if (document.customerInfo.pr.checked == true)
  parent.topframe.document.hiddenElements.pr.value = true;
```

5 Finally, add the following statements that copy the values of the location and comment fields.

```
parent.topframe.document.hiddenElements.location.value =
    document.customerInfo.location.value;
parent.topframe.document.hiddenElements.comments.value =
    document.customerInfo.comments.value;
```

6 Save the **CustomerInfo.html** file.

Next you will add code that confirms that users have entered data into several required fields before they pressed the Next button. The required fields are name, address, city, state, zip, and password.

To add code that confirms that users have entered data into several required fields before they pressed the Next button:

1 Return to the **CustomerInfo.html** file in your text editor or HTML editor.

2 Add the following statements just above the statement that reads location.href="ProductInfo.html";. The `if` statement uses the logical or operator, ||, to make sure all the required fields are entered. If any one of the fields is equal to an empty string, "", then an alert dialog box appears informing users that they must fill in all the fields. If all the fields have been entered, then the else clause executes the location.href="ProductInfo.html"; statement.

```
if (parent.topframe.document.hiddenElements
     .name.value == ""
|| parent.topframe.document.hiddenElements
     .address.value == ""
|| parent.topframe.document.hiddenElements
     .city.value == ""
|| parent.topframe.document.hiddenElements
     .state.value == ""
|| parent.topframe.document.hiddenElements
     .zip.value == ""
|| parent.topframe.document.hiddenElements
     .password.value == "")
     alert("You must fill in the name, address, city,
          state, zip, and password fields.");
else
```

3 Save the **CustomerInfo.html** file.

4 Open the **ProductRegistration.html** file in your Web browser. Leave several of the required fields blank and click the **Next** button to see if you receive the alert dialog box.

5 Click **OK** to close the alert dialog box.

6 Fill in all the required fields and check to see if the ProductInfo.html file loads properly after you press the **Next** button.

7 Close the Web browser window.

You also need to add code that copies the field values from the ProductInfo.html file to the corresponding hidden fields in TopFrame.html and confirms that any required fields are not empty. Since the ProductInfo.html file does not contain a Next button, as does the CustomerInfo.html file, you need to add the code that copies the field values to an onSubmit event handler, which you will learn about next.

Form Event Handlers

In Tutorial 2, you learned about many of the event handlers that can be used in JavaScript. Two additional event handlers, onSubmit and onReset, are available for use with the <FORM> tag. The **onSubmit event handler** executes when a form is submitted to a CGI script using a submit <INPUT> tag or an image <INPUT> tag. The onSubmit event handler is often used to verify or validate form data before it is sent to a server. The **onReset event handler** executes when a reset button is selected on a form. You use the onReset event handler to confirm that a user really wants to reset the contents of a form. Both the onSubmit and the onReset event handlers are placed before the closing bracket of a <FORM> tag. The following code shows how a form tag with onSubmit and onReset event handlers is written:

```
<FORM ACTION="http://exampleurl/cgi-bin/cgi_program"
    METHOD="post" NAME="exampleForm"
    onSubmit="JavaScript statements;"
    onReset="JavaScript statements;">
```

When you use the onSubmit and onReset event handlers, you need to return a value of true or false, depending on whether the form should be submitted or reset. For example, the following code returns a value of true or false, depending on whether the user presses the OK button or the Cancel button in the confirm dialog box. If the user presses the OK button, the confirm dialog box returns a value of true, and the onReset event executes. If the user presses the Cancel button, the confirm dialog box returns a value of false, and the onReset event does not execute.

```
<FORM ACTION="http://exampleurl/cgi-bin/cgi_program"
    METHOD="post" NAME="exampleForm"
    onReset="return confirm(
    'Are you sure you want to reset the form?')">
```

Figure 6-33 shows a program that includes both the onSubmit and the onReset event handlers. The program uses one function to validate the form data when the onSubmit event handler executes, and uses another function to confirm whether the user really wants to reset a form.

```
<SCRIPT LANGUAGE="JavaScript">

<!-- HIDE FROM INCOMPATIBLE BROWSERS

function confirmSubmit() {

    var sendForm = confirm(
        "Are you sure you want to submit the form?");

    if (sendForm == true)

        return true;

    return false;

}
```

Figure 6-33: Program with onSubmit and onReset event handlers

```
function confirmReset() {

    var resetForm = confirm(
        "Are you sure you want to reset the form?");

    if (resetForm == true)

        return true;

    return false;

}
// STOP HIDING FROM INCOMPATIBLE BROWSERS -->
</SCRIPT>
<FORM ACTION="http://exampleurl/cgi-bin/cgi_program"

    METHOD="post" NAME="exampleForm"

    onSubmit="return confirmSubmit();"

    onReset="return confirmReset();">
Name<BR>
<INPUT TYPE="text" NAME="name" SIZE=50><BR>
Address<BR>
<INPUT TYPE="text" NAME="address" SIZE=50><BR>
City, State, Zip<BR>
<INPUT TYPE="text" NAME="city" SIZE=38>
<INPUT TYPE="text" NAME="state" SIZE=2 MAXLENGTH=2>
<INPUT TYPE="text" NAME="zip" SIZE=5 MAXLENGTH=5><BR>
<INPUT TYPE="reset">
<INPUT TYPE="submit">
</FORM>
```

Figure 6-33: Program with onSubmit and onReset event handlers (continued)

Next you will add an onReset event handler to confirm that users really want to reset the CustomerInfo.html and ProductInfo.html forms.

To add an onReset event handler to confirm that users really want to reset the CustomerInfo.html and ProductInfo.html forms:

1   Return to the **CustomerInfo.html** file in your text editor or HTML editor.

2 Add the following confirmReset() function above the nextForm() function in the <SCRIPT>...</SCRIPT> tag pair in the <HEAD> section:

```
function confirmReset() {
     var resetForm = confirm(
          "Are you sure you want to reset the form?");
     if (resetForm == true)
          return true;
     return false;
}
```

3 Next, before the closing bracket of the <FORM> tag, add `onReset="return confirmReset();"`.

4 Save and close the **CustomerInfo.html** file.

5 Open the **ProductInfo.html** file in your text editor or HTML editor and add a <SCRIPT>...</SCRIPT> tag pair to the <HEAD> section. Between the <SCRIPT>...</SCRIPT> tag pair, add the same confirmReset() function you added to the CustomerInfo.html file.

6 Add the event handler `onReset="return confirmReset();"` before the closing bracket of the <FORM> tag.

7 Save and close the **ProductInfo.html** file.

8 Open the **ProductRegistration.html** file in your Web browser. Enter some data into the fields in the Customer Information form, and then click the **Reset** button to see if you receive the warning. Click **OK** to close the alert dialog box. Fill in the required information on the Customer Information form, and click **Next**. Then test the Reset button in the ProductInfo.html file. Click **OK** to close the alert dialog box.

9 Close the Web browser window.

Next you will add to the ProductInfo.html file an onSubmit event that validates the fields in ProductInfo.html and then copies the data from each field to the corresponding hidden form fields in TopFrame.html.

To add an onSubmit event and code to the ProductInfo.html file:

1 Open the **ProductInfo.html** file in your text editor or HTML editor.

2 Add an onSubmit event `onSubmit="return submitForm();"` to the <FORM> tag just before the closing bracket.

3 In the <SCRIPT>...</SCRIPT> tag pair, add `function submitForm() {` above the confirmReset() function, to create the opening lines of the submitForm() function.

4   Next add to the submitForm() function the following statements, which copy the ProductInfo.html fields to the corresponding hidden fields in TopFrame.html:

```
parent.topframe.document.hiddenElements.serial.value =
    document.productInfo.serial.value;
parent.topframe.document.hiddenElements.date.value =
    document.productInfo.date.value;
if (document.productInfo.where[0].checked == true)
  parent.topframe.document.hiddenElements.where.value =
    document.platformInfo.where[0].value;
if (document.productInfo.where[1].checked == true)
  parent.topframe.document.hiddenElements.where.value =
    document.platformInfo.where[1].value;
if (document.productInfo.where[2].checked == true)
  parent.topframe.document.hiddenElements.where.value =
    document.platformInfo.where[2].value;
if (document.productInfo.where[3].checked == true)
  parent.topframe.document.hiddenElements.where.value =
    document.platformInfo.where[3].value;
```

5   Following the lines that copy fields from ProductInfo.html to TopFrame.html, add the following if statement to confirm that users have filled in all the required fields. For the ProductInfo.html file, the serial number and date fields must be filled in. If the required fields are filled in, a value of true is returned, and the form is submitted. If a value of false is returned, the onSubmit event is cancelled.

```
if (
    parent.topframe.document.hiddenElements.serial.value
== "" ||
    parent.topframe.document.hiddenElements.date.value
== "") {
    alert(
    "You must fill in the date and serial number.");
    return false;
}
```

6   Add the closing bracket } for the submitForm() function.

7   Save **ProductInfo.html**. Remember that the TopFrame.html file contains the hidden form fields that the form uses to gather data from both the CustomerInfo.html and the ProductInfo.html files. Before you can test the submitForm() function, you must add a statement that submits the hidden form fields in TopFrame.html. To submit the contents of a form from JavaScript, you need to learn about form methods, which are covered next.

Form Methods

The Form object contains only two methods: submit() and reset(). The **submit() method** is used to submit a form without the use of a submit <INPUT> tag. The **reset() method** is used to clear a form without the use of a reset <INPUT> tag. The submit() and reset() methods perform the same functions as the submit and reset buttons. However, the onSubmit and onReset event handlers do not execute when you use the submit() and reset() methods. Any validation that needs to be performed must be included in the code that calls the submit() and reset() methods.

The submit() and reset() methods are used with forms that do not include submit or reset buttons. Figure 6-34 shows a program that uses the submit() and reset() methods. The program consists of a game in which the user must correctly count several groups of items. If a user counts one group of items incorrectly, the reset() method clears the form, and the user must start over. Once a user enters each item count correctly, the form is automatically submitted. The program uses the onChange event handler to call the confirmAnswers() function. The confirmAnswers() function checks the picture and answer arguments that are passed to it, then takes the appropriate action, using if statements. The last if statement in the confirmAnswers() function checks whether the three global variables for the three items have all been set to true. If all three global variables have been set to true, then the form is submitted. Figure 6-35 shows the program output in a Web browser window.

```
<HTML>

<HEAD>

<TITLE>Counting Contest</TITLE>

<SCRIPT LANGUAGE="JavaScript">

<!-- HIDE FROM INCOMPATIBLE BROWSERS

var applesCorrect; var orangesCorrect; var nutsCorrect;

function confirmAnswers(picture, answer) {

    if (picture == "apples") {

        if (answer == 9)

           applesCorrect = true;

        else {

            alert("Sorry! You must start over.");

            document.contestForm.reset();

        }

    }
```

Figure 6-34: Program with submit() and reset() methods

```
        if (picture == "oranges") {

            if (answer == 5)

               orangesCorrect = true;

            else {

                alert("Sorry! You must start over.");

                document.contestForm.reset();

            }

  }

    if (picture == "nuts") {

            if (answer == 56)

               nutsCorrect = true;

            else {

                alert("Sorry! You must start over.");

                document.contestForm.reset();

            }

    }

    if (applesCorrect == true && orangesCorrect == true
         && nutsCorrect == true) {

        alert("Congratulations! You will be entered in the contest.");
            document.contestForm.submit();

    }

}
// STOP HIDING FROM INCOMPATIBLE BROWSERS -->

</SCRIPT>

</HEAD>

<BODY>

<H1>How Many Items Can You Count?</H1>

<STRONG>If you count all the items correctly, you will automatically
be entered into a drawing to win a free grocery shopping spree.
Watch out! If you enter the wrong number of items for any picture,
you will need to start over from the beginning.</STRONG>

<FORM ACTION="http://exampleurl/cgi-bin/cgi_program"

    METHOD="post" NAME="contestForm">

<P>First enter your e-mail address: <INPUT TYPE="text"
    NAME="email" SIZE="50"></P>
```

Figure 6-34: Program with submit() and reset() methods (continued)

```
<P>Now count the number of items in each picture:</P>

<P><IMG SRC="apples.jpg" HEIGHT=150>

<IMG SRC="oranges.jpg" HEIGHT=150>

<IMG SRC="nuts.jpg" HEIGHT=150></P>

Apples: <INPUT TYPE="text" SIZE="15"

          onChange="confirmAnswers('apples', this.value);">

Oranges: <INPUT TYPE="text" SIZE="15"

          onChange="confirmAnswers('oranges', this.value);">

Nuts: <INPUT TYPE="text" SIZE="15"

          onChange="confirmAnswers('nuts', this.value);">

</FORM>

</BODY>

</HTML>
```

Figure 6-34: Program with submit() and reset() methods (continued)

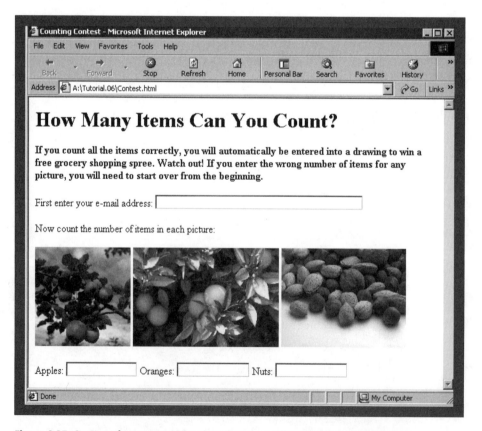

Figure 6-35: Output of program with submit() and reset() methods in a Web browser

Next you will add to the ProductInfo.html file statements that submit the contents of TopFrame.html using the submit() method.

To add statements to the ProductInfo.html file that submit the contents of TopFrame.html using the submit() method:

1   Return to the **ProductInfo.html** file in your text editor or HTML editor.

2   Before the closing bracket of the submitForm() function, add the following else clause that submits the hidden form fields in TopFrame.html. Note that false is returned to the onSubmit event handler to prevent the ProductInfo.html file from also submitting its own form fields.

```
else {
parent.topframe.document.hiddenElements.submit();
return false;
}
```

3   Save and close **ProductInfo.html**.

4   Open the **ProductRegistration.html** file in your Web browser. Enter data into the required fields in the Customer Information form, and then click the **Next** button. Click the **Submit Query** button without entering any data into the Product Information form. You should receive an alert dialog box.

> If you enter data and click the Submit button, nothing will happen since you are not working with a Web server. At the end of this section you will add code that submits the form data to an e-mail address.

5   Click **OK** to close the alert dialog box, and then close the Web browser window.

Form Properties

The Form object includes several properties that correspond to the attributes of the <FORM> tag. It also includes properties containing information about form elements. Properties of the Form object are listed in Figure 6-36. You should be familiar with most of these properties from Section A.

Property	Description
action	The URL to which form data will be submitted
method	The method by which form data will be submitted: GET or POST
enctype	The format of the data being submitted

Figure 6-36: Properties of the Form object

Property	Description
target	The window in which any results returned from the server are displayed
name	The name of the form
elements[]	An array representing a form's elements
length	The number of elements on a form

Figure 6-36: Properties of the Form object (continued)

 tip

All the properties of the Form object, with the exception of the name, elements[], and length properties, can be modified in JavaScript code.

The length property is useful for retrieving the number of elements on a form. Figure 6-37 contains a program that uses the length property to determine if form fields have been filled out. The program's onSubmit event calls a function named confirmFields(). The confirmFields() function uses a `while` statement to loop through the elements[] array. If an element in the elements[] array is empty, then a variable named missingFields increments by one. When the `while` statement finishes, an `if` statement checks whether the missingFields variable is greater than zero. If it is, then an alert dialog box appears telling the user how many fields are missing. Notice that one is being subtracted from the length property, since you do not want to count the submit button as one of the fields that needs to be filled out.

```
<SCRIPT LANGUAGE="JavaScript">

<!-- HIDE FROM INCOMPATIBLE BROWSERS

function confirmFields() {

    var count = 0;

    var missingFields = 0;

    while (count < document.exampleForm.length - 1) {

        if (document.exampleForm.elements[count].value == "")

            missingFields = ++missingFields;

        ++count;

    }
```

Figure 6-37: Confirm fields program

```
      if (missingFields > 0) {

            alert("You are missing " + missingFields + " out of " +
                  (document.exampleForm.length - 1) + " fields.");

            return false;

      }

      else

            return true;

}
// STOP HIDING FROM INCOMPATIBLE BROWSERS -->

</SCRIPT>

<FORM ACTION="http://exampleurl/cgi-bin/cgi_program"

      METHOD="post" NAME="exampleForm"

      onSubmit="return confirmFields();">

Name<BR>

<INPUT TYPE="text" NAME="name" SIZE=50><BR>

Address<BR>

<INPUT TYPE="text" NAME="address" SIZE=50><BR>

City, State, Zip<BR>

<INPUT TYPE="text" NAME="city" SIZE=38>

<INPUT TYPE="text" NAME="state" SIZE=2 MAXLENGTH=2>

<INPUT TYPE="text" NAME="zip" SIZE=5 MAXLENGTH=5><BR>

<INPUT TYPE="submit">

</FORM>
```

Figure 6-37: Confirm fields program (continued)

E-Mailing Form Data

Most of the forms you have seen so far have contained data that is transmitted to a CGI script on a server. Instead of submitting form data to a CGI script, another option is to send the form data to an e-mail address. Sending form data to an e-mail address is a much simpler process than creating and managing a CGI script. Instead of relying on a complex CGI script on a server to process the data, you rely on the recipient of the e-mail message to process the data. For instance, a Web site may contain an online order form for some type of product. After the user clicks the Submit button, the data for the order can be sent to the e-mail address of whomever is responsible for filling the order. For large organizations that deal with hundreds or thousands of orders a day, e-mailing each order to a single individual is not the ideal solution. But, for smaller companies or Web sites that do not have a high volume of orders, e-mailing form data is a good solution.

To e-mail form data instead of submitting it to a CGI script, you replace the CGI script's URL in the <FORM> tag's ACTION attribute with mailto:*email_address*. Figure 6-38 shows an example of code that generates a form whose data will be e-mailed to a fictitious e-mail address, john_howe@exampledomain.com.

```
<HTML>

<HEAD>

<TITLE>Customer Information</TITLE>

</HEAD>

<BODY>

<H2>Customer Information</H2>

<FORM ACTION="mailto:john_howe@exampledomain.com"

    METHOD="post" ENCTYPE="text/plain" NAME="customer_information">

Name<BR>

<INPUT TYPE="text" NAME="name" SIZE=50><BR>

Address<BR>

<INPUT TYPE="text" NAME="address" SIZE=50><BR>

City, State, Zip<BR>

<INPUT TYPE="text" NAME="city" SIZE=38>

<INPUT TYPE="text" NAME="state" SIZE=2 MAXLENGTH=2>

<INPUT TYPE="text" NAME="zip" SIZE=5 MAXLENGTH=5><BR>

E-Mail<BR>

<P><INPUT TYPE="text" NAME="email" SIZE=50></P>

<INPUT TYPE="reset">

<INPUT TYPE="submit">

</BODY>

</HTML>
```

Figure 6-38: Form code with an ACTION attribute of mailto

When you send form data to an e-mail address, use the ENCTYPE of *text/plain*. The ENCTYPE of *text/plain* ensures that the data arrives at the e-mail address in a readable format. Figure 6-39 shows an example of the e-mail message received by john_howe@exampledomain.com after the form generated by the code in Figure 6-38 is submitted. The e-mail message appears in Outlook Express.

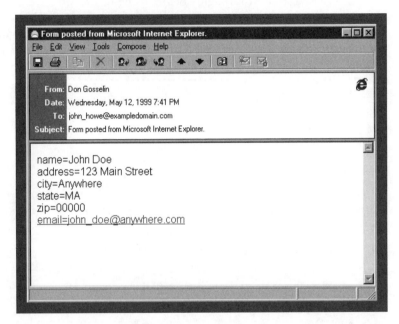

Figure 6-39: Data in Outlook Express after being e-mailed with an ENCTYPE of *text/plain*

If you omit the ENCTYPE of *text/plain*, the form data is sent using the default type of *application/x-www-form-urlencoded*. When form data is sent via e-mail using ENCTYPE *application/x-www-form-urlencoded*, it can be difficult to read and work with. Figure 6-40 shows the data sent from the same program when the form is submitted with an ENCTYPE of *application/x-www-form-urlencoded*.

```
name=John+Doe&address=123+Main+Street&city=Anywhere&state=MA

&zip=00000&email=john_doe@anywhere.com
```

Figure 6-40: Data e-mailed with an ENCTYPE of *application/x-www-form-urlencoded*

You can use the data shown in the e-mail in Figure 6-40. However, you would need to write a special program that converts the data to a readable format.

The drawback to e-mailing form data is that not all Web browsers support the mailto:email_address option with the <FORM> tag ACTION attribute. In addition, the performance of the mailto:email_address option is unreliable. Some Web browsers that do support the e-mailing of form data do not properly place the data within the body of an e-mail message. If you write a Web page that e-mails form data, be sure to test it thoroughly before using it.

tip

....

When users click the Submit button for a form that is e-mailed, they may receive a security warning or be given a chance to edit the e-mail, depending on how their e-mail application is configured.

....

Next you will change the <FORM> tag of the Product Registration program so that the form data is e-mailed to your e-mail address whenever it is submitted. In order to be sure this exercise works properly, you must be using Internet Explorer 4.0 or higher or Navigator 4.0 or higher.

To change the <FORM> tag of the Product Registration program so that the form data is e-mailed to your e-mail address whenever it is submitted:

1 Open the **TopFrame.html** file in your text editor or HTML editor.

2 Add the following attributes just before the closing bracket of the <FORM> tag. Replace *email_address* with your own e-mail address.

  ACTION="mailto:*email_address*" METHOD="post" ENCTYPE="text/plain"

3 Save and close **TopFrame.html**, then open the **ProductRegistration.html** file in your Web browser. Fill in the fields for each form, then submit it. Depending on your e-mail configuration, you may receive warning dialog boxes or be given a chance to edit the e-mail message.

4 Wait several minutes before retrieving the new message from your e-mail, since transmission time on the Internet can vary. After you receive the e-mail, examine the message to see how the form data appears.

5 Close your e-mail program, the Web browser window, and your text or HTML editor.

S U M M A R Y

- Hidden form fields are created with the <INPUT> tag and are used to hide information from users.

- You use the properties, methods, and events of the Form object to verify form information with JavaScript.

- The Document object includes a forms[] array that contains all of an HTML document's forms.

- Each element on a form can be referenced using the elements[] array of the Form object.

- When multiple form elements share the same name, JavaScript creates an array out of the elements using the shared name.

- The checked property corresponds to the HTML CHECKED attribute and returns a value of true if a check box or radio button is selected and a value of false if it is not.

- The onSubmit event handler executes when a form is submitted to a CGI script, using a submit <INPUT> tag or an image <INPUT> tag.

- The onReset event handler executes when a reset button on a form is clicked.

- The submit() method is used to submit a form in JavaScript without the use of a submit <INPUT> tag.

- The reset() method is used to clear a form in JavaScript without the use of a reset <INPUT> tag.

- The Form object includes several properties that correspond to the attributes of the <FORM> tag, as well as properties containing information about form elements.

- The length property is useful for retrieving the number of elements on a form.

- Form data can be submitted to an e-mail address instead of a CGI script by using an ACTION attribute of mailto.

QUESTIONS

1. What is the correct syntax for creating a hidden form field?
   a. <HIDDEN VALUE=" *text to be hidden*">
   b. <HIDDEN>*text to be hidden*</HIDDEN>
   c. <INPUT TYPE="hidden" NAME="storedValue">
   d. <INPUT TYPE="hide" NAME="storedValue">

2. In order to perform a floating-point calculation using a number retrieved from a text box, you must convert the number using the _____ built-in function.
   a. parseInt()
   b. parseFloat()
   c. toString()
   d. typeOf()

3. Form data can be verified in JavaScript using the properties, methods, and events of the _____ object.
   a. Form
   b. Document
   c. Window
   d. Data

4. If the first form in an HTML document is named myForm, which of the following can be used to refer to the form in JavaScript code?
   a. myForm.document
   b. document.frames[1]
   c. document.forms[0]
   d. document.forms[1]

5. Each element on a form can be referenced using the _____ array.
   a. elements[]
   b. input[]
   c. components[]
   d. forms[]

6. If you have a set of six radio buttons named size on a form named measurements, how can you assign the value of the third radio button to a variable named shirtSize?
   a. `var shirtSize = document.measurements.elements[2].value;`
   b. `var shirtSize = document.measurements.size.value;`
   c. `var shirtSize = document.measurements.size[2].value;`
   d. `var shirtSize = document.measurements.size[3].value;`

7. Which of the following statements is true about the NAME attribute of the <FORM> tag?
   a. You cannot include a NAME attribute with the <FORM> tag.
   b. The NAME attribute of the <FORM> tag is required if the form will be submitted to a CGI script.
   c. You cannot refer to a form in JavaScript if it does not include the NAME attribute.
   d. The NAME attribute of the <FORM> tag is used only to make it easier to refer to the form in JavaScript.

8. An HTML document contains two frames. The first frame is named leftFrame, and the second frame is named rightFrame. The right frame contains a form named myForm with a checkbox <INPUT> tag named myCheckbox. The myCheckbox element is the second element on the form. Which statement can be used *from the leftFrame* to change the value of myCheckbox to true?
   a. `parent.rightFrame.elements[0].checked = true;`
   b. `parent.rightFrame.myForm.elements[0].checked = true;`
   c. `myForm.myCheckbox.value = true;`
   d. `myForm.myCheckbox.checked = true;`

9. What is the onSubmit event handler often used for?
   a. saving a form to a local file before it is submitted to a CGI program
   b. periodically refreshing a Web browser window in order to show the most current form data
   c. checking for new e-mail messages when a Web browser window opens or closes
   d. verifying or validating form data before it is sent to a server

10. Which of the following is the correct syntax for an onReset event handler?
    a. `<BUTTON onReset="functionName()";>`
    b. `<RESET onReset="functionName()";>`
    c. `<FORM onReset="functionName()";>`
    d. `<SUBMIT onReset="functionName()";>`

11. In order to cancel the onSubmit or onReset event handlers, what does a JavaScript function or code need to do?

    a. return a value of `false`

    b. return a value of `true`

    c. execute the stop or quit methods

    d. Nothing. The onSubmit and onReset events are canceled as soon as a corresponding event handler is encountered by the JavaScript interpreter.

12. The Form object contains two methods: the submit() method and the _____ method.

    a. resubmit()

    b. execute()

    c. process()

    d. reset()

13. The _____ property returns the number of form elements.

    a. length

    b. number

    c. elements

    d. fields

14. Which ENCTYPE should be used to send form data to an e-mail address?

    a. *application/jpeg/gif*

    b. *cgi.bin*

    c. *application/x-www-form-urlencoded*

    d. *text/plain*

E X E R C I S E S

Save all files you create in the Tutorial.06 folder on your Data Disk.

1. Add event handlers to the following code that prompt the user to confirm whether he or she wants to submit or reset the form. Save the HTML document as ConfirmForm.html.

```
<HTML>
<HEAD>
<TITLE>Confirm Firm</TITLE>
</HEAD>
<BODY>
<FORM NAME="enroll">
<P>First name: <INPUT TYPE="text"
     NAME="first"SIZE=50></P>
<P>Last name: <INPUT TYPE="text"
     NAME="last"SIZE=50></P>
<P>Address: <INPUT TYPE="text"
     NAME="address"SIZE=50></P>
<P>City: <INPUT TYPE="text"
     NAME="city" SIZE=15>
```

```
State: <INPUT TYPE="text"
     NAME="state" SIZE=2>
Zip: <INPUT TYPE="text"
     NAME="zip" SIZE=10></P>
<P>E-mail: <INPUT TYPE="text"
     NAME="email"SIZE=50></P>
<P><INPUT TYPE="submit" VALUE="Enroll">
<INPUT TYPE="reset"></P>
</FORM>
</BODY>
</HTML>
```

2. Modify the program you created in Exercise 1 so that the form is submitted and reset from within a JavaScript section—not by returning values to the onSubmit and onReset event handling functions. Save the modified program as ConfirmForm2.html

3. Modify the following program so that it sends the form data to your personal e-mail account. Be sure to include the correct METHOD and ENCTYPE attributes. Save the HTML document as InfoRequest.html.

```
<FORM NAME="info">
<P>First name: <INPUT TYPE="text"
     NAME="first"SIZE=50></P>
<P>Last name: <INPUT TYPE="text"
     NAME="last" SIZE=50></P>
<P>Company: <INPUT TYPE="text"
     NAME="company" SIZE=50></P>
<P>Address: <INPUT TYPE="text"
     NAME="address"SIZE=50></P>
<P>City: <INPUT TYPE="text"
     NAME="city" SIZE=15>
State: <INPUT TYPE="text"
     NAME="state" SIZE=2>
Zip: <INPUT TYPE="text"
     NAME="zip" SIZE=10></P>
<P>Telephone: <INPUT TYPE="text"
     NAME="telephone" SIZE=50></P>
<P>E-mail: <INPUT TYPE="text"
     NAME="email" SIZE=50></P>
<P><INPUT TYPE="checkbox"
     NAME="sendinfo" VALUE="true">Send me information<BR>
<INPUT TYPE="checkbox"
     NAME="contactme" VALUE="true">Contact me<BR>
<INPUT TYPE="checkbox"
     NAME="mailinglist" VALUE="true">Put me on your mailing list</P>
<P><INPUT TYPE="submit" VALUE="Send">
<INPUT TYPE="reset"></P>
</FORM>
```

4. Create a purchase order form for a hardware store. Include selection lists for standard items such as hammers, wrenches, and other tools. Use JavaScript to verify that customers fill out required information such as billing and shipping information. Save the HTML document as PurchaseOrder.html in the Tutorial.06 folder on your Data Disk.

5. Create a math quiz for a 6th grade class. Use hidden fields for the answers to the quiz. Use *Score Quiz* for the label of the submit button. When students click the submit button, execute the onSubmit event handler and determine if they have answered all the questions. If they have answered all the questions, score the quiz using the answers in the hidden fields. If they have not answered all the questions, cancel the onSubmit event and use an alert dialog box to instruct them to answer all the questions before selecting the Score Quiz button. Save the HTML document as MathQuiz.html in the Tutorial.06 folder on your Data Disk.

6. Create a form to allow users to sign up for a professional conference. Have the forms submitted to your e-mail address. Save the HTML document as Conference.html in the Tutorial.06 folder on your Data Disk.

7. Create an RSVP form for a party you are hosting. Your guests should fill out the form and submit it to your e-mail address. Save the HTML document as RSVP.html in the Tutorial.06 folder on your Data Disk.

8. Create a form for processing vacation requests from employees. Use JavaScript to verify that employees fill out required information such as the dates they will be taking their vacations. Use *Submit Request* for the submit button label. Find someone in your class who can act as your manager and submit the form to his or her e-mail address. Save the HTML document as VacationRequest.html in the Tutorial.06 folder on your Data Disk.

9. Guest book applications are widely used on the Web to gather information about visitors to a Web site. Create a simple guest book that sends a visitor's registration information to your e-mail address. Include fields such as name, e-mail address, city, country, and a comment. Save the HTML document as GuestBook.html.

10. A useful interface element is a read-only text field that only displays information, such as the result of a calculation. Unfortunately, HTML does not have any sort of read-only form field. Text fields are always accessible to the user, and hidden fields are not visible to the user. You can simulate a read-only text field by using the onFocus event handler to call the text field blur() method. Several of the event handlers discussed throughout this book also have a corresponding method that you can use to execute the event with JavaScript. The click event has a corresponding click() method, the focus event has a corresponding focus() method, and so on. For example, if you want to use JavaScript to change focus to a text box named address on a form named personalInfo, you can use the statement `document.personalInfo.address.focus();`. To simulate a read-only field, you call the text field blur() method from its onFocus() event handler. All this technique does is immediately remove the focus from the text field. The text field is not truly read-only, but nevertheless, users will not be able to modify it. The Calculator program you created in Tutorial 3 can make good use of a read-only text field. Users should never manually type into the text box that displays the results of the calculations. See if you can modify the text field of the Calculator program so that it is read-only. You can find a copy of the Calculator program in the Tutorial.06 folder on your Data Disk.

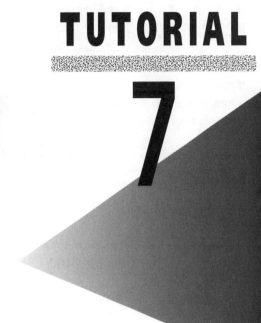

## 7

Debugging JavaScript

case ▶ The more JavaScript programs you write, the more likely you are to receive error messages. In addition, your programs may never seem to function quite the way you want them to. Because you now understand most of the basics of JavaScript programming, and WebAdventure has you constantly writing JavaScript programs for their clients, it is time you looked into some JavaScript debugging techniques.

In this section you will learn:

- About debugging concepts
- How to interpret error messages
- How to trace errors with the alert() method
- How to trace errors with the write() and writeln() methods
- How to use comments to locate bugs
- About additional debugging techniques

Basic Debugging Techniques

Understanding Debugging

Regardless of experience, knowledge, and ability, all programmers create errors in their programs at one time or another. As you learned at the start of this book, debugging is the act of tracing and resolving errors in a program. Debugging is an essential skill for any programmer, regardless of the programming language. In this tutorial, you will learn techniques and tools to help you trace and resolve errors in your JavaScript programs.

Three types of errors can occur in a program: syntax errors, run-time errors, and logic errors. **Syntax errors** occur when you enter code that the interpreter does not recognize. Syntax errors in JavaScript include invalid statements or statements that are entered incorrectly, for example, when a closing parenthesis for a method is missing. Other types of syntax errors include incorrectly spelled or mistyped words. For example, if you were to enter the statement `document.writln("Hello World");`, you would receive a syntax error when you ran the program because the writeln() method is incorrectly spelled as *writln()*. Similarly, the statement `Document.writeln("Hello  World");` causes a syntax error because the Document object is incorrectly entered with an uppercase *D*. (Remember that most JavaScript objects, such as the Document object, are entered in a statement with lowercase letters.)

 tip

Syntax errors in compiled languages, such as C++, are also called compile-time errors, since they are usually discovered when a program is compiled. Since JavaScript is an interpreted language, syntax errors are not discovered until a program executes.

If the JavaScript interpreter encounters a problem while a program is executing, that problem is called a **run-time error**. Run-time errors differ from syntax errors in that they do not necessarily represent JavaScript language errors. Instead, run-time errors occur when the interpreter encounters code that it cannot handle. For example, the statement `customFunction();` calls a custom JavaScript function named customFunction(). This is not a syntax error, since it is legal (and usually necessary) to create custom functions in a JavaScript program. However, if you fail to create the function and your program attempts to call it during execution, then a run-time error occurs, since the interpreter cannot find the function. The following code shows another example of a run-time error. In the example, a writeln() method attempts to print the contents of a variable named messageVar. Since the messageVar variable is not declared (assuming that it has not been declared in another script section elsewhere in the document), a run-time error occurs.

```
<SCRIPT LANGUAGE="JavaScript">
document.writeln(messageVar);
</SCRIPT>
```

Logic errors are problems in the design of a program that prevent it from running as you anticipate it will run. The logic behind any program involves executing the various statements and procedures in the correct order to produce the desired results. For example, when you do the laundry, you normally wash, dry, iron, and then fold. If a laundry program irons, folds, dries, then washes, you have a logic error, and the program executes incorrectly. One example of a logic error in a computer program is multiplying two values when you mean to divide them, as in the following code:

```
<SCRIPT>
var divisionResult = 10 * 2;
document.write("Ten divided by two is equal to "
    + divisionResult);
</SCRIPT>
```

Another example of a logic error is the creation of an infinite loop, in which a looping statement never ends because its conditional expression is never updated or is never false. The following code creates a `for` statement that results in the logic error of an infinite loop, since the third argument in the `for` statement constructor never changes the value of the count variable.

```
for(var count = 10; count >= 0; count) {
    alert("We have liftoff in " + count);
}
```

Since the count variable is never updated in the preceding example it will continue to have a value of 10 through each iteration of the loop, resulting in the repeated display of an alert dialog box containing the text *We have liftoff in 10*. To correct this logic error, you add a decrement operator to the third argument in the for statement constructor, as follows:

```
for(var count = 10; count >= 0; --count) {
    alert("We have liftoff in " + count);
}
```

Error Messages

The first line of defense in locating bugs, or errors, in JavaScript programs are the error messages you receive when the JavaScript interpreter encounters a syntax or run-time error. Two important pieces of information displayed in error message dialog boxes by both Netscape and Internet Explorer are the line number in the document where the error occurred and a description of the error. Note that the line number in an error message is counted from the start of the HTML document, not just from the start of a script section. In addition to the line number and a description of the error, Netscape displays a snippet of the offending code. Internet Explorer points you to the character in the line where the error occurred and also tells you if it was a run-time error. All errors that are not run-time errors are syntax errors. For an example of the error messages that appear in Netscape and Internet Explorer, consider the following function, which causes a syntax error because it is missing the closing brace (}).

```
function missingClosingBrace() {
    var message =
        "This function is missing a closing brace.";
    alert(message);
```

Figure 7-1 shows the Netscape error message generated by the preceding code, and Figure 7-2 shows the Internet Explorer error message.

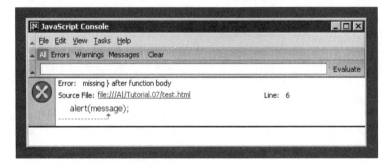

Figure 7-1: Netscape error message

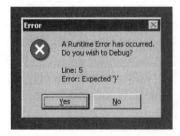

Figure 7-2: Internet Explorer error message

If you are using a version of Internet Explorer higher than 4, you need to turn on error notification by selecting Internet Options from the Tools menu and clicking the Advanced tab. In the Browsing category on the Advanced tab, make sure the Display a notification about every script error check box is selected, and click the OK button to close the dialog box. In versions of Netscape that support JavaScript 1.3 and higher, to view error messages you must point to Tools on the Tasks menu and select JavaScript Console. Depending on the browser version you are using, the error messages you see may appear differently from the error messages you see in the figures in this book.

▶ **tip**

Notice that the Netscape error message points you to line six, while the Internet Explorer error message points you to line five. Netscape points you to the line where the brace should be placed following the function body. Internet Explorer points you to the line that should be followed by the brace.

Regardless of which browser you use, you should use error messages only to find the general location of an error in a program and not as the exact indicator of an error. You cannot always assume that the line specified by an error message is the actual problem in your program. For example, the `var result = amount * percentage;` statement in the following code causes a run-time error because it cannot locate the percentage and amount variables. Since the percentage and amount variables are not global because they are declared inside the variableDeclarations() function, they are not visible to the calculatePercentage() function, and this causes a run-time error. Although the `var result = amount * percentage;` statement generates the run-time error, since it attempts to access variables that are local to another function, the real bug in the code is that the percentage and amount variables are not declared at a global level.

```
<SCRIPT LANGUAGE="JavaScript">
function variableDeclarations() {
     var percentage = .25;
     var amount = 1600;
}
function calculatePercentage() {
     var result = amount * percentage;
     document.write("Twenty-five percent of 1,600 is ");
     document.write(result);
}
</SCRIPT>
```

Note that you do not receive error messages for logic errors, since computers are not smart enough (yet) to identify a flaw in your logic. For example, if you create an infinite loop with a `for` statement, the interpreter has no way of telling whether you really wanted to continually execute the `for` statement code. Later in this tutorial, you will learn how to trace the flow of program execution in order to locate logic errors.

When debugging JavaScript, it is important that you understand how a browser interprets an HTML document and JavaScript code. A common complaint among professional programmers is that Web browsers do not strictly enforce JavaScript syntax. For example, you are not required to end a JavaScript statement with a semicolon. In contrast, in high-level languages such as C++ and Java, you *must* end a statement or you will receive an error. You can compare how Web browsers render HTML and interpret JavaScript to how human beings comprehend language. Someone can speak to you using poor grammar or with a strong regional or foreign accent. Yet, provided the other person is speaking to you in the same root language, you can usually understand what he or she is saying. The same applies to a Web browser and JavaScript: Even if you use sloppy JavaScript code, the Web browser can often (but not always) figure out what the code is supposed to do. This means that a Web browser can run JavaScript code and render HTML, even though your program contains bugs. In fact, a bug that generates an error message in one browser may be ignored altogether in another browser. For example, you typically use a statement similar to `// STOP HIDING FROM INCOMPATIBLE BROWSERS -->` to end the HTML comments that you use to hide JavaScript sections from incompatible browsers. The two slashes that begin the statement create a line comment that you use to describe the purpose of the statement. Technically, if you do not include the line comment, your browser should generate an error message, since the text *STOP HIDING FROM INCOMPATIBLE BROWSERS* is not valid JavaScript syntax. However, Internet Explorer will correctly interpret the statement `STOP HIDING FROM INCOMPATIBLE BROWSERS -->` as a closing HTML comment tag, even if it is contained within a JavaScript section and is technically a bug. Netscape, on the other hand, will interpret the statement as a bug and generate an error message.

This lack of common bug enforcement makes writing and debugging programs more difficult. What can you do to mitigate bugs in your JavaScript programs? First, always use good syntax, such as ending statements with semicolons and declaring variables with **var** keywords. The more disciplined you are in your programming technique, the fewer bugs you will find in your programs. Second, be sure to thoroughly test your JavaScript programs with every browser type and version on which you anticipate your program will run. At the time of this writing, Internet Explorer had the lion's share of the browser market. For this reason, some JavaScript programmers ignore Netscape and other browsers altogether. Yet, it is difficult to predict how long Microsoft will dominate the browser market. Netscape still holds 10% to 20% of the browser market, and other browsers, such as Opera and HotJava, are gaining in popularity. One rule of thumb is that if a browser is used by more than 1% of the market, then you need to write and debug your JavaScript programs for that browser.

 tip

A popular site for finding browser usage statistics is the Internet.com BrowserWatch Web site at *browserwatch.internet.com/.*

Next you will use error messages to help locate bugs in a JavaScript program. You can use either Netscape or Internet Explorer for the exercises in this section. If you have both browsers, try performing the exercises in each of them to try to locate bugs that may be ignored by only one of the browsers.

To use error messages to help locate bugs in a JavaScript program:

1 In your Web browser, open the **FavoriteFoods.html** file from the **Tutorial.07** folder on your Data Disk. The file uses several functions to print a list of favorite foods. As soon as you open the file, you should receive an error message. If you are using a version of Navigator higher than version 4, remember to point to **Tools** on the Tasks menu, and then select **JavaScript Console**. You can clear old error messages from the JavaScript Console by clicking the Clear button.

2 Close your Web browser and open **FavoriteFoods.html** in your text editor or HTML editor.

3 Locate and correct the errors specified by the error messages, and then save the file as **FavoriteFoodsDebug.html** in the **Tutorial.07** folder on your Data Disk. If you have trouble locating the bugs, a corrected version of the file named FavoriteFoodsCorrect.html is located in the Tutorial.07 folder on your Data Disk.

4 Open **FavoriteFoodsDebug.html** in your Web browser, and check for errors.

5 Continue correcting errors in your text editor or HTML editor until the file opens without any error messages.

6 Close the Web browser and editing windows.

Tracing Errors with the alert() Method

When you are unable to locate a bug in your program by using error messages, or if the bug is a logic error that does not generate error messages, then you must trace your code. **Tracing** is the examination of individual statements in an executing program. The alert() method provides one of the most useful ways to trace JavaScript code. You place an alert() method at different points in your program and use it to display the contents of a variable, an array, or the value returned from a function. Using this technique, you can monitor values as they change during program execution. For example, examine the function in Figure 7-3, which calculates weekly net pay, rounded to the nearest integer. The program is syntactically correct and does not generate an error message. However, the function is not returning the correct result, which should be 485. Instead, the function is returning a value of 5169107.

```
function calculatePay() {

    var payRate = 15; numHours = 40;

    var grossPay = payRate * numHours;

    var federalTaxes = grossPay * .06794;

    var stateTaxes = grossPay * .0476;

    var socialSecurity = grossPay * .062;

    var medicare = grossPay * .0145;

    var netPay = grossPay - federalTaxes;

    netPay *= stateTaxes;

    netPay *= socialSecurity;

    netPay *= medicare;

    return Math.round(netPay);

}
```

Figure 7-3: calculatePay() function with a logic error

To trace the problem, you place an alert() method at the point in the program where you think the error may be located. For example, the first thing you may want to check in the calculatePay() function is whether the grossPay variable is being calculated correctly. To check whether the program calculates grossPay correctly, place an alert() method in the function following the calculation of the grossPay variable as shown in Figure 7-4.

```
function calculatePay() {

    var payRate = 15; numHours = 40;

    var grossPay = payRate * numHours;

alert(grossPay);

    var federalTaxes = grossPay * .06794;

    var stateTaxes = grossPay * .0476;

    var socialSecurity = grossPay * .062;

    var medicare = grossPay * .0145;

    var netPay = grossPay - federalTaxes;
```

Figure 7-4: calculatePay() function with an alert() method to trace program execution

```
        netPay *= stateTaxes;

        netPay *= socialSecurity;

        netPay *= medicare;

        return Math.round(netPay);

}
```

Figure 7-4: `calculatePay( )` function with an alert() method to trace program execution (continued)

tip

It is helpful to place any alert methods you use to trace program execution at a different level of indentation to clearly distinguish them from the actual program.

Since the grossPay variable calculated correctly as 600, change the alert() method to start checking the value of the netPay variable, and move it down a line. Continue with this technique until you discover the error. The calculatePay() function does not perform properly because the lines that add the stateTaxes, socialSecurity, and medicare variables to the netPay variable are incorrect, since they use the multiplication assignment operator (*=) instead of the subtraction assignment operator (-=). A correct version of the program, named CalculatePayCorrect.html, is located in the Tutorial.07 folder on your Data Disk.

tip

Instead of using the alert() method, you can write information to the status bar, using the status property of the Window object.

An alternative to using a single alert() method is to place multiple alert() methods throughout your code to check values as the code executes. For example, you could trace the calculatePay() function by using multiple alert() methods, as shown in Figure 7-5.

```
function calculatePay( ) {

    var payRate = 15; numHours = 40;

    var grossPay = payRate * numHours;

alert(grossPay);

    var federalTaxes = grossPay * .06794;

    var stateTaxes = grossPay * .0476;

    var socialSecurity = grossPay * .062;

    var medicare = grossPay * .0145;

    var netPay = grossPay - federalTaxes;
```

Figure 7-5: `calculatePay( )` function with multiple alert() methods to trace program execution

```
alert(netPay);

    netPay *= stateTaxes;

alert(netPay);

    netPay *= socialSecurity;

alert(netPay);

    netPay *= medicare;

alert(netPay);

    return Math.round(netPay);

}
```

Figure 7-5: `calculatePay( )` function with multiple alert() methods to trace program
execution (continued)

One drawback to using multiple alert() methods to trace values is that you
must close each dialog box for your code to continue executing. However, using
multiple alert() methods is sometimes more efficient than moving a single alert()
method. The key to using multiple alert() methods to trace program values is using
them selectively at key points throughout a program. Consider a large accounting
program with multiple functions that is not executing properly. Place an alert()
method at key positions within the program, such as wherever a function returns a
value or a variable is assigned new data. In this way, you can get the big picture of
what portion of your program contains the bug. Once you discover the approxi-
mate location of the bug—for instance, in a particular function—you can then
concentrate your debugging efforts on that one function.

Next you will use alert dialog boxes to help locate bugs in a JavaScript program.

To use alert dialog boxes to help locate bugs in a JavaScript program:

1 In your Web browser, open the **VitalInfo.html** file from the **Tutorial.07** folder
on your Data Disk. The file is an online application that asks for various
types of personal information. Fill in each prompt dialog box with the
appropriate information. After entering information into all of the prompt
dialog boxes, you will see that the alert dialog box that appears does not display the correct information. At several points in the file, variables are being
assigned incorrect values.

2 Now open the **VitalInfo.html** file in your text editor or HTML editor, but
leave the file open in your Web browser window.

3   After the first variable declaration, `var name = prompt("Please enter your name.", "");` that assigns values to the name variable, add an alert() method: `alert(name);`. Then save the file.

4   Switch to your Web browser window, then click **Reload** or **Refresh**. After you enter information in the first text box, an alert dialog box should display the name variable.

5   To find the error, switch to your editor and move the alert() method so you can view the name of each variable as it is assigned. Be sure to change the variable name that is passed as the alert() method argument to the variable name you want to trace. When you find an error, correct it in the file. Note that there are multiple errors in the file. A corrected version of the file, named VitalInfoCorrect.html, is located in the Tutorial.07 folder on your Data Disk. Your corrected file should display a final dialog box similar to Figure 7-6.

Figure 7-6: Final dialog box in corrected VitalInfo.html file

6   Close the Web browser and editing windows.

Tracing Errors with the write() and writeln() Methods

There may be situations in which you want to trace a bug in your program by analyzing a list of values rather than by trying to interpret the values displayed in alert dialog boxes on a case-by-case basis. You can create such a list by opening a new browser window and using the write() and writeln() methods to print values to this separate window. Figure 7-7 shows an example of the calculatePay() function printing values to a separate window. The separate window is created at the beginning of the function, using the statement `valueWindow = window.open("","","height=300, width=400");`. The valueWindow variable is used to refer to the newly created window. Write() methods that print values to valueWindow are placed throughout the function. Figure 7-8 shows the contents of valueWindow after executing the calculatePay() function.

```
function calculatePay() {

valueWindow = window.open("","","height=300,width=400");

    var payRate = 15; numHours = 40;

    var grossPay = payRate * numHours;

valueWindow.document.write("grossPay is "
+ grossPay + "<BR>");

    var federalTaxes = grossPay * .06794;

    var stateTaxes = grossPay * .0476;

    var socialSecurity = grossPay * .062;

    var medicare = grossPay * .0145;

    var netPay = grossPay - federalTaxes;

valueWindow.document.write("netPay minus Federal taxes is "
+ netPay + "<BR>");

    netPay *= stateTaxes;

valueWindow.document.write("netPay minus State taxes is "
+ netPay + "<BR>");

    netPay *= socialSecurity;

valueWindow.document.write("netPay minus Social Security is "
+ netPay + "<BR>");

    netPay *= medicare;

valueWindow.document.write("netPay minus Medicare is "
+ netPay + "<BR>");

    return Math.round(netPay);

}
```

Figure 7-7: `calculatePay()` function printing values to a separate browser window

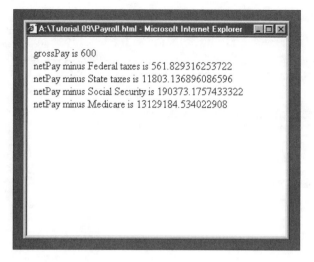

Figure 7-8: Contents of valueWindow after executing the `calculatePay()` function

Using the contents of the window in Figure 7-8, you can evaluate each variable in the calculatePay() function as values change throughout the function execution.

Next, you will use write() methods and a separate browser window to help locate bugs in a JavaScript program.

To use write() methods and a separate browser window to help locate bugs in a JavaScript program:

1 In your Web browser, open the **Questionnaire.html** file from the **Tutorial.07** folder on your Data Disk and fill in the appropriate information for each prompt. The file prompts users for their name, address, city, state, zip, and telephone number, assigns the information to an array named info, and then prints the information to the screen. However, *undefined* is being printed first, and the telephone number is not printing at all.

2 Open the **Questionnaire.html** file in your text editor or HTML editor, but leave the file open in your Web browser window.

3 After the for loop that prints the information to the screen, add the following code. The first statement creates a new, empty window. To allow you to clearly see the value assigned to each element in the info array, the new for loop prints the element number of the info array, along with the contents of each element.

```
valueWindow = window.open("","","height=300,width=400");
for(var i = 0; i < 4; ++i) {
    valueWindow.document.write("info[" + i + "]="
        + info[i] + "<BR>");
    }
```

4   Save the file, then switch to your Web browser window, and click **Reload** or **Refresh**. After you enter information in the text boxes and the lines are written to the screen, the new window opens displaying each array element number and its contents. Figure 7-9 shows an example of the new window.

```
A:\Tutorial.09\Questionnaire.html - Microsoft Internet E...

info[0]=undefined
info[1]=Don Gosselin
info[2]=49 Cranberry Meadow Road
info[3]=Spencer, MA 01562
```

Figure 7-9: Window containing the array elements

5   Find and correct the source of the error in the document by comparing the results written to the new window to the values as they are assigned to array elements. A corrected version of the file named QuestionnaireCorrect.html is located in the Tutorial.07 folder on your Data Disk.

6   Close the Web browser and editing windows.

Using Comments to Locate Bugs

Another method of locating bugs in a JavaScript program is to comment out lines that you think may be causing the problem. You can comment out individual lines that may be causing the error or comment out all lines except the lines that you know work. When you receive an error message, start by commenting out only the statement specified by the line number in the error message. Save the document, and then open it again in your Web browser to see if you receive another error. If you receive additional error messages, then comment out those statements as well. Once you eliminate the error messages, examine the commented out statements for the cause of the bug.

tip

••

The cause of an error in a particular statement is often the result of an error in a preceding line of code.

••

The last five statements in Figure 7-10 are commented out, since they generate error messages stating that yearlyIntrest is not defined. The problem with the code is that the yearlyInterest variable is incorrectly spelled as yearlyIntrest in several of the statements. Commenting out the lines isolates the problem statements.

```
var amount = 100000;

var percentage = .08;

document.write("The interest rate for a loan in the amount of "
     + amount + " is " + percentage);

var yearlyInterest = amount * percentage;

// document.writeln("The amount of interest for one year is "
     + yearlyIntrest);

// var monthlyInterest = yearlyIntrest / 12;

// document.writeln("The amount of interest for one month is "
     + monthlyInterest);

// var dailyInterest = yearlyIntrest / 365;

// document.writeln("The amount of interest for one day is "
     + dailyInterest);
```

Figure 7-10: Code using comments to trace errors

Although the error in Figure 7-10 may seem somewhat simple, it is typical of the types of errors you will encounter. Often you will see the error right away and not need to comment out code or use any other tracing technique. However, when you have been staring at the same code for long periods of time, simple spelling errors, like yearlyIntrest, are not always easy to spot. Commenting out the lines you know are giving you trouble is a good technique for helping you isolate and correct even the simplest types of bugs.

You can combine debugging techniques to aid in your search for errors. Figure 7-11 uses the calculatePay() function as an example of how to use comments combined with an alert dialog box to trace errors. You know that the `var grossPay = payRate * numHours;` statement is the last statement in the function that operates correctly. Therefore, all of the lines following that statement are commented out. You would then use an alert dialog box to check the value of each statement, removing comments from each statement in a sequential order, checking and correcting syntax as you go.

```
function calculatePay() {
    var payRate = 15; numHours = 40;
    var grossPay = payRate * numHours;
alert(grossPay);
//   var federalTaxes = grossPay * .06794;
//   var stateTaxes = grossPay * .0476;
//   var socialSecurity = grossPay * .062;
//   var medicare = grossPay * .0145;
//   var netPay = grossPay - federalTaxes;
//   netPay *= stateTaxes;
//   netPay *= socialSecurity;
//   netPay *= medicare;
//   return Math.round(netPay);
}
```

Figure 7-11: calculatePay() function with comments and an alert() method to trace program execution

Next you will use comments to help locate bugs in a JavaScript program.

To use comments to help locate bugs in a JavaScript program:

1 In your Web browser, open the **ComparisonExamples.html** file from the **Tutorial.07** folder on your Data Disk. The file contains various logical comparisons of two numbers. However, most of the statements contain errors. You will receive an error message when you open the file. Your goal in this exercise is to fix each of the errors so that the final output resembles Figure 7-12.

value1 equal to value2: false
value1 equal to value2: false
value1 not equal to value2: true
value1 greater than value2: false
value1 less than value2: true
value1 greater than or equal to value2: false
value1 less than or equal to value2: true

Figure 7-12: Correct output of ComparisonExamples.html

2 Next open the **ComparisonExamples.html** file in your text editor or HTML editor, but leave the file open in your Web browser window.

3 Start by commenting out all the lines in the script section.

4 Next remove the comments one line at time. Each time you remove a comment, save the file, switch to your Web browser, and then reload or refresh the file. Fix each error as you encounter it.

5 Once you have fixed all the errors and your output resembles Figure 7-12, close the Web browser and editing windows. A corrected version of the file named ComparisonExamplesCorrect.html is located in the Tutorial.07 folder on your Data Disk.

Additional Debugging Techniques

The rest of this section discusses additional methods and techniques for locating and correcting errors in your JavaScript programs, including checking your HTML code, analyzing your logic, testing statements with JavaScript URLs, and reloading an HTML document.

Checking HTML Tags

There will be occasions when you cannot locate the source of a bug, no matter how long you search. In such cases, the simplest element is usually causing the problem. Sometimes it is not a problem with your JavaScript code at all, but a problem with your HTML tags. If you cannot locate a bug using any of the methods described in this section, then perform a line-by-line analysis of your HTML code, making sure that all tags have opening and closing brackets. Also, be sure that all necessary opening and closing tags, such as the <SCRIPT>...</SCRIPT> tag pair are included. For an example of a problem with HTML tags that can cause problems with JavaScript, examine the following code. The code contains an error that can be difficult to spot:

```
<HTML>
<HEAD>
<TITLE>Error Example</TITLE>
<SCRIPT LANGUAGE="JavaScript"
    document.writeln("Hello World");
</SCRIPT>
</HEAD>
<BODY>
<H2>Error Example</H2>
</BODY>
</HTML>
```

The problem with the preceding code is that the <SCRIPT> tag is missing a closing bracket. Without the closing bracket, the browser sees only the script section that you want to include in the head section of the document. Since the contents of the head section are not rendered, you never receive an error message, nor do you see the output from the writeln() method. In your debugging efforts, you may think the JavaScript code is not functioning properly when actually it does not function at all.

Next you will find and correct HTML errors that are preventing a JavaScript program from running.

To find and correct HTML errors that are preventing a JavaScript program from running:

1   In your Web browser, open the **PrintDate.html** file from the **Tutorial.07** folder on your Data Disk. The PrintDate.html file is not working. It is supposed to display the date in an alert dialog box.

2   Next open the **PrintDate.html** file in your text editor or HTML editor, but leave the file open in your Web browser window.

3   Locate and correct each of the HTML errors, then save the file. Switch to your Web browser, and then click **Reload** or **Refresh**.

> **4** Once you have fixed the errors and the date prints to the screen, close the Web browser and editing windows. A corrected version of the file named PrintDateCorrect.html is located in the Tutorial.07 folder on your Data Disk.

Analyzing Your Logic

At times, errors in your JavaScript code will be logic problems that are difficult to spot using tracing techniques. When you suspect that your code contains logic errors, you must analyze each statement on a case-by-case basis. For example, the following code contains a logic flaw that prevents it from functioning correctly:

```
var displayAlert = false, conditionTrue;
if (displayAlert == true)
    conditionTrue = "condition is true";
    alert(conditionTrue);
```

If you were to execute the preceding code, you would always see the alert dialog box, although it should not appear, since the displayAlert variable is set to false. However, if you examine the `if` statement more closely, you will see that the `if` statement ends after the declaration of the conditionTrue variable. The alert() method following the variable declaration is not part of the `if` structure, since the `if` statement does not include a set of braces to enclose the lines it executes when the conditional evaluation returns true. The alert() method will also display the value *undefined*, since the statement that assigns the value *condition is true* to the conditionTrue variable is bypassed when the `if` statement conditional expression evaluates to false. For the code to execute properly, the `if` statement must include braces as follows:

```
var displayAlert = false, conditionTrue;
if (displayAlert == true) {
    conditionTrue = "condition is true";
    alert(conditionTrue);
}
```

The following code shows another example of an easily overlooked logic error, using a `for` statement:

```
var count = 0;
for (var count = 1; count < 6; ++count);
    document.writeln(count);
```

The code should print the numbers 1 through 5 to the screen. However, the line `for (var count = 1; count < 6; ++count);` contains an ending semicolon, which marks the end of the `for` loop. The loop executes five times and changes the value of count to 6, but does nothing else, since there are no statements before its ending semicolon. The line `document.writeln(count);` is a separate statement that executes only once, printing the number 6 to the screen. The code is syntactically correct, but does not function as you anticipated. As you can see from these examples, it is easy to overlook very minor logic errors in your code.

Testing Statements with JavaScript URLs

If you find that the error in your code is the result of a single statement, you can test the statement using a JavaScript URL without rerunning the entire program. A **JavaScript URL** is used for testing and executing JavaScript statements without an HTML document or JavaScript source file. The syntax for a JavaScript URL is `javascript:statement(s)`. You enter a JavaScript URL into the Netscape Location box or the Internet Explorer Address box, just like a normal URL. When your browser sees the URL's javascript: protocol, it executes the JavaScript statements that follow. For example, to display an alert dialog box without executing a script, enter `javascript:alert("Hello World")` into your browser Location or Address box. You can include multiple statements in a JavaScript URL if a semicolon separates them. To declare a variable and display its value using an alert dialog box, you use the syntax `javascript:var stringVar="Hello World";alert(stringVar)`.

JavaScript URLs are particularly useful if you are trying to construct the correct syntax for a mathematical expression. The following code calculates the total amount due on a mortgage of $100,000. The calculation adds 8% interest and a $35 late fee. However, the calculation does not function correctly because of an order of precedence problem.

```
mortgageBalance = 100000;
interest = .08;
lateFees = 35;
document.write(mortgageBalance + lateFees * 1 + interest);
```

Although you can modify the structure of the formula directly within a JavaScript program, you can also use a JavaScript URL to test the calculation. The following statement displays the result of the formula in an alert dialog box, using a JavaScript URL. Parentheses that correct the order of precedence problem have been added to the formula.

```
javascript:mortgageBalance=100000;
interest=.08; lateFees=35;
alert((mortgageBalance + lateFees) * (1 + interest));
```

 tip

The preceding code example is broken onto multiple lines due to space limitations in this book. To check code using a JavaScript URL, you must enter the code all on one line before pressing Enter.

Reloading an HTML Document

When you edit the JavaScript code in an HTML document, it is usually sufficient to save the document and click the Reload or Refresh button in your browser to test your changes. However, it is important to understand that with complex scripts, a Web browser cannot always completely clear its memory of the remnants of an old bug, even though you have fixed the code. Therefore, it is sometimes necessary to completely reopen the document, using the Open or Open Page command on your browser File menu. At times, however, even reopening the file will not completely clear the browser memory of the old JavaScript code. Instead, you must close the browser window completely and start a new session. You may also find it necessary to delete the frequently visited Web pages that your browser temporarily stores either in your computer's memory or on the hard drive. You delete temporary files in Netscape by selecting Preferences from the Edit menu to display the Preferences dialog box. In the Preferences dialog box, expand the Advanced category, click the Cache option, and then click the Clear Memory Cache and Clear Disk Cache buttons. The Clear Memory Cache button deletes Web pages that are stored in memory, and the Clear Disk Cache button deletes Web pages that are stored on your hard drive. To delete temporary Web pages in Internet Explorer, select Internet Options from the Tools menu and click the Delete Files button on the General tab. Do not forget to perform these tasks if you are certain that you have fixed an error in your code, but are unable to get your program to perform properly.

 **S U M M A R Y**

- Syntax errors occur when you enter code that the interpreter does not recognize.

- If the JavaScript interpreter encounters a problem while a program is executing, that problem is called a run-time error.

- Run-time errors differ from syntax errors in that they do not necessarily represent JavaScript language errors. Instead, run-time errors occur when the interpreter encounters code that it cannot handle.

- Logic errors are problems in the design of a program that prevent it from running as you anticipate. The logic behind any program involves executing the various statements and procedures in the correct order to produce the desired results.

- The first line of defense in locating bugs in JavaScript programs is the error messages you receive when the JavaScript interpreter encounters a syntax or run-time error.

■ Error messages should only be used to find the general location of an error in a program, not as the exact indicator of an error. You cannot always assume that the line specified by an error message contains the actual problem in your program.

■ Tracing is the examination of individual statements in an executing program.

■ The alert() method provides one of the most useful ways to trace JavaScript code. You place an alert() method at different points in your program and use it to display the contents of a variable or array, or the value returned from a function.

■ Using multiple alert() methods to trace an error is sometimes more efficient than moving a single alert() method.

■ You can create a list of values assigned to a variable by opening a new browser window and printing values using the write() and writeln() methods.

■ Comments are often used to help locate bugs in a JavaScript program. You can comment out individual lines that may be causing the error, or comment out all lines except the lines that you know work.

■ If you cannot locate a bug by using error messages, tracing, or comments, then perform a line-by-line analysis of your HTML code, making sure that all tags have opening and closing brackets.

■ A JavaScript URL is used for testing and executing JavaScript statements without an HTML document or JavaScript source file.

■ It is sometimes necessary to completely reopen an HTML document or restart your browser for changes to JavaScript code to take effect.

Q U E S T I O N S

1. _____ errors occur when you enter code that the interpreter does not recognize.
    a. Application
    b. Logic
    c. Run-time
    d. Syntax

2. If the JavaScript interpreter encounters a problem while a program is executing, that problem is called a(n) _____ error.
    a. application
    b. logic
    c. run-time
    d. syntax

3. _____ errors are problems in the design of a program that prevent it from running as you anticipate.

a. Application

b. Logic

c. Run-time

d. Syntax

4. Which of the following statements would cause a syntax error?

a. `alert("Hello World.");`

b. `document.writeln("Hello World")`

c. `Return true;`

d. `myDate = new Date();`

5. Which of the following scripts would cause a run-time error, assuming that the script section is the only one in a document?

a.
```
<SCRIPT LANGUAGE="JavaScript">
var greeting = "Welcome to my Web page!";
alert(greeting);
</SCRIPT>
```

b.
```
<SCRIPT LANGUAGE="JavaScript">
var greeting = "Welcome to my Web page!";
alert("greeting");
</SCRIPT>
```

c.
```
<SCRIPT LANGUAGE="JavaScript">
var greeting = "Welcome to my Web page!";
alert("" + greeting);
</SCRIPT>
```

d.
```
<SCRIPT LANGUAGE="JavaScript">
alert(greeting);
</SCRIPT>
```

6. Which of the following `if` statements is logically incorrect?

a.
```
if (count < 5)
        document.write(count);
```

b.
```
if (count =< 5)
        document.write(count);
```

c.
```
if (count = 5);
        document.write(count);
```

d.
```
if (count = 5) {
        document.write(count);
}
```

7. Which of the following types of errors is caught by error messages?

a. application

b. logic

c. run-time

d. breakpoint

8. _____ refers to the examination of individual statements in an executing program.
   a. Trailing
   b. Tracing
   c. Tracking
   d. Auditing

9. Which of the following JavaScript elements is *not* used in debugging?
   a. `switch` statements
   b. the alert() method
   c. the write() and writeln() methods
   d. comments

10. Which of the following code structures prints the text *Hello World* five times?

```
a. for (var count = 1; count < 6; ++count);
        document.writeln("Hello World");
        document.writeln("Hello World");
        document.writeln("Hello World");
        document.writeln("Hello World");
        document.writeln("Hello World");
b. for (var count = 0; count < 6; ++count)
        document.writeln("Hello World");
c. for (var count = 0; count < 6; ++count) {
        document.writeln("Hello World");
   }
d. for (var count = 0; count < 6; ++count);
        document.writeln("Hello World");
```

11. Which of the following is the correct syntax for executing a JavaScript URL?

```
a. javascriptURL:alert("Hello World");
b. javascript:"alert('Hello World');"
c. javascript:"alert("Hello World");"
d. javascript:alert("Hello World");
```

E X E R C I S E S

Save all files you create in the Tutorial.07 folder on your Data Disk.

1. The following code contains syntax errors. Fix the bugs and save the HTML document as StringProblem_Correct.html.

```
<SCRIPT LANGUAGE="JavaScript">
document.writeln(This is a text string.);
document.writeln("This is another text string.');
document.writeln("This should be a "quoted" text string.");
</SCRIPT>
```

2. The following code contains a syntax error. Fix the bug and save the HTML document as IfElse_Correct.html.

```
<SCRIPT LANGUAGE="JavaScript">
var iNumber = prompt("Please enter a number.", "");
if (iNumber <= 100) {
   document.writeln("The number you entered is " + iNumber);
   document.writeln(iNumber + " is between 0 and 100");
else if (iNumber > 100)
   document.writeln("The number you entered is " + iNumber);
   document.writeln(iNumber + " is greater than 100");
}
</SCRIPT>
```

3. The following code generates error messages in both Internet Explorer and Navigator. Fix the bug and save the HTML document as Stocks_Correct.html.

```
<SCRIPT LANGUAGE="JavaScript">
var stockShares == 100;
var stockValue == 22.75;
document.write("Current stock value: ");
document.write(stockShares * stockValue);
</SCRIPT>
```

4. The following code will cause your browser to enter an infinite loop. Fix the problem and save the HTML document as InfiniteLoop_Correct.html.

```
var count = 1;
while (count <= 10) {
     alert("The number is " + count);
}
```

5. At an interest rate of 8%, the first year's interest on a mortgage of 120000 is 9600. However, the following code is printing NaN as the total yearly interest. Correct the errors and save the HTML document as InterestRate_Correct.html.

```
<SCRIPT LANGUAGE="JavaScript">
var mortgage = 120000;
var interest = .08;
document.write("At an interest rate of " + interest
   + ", the first year's interest on a mortgage of "
   + mortgage + " is " + "mortgage" * "interest");
</SCRIPT>
```

6. The following code should print the values 1, 2, 4, and 5 to the screen. Instead, the code prints only 1 and 2 to the screen. Locate and correct the error. Save the HTML document as For_Correct.html.

```
for(var count = 1; count <=5; ++count) {
  if(count == 3)
          break;
  document.writeln(count);
}
```

7. The following program illegally uses a reserved word that causes several syntax errors when you attempt to open it in a Web browser. Fix the errors and save the HTML document as ReturnValue_Correct.html.

```
<HTML>
<HEAD>
<TITLE>Return Value</TITLE>
<SCRIPT LANGUAGE="JavaScript">
function average_numbers(a, b, c) {
  var sum_of_numbers = a + b + c;
  var return = sum_of_numbers / 3;
  return return;
}
</SCRIPT>
</HEAD>
<BODY>
<PRE>
<SCRIPT LANGUAGE="JavaScript">
document.write(
        "<P>The average of the numbers 4, 18, and 32 is ");
document.write(
        average_numbers(4, 18, 32) + "</P>");
</SCRIPT></P>
</PRE>
</BODY>
</HTML>
```

8. The following code should print *condition is false* to the screen. However, although the displayAlert variable holds a value of false, the code prints *condition is true* to the screen. Fix the bug and save the HTML document as Condition_Correct.html.

```
<SCRIPT LANGUAGE="JavaScript">
var displayAlert = false;
var conditionState;
if (displayAlert = true) {
  conditionState = "condition is true";
  document.write(conditionState);
}
else if (displayAlert = false) {
  conditionState = "condition is false";
  document.write(conditionState);
}
else {
  conditionState = "no condition";
  document.write(conditionState);
}
</SCRIPT>
```

9. The following code should print *My Company* to the screen, but nothing happens when you open the document in a Web browser. Fix the bug and save the HTML document as CompanyName_Correct.html.

```
<HTML>
<HEAD>
<TITLE>Print Company Name Function</TITLE>
<SCRIPT LANGUAGE="JavaScript">
<!-- HIDE FROM INCOMPATIBLE BROWSERS
function print_company_name() {
     var company_name = "My Company";
     document.writeln(company_name);
}
// STOP HIDING FROM INCOMPATIBLE BROWSERS -->
</SCRIPT>
</HEAD>
<BODY>
<SCRIPT LANGUAGE="JavaScript">
<!-- HIDE FROM INCOMPATIBLE BROWSERS
print_company_name;
// STOP HIDING FROM INCOMPATIBLE BROWSERS -->
</SCRIPT>
</BODY>
</HTML>
```

10. The following code should display an alert box after five seconds (using the setInterval() method), or after the user clicks the command button. However, if you execute the code and click the command button before five seconds has elapsed, a second alert box displays after you close the first alert box, even though the displayAlert() function calls the clearTimeout() method. In other words, the clearTimeout() method is not being called properly after the user clicks the command button. Locate and correct the error. Save the HTML document as AlertCode_Correct.html.

```
<HTML>
<HEAD>
<TITLE>Exercise 2A</TITLE>
<SCRIPT LANGUAGE="JavaScript">
var showAlert;
function displayAlert() {
  clearTimeout(showAlert);
  alert("Hello World.");
}
</SCRIPT>
</HEAD>
<BODY onLoad=
       "var showAlert=setTimeout('displayAlert()',5000);">
<FORM>
<INPUT TYPE="button"
       VALUE="Click here to show an alert dialog box"
  onClick="displayAlert();">
</FORM>
</BODY>
</HTML>
```

11. The following code should print the days of the week. Instead, only Tuesday through Sunday print, and an indecipherable value prints after *Sunday*. Locate and correct the error. Save the HTML document as Array_Correct.html.

```
daysOfWeek = new Array(7);
daysOfWeek[0] = "Monday";
daysOfWeek[1] = "Tuesday";
daysOfWeek[2] = "Wednesday";
daysOfWeek[3] = "Thursday";
daysOfWeek[4] = "Friday";
daysOfWeek[5] = "Saturday";
daysOfWeek[6] = "Sunday";
var count = 1;
do {
   document.writeln(daysOfWeek[count]);
   ++count;
} while (count <= 7);
```

12. When you pass your mouse over the link in the following code, the status bar text should change to *Course Technology Home Page*, but nothing happens. Locate and correct the error. Save the HTML document as MouseOver_Correct.html.

```
<HTML>
<HEAD>
<TITLE>MouseOver</TITLE>
<SCRIPT LANGUAGE="JavaScript">
defaultStatus = "";
</SCRIPT>
</PRE>
</HEAD>
<BODY>
<A HREF="http://www.course.com"
      onMouseOver=
      "status='Course Technology Home Page';return true">
      Course Technology</A>
</BODY>
</HTML>
```

In this section you will learn:

■ How to use a `for...in` statement to check object properties

■ How to use watch points in Netscape

■ How to use the Netscape JavaScript Debugger

■ How to use the Microsoft Script Debugger

■ About JavaScript language bugs and debugging resources

Advanced Debugging Techniques and Resources

Using a `for...in` Statement to Check Object Properties

Sometimes program errors are caused by using the wrong object properties or by assigning the wrong value to an object property. Recall that the `for...in` statement is a looping statement that executes the same statement or command block for all of the properties within an object. You can use a `for...in` loop to determine if values are being assigned to the correct properties in an object. This technique is useful when you have an object with many properties, and you cannot trace the cause of incorrect values being assigned to properties. Consider the following constructor function, which instantiates a Car object:

```
function Car(make, model, color) {
    this.car_make = make;
    this.car_model = model;
    this.car_color = color;
}
```

When you instantiate a new Car object using the statement `myCar = new Car("Jeep", "Gray", "CJ7");`, you discover that the color of the car is being assigned to the car_model property, and the model of the car is being assigned to the car_color property. To help trace the problem, you can use the following `for...in` statement to loop through the properties in the Car object and display their values in an alert dialog box:

```
myCar = new Car("Jeep", "Gray", "CJ7");
var propertiesList = "";
```

```
for (prop in myCar) {
    propertiesList += prop + "=" + myCar[prop] + "\n";
}
alert(propertiesList);
```

The preceding code creates the dialog box displayed in Figure 7-13.

Figure 7-13: Alert dialog box created with a for...in statement

From the values listed in the alert box, you can see that car_color and car_make are assigned the wrong values because the argument list in the statement that instantiates the myCar object is incorrect. Instead of `myCar = new Car("Jeep", "Gray", "CJ7");`, the statement should be `myCar = new Car("Jeep", "CJ7", "Gray");`. Although this example of using the `for...in` statement to track down property values is fairly simple, it gives you an idea of how to use this technique to locate bugs in the assignment of object properties.

Watch Points in Netscape

Another technique for monitoring object properties is to use watch points. A **watch point** is a specific object property that you monitor for changes during program execution. Netscape includes two methods, watch() and unwatch(), that are used for setting and removing watch points for a particular object. The **watch() method** sets a watch point for an object property. To watch the property of a particular object, you include a statement that appends the watch() method to the object name and place it following the statement that instantiates the object. The watch() method receives two arguments: the name of the property to watch enclosed in quotation marks and the name of a function to execute when the property changes. The syntax for the watch() method is `object.watch("property", function name);`. For example, to set a watch point that executes a function named watchColor() for the car_color property of an object named myCar, you use the statement `myCar.watch("car_color", watchColor);` following the line that instantiates myCar from the Car object. Notice that the watchColor() function in the watch() statement does not include parentheses like most other functions. You exclude the parentheses from the function you are calling from the watch() method, similarly to the way you exclude the parentheses from an object method you add to a constructor function.

Later in this section, you will learn how to use the Netscape JavaScript Debugger and the Microsoft Script Debugger to set watch points.

The function you call with the watch() method has automatically passed three arguments: the name of the property, the original value of the property, and the new value being assigned to the property. You need to include three variables in the function header to receive the arguments. The following function is an example of the watchColor() function that executes whenever the car_color property changes:

```
function watchColor(prop, oldValue, newValue) {
    alert("The " + prop + " property has changed from "
        + oldValue + " to " + newValue);
    return newValue;
}
```

Notice that the watchColor() function header includes three variables, prop, oldValue, and newValue, to receive the property name, old value, and new value arguments. Also notice that the function returns the newValue variable. You must return a value, or the watched property will be assigned a value of *undefined*. Figure 7-14 shows a complete example of the program that monitors the car_color property.

Notice in Figure 7-14 that the watch() method statement is placed after the statement that declares the myCar object. Placing the watch() method before the declaration of an object causes an error. Executing the program would display three alert dialog boxes, one for each time the car_color property changes.

The **unwatch() method** cancels a previously declared watch. The syntax for the unwatch() method is `object.unwatch("property");`. For example, if you want to cancel the watch() method in Figure 7-14 after the car_color property changes to black, you add the statement `myCar.unwatch("car_color");` before the statement that changes the car_color property to red.

```
<HTML>

<HEAD>

<TITLE>Car Properties</TITLE>

<SCRIPT LANGUAGE="JavaScript">

function Car(make, model, color) {

    this.car_make = make;

    this.car_model = model;

    this.car_color = color;

}
```

Figure 7-14: car_color property of the myCar object being monitored with a watch() method

```
function watchColor(prop, oldValue, newValue) {

    alert("The " + prop + " property has changed from "
        + oldValue + " to " + newValue);

    return newValue;

}

myCar = new Car("Jeep", "CJ7", "Gray");

myCar.watch("car_color", watchColor);

myCar.car_color = "blue";

myCar.car_color = "black";

myCar.car_color = "red";

</SCRIPT>

<BODY>

</BODY>

</HTML>
```

Figure 7-14: car_color property of the myCar object being monitored with a watch() method
(continued)

To use watch points to monitor a changing variable in Netscape:

1 In Netscape, open the **FootballTeams.html** file from the **Tutorial.07** folder on your Data Disk. The FootballTeams.html file creates an object from the Football constructor function, and then prints the properties of the object.

2 Next, open the **FootballTeams.html** file in your text editor or HTML editor, but leave the file open in your Web browser window. You will add watch statements to monitor when the teamName property of the favoriteTeam object changes.

3 Just after the statement that instantiates the favoriteTeam object (favoriteTeam = new FootballTeam("Patriots", "New England"), add the statement **favoriteTeam.watch("teamName", watchName);**.

4 Next add the following watchName() function before the FootballTeam() constructor function. The watchName() function will be called each time the teamName property changes.

```
function watchName(prop, oldValue, newValue) {
    alert("The " + prop +
    " property has changed from "
    + oldValue + " to " + newValue);
    return newValue;
}
```

5   Save the file, return to Netscape, and then reload the **FootballTeam.html** file. You should see two dialog boxes, one for each time the teamName property changes.

6   Close the Web browser and editing windows.

Netscape JavaScript Debugger

Many high-level programming languages such as Visual C++ have debugging capabilities built directly into their development environments. These built-in debugging capabilities provide sophisticated commands for tracking errors. The JavaScript programming language does not have a development environment other than your text editor or HTML editor. The only true debugging tools you have in JavaScript are the error messages generated by a browser, unless you count the watch() and unwatch() methods, which are specific to Netscape. To provide JavaScript with debugging capabilities, both Netscape and Microsoft developed debugging tools that can be used with their browsers to debug JavaScript code. First we will discuss the Netscape tool, called the JavaScript Debugger.

Note that at the time of this writing, a Netscape 6 version of the JavaScript Debugger was not available since the Netscape 6 browser had only recently been released. Therefore, this section uses an older version of the JavaScript Debugger that is compatible with versions of Netscape Navigator earlier than 4.7. The examples shown in this section are created using Navigator version 4.7. When the JavaScript Debugger for Netscape 6 becomes available, it will, more than likely, differ only slightly from the version discussed in this book; the installation and configuration instructions are most likely to change. However, most of the debugging principles discussed here should apply to the new version.

Up to this point, you have learned how to interpret error messages and correct the statements that cause the errors. As helpful as they are, error messages are useful only in resolving syntax and run-time errors. You have also learned some techniques that assist in locating logic errors. Examining your code manually is usually the first step to take when you have a logic error, or you may use an alert dialog box to track values. These techniques work fine with smaller programs. However, when you are creating a large program that includes multiple objects, methods, and functions, logic errors can be very difficult to spot. For instance, you may have a function that instantiates objects from several different constructor functions. Each instantiated object may then call methods or use properties from its parent object or from other ancestor objects. Attempting to trace the logic and flow of such a program using simple tools such as the alert dialog box can be difficult. The Netscape JavaScript Debugger provides several tools that can help you trace each line of code, creating a much more efficient method of finding and resolving logic errors.

••

In versions of Navigator between 4.5 and 6, brief descriptions of JavaScript errors appear in the status bar. You can access more information on JavaScript errors in these versions of Navigator by typing "javascript:" into the Location box, without any code following it.

••

Before you can use the JavaScript Debugger, you must download and install it from *developer.netscape.com/software/jsdebug.html*. Follow the instructions there for installing the program. During the installation process, you will be prompted to grant several privileges. If you like, click the Certificate button to make sure Netscape signed the document. You will not be able to use the JavaScript Debugger unless you grant access to the privileges. Note that you will be prompted to grant the privileges each time you open the debugger unless you click the Remember this decision button.

••

Do not change pages in Navigator during installation of the JavaScript Debugger or the installation will fail.

••

The JavaScript Debugger is an applet that starts automatically during the download process. To start the debugger in subsequent Navigator sessions, you must open the Jsdebugger.html file from the \JSDebug folder, which is installed somewhere in the Netscape folder on your computer. Therefore, as soon as the installation is complete, you should create a bookmark to the Jsdebugger.html file. Opening the Jsdebugger.html file actually creates three windows: a Navigator window containing the JavaScript Debugger start page, another Navigator "applet stub" window that executes the JavaScript Debugger applet, and an applet window containing the JavaScript Debugger program. Open a document you want to debug in the window containing the JavaScript Debugger start page, then use the JavaScript Debugger commands in the applet window. Once the applet loads, you can use the Exit Debugger link in the applet stub window to close the applet.

You create a bookmark in Navigator by opening the page you want to bookmark, then pressing Ctrl+D.

When you first open the Jsdebugger.html file in a Navigator session, it usually takes a few moments for the applet to start, during which time the applet stub window displays the message *Loading Debugger*. Figure 7-15 shows an example of the start page and applet stub window before the applet opens. Figure 7-16 shows an example of the JavaScript Debugger applet window before a document is opened for debugging.

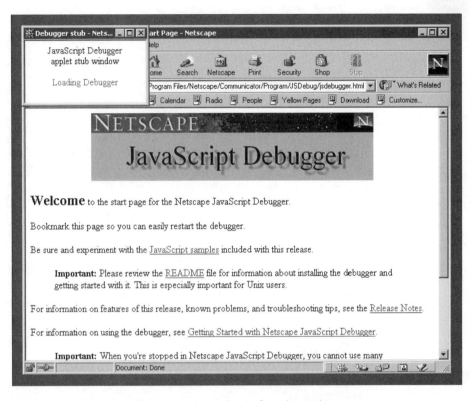

Figure 7-15: Start page and applet stub window before the applet opens

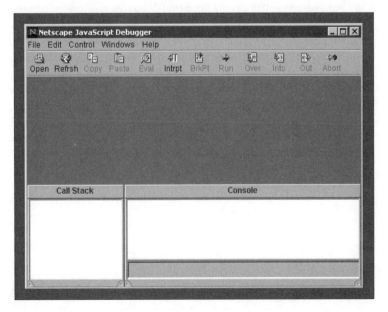

Figure 7-16: JavaScript Debugger applet window before a document is opened for debugging

When the applet first loads, the JavaScript Debugger window contains a Call Stack window and a Console window. You will learn how to work with these windows later in this section.

Source View

The Control menu in the JavaScript debugger contains several commands for entering and working in break mode. **Break mode** temporarily suspends, or pauses, program execution so that you can monitor values and trace program execution. Before you can enter break mode and use any of the tools on the Control menu, you must open a document in a Source View window. A **Source View** window is a separate debugging window for each HTML page opened in the JavaScript Debugger. You can have multiple Source View windows open at the same time. To open an HTML document in Source View, you must:

1. Select the Set Interrupt command from the Control menu. The Set Interrupt command instructs the JavaScript Debugger to enter break mode as soon as it encounters JavaScript code.
2. Switch to the Navigator window containing the JavaScript Debugger start page, and open the HTML page you want to debug. As soon as JavaScript code is encountered, Navigator pauses execution and switches to the JavaScript Debugger.

• •
To clear an interrupt that is set for an HTML document, select Clear Interrupt from the Control menu.
• •

This book instructs you to use the JavaScript Debugger menu to execute commands. However, many of the commands are also available as icons on the JavaScript Debugger toolbar.
• •

Once you open a document in the JavaScript Debugger, colors and icons appear in the left margin to indicate various elements of the JavaScript program. For example, an orange bar appears to the left of a function body, and a yellow bar indicates the main <SCRIPT> section of the document. An arrow in the margin designates the JavaScript statement at which the debugger is currently paused. Figure 7-17 shows an example of an HTML document opened in Source View. Notice that the name of the file appears at the top of the Source View window.

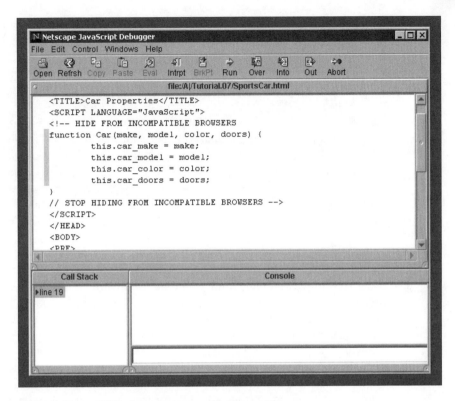

Figure 7-17: An HTML document opened in Source View

tip

If you would like the JavaScript Debugger to display line numbers in the left margin, select Preferences from the Edit menu, then select Show Line Numbers. You can turn off line numbers by selecting Preferences from the Edit menu, then selecting Hide Line Numbers.

Next you will open an HTML document in Source View for debugging. The HTML document you will work with for the rest of this section is named CompanyObjects.html. The CompanyObjects.html file contains several functions and constructor functions that print information about a company. The document does not contain any errors—the purpose of most of the exercises in this section is for you to become accustomed to working with the Netscape JavaScript Debugger and with the Microsoft Script Debugger.

help

Remember, the steps in this section use Navigator 4.7. If you are not using Navigator 4.7, when the debugger enters break mode, the statements referenced in the following steps may not directly correspond to the location at which your version of Navigator enters break mode.

To open an HTML document in Source View for debugging:

1   Open **Navigator**, then open the **Jsdebugger.html** file. If necessary, grant any privileges. (You will learn about privileges in the next chapter.)

2   After the JavaScript Debugger applet opens, select **Set Interrupt** from the **Control** menu.

3   Switch to the Navigator window containing the JavaScript Debugger start page and open the **CompanyObjects.html** file from the **Tutorial.07** folder on your Data Disk. As soon as the debugger encounters JavaScript code, the program pauses, and the CompanyObjects.html file opens in a Source View window in break mode. The debugger stops at the `function company( ) {` line, since it is the first JavaScript code to execute.

Step Commands

The Step Into, Step Over, and Step Out commands on the Control menu are used for continuing program execution once you enter break mode. The **Step Into command** executes an individual line of code and then pauses until you instruct the debugger to continue. This feature gives you an opportunity to evaluate program flow and structure as it is being executed.

As you use the Step Into command to move through code, the debugger stops at each line within every function of the JavaScript program. When stepping through a program to trace a logical error, it is convenient to be able to skip functions that you know are functioning correctly. The **Step Over command** allows you to skip function calls. The program still executes the function that you step over, but it appears in the debugger as if a single statement executes.

The Step Out command executes all remaining code in the current function. If the current function were called from another function, all remaining code in the current function executes and the debugger stops at the next statement in the calling function.

When a program enters break mode, program execution is not stopped—it is only suspended. To resume program execution after entering break mode, select Run from the Control menu. The Run command ends the debugging session and executes the rest of the program normally. You can also end a debugging session by selecting the Abort command from the Control menu. The Abort command stops execution of the current function and continues executing the rest of the program.

help

Again remember, the steps in this section use Navigator 4.7. If you are not using Navigator 4.7 when you use the step commands, your version of Navigator may not pause at the statements listed in the following steps.

Next you will practice tracing program execution using the step commands.

To practice tracing program execution using the step commands:

1 Return to the **CompanyObjects.html** document in the JavaScript Debugger.

2 Select **Step Into** from the **Control** menu. Since the Company() constructor function is not actually being called, the JavaScript Debugger skips the function and moves to the first line in the Sales() constructor function.

3 Select **Step Into** again, and the program skips over the Sales() constructor function and pauses at the `Sales.prototype = new Company;` statement.

4 Select **Step Into** again. Since the `Sales.prototype = new Company;` statement uses the prototype property to extend the Company object definition, program execution transfers to the first statement in the Company() constructor function.

5 Next select **Step Out** from the Control menu. The Step Out command executes the remaining statement in the Company() constructor function, then moves back to the `Sales.prototype = new Company;` statement.

6 Select **Step Into**, and program execution moves to the next line, `function Production() {`, which is the first line in the Production() constructor function. Select **Step Into** again and the program skips over the Production() constructor function and pauses at the `Production.prototype = new Company;` statement, which also uses the prototype property to extend the Company object definition.

7 Next select **Step Over** from the **Control** menu. The Step Over command executes all of the commands in the Company constructor function, then moves to the next line, `function displaySalesInfo() {`.

8 Finally, since you know that there is no problem with the program, select **Run** from the **Control** menu to finish executing the rest of the JavaScript code.

9 Close Navigator and the JavaScript Debugger windows.

Breakpoints

Another method of tracing program execution in the JavaScript Debugger involves inserting breakpoints into code. A **breakpoint** is a statement in the code at which program execution enters break mode. Once a program is paused at a breakpoint, you can use the Step Into, Step Over, and Step Out commands to trace program execution, or you can use the Run or Abort commands to complete program execution and run to the next breakpoint. Multiple breakpoints provide a convenient way to pause program execution at key positions in your code where you think there may be a bug.

The steps for opening an HTML document you want to debug with break-points are somewhat different from the steps you use with the Set Interrupt command. You must open the document in Navigator, and then open it again in the JavaScript Debugger. The specific steps are as follows:

1. Start Navigator, then open the Jsdebugger.html page to start JavaScript Debugger. Then open the HTML document you want to debug.
2. Switch to the JavaScript Debugger and select the Open command from the File menu. The Open dialog box that appears contains a list of HTML documents you have opened since starting the JavaScript Debugger. Select the document you opened in Navigator in Step 1.
3. In the Source View window that opens, place your insertion point on the line where you want to pause program execution, and select Set Breakpoint from the Control menu.
4. Switch to Navigator and click the Reload button or click a form button that executes JavaScript code.

Next you will practice using breakpoints.

To practice using breakpoints:

1 In Navigator, open the **Jsdebugger.html** page to start JavaScript Debugger, and then open **CompanyObjects.html** from the **Tutorial.07** folder on your Data Disk.

2 Switch to **JavaScript Debugger** and select the **Open** command from the **File** menu. The Open dialog box that appears contains a list of HTML documents you have opened since starting the JavaScript Debugger. Select **CompanyObjects.html** from the Open dialog box, and click the **Open** button.

Position the insertion point anywhere in the line that reads `this.territory = "North America";` and select **Set Breakpoint** from the **Control** menu. A red circle appears in the margin of the Source View window next to the line containing the breakpoint.

tip

> You can also insert a breakpoint by clicking once in the left margin, next to the line at which you want to pause program execution.

4 Add another breakpoint in the line that reads `this.facilities = "New York, Chicago, and Los Angeles";`. Figure 7-18 shows how the Source View window appears with the two breakpoints set.

5 Switch to **Navigator**, and click the **Reload** button. The program starts running, then switches to the JavaScript Debugger and pauses at the first breakpoint.

6 Select **Run** from the **Control** menu. The statements between the two break-points execute, then the program pauses at the second breakpoint.

7 At this point, you can continue program execution by selecting the **Run** command again, set additional breakpoints, or use any of the other debug commands.

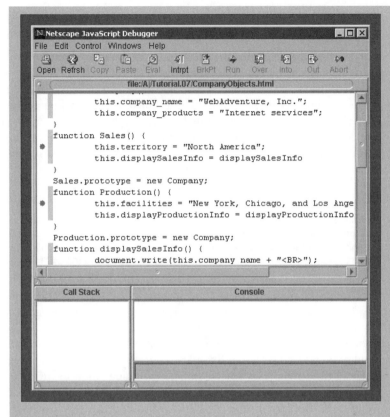

Figure 7-18: Breakpoints in the Source View window

To remove breakpoints:

1 Place the insertion point anywhere in the line containing the first breakpoint and select **Clear Breakpoint** from the **Control** menu. The red circle in the margin of the Source View window is removed.

> **tip**
>
> You can also remove a breakpoint by clicking a red circle in the margin of the Source View window.

2 Repeat Step 1 to remove the second breakpoint in the file.

> **tip**
>
> You can add and delete breakpoints using the Breakpoints dialog box. To access the Breakpoints dialog box, select Breakpoints from the Windows menu. You can also use the Breakpoints dialog box to set the conditions for which a program should pause at a breakpoint. For example, you can set a breakpoint to occur only when the contents of a variable match a specific value.

Tracing Variables and Expressions

As you trace program execution using step commands and breakpoints, you may also need to trace how variables and expressions change during the course of program execution. For example, you may have a statement that reads `resultNum = firstNum / secondNum;`. You know this line is causing a divide-by-zero error, but you do not know exactly when secondNum is being changed to a zero value. The ability to trace program execution and locate the exact location at which secondNum is being changed to a zero value allows you to pinpoint the cause of the logic problem. You can monitor variables and expressions in break mode during a debugging session by using the Console window, the Watches window, and the Evaluate command.

You can monitor properties of objects in the JavaScript Debugger by using the Inspector window. To display the Inspector window, select Inspector from the Windows menu. You can also display the value of a specific object property in the Inspector window by highlighting the object and property in the Source View window and selecting Inspect from the Edit menu.

The upper portion of the Console window, which automatically appears in the lower-right corner of the JavaScript Debugger, displays the values of variables and expressions when you are debugging an HTML document. When the JavaScript Debugger is in break mode, you can display the value of a variable or expression by highlighting it and selecting Evaluate from the Edit menu. The lower portion of the Console window allows you to change variable values during a debugging session. Changing variable values in the Console window allows you to see how a different value may affect the rest of your program. Figure 7-19 shows an example of the JavaScript Debugger after an expression is highlighted and evaluated. The result of the evaluation is displayed in the upper portion of the Console window. The lower portion of the Console window shows an example of how to change the value of a variable during a debugging session.

During a debugging session, you can clear the values and results in the Console window by selecting Clear Console from the Edit menu.

The Watches window is used for monitoring specific variables and expressions that you enter. For example, you can enter the name of a variable or expression into the Watches window and monitor how the variable or expression changes during the course of program execution. You can also enter custom expressions in the Watches window and observe how their values change as the program executes. If you place the expression `sampleVariable * 2` in the Watches window, for instance, its value changes as sampleVariable changes.

Figure 7-19: Console window

The easiest method of adding a variable or expression to the Watches window is to highlight the variable or expression when you are in break mode, then select Copy to Watch from the Edit menu. You can also display the Watches window by selecting Watches from the Window menu. Figure 7-20 displays an example of the Watches window.

Watches	
value1	New
value2	
returnValue	Edit
value1 * 2	
(value1 * value2) / 10	Move Up
	Move Down
	Delete
	Eval
	Done

Figure 7-20: Watches window

Next you will practice tracing variables.

To practice tracing variables:

1   Return to the **CompanyObjects.html** document in the JavaScript Debugger.

2   In the script section in the body of the document, highlight the variable name **personnel** in the `var personnel;` statement and select **Copy to Watch** from the **Edit** menu.

3   Place a breakpoint in the `personnel = 50;` statement in the displaySalesInfo() function, and place another breakpoint in the `personnel = 100;` statement in the displayProductionInfo() function.

4   Switch to **Navigator,** and click the **Reload** button. The program starts to execute, then pauses at the first breakpoint. Notice that the value of the personnel variable is null, since it was not assigned an initial value upon declaration.

5   Select **Step Into** from the **Control** menu to execute the `personnel = 50;` statement. The new value of the personnel variable is printed to the Console window.

6   Select **Run** from the **Control** menu. The program executes and stops at the next breakpoint. The current value of the personnel variable, 50, is printed again to the Console window. Select **Step Into** from the **Control** menu to execute the `personnel = 100;` statement. The new value of the personnel variable is printed to the Console window.

7   Place the insertion point in the lower portion of the Console window and type **personnel = 200**, then press **Enter.** The value of the personnel variable changes to 200 and is printed to the upper portion of the Console window.

8   Select the **Run** command to execute the remainder of the program.

The Call Stack Window

When you are working with a JavaScript program that contains multiple functions, the computer must remember the order in which functions are executed. For example, if you have an accountsPayable() function that calls an accountsReceivable() function, the computer must remember to return to the accountsPayable() function once the accountsReceivable() function finishes executing. Similarly, if the accountsReceivable() function calls a depositFunds() function after it has been called by the accountsPayable() function, then the computer must remember to return to the accountsReceivable() function when the depositFunds() function finishes executing, then return to the accountsPayable() function once the accountsReceivable() function finishes executing. The **call stack** refers to the order in which procedures, such as functions, methods, or event handlers, execute in a program. Each time a program calls a procedure, the procedure is added to the top of the call stack, and then removed once it finishes executing.

The ability to view the contents of a call stack is very useful when tracing logic errors in large programs with multiple functions. For example, you may have a variable that is passed as an argument among several functions. At some point, the variable is being assigned the wrong value. Viewing the call stack, along with using tracing commands, makes it easier to locate the specific function causing the problem. The Call Stack window opens when you first start the JavaScript Debugger. When you enter break mode to debug a program, procedures are automatically added to and removed from the Call Stack window as you step through your program.

Next you will step through some of the functions in CompanyObjects.html to observe the contents of the Call Stack window.

help

As with the step commands, if you are not using Navigator 4.7, when you use the Call Stack window your version of Navigator may not display the same line numbers in the call stack as are listed in the following steps.

To observe the contents of the Call Stack window:

1 Return to the **CompanyObjects.html** document in the JavaScript Debugger.

2 Clear the breakpoints you set in the last exercise. Set a new breakpoint in the JavaScript section in the body at the statement that reads `sales_object = new Sales();`.

3 Switch to **Navigator** and reload the document. The program starts executing, then switches to JavaScript Debugger and pauses at the first statement. Notice that *line 41* is added to the Call Stack window. This is the first call in the current call stack.

4 Select **Step Into** from the Control menu. Control transfers to the Sales() function, and *Sales() line 11* is added to the Call Stack window above the first call, *line 41*. It is now the first call in the current call stack.

5 Select **Step Out** from the **Control** menu. The remainder of the Company() function executes, program control returns to line 41, and *Sales() line 11* is removed from the call stack.

6 Execute the **Step Into** command again and *line 41* is replaced in the call stack by *line 42*, which is the next statement to execute. Selecting the Step Into command again would add the displaySalesInfo() function onto the call stack, since that is the function called by the statement in line 42.

7 Select the **Run** command to execute the remainder of the program.

8 Close Navigator and the JavaScript Debugger.

Microsoft Script Debugger

Microsoft Script Debugger is surprisingly similar to Netscape JavaScript Debugger. One major difference between the two programs is that Script Debugger allows you to debug VBScript, Java applets, JavaBeans, and ActiveX components in addition to JavaScript programs. In comparison, JavaScript Debugger debugs only JavaScript and Java programs. This section will discuss how to debug only JavaScript programs. Note that Script Debugger refers to JavaScript as JScript. This book, however, always uses the original name of the language, JavaScript, as created by Netscape.

You can download Script Debugger from the Microsoft Windows Script Technologies Web site at *msdn.microsoft.com/scripting/default.htm*. Windows 95, Windows 98, and Windows Millennium Edition users should download version 1.0, while Windows NT 4.0 and Windows 2000 users should download version 1.0a. Before installing the program, be sure to thoroughly read the installation instructions, especially if you are working with Windows 95, Windows 98, or Windows ME. A bug exists in the Script Debugger version for those operating systems and special installation procedures are required for the program to run properly. Installation instructions for Script Debugger are also available at the Microsoft Windows Script Technologies Web site.

The Script Debugger Window

You do not need to open a separate HTML document to start Script Debugger, as you do with JavaScript Debugger. Instead, you open the document you want to debug in Internet Explorer and use the Script Debugger submenu on the View menu. The Script Debugger submenu contains two commands: Open and Break at Next Statement. The Open command opens the current document in the Script Debugger window. The Break at Next Statement command is the equivalent of the JavaScript Debugger Set Interrupt command. It instructs Script Debugger to enter break mode as soon as it encounters JavaScript code. The steps for opening an HTML document in the Script Debugger window and entering break mode at the first statement are as follows:

1. Open the HTML document in Internet Explorer, and then select Break at Next Statement from the Script Debugger submenu on the View menu. This command instructs Internet Explorer that you want to debug the current document.
2. In Internet Explorer, click the Refresh button or click a form button that executes JavaScript code. The document opens in the Script Debugger window at the first executed JavaScript statement.

This book instructs you to use the Script Debugger menu to execute commands. However, many of the commands are also available as icons on the Script Debugger toolbar.

Alternately, you can open the HTML document in the Script Debugger window and select Break at Next Statement from the Script Debugger Debug menu. Then switch back to Internet Explorer and click the Refresh button or a form button that executes JavaScript code.

Once you open a document in the Script Debugger, icons appear in the left margin to indicate various elements. For example, a yellow arrow indicates the next statement to execute. The various types of code elements in a JavaScript program are distinguished by syntax color coding. This color coding makes it easier to understand the structure and code in a JavaScript program. For example, the default syntax coloring for JavaScript keywords is blue. Figure 7-21 shows an example of a document in the Script Debugger window in break mode.

```
Microsoft Script Debugger - [Read only: file://A:\Tutorial.07\SportsCar.html [break]]   _ □ ×
 File   Edit   View   Debug   Window   Help                                          _ ð ×

 File  🗋 📂  📄  Edit  ✂ 📋 📋 ✕ 🔳  Debug 📊 📊 📊 📊 📊 📊  🖐 🔍  📊 📊 📊

  <HTML>
  <HEAD>
  <TITLE>Car Properties</TITLE>
  <SCRIPT LANGUAGE="JavaScript">
  <!-- HIDE FROM INCOMPATIBLE BROWSERS -->
  function Car(make, model, color, doors) {
⇨     this.car_make = make;
      this.car_model = model;
      this.car_color = color;
      this.car_doors = doors;
  }
  // STOP HIDING FROM INCOMPATIBLE BROWSERS -->
  </SCRIPT>
  </HEAD>
  <BODY>
  <PRE>
  <SCRIPT LANGUAGE="JavaScript">
  <!-- HIDE FROM INCOMPATIBLE BROWSERS -->
  sports_car = new Car();
  sports_car.car_make = "Triumph";
  sports_car.car_model = "Spitfire";
  sports_car.car_color = "Yellow";
  sports_car.car_doors = 2;

 Ready                                              Ln 7
```

Figure 7-21: An HTML document in break mode in the Script Debugger window

tip

Your Script Debugger window may not appear the same as the example in Figure 7-21, since the Call Stack and Command windows do not open automatically. You can display the Call Stack and Command windows by selecting Call Stack or Command Window from the View menu.

To open an HTML document in Source View for debugging:

1 In Internet Explorer, open the **CompanyObjects.html** file from the **Tutorial.07** folder on your Data Disk.

2 Select **Break at Next Statement** from the **Script Debugger** submenu on the **View** menu.

3 Click the **Refresh** button. The document opens in the Script Debugger window at the first executed JavaScript statement, `Sales.prototype = new Company;`.

Step Commands

The Step Into, Step Over, and Step Out commands in Script Debugger are identical to these same commands in JavaScript debugger. They are used for continuing program execution once you enter break mode. In Script Debugger, these commands are located on the Debug menu. To resume program execution after entering break mode, select Run from the Debug menu. The Run command on the Debug menu ends the debugging session and executes the rest of the program normally. You can end a debugging session in Script Debugger by selecting the Stop Debugging command from the Debug menu.

Next you will practice tracing program execution using the step commands.

To practice tracing program execution using the step commands:

1 Return to the **CompanyObjects.html** document in the Script Debugger window.

2 Select **Step Into** from the **Debug** menu. Since the `Sales.prototype = new Company;` statement uses the prototype property to extend the Company object definition, program execution transfers to the first statement in the Company() constructor function.

3 Select **Step Into** again, and the program executes the first statement in the Company() constructor function and moves to the second statement.

4 Next select **Step Out** from the **Debug** menu. The Step Out command executes the remaining statement in the Company() constructor function, then moves to the next statement, `Production.prototype = new Company;`, which uses the prototype property to extend the Company object definition.

5 Again select **Step Over** from the **Debug** menu. The Step Over command executes all of the commands in the Company construction function, then moves to the next statement, `sales_object = new Sales();`.

6 Finally, since you know that there is no problem with the program, select **Run** from the **Debug** menu to finish executing the rest of the JavaScript code.

7 Close **Script Debugger**, but leave CompanyObjects.html open in Internet Explorer.

Breakpoints

Working with breakpoints in Script Debugger is very similar to working with breakpoints in JavaScript Debugger. The breakpoint commands are located on the Debug menu, and there are some differences in opening a document for debugging. The steps in Script Debugger for opening an HTML document you want to debug with breakpoints are as follows:

1. Open the HTML document you want to debug in Internet Explorer, select Break at Next Statement from the Script Debugger submenu on the View menu, and then click the Refresh button.
2. In Script Debugger, place the insertion point on the line at which you want to pause program execution, and select Toggle Breakpoint from the Debug menu.
3. Select the Run command from the Debug menu to execute the code up to the breakpoint.

   Next you will practice using breakpoints.

To practice using breakpoints:

1 Return to the **CompanyObjects.html** document in Internet Explorer.

2 Select **Break at Next Statement** from the **Script Debugger** submenu on the **View** menu, and then click the **Refresh** button.

3 After the Script Debugger pauses at the first statement, position the insertion point anywhere in the line that reads `this.territory = "North America";` and select **Toggle Breakpoint** from the **Debug** menu. A red circle appears in the margin of the Script Debugger window next to the line containing the breakpoint.

4 Add another breakpoint in the line that reads `this.facilities = "New York, Chicago, and Los Angeles";`. Figure 7-22 shows how the Script Debugger window appears with the two breakpoints.

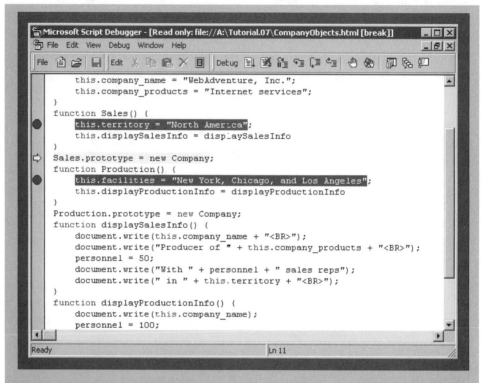

```
Microsoft Script Debugger - [Read only: file://A:\Tutorial.07\CompanyObjects.html [break]]
File  Edit  View  Debug  Window  Help

    this.company_name = "WebAdventure, Inc.";
    this.company_products = "Internet services";
}
function Sales() {
    this.territory = "North America";
    this.displaySalesInfo = displaySalesInfo
}
Sales.prototype = new Company;
function Production() {
    this.facilities = "New York, Chicago, and Los Angeles";
    this.displayProductionInfo = displayProductionInfo
}
Production.prototype = new Company;
function displaySalesInfo() {
    document.write(this.company_name + "<BR>");
    document.write("Producer of " + this.company_products + "<BR>");
    personnel = 50;
    document.write("With " + personnel + " sales reps");
    document.write(" in " + this.territory + "<BR>");
}
function displayProductionInfo() {
    document.write(this.company_name);
    personnel = 100;
```

Ready   Ln 11

Figure 7-22: Breakpoints in the Script Debugger window

5 Select **Run** from the **Debug** menu. The program starts executing, and then pauses at the first breakpoint.

6 Select **Run** from the **Debug** menu again. The statements between the two breakpoints execute, then the program pauses at the second breakpoint.

7 At this point, you can continue program execution by selecting the **Run** command again, set additional breakpoints, or use any of the other debug commands.

To remove breakpoints:

1 Place the insertion point anywhere in the line containing the first breakpoint and select **Toggle Breakpoint** from the **Debug** menu. The red circle in the margin of the Script Debugger window is removed.

2 Repeat Step 1 to remove the second breakpoint in the file.

3 Select **Exit** from the **File** menu to close Script Debugger.

> **tip**
>
> You can remove all breakpoints in an HTML document in Script Debugger by selecting the Clear All Breakpoints command from the Debug menu.

Tracing Variables and Expressions

A major difference between Script Debugger and JavaScript Debugger is that Script Debugger does not contain the equivalent of a Watches window to monitor how a variable or expression changes during the course of program execution. Script Debugger uses only a Command window, which is comparable to the JavaScript Debugger Console window. You display the Command window by selecting Command Window from the View menu.

The Command window does not contain an upper portion and a lower portion like the JavaScript Debugger Console window. Instead, the Command window consists of a single area in which you can view and change the value of a variable or expression when in break mode during a debugging session. To display the value of a variable or expression in the Command window, you enter the variable or expression and press Enter. The value prints directly beneath the variable or expression in the Command window. To change the value of a variable, type the variable name in the Command window followed by an equal sign and the new value, and then press Enter. The new value prints beneath the statement you entered. The Command window in Figure 7-23 contains an example of how to view a value and an example of how to change a value.

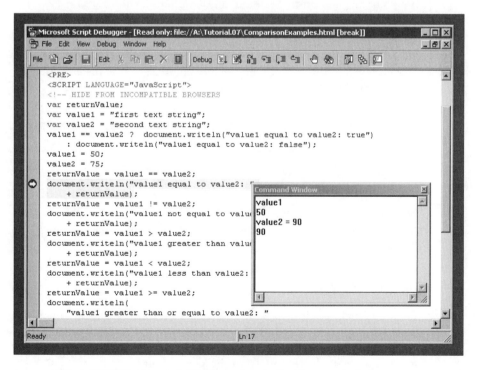

Figure 7-23: Viewing and changing values in the Command window

tip

> The Command window also allows you to change the value of Object properties during a debugging session. For example, if you want to change the car_color property of the myCar object to blue during a debugging session, type `myCar.car_color = "blue"` in the Command window and press Enter.

Next you will practice tracing variables.

To practice tracing variables:

1   Return to the **CompanyObjects.html** document in Internet Explorer.

2   Select **Break at Next Statement** from the **Script Debugger** submenu on the **View** menu, and then click the **Refresh** button.

3   After the Script Debugger pauses at the first statement, place one breakpoint in the `personnel = 50;` statement in the displaySalesInfo() function, and another breakpoint in the `personnel = 100;` statement in the displayProductionInfo() function.

4   Select **Run** from the **Debug** menu to execute the code up to the first breakpoint, then select the **Step Into** command from the **Debug** menu to execute the `personnel = 50;` statement.

5   Select **Command Window** from the **View** menu to display the Command window.

6   Place the insertion point in the Command window and type **personnel**, and then press **Enter**. The personnel variable value of 50 is printed to the Command window.

7   Select **Run** from the **Debug** menu. The program executes and stops at the next breakpoint. Select the **Step Into** command from the **Debug** menu to execute the `personnel = 100;` statement.

8   Place the insertion point in the Command window and type **personnel**, then press **Enter**. The personnel variable new value of 100 is printed to the Command window.

9   While the insertion point is still in the Command window type **personnel = 200**, then press **Enter**. The value of the personnel variable changes to 200 and is printed to the upper portion of the Command window.

10   Select the **Run** command to execute the remainder of the program.

11   Select **Exit** from the **File** menu to close **Script Debugger**.

The Call Stack Window

The Call Stack window in Script Debugger performs the same function as the Call Stack window in JavaScript Debugger. It provides the ability to view the contents of a call stack when debugging a program. You display the Call Stack window by selecting Call Stack window from the View menu.

Next you will step through some of the functions in CompanyObjects.html to observe the contents of the Call Stack window.

To observe the contents of the Call Stack window:

1 Return to the **CompanyObjects.html** document in Internet Explorer.

2 Select **Break at Next Statement** from the **Script Debugger** submenu on the **View** menu, and then click the **Refresh** button. The program starts executing, then switches to Script Debugger and pauses at the first statement.

3 If necessary, display the Call Stack window by selecting **Call Stack** from the **View** menu. Notice that *<JScript> -JScript global code* is added to the Call Stack window. This text represents the first JavaScript statement in the current call stack, `sales.prototype = new Company;`.

4 Select **Step Into** from the **Debug** menu. Control transfers to the Company() function, and *<JScript> -Company* is added to the Call Stack window before the first call.

5 Select **Step Out** from the **Debug** menu. The remainder of the Company() function executes, program control transfers to the next statement, `Production.prototype = new Company;`, and *<JScript> Company* is removed from the call stack. Selecting the Step Into command again would add the Company() function back onto the call stack, since that is the function called by the `Production.prototype = new Company;` statement.

6 Select the **Run** command to execute the remainder of the program.

7 Close Internet Explorer and Script Debugger.

JavaScript Language Bugs and Debugging Resources

If you have tried everything you can think of to fix a bug in your program, consider the possibility that you may be encountering one of the known bugs in the JavaScript language itself. For example, one known bug is that the onSelect event handler, which occurs when a user selects a form field, does not work on Windows platforms. No matter what you try, the following code will *not* work on Windows platforms due to a JavaScript language bug:

```
<FORM>
<INPUT TYPE="text" onSelect="alert('This alert method does
not execute on Windows platforms');">
</FORM>
```

To see a list of known JavaScript bugs, visit the Netscape JavaScript Known Bugs page at *developer.netscape.com/support/bugs/known/index.html*. Note, however, that the manufacturer of a software program is not always the first to know about a bug in its product. Innovative users often discover bugs first, and then report them to the program creator. These users also usually love to share their bug discoveries with other users. Take advantage of the many JavaScript programmers who are often more than happy to help you solve a problem or track down a bug. You can find help on many different Web sites, in newsgroups, and in special forums of Internet service providers such as CompuServe, Prodigy, and America Online. Figure 7-24 lists some Internet debugging resources.

Resource	Address
Netscape JavaScript Newsgroup (requires a subscription to the Netscape developer program)	*developer.netscape.com/members/ doc/subscriber/doc/newsgroups/ javascript.html*
Netscape JavaScript Frequently Asked Questions (FAQ)	*developer.netscape.com/support/ faqs/index.html? content=champions/javascript.html*
Doc JavaScript	*www.webreference.com/js/*
Usenet JavaScript Newsgroup	*comp.lang.javascript*
Website Abstraction	*wsabstract.com/*
JavaScripts.com	*www.javascripts.com*
JavaScript Source	*javascript.internet.com/*
ZDNet Developer	*www.zdnet.com/devhead/resources/ scriptlibrary/javascript/*
WebDeveloper	*webdeveloper.com/javascript/*

Figure 7-24: Internet debugging resources

The addresses in Figure 7-24 were current as of June 2001. As you access the addresses, keep in mind that the Internet is an ever-changing place. Just like other businesses, Web sites may change their addresses over time or close altogether.

 # S U M M A R Y

- You can use a `for...in` loop to determine if values are being assigned to the correct properties in an object.

- Navigator includes two methods, watch() and unwatch(), that are used for setting and unsetting watch points for a particular object.

- A watch point is a specific property that you monitor for changes during program execution.

- The watch() method sets a watch point for an object property.

- The unwatch() method cancels a previously declared watch.

- JavaScript Debugger is the Netscape tool for debugging JavaScript.

- Script Debugger is the Microsoft tool for debugging scripting languages, including JavaScript and VBScript.

- Break mode temporarily suspends, or pauses, program execution so that you can monitor values and trace program execution.

- The Step Into command executes an individual line of code, then pauses until you instruct the debugger to continue.

- The Step Over command allows you to skip function calls.

- The Step Out command executes all remaining code in the current function.

- A breakpoint is a statement in the code at which program execution enters break mode.

- Tracing program execution allows you to identify the exact location where a value changes, to pinpoint the cause of logic problems.

- During a debugging session in JavaScript Debugger, you can monitor variables and expressions in break mode with the Console window, the Watches window, and the Evaluate command.

- The order in which a procedure, such as a function, a method, or an event handler, executes in a program is the call stack.

- During a debugging session in Script Debugger, you can monitor variables and expressions in break mode with the Command window.

- JavaScript Debugger and Script Debugger both monitor the call stack using a Call Stack window.

- If you have tried everything you can think of to fix a bug in your program, consider the possibility that you may be encountering one of the known bugs in the JavaScript language itself.

Q U E S T I O N S

1. What is the best way to discover the values assigned to object properties?
   a. an `if...else` statement
   b. a `for...in` statement
   c. a `switch` statement
   d. the internal JavaScript Properties object

2. What is the correct syntax in Navigator for adding a watch point to the slogan property of a companyInfo object that executes a function named changedSlogan()?
   a. `changeSlogan() = companyInfo.watch("slogan");`
   b. `companyInfo.watch("slogan" = changeSlogan();`
   c. `companyInfo.watch("slogan", changeSlogan());`
   d. `companyInfo.watch("slogan", changeSlogan);`

3. How do you cancel a watch point in Navigator?
   a. the unwatch() method
   b. the stop() method
   c. the stopWatch() method
   d. Delete the statement containing the watch() method.

4. _____ mode temporarily suspends, or pauses, program execution so that you can monitor values and trace program execution.
   a. Break
   b. Stop
   c. Suspend
   d. Wait

5. In JavaScript Debugger, the _____ command instructs the JavaScript Debugger to enter break mode as soon as it encounters JavaScript code.
   a. Stop Execution
   b. Set Interrupt
   c. Break at Next Statement
   d. Pause Program

6. Which debugger command executes the next line of code?
   a. Step Into
   b. Step Out
   c. Step Over
   d. Continue

7. Which debugger command executes all the statements in the next function?
   a. Step Into
   b. Step Out
   c. Step Over
   d. Continue

8. Which debugger command executes the rest of the commands in a function and moves to the next statement following the statement that called the current function?
   a. Step Into
   b. Step Out
   c. Step Over
   d. Continue

9. Which debugger command proceeds with the normal execution of a program?
   a. Continue
   b. Proceed
   c. Exit Debug
   d. Run

10. A(n) _____ is a statement in the code at which program execution enters break mode.
   a. stop marker
   b. breakpoint
   c. pause position
   d. interrupt

11. The JavaScript Debugger allows you to monitor variables and expressions using the _____ window.
   a. Console
   b. Command
   c. Values
   d. Expressions

12. The Script Debugger allows you to monitor variables and expressions using the _____ window.
   a. Console
   b. Command
   c. Values
   d. Expressions

13. The order in which a procedure, such as a function, a method, or an event handler, executes in a program is the _____.
   a. execution chain
   b. procedure heap
   c. call stack
   d. method batch

14. Which of the following event handlers does *not* work on Windows platforms?
   a. onChange
   b. onFocus
   c. onClick
   d. onSelect

E X E R C I S E S

For the following exercises, use the Netscape JavaScript Debugger or the Microsoft Script Debugger, depending on which browser you are using. Save all files you create in the Tutorial.07 folder on your Data Disk.

1. The Calculator.html file in the Tutorial.07 folder on your Data Disk is the same program you created earlier in this book. The program contains a very common bug that has to do with referencing forms. Note that Internet Explorer ignores the bug and runs the program successfully. However, the program does not run in Netscape. Even if you do not use Netscape, see if you can identify the problem. Fix the bug and save the HTML document as Calculator_Correct.html.

2. The PrintDays.html document in the Tutorial.07 folder on your Data Disk contains a function named printDays() in one JavaScript section that should be called from another JavaScript section when the document first loads. However, the program is generating an error message. Fix the bug and save the HTML document as PrintDays_Correct.html.

3. The Tutorial.07 folder on your Data Disk contains a document named MovingEstimator.html that calculates the costs of moving a household from one location to another, based on distance, weight, and several other factors. The program is fairly simple and uses various functions to calculate the types of moving costs, along with a function named calcTotalEstimate() that totals the estimate. Calculations are called by onChange events in the document form. However, if you open the program in a Web browser, the calculations do not function. Use the tracing abilities in Netscape JavaScript Debugger or the Microsoft Script Debugger to determine why the program is not functioning properly. Fix the corrected HTML document as MovingEstimator_Correct.html.

4. The Tutorial.07 folder on your Data Disk contains copies of some of the programs you created earlier in this book. However, all of the programs contain errors. Use any of the debugging skills you have learned in this tutorial to correct the errors. You may review earlier tutorials to see how the program should function—but *not* to copy or review the correct syntax. Use these exercises as an opportunity to test and improve your debugging skills. The tutorial number in which you created each program is appended to the name of the file. After you fix each file, rename the file by replacing the _Tutorial0*x* portion of the filename with _Correct, and save the file. The files for you to correct are as follows:

   - GreetVisitor_Tutorial02.html

   - PoliticalSurvey_Tutorial02.html

   - TwoFunctionsProgram_Tutorial02.html

   - CarpetCost_Tutorial03.html

   - ConvertTemperature_Tutorial03.html

   - DailySpecials_Tutorial03.html

   - Regions_Tutorial04.html

   - About_Tutorial05.html and AboutExercise_Tutorial05.html

   - FlashGreeting_Tutorial05.html

   - GuestBook_Tutorial06.html

   - MathQuiz_Tutorial06.html

5. One of the most important aspects of creating a good program is the design and analysis phase of the project. Conducting a good design and analysis phase is critical to minimizing bugs in your program. Search the Internet or your local library for information on this topic. Explain how you think you should handle the design and analysis phase of a software project.

6. During software development, the testing phase also is an important time to minimize bugs. Search the Internet or your local library for information on software testing. Then design a plan for thoroughly testing your JavaScript programs before deploying them on the Web.

7. Visit the Netscape bug list at *developer.netscape.com/support/bugs/known/index.html*. Study the different types of bugs and errors in the JavaScript programming language that are currently known. Write an analysis of the different categories of bugs and include information such as the category of error, what platforms and browsers the bug affects, and what sort of workaround, if any, exists for each bug.

8. Many advanced programming languages, including ECMAScript Edition 3, include a feature known as exception handling, which allows programs to handle errors as they occur in the execution of a program. Search the MSDN Library and the Netscape developer site, (*developer.netscape.com*) for exception-handling topics, and explain how you would use exception handling in your projects.

TUTORIAL

8

Dynamic HTML and Animation

case ▶ More and more of WebAdventure's clients are asking if their Web sites can include formatting and images that can be updated without having to reload an HTML document from the server. They also want to find innovative ways to use animation and interactivity to attract and retain visitors and make their Web sites effective and easy to navigate. Since standard HTML cannot perform these types of effects, your manager has asked that you learn how to use dynamic HTML (DHTML) to better serve their clients' needs. One client, Rocking Horse Toys, Inc., wants to include an animated rocking horse on their Web page as a corporate logo. Your manager also wants you to use your DHTML skills to create an animated logo for WebAdventure.

Previewing the Animation Files

Dynamic HTML allows HTML tags to be changed after a Web page is rendered by a browser. The ability to render HTML tags dynamically allows you to add animation, games, multimedia presentations, and other features to Web pages. This tutorial uses animation to study dynamic HTML techniques. You will create two different animations while learning about dynamic HTML: a rocking horse and the Earth revolving around the sun. Both animation sequences are examples that could be used for advertising purposes or as visually appealing effects to draw visitors to a Web page.

To preview the rocking horse animation:

1 In your Web browser, open the **Tutorial8_RockingHorse.html** file from the **Tutorial.08** folder on your Data Disk. Figure 8-1 displays an example of the Tutorial8_RockingHorse.html file in Navigator.

Figure 8-1: Tutorial8_RockingHorse.html in Navigator

2 Click the **Start Rocking** button to begin the animation. After you have viewed the animation, click the **Stop Rocking** button.

3 Close the Web browser window.

4 Next examine the code for the Tutorial8_RockingHorse.html file in your text editor or HTML editor. The <SCRIPT> section contains several global variables used in the animation. The animation itself is executed using the rockHorse() function, which is called by the startRocking() function. The button in the body of the document uses an onClick method to call the startRocking() function.

5 Close your text editor or HTML editor when you are finished examining the code.

Now you will preview the orbit animation.

To preview the orbit animation:

1 In your Web browser, open the **Tutorial8_OrbitMaster.html** file from the **Tutorial.08** folder on your Data Disk. Note that the Tutorial8_OrbitMaster.html file opens Tutorial8_OrbitIE.html if you are using an older version of Internet Explorer. It opens Tutorial8_OrbitNavigator.html if you are using an older version of Navigator. Tutorial8_OrbitMaster.html opens Tutorial8_OrbitW3C.html if you are using a W3C DOM-compatible browser; the W3C DOM and W3C DOM-compatible browsers will be discussed later in this tutorial. Figure 8-2 displays an example of the orbit animation as it appears in Navigator 6.

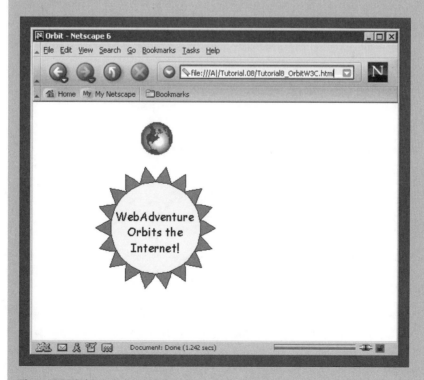

Figure 8-2: Orbit animation in Navigator 6

2   Close the Web browser window.

3   Examine the code for the Tutorial8_OrbitMaster.html file in your text editor or HTML editor. The onLoad event in the <BODY> tag calls a checkBrowser() function that opens a different version of the animation file, Tutorial8_OrbitIE.html, Tutorial8_OrbitNavigtor.html, or Tutorial8_OrbitW3C.html, depending on which browser is running.

4   Next compare the code for the Tutorial8_OrbitIE.html, Tutorial8_Orbit Navigator.html, and Tutorial8_OrbitW3C.html files. All three files contain an orbit() function. Notice the differences in the statements for each file. Also notice that each file uses different HTML tags. Section B explains why older versions of Internet Explorer, Navigator, and W3C DOM-compliant browsers require different JavaScript syntax and HTML tags for dynamic HTML files.

In this section you will learn:

- About dynamic HTML
- About the Document Object Model
- About Document object properties
- About Document object methods
- About the Image object
- About animation with the Image object
- About image caching

Dynamic HTML

Introduction

The Web is used for many purposes. Researchers, scientists, and others in academic settings use the Web to display, search for, and locate information. Commercial applications of the Web include publishing, advertising, and entertainment. Many businesses today have Web sites, and in the future many more businesses will probably have a presence on the Web. To attract and retain visitors, Web sites must be exciting and visually stimulating. Businesses, in particular, want their Web sites to include advertising, animation, interactivity with users, intuitive navigation controls, and many other types of effects that will help sell their products.

In addition to business sites, the Web has many forms of entertainment, including games, animation, and multimedia presentations. Animations and multimedia presentations need to load quickly to keep users interested. Games must be exciting and interactive. For example, visitors to a Web site that features a chess game must be able to move the chess pieces.

HTML would be much more useful if it were dynamic. In Internet terminology the word *dynamic* means several things. Primarily, dynamic refers to Web pages that respond to user requests through buttons or other types of controls. For example, a dynamic Web page may allow a user to change the document background color, process a query when a user submits a form, or interact with a user in other ways, such as through an online game or quiz. The term dynamic also refers to various types of effects such as animation that appear automatically in a Web browser.

You can simulate limited dynamism and interactivity with hypertext links. Consider the Web page shown in Figure 8-3, which displays a photo of a WebAdventure programmer. This single Web page has links to seven other Web pages that are identical except for the picture that appears. Figure 8-4 shows the tags for the HTML file that displays Erica Miller's page.

Figure 8-3: Miller.html in a browser

Hypertext links do not change the currently displayed document, but load new ones from the server instead, so they cannot produce true dynamic effects. When a user clicks a link on the Programmers Web page, it appears as if only the graphic changes. In reality, the entire page is replaced. The Web browser has to find the correct Web page on the server, transfer that file to your computer, and then render the new document. Although you might not notice the time it takes for these steps to occur in this simple example, the transfer and rendering time for a large, complex Web page could be significant. If this Web page were dynamic, only the file displayed by the <IMG> tag would change, and the work would be performed locally by a Web browser rather than by a server. Changing only the image would be much more effective and efficient.

```
<HTML>

<HEAD>

<TITLE>Programmers</TITLE>

</HEAD>

<BODY>

<H1>WebAdventure Programmers</H1>
```

Figure 8-4: Miller.html

```
<H2>Click a link to meet one of

WebAdventure's programmers</H2>

<P><IMG NAME="programmer_pic" SRC="Miller.jpg"></P>

<H3>

<A HREF="Blair.html">Dennis Blair</A>

<A HREF="Hernandez.html">Louis Hernandez</A>

<A HREF="Miller.html">Erica Miller</A>

<A HREF="Morinaga.html">Scott Morinaga</A>

<A HREF="Picard.html">Raymond Picard</A>

</H3>

</BODY>

</HTML>
```

Figure 8-4: Miller.html (continued)

You can find copies of the WebAdventure programmer pages in the Tutorial.08 folder on your Data Disk.

Several combined Internet technologies, called dynamic HTML or DHTML, allow HTML tags to change dynamically and allow Web pages to be rendered dynamically. The term DHTML can refer to different combinations of technologies that give a dynamic quality to HTML pages. Technologies used for creating DHTML include JavaScript, VBScript, CGI, Java, Active Server Pages, and others. For our purposes, DHTML includes the following technologies:

- JavaScript
- HTML
- The Document Object Model
- Cascading style sheets

As you work through this tutorial, remember that DHTML does not refer to a single technology, but to several technologies combined.

Cascading style sheets are used to manage the formatting information of HTML documents. You will learn about cascading style sheets in Section B.

Figure 8-5 displays two popular DHTML features: a slider menu that "pops out" when a user holds his or her mouse over it, and marquee text that scrolls a message across the screen. The marquee text appears at the bottom of the browser window, just beneath the text *WebAdventure's Mission*.

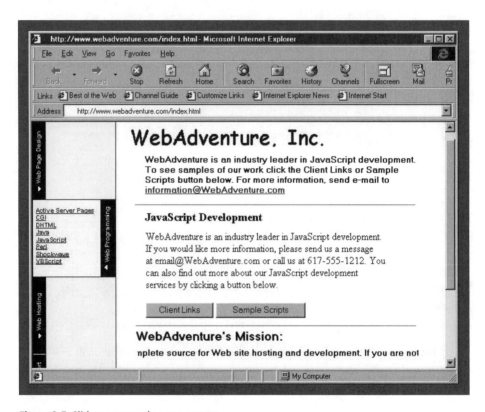

Figure 8-5: Slider menu and marquee text

Figure 8-6 displays a game written in DHTML. The game is a version of the classic Tetris game and combines animation (the movement of game pieces) with interactivity (keys that rotate and move each piece).

The TetriScript game in Figure 8-6 was created by Kazuhiro Moriyama of Tochigi, Japan. You can find many of his other excellent JavaScript games at *plaza.harmonix.ne.jp/~jimmeans/*.

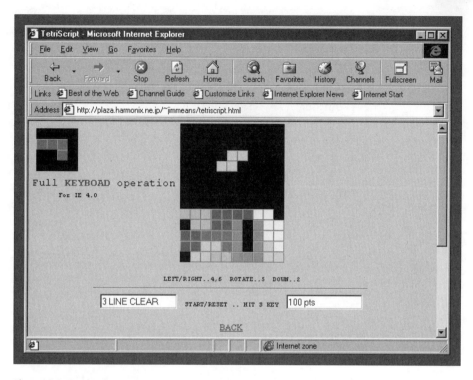

Figure 8-6: TetriScript game

Document Object Model

At the core of DHTML is the Document Object Model. The **Document Object Model**, or **DOM**, represents the HTML document displayed in a window and provides programmatic access to HTML elements through various events, properties and methods. The DOM is actually the Document object branch of the browser object model you learned about in Tutorial 5. Whenever you have used images and forms or have referred to the Document object, you have used the DOM. You have used two methods of the Document object, write() and writeln(), extensively. Figure 8-7 shows the object model of the HTML elements that make up the DOM.

 tip

The Document object refers not only to HTML documents, but also to other file types that are displayed in a Web browser, such as .jpg, .gif, and .xml. .jpg and .gif are image file formats. .xml is a file format for structured documents that uses tags similar to HTML.

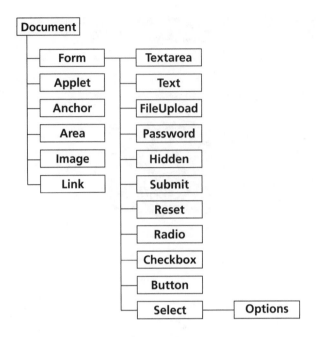

Figure 8-7: Document Object Model

The DOM enables JavaScript to access individual HTML elements by turning each tag in an HTML document into its own programmatic object. This functionality lets you change individual HTML elements dynamically after a page has been rendered, without having to reload the page from the server. You refer to an HTML tag using its NAME attribute or by referring to an element number in an Array object. The following code shows a simple form that dynamically changes the text displayed in a text <INPUT> tag when a user clicks a button. Figure 8-8 shows the output of the program in a Web browser. In the onClick event, the code uses the `this` reference with the Form object and with the elements[] array. Note that the code does not load a new HTML document or reload the original document, but *dynamically* changes only the value of the text box. This type of functionality is not possible without DHTML.

```
<H2>Click to display each New England state capital</H2>
<FORM NAME="states">
<P><INPUT TYPE="text"></P>
<P><INPUT TYPE="button" VALUE="Maine"
     onClick="this.form.elements[0].value='Augusta';">
<INPUT TYPE="button" VALUE="Massachusetts"
     onClick="this.form.elements[0].value='Boston';">
<INPUT TYPE="button" VALUE="Connecticut"
     onClick="this.form.elements[0].value='Hartford';"><BR>
```

```
<INPUT TYPE="button" VALUE="Rhode Island"
    onClick="this.form.elements[0].value='Providence';">
<INPUT TYPE="button" VALUE="Vermont"
    onClick="this.form.elements[0].value='Montpelier';">
<INPUT TYPE="button" VALUE="New Hampshire"
    onClick="this.form.elements[0].value='Concord';"></P>
</FORM>
```

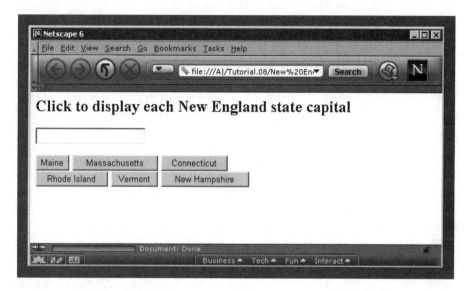

Figure 8-8: State capitals program

Although the individual technologies that make up DHTML have been accepted standards for some time, the implementation of DHTML has evolved slowly. One of the main reasons for the slow implementation of DHTML has to do with the DOM. Earlier versions of Internet Explorer and Navigator included document object models that were almost completely incompatible with each other. In one of the most important battles of the so-called browser wars, Microsoft and Netscape each wanted their version of the DOM to become the industry standard. To settle the argument, the World Wide Web Consortium (W3C) set out to create a platform-independent and browser-neutral version of the DOM. The W3C's first standardized DOM effort, a primitive version known as Level 0, was first supported by versions 3 of both Internet Explorer and Navigator. However, versions 4 of both Internet Explorer and Navigator added a number of proprietary DOM objects that were completely incompatible with the other browser. These incompatibilities meant that for advanced DHTML techniques, such as animation, you had to write a different set of JavaScript code for each browser type. Subsequent releases of each browser have become more compatible with each other as they provide greater support for the W3C specification.

Currently, there are two levels to the W3C DOM. DOM Level 1 first defined basic document functionality, such as navigation and HTML element manipulation. DOM Level 2 introduced style sheet functionality and event handling. This section discusses DOM Level 1 concepts that can be used for basic manipulation of HTML elements, and Section B covers some of the more advanced DOM Level 2 style sheet techniques that are used for animation. Although versions 6 and later of Internet Explorer and Navigator both provide full support for the W3C DOM, you need to keep in mind that earlier versions of each browser were not 100% compliant with the W3C DOM. Internet Explorer has supported DOM Level 1 since version 4 and DOM Level 2 since version 5. Netscape, on the other hand, did not become completely compliant with DOM Levels 1 or 2 until Navigator version 6. You cannot automatically assume that everyone who accesses your JavaScript program will be using the latest version of each browser type (unless of course you are working in a private setting such as a corporate Intranet). This means that depending on the DHTML technique you use, you may need to write different code sections for each browser type and version that you want your program to be compatible with. Throughout this tutorial it will be noted which DOM techniques function with which browser type and version. Additionally, Section B will present how to write different DHTML code segments for each browser type and version in which you anticipate your JavaScript program will run.

....

At the time of this writing, the W3C is drafting a new level of the DOM, Level 3, which will specify, among other items, document loading and saving techniques. Future levels of the DOM may also be drafted to specify additional advanced programming techniques and concepts.

....

This tutorial discusses only methods and properties of the Document object that conform to the WC3 DOM specifications. Even though versions 6 of Internet Explorer and Navigator conform to the WC3 DOM specification, both browsers also support additional Document object methods and properties that may or may not be compatible with each other. For example, both browsers support the lastModified property, which returns the date the document was last modified. Although both browsers support the lastModified property, this property is not part of the WC3 DOM specification. Other Document object methods and properties, such as the Internet Explorer fileCreatedDate property (which returns the document creation date) and the Navigator height property (which returns the document height in pixels) are not available in the other browser.

....

Document Object Properties

The Document object contains various properties used for manipulating HTML objects. Figure 8-9 lists the properties of the Document object that are specified in the WC3 DOM.

Property	Description
anchors[]	An array referring to document anchors
applets[]	An array referring to document applets
body	The element that contains the content for the document
cookie	The current document cookie string
domain	The domain name of the server where the current document is located
forms[]	An array referring to document forms
images[]	An array referring to document images
links[]	An array referring to document links
referrer	The URL of the document that provided a link to the current document
title	The title of the document as specified by the <TITLE>...</TITLE> tag pair in the document <HEAD> section
URL	The URL of the current document

Figure 8-9: Document object properties

In Navigator 4, the majority of the Document object properties can be set only *before* the document is rendered. Therefore, in DOM Level 0, many Document object properties are of limited use in creating dynamic documents. The properties are more useful for retrieving information about the current document. For example, the following function displays the title, URL, and date of last modification of a document in an alert dialog box:

```
function documentStatistics() {
    alert(document.title + "\n" + document.URL + "\n"
        + document.lastModified);
}
```

In contrast to DOM Level 0, DOM Level 1-compatible browsers allow you to dynamically change many of the Document object properties after the document is rendered. For example, the following statement can be used to change the text displayed in the title bar after the Web page is rendered:

```
document.title = "WebAdventure, Inc.";
```

If you decide to dynamically change properties of the Document object, keep in mind that JavaScript programs that dynamically change Document object properties may not function with older browsers (such as Navigator 4) that do not support DOM Level 1.

Document Object Methods

As you create Web pages, you may want to dynamically create a new HTML document. For example, after running a CGI script that processes an online order, you may want to dynamically generate a new HTML document that confirms the order. The DOM methods listed in Figure 8-10 can be used for dynamically generating and manipulating Web pages.

Methods	Description
close()	Closes a new document that was created with the open() method
open()	Opens a new document in a window or frame
write()	Adds new text to a document
writeln()	Adds new text to a document, followed by a line break

Figure 8-10: Document object methods for dynamically generating Web pages

You have used the write() and writeln() methods throughout this book to add content to a new Web page as it is being rendered. A limitation of the write() and writeln() methods is that they cannot be used to change content after a Web page has been rendered. You can execute the write() and writeln() methods in the current document after it is rendered, but doing so will overwrite the existing content. Although the write() and writeln() methods are not used for dynamically changing an existing Web page, they are used for dynamically creating new windows or frames. You use the Document object open() method to create a new document in a specified window or frame, and then use the write() and writeln() methods to add content to the new document. You can include an argument with the open() method specifying the MIME type of the document to be displayed. (You learned about MIME types in Tutorial 6.) If you do not include an argument, a default MIME type of text/html is used. The close() method notifies the Web browser that you are finished writing to the window or frame and that the document should be displayed. If you use the write() and writeln() methods without using the open() method, the contents of the current window are overwritten.

You may discover on your own that you can omit the Document open() and close() method and add content to a new window or frame by just using the write() and writeln() methods. Although later versions of Navigator and Internet Explorer do not require you to use these methods, some older browsers will not display any content in the new window until you execute the close() method. In addition, some older browsers will not stop the spinning icon in the upper-right browser corner that indicates that a document is loading until you execute the close() method. If you expect your JavaScript code to run on older browsers, then you should use the open() and close() methods when dynamically creating document content.

As you know, the write() and writeln() methods of the Document object require a text string as an argument. The only difference between the write() and writeln()

methods is that the writeln() method adds a carriage return after the line. For a Web browser to recognize the line break following the writeln() method, you must enclose the <SCRIPT>...</SCRIPT> tag pair containing the writeln() method within a <PRE>...</PRE> tag pair. You can include line breaks without the <PRE> tag and writeln() method by including the escape character (\n) within the text argument of the write() method. The following code illustrates how the write() method and escape character work:

```
<SCRIPT LANGUAGE="JavaScript">
document.write("Hello World\n")
document.write("This line prints
    below the 'Hello World' line.")
</SCRIPT>
```

Rather than using separate write() and writeln() line methods, you can generate multiple lines of text with a single write() method by including each text string as an argument, separated by commas. The following code performs the same function as the preceding example, but this time using only a single write() method:

```
<SCRIPT LANGUAGE="JavaScript">
document.write("Hello World\n", "This line prints
    below the 'Hello World' line.")
</SCRIPT>
```

The code in Figure 8-11 generates a new window that displays basic Web page statistics using Document object properties. When the user clicks a command button, the showStats() function executes, which first builds a string containing the Web page statistics. Then a new window named statWindow is opened using the Window object open() method. Using the statWindow variable that represents the new window, a document is opened in the new window using the Document object open() method. The write() method then adds the string to the new document. Once the write() method is finished, the Document close() method executes and displays the page in the new window. Since both the Window and Document objects contain open() and close() methods, the code includes each object reference, to differentiate between the two. Figure 8-12 shows how the new window appears.

```
<HTML>

<HEAD>

<TITLE>WebAdventure Home Page</TITLE>

<SCRIPT LANGUAGE="JavaScript">

function showStats() {

    var message = "<H2>Web Page Statistics</H2>";

    var stats = "<STRONG>Document title:</STRONG> ";
```

Figure 8-11: Web Page Statistics program

```
        stats += document.title;

        stats += "<BR><STRONG>Document URL:</STRONG> ";

        stats += document.URL;

        stats += "<BR><STRONG>Last modified:</STRONG> ";

        stats += document.lastModified;

        var statWindow = window.open("", "Ad", "height=200,width=500");

        statWindow.document.open("text/html");

        statWindow.document.write(message, stats);

        statWindow.document.close();

}

</SCRIPT>

</HEAD>

<BODY>

<FORM>

<INPUT TYPE="button" VALUE="Web Page Statistics"

        onClick="showStats();">

</FORM>

</BODY>

</HTML>
```

Figure 8-11: Web Page Statistics program (continued)

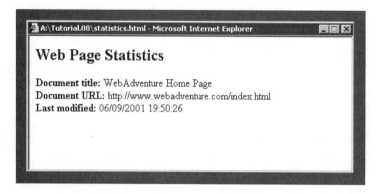

Figure 8-12: Web Page Statistics program in a browser

The Image Object

One of the most visually pleasing parts of a Web page is its images. Without images, a Web page is nothing more than a collection of text and hypertext links. Web pages today include images in the form of company logos, photographs of products, drawings, animation, image maps like the one you created in Tutorial 2, and other types of graphics. Commerce-oriented Web pages that did not include images would be hard pressed to attract—and keep—visitors.

The ability to include images in a Web page is not new. You simply include an <IMG> tag with the SRC attribute set to the URL of the image you want to display. Each <IMG> tag in an HTML document is represented in the DOM images[] array by an Image object. An `Image object` represents images created using the <IMG> tag. If you want to change an image on the basis of a user's selection, as part of a timed advertising routine, or for simple animation, you must use JavaScript with an Image object.

Figure 8-13 lists frequently used Image object properties, and Figure 8-14 lists frequently used Image object events.

Property	Description
border	A read-only property containing the border width, in pixels, as specified by the BORDER attribute of the <IMG> tag
complete	A Boolean value that returns true when an image is completely loaded
height	A read-only property containing the height of the image as specified by the HEIGHT attribute of the <IMG> tag
hspace	A read-only property containing the amount of horizontal space, in pixels, to the left and right of the image, as specified by the HSPACE attribute of the <IMG> tag
lowsrc	The URL of an alternate image to display at low resolution
name	A name assigned to the tag
src	The URL of the displayed image
vspace	A read-only property containing the amount of vertical space, in pixels, above and below the image, as specified by the VSPACE attribute of the <IMG> tag
width	A read-only property containing the width of the image as specified by the WIDTH attribute of the <IMG> tag

Figure 8-13: Image object properties

Event	Description
onLoad	Executes after an image is loaded
onAbort	Executes when the user cancels the loading of an image, usually by clicking the Stop button
onError	Executes when an error occurs while an image is loading

Figure 8-14: Image object events

One of the most important elements of the Image object is the src property, which allows JavaScript to change an image dynamically. Figure 8-15 shows a modified version of the Programmers.html program you saw in Figure 8-4 and illustrates the use of the src property. In this case, form buttons replace the hypertext links for each programmer. What is most important, the HTML document is not replaced when the user clicks a different programmer. Instead, the picture displayed by the <IMG> tag is replaced dynamically, by means of the src property of the Image object. This new program is much more efficient than loading a new HTML document each time you want to display a new picture, as was the case in the earlier example. The default image in the program is the first programmer in the list, Dennis Blair. Figure 8-16 shows the program in a Web browser.

```
<HTML>

<HEAD>

<TITLE>Programmers</TITLE>

</HEAD>

<BODY>

<H1>WebAdventure Programmers</H1>

<H2>Click a button to meet one of

WebAdventure's programmers</H2>

<P><IMG NAME="programmer_pic" SRC="blair.jpg"></P>

<FORM NAME="programmer_list">

    <INPUT TYPE="button" VALUE="Dennis Blair"

        onClick="document.programmer_pic.src='blair.jpg'">

    <INPUT TYPE="button" VALUE="Louis Hernandez"

        onClick="document.programmer_pic.src='hernandez.jpg'">
```

Figure 8-15: Programmers.html

```
        <INPUT TYPE="button" VALUE="Erica Miller"

            onClick="document.programmer_pic.src='miller.jpg'">

        <INPUT TYPE="button" VALUE="Scott Morinaga"

            onClick="document.programmer_pic.src='morinaga.jpg'">

        <INPUT TYPE="button" VALUE="Raymond Picard"

            onClick="document.programmer_pic.src='picard.jpg'">

    </FORM>

    </BODY>

    </HTML>
```

Figure 8-15: Programmers.html (continued)

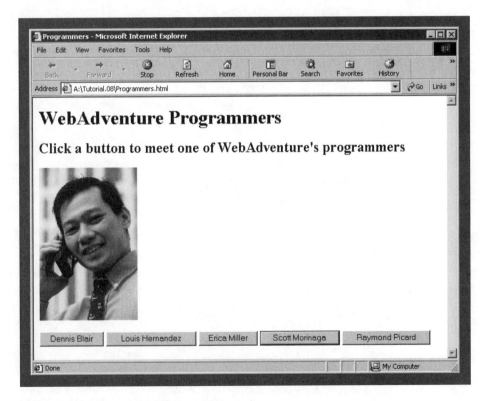

Figure 8-16: Programmers.html in a Web browser

tip

··

You can find a copy of Programmers.html in the Tutorial.08 folder on your Data Disk.

··

Next you will create a document that allows users to dynamically change the image displayed with an <IMG> tag. You will create three buttons that allow users to display different sized versions of the same image. The images you will use in the document are located in the Tutorial.08 folder on your Data Disk.

To create a document that allows users to dynamically change the image displayed with an <IMG> tag:

1 Start your text editor or HTML editor and create a new document.

2 Type the <HTML> and <HEAD> sections of the document:

```
<HTML>
<HEAD>
<TITLE>Image Options</TITLE>
</HEAD>
```

3 Add **<BODY>** to start the body section, and then type **<FORM>** to start a form.

4 Create the following <INPUT> tags that will change the image of a bird to small, medium, or large. The tags use the onClick event handler to change the height and width properties of the Image object.

```
<INPUT TYPE="button" VALUE=" Small Bird "
    onClick="document.bird.src='smallbird.gif';">
<INPUT TYPE="button" VALUE=" Medium Bird "
    onClick="document.bird.src='mediumbird.gif';">
<INPUT TYPE="button" VALUE=" Big Bird "
    onClick="document.bird.src='largebird.gif';">
```

5 Type the closing **</FORM>** tag.

6 Next add the following line, which adds the <IMG> tag. The image is initially set to smallbird.gif.

```
<IMG SRC="smallbird.gif" NAME="bird">
```

7 Type the closing **</BODY>** and **</HTML>** tags.

8 Save the file as **ChangeImage.html** in the **Tutorial.08** folder on your Data Disk. Open the **ChangeImage.html** file in your Web browser. Figure 8-17 shows how the document appears in a Web browser after the user selects the Medium Bird button.

Figure 8-17: ChangeImage.html

9 Close the Web browser window.

Animation with the Image Object

In Tutorial 5, you learned how to use the setTimeout() and setInterval() methods to automatically execute JavaScript code. By combining the src attribute of the Image object with the setTimeout() or setInterval() methods, you can create simple animation in an HTML document. What animation means in this context is not necessarily a complex cartoon character, but any situation in which a sequence of images changes automatically. Web animation can also include traditional animation involving cartoons and movement. Examples of JavaScript programs that use animation include a simple advertisement in which two images change every couple of seconds and the ticking hands of an online clock (each position of the clock hands requires a separate image). Figure 8-18 contains a program that uses the setInterval() method to automatically swap two advertising images every couple of seconds. Figure 8-19 shows the two images.

```
<HTML>

<HEAD>

<TITLE>Advertisement</TITLE>

<SCRIPT LANGUAGE="JavaScript">

<!-- HIDE FROM INCOMPATIBLE BROWSERS

var qa = "q";

function changeImage() {

    if (qa == "q") {

            document.animation.src = "answer.jpg";

            qa = "a";

    }

    else {

            document.animation.src = "question.jpg";

            qa = "q";

    }

}

// STOP HIDING FROM INCOMPATIBLE BROWSERS -->

</SCRIPT>

</HEAD>

<BODY onLoad="var begin=setInterval('changeImage()',2000);">

<P><IMG SRC="question.jpg" NAME="animation"></P>

</BODY>

</HTML>
```

Figure 8-18: Changing images program

Figure 8-19: Advertising images

If you would like to see how the flashing advertising program functions, a copy of it named **Advertisement.html is in the Tutorial.08 folder on your Data Disk.**

True animation involving movement requires a different graphic, or frame, for each movement that a character or object makes. This book does not teach the artistic skills necessary for creating frames in an animation sequence. Instead, the goal is to show how to use JavaScript and the Image object to perform simple animation by swapping frames displayed by an <IMG> tag.

Do not confuse animation frames with frames created with the <FRAMESET> and <FRAME> tags.

As an example of frames in an animation sequence, Figure 8-20 shows six frames, each frame containing a motion that a runner goes through.

Figure 8-20: Animation frames

You create an animated sequence with JavaScript by using the setInterval() or setTimeout() methods to cycle through the frames in an animation series. Each iteration of a setInterval() or setTimeout() method changes the frame displayed by an <IMG> tag. The speed of the animation depends on how many milliseconds are passed as an argument to the setInterval() or setTimeout() methods.

When creating animation sequences, it is important to make sure that each frame of the animation is created with the same HEIGHT and WIDTH attributes of the <IMG> tag, so all images in the sequence will be displayed in the same size.

Figure 8-21 contains code that animates the frames in Figure 8-20. The code assigns the frames to a runner[] array. Once the Run button is clicked, a setInterval() method executes an `if` statement that changes the displayed frame based on the curRunner variable. Once the curRunner variable reaches five (the highest element in an array with six elements), it resets to zero (the first element in the array), and the animation sequence starts over from the beginning. The name of each graphic for the frames shown in Figure 8-20 corresponds to an element number in the runner[] array. The Stop button uses the clearInterval() method to stop the startInterval() method. Figure 8-22 shows an example of the program in a Web browser.

```
<HTML>

<HEAD>

<TITLE>Runners</TITLE>

<SCRIPT LANGUAGE="JavaScript">

<!-- HIDE FROM INCOMPATIBLE BROWSERS

var runner = new Array(6);

var curRunner = 0;

var startRunning;

runner[0] = "runner0.jpg";

runner[1] = "runner1.jpg";

runner[2] = "runner2.jpg";

runner[3] = "runner3.jpg";

runner[4] = "runner4.jpg";

runner[5] = "runner5.jpg";

function marathon() {

    if (curRunner == 5)

        curRunner = 0;
```

Figure 8-21: Runner animation code

```
        else

              ++curRunner;

        document.animation.src = runner[curRunner];

}

// STOP HIDING FROM INCOMPATIBLE BROWSERS -->

</SCRIPT>

</HEAD>

<BODY>

<P><IMG SRC="runner0.jpg" NAME="animation"></P>

<FORM>

<INPUT TYPE="button" NAME="run" VALUE=" Run "
onClick="startRunning=setInterval('marathon()',100);">
<INPUT TYPE="button" NAME="stop" VALUE=" Stop "

      onClick="clearInterval(startRunning);">

</FORM>

</BODY>

</HTML>
```

Figure 8-21: Runner animation code (continued)

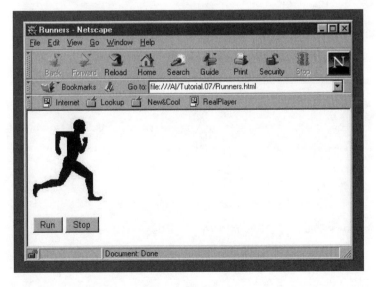

Figure 8-22: Runner animation in a Web browser

Although the runner animation adds a dynamic aspect to images, it does have one shortcoming: The animation does not actually move across the screen, but takes place within the confines of the space taken up by the single <IMG> tag. The runner is animated, but appears as if he is running in place. In Section B, you will learn how to use style sheets to change the position of an image onscreen, so that animation actually appears to be traveling.

Next you will create an animated rocking horse. The six images required for the animation are located in the Tutorial.08 folder on your Data Disk. Figure 8-23 shows the figures.

The rocking horse animation will be similar to the runner animation. However, unlike the runner animation, the rocking horse animation cannot redisplay the first frame, rockinghorse0.jpg, after displaying the last frame, rockinghorse5.jpg. If it did, the animation would not run smoothly. The rocking horse animation must cycle back down through each frame after the last frame is reached, instead of starting over again at the first frame.

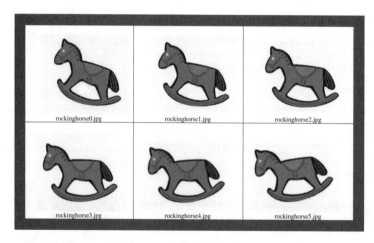

rockinghorse0.jpg rockinghorse1.jpg rockinghorse2.jpg

rockinghorse3.jpg rockinghorse4.jpg rockinghorse5.jpg

Figure 8-23: Rocking horse frames

To create the rocking horse animation:

1 Create a new document in your text editor or HTML editor.

2 Type the <HTML> and <HEAD> sections of the document:

```
<HTML>
<HEAD>
<TITLE>Rocking Horse</TITLE>
```

3 Add the opening statements for a JavaScript section:

```
<SCRIPT LANGUAGE="JavaScript">
<!-- HIDE FROM INCOMPATIBLE BROWSERS
```

4 Type the following four variables. The horses variable will contain the names of the six image files. The curHorse variable will be used in an `if` statement as a counter. The direction variable will be used to determine if the horse should "rock" right or left. The begin variable will be assigned to the setInterval() method that starts the animation.

```
var horses = new Array(5);
var curHorse = 0;
var direction;
var begin;
```

5 Assign the image files to the corresponding elements in the horses array:

```
horses[0] = "rockinghorse0.jpg";
horses[1] = "rockinghorse1.jpg";
horses[2] = "rockinghorse2.jpg";
horses[3] = "rockinghorse3.jpg";
horses[4] = "rockinghorse4.jpg";
horses[5] = "rockinghorse5.jpg";
```

6 The following function actually performs the animation. The first `if` statement checks the curHorse variable to see if it is equal to 0 or 5. If the variable is equal to 0, the direction variable is set to *right*, if it is equal to 5, the direction variable is set to *left*. The next `if` statement then checks the direction variable to determine whether to increment or decrement the curHorse variable. The final statement in the function changes the image displayed by an <IMG> tag named *animation* to the image that corresponds to the element in the horses[] array that matches the curHorse variable. You will create the animation <IMG> tag in Step 9.

```
function rockHorse() {
    if (curHorse == 0)
        direction = "right";
    else if (curHorse == 5)
        direction = "left";
    if (direction == "right")
        ++curHorse;
    else if (direction == "left")
        --curHorse;
    document.animation.src = horses[curHorse];
}
```

7 Next add the following function, which will be called from a Start Rocking button in the body of the document. The `if` statement checks whether the animation is already running. Notice that the `if` statement conditional expression includes the only name of the begin variable, without any other operators.

This technique enables you to quickly check whether an object exists or if a variable has been initialized. If the setInterval() method has been called and assigned to the begin variable, then the conditional expression returns a value of true, which causes the `if` statement to execute the clearInterval() method to cancel the animation. If you do not include the `if` statement, then the user could click the Start Rocking button several times, which would cause multiple instances of the setInterval() method to occur. Multiple instances of the same setInterval() method will cause your computer to execute as many animation sequences as there are instances of the setInterval() method, which could make the animation appear to run faster than desired or function erratically. The last statement in the function is the setInterval() method that runs the rockHorse function() you created in Step 6.

```
function startRocking() {
    if (begin)
        clearInterval(begin);
    begin = setInterval("rockHorse()",100);
}
```

8   Add the following code to close the <SCRIPT> and <HEAD> tags:

```
// STOP HIDING FROM INCOMPATIBLE BROWSERS -->
</SCRIPT>
</HEAD>
```

9   Add the following body section to the document. The <IMG> tag, named *animation*, opens the first frame in the animation, rockinghorse0.jpg. The Start Rocking button uses the onClick event handler to execute the startRocking() function, and the Stop Rocking button clears the setInterval() method executed by the startRocking() function.

```
<BODY>
<H1>Rocking Horse Toys, Inc.</H1>
<P><IMG SRC="rockinghorse0.jpg" NAME="animation"></P>
<FORM>
<INPUT TYPE="button" NAME="run" VALUE=" Start Rocking "
    onClick="startRocking();">
<INPUT TYPE="button" NAME="stop" VALUE=" Stop Rocking "
    onClick="clearInterval(begin);">
</FORM>
</BODY>
```

10 Type a closing </HTML> tag.

11 Save the file as **RockingHorse.html** in the **Tutorial.08** folder on your Data Disk. Open the **RockingHorse.html** file in your Web browser and see if it functions correctly.

12 Close the Web browser window.

Image Caching

In the rocking horse program, you may have noticed that the loading of each image appears to be jerky, erratic, or slow, and that the URL for each image flickers in the status bar each time the image changes. This effect happens because JavaScript does not save a copy of the image in memory that can be used whenever necessary. Instead, each time a different image is loaded by an <IMG> tag, JavaScript must physically open or reopen the image from its source. You probably accessed the rocking horse image files directly from the Data Disk on your local computer, and if you have a particularly fast computer, you may not have noticed a loading problem. If you did experience erratic loading of the images, then you can imagine how erratic and slow the animation would appear if you had to download the images from the Web server *each time they are loaded*. A technique for eliminating multiple downloads of the same file is called image caching. **Image caching** temporarily stores image files in memory on a local computer. This technique allows JavaScript to store and retrieve an image from memory rather than download the image each time it is needed.

Images are cached using the Image() constructor of the Image object. The Image() constructor creates a new Image object. There are three steps for caching an image in JavaScript:

- Create a new object using the Image() constructor
- Assign a graphic file to the src property of the new Image object
- Assign the src property of the new Image object to the src property of an <IMG> tag

In the following code, the SRC attribute of the <IMG> tag named myImage is initially set to an empty string "". In the <SCRIPT> section, a new Image object named newImage is created. The newImage object is used to save and access the memory cache containing the image file. A file named graphic.jpg is assigned to the src property of the newImage object. The src property of the newImage object is then assigned to the src property of the <IMG> tag.

```
<BODY>
<IMG NAME="myImage" SRC="">
<SCRIPT LANGUAGE="JavaScript">
<!-- HIDE FROM INCOMPATIBLE BROWSERS
newImage = new Image()
newImage.src = "graphic.jpg"
document.myImage.src = newImage.src
// STOP HIDING FROM INCOMPATIBLE BROWSERS -->
</SCRIPT>
</BODY>
```

Be sure to understand that in the preceding code, the graphic.jpg file is *not* assigned directly to the src property of the <IMG> tag. Instead, the *newImage object* is assigned to the src property of the <IMG> tag. If you assigned the graphic.jpg file directly to the src property of the <IMG> tag using the statement document.myImage.src = "graphic.jpg";, then the file would reload from its source each time it was needed. The newImage object opens the file once and saves it to a memory cache.

Figure 8-24 shows a version of the runner animation code modified to use image caching. The lines that add each image file to the runner[] array have been replaced by a for loop. As you learned in Tutorial 4, the for statement is used to repeat a statement or series of statements as long as a given conditional expression evaluates to true. The for loop in Figure 8-24 assigns a new object to each element of the runner[] array until the counter *i* is greater than six, which represents the highest element in the array. Each object in the runner[] array is then assigned an image file using the src property. In the marathon() function, the runner[curRunner] operator in the statement document.animation.src = runner[curRunner]; now includes the src property so that the statement reads document.animation.src = runner [curRunner].src;.

```
<HTML>

<HEAD>

<TITLE>Runners</TITLE>

<SCRIPT LANGUAGE="JavaScript">

<!-- HIDE FROM INCOMPATIBLE BROWSERS

var runner = new Array(6);

var curRunner = 0;

var startRunning;

for(var i = 0; i < 6; ++i) {

     runner[i] = new Image();

     runner[i].src = "runner" + i + ".jpg";

}

function marathon() {

     if (curRunner == 5)

          curRunner = 0;

     else

          ++curRunner;

     document.animation.src = runner[curRunner].src;

}
```

Figure 8-24: Runner animation code after adding caching

```
// STOP HIDING FROM INCOMPATIBLE BROWSERS -->

</SCRIPT>

</HEAD>

<BODY>

<P><IMG SRC="runner1.jpg" NAME="animation"></P>

<FORM>

<INPUT TYPE="button" NAME="run" VALUE=" Run "
onClick="startRunning=setInterval('marathon()',100);">

<INPUT TYPE="button" NAME="stop" VALUE=" Stop "
        onClick="clearInterval(startRunning);">

</FORM>

</BODY>

</HTML>
```

Figure 8-24: Runner animation code after adding caching (continued)

Next you will modify the rocking horse program so that it includes image caching.

To add image caching to the RockingHorse.html document:

1 Return to the RockingHorse.html file in your text editor or HTML editor, then save it as a new file named **RockingHorseCache.html** in the **Tutorial.08** folder on your Data Disk.

2 Locate the following six statements that assign each rocking horse frame to the horses[] array:

```
horses[0] = "rockinghorse0.jpg";
horses[1] = "rockinghorse1.jpg";
horses[2] = "rockinghorse2.jpg";
horses[3] = "rockinghorse3.jpg";
horses[4] = "rockinghorse4.jpg";
horses[5] = "rockinghorse5.jpg";
```

3 Replace the preceding statements with the following for statement. The for statement creates a new Image object within each element of the horses[] array. Each object in the horses[] array is then assigned an image file using the src property.

```
for(var i = 0; i < 6; ++i) {
     horses[i] = new Image();
     horses[i].src = "rockinghorse" + i + ".jpg";
}
```

4 Add the src property to the `document.animation.src = horses[curHorse];` statement in the rockHorse() function so that it reads `document.animation.src = horses[curHorse].src;`.

5 Save the document and open it in your Web browser. If you previously experienced erratic animation, the new animation should appear much smoother.

6 Close the Web browser window.

Even when you use image caching, the images must all be loaded into an Image object before the animation will function correctly. Often, you will want animation to start as soon as a page finishes loading. The rocking horse program is designed to start as soon as a page finishes loading. However, although a page has finished loading, all the images may not have finished downloading and may not be stored in image caches. If you run the rocking horse program across an Internet connection, the onLoad event handler of the <BODY> tag may execute the animation sequence before all the frames are transferred and assigned to Image objects (depending on Internet connection speed). The animation will still function, but will be erratic until all the images have been successfully stored in Image objects. To be certain that all images are downloaded into a cache before commencing an animation sequence, you use the onLoad event handler of the Image object.

Figure 8-25 shows another modified version of the runner program. This time the program does not include a Run or Stop button. Instead, a `for` loop in the <SCRIPT> section executes each Image object onLoad event. First, each element in the runner[] array is assigned a new Image object. Next, each Image object in the runner[] array is assigned a corresponding frame of runner animation images. The statement runner[i].onload = runMarathon; assigns the runMarathon() function to each Image object onLoad event. After the image assigned to each Image object in the runner[] array finishes loading, its onLoad event executes the runMarathon() function, which increments the imagesLoaded variable by one each time an image loads into the runner[] array. Once the imagesLoaded variable equals six (which indicates that all the images have been downloaded), the marathon() function executes using the same setInterval() statement that was originally located in the onClick event for the Run button.

```
<HTML>

<HEAD>

<TITLE>Runner</TITLE>

<SCRIPT LANGUAGE="JavaScript">
```

Figure 8-25: Runner animation code after adding an onLoad event

```
<!-- HIDE FROM INCOMPATIBLE BROWSERS

var runner = new Array(6);

var curRunner = 0;

var startRunning;

var imagesLoaded = 0;

for(var i = 0; i < 6; ++i) {

    runner[i] = new Image();

    runner[i].src = "runner" + i + ".jpg";

    runner[i].onload = runMarathon;

}

function runMarathon() {

    ++imagesLoaded;

    if (imagesLoaded == 6)

        startRunning=setInterval("marathon()",100);

}

function marathon() {

    if (curRunner == 5)

        curRunner = 0;

    else

        ++curRunner;

    document.animation.src = runner[curRunner].src;

}

// STOP HIDING FROM INCOMPATIBLE BROWSERS -->

</SCRIPT>

</HEAD>

<BODY>

<P><IMG SRC="runner1.jpg" NAME="animation"></P>

</BODY>

</HTML>
```

Figure 8-25: Runner animation code after adding an onLoad event (continued)

You can find a completed version of the runner animation program, named Runner.html, in the Tutorial.08 folder on your Data Disk.

Next you will add to the rocking horse program an image onLoad event that executes the animation after all the images load. You will also modify the program so that the animation executes as soon as all the images load.

To add an image onLoad event to the rocking horse program and to modify it so that the animation executes as soon as all the images load:

1 Return to the RockingHorseCache.html file in your text editor or HTML editor, then save it as a new file named **RockingHorseImageLoad.html** in the **Tutorial.08** folder on your Data Disk.

2 Add `var imagesLoaded = 0;` after the `var begin;` statement. The imagesLoaded variable will keep a count of the number of images loaded.

3 Add the statement `horses[i].onload = loadImages;` just before the closing brace in the `for` loop that assigns each rocking horse image file to the horses[] array. As each image is loaded, its onLoad event calls the loadImages() function.

4 After the `for` loop, create the following loadImages() function, which is called from the `horses[i].onload = loadImages;` statement you added in Step 3. The function increments the imagesLoaded variable each time it is called. After the imagesLoaded variable equals six, a setInterval() method executes the rockHorse() function.

```
function loadImages() {
    ++imagesLoaded;
    if (imagesLoaded == 6)
        begin=setInterval("rockHorse()",100);
}
```

5 Delete the startRocking() function from the <SCRIPT> section, and delete the form from the body of the document.

6 Save the document and open it in your Web browser. The animation should begin as soon as all the images load.

7 Close the Web browser window and your text or HTML editor.

In the next section, you will learn how to use cascading style sheets to create more complex types of animation.

S U M M A R Y

- Dynamic HTML (DHTML) combines several Internet technologies, including JavaScript, HTML, the Document Object Model, and cascading style sheets, to allow HTML tags to change dynamically, Web pages to be rendered dynamically, and users to interact with Web pages.

- The Document Object Model (DOM) represents the HTML document displayed in a window and provides programmatic access to document elements.

- The World Wide Web Consortium (W3C) is responsible for defining a platform-independent and browser-neutral version of the DOM.

- The open() method opens a window or frame other than the current window or frame, to update its contents with the write() and writeln() methods.

- The close() method notifies the Web browser that you are finished writing to the window or frame and that the document should be displayed.

- The images[] array contains all of an HTML document's images in the same manner that the forms[] array contains all of an HTML document's forms. If an HTML document does not contain any images, then the images[] array is empty.

- An Image object represents images created using the <IMG> tag.

- One of the most important elements of the Image object is the src property, which allows JavaScript to change an image dynamically.

- By combining the src attribute of the Image object with the setTimeout() or setInterval() methods, you can create simple animation in an HTML document.

- You create an animated sequence with JavaScript by using the setInterval() or setTimeout() methods to cycle through the frames in an animation series.

- Image caching, which temporarily stores image files in memory, is a technique for eliminating multiple downloads of the same file. This technique allows JavaScript to store and retrieve an image from memory rather than download the image each time it is needed.

- You use the onLoad event handler of the Image object to be certain that all images are downloaded into a cache before commencing an animation sequence.

 Q U E S T I O N S

1. Which of the following programming languages cannot be used to interact with users?
   a. Java
   b. CGI
   c. Perl
   d. HTML

2. DHTML is created using JavaScript and _____.
   a. the Document Object Model
   b. HTML
   c. cascading style sheets
   d. all of the above

3. Which version of the DOM is supported by both Navigator 3 and Internet Explorer 3?
   a. Level 0
   b. Level 1
   c. Level 2
   d. none of the above

4. Which is the first version of Internet Explorer to support both DOM Level 1 and Level 2?
   a. 4
   b. 5
   c. 5.5
   d. 6

5. Which is the first version of Netscape to support both DOM Level 1 and Level 2?
   a. 3
   b. 4
   c. 4.7
   d. 6

6. _____ represents the HTML document displayed in a window and provides programmatic access to document elements.
   a. The Window object
   b. JavaScript
   c. The DOM
   d. The Frame object

7. Which Document object property returns the URL of the current document?
   a. URL
   b. src
   c. href
   d. protocol

8. Which Document object property returns the text that appears in the Web browser title bar?
   a. title
   b. head
   c. heading
   d. name

9. The _____ method opens a window or frame other than the current window or frame, in order to update its contents with the write() and writeln() methods.
   a. draw()
   b. get()
   c. update()
   d. open()

10. The _____ method notifies the Web browser that you are finished writing to the window or frame and that the document should be displayed.
    a. complete()
    b. close()
    c. update()
    d. refresh()

11. The _____ array contains all of an HTML document's images.
    a. images[]
    b. pictures[]
    c. graphics[]
    d. figures[]

12. Each image in an HTML page is represented in JavaScript by the _____ object.
    a. Picture
    b. Graphic
    c. Image
    d. Figure

13. Simple animation can be created with JavaScript using the setInterval() or setTimeout() methods and the _____ property of an image.
    a. GIF
    b. JPG
    c. BMP
    d. SRC

14. The speed of animation in JavaScript depends on _____.
    a. the animation speed option, which is set in the Options dialog box in Internet Explorer or the Preferences dialog box in Navigator
    b. the speed of a computer's microprocessor
    c. how many frames are used in the animation sequence
    d. how many milliseconds are passed as an argument to the setInterval() or setTimeout() methods

15. Which of the following is an unnecessary step in image caching?
    a. Create a new object using the Image() constructor.
    b. Assign a graphic file to the src property of the new Image object.
    c. Assign the src property of the new Image object to the src property of an <IMG> tag.
    d. Download a copy of an image file to a local hard drive.

16. To be certain that all images are downloaded into a cache before commencing an animation sequence, you use the _____ of the Image object.
    a. onLoad event handler
    b. animation property
    c. loadImages() method
    d. images[] array

E X E R C I S E S

Save all files you create in the Tutorial.08 folder on your Data Disk.

1. Create a document with two vertical frames. Create a series of buttons in the left frame. Each button should represent the name of a state in your area. Use a dictionary, an encyclopedia, or the Internet to look up statistical information on each state, such as the name of the capital, the name of the governor, population, and so on. Use the open(), close(), and writeln() methods to write the information to the right frame when a user clicks a state button. Save the document as StateStatistics.html.

2. The following program is missing two important statements that may prevent the program from functioning properly in older browsers. Add the missing statements and save the document as NewDocument.html.

```
<HTML>
<HEAD>
<TITLE>Document Statistics</TITLE>
<SCRIPT LANGUAGE="JavaScript">
var newWindow = window.open();
newWindow.document.write("Document title: ");
newWindow.document.write(document.title + "<BR>");
newWindow.document.write("Document URL: ");
newWindow.document.write(document.URL + "<BR>");
newWindow.document.write("Last modified: ");
newWindow.document.write(document.lastModified);
</SCRIPT>
</HEAD>
<BODY>
</BODY>
</HTML>
```

3. The following program is a partially completed animation program of a fat cat dancing. The three images required for the program, fatcat0.gif, fatcat1.gif, and fatcat2.gif are in the Tutorial.08 folder on your Data Disk. Complete the program so that the fat cat images change every 200 milliseconds. Save the HTML document as FatCatDancing.html.

```
<HTML>
<HEAD>
<TITLE>Fat Cat Dancing</TITLE>
<SCRIPT LANGUAGE="JavaScript">
<!-- HIDE FROM INCOMPATIBLE BROWSERS
var cats = new Array(3);
var fatCat = 0;
var direction;
var begin;
cats[0] = "fatcat0.gif";
cats[1] = "fatcat1.gif";
```

```
cats[2] = "fatcat2.gif";
function dance() {
   if (fatCat == 0)
                direction = "right";
   else if (fatCat == 2)
                direction = "left";
   if (direction == "right")
                ++fatCat;
   else if (direction == "left")
                --fatCat;
   document.animation.src = cats[fatCat];
}
// STOP HIDING FROM INCOMPATIBLE BROWSERS -->
</SCRIPT>
</HEAD>
<BODY>
<H1>Fat Cat Dancing</H1>
<P><IMG SRC="fatcat1.gif" NAME="animation"></P>
<FORM>
<INPUT TYPE="button" NAME="run" VALUE=" Start Dancing ">
<INPUT TYPE="button" NAME="stop" VALUE=" Stop Dancing "
   onClick="clearInterval(begin);">
</FORM>
</BODY>
</HTML>
```

4. Add image caching to the FatCatDancing program. Also, delete the control buttons and modify the program so that the cat starts dancing as soon as the images finish loading. Save the modified HTML document as FatCatDancingCache.html.

5. Use Paint or another graphics program to create a series of frames in which a stick figure performs jumping jacks. In each frame, position the stick figure in one step or stage of performing a jumping jack. Use JavaScript to animate the frames. Save the document as JumpingJacks.html.

6. The Tutorial.08 folder on your Data Disk contains six images of a windmill: windmill0.gif through windmill5.gif. Use JavaScript to animate the images. Save the document as Windmill.html.

7. Use Paint or another graphics program to create three pictures of a traffic light. One image should have the green light illuminated, one image should have the yellow light illuminated, and one image should have the red light illuminated. Use JavaScript to cycle through the images. Save the document as TrafficLight.html.

8. The Tutorial.08 folder on your Data Disk contains two images of a pennant: pennant1.gif and pennant2.gif. Use JavaScript to animate the images so that the pennant appears to be blowing in the wind. Save the document as Pennant.html.

9. The Tutorial.08 folder on your Data Disk contains five images of a basketball: basketball1.gif through basketball5.gif. Animate the images so that the basketball appears to bounce up and down on the screen. Save the document as Dribble.html.

10. Using an Internet search engine, such as Yahoo!, or a graphics program to which you have access, locate an animal image for each letter of the alphabet, such as aardvark for A, beaver for B, and so on. (To search for images, use keywords such as clip art, images, pictures, .jpg, or .gif. Make sure the images you find are in the public domain.) Use Paint or another graphics program to add a corresponding letter of the alphabet to each image. Use JavaScript to write a program that cycles through the letters of the alphabet. Save the document as AnimalAlphabet.html.

In this section you will learn:

- About cascading style sheets
- How to use JavaScript with styles in Netscape and Internet Explorer
- About cascading style sheet positioning
- How to use positioning in Netscape and Internet Explorer
- About cross-browser compatibility

Animation and Cascading Style Sheets

Cascading Style Sheets

Cascading style sheets are one of the three technologies used for creating DHTML. **Cascading style sheets (CSS)**, also called style sheets, are a standard set by the W3C for managing the formatting information of HTML documents. Formatting information includes fonts, backgrounds, colors, layout, and other aspects of the appearance of an HTML document, as opposed to its content. A single piece of formatting information is called a **style**. Prior to styles, Web page designers applied formatting to individual HTML tags to control the appearance of a Web page. With CSS, Web page designers can centrally manage styles for a single HTML page and create a consistent look across different Web pages. In essence, CSS separates document content from its appearance.

The W3C offers a free utility, CSS Validator, that you can use to check the CSS tags in your HTML documents. You can download the CSS Validator at *jigsaw.w3.org/css-validator/*.

DHTML uses JavaScript to manipulate CSS to dynamically change the appearance of tags and the position of elements in an HTML document. For example, your Web page may have a series of buttons that users can click to change the appearance of the page according to their personal tastes. Later in this section, you will see how CSS is used to create traveling animation by allowing HTML elements to be dynamically repositioned on a page.

CSS is of most interest to Web page designers, since it allows much greater control and management of the visual aspects of a Web page than is possible with HTML. Our purpose in looking at CSS is to see how to make Web pages more dynamic using JavaScript and DHTML. Therefore, this section includes only a cursory overview of CSS styles and syntax. If you would like more information on CSS, visit the World Wide Web Consortium Web site at *www.w3.org*.

CSS styles are created using name/value pairs separated by a colon. The name portion of the name/value pair refers to a specific CSS style attribute known as a **property.** Each CSS property can be formatted with different values, depending on the property. Figure 8-26 contains examples and descriptions of common CSS properties.

CSS Property	Description	Code Example
background-color	Specifies a background color for the document	`background-color: blue;`
border-color	Specifies a border color for an element	`border-color: blue;`
font-family	Specifies the font name	`font-family: arial;`
font-style	Specifies the font style: normal, italic, or oblique	`font-style: italic;`
font-weight	Specifies font weight: normal, bold, bolder, lighter, or a number between 100 and 900; 400 is the equivalent of normal, and 700 is the equivalent of bold	`font-weight: bold;`
margin-left	Adjusts the left margin	`margin-left: 1in;`
margin-right	Adjusts the right margin	`margin-right: 1in;`
text-align	Determines the alignment of text: center, justify, left, or right	`text-align: center;`

Figure 8-26: Common CSS properties

There are two types of CSS styles: inline styles and document-level style sheets. **Inline styles** determine the appearance of individual tags in an HTML document. You define inline styles using the STYLE attribute along with a string containing the name/value pairs for each style you want to include. Multiple properties are separated by semicolons. The following code shows an <H1> tag with an inline style that changes the font-family to *serif*, the font-weight to *bold*, and the font-style to *italic*:

```
<H1 STYLE="font-family: serif; font-weight: bold;
    font-style: italic">
        H1 tag formatted with inline styles</H1>
```

Document-level style sheets determine global formatting for HTML tags. You create document-level style sheets within a set of <STYLE>...</STYLE> tag pairs placed in the <HEAD> section of a document. Any style instructions for a specific tag are applied to all associated tags contained in the body of the document. The tag to which specific style rules in a style sheet apply is called a **selector**. You can include multiple selectors within a style sheet if the rules for each selector are enclosed in a pair of braces {}. As with inline styles, multiple properties for a selector are separated by semicolons. The following code shows an example of a style sheet for the <H1>, <H2>, and <BODY> tags. Each tag is followed by a pair of braces containing style instructions. All instances of the tags in the body of the document are formatted using these style instructions.

```
<STYLE>
H1 {color: red; font-family: "ms sans serif";
    font-size: 24pt; font-weight: bold;}
H2  {color: black; font-family: "ms sans serif";
     font-size: 18pt; margin-top: 0.25in;
     margin-left: 1in;}
BODY {color: blue; font-family: "arial";
     font-size: 12pt; font-weight: medium;}
</STYLE>
<H1>H1 tag formatted with a style sheet</H1>
<H2>H2 tag formatted with a style sheet</H2>
<BODY>Body text formatted with a style sheet</BODY>
```

Another method of applying styles to tags in an HTML document is by using the CLASS attribute. The **CLASS attribute** can be applied to any HTML tag and identifies various elements as part of the same group. The syntax for the CLASS attribute is *<TAG CLASS="class name">*. You replace the TAG portion of the syntax with an HTML tag you want to include as part of the class. To include an <H1> tag and a <P> tag as part of a class named myClass, you use the syntax <H1 CLASS="myClass"> and <P CLASS="myClass">. You can create two types of CSS classes in an HTML document: a regular class and a generic class. A **regular class** is used to define different style instructions for the same tag. For example, you may need two or more different versions of the <H1> tag in a document. You create a regular class within the <STYLE>...</STYLE> tag pair by appending a class name to a style with a period. You then include the appropriate class name within the necessary tags in the document body section. The following code contains two regular classes, level1 and level2, that define the formatting instructions for different instances of the <P> tag.

```
<STYLE>
P.level1 {color: black; font-family: "serif";
     font-size: 10pt; font-weight: medium;
     text-indent: 1in}
P.level2 {color: green; font-family: "serif";
     font-size: 8pt; font-style: italic;
     text-indent: 2in}
</STYLE>
<BODY>
<P CLASS="level1">This is the level1 class</P>
<P CLASS="level2">This is the level2 class</P>
</BODY>
```

A **generic class** is similar to a regular class, except that it is not associated with any particular tag. You create a generic class within the <STYLE>...</STYLE> tag pair using a class name preceded by a period, but without appending it to a tag. The following code shows an example of a generic class named *highlight* that formats text in yellow, Arial, and with a blue background. Notice that in the body section, the generic class is applied to two different styles: bold <B> and strong <STRONG>.

```
<STYLE>
.highlight {color: yellow; font-family: arial;
     background: blue}
</STYLE>
<BODY>
<P>This <B CLASS="highlight">line</B> contains two
<STRONG CLASS="highlight">examples</STRONG>
of a generic class.</P>
</BODY>
```

The ID attribute is also used to apply styles. The value of an `ID attribute` uniquely identifies individual tags in an HTML document. The syntax for the ID attribute is *<TAG* ID="*unique name*">. An ID is similar to a class, except that it is applied only to a single occurrence of a specific ID attribute in the body of an HTML document. You create ID attributes within <STYLE>...</STYLE> tag pairs, and the name of an ID is preceded by the number sign #, as in the following example:

```
<STYLE>
#bigGreenLine {color: green; font-family: arial;
     font-size: 36pt}
</STYLE>
<BODY>
<P ID="bigGreenLine">The formatting for this
     ID class applies only to this line.</P>
</BODY>
```

tip

••

Many browsers will allow you to apply the same ID attribute to multiple tags within the same document. However, using the same ID attribute multiple times in the same document is an illegal use of HTML and you should avoid doing it, even if some browsers let you get away with it. If you need to apply the same style instructions to multiple tags, use the class attribute.

••

To give you an idea of how much easier it is to manage HTML document appearance using styles, Figure 8-27 shows an example of an HTML document created without a style sheet. Notice that the formatting for the <H1> and <H2> tags repeats with each recurrence of the tag.

```
<HTML>

<HEAD>

<TITLE>Example of Individually Formatted Tags</TITLE>

</HEAD>

<BODY>

<H1><FONT SIZE=6 COLOR="red" FACE="arial">

First instance of Heading 1</FONT></H1>

<H2><FONT SIZE=5 COLOR="black" FACE="arial"><I>

First instance of Heading 2</FONT></I></H2>

<H1><FONT SIZE=6 COLOR="red" FACE="arial">

Second instance of Heading 1</FONT></H1>

<H2><FONT SIZE=5 COLOR="black" FACE="arial"><I>

Second instance of Heading 2</FONT></I></H2>

</BODY>

</HTML>
```

Figure 8-27: Individually formatted tags

Now examine the same document with CSS styles in Figure 8-28. Notice how the style sheet separates the document content from its appearance. If you want to change the appearance of an element, such as the color of the <H1> tag, you need to change it only once in the style sheet, instead of changing it whenever the tag occurs in the document. The output for both versions of the document is shown in a Web browser in Figure 8-29.

```
<HTML>

<HEAD>

<TITLE>Example of Style Sheet Heading Tags</TITLE>

</HEAD>

<STYLE>
```

Figure 8-28: Style sheet heading tags

```
H1 {color: red; font-family: "arial";
    font-size: "x-large";}

H2  {color: black; font-family: "arial";
     font-size: "large"; font-style: italic}

</STYLE>

<BODY>

<H1>First instance of Heading 1</H1>

<H2>First instance of Heading 2</H2>

<H1>Second instance of Heading 1</H1>

<H2>Second instance of Heading 2</H2>

</BODY>

</HTML>
```

Figure 8-28: Style sheet heading tags (continued)

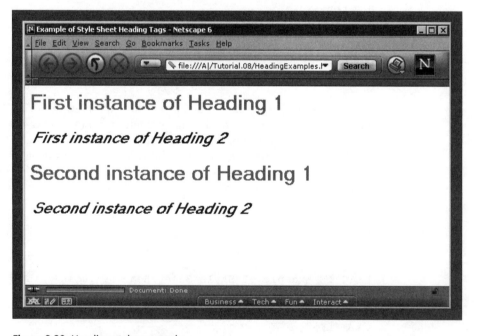

Figure 8-29: Heading styles example

Using JavaScript with CSS Styles

CSS styles determine the formatting of HTML document elements. You use JavaScript to modify CSS styles after a Web browser renders a document. As mentioned in Section A, prior to the release of the W3C standardized DOM specification, there was no compatible DHTML standard that worked with both Internet Explorer and Netscape Navigator. This incompatibility was particularly evident when using JavaScript to manipulate CSS styles. Earlier versions of Internet Explorer and Navigator supported incompatible Document object properties and methods. Because JavaScript uses Document object properties and methods to access CSS styles, if you wanted to use JavaScript code to manipulate CSS in older browsers, you had three options:

- Write code that functioned only in Navigator.
- Write code that functioned only in Internet Explorer.
- Write both sets of code and execute the correct set depending on which Web browser was in use.

In contrast, today you can write one set of code that runs on any browser that complies with the W3C DOM. However, you need to understand the incompatibilities among older browsers because, at the time of this writing, versions of Internet Explorer earlier than 5 and versions of Netscape Navigator earlier than 6 are still widely in use. Recall that style sheet functionality was not standardized in the DOM until Level 2. Also recall that Netscape Navigator did not support DOM Level 2 until version 6, and Internet Explorer did not support DOM Level 2 until version 5. Although you can write one set of code that will run on the most recent versions of both browsers, you may need to write other sets of code to run on earlier browser versions. Therefore, this section briefly explains how to use JavaScript to refer to CSS styles and presents some techniques for writing DHTML code that functions in older versions of each browser as well as current versions of each browser that support the W3C DOM Level 2.

Using JavaScript and Styles in Older Versions of Navigator

The Navigator Document Object Model in older versions of Navigator accesses the styles for selectors using the tags, classes, and ID properties of the Document object. The **tags** property provides access to the styles of tags in an HTML document. The **classes** property provides access to the styles of classes in an HTML document. The **ids** property provides access to the styles of **ID** attributes in an HTML document.

The Document object tags, classes, and ID properties are available only in Navigator 4.7 and earlier.

To refer to a CSS style in Navigator, you append the tags, classes, or ids property to the Document object with a period. For the tags and ids properties, you then append the name of a CSS selector, followed by another period and a CSS property. For example, to modify the font color for the H1 tag to blue, you use the statement `document.tags.H1.fontColor = "blue";`. To modify the font color for the ID named bigGreenLine to blue, you use the statement `document.ids.bigGreenLine.fontColor = "blue";`. For the classes property, you must append either the *all* property to modify all instances of the class or the name of a CSS selector, followed by another period and a CSS property. For example, to change the font color for all HTML tags that include the level1 CLASS attribute, you use the statement `document.classes.level1.all.fontColor = "blue";`. To change just the H1 tags that include the level1 CLASS attribute, you use the statement `document.classes.level1.H1.fontColor = "blue";`. Notice that when you refer to a CSS property containing a hyphen in JavaScript code, you remove the hyphen, convert the first word to lowercase, and convert the first letter of subsequent words to uppercase. CSS properties without hyphens are referred to with all lowercase letters. Border is referred to as `border`, border-color is referred to as `borderColor`, font-size is referred to as `fontSize`, and so on. For example, to modify the font size of the H1 tag to 18pt, you use the statement `document.tags.H1.fontSize = "18pt";`.

The following example uses JavaScript syntax to define styles for tags, classes, and ID attributes. This code performs the same function of defining styles as standard CSS syntax located between <STYLE>...</STYLE> tag pairs. Note that although older versions of Navigator allow you to define styles using JavaScript, you cannot easily change style values dynamically. Therefore, using JavaScript with styles in older versions of Navigator is of most use in defining new styles before an HTML element that uses that style is rendered. In the following example, new styles are defined before they are used in an HTML element.

```
<SCRIPT LANGUAGE="JavaScript">
<!-- HIDE FROM INCOMPATIBLE BROWSERS
document.write(
    "<H1>H1 tag before defining style properties</H1>");
document.tags.H1.color = "red";
document.tags.H1.fontSize = "24pt";
document.tags.H1.fontFamily = "arial";
document.write(
    "<H1>H1 tag after defining style properties</H1>");
document.write(
    "<P CLASS='level1'>level1 class before defining style
    properties</P>");
document.classes.level1.all.color = "blue";
document.classes.level1.all.fontSize = "18pt";
document.classes.level1.all.fontFamily = "serif";
document.write(
    "<P CLASS='level1'>level1 class after defining style
    properties</P>");
document.write(
    "<P ID='bigGreenLine'>bigGreenLine ID before defining
    style properties </P>");
document.ids.bigGreenLine.color = "green";
```

```
document.ids.bigGreenLine.fontSize = "36pt";
document.ids.bigGreenLine.fontFamily = "arial";
document.write(
    "<P ID='bigGreenLine'>bigGreenLine ID after
    defining style properties </P>");
// STOP HIDING FROM INCOMPATIBLE BROWSERS -->
</SCRIPT>
```

The text strings in the preceding code are broken due to space limitations.

Figure 8-30 shows the output of the preceding code in Navigator 4.7.

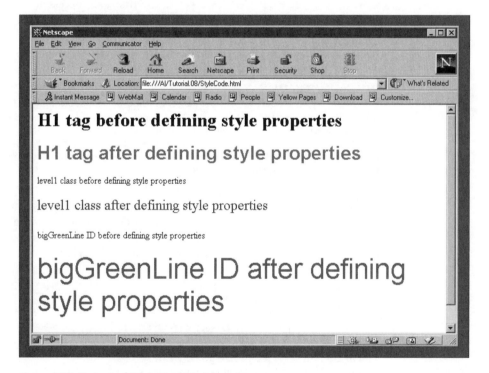

Figure 8-30: Output of Navigator 4.7 style code

You can use JavaScript code to change the value of a style after it has been rendered by a Web browser, but the change does not appear until the user resizes the screen.

Using JavaScript and Styles in Older Versions of Internet Explorer

The Internet Explorer Document Object Model accesses the styles for selectors using the all property of the Document object. The **all property** is an array of all the elements in an HTML document. The all property is appended with a period to the Document object. If you want to modify the styles for a CSS selector, you then append another period and the name of a specific CSS selector. You then append a period and the style property, followed by a period and a specific CSS property. The **style** property represents the CSS styles for a particular tag or ID attribute. As in Navigator, when you refer to a CSS property in JavaScript code in Internet Explorer, you remove the hyphen from the property name and convert the property to mixed case. For example, to modify the font size for the ID attribute named bigGreenLine tag to 36pt, you use the statement `document.all.bigGreenLine.style.fontSize = "36pt";`. To modify the styles for a specific HTML tag, you must first gain access to the styles using the tags(*tag name*) method. The **tags(*tag name*) method** returns an array of HTML elements represented by *tag name*. You append the tags() method to the all property (which is appended to the Document object) with a period, and then pass the tag name enclosed in quotation marks to the tags() method.

▶ **tip**

The all and style properties and the tags() method are available only in Internet Explorer. Unlike the Navigator Document Object Model, which is only available in Navigator versions 4.7 and earlier, the Internet Explorer Document Object Model is available in all versions of Internet Explorer, including version 6. However, keep in mind that if you use the all and style properties in your JavaScript programs, they will not be compatible with the W3C DOM, and therefore, they are not cross-browser compatible.

With the tags() method, the HTML tags that match a specific tag name are assigned to the elements of an array in the order in which they are encountered in a document. The following code shows how to use the tags() method to return all of the <H1> tags in a document to an array named allH1Tags[]. Text placed within the <H1>...</H1> tag pairs shows the element number that each <H1> tag is assigned to in the allH1Tags[] array.

```
<BODY>
<H1>Assign to allH1Tags[0]</H1>
<H1>Assign to allH1Tags[1]</H1>
<H1>Assign to allH1Tags[2]</H1>
<H1>Assign to allH1Tags[3]</H1>
<SCRIPT LANGUAGE="JavaScript">
<!-- HIDE FROM INCOMPATIBLE BROWSERS
var allH1Tags = document.all.tags("H1");
// STOP HIDING FROM INCOMPATIBLE BROWSERS -->
</SCRIPT>
</BODY>
```

You append a period and the style property to the array returned by the tags() method, followed by a period and a specific CSS property, the same as when you modify an ID attribute. However, you must use the element number to access a specific tag in the returned array. For example, the following code shows how to modify the color CSS property for the third <H1> tag found in a document using the allH1Tags[] array:

```
allH1Tags[2].style.color = "red";
```

You can also use the Document object with the tag() method directly in a statement that modifies a CSS style, the same as you can with an ID attribute, although the statement may get somewhat cumbersome, as shown in the following statement:

```
document.all.tags("H1")[2].style.color = "red";
```

In order to change style properties for all of the tags in an array returned by the tags() method at the same time, you must use a looping statement, such as a for statement, as follows:

```
var allH1Tags = document.all.tags("H1")
for (var i=0; i < allH1Tags.length; ++i) {
    allH1Tags[i].style.color = "red";
    allH1Tags[i].style.fontFamily = "arial";
    allH1Tags[i].style.fontSize = "24pt";
}
```

One of the advantages to the Internet Explorer Document Object Model is that you can use JavaScript to dynamically change styles in Internet Explorer. When you change a style in Internet Explorer using JavaScript, the changes appear immediately in the browser, whereas in Navigator you must resize the screen.

tip

Modifying the CSS styles for a particular class with JavaScript in older versions of Internet Explorer is somewhat advanced for our purposes, so these techniques will not be discussed here. If you would like to learn how to use JavaScript to modify CSS styles for a particular class in older versions of Internet Explorer see the topic *Dynamic Styles* and its subtopics in the MSDN Library at *msdn.microsoft.com/ library/default.asp?url=/workshop/author/dynstyle/ changing.asp*. Also see the MSDN Library article "Scripting with Elements and Collections" at *msdn.microsoft.com/library/default.asp?url=/workshop/author/om/scripting_elements_ collections.asp*.

Using JavaScript and Styles with the W3C DOM

In order to manipulate CSS styles with the W3C DOM, you must first gain access to the styles using either the getElementByID(*ID*) method or the getElementsByTagName(*tag name*) method. The **getElementByID(*ID*) method** returns the HTML element represented by *ID*. The **getElementsByTagName(*tag name*) method** returns an array of HTML elements represented by *tag name*. You append each of the methods to the Document object with a period, and then pass the appropriate argument to the method you are using. The following statement shows how to use the getElementByID() method to access the tag with an ID of *bigGreenLine* and assign it to a variable named curStyle:

```
var curStyle = document.getElementById("bigGreenLine");
```

After using the getElementByID() method to assign a tag to a variable, you then append a period and the style property to the variable, followed by a period and a specific CSS property. The style property represents the CSS styles for a particular tag, class, or ID, the same as in the Internet Explorer Document Object Model. The following code shows how to modify CSS properties using the curStyle variable, which contains the tag returned by the getElementByID() method for the *bigGreenLine* ID.

```
curStyle.style.color = "green";
curStyle.style.fontFamily = "arial";
curStyle.style.fontSize = "36pt";
```

Instead of assigning the tag returned by the getElementByID() method to a variable, you can use the Document object and getElementByID() method directly in a statement that modifies a CSS style, as follows:

```
document.getElementById("bigGreenLine").style.color
    = "green";
document.getElementById("bigGreenLine").style.fontFamily
    = "arial";
document.getElementById("bigGreenLine").style.fontSize
    = "36pt";
```

With the getElementsByTagName() method, the HTML tags that match a specific tag name are assigned to the elements of an array in the order in which they are encountered in a document. The following code shows how to use the getElementsByTagName() method to return all of the <H1> tags in a document to an array named allH1Tags[]. Text placed within the <H1>...</H1> tag pairs shows the element number that each <H1> tag is assigned to in the allH1Tags[] array.

```
<BODY>
<H1>Assign to allH1Tags[0]</H1>
<H1>Assign to allH1Tags[1]</H1>
<H1>Assign to allH1Tags[2]</H1>
<H1>Assign to allH1Tags[3]</H1>
<SCRIPT LANGUAGE="JavaScript">
<!-- HIDE FROM INCOMPATIBLE BROWSERS
var allH1Tags = document.getElementsByTagName("H1")
// STOP HIDING FROM INCOMPATIBLE BROWSERS -->
</SCRIPT>
</BODY>
```

You append a period and the style property to the array returned by the getElementsByTagName() method, followed by a period and a specific CSS property, the same as when you use a variable returned with the getElementByID() method. However, you must use the element number to access a specific tag in the returned array. For example, the following code shows how to modify the color CSS property for the third <H1> tag found in a document using the allH1Tags[] array:

```
allH1Tags[2].style.color = "red";
```

You can also use the Document object with the getElementsByTagName() method directly in a statement that modifies a CSS style, the same as you can with the getElementByID() method, although the statement may get somewhat cumbersome, as shown in the following statement:

```
document.getElementsByTagName("H1")[2].style.color = "red";
```

In order to change style properties for all of the tags in an array returned by the getElementsByTagName() method at the same time, you must use a looping statement, such as a `for` statement, as follows:

```
var allH1Tags = document.getElementsByTagName("H1")
for (var i=0; i < allH1Tags.length; ++i) {
    allH1Tags[i].style.color = "red";
    allH1Tags[i].style.fontFamily = "arial";
    allH1Tags[i].style.fontSize = "24pt";
}
```

Modifying the CSS styles for a particular class with JavaScript and the W3C DOM is also somewhat advanced for our purposes, so these techniques will not be discussed here. If you would like to learn how to use JavaScript to modify CSS styles for a particular class in the W3C DOM, see the article "How to dynamically change an Element's Style by its Class Attribute" at the Markup for hand coders Web site at *www.markup.co.nz/dom/styleClass_with_dom.htm*.

CSS Positioning

In Section A, you used the <IMG> tag to create simple animations with JavaScript. The <IMG> tag is limited, however, because the only type of animation you can perform with it is stationary. That is, an animation created with the <IMG> tag does not travel across the screen. Actually, there is no way to reposition an image on a Web page unless you use **CSS positioning**, which is used to position or lay out elements on a Web page. CSS positioning is supported in W3C DOM-compliant browsers as well as older versions of both Navigator and Internet Explorer. Because of the Document object incompatibilities between the two older browsers, however, you cannot write JavaScript code that works in both older browsers and in W3C DOM-compliant browsers. You must design your program for either older versions of Navigator, older versions of Internet Explorer, W3C DOM-compliant browsers, or write three sets of code and execute the correct set depending on which Web browser is in use.

There are two types of CSS positioning: relative and absolute. **Relative positioning** places an element according to other elements on a Web page. **Absolute positioning** places elements in a specific location on a Web page. Relative positioning is mainly used for the design and layout of Web pages and is beyond the scope of this text. Absolute positioning is used with JavaScript to create full animation, among other purposes.

You usually add positioning to tags with inline styles. You can also use CSS positioning in a document-level style sheet. However, if you apply positioning to a tag, such as <H1>, in a document-level style sheet, then all instances of the <H1> tag in the document will be positioned in exactly same place. In contrast, using positioning for IDs in document-level style sheets works fine. It is usually easier, however, to add positioning directly to an element as an inline style.

Several common CSS positioning properties are listed in Figure 8-31.

Property	Description	Values
position	Determines how an element is to be positioned	*absolute* or *relative*
left	The horizontal distance from the upper-left corner of the window	A value in pixels
top	The vertical distance from the upper-left corner of the window	A value in pixels
width	The width of the boundary box	A value in pixels
height	The height of the boundary box	A value in pixels
visibility	Determines if an element is visible	*visible* or *hidden*

Figure 8-31: Common CSS positioning properties

Older Navigator versions do not recognize CSS positioning for elements that are not container elements—that is, elements without a closing tag. For instance, you cannot use CSS positioning on an <IMG> tag, since it does not include a closing tag. To maintain cross-browser compatibility, elements that are to be positioned are usually placed within <SPAN>...</SPAN> or <DIV>...</DIV> tag pairs. The <SPAN> tag is used for applying formatting to sections of an HTML document, while the <DIV> tag breaks a document into distinct sections. Specific CSS positioning properties are placed inside the closing bracket of an opening <SPAN> or <DIV> tag.

The following code absolutely positions an image contained within a <SPAN> tag pair. The resulting image is displayed in a Web browser in Figure 8-32.

```
<SPAN STYLE="position:absolute; left:150; top:165">
<IMG SRC="sun.gif">
</SPAN>
```

Figure 8-32: CSS positioning

Next you will position two images in an HTML document. The images, named up.gif and down.gif, are located in the Tutorial.08 folder on your Data Disk. The up.gif file contains an image of a bird with its wings lifted, and the down.gif file contains an image of the same bird with its wings down. The Web page you create will contain the up.gif image twice and the down.gif image once. You will position the three images so the bird appears to be taking off.

To position two images in an HTML document:

1 Create a new document in your text editor or HTML editor.

2 Type the <HTML> and <HEAD> sections of the document:

```
<HTML>
<HEAD>
<TITLE>Two Birds</TITLE>
</HEAD>
```

3 Type **<BODY>** to start the body section.

4 Add the following lines to create the first absolutely positioned image. The image, up.gif, is contained within a <SPAN>...</SPAN> tag pair. You use the STYLE attribute to absolutely position the image at 40 pixels from the left and 200 pixels from the top.

```
<SPAN STYLE="position:absolute; left:40; top:200">
<IMG SRC="up.gif">
</SPAN>
```

5 Add the following lines to create the second absolutely positioned image. The image, down.gif, is also contained within a <SPAN>...</SPAN> tag pair. You use the STYLE attribute to absolutely position the image at 250 pixels from the left and 80 pixels from the top.

```
<SPAN STYLE="position:absolute; left:250; top:80">
<IMG SRC="down.gif">
</SPAN>
```

6 Now add the following lines to create the third absolutely positioned image. The up.gif image is used again and is absolutely positioned at 480 pixels from the left and 10 pixels from the top.

```
<SPAN STYLE="position:absolute; left:480; top:10">
<IMG SRC="up.gif">
</SPAN>
```

7 Add the following code to close the <BODY> and <HTML> tags:

```
</BODY>
</HTML>
```

8 Save the file as **ThreeBirds.html** in the **Tutorial.08** folder on your Data Disk. Open the **ThreeBirds.html** file in your Web browser. Figure 8-33 shows the output.

Figure 8-33: Output of ThreeBirds.html

9 Close the Web browser window.

Next you will learn how to create traveling images by dynamically positioning images with JavaScript. Because of the incompatibilities between older versions of Navigator and Internet Explorer, you will learn how to achieve dynamic positioning for each older browser, as well as how to perform dynamic positioning in W3C DOM-compatible browsers. First you will learn about dynamic positioning in older versions of Internet Explorer.

Dynamic Positioning in Older Versions of Internet Explorer

As you learned earlier, older versions of Internet Explorer allow you to use JavaScript to dynamically change CSS styles. Changes to document appearance are displayed immediately. You dynamically position an element in Internet Explorer by appending the all property to the Document object, followed by a period and the name of a specific CSS selector, followed by the style property. Finally, you append another period and the left or top CSS properties. For example, the statement `document.all.sampleimage.style.left = "3.00in";` moves an element with an ID of *sampleimage* three inches to the right by changing its left property to "3.00in". Combining the left and top CSS properties with a setTimeout() or setInterval() method allows you to create traveling animation.

As an example of CSS traveling animation in Internet Explorer, you are going to look at a simple animation of the birds you used in the last exercise. The program animates the two pictures of the birds using the setInterval() method with absolute positioning. Since the program only includes two frames in three different positions, it is not very exciting. However, it gives you a good idea of how to create traveling animation.

The code for the bird animation program is shown in Figure 8-34. Two Image objects, *up* and *down*, are created to hold each image file. Users click a Fly button to start the traveling animation. The onClick event of the Fly button event handler calls the setInterval method, which executes the fly() function. The fly() function performs the animation using three if statements. Each if statement checks the value of a variable named position. If the position property is equal to 1 or 3, then the src property of the <IMG> tag named birdImage is changed to up.gif using the statement document.birdimage.src = up.src;. If the position property is equal to 2, then the src property of the <IMG> tag named birdImage is changed to down.gif using the statement document.birdimage.src = down.src;. Each if statement also changes the left and top properties of the absolutely positioned <SPAN> tag named bird, which contains the image. The position variable is then set to the next number: 2 or 3. After the third position appears, the position property resets to 1, and the animation starts over.

```
<HTML>

<HEAD>

<TITLE>Flying Bird</TITLE>

<SCRIPT LANGUAGE="JavaScript">

<!-- HIDE FROM INCOMPATIBLE BROWSERS

var startFlying;

var updown = 0;

var horizontalPosition = 10;

var up = new Image();

up.src = "up.gif";

var down = new Image();

down.src = "down.gif";

position = 1;

function fly() {

      if (position == 1) {

            document.birdimage.src = up.src;

            document.all.bird.style.left = 40;
```

Figure 8-34: Bird animation document

```
                        document.all.bird.style.top = 200;

                        position = 2;

                }

        else if (position == 2) {

                        document.birdimage.src = down.src;

                        document.all.bird.style.left = 250;

                        document.all.bird.style.top = 80;

                        position = 3;

                }

        else if (position == 3) {

                        document.birdimage.src = up.src;

                        document.all.bird.style.left = 480;

                        document.all.bird.style.top = 10;

                        position = 1;

                }

}
// STOP HIDING FROM INCOMPATIBLE BROWSERS -->
</SCRIPT>
</HEAD>
<BODY>
<SPAN ID="bird" STYLE="position:absolute; left:40; top:200">
<IMG NAME="birdimage" SRC="up.gif" HEIGHT=200 WIDTH=200>
</SPAN>
<FORM>
<INPUT TYPE="button" NAME="fly" VALUE=" Fly "
     onClick="startFlying=setInterval('fly()',500);">
<INPUT TYPE="button" NAME="stop" VALUE=" Stop "
     onClick="clearInterval(startFlying);">
</FORM>
</BODY>
</HTML>
```

Figure 8-34: Bird animation document (continued)

Next, to show how simple traveling animation is accomplished, you are going create an animation of the Earth revolving around the sun, for Internet Explorer. The coordinates of the orbit that the Earth will take are plotted in Figure 8-35. Note that the positions around the sun are not exact. To calculate exact positions you would need a complicated formula to calculate the radius of the orbit. Also, note that smoother animation can be created by using more positions in the Earth's orbit.

Create the program even if you do not have a copy of Internet Explorer, since you will use the program later in this section when you learn about cross-browser compatibility.

To create the orbit animation for Internet Explorer:

1 Create a new document in your text editor or HTML editor.

2 Type the <HTML> and <HEAD> sections of the document:

```
<HTML>
<HEAD>
<TITLE>Orbit</TITLE>
```

3 Add the opening statements for a JavaScript section:

```
<SCRIPT LANGUAGE="JavaScript">
<!-- HIDE FROM INCOMPATIBLE BROWSERS
```

4 To create a variable to track which of the 16 orbit positions is current, add the statement `position = 0;`.

5 Create the following array to hold the 16 positions corresponding to the left position of the image. The positions correspond to the first position in each set of positions plotted in Figure 8-35.

```
leftEarth = new Array(16);
leftEarth[0] = 165; leftEarth[1] = 215;
leftEarth[2] = 260; leftEarth[3] = 290;
leftEarth[4] = 300; leftEarth[5] = 290;
leftEarth[6] = 260; leftEarth[7] = 215;
leftEarth[8] = 165; leftEarth[9] = 115;
leftEarth[10] = 70; leftEarth[11] = 40;
leftEarth[12] = 30; leftEarth[13] = 40;
leftEarth[14] = 70; leftEarth[15] = 115;
```

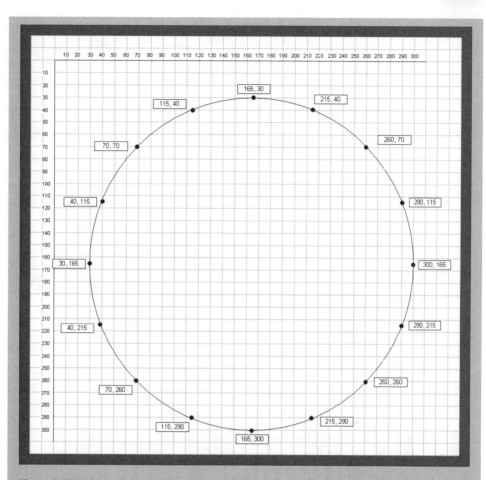

Figure 8-35: Orbit animation coordinates

6 Create the following array to hold the 16 positions corresponding to the top position of the image. The positions correspond to the second position in each set of positions plotted in Figure 8-35.

```
topEarth = new Array(16);
topEarth[0]  = 30;  topEarth[1]  = 40;
topEarth[2]  = 70;  topEarth[3]  = 115;
topEarth[4]  = 165; topEarth[5]  = 215;
topEarth[6]  = 260; topEarth[7]  = 290;
topEarth[8]  = 300; topEarth[9]  = 290;
topEarth[10] = 260; topEarth[11] = 215;
topEarth[12] = 165; topEarth[13] = 115;
topEarth[14] = 70;  topEarth[15] = 40;
```

7 Add the following orbit() function, which cycles the image of the Earth through the sixteen positions of the leftEarth and topEarth arrays. Each position is tracked by the position variable. The orbit() function will be called using a setInterval() method from the onLoad event handler in the <BODY> tag.

```
function orbit() {
    document.all.earth.style.left
        = leftEarth[position];
    document.all.earth.style.top
        = topEarth[position];
    ++position;
    if (position == 16)
        position = 0;
}
```

8 Add the following code to close the <SCRIPT> and <HEAD> sections:

```
// STOP HIDING FROM INCOMPATIBLE BROWSERS -->
</SCRIPT>
</HEAD>
```

9 Add the following opening <BODY> tag, which uses the setInterval() method to execute the orbit() function with the onLoad event handler:

```
<BODY onLoad="setInterval('orbit()',200)">
```

10 Type the following <SPAN> section, which contains and positions the image of the sun:

```
<SPAN STYLE="position:absolute; left:95; top:95">
<IMG SRC="sun.gif">
</SPAN>
```

11 Add another <SPAN> section to contain and initially position the image of the Earth. Since you will be animating the Earth using CSS positioning, the <SPAN> section is given an ID of *earth*.

```
<SPAN ID="earth" STYLE="position:absolute; left:165;
        top:30">
<IMG SRC="earth.gif">
</SPAN>
```

12 Type the closing **</BODY>** and **</HTML>** tags.

13 Save the file as **OrbitIE.html** in the **Tutorial.08** folder on your Data Disk. If you have a copy of Internet Explorer, open the file and see if the animation functions properly. Figure 8-36 shows the program output in Internet Explorer as it appears before the animation begins.

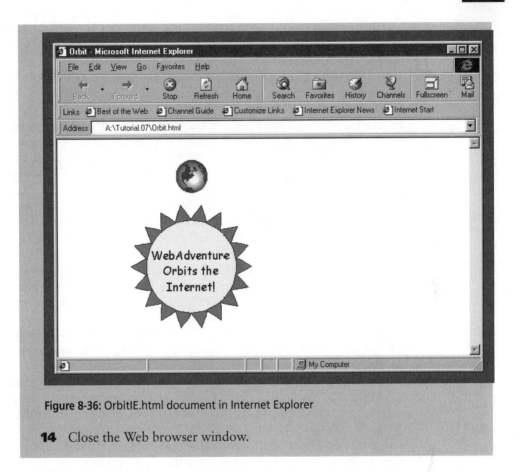

Figure 8-36: OrbitIE.html document in Internet Explorer

14 Close the Web browser window.

Dynamic Positioning in Navigator

Older versions of Navigator do not use CSS positioning for dynamic animation. Instead, you must use layers. **Layers** are used in Navigator to arrange HTML elements in sections that can be placed on top of one another and moved individually. You can still use CSS positioning with Navigator, but not for traveling animation. Although layering is not part of the CSS protocol, you need to understand layers to be able to create animation that functions in Navigator. Layering is a large topic that deals not only with animation, but also with other HTML design issues in Navigator. However, you will learn only the aspects of layering that relate to animation.

You create a layer in an HTML document using a <LAYER>...</LAYER> tag pair. You use LEFT and TOP attributes of the <LAYER> tag to specify an initial position for a layer. You can also include the NAME attribute in a <LAYER> tag.

JavaScript accesses each <LAYER> tag using a Layer object. The **Layer object** contains several properties and methods for manipulating layers in JavaScript. The two methods of the Layer object that create traveling animation in Navigator are the moveTo() method and the offset() method. The **moveTo() method** moves a layer to a specified position, and it accepts two arguments. The first argument represents the number of pixels from the left side of the window, and the second argument represents the number of pixels from the top of the window. The **offset() method** moves a layer a specified number of pixels horizontally and vertically from its current position. The offset() method also accepts two arguments. The first argument represents the number of pixels to move horizontally, and the second argument represents the number of pixels to move vertically.

You refer to a specific layer in JavaScript by using its position in the layers[] array or by using the value assigned to the <LAYER> tag NAME attribute. As with other arrays in JavaScript, such as the forms[] array, layers are assigned to the layers[] array in the order in which they are encountered by the JavaScript interpreter. To refer to the first layer in a document, you use the statement `document.layers[0];`. However, it is usually easier to refer to a layer using the value assigned to its NAME attribute. For example, to refer to an array named animation, you use the statement `document.animation;`. Each layer contains its own Document object that you must also include in order to refer to layer elements. Therefore, you use the Document object twice. For example, to change the src property of an image named myImage on a layer named animation, you use the statement `document.animation.document.myImage.src = "new_image.jpg;"`.

Figure 8-37 displays the same bird animation document you saw in Figure 8-33, but modified for use with Navigator. The displayed image is changed in the fly() function using the statements `document.bird.document.birdimage.src = up.src;` and `document.bird.document.birdimage.src = down.src;`. A single statement within each `if` statement uses the moveTo() method to move the layer named *bird*, which contains the image.

```
<HTML>

<HEAD>

<TITLE>Flying Bird</TITLE>

<SCRIPT LANGUAGE="JavaScript">

<!-- HIDE FROM INCOMPATIBLE BROWSERS

var startFlying;

var updown = 0;

var horizontalPosition = 10;

var up = new Image();
```

Figure 8-37: Bird animation document modified for use with Navigator

```
up.src = "up.gif";

var down = new Image();

down.src = "down.gif";

position = 1;

function fly() {

    if (position == 1) {

        document.bird.document.birdimage.src = up.src;

        document.bird.moveTo(40, 200);

        position = 2;

    }

    else if (position == 2) {

        document.bird.document.birdimage.src = down.src;

        document.bird.moveTo(250, 80);

        position = 3;

    }

    else if (position == 3) {

        document.bird.document.birdimage.src = up.src;

        document.bird.moveTo(480, 10);

        position = 1;

    }

}
// STOP HIDING FROM INCOMPATIBLE BROWSERS -->
</SCRIPT>
</HEAD>
<BODY>
<LAYER NAME="bird" LEFT=40 TOP=200>
<IMG NAME="birdimage" SRC="up.gif" HEIGHT=200 WIDTH=200>
</LAYER>
```

Figure 8-37: Bird animation document modified for use with Navigator (continued)

```
<FORM>

<INPUT TYPE="button" NAME="fly" VALUE=" Fly "
onClick="startFlying=setInterval('fly()',500);">

<INPUT TYPE="button" NAME="stop" VALUE=" Stop "
     onClick="clearInterval(startFlying);">

</FORM>

</BODY>

</HTML>
```

Figure 8-37: Bird animation document modified for use with Navigator (continued)

tip

If you would like to see how the flying bird animation functions in Navigator, a copy of it named **FlyingBirdNavigator.html** is in the Tutorial.08 folder on your Data Disk. Remember that you can open this file only in Navigator version 4.7 or earlier. If you attempt to open and run it in Internet Explorer or a W3C DOM-compliant browser, you will receive an error message.

Next you will modify the orbit program so that it functions in Navigator. As with the Internet Explorer version, create the program even if you do not have a copy of Navigator, since you will need it when you learn about cross-browser compatibility.

To modify the orbit animation program so that it functions in Navigator:

1 Open the **OrbitIE.html file** in your text editor or HTML editor and immediately save it as **OrbitNavigator.html** in the **Tutorial.08** folder on your Data Disk.

2 In the orbit() function, replace the two statements that modify the left and top properties of the <SPAN> tag for the Earth image with the following single statement. The new statement uses the Navigator moveTo() method to change the position of the earth layer, which you will add next:

```
document.earth.moveTo(leftEarth[position],
     topEarth[position]);
```

3 Replace the <SPAN> section for the Earth image with the following layer tags:

```
<LAYER NAME="earth" LEFT=165 TOP=30>
<IMG SRC="earth.gif">
</LAYER>
```

4 Save the document. If you have a copy of Navigator 4.7 or earlier, open the document and see if it functions correctly. Figure 8-38 shows the program output as it appears in Navigator before the animation begins.

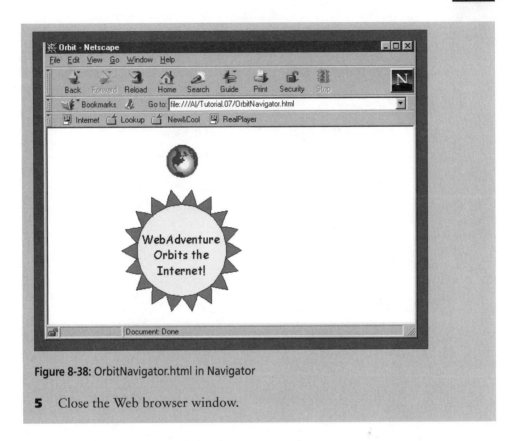

Figure 8-38: OrbitNavigator.html in Navigator

5 Close the Web browser window.

Dynamic Positioning with W3C DOM-Compliant Browsers

Dynamic positioning with JavaScript in W3C DOM-compliant browsers is quite similar to positioning with JavaScript in the Internet Explorer Document Object Model. You move an element using the style property and the left and top CSS properties. The only difference is that you replace the Internet Explorer all property with a call to the getElementByID() or getElementsByTagName() methods, or with a variable that has been assigned the return value from one of those methods. For example, the statement `document.getElementByID("sampleimage").style.left = "3.00in";` moves an element with an ID of *sampleimage* three inches to the right by changing its left property to "3.00in".

Figure 8-39 displays the bird animation document you saw for earlier versions of Navigator and Internet Explorer, but modified for use with W3C DOM-compatible browsers. The birdTag variable is assigned the return value from the getElementByID() method, and then used in the `if...else` statement to change the displayed image. Each `if` statement uses the birdTag variable twice to change the left and top properties of the absolutely positioned <SPAN> tag.

```
<HTML>

<HEAD>

<TITLE>Flying Bird W3C</TITLE>

<SCRIPT LANGUAGE="JavaScript">

<!-- HIDE FROM INCOMPATIBLE BROWSERS

var startFlying;

var updown = 0;

var horizontalPosition = 10;

var up = new Image();

up.src = "up.gif";

var down = new Image();

down.src = "down.gif";

position = 1;

function fly() {

    var birdTag = document.getElementById("bird");

    if (position == 1) {

            document.birdimage.src = up.src;

            birdTag.style.left = 40;

            birdTag.style.top = 200;

            position = 2;

    }

    else if (position == 2) {

            document.birdimage.src = down.src;

            birdTag.style.left = 250;

            birdTag.style.top = 80;

            position = 3;

    }
```

Figure 8-39: Bird animation document modified for use with W3C DOM-compliant browsers

```
        else if (position == 3) {

                document.birdimage.src = up.src;

                birdTag.style.left = 480;

                birdTag.style.top = 10;

                position = 1;

        }

}
// STOP HIDING FROM INCOMPATIBLE BROWSERS -->
</SCRIPT>
</HEAD>
<BODY>
<SPAN ID="bird" STYLE="position:absolute; left:40; top:200">
<IMG NAME="birdimage" SRC="up.gif" HEIGHT=200 WIDTH=200>
</SPAN>
<FORM>
<INPUT TYPE="button" NAME="fly" VALUE=" Fly "
onClick="startFlying=setInterval('fly()',500);">
<INPUT TYPE="button" NAME="stop" VALUE=" Stop "
     onClick="clearInterval(startFlying);">
</FORM>
</BODY>
</HTML>
```

Figure 8-39: Bird animation document modified for use with W3C DOM-compliant browsers (continued)

tip

If you would like to see how the flying bird animation functions in W3C DOM-compliant browsers, a copy of it named FlyingBirdW3C.html is in the Tutorial.08 folder on your Data Disk. Remember that you can open this file only in W3C DOM-compliant browsers. If you attempt to open it in earlier versions of Internet Explorer or Navigator, you will receive an error message.

Next you will modify the orbit program so that it functions in W3C DOM-compliant browsers.

To modify the orbit animation program so that it functions in W3C DOM-compliant browsers:

1   Open the **OrbitIE.html file** in your text editor or HTML editor and immediately save it as **OrbitW3C.html** in the **Tutorial.08** folder on your Data Disk.

2   In the orbit() function, replace the two statements that modify the left and top properties of the <SPAN> tag for the Earth image with the following statements. The new statements use the getElementById() method to access the <SPAN> tag with the earth ID attribute.

```
document.getElementById("earth").style.left
     = leftEarth[position];
document.getElementById("earth").style.top
     = topEarth[position];
```

3   Save the document, open it in Internet Explorer 6 or Navigator 6, and see if it functions correctly.

4   Close the Web browser window.

Cross-Browser Compatibility

People and companies want to attract visitors to their Web pages, and they want their Web pages to be as appealing and interesting as possible. However, both Navigator and Internet Explorer are widely used, along with other browsers such as Opera and HotJava. If developers were forced to choose a single Web browser, then a significant portion of Internet users would not be able to visit their Web sites. The best solution is to create DHTML code for each Document Object Model in which you expect your program will run. You could place all of this code in the same document, but that could make your program difficult to work with since you would need to write numerous conditional expressions for each browser type.

An easier solution is to create separate documents for each Document Object Model: one for older Netscape browsers, one for older Internet Explorer browsers, and one for W3C DOM-compliant browsers. You can then use a "master" document that checks which browser is running when users open the file. After the master document learns which browser is running, it opens the appropriate Web page. A JavaScript program that checks which type of browser is running is commonly called a **browser sniffer**.

Although there are several ways to check which browser is running, including using properties of the Navigator object, many JavaScript programmers prefer to test which DOM is being used. You can test which DOM is being used by checking whether the Document object has a layers property (for older Navigator versions), an all property (for older Internet Explorer versions), or the getElementByID() method (for W3C DOM-compliant browsers). You can check for the layers property, the all property, and the getElementByID() method using conditional statements such as `if (document.layers)`, `if (document.all)`, and `if (getElementByID)`. If the property or method is available in the browser, then a value of true is returned. For example, since only the Navigator Document object includes a layers object, the statement `if (document.layers)` checks if the object exists and returns true if executed in an older version of Navigator or false if executed in Internet Explorer or a W3C DOM-compliant browser. Similarly, since only W3C DOM-compliant browsers support the getElementByID() method, the statement `if (document.getElementByID)` returns true only if executed in a W3C DOM-compliant browser and false if executed in earlier versions of Internet Explorer or Navigator. Note that when checking for the existence of a method, you do not include the method parentheses in the conditional expression.

The browser sniffer program in Figure 8-40 opens a browser-specific version of the flying bird animation program. The onLoad() event handler in the <BODY> tag calls a checkBrowser() function. The checkBrowser() function checks for the getElementByID() method, the layers property, and the all property to see which browser is running, then uses the `document.location.href;` statement to open the correct file. Notice that the program first checks if the browser is W3C DOM-compliant. Remember that Internet Explorer 6 supports both its own Document Object Model (which uses the all property) and the W3C DOM. In order to make sure that the W3C DOM version of your program opens, you need to place the conditional statement that checks for the getElementById() before the conditional statement that checks for the all property. If the order were reversed, then your program would always open the older Internet Explorer Document Object Model version instead of the current W3C DOM version. Also notice that the checkBrowser() function includes a final `else` clause that prints a message informing users that they are using an unsupported browser.

```
<HTML>

<HEAD>

<TITLE>Flying Bird</TITLE>

<SCRIPT LANGUAGE="JavaScript">

<!-- HIDE FROM INCOMPATIBLE BROWSERS

function checkBrowser() {

    if (document.getElementById)

        document.location.href = "FlyingBirdW3C.html";

    else if (document.layers)

        document.location.href = "FlyingBirdNavigator.html";

    else if (document.all)

        document.location.href = "FlyingBirdIE.html";
```

Figure 8-40: Browser sniffer program

```
    else

        document.write("Sorry! Your browser type is not supported.")

}

// STOP HIDING FROM INCOMPATIBLE BROWSERS -->

</SCRIPT>

</HEAD>

<BODY onLoad="checkBrowser();">

</BODY>

</HTML>
```

Figure 8-40: Browser sniffer program (continued)

Next you will create a browser sniffer that opens a browser-specific version of the orbit program.

To create a browser sniffer that opens a browser-specific version of the orbit program:

1 Create a new document in your text editor or HTML editor.

2 Type the opening <HTML>, <HEAD>, and <TITLE> sections of the document:

```
<HTML>
<HEAD>
<TITLE>Orbit</TITLE>
```

3 Add the opening statements for a JavaScript section within the <HEAD> section:

```
<SCRIPT LANGUAGE="JavaScript">
<!-- HIDE FROM INCOMPATIBLE BROWSERS
```

4 Create the following function to check which browser is being used. The function will be called from the onLoad event in the <BODY> tag:

```
function checkBrowser() {
    if (document.getElementById)
        document.location.href
        = "OrbitW3C.html";
    else if (document.layers)
        document.location.href
        = "OrbitNavigator.html";
    else if (document.all)
        document.location.href
        = "OrbitIE.html"; else
```

```
              document.write(
          "Sorry! Your browser type is not supported.")
        }
```

5   Add the following code to close the <SCRIPT> and <HEAD> sections:

```
// STOP HIDING FROM INCOMPATIBLE BROWSERS -->
</SCRIPT>
</HEAD>
```

6   Type the following <BODY> tag that includes an onLoad event, which calls the checkBrowser() function:

```
<BODY onLoad="checkBrowser()">
```

7   Add the closing **</BODY>** and **</HTML>** tags.

8   Save the file as **OrbitMaster.html** in the **Tutorial.08** folder on your Data Disk. Open the **OrbitMaster.html** file from either Navigator, Netscape, or Internet Explorer to see if the correct version of the program opens. The name of the document that opens appears in the Address box in Internet Explorer, in the Location box in Navigator, or in the Search box in Netscape.

9   Close the Web browser window.

S U M M A R Y

- Cascading style sheets (CSS, also called style sheets) are a standard set forth by the World Wide Web Consortium for managing the formatting information of HTML documents.

- A single piece of formatting information is called a style.

- CSS styles are created using name/value pairs separated by a colon. The name portion of the name/value pair refers to a specific CSS style attribute known as a property.

- Inline styles determine the appearance of individual tags in an HTML document. You define inline styles using the STYLE attribute along with a string containing the name/value pairs for each style you want to include. Multiple properties are separated by semicolons.

- Document-level style sheets determine formatting for instances of a specific HTML element, such as the <H1> tag, and for specific CLASS and ID attributes.

- The CLASS attribute can be applied to any HTML tag, identifying various elements as part of the same class.

- The value of an ID attribute uniquely identifies individual tags in an HTML document.

- The tag, class, or ID to which specific style rules in a style sheet apply is called a selector.

■ A regular class is used to define different style instructions for the same tag.

■ A generic class is similar to a regular class, but it is not associated with any particular tag.

■ The Netscape Document Object Model accesses the styles for selectors using the tags, classes, and ID properties of the Document object in older versions of Navigator. The tag property provides access to the styles of tags in an HTML document. The classes property provides access to the styles of classes in an HTML document. The ID property provides access to the styles of ID attributes in an HTML document.

■ When you refer to a CSS property in JavaScript code, you remove the hyphen, use a lowercase letter for the first letter of the first word, and use an uppercase letter for the first letter of subsequent words.

■ The Internet Explorer Document Object Model accesses the styles for selectors using the all and style properties and the tags() method of the Document object in older versions of Internet Explorer. The all property is an array of all the elements in an HTML document. The style property represents the CSS styles for a particular tag, class, or ID attribute. The tags(*tag name*) method returns an array of HTML elements represented by *tag name*.

■ In order to manipulate CSS styles with the W3C DOM, you must first gain access to the styles using either the getElementByID(*ID*) method or the getElementsByTagName(*tag name*) method.

■ CSS positioning is used to position or lay out elements on a Web page.

■ Relative positioning places an element according to other elements on the Web page.

■ Absolute positioning places elements in a specific location on a Web page.

■ You dynamically position an element in older versions of Internet Explorer by appending the all property to the Document object, followed by a period and the name of a specific CSS selector, followed by the style property. Finally, you append another period and the left or top CSS properties.

■ Layers are used in Navigator to arrange HTML elements in sections that can be placed on top of one another and moved individually.

■ You use the moveTo() and offset() methods of the Layer object to dynamically position elements in older versions of Navigator.

■ You dynamically position an element with JavaScript in W3C DOM-compliant browsers by accessing a tag using the getElementByID() or getElementsByTagName() methods, and then by using the style property and the left and top CSS properties.

■ A JavaScript program that checks which type of browser is running is commonly known as a browser sniffer. After a master document learns which browser is running, it opens the appropriate Web page.

■ You can test which DOM is being used by checking whether the Document object has a layers property (for older Navigator versions), an all property (for older Internet Explorer versions), or the getElementByID() method (for W3C DOM-compliant browsers).

Q U E S T I O N S

1. The name portion of the name/value pair refers to a specific CSS style attribute known as a _____.
   a. property
   b. key
   c. definition
   d. style module

2. _____ styles determine the appearance for individual tags in an HTML document.
   a. Tag
   b. Line
   c. Inline
   d. Instance

3. _____ style sheets determine formatting for instances of a specific HTML element, such as the <H1> tag, and for specific CLASS and ID attributes.
   a. Global
   b. Document-level
   c. Class
   d. Inline

4. The CLASS attribute _____.
   a. contains a grouping of JavaScript functions
   b. manages all the arrays within a given <SCRIPT>...</SCRIPT> tag pair
   c. determines whether Internet Explorer or Navigator is the browser platform
   d. identifies different HTML elements as part of the same class

5. The value of an ID attribute _____.
   a. contains a color identifier used for changing background colors
   b. uniquely identifies individual tags in an HTML document
   c. is a type of label used within JavaScript code
   d. is only used with images in an HTML document

6. The tag, class, or ID to which specific style rules in a style sheet apply is called a _____.
   a. label
   b. marker
   c. indicator
   d. selector

7. A _____ class is used for defining different style instructions for the same tag.
   a. regular
   b. standard
   c. style
   d. JavaScript

8. A class that is not associated with any particular style is referred to as a(n) _____ class.
   a. irregular
   b. generic
   c. independent
   d. floating

9. What happens when you change the formatting of a style contained in a style sheet?
   a. Nothing. You must reload the HTML document from the server in order for the changes to take effect.
   b. All tags in the document that are associated with the style are automatically updated.
   c. Only the first instance of a tag associated with the style is automatically updated.
   d. You must right-click each tag associated with the style and select Update from the shortcut menu.

10. How is the CSS property font-weight written in JavaScript?
    a. font-weight
    b. fontweight
    c. FontWeight
    d. fontWeight

11. When does a change to a style value using JavaScript code appear in older versions of Navigator?
    a. immediately
    b. after the HTML document is reloaded from the server
    c. after the user resizes the window
    d. You cannot use JavaScript to change style values in Navigator.

12. How do you change the color style for the companyLogo ID using JavaScript code in older versions of Internet Explorer?
    a. `document.companyLogo.style.color = "red";`
    b. `document.all.companyLogo.style.color = "red";`
    c. `document.all.companyLogo.color = "red";`
    d. `document.companyLogo.color = "red";`

13. When does a change to a style value using JavaScript code appear in older versions of Internet Explorer?
    a. immediately
    b. after the HTML document is reloaded from the server
    c. after the user resizes the screen
    d. You cannot use JavaScript to change style values in Internet Explorer.

14. Which W3C DOM method do you use for manipulating HTML tags that are represented by an ID attribute?
    a. getElement()
    b. getElementID()
    c. getElementById()
    d. getElementByID()

15. Which W3C DOM method returns an array of HTML elements that represents all instances of a particular tag in a document?
    a. getElementName()
    b. getElementTagName()
    c. getElementByTag ()
    d. getElementByTagName()

16. _____ positioning places an element according to the positions of other elements on the Web page.
    a. Relative
    b. Absolute
    c. Inline
    d. Frame

17. _____ positioning places elements in a specific location on a Web page.
    a. Relative
    b. Absolute
    c. Inline
    d. Frame

18. Which properties are used with the STYLE attribute of inline styles for CSS positioning?
    a. left and top
    b. x and y
    c. horizontal and vertical
    d. x-axis and y-axis

19. Which HTML tag pairs are used exclusively by older versions of Navigator for positioning?
    a. <SPAN>...</SPAN>
    b. <DIV>...</DIV>
    c. <LAYERS>...</LAYERS>
    d. <POSITION>...</POSITION>

20. What method is—or what methods are—used in older versions of Navigator for positioning with JavaScript?
    a. the setAt() method
    b. the top() and bottom() methods
    c. the left() and right() methods
    d. the moveTo() method

21. A JavaScript program that checks which type of browser is running is commonly referred to as a _____.
    a. browser sniffer
    b. browser rooter
    c. Web check routine
    d. branching browser program

E X E R C I S E S

For the following exercises, locate the necessary images on the Internet or from a graphics program to which you have access. Create versions for older versions of Navigator and Internet Explorer as well as for the W3C DOM. Also create a browser sniffer for each program. Save all files you create in the Tutorial.08 folder on your Data Disk.

1. The Tutorial.08 folder on your Data Disk contains three images of snowflakes: snowflake1.gif, snowflake2.gif, and snowflake3.gif. Use each image as many times as you like to create a snowstorm effect on a Web page. It should "snow" from the top of the screen to the bottom. Save the document as Blizzard.html.

2. The Tutorial.08 folder on your Data Disk contains an image of a kangaroo, kangaroo.gif. Animate the image so that the kangaroo appears to hop up and down and across your screen. Save the document as Kangaroo.html.

3. The Tutorial.08 folder on your Data Disk contains three images of fish: fish1.gif, fish2.gif, and fish3.gif. Use the fish images to create a fish tank in a Web page. The fish should swim across the screen from both directions. Use as many copies of the images as you think necessary. Save the document as FishTank.html.

4. The Tutorial.08 folder on your Data Disk contains an image of a racecar, racecar.gif. Animate the image so that the racecar appears to drive around a Web page on an oval racetrack. Add buttons that start and stop the animation. Use several start buttons that drive the car at different speeds. Save the document as RaceTrack.html.

5. The Tutorial.08 folder on your Data Disk contains an image of an airplane, airplane.gif. Create a Web page that includes the airplane image. Create several buttons that make the airplane fly. Create one button for takeoff, one button to land, another button that flies a loop-the-loop, and so on. Save the document as Pilot.html.

Cookies and Security

case ▶ As you create more and more JavaScript programs, you are frustrated that you cannot save any information about people who visit your Web site. Your manager at WebAdventure has recommended that you learn about cookies so you will be able to save visitor information. Cookies are small pieces of information that are saved to a user's computer. However, when you learn that cookies actually get saved on a user's computer, you become concerned about security issues, especially given the problems you have been hearing about in the news. So, your next task at WebAdventure is to learn how to create cookies and how to implement JavaScript security features.

Previewing the Product Registration and Home Page Programs

In this tutorial you will work on two separate projects. The first project modifies the Product Registration program you created in Tutorial 6 so that its form information is saved in cookies instead of in hidden form fields. The second project is a Navigator-specific program that changes a user's default home page. You will need Navigator 4.7 or earlier to run the program. It is an example of a program that you should not write, because it intrudes into an area normally off limits to JavaScript programs. However, creating the program will allow you to understand how JavaScript security prevents programs such as these from tampering with a user's system. The security program that you create will be signed with a digital certificate, which identifies the creator of a JavaScript program. You will not be able to preview the security program because you must first create a test certificate. You will, however, preview the code that creates the program.

To preview the Product Registration program:

1 In your Web browser, open the **ProductRegistration.html** file from the **Tutorial9_ProductRegistration** folder in the **Tutorial.09** folder on your Data Disk. The program works the same way it did in Tutorial 6, except that the form data is now stored in cookies on the local computer instead of in hidden form fields.

2 Close the Web browser window.

3 Now in your text editor or HTML editor, open the **CustomerInfo.html** file from the **Tutorial9_ProductRegistration** folder in the **Tutorial.09** folder on your Data Disk. The nextForm() function builds name=value pairs for each field on the form and uses the encodeURI() method to encode each text string into a value URI. The encoded text string is then assigned to the cookie property of the Document object.

4 Close **CustomerInfo.html**.

To preview the Home Page program code:

1 In your text editor or HTML editor, open the **HomePage.html** file from the **Tutorial9_Homepage** folder in the **Tutorial.09** folder on your Data Disk.

Notice that an ARCHIVE attribute in the script section refers to a HomePage.jar file. A file with an extension of .jar is a special kind of compressed file that contains signed script information. Also notice that the <SCRIPT> tag and the form button contain unique ID tags. The ARCHIVE and ID attributes are used for digitally signing a JavaScript program. The HomePage.html file is digitally signed with a test certificate named *dongosselin*. The test certificate is just for testing purposes and is not issued by a valid Certificate Authority (CA). Because the test certificate is not recognized by a valid CA, if you attempt to open the file in your version of Navigator, it will be treated as if it were unsigned. (Remember you will need Navigator 4.7 or earlier to run the program.)

However, if the program were signed with a valid digital certificate (issued by a recognized CA) and you were to run it and click the button, a dialog box would appear prompting you to grant or deny permission to read your personal preferences. The dialog box would inform you that JavaScript or a Java applet from *dongosselin* is requesting additional privileges. To view the certificate, you would click the Certificate button. Figure 9-1 shows an example of the dongosselin digital certificate. Remember that you will not be able to see the digital certificate shown in Figure 9-1 because it is not issued by a valid CA. However, in Section B you will create your own test certificate, similar to the one shown in Figure 9-1, that you can use for testing purposes to digitally sign your JavaScript files.

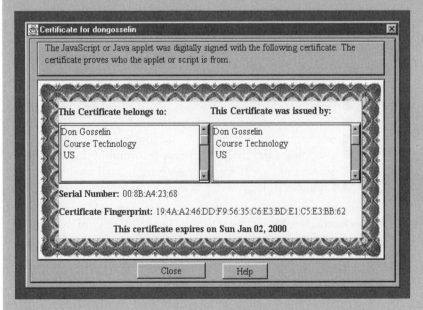

Figure 9-1: Digital certificate

2 Close the **HomePage.html** file.

In this section you will learn:
■ About state information
■ About the String object
■ How to save state information with query strings
■ How to create and read cookies

State Information and Cookies

State Information

Hypertext Transfer Protocol (HTTP) manages the hypertext links used to navigate the Web and ensures that Web browsers correctly process and display the various types of information contained in Web pages. HTTP was originally designed to be **stateless**, and no persistent data was stored about a visit to a Web page. The original stateless design of the Web allowed early Web servers to quickly process requests for Web pages, because they did not need to remember any unique requirements for different clients. Similarly, Web browsers did not need to know any special information to load a particular Web page from a server. Although this stateless design was efficient, it was also limiting, because a Web server could not remember individual user information. Web browsers treated every visit to a Web page as an entirely new session, regardless of whether users opened a different Web page on the same server, navigated to a different Web site, or closed their Web browser entirely. This design hampered interactivity and limited the personal attention a Web site could provide. Today, there are many reasons for maintaining state information, including:

■ Individual Web page customization based on user preferences
■ Temporary storage of information when navigating within a multipart form
■ Bookmarks for returning to specific locations within a Web site
■ Shopping carts that store order information for commercial Web sites
■ Storage of user IDs and passwords
■ Counters to keep track of how many times a user has visited a site

There are several methods of maintaining state information. One of the most common methods is hidden form fields. Two other ways of maintaining state information are query strings and cookies. To learn about query strings and cookies, you will work with the Product Registration program you created in Tutorial 6. The Product Registration program consists of two frames created in the ProductRegistration.html file. The bottom frame is used for navigating between two Web pages, ProductInfo.html and CustomerInfo.html. To record state information when a user navigates between ProductInfo.html and CustomerInfo.html, the contents of the forms on each Web page are copied into hidden form fields in the frame at the top of ProductRegistration.html. First, you will modify the Product Registration program to maintain state information using query strings. Then you will modify the program to maintain state information using cookies.

Saving State Information with Query Strings

One way to preserve information following a user's visit to a Web page is to append a query string to the end of a URL. A query string is a set of *name=value* pairs appended to a target URL and consists of a single text string containing one or more pieces of information. You can use a query string to pass information, such as search criteria, from one Web page to another. To pass information from one Web page to another using a query string, add a question mark (?) immediately after a URL, followed by the query string (in *name=value* pairs) for the information you want to preserve. In this manner, you are passing information to another Web page, similarly to the way you can pass arguments to a function or method. You separate individual *name=value* pairs within the query string using ampersands (&). The following code provides an example of an <A>...</A> tag pair that contains a query string consisting of three *name=value* pairs:

```
<A HREF="http://www.URL.com/TargetPage.html?firstName=Don
&lastName=Gosselin&occupation=writer">Link Text</A>
```

The passed query string is then assigned to the search property of the target Web page Location object. The search property of the Location object contains a URL's query or search parameters. To use the data contained in a query string, you must parse the string contained in the search property using the String object methods and length property. (You will see some examples of parsing later in this tutorial.) For the preceding example, after the TargetPage.html file opens, the query string ?firstName=Don&lastName=Gosselin&occupation=writer will be available in the search property of the Location object.

tip If the target Web page is a CGI script, then the query string is assigned to the QUERY_STRING environment variable.

tip The search property of the Location object gets its name because many Internet search engines use the query string the property contains to store search criteria.

Next you will modify the Product Registration program you created in Tutorial 6 so that customer information is passed as query strings instead of being stored in hidden form fields.

To modify the Product Registration program so that customer information is passed as query strings instead of being stored in hidden form fields:

1 Create a folder named **ProductRegistration** in the **Tutorial.09** folder on your Data Disk. Although you do not usually need to create JavaScript programs in separate folders, several of the programs you work on in this tutorial will include cookies. By default, a cookie is available to all Web pages in the same directory. To avoid conflicts among the cookies stored by the programs you create in this tutorial, you will create each program in a separate folder.

2 Copy the **ProductRegistration.html, ProductInfo.html, CustomerInfo.html,** and **TopFrame.html** files you created in Tutorial 6 from the Tutorial.06 folder to the ProductRegistration folder in the Tutorial.09 folder on your Data Disk.

3 Open **TopFrame.html** in your text editor or HTML editor. Delete the form containing the hidden form fields. You do not need the form because the data will be saved in a query string.

4 Save and close **TopFrame.html**.

5 Open **CustomerInfo.html** in your text editor or HTML editor.

6 Replace all of the statements in the nextForm() function with the following code, which builds the query string using each form element name and value in a variable named savedData. The name of each form element is entered as a literal string and concatenated with the value property of each element, using the + and += assignment operators. All of the *name=value* pairs are concatenated into a single string that is assigned to the savedData variable. Notice that each *name=value* pair is separated by an ampersand. The last statement appends a question mark along with the savedData query string to the CustomerInfo.html URL.

```
var savedData;
savedData = "name=" +
    document.customerInfo.name.value;
savedData += "&address=" +
    document.customerInfo.address.value;
savedData += "&city=" +
    document.customerInfo.city.value;
savedData += "&state=" +
    document.customerInfo.state.value;
savedData += "&zip=" +
    document.customerInfo.zip.value;
savedData += "&email=" +
    document.customerInfo.email.value;
```

```
savedData += "&password=" +
    document.customerInfo.password.value;
if (
    document.customerInfo.platform[0].checked == true)
    savedData += "&platform=" +
document.customerInfo.platform[0].value;
else if (
    document.customerInfo.platform[1].checked == true)
    savedData += "&platform=" +
document.customerInfo.platform[1].value;
else if (
    document.customerInfo.platform[2].checked == true)
    savedData += "&platform=" +
document.customerInfo.platform[2].value;
else if (
    document.customerInfo.platform[3].checked == true)
    savedData += "&platform=" +
document.customerInfo.platform[3].value;
else if (
    document.customerInfo.platform[4].checked == true)
    savedData += "&platform=" +
document.customerInfo.platform[4].value;
else if (
    document.customerInfo.platform[5].checked == true)
    savedData += "&platform=" +
document.customerInfo.platform[6].value;
if (document.customerInfo.wp.checked == true)
    savedData += "&wp=true";
if (document.customerInfo.ss.checked == true)
    savedData += "&ss=true";
if (document.customerInfo.db.checked == true)
    savedData += "&db=true";
if (document.customerInfo.gr.checked == true)
    savedData += "&gr=true";
if (document.customerInfo.pr.checked == true)
    savedData += "&pr=true";
savedData += "&location=" +
    document.customerInfo.location.value;
savedData += "&comments=" +
    document.customerInfo.comments.value;
location.href="ProductInfo.html" + "?" + savedData;
```

7 Save and close **CustomerInfo.html.**

Next you will modify the ProductInfo.html file, which contains a Submit button that transmits the form data to an imaginary server. In this exercise, you append a query string to a URL and do not submit form data to a server. Therefore, you need to modify the submitForm() function so that a query string is appended to the URL of an imaginary CGI script. In a working environment, you would write a CGI script that further manipulates or processes the *name=value* pairs in the query string.

To modify the ProductInfo.html file:

1 Open **ProductInfo.html** in your text editor or HTML editor.

2 Delete all of the statements in the submitForm() function. Then, add the following code, which creates a new savedData variable.

```
var savedData = location.search;
savedData += "&serial=" +
    document.productInfo.serial.value;
savedData += "&date=" +
    document.productInfo.date.value;
if (document.productInfo.where[0].checked == true)
    savedData += "&where=" +
    document.productInfo.where[0].value;
else if (
    document.productInfo.where[1].checked == true)
    savedData += "&where=" +
    document.productInfo.where[1].value;
else if (
    document.productInfo.where[2].checked == true)
    savedData += "&where=" +
    document.productInfo.where[2].value;
else if (
    document.productInfo.where[3].checked == true)
    savedData += "&where=" +
    document.productInfo.where[3].value;
```

3 Press **Enter** and type **// location.href="ProcessOrder.cgi" + "?" + savedData;**. Be sure to include the two forward slashes in front of the statement that changes the href property of the Location object. These slashes change the statement into a comment that will not be executed. This exercise illustrates appending a query string to any type of URL, and the program ProcessOrder.cgi does not really exist. Because the CGI program does not actually exist, you will receive an error message if you submit the form without commenting out the statement that changes the href property of the Location object. To simulate how a CGI script might handle the query string, you will display the *name=value* pairs in an alert dialog box in the next exercise.

4 Press **Enter** again and add the statement `return false;` to prevent the form from actually being submitted.

5 Save **ProductInfo.html**. Before you open the file and run the program, you need to add code that parses the query string and displays its contents in an alert dialog box.

Parsing a String

For a Web page to use the information in a query string, you must first parse the string, using a combination of several methods and the length property of the String object. The first parsing task is to remove the question mark at the start of the query string, using the substring() method combined with the length property. The substring() method takes two arguments: a starting index number and an ending index number. The first character in a string has an index number of 0, similar to the first element in an array. Because you want to exclude the first character of the string (the question mark), which has an index of 0, you will use a starting index of 1. For the ending index number, you will use the length property, which tells the substring() method to include the rest, or *length*, of the string. The following code assigns the search property of the Location object to a variable named queryData and uses the substring() method and length property to remove the starting question mark.

```
// Assigns the query string to the queryData variable
var queryData = location.search;
// Removes the opening question mark from the string
queryData = queryData.substring(1, queryData.length);
```

The next step is to convert the individual pieces of information in the queryData variable into array elements using the split() method. The split() method takes a single argument representing the character that separates each individual piece of information in a string. You will use an ampersand, because that is what separates the *name=value* pairs in the query string. However, keep in mind that you can split a string at whatever character is necessary. The code to convert the information in the queryData variable into an array named queryArray is as follows:

```
// splits queryData into an array
var queryArray = queryData.split("&");
```

Figure 9-2 shows a completed version of the parsing program.

```
<HTML>
<HEAD>
<TITLE>Parsing Query Strings</TITLE>
</HEAD>
<BODY>
<PRE>
<SCRIPT LANGUAGE="JavaScript">
<!-- HIDE FROM INCOMPATIBLE BROWSERS
// Assigns the query string to the queryData variable
var queryData = location.search;
// Removes the opening question mark from the string
queryData = queryData.substring(1, queryData.length);
// splits queryData into an array
var queryArray = queryData.split("&");
document.writeln(queryArray[0]);
document.writeln(queryArray[1]);
document.writeln(queryArray[2]);
// STOP HIDING FROM INCOMPATIBLE BROWSERS -->
</SCRIPT>
</PRE>
</BODY>
</HTML>
```

Figure 9-2: Parsing program

Next you will parse the *name=value* pairs in the ProductInfo.html query string and display them in an alert dialog box.

To parse the *name=value* pairs in the ProductInfo.html query string and display them in an alert dialog box:

1   Return to **ProductInfo.html** in your text editor or HTML editor.

2   Replace the statement   `// location.href="ProcessOrder.cgi" +` `"?" +  savedData;` at the end of the submitForm() function with the statement
`savedData = savedData.substring(1, savedData.length);`,
which uses the substring() method to remove the opening question mark of the query string.

3   Press **Enter** and type `var dataArray = savedData.split("&");` to split the query string into an array named dataArray[].

4   Add the following statements that use a `for` loop to display the contents of dataArray[] in an alert dialog box. Each *name=value* pair will be separated in the alert dialog box by a new line escape character (\n).

```
var messageString = "";
for (var i = 0; i < dataArray.length; ++i) {
    messageString += dataArray[i] + "\n";
}
alert(messageString);
```

5   Save and close **ProductInfo.html**, then open **ProductRegistration.html** in your Web browser. Fill in the fields in the Customer Information form and click the **Next** button. Then fill in the fields in the Product Information form and click the **Submit Query** button. The *name=value* pairs for both forms should appear in an alert dialog box. If you added any spaces to the values you entered in the forms, they will appear in the alert dialog box as %20, which is a special type of encoding that is required for transmitted URLs. You will learn how to handle encoded characters in the next section.

6   Close the Web browser window.

Saving State Information with Cookies

Query strings do not permanently maintain state information. The information contained in a query string is available only during the current session of a Web page. Once a Web page that reads a query string closes, the query string is lost. Hidden form fields maintain state information between Web pages, but the data they contain are also lost once the Web page that reads the hidden fields closes. You can save the contents of a query string or hidden form fields by using a CGI script, but that method requires a separate server-based application. To be able to store state information beyond the current Web page session, Netscape created cookies. **Cookies**, or magic cookies, are small pieces of information about a user that are stored by a Web server in text files on the user's computer. The W3C DOM Level 1 defines cookie specifications.

Each time the Web client visits a Web server, saved cookies for the requested Web page are sent from the client to the server. The server then uses the cookies to customize the Web page for the client. Cookies were originally created for use with CGI scripts, but are now commonly used by JavaScript. Consider visiting a Web site and being asked to enter a username in a prompt dialog box or in a text field. With each subsequent visit to the same Web site, whether during the same browser session or during a different browser session days or weeks later, you are greeted with the username you entered. The Web page remembers this information by storing it locally on your computer in a cookie. Another example of a typical cookie you may have seen is a counter that counts the number of times an individual user has visited a Web site.

Cookies can be temporary or persistent. Temporary cookies remain available only for the current browser session. Persistent cookies remain available beyond the current browser session and are stored in a text file on a client computer. In this section, you will create both persistent and temporary cookies.

There are a number of limitations on the use of cookies. Each individual server or domain can store only a maximum of 20 cookies on a user's computer. In addition, the total cookies per browser cannot exceed 300, and the largest cookie size is 4 kilobytes. If these limits are exceeded, a Web browser may start discarding older cookies.

Creating Cookies

You use the cookie property of the Document object to create cookies in *name=value* pairs, the same way you used *name=value* pairs with a query string. The syntax for the cookie property is `document.cookie = name + value;`. The cookie property is created with a required name attribute and four optional attributes: expires, path, domain, and secure.

Name Attribute The only required parameter of the cookie property is the name attribute, which specifies the cookie name=value pair. Cookies that are created with only the *name=value* parameter are called transient, or temporary, because they are available for only the current browser session. The following code creates a cookie with a *name=value* pair of *firstName=Don*:

```
document.cookie = "firstName=" + "Don";
```

The cookie property of the Document object can be confusing. For other JavaScript properties, assigning a new value to a property *replaces* the old value. In contrast, assigning a new value to the cookie property builds a list of cookies, rather than replacing the last value. The following example builds a list of cookies:

```
document.cookie = "firstName=" + "Don";
document.cookie = "lastName=" + "Gosselin";
document.cookie = "occupation=" + "writer";
```

A Web browser automatically separates each *name=value* pair in the cookie property with a semicolon and a space. In Internet Explorer (including version 6) and older versions of Navigator, you can build a string containing multiple *name=value* pairs separated by semicolons, and then assign the string to the cookie property of the Document object. Each statement in the string would then be assigned to the cookie property as a separate cookie. However, later versions of JavaScript impose a much stricter syntax when assigning cookies: Only the first statement in a string is assigned to the cookie property; the rest of the statements in the string are ignored. Netscape 6 is an example of a browser that imposes this stricter syntax. For example, in Navigator only the firstName cookie in the following code is assigned to the cookie property of the Document object:

```
document.cookie = "firstName=" + "Don" + "; lastName=" +
    "Gosselin"
+ "; occupation=" + "writer";
```

Due to the stricter cookie syntax in Netscape and later versions of JavaScript, you should avoid assigning cookies by building a string of multiple name = value pairs, and instead assign each cookie individually.

By default, cookies themselves cannot include semicolons or other special characters, such as commas or spaces. Cookies cannot include special characters because they are transmitted between Web browsers and Web servers using HTTP, which does not allow certain nonalphanumeric characters to be transmitted in their native format. However, you can use special characters in your cookies if you use encoding, which involves converting special characters in a text string to their corresponding hexadecimal ASCII value, preceded by a percent sign. For example, 20 is the hexadecimal ASCII equivalent of a space character, and 25 is the hexadecimal ASCII equivalent of a percent sign (%). In URL encoded format, each space character is represented by %20, and each percent sign is represented by %25. After encoding, the contents of the string *tip=A standard tip is 15%* would read *tip=A%20standard%20tip%20is%2015%25*.

The **encodeURI() method** is used in JavaScript for encoding text strings into a valid URI. More specifically, the encodeURI() method converts special characters in a text string to their corresponding hexadecimal ASCII value, preceded by a percent sign. The syntax for the encodeURI() method is `encodeURI(text);`. The encodeURI() method does not encode standard alphanumeric characters such as A, B, C, or 1, 2, 3, or any of the following special characters: - _ . ! ~ * ' ( ). It also does not encode the following characters which have special meaning in a URI: ; / ? : @ & = + $,. When you read a cookie or other text string encoded with the encodeURI() method, you must first decode it with the **decodeURI() method**. The syntax for the decodeURI() method is `decodeURI(text);`. The following code encodes several cookies with the encodeURI() method and assigns them to the cookie property of the Document object.

```
document.cookie = encodeURI("firstName=" + "Don");
document.cookie = encodeURI("lastName=" + "Gosselin");
document.cookie = encodeURI("occupation=" + 'writer");
```

If you transmit a URI containing spaces in versions 6 or higher of Internet Explorer or Netscape, the Web browser automatically encodes the spaces for you before transmitting the cookie. However, special characters such as the percent sign are not automatically encoded. This can cause problems with older browsers and Web servers that do not recognize certain special characters unless they are encoded. Additionally, older Web browsers do not automatically encode spaces in URIs. For these reasons, you should always manually encode cookies using the encodeURI() method.

 tip

••

Older versions of JavaScript use the obsolete escape() and unescape() methods for encoding and decoding text strings.

••

Next, you will modify the Product Registration program so that customer information is saved in transient cookies.

To modify the Product Registration program so that customer information is saved in transient cookies:

1 Open **CustomerInfo.html** in your text editor or HTML editor.

2 Delete the first two statements in the nextForm() function that declare the savedData variable and assign an initial value to it.

3 Next, in each of the lines that builds the savedData variable, replace the `savedData +=` portion with `document.cookie =`. Also, encode each of the values that are assigned as cookies using the encodeURI() method. Finally, delete the portions of the location.href statement that append the query string, so that it reads `location.href="ProductInfo.html";`. The modified nextForm() function should appear as follows:

```
function nextForm() {
        document.cookie = encodeURI("name=" +
document.customerInfo.name.value);
        document.cookie = encodeURI("address=" +
document.customerInfo.address.value);
        document.cookie = encodeURI("city=" +
document.customerInfo.city.value);
        document.cookie = encodeURI("state=" +
document.customerInfo.state.value);
        document.cookie = encodeURI("zip=" +
document.customerInfo.zip.value);
        document.cookie = encodeURI("email=" +
document.customerInfo.email.value);
        document.cookie = encodeURI("password=" +
document.customerInfo.password.value);
```

```
                if (
document.customerInfo.platform[0].checked == true)
        document.cookie = encodeURI("platform=" +
document.customerInfo.platform[0].value);
                if (
document.customerInfo.platform[1].checked == true)
        document.cookie = encodeURI("platform=" +
document.customerInfo.platform[1].value);
                if (
document.customerInfo.platform[2].checked == true)
        document.cookie = encodeURI("platform=" +
document.customerInfo.platform[2].value);
                if (
document.customerInfo.platform[3].checked == true)
        document.cookie = encodeURI("platform=" +
document.customerInfo.platform[3].value);
                if (
document.customerInfo.platform[4].checked == true)
        document.cookie = encodeURI("platform=" +
document.customerInfo.platform[4].value);
                if (
document.customerInfo.platform[5].checked == true)
        document.cookie = encodeURI("platform=" +
document.customerInfo.platform[5].value);
        if (document.customerInfo.wp.checked == true)
                document.cookie = encodeURI("wp=true");
        if (document.customerInfo.ss.checked == true)
                document.cookie = encodeURI("ss=true");
        if (document.customerInfo.db.checked == true)
                document.cookie = encodeURI("db=true");
        if (document.customerInfo.gr.checked == true)
                document.cookie = encodeURI("gr=true");
        if (document.customerInfo.pr.checked == true)
                document.cookie = encodeURI("pr=true");
        document.cookie = encodeURI("location=" +
document.customerInfo.location.value);
        document.cookie = encodeURI("comments=" +
document.customerInfo.comments.value);
        location.href="ProductInfo.html";
}
```

4   Save and close **CustomerInfo.html**.

Next you will modify the ProductInfo.html file so that it adds its fields to transient cookies.

To modify the ProductInfo.html file:

1 Open **ProductInfo.html** in your text editor or HTML editor.

2 Locate the following statements in the submitForm() function:

```
var savedData = location.search;
savedData += "&serial=" +
    document.productInfo.serial.value;
savedData += "&date=" +
    document.productInfo.date.value;
if (document.productInfo.where[0].checked == true)
    savedData += "&where=" +
    document.productInfo.where[0].value;
else if (
    document.productInfo.where[1].checked == true)
    savedData += "&where=" +
document.productInfo.where[1].value;
else if (
    document.productInfo.where[2].checked == true)
    savedData += "&where=" +
document.productInfo.where[2].value;
else if (
    document.productInfo.where[3].checked == true)
    savedData += "&where=" +
document.productInfo.where[3].value;
```

3 Replace the statements located in the preceding step with the following statements, which add the ProductInfo.html form fields to cookies:

```
document.cookie = encodeURI("serial=" +
document.productInfo.serial.value);
document.cookie = encodeURI("date=" +
document.productInfo.date.value);
if (document.productInfo.where[0].checked == true)
    document.cookie = encodeURI("where=" +
document.productInfo.where[0].value);
else if (document.productInfo.where[1].checked == true)
    document.cookie = encodeURI("where=" +
    document.productInfo.where[1].value);
else if (document.productInfo.where[2].checked == true)
    document.cookie = encodeURI("where=" +
```

```
        document.productInfo.where[2].value);
    else if (document.productInfo.where[3].checked == true)
        document.cookie = encodeURI("where=" +
        document.productInfo.where[3].value);
```

4   Save and close **ProductInfo.html**. Although you can open the form and enter data, you will not be able to see that the data is available between the forms until you learn how to read cookies. Before you learn how to read cookies, you will learn about other cookie parameters.

Expires Attribute   For a cookie to persist beyond the current browser session, you must use the expires attribute of the cookie property. The **expires attribute** of the cookie property determines how long a cookie is to remain on a client system before it is deleted. Cookies created without an expires attribute are available for only the current browser session. The syntax for assigning the expires attribute to the cookie property, along with an associated *name=value* pair, is *expires=date*. The *name=value* pair and the *expires=date* pair are separated by a semicolon and a space. The *date* portion of the expires attribute must be a text string in Coordinated Universal Time (usually abbreviated as UTC) format as follows:

`Weekday Mon DD HH:MM:SS Time Zone YYYY`

The following is an example of Coordinated Universal Time:

`Mon Dec 27 14:15:18 PST 2003`

Coordinated Universal Time is also known as Greenwich Mean Time, Zulu Time, and World Time.

Be sure not to encode the expires attribute using the encodeURI() method. JavaScript does not recognize a UTC date when it is in URI encoded format. If you use the encodeURI() method with the expires attribute, JavaScript will not be able to set the cookie expiration date.

You can manually type a string in UTC format, or you can create the string with the Date object. The **Date object** is used for manipulating the date and time. Creating a new Date object copies the current date and time from the local computer into a specified object name. You can then manipulate the date and time in the variable, using the methods of the Date object. Note that the date and time in a Date object are not updated over time like a clock. Instead, a Date object contains the static date and time *as of the moment the JavaScript code executes*. You create a new instance of the Date object by using the syntax `var variable = new Date();`. Figure 9-3 lists frequently used methods of the Date object.

Method	Description
getDate()	Returns the date of a Date object
getDay()	Returns the day of a Date object
getFullYear()	Returns the year of a Date object in four-digit format
getHours()	Returns the hour of a Date object
getMinutes()	Returns the minutes of a Date object
getMonth()	Returns the month of a Date object
getSeconds()	Returns the seconds of a Date object
getTime()	Returns the time of a Date object
setDate()	Sets the date of a Date object
setFullYear()	Sets the four-digit year of a Date object
setHours()	Sets the hours of a Date object
setMinutes()	Sets the minutes of a Date object
setMonth()	Sets the month of a Date object
setSeconds()	Sets the seconds of a Date object
setTime()	Sets the time of a Date object
toUTCString()	Converts a Date object to a string, set to the UTC time zone
ToLocaleString()	Converts a Date object to a string, set to the local time zone

Figure 9-3: Commonly used Date object methods

Each portion of a Date object, such as the day, month, year, and so on, can be retrieved and modified using the Date object methods. For example, if you create a new Date object, using the statement var myDate = new Date();, you can retrieve just the date portion stored in the myDate object by using the statement myDate.getDate();.

To use a Date object with the expires attribute, you add the specified amount of time for which you want a cookie to be valid by using a combination of the set() and get() methods of the Date object. The following example changes the date portion of myDate using the setDate() and getDate() methods. Notice that you can nest Date object methods inside other Date object methods. In the example, the setDate() method sets the date portion of myDate by using the getDate() method to retrieve the date, and adding seven to increase the date by one week.

```
myDate.setDate(myDate.getDate() + 7);
```

The following code creates a new cookie and assigns an expiration date one year from now. Before the expires attribute is assigned to the cookie property, the Date object uses the toUTCString() method to ensure that the date is in Coordinated Universal Time.

```
var expiresDate = new Date();
expiresDate.setFullYear(expiresDate.getFullYear() + 1);
document.cookie = encodeURI("firstName=Don") + "; expires=" +
 expiresDate.toUTCString();
```

To delete a cookie, you reassign its name and an arbitrary value to the cookie property and set its expiration date to sometime in the past. The following code deletes the firstName cookie by setting its expires attribute to one year ago:

```
var expiresDate = new Date();
expiresDate.setFullYear(expiresDate.getFullYear() - 1);
document.cookie = encodeURI("firstName=delete") + ";
expires=" + expiresDate.toUTCString();
```

> During the development process, you may accidentally create persistent cookies that your program does not need, but you never delete. Unused persistent cookies can sometimes interfere with the execution of a JavaScript cookie program. For this reason, you may periodically want to delete your browser cookies, especially while developing a JavaScript program that uses cookies. To delete cookies in Internet Explorer, select Internet Options from the Tools menu. On the General tab of the Internet Options dialog box that appears, click the Delete Cookies button. To delete cookies in Netscape, point to the Privacy and Security submenu on the Tasks menu, then point to the Cookie Manager submenu, and select the View Stored Cookies command. In the Cookie Manager dialog box that appears, you can either delete individual cookies using the Remove Cookie button, or delete all cookies by using the Remove All Cookies button.

Next you will create a document that stores a user's name and favorite background color in a persistent cookie. In the exercise, you will first create a function that references a form in the document body. After creating the function, you will then create the body and form section of the document.

To create a file that stores a user's name and favorite background color in a persistent cookie:

1 Create a new document in your text editor or HTML editor.

2 Type the opening <HTML>, <HEAD>, and <SCRIPT> sections of the document:

```
<HTML>
<HEAD>
<TITLE>Personal Preferences</TITLE>
<SCRIPT LANGUAGE="JavaScript">
<!-- HIDE FROM INCOMPATIBLE BROWSERS
```

3 Add the following setCookie() function that creates cookies containing the user's name and favorite color from the values entered into the user_name and user_color form fields. Each cookie is set to expire in one year.

```
function setCookie() {
  var expiresDate = new Date();
  expiresDate.setFullYear(expiresDate.getFullYear() + 1);
  document.cookie = encodeURI("user_name="
        + document.user_prefs.user_name.value) + ";
expires=" + expiresDate.toUTCString();
  document.cookie = encodeURI("user_color="
        + document.user_prefs.user_color.value) + ";
expires=" + expiresDate.toUTCString();
  alert("Your name and favorite color have been saved
  in a cookie.");
  }
```

4 Type the closing <SCRIPT> and <HEAD> tags and the opening <BODY> tag. The opening <BODY> tag includes an ID of docBody, which you will use later to programmatically change the document background color, based on a user's selection.

```
// STOP HIDING FROM INCOMPATIBLE BROWSERS -->
</SCRIPT>
</HEAD>
<BODY ID="docBody">
```

5 Add the following form, which users will use to store their name and favorite color in a cookie. The buttons use onClick event handlers to call the functions in the head section.

```
<FORM NAME="user_prefs">
<P>Name  <INPUT TYPE="text" NAME="user_name"><BR>
Color  <INPUT TYPE="text" NAME="user_color"></P>
<P><INPUT TYPE="button" VALUE=" Set Cookie "
        onClick="setCookie();"></P>
</FORM>
```

6 Add the following code to close the \<BODY\> and \<HTML\> tags:

```
</BODY>
</HTML>
```

7 Save the file as **PersonalPrefs.html** in a new folder named **PersonalPrefs** in the **Tutorial.09** folder on your Data Disk, close it, and then open the file in your Web browser. Enter your name and favorite background color, and click the Set Cookie button. Although the file saves the cookie, you need to learn how to read cookies with JavaScript before you can write code that displays a user's personal options on returning to the Web page. You will learn how to read cookies later in this section.

8 Close the Web browser window.

Path Attribute The path attribute determines the availability of a cookie to other Web pages on a server. The path attribute is assigned to the cookie property, along with an associated *name=value* pair, using the syntax `path=`*`path name`*. By default, a cookie is available to all Web pages in the same directory. However, if you specify a path, then a cookie is available to all Web pages in the specified path as well as to all Web pages in all subdirectories in the specified path. For example, the following statement makes the cookie named firstName available to all Web pages located in the MyFiles directory or any of its subdirectories:

```
document.cookie = "firstName=Don" + "; path=/MyFiles");
```

To make a cookie available to all directories on a server, use a slash to indicate the root directory, as in the following example:

```
document.cookie = "firstName=Don" + "; path=/");
```

When you are developing JavaScript programs that contain cookies, your programs may not function correctly if the directory containing your Web page contains other programs that set cookies. Cookies from other programs that are stored in the same directory along with unused cookies you created during development can cause your JavaScript cookie program to run erratically. Therefore, it is a good idea to always place JavaScript cookie programs in their own directory and use the path attribute to specify any subdirectories your program requires.

Domain Attribute Using the path attribute allows cookies to be shared across a server. Some Web sites, however, are very large and use a number of servers. The **domain attribute** is used for sharing cookies across multiple servers in the same domain. Note that you cannot share cookies outside a domain. The domain attribute is assigned to the cookie property, along with an associated *name=value* pair, using the syntax `domain=`*`domain name`*. For example, if the Web server `programming.gosselin.com` needs to share cookies with the Web server `writing.gosselin.com`, the domain attribute for cookies set by `programming.gosselin.com` should be set to `gosselin.com`.

That way, cookies created by programming.gosselin.com are available to `writing.gosselin.com` and to all other servers in the domain gosselin.com.

If your domain ends in one of the nine top-level domain identifiers, .biz, .com, .edu, .info, .net, .org, .gov, .mil, or .int, then you are required to use two periods in the domain name. For example, to use the domain attribute for `gosselin.com`, you use the statement `domain=.gosselin.com` because .com is one of the nine top-level domain identifers. If your domain does not end in one of the nine top-level identifiers, then you must use three periods and include a sub-domain. For example, if your domain ends in .ca (for Canada) then you must use a statement similar to `domain=.subdomain.domain.ca`.

The following code shows how to make a cookie at `programming.gosselin.com` available to all servers in the gosselin.com domain:

```
document.cookie = "firstName=Don" + "; domain=.gosselin.com";
```

Secure Attribute Standard Internet connections are not always considered safe for transmitting sensitive information. It is possible for unscrupulous people to steal personal information, such as credit card numbers, passwords, Social Security numbers, and other types of private information online. To protect private data transferred across the Internet, Netscape developed Secure Sockets Layer, or SSL, to encrypt data and transfer it across a secure connection. Web sites that support SSL usually start with HTTPS instead of HTTP. The **secure attribute** indicates that a cookie can only be transmitted across a secure Internet connection using HTTPS or another security protocol. Generally when working with client-side JavaScript, the secure attribute should be omitted. However, if you wish to use this attribute, you assign it to the cookie property with a Boolean value of true or false, along with an associated *name=value* pair, using the syntax `secure=boolean value`. For example, to activate the secure attribute for a cookie, you use a statement similar to the following:

```
document.cookie = "firstName=Don" + "; secure=true");
```

Reading Cookies

The cookies for a particular Web page are available in the cookie property of the Document object. So far, you have stored both temporary and persistent cookies. Next you need to learn how to retrieve stored cookie values. Cookies consist of one continuous string that must be parsed before the data they contain can be used. To parse a cookie, you must first unencode it using the decodeURI() function. Then, you must use the methods of the String object to extract individual *name=value* pairs. To give you an idea of what is involved in extracting data from cookies, the following code creates three encoded cookies, then reads them from the cookie property and unencodes them. The split() method is then used to copy each *name=value* pair into the elements of an array named cookieArray.

```
document.cookie = encodeURI("city=Boston");
document.cookie = encodeURI("team=Red Sox");
document.cookie = encodeURI("sport=baseball");
var cookieString = decodeURI(document.cookie);
var cookieArray = cookieString.split("; ");
```

Notice that the split() method in the preceding code splits the cookies using two characters: a semicolon and a space. Recall that when you assign a *name=value* pair to the cookie property of the Document object, JavaScript automatically separates cookies with a semicolon and space. If you do not include the space in the split() method, then the name portion of each *name=value* pair in the new array will have an extra space before it. Once you split the cookies into separate array elements, you still need to determine which cookie holds the value you need. The following for loop cycles through each element in the array and uses an if statement and several string methods to check if the name portion of each *name=value* pair is equal to *team*. The conditional expression in the if statement uses the substring() method to return the name portion of the *name=value* pair in the variable named yourTeam. The first argument in the substring() method specifies the starting point of the substring as the first character (0). The second argument in the substring() method is the indexOf() method appended to the yourTeam variable, which returns the index number of the equal sign. If the substring is equal to *team*, then the for loop ends using a break statement, and the text *Your team is the* is written to the browser along with the value portion of the *name=value* pair. The statements that return the value portion of the *name=value* pair also use the substring() method along with the indexOf() method. However, this time the first argument starts the substring at the index number of the equal sign plus one, which is the character following the equal sign. The second argument in the substring() method specifies the ending point of the substring to be the length of the data variable.

```
var yourTeam;
for (var count = 0; count < 3; ++count) {
    yourTeam = cookieArray[count];
    if (yourTeam.substring(0,yourTeam.indexOf("="))
            == "team") {
        document.writeln("Your team is the "
        + yourTeam.substring(yourTeam.indexOf("=") + 1,
            yourTeam.length));
        break;
    }
}
```

The preceding code is difficult to understand at first. If you are having trouble understanding how to manipulate strings, try experimenting with different String methods and see what you come up with. Using string methods to parse a cookie is the only way to extract individual pieces of information from a long cookie string, so it is important that you understand how they work.

Next you will add code to the submitForm() function in the ProductInfo.html file that reads and displays the contents of the cookies created by the Product Registration program.

To add code to the submitForm() function in the ProductInfo.html file that reads and displays the contents of the cookies created by the Product Registration program:

1   Open the **ProductInfo.html** file in your text editor or HTML editor.

2   Within the submitForm() function, delete the statement **savedData = saved Data.substring(1, savedData.length);**, which removed the question mark from the start of the query string. Because cookies do not include an opening question mark, this statement is no longer necessary.

3   Add to the submitForm() function above the statement **var dataArray = savedData.split(";");** the following statement that assigns the unencoded cookie value to the savedData variable:

```
var savedData = decodeURI(document.cookie);
```

4   In the statement that splits the savedData variable into the dataArray, change the ampersand in the split() method arguement to a semicolon and space so that the statement reads **var dataArray = savedData.split (";") ;**.

5   Save and close **ProductInfo.html**, then open **ProductRegistration.html** in your Web browser. Fill in the fields in the Customer Information form and click the **Next** button, then fill in the fields in the Product Information form and click the **Submit Query** button. The *name=value* pairs for both forms should appear in an alert dialog box, as they did with the query string.

6   Close the Web browser window.

Now you will modify the PersonalPrefs.html file so that a user's personal options are read from the stored cookies.

To modify the PersonalPrefs.html file so that a user's personal options are read from the stored cookies:

1 Open **PersonalPrefs.html** in your text editor or HTML editor.

2 To the script section, add the following function after the setCookie() function. The new function will be called with the document onLoad event handler in the <BODY> tag. An `if` statement uses the String object length property to check if any values are stored in the document cookie. If no values are stored, then the statements that read the cookie are bypassed. If the cookie contains values, then an alert dialog box greets users by name and sets the background color of the document to their favorite color. Both pieces of information are stored in persistent cookies that are created by using form elements. First, the cookie is unencoded with the decodeURI() method and assigned to a variable named curCookie. Then, the function uses the indexOf() and substring() methods along with the length method of the String object to locate the value portion of each *name=value* pair. The last statement uses the **getElementByID()** method to change the CSS backgroundColor style of the <BODY> tag, which has been assigned an ID of *docBody*, to the user's favorite color.

```
function getUserPrefs() {
  var userPrefs = decodeURI(document.cookie);
  if (userPrefs.length != 0) {
        var prefsArray = userPrefs.split("; ");
        var curCookie;
        for (var count = 0; count < prefsArray.length;
                  ++count) {
              curCookie = prefsArray[count];
if (curCookie.substring(0,curCookie.indexOf("="))
                  == "user_name") {
var user_name = curCookie.substring(curCookie.indexOf("=")
+ 1, curCookie.length);
              }
if (curCookie.substring(0,curCookie.indexOf("="))
   == "user_color")
   var user_color =
curCookie.substring(curCookie.indexOf("=")
+ 1, curCookie.length);
        }
        alert("Welcome " + user_name +
". Click OK and I will set your favorite color.");
document.getElementById("docBody").style.backgroundColor =
   user_color;
  }
}
```

3 To the <BODY> tag, add an onLoad event to call the getUserPrefs() function. The modified tag should appear as follows: **<BODY onLoad="getUserPrefs();" ID="docBody">**. The ID attribute of *docBody* enables you to programmatically control the <BODY> tag CSS elements, including background color, using the getUserPrefs() function.

4 Save and close **PersonalPrefs.html**, then open the document in your Web browser. The name you entered earlier should appear in an alert dialog box. Once you close the alert dialog box, the document background should change to your color choice.

5 Close the Web browser window.

S U M M A R Y

■ HTTP was originally designed to be stateless, and no persistent data could be stored about a visit to a Web page.

■ State information refers to any stored information about a previous visit to a Web site.

■ A query string is a set of *name=value* pairs appended to a target URL and consists of a single text string containing one or more pieces of information.

■ The search property of the Location object contains URL query or search parameters.

■ For a Web page to use the information in a query string, you must first parse the string, using a combination of several methods and the length property of the String object.

■ Cookies, or magic cookies, are small pieces of information about a user that are stored by a Web server in text files on the user's computer.

■ Cookies can be temporary or persistent. Temporary cookies are available only for the current browser session. Persistent cookies are available beyond the current browser session and are stored in a text file on a client computer.

■ You create cookies in *name=value* pairs, the same way you use *name=value* pairs in a query string, using the cookie property of the Document object.

■ The only required attribute of the cookie property is the name attribute, which specifies the cookie *name=value* pair.

■ The encodeURI() method is used in JavaScript for encoding a text strings into a valid URI.

■ When you read a cookie or other text string encoded with the encodeURI() method, you must first unencode it with the decodeURI() method.

- The expires attribute of the cookie property determines how long a cookie is to remain on a client system before it is deleted.

- The path attribute determines the availability of a cookie to other Web pages on a server.

- The domain attribute is used for sharing cookies across multiple servers in the same domain.

- The secure attribute designates that a cookie can only be transmitted across a secure Internet connection using HTTPS or another security protocol.

- The cookies for a particular Web page are available in the cookie property of the Document object; they consist of one continuous string that must be parsed before the data they contain can be used.

 **Q U E S T I O N S**

1. Stored information about a previous visit to a Web site is called _____ information.
   a. HTTP
   b. client-side
   c. state
   d. prior

2. In what format are items in a query string appended to a target URL?
   a. in comma-delimited format
   b. as *name&value* pairs
   c. as *name=value* pairs
   d. in *name, value, length* format

3. What character is used for appending a query string to a URL?
   a. ?
   b. &
   c. $
   d. %

4. Where in the target URL is a query string stored?
   a. the queryString property of the Document object
   b. the query property of the Window object
   c. at the end of the query string
   d. the search property of the Location object

5. What character separates entries in a query string?
   a. ?
   b. &
   c. $
   d. %

6. The _____ method separates individual pieces of information in a query string into array elements.
    a. divide()
    b. toArray()
    c. queryToArray()
    d. split()

7. Where are cookies stored?
    a. on a Web client
    b. on a Web server
    c. within an HTTP connection
    d. Cookies are never stored

8. What is the correct syntax to create a cookie?
    a. `cookie = name + value;`
    b. `document.cookie = name + value;`
    c. `window.cookie = name + value;`
    d. `this.cookie = name + value;`

9. What is the only required attribute of the cookie property?
    a. name
    b. domain
    c. expires
    d. path

10. The _____ method is used in JavaScript for encoding text strings.
    a. protect()
    b. encode()
    c. encrypt()
    d. encodeURI()

11. Cookies created without the expires attribute are called _____.
    a. transient
    b. temporary
    c. permanent
    d. persistent

12. The *date* portion of the expires attribute must be a text string in which format?
    a. `DD-Mon-YY`
    b. `HH:MM:SS`
    c. Coordinated Universal Time (UTC)
    d. It can be in any time format.

13. When is the date and time in a new Date object updated?

a. every millisecond

b. every second

c. according to its time interval argument

d. never

14. The availability of a cookie to other Web pages on a server is determined by the _____ attribute.

a. path

b. directory

c. system

d. server

15. Which attribute is used for sharing cookies outside a domain?

a. domain

b. share

c. secure

d. You cannot share cookies outside a domain.

16. The_____ attribute designates that a cookie can be transmitted only across a secure Internet connection using HTTPS or another security protocol.

a. domain

b. share

c. secure

d. expires

E X E R C I S E S

Remember that, by default, a cookie is available to all Web pages in the same directory. To avoid conflicts with the cookies you created in this tutorial, save the solution files for each of the following exercises in their own folders within the Tutorial.09 folder on your Data Disk. Name each exercise folder as Exercise_A*x*, replacing *x* with the appropriate exercise number. Exercise 1, for example, should be saved in a folder named \Exercise_A01 in the Tutorial.09 folder on your Data Disk.

1. The following HTML document displays a simple form in which a user can enter his or her name and occupation:

```
<HTML>
<HEAD>
<TITLE>ClientDoc</TITLE>
</HEAD>
<BODY>
<FORM NAME="info">
<P>First Name  <INPUT TYPE="text" NAME="firstName"><BR>
Last Name  <INPUT TYPE="text" NAME="lastName"></P>
<P>Occupation  <INPUT TYPE="text" NAME="occupation"></P>
<P><INPUT TYPE="submit"></P>
</FORM>
</BODY>
</HTML>
```

   a. Add a JavaScript section to the preceding HTML document. The JavaScript section should open a new Web page named ServerDoc.html when you click the Submit button. Append the values of each form element to the ServerDoc.html URL as a query string. Save the document as ClientDoc.html.

   b. Create the ServerDoc.html file referred to in Exercise 1a. Include in the ServerDoc.html file the same form and form elements as the ClientDoc.html file. Although the values you pass to a server-based program are normally stored in a database, you are using a form just to practice passing values using a query string. When the ServerDoc.html file loads, parse the query string and place the value portion of each *name=value* pair in the appropriate form element. Next, open the ClientDoc.html file in your Web browser, enter some data into the form, and then click the Submit button. When the ServerDoc.html file loads, the values you entered in the form in the ClientDoc.html file should be filled into the form in ServerDoc.html.

2. Modify the ClientDoc.html and ServerDoc.html files from Exercise 1 so that the query string data is stored in transient cookies. Be sure to encode the cookie data. Save the modified files in their own folder named Exercise_A02.

3. When you run the following program in Netscape 6, only the first cookie named
    itemCookie is saved. Fix the problem and save the document as
    PurchaseCookies.html.

```
<HTML>
<HEAD>
<TITLE>Purchase Cookies</TITLE>
<SCRIPT LANGUAGE="JavaScript">
<!-- HIDE FROM INCOMPATIBLE BROWSERS
function storePurchaseData() {
   itemCookie = "item=sports coat";
   styleCookie = "; style=double breasted";
   sizeCookie = "; size=44 Regular";
   document.cookie = itemCookie + styleCookie + sizeCookie;
   // test the cookies
   var purchaseData = decodeURI(document.cookie);
   var cookieString = "";
   if (purchaseData.length > 0) {
           purchaseArray = purchaseData.split("; ");
           for (var i = 0; i < purchaseArray.length; ++i) {
                   cookieString += purchaseArray[i] + "<BR>";
           }
           document.write(cookieString);
   }
   else
           document.write("No stored purchase data.");
}
// STOP HIDING FROM INCOMPATIBLE BROWSERS -->
</SCRIPT>
</HEAD>
<BODY onLoad="storePurchaseData();">
</BODY>
</HTML>
```

4. The following program should save the date and time of your last visit to the Web
    page in a cookie using the onUnload event handler in the <BODY> tag, then display
    the saved cookie information whenever you close and then reopen the Web page.
    However, each time you open the document, you receive the message *This is your first
    visit*. Fix the problem and save the document as LastVisit.html. (*Hint*: there is more
    than one error in the program.)

```
<HTML>
<HEAD>
<TITLE>Last Visit</TITLE>
<SCRIPT LANGUAGE="JavaScript">
<!-- HIDE FROM INCOMPATIBLE BROWSERS
function storeLastVisit() {
   var currentDate = new Date();
   var expiresDate = new Date();
```

```
        expiresDate.setFullYear(expiresDate.getFullYear() - 1);
        document.cookie = encodeURI("lastVisit="
                + currentDate.toUTCString()
                + ";expires=" + expiresDate.toUTCString());
    }
    // STOP HIDING FROM INCOMPATIBLE BROWSERS -->
    </SCRIPT>
    </HEAD>
    <BODY onUnload="storeLastVisit();">
    <SCRIPT LANGUAGE="JavaScript">
    <!-- HIDE FROM INCOMPATIBLE BROWSERS
    var visitData = decodeURI(document.cookie);
    if (visitData.length > 0) {
        var lastVisit = visitData.substring(visitData.indexOf("=")
                + 1,visitData.length)
        document.write("Last visit: " + lastVisit);
    }
    else
        document.write("This is your first visit.");
    // STOP HIDING FROM INCOMPATIBLE BROWSERS -->
    </SCRIPT>
    </BODY>
    </HTML>
```

5. Create a document that stores and reads cookies containing a user's name and the number of times he or she has visited your Web site. Whenever a user visits the site, display the cookies in an alert dialog box, increment the counter cookie by one, and then reset the counter cookie expiration date to one year from the current date. Save the document as Counter.html.

6. Create a document with a "nag" counter that reminds users to register. Save the counter in a cookie and display a message reminding users to register every fifth time they visit your site. Create a form in the body of the document that includes text boxes for a user's name and e-mail address along with a Registration button. Once a user fills in the text boxes and clicks the Registration button, delete the nag counter cookie and replace it with cookies containing the user's name and e-mail address. After registering, display the name and e-mail address cookies in an alert dialog box whenever the user revisits the site. Save the document as NagCounter.html.

7. Create a document that prompts a user for a username and password, and then stores the information in cookies. When the user visits the Web page again, prompt him or her to enter the stored username and password. If the user does not enter the correct information within three tries, allow him or her to enter a new username and password. Save the document as Password.html.

8. Create a document that contains a form with buttons representing different colors such as red, blue, yellow, and so on. When a user clicks a color button on the form, change the document background to the appropriate color and save the color in a cookie. Whenever the user revisits the Web page, reset the background to the color stored in the cookie. Save the document as FavoriteBackground.html.

9. Create a document with a form that registers users for a professional conference. When a user submits the registration form, store cookies containing the user's information such as name, company, and so on. If a user attempts to register a second time with the same name, display a confirm dialog box asking if he or she wants to register again. Save the document as ConferenceRegistration.html.

10. Create a document with a form that reserves hotel rooms. As a user creates a reservation, store cookies containing the user's itinerary. Also, create buttons that redisplay a user's itinerary in an alert dialog box. Set the cookies so that they expire one day after a visit. Save the document as HotelReservations.html.

11. Recall that the date and time in a Date object contain the static date and time as of the moment the JavaScript code executes. Although the Date object does not give you a true "clock," you can use the setInterval() method to continually retrieve the current date and time from your computer's system clock. Use the Date object to create a form-based digital clock. The clock should display the time to the second, so you will need to use the getHours(), getMinutes(), and getSeconds() methods of the Date object. Save the HTML document as DigitalClock.html

In this section you will learn:
- About JavaScript security concerns
- About the same origin policy
- About signed scripts and digital certificates
- How to create a test certificate
- How to work with privileges
- How to sign a JavaScript program
- How to enable codebase principals

Security

JavaScript Security Concerns

Today it is common to read about security breaches on the Internet. Corporate and government Web sites seem to be routinely invaded by unauthorized visitors, and credit card numbers and other personal information are often stolen during Internet transactions. To combat security violations, technologies, such as firewalls, have been developed that use combinations of software and hardware to prevent access to private networks connected to the Internet. Additionally, to safeguard information, Netscape developed the Secure Sockets Layer protocol to encrypt data and transfer it across a secure connection. These types of security technologies work well in the realm of the Internet. However, JavaScript programs are downloaded and execute locally, within the Web browser of a client computer, and are not governed by security technologies such as firewalls and Secure Sockets Layer.

tip

● ●

Internet security is a large and evolving issue. This tutorial discusses security only as it relates to Web browsers and client-side JavaScript.

● ●

The Web was originally designed to be read-only; its primary purpose was to locate and display documents that existed on other areas of the Web. With the development of programming languages such as Java and JavaScript, Web pages can now contain programs in addition to static content. This ability to execute programs within a Web page raises several security concerns. The security areas of most concern to JavaScript programmers are:

- Protection of a Web page and JavaScript program against malicious tampering
- Privacy of individual client information
- Protection of the local file system of the client or Web site from theft or tampering

Due to the open nature of HTML and JavaScript programming code, anyone can read your JavaScript code simply by selecting Page Source from the Netscape View menu or by selecting Source from the Internet Explorer View menu. You can use a JavaScript source file to hide your code, although clients can also view source files. For example, consider the following <SCRIPT> tag, which loads a source file named HiddenScript.js:

```
<SCRIPT LANGUAGE="JavaScript"
SRC="http://www.dongosselin.com/javascript/HiddenScript.js"
```

The preceding <SCRIPT> tag could be embedded within an HTML document, preventing clients from directly seeing the JavaScript code in the HiddenScript.js file. However, anyone can view the contents of HiddenScript.js by opening its URL in a Web browser and viewing the source file. There is no way to hide your JavaScript code. The potential theft of your hard work and intellectual property is no small concern. However, a larger security issue is raised when you cannot control access to your code. When someone can access your code, an unethical person can alter it and use it to steal information or cause damage on a client system. Two security features, the same origin policy and digital signing of scripts, are used to ensure that a script is not tampered with. In addition to providing security features, digital signing also verifies the trustworthiness of the creator of a script, using a technology called digital certificates.

Another security concern is the privacy of individual client information in the Web browser window. Your e-mail address, bookmarks, and history list are valuable pieces of information that many direct marketers would love to get their hands on in order to bombard you with advertising geared toward your likes and dislikes. Without security restrictions, a JavaScript program could read this information from your Web browser. To protect private information, JavaScript includes a feature called privileges, which determines what types of browser information are available to a script. You use privileges with signed scripts to designate the types of information a script can access.

Internet Explorer does not directly support digital signing of JavaScript programs and the manipulation of privileges with JavaScript code. Because Internet Explorer supports only some JavaScript security features, such as the same origin policy, this section is geared primarily toward Netscape.

One of the most important JavaScript security features is its *lack* of certain types of functionality. For example, many programming languages include objects and methods that allow you to read, write, and delete files. To prevent mischievous scripts from stealing information or causing damage by changing or deleting files, JavaScript does not allow any file manipulation whatsoever. Similarly, JavaScript does not include any sort of mechanism for creating a network connection. This limitation prevents JavaScript programs from infiltrating a private network or intranets from which information may be stolen or damaged. JavaScript also cannot run system commands or execute programs on a client. The ability to read and write cookies is the only type of access to a client that JavaScript has. Web browsers, however, strictly govern cookies and do not allow access to cookies from outside the domain that created them.

●●●

Another JavaScript security feature you may hear about is *data tainting*, which marks specific properties as private or secure. Data tainting was available in Navigator 3, but discontinued in Navigator 4.

●●●

The Same Origin Policy

The **same origin policy** restricts how JavaScript code in one window or frame accesses a Web page in another window or frame on a client computer. For windows and frames to view and modify important properties of documents displayed in other windows and frames, they must have the same protocol (such as HTTP) and exist on the same Web server. For example, documents from the following two domains cannot access each others' properties because they use different protocols. The first domain's protocol is HTTP and the second domain's protocol is HTTPS, which is used on secure networks.

```
http://www.gosselin.com
https://www.gosselin.com
```

The same origin policy applies not only to the domain name, but also to the server on which a document is located. Therefore, documents from the following two domains cannot access each others' properties, because they are located on different servers, even though they exist in the same domain of `gosselin.com`:

```
http://www.programming.gosselin.com
http://www.writing.gosselin.com
```

The same origin policy prevents malicious scripts from modifying the content of other windows and frames and prevents the theft of private browser information and information displayed on secure Web pages. Figure 9-4 shows the JavaScript objects and properties that are subject to the same origin policy.

Object	Properties
Document	Read and write restrictions: anchors, applets, cookies, domain, embeds, forms, lastModified, length, links, referrer, title, URL, form names
	Write restrictions only: all other properties
Form	elements
Image	src, lowsrc
Layer	src
Location	All properties except x and y
Window	find

Figure 9-4: Objects and properties subject to the same origin policy

tip

Same origin policy restrictions can be bypassed by using signed scripts and privileges, which you will study later in this section.

As an example of what could happen *without* the same origin policy, consider the src attribute of the Document object, which determines the URL displayed in a window or frame. If a client had multiple windows or frames open on its system and the same origin policy did not exist, then a Web page in one window or frame could change the Web pages displayed in other windows or frames. There are plenty of unscrupulous or simply malicious advertisers who would try to force you to view only their Web pages. The security of private networks and intranets would also be at risk without the same origin policy. Consider a user who has one Web browser open to a page on the Internet and another Web browser open to a secure page from his or her private network or intranet. Without the same origin policy, the Internet Web page would have access to the information displayed on the private Web page.

The same origin policy also protects the integrity of the design of your Web page. For example, without the same origin policy, a frame in one window or frame could modify properties of JavaScript objects and HTML code in other windows and frames. To give you an idea of how the same origin policy prevents this type of scenario from occurring, you will now create a frame set in which one frame uses JavaScript code to try to change the background color of the Yahoo! Web page, using the bgColor property of the Document object. There are no restrictions on reading the bgColor property of the Document object of documents from different origins. However, *changing* the bgColor property is governed by the same origin policy. Because your document is not part of the Yahoo! domain, you will receive an error message when you try to execute the code.

To create a frame set that demonstrates the wrong origin policy:

1 Start your text editor or HTML editor and create a new document.

2 Type the following lines to create a frame set with two frames. The code causes the Yahoo! Web page to appear in the second frame.

```
<HTML>
<FRAMESET COLS="20%,*">
    <FRAME NAME="wrongframe" SRC="WrongOrigin.html">
    <FRAME NAME="yahooframe"
        SRC="http://www.yahoo.com/">
</FRAMESET>
</HTML>
```

3   Save the file as **MainFrame.html** in the **Tutorial.09** folder on your Data Disk.

4   Next create another new document in your text editor or HTML editor.

5   Add the following simple form that contains a single button called Change Color. The button uses an onClick event that tries to change the background color of the frame containing the Yahoo! Web page.

```
<HTML>
<FORM>
<INPUT TYPE="button" VALUE=" Change Color "
    onClick="parent.yahooframe.document.bgColor =
        'yellow';">
</FORM>
</HTML>
```

6   Save the document as **WrongOrigin.html**, and then close it. Open **MainFrame.html** in your Web browser. After Yahoo! loads, click the **Change Color** button in the left frame. You should receive an error message. Figure 9-5 shows the error message generated by Navigator.

> If you are working with Internet Explorer 5 or Navigator versions 4.0 through 4.7, to view an error message you will need to type javascript: in the address box in Internet Explorer or in the location box in Navigator.

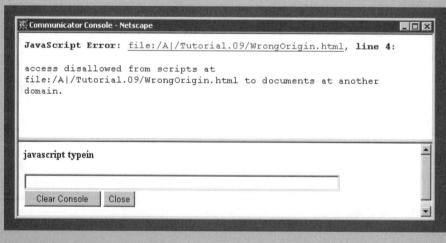

Figure 9-5: Wrong origin error message in Navigator

7   Close the Web browser window.

There are circumstances in which you want two documents from related Web sites on different servers to be able to access each other's properties. Consider a situation in which a document from `programming.gosselin.com` and a document from `writing.gosselin.com` are used within the same frame set, and one of the documents is designed to update properties of the other document. To allow documents from different origins in the same domain to access each other's properties, you use the domain property of the Document object. The **domain property** of the Document object changes the origin of a document to its root domain name using the statement `document.domain = "domain";`. Adding the statement `document.domain = "gosselin.com";` to documents from both `programming.gosselin.com` and `writing.gosselin.com` allows the documents to access each other's properties, even though they are located on different servers.

tip

You can set the domain property only to the domain of a document's origin and not to any domains outside its origin.

Signed Scripts and Digital Certificates

At the time of this writing, the tools necessary for digitally signing scripts in Netscape 6 were not yet available. Therefore, the remainder of this section uses Navigator 4.7. However, you should be able to apply most of the Navigator 4.7 concepts and skills that are discussed here to the tools for digitally signing scripts in Netscape 6, once they become available.

JavaScript code essentially creates miniprograms within a Web browser window that can be written by anyone with knowledge of JavaScript syntax. Unlike commercial software programs you buy in a shrink-wrapped box, you have no way of knowing who created a JavaScript program and whether it has been modified in some way not intended by the author. The possibility of tampering is especially likely with JavaScript, because anyone can copy a JavaScript program to their own server and make any modifications they like. There are two dangers in running a program on your computer that you did not intentionally install. First, you never have the opportunity to make decisions about what you want to allow the program to do. Second, you do not know whether you can trust the author of such a program. When you install a new program on your computer, such as a word-processing program, you are usually presented with a number of installation options. You may be asked where you want to install the program, whether it should be your default word-processing program, and so on. If a well-known company such as Microsoft or Netscape writes the program, you can be fairly certain that it is trustworthy and safe (provided you purchased the software in a shrink-wrapped box from a reputable dealer).

Although JavaScript programs are not installed like traditional software, there are strict rules that govern the access JavaScript programs have to a client Web browser and computer system. For example, a JavaScript program cannot close your Web browser or access your personal preferences unless you grant it a privilege. A **privilege** refers to permission that is granted to access a restricted feature or information that is not normally available to a JavaScript program. For a

JavaScript program to access a privilege, it must make a request to the user, who has the option of granting or denying the request. With this security model, the decision about how much security access to grant a JavaScript program is placed in the hands of the client. Consider what happens when you attempt to submit a form to an e-mail address. When you attempt to e-mail a form, you are presented with a dialog box asking whether you want to grant e-mail permission to the JavaScript program. Other types of privileges include access to your history list and access to your preferences.

▶ **tip**

The rules under which JavaScript programs operate are known as the "sandbox." The term sandbox comes from Java programming and defines a carefully controlled environment in which a programming language can operate.

Normally, privileges are off-limits to a JavaScript program. However, there are situations in which a client should grant permission to use a privilege, such as when form data is being e-mailed. In situations in which a JavaScript program requests privileges, it is dangerous to grant permission unless you know who authored the program. To identify the author of a JavaScript program, Navigator supports digital signing of scripts. **Digital signing** clearly identifies the author of a JavaScript program and ensures that a JavaScript program has not been modified from its original format. A digital certificate identifies the author of a digitally signed script. A **digital certificate** is an electronic identification that the creator of a JavaScript program attaches to a signed script. Trusted organizations known as Certificate Authorities, or CAs, issue digital certificates. A Certificate Authority verifies the identity of an owner, or principal, of a digital certificate. A **principal**, or **entity**, refers to the owner of a digital certificate. Some of the better-known Certificate Authorities include VeriSign, Equifax, and GlobalSign.

▶ **tip**

Although a digital certificate does not necessarily ensure that you can trust its principal, it is safe to assume that a Certificate Authority has verified the principal's identity.

The Security Info dialog box provides information on digital certificates and other security information for your installation of Navigator. To access the Security Info dialog box in Navigator 4.7, select Security Info from the Tools sub-menu on the Communicator menu. The Certificates menu lets you manage the certificates that are registered with your copy of Navigator, including your personal certificates and Web site certificates. You can also view the Certificate Authorities recognized by Netscape by clicking on the Signers menu beneath the Certificates menu. Figure 9-6 shows an example of the Security Info dialog box opened to the Yours option on the Certificates menu.

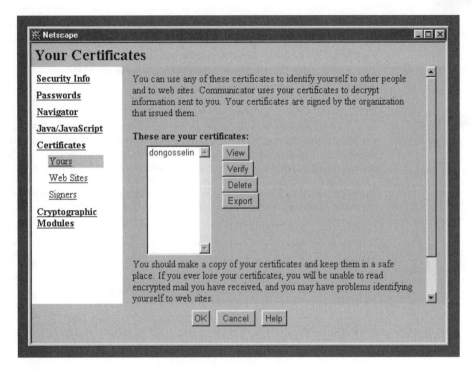

Figure 9-6: Certificates menu of the Security Info dialog box

••

If you scroll to the bottom of the Yours option on the Certificates menu, you will see a Get a Certificate button that brings you to a Web site that can help you obtain your own digital certificate. You can also import existing certificates, using the Import a Certificate button.

••

The following steps are required to create a signed script:

1. Obtain a digital certificate or generate a test certificate.
2. Write the JavaScript program and include requests for privileges.
3. Prepare a JavaScript program for signing.
4. Sign the JavaScript program, using the Netscape Sign Tool program.

This section applies only to Navigator, because Internet Explorer does not support digital signing of JavaScript code. To perform the exercises in this section, you will need Navigator and a copy of the Netscape Signing Tool, or Signtool, program. **Signtool** is a Perl program created by Netscape that is necessary for generating signed scripts. You can download Signtool from *developer.netscape.com/software/signedobj*. The most recent version of Signtool is 1.3, although different implementations exist for different operating systems. The Signtool program is downloaded as a compressed ZIP file. Once you finish downloading the ZIP file, place it in a directory where you want to install the Signtool program and decompress it using PKUNZIP or any other compression/decompression utility capable of working with ZIP files. Decompressing the ZIP file is the only step needed to install the Signtool program. The steps in this section explain how to use Signtool on Windows operating systems. To easily access the Signtool program from a command prompt from Windows operating systems, you may want to add to your PATH statement the directory where Signtool is installed. If you use another type of operating system, such as Macintosh or UNIX, refer to the Signtool online documentation.

The PATH statement notifies your operating system where to search for files when commands are executed at the command prompt. Different platforms have different methods of setting the PATH statement. For example, in Windows NT, you place a PATH statement in your AUTOEXEC.NT file to notify Windows where to search for files. A PATH statement similar to PATH=c:\dos;c:\winnt in the AUTOEXEC.NT file instructs Windows NT to look in the c:\dos and c:\winnt folders each time you execute a command at the command prompt. See your operating system documentation for information on setting the PATH statement.

This section includes only basic information on using Signtool. Complete documentation for Signtool can be downloaded from *developer.netscape.com/software/signedobj/*.

Creating a Test Certificate

To learn how to use digital certificates, you will use Signtool to generate a test certificate. Without a test certificate created by Signtool, to perform the exercises in this section, you would need to purchase a real certificate from a Certificate Authority. The test certificate you create is only for testing purposes and will not be recognized as a certificate issued by a Certificate Authority. If you digitally sign a program with a test certificate and then make the program available on the Web, any Navigator browser that runs the program will treat it as unsigned because your test certificate will not have been issued by any of the CAs listed in the Signers menu in the Navigator Security Info dialog box. If you want to legitimately sign your JavaScript programs, you will need to purchase your own certificate.

For Windows operating systems, Signtool is a command-line program. The command-line syntax for creating a test certificate is signtool -G *certificate name* -d *certificates directory*. You *must* exit Navigator before creating a test certificate, or you may corrupt the certificates database. If you include spaces in the certificate name, the name must be enclosed in quotation marks. Similarly, if your certificate directory includes spaces, its name must also be enclosed in quotation marks.

The certificate directory is the location of your certificate database. The certificate directory on Windows systems is usually located somewhere within c:\Program Files\Netscape\Users. On UNIX systems, the directory is ~/.netscape. If you have trouble locating your certificate directory, look for a directory containing the files Cert7.db and Key3.db. The following code creates a certificate named *dongosselin* on a Windows 98 operating system:

```
signtool -G dongosselin -d 'c:\ProgramFiles
  \Netscape\Users\default\"
```

tip

The preceding example is broken into two lines because of space limitations. When you type the command, be sure to enter the entire command on a single line before pressing Enter.

Signtool parameters are case-sensitive. Therefore, the -G parameter (for *generate*) in the preceding code must be typed as an uppercase letter, and the -d parameter (for *directory*) must be typed as a lowercase letter.

Certificates in Navigator are protected by passwords. To create a test certificate, you must first designate a certificate password for your installation of Navigator.

Next you will create a certificate password. If you have already entered a certificate password, skip the following steps.

To create a certificate password:

1 If necessary, start Navigator 4.7.

2 Point to the Tools menu on the Communicator menu and select **Security Info** to display the Security Info window, and then select the **Passwords** menu. Figure 9-7 shows an example of the Passwords menu in the Security Info window.

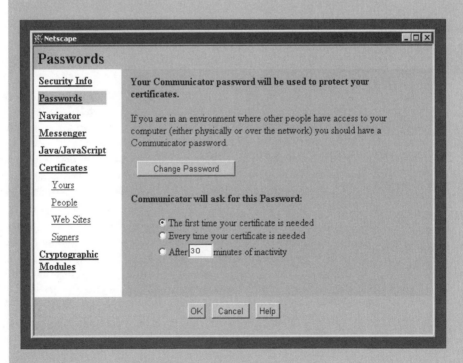

Figure 9-7: The Passwords menu in the Security Info window

3 Click the **Change Password** button or **Set Password** button, depending on your version of Navigator, to display the Setting Up Your Password dialog box. Type a password in the Password text box, then retype it in the Type it again to confirm box. Write down the password because you will need it to create the test certificate.

4 Click **OK** to close the Setting Up Your Navigator Password dialog box. In the group of radio buttons at the bottom of the Passwords options dialog box, make sure the first radio button is selected. The first radio button prompts you for your Navigator password only the first time your certificate is needed.

5 Click **OK** to close the Security Info window.

6 Close all instances of Navigator. Remember, if Navigator is running when you create a test certificate, you may corrupt the certificate database.

Next you will create a test certificate with Signtool.

To create a test certificate with Signtool:

1 Select **Run** from the Windows Start menu, then type **command** on Windows 95/98 or **cmd** on Windows NT/2000, and press **Enter**. A command-line window will open.

2 If the directory containing Signtool is not part of your system path, change to the directory where you installed Signtool.

3 Type `signtool -G your name -d certificate directory` and press **Enter**. If you include spaces in your name, or if there are spaces in the name of your certificate directory, be sure to enclose the names in quotation marks. Remember that the -G and -d parameters are case-sensitive. For example, if your certificates directory is c:\Program Files\Netscape\Users\default, to create a certificate named dongosselin you type the statement `signtool -G dongosselin -d "c:\Program Files\Netscape\Users\default"`. Also, remember to write down the name of your certification in case you forget it.

4 Signtool will warn you that Communicator must be closed before running this command, then prompt you to type **y** to continue or any other key to cancel. Type **y** to continue, if you are sure you do not have any instances of Communicator running. Signtool then prompts you for several other types of optional information, such as a common name for the certificate, organization, state or province. The only option you must enter is the certificate database password. Simply press **Enter** to move through the optional information prompts without entering any information. After you enter the certificate database password, Signtool generates several lines on the screen, including a line stating `certificate "certificatename" added to database`.

5 Type **exit** and press **Enter** to close the command-line window.

6 To check your certificate, start Netscape. Point to **Tools** on the **Communicator** menu, and then click **Security Info** to display the Security Info window. Click the **Yours** menu in the Security Info window, click your certificate name, and then click the View button to display a window containing information about your certificate. Figure 9-8 shows an example of a test certificate.

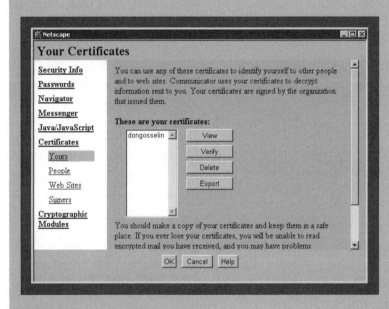

Figure 9-8: Test certificate

7 Click **OK** to close the certificate window, and then click **OK** again to close the Security Info window.

You will not be able to view the "official" version of the certificate (like the one you saw in the preview) until a signed script to which it is attached requests a privilege.

Working with Privileges

To use a restricted privilege in JavaScript, you must access its target. A **target** is a category containing related types of privileges. With the exception of CapabilityPreferencesAccess, target names begin with the word *Universal*. For example, to send e-mail from JavaScript, you request access to the UniversalSendMail target. Figure 9-9 lists the targets used for requesting privileges with JavaScript and describes the privileges available with each target.

Target	Privilege
CapabilityPreferencesAccess	Modify the preferences that define security policy, including privileges that have been granted or denied to programs
UniversalBrowserRead	Retrieve the value of any property of the History object
	Use an about:URL other than about:blank
UniversalBrowserWrite	Capture events in pages loaded from different servers using the enableExternalCapture() method of the Window object
	Read from or write to any of the following properties of the Window object: locationbar, menubar, personalbar, scrollbars, statusbar, and toolbar
	Unconditionally close a browser window using the close() method of the Window object
	Move a window offscreen using the moveBy() or moveTo() methods of the Window object
	Use the innerWidth(), innerHeight(), outerWidth(), and outerHeight() methods and the innerWidth and innerHeight properties of the Window object to set the inner width and height of a window to a size smaller than 100 x 100 or larger than the screen can accommodate
	Use the open() method of the Window object to create a window without a title bar
	Use the open() method of the Window object to create a window smaller than 100 x 100 pixels or larger than the screen can accommodate
	Use the alwaysRaised, alwaysLowered, or z-loc properties of the Window object open() method
	Use the screenX and screenY properties of the Window object to place a window off-screen
	Use the resizeTo() or resizeBy() methods of the Window object to resize a window smaller than 100 x 100 pixels or larger than the screen can accommodate

Figure 9-9: Targets and associated privileges

Target	Privilege
UniversalFileRead	Read any file in the local file system
UniversalPreferencesRead	Read any preferences, using the preferences() method of the Navigator object
UniversalPreferencesWrite	Write any preferences, using the preferences() method of the Navigator object
UniversalXPConnect	Use XPConnect to gain unrestricted access to the browser API

Figure 9-9: Targets and associated privileges (continued)

tip

Many of the properties and methods listed in Figure 9-9 are available only in Navigator and not Internet Explorer.

JavaScript uses a Java class, netscape.security.PrivilegeManager, to request privileges. The netscape.security.PrivilegeManager class contains two methods, enablePrivilege() and revertPrivilege(). The **enablePrivilege() method** requests a privilege of the client, using a dialog box. The client has the option of granting or denying a privilege request. The enablePrivilege() method receives a single argument in quotation marks, containing the name of the target. If a privilege is granted, the **revertPrivilege() method** can be used to revoke the privilege. The first statement in the following code grants access to the UniversalFileRead target using the enablePrivilege() method. The second statement revokes access to the UniversalFileRead target, using the revertPrivilege() method.

```
netscape.security.PrivilegeManager.
    enablePrivilege("UniversalFileRead");
netscape.security.PrivilegeManager.
    revertPrivilege("UniversalFileRead");
```

In the preceding example, if a user grants the request for the UniversalFileRead privilege, the JavaScript program can read local files. If the user denies the request, a Navigator error message is displayed. Note that a client evaluates each privilege request on a case-by-case basis. In this manner, a client builds his or her own security database for each principal. A privilege lasts only for the current browser session, unless the user clicks the *Remember this decision* check box contained in the privilege request dialog box, or the privilege is revoked using the revertPrivilege() method. If the user does click the *Remember this decision* check box, then the privilege is automatically granted to that particular principal for any future requests.

You should use only the minimum target type necessary to accomplish your task. For instance, if you only need to read a browser setting, then you should use the UniversalBrowserRead target rather than the UniversalBrowserWrite target. If you use the UniversalBrowserWrite target, you open the door for someone to use your program to tamper with a user's system. Using the read-only UniveralBrowserRead target reduces this risk. For all target types, but especially for those types that can actually write to a user's system, it is considered good practice to revoke a privilege as soon as you are finished using it. Revoking a privilege as soon as you are finished using it also helps reduce the risk of someone using your program to steal information or tamper with a user's system.

If a user has selected the *Remember this decision* check box for a particular privilege, then only the user can revoke the privilege. A user revokes a privilege from a principal by editing the principal's list of privileges using the Java/JavaScript menu in the Security Info window.

Next you will start building the program you saw in the preview that attempts to change a user's home page to the Course Technology home page. To build the program, you will use the UniversalPreferencesRead and UniversalPreferencesWrite targets. You can access the Navigator preference settings with these targets. To change a user's home page, you will modify the browser.startup.homepage preference setting.

Many types of preferences can be set in Navigator. For a complete list of Navigator preferences, visit *developer.netscape.com/docs/manuals/communicator/preferences/*.

To start building the program to change a user's home page:

1 Start your text editor or HTML editor and create a new document.

2 Type the opening <HTML>, <HEAD>, and <SCRIPT> sections of the document:

```
<HTML>
<HEAD>
<TITLE>Change Home Page</TITLE>
<SCRIPT LANGUAGE="JavaScript">
<!-- HIDE FROM INCOMPATIBLE BROWSERS
```

3 Add the following function, which reads the user's home page setting (provided permission is granted to the UniversalPreferencesRead target), then prompts the user with a confirm dialog box, asking if he or she wants his or her home page changed to Course Technology's home page. If the user clicks OK, then a function named writeHomePage() is called.

```
function readHomePage() {
    netscape.security.PrivilegeManager.enablePrivilege(
        "UniversalPreferencesRead");
    var curHomePage =
        navigator.preference(
    "browser.startup.homepage");
    var changePage = confirm (
    "Do you want to change your personal home page from "
    + curHomePage +
    " to Course Technology's home page?");
    if (changePage == true)
        writeHomePage();
}
```

4 Next type the writeHomePage() function that changes the user's home page to the Course Technology home page, if permission is granted to the UniversalPreferencesWrite target.

```
function writeHomePage() {
netscape.security.PrivilegeManager.enablePrivilege(
"UniversalPreferencesWrite");
navigator.preference("browser.startup.homepage",
"http://www.course.com");
alert(
"Your home page has been changed to Course Technology.");
}
```

5 Type the closing <HEAD> and <SCRIPT> tags along with the opening <BODY> tag:

```
// STOP HIDING FROM INCOMPATIBLE BROWSERS -->
</SCRIPT>
</HEAD>
<BODY>
```

6 Type the following form section, which contains a single button that uses an onClick event handler to call the readHomePage() function:

```
<FORM>
<INPUT TYPE="button"
          VALUE=" Change Home Page to Course Technology "
     onClick="readHomePage();">
</FORM>
```

7 Add the following code to close the <BODY> and <HTML> tags:

```
</BODY>
</HTML>
```

8 To save the file, create a folder named **Homepage** in the **Tutorial.09** folder on your Data Disk. Then save the file as **HomePage.html** in this new Homepage folder on your Data Disk. Before you can try the program, it must be signed with your digital test certificate.

Signing a JavaScript Program

Signing a program creates a separate JAR file that contains the digital signatures of the program's JavaScript code. A **JAR file** is a special kind of compressed file that has an extension of .jar and that contains signed script information. Signing a JavaScript program does not change the original HTML or JavaScript source files. Instead, signed versions of the JavaScript code are placed in the JAR file along with the principal's certificate information. The original HTML and JavaScript source files, along with the JAR file, are deployed together on a Web server. When a signed program requests privileged information from a client, Navigator locates the program's JAR file and compares the signed version of the JavaScript code with the JavaScript code in the HTML and JavaScript source files. If they do not match, Navigator ignores the request for privileges, because it is possible the code has been tampered with or corrupted. If the code and signatures match, Navigator presents the principal's certificate information in the request for privileges dialog box.

tip

You can view the digital certificate for a Web page before it requests privileges by selecting Page Info from the Navigator View menu.

Signing a JavaScript program consists of two steps: preparing the program for signing and running the Signtool program, which creates the JAR file. You prepare a JavaScript program for signing using the ARCHIVE and ID attributes of the <SCRIPT> tag. The ARCHIVE attribute designates the name you want to use for the JAR file of a signed script. You must include the ARCHIVE attribute in the first <SCRIPT> tag in a document, and you include it only once. You must assign a unique ID label to each section of JavaScript code in a signed script, or

Navigator treats the entire script as if it were unsigned. Event handlers contained within HTML tags and the code contained in <SCRIPT>...</SCRIPT> tag pairs are all JavaScript code sections and must include ID attributes. Figure 9-10 shows a program that is prepared for signing. Notice that the <SCRIPT>...</SCRIPT> tag containing the JavaScript source file, the embedded <SCRIPT>...</SCRIPT> section, and the event handler all have ID attributes.

```
<HTML>

<HEAD><TITLE>Signing</TITLE>

<SCRIPT LANGUAGE="JavaScript" ARCHIVE="SignedFile.jar"
     SRC="SourceFile.js" ID="s1">

</SCRIPT>

<SCRIPT ID="s2">

function hideElements() {

      netscape.security.PrivilegeManager.
           enablePrivilege("UniversalPreferencesWrite");

      navigator.preference(
           "browser.background_color", "blue");

}

</SCRIPT>

</HEAD>

<BODY>

<FORM>

<INPUT TYPE="button" VALUE=" Hide Screen Elements "
     ID="bt1" onClick="hideElements();">

</FORM>

</BODY>

</HTML>
```

Figure 9-10: JavaScript program prepared for signing

If you want to sign a document that does not include a <SCRIPT>...</SCRIPT> tag pair, you must create an empty <SCRIPT>...</SCRIPT> tag pair to hold the ARCHIVE attribute. Unlike the ID attribute, the ARCHIVE attribute is valid only within the <SCRIPT> tag. The following code contains a single button that displays an alert dialog box. The empty <SCRIPT>...</SCRIPT> tag pair above the button is necessary for the document to be signed.

```
<HTML>
<HEAD><TITLE>Signing</TITLE>
<SCRIPT LANGUAGE="JavaScript" ARCHIVE="SignedFile.jar"
    ID="s1">
</SCRIPT>
</HEAD>
<BODY>
<FORM>
<INPUT TYPE="button" VALUE=" Display Alert " ID="bt1"
    onClick="alert("You clicked a button.");>
</FORM>
</BODY>
</HTML>
```

tip

Remember that the ARCHIVE attribute needs to appear only once, must be placed in the first <SCRIPT> tag in your document, and is valid only within the <SCRIPT> tag.

Next you will prepare the HomePage.html file for signing.

To prepare HomePage.html for signing:

1   Return to HomePage.html in your text editor or HTML editor.

2   Add the attribute **ARCHIVE="homepage.jar"** to the <SCRIPT> tag in the head section to designate the JAR file for the signed script. Also add the attribute **ID="s1"** to create a unique ID for the tag.

3   Add an ID attribute named **b1** to the button <INPUT> tag in the form.

4   Save and close **HomePage.html**.

Now that the HomePage.html file is prepared for signing, it can be signed using Signtool. You use the syntax `signtool -J -k certificate_name files_path -d certificates_path` to sign a JavaScript program. The -J parameter indicates that you are signing JavaScript files, the -k parameter specifies the certificate to use, and -d specifies the location of your certificates directory. You also include the certificate name, the path to the files you want to sign, and the path to your certificates directory. Note that Signtool digitally signs *all* of the files in the designated directory.

To sign HomePage.html:

1 Select **Run** from the Windows Start menu, then type **command** on Windows 95/98 or **cmd** on Windows NT, and press **Enter**. A command-line window will open.

2 Change to the directory where you installed Signtool, or skip to the next step if the directory containing Signtool is part of your system path.

3 Type **signtool -J -k** *certificate name* **-d** *"certificates directory" "files directory"*, replacing *certificate name* with the name of the certificate you created earlier in this section, and *certificates directory* with the path to the directory containing your certificates database. (You may find it helpful to write down on a piece of paper the names of your certificates directory and files directory so they are easy to refer to.) Also replace *files directory* with the directory containing the HomePage.html file. For example, to sign the HomePage.html file in the homepage folder in the Tutorial.09 folder on my Data Disk in my A: drive, I would type `signtool -J -k dongos-selin -d "c:\Program Files\Netscape\Users\default" a:\Tutorial.08\homepage`. Be sure to include quotation marks around your directory names if they include spaces. Signtool will begin generating the signatures, then prompt you for your certificates password. Enter your password and press **OK**. The last line should say that the directory was signed successfully.

4 Type **exit** and press **Enter** to close the command-line window.

5 Open **HomePage.html** in Navigator from the **Tutorial.09** folder on your Data Disk. (Remember, the signed files must be in the same location as the JAR file.) Click the **Change Home Page to Course Technology** button. You should receive a prompt, asking for additional privileges to read your preferences. If you grant the privilege, you will receive an alert dialog box asking if you want to change your home page to the Course Technology home page. Clicking the OK button displays another prompt, asking for additional privileges to modify your preferences. Granting the additional privileges changes your personal home page. With either request for privileges, if you deny the request, you will receive a Netscape error message and the code will stop. You can view your digital certificate before granting or denying the privilege by clicking the Certificate button.

After signing a JavaScript program, you deploy the HTML files, JavaScript source files, and the JAR file to a server. A very important point to remember is that if you make changes to any of the code in your signed program, you must rerun Signtool. Because Navigator compares each code section to its digital signature in the JAR file, even the slightest change to your JavaScript will cause Navigator to treat your program as unsigned.

Enabling Codebase Principals

As you are developing JavaScript programs that will be digitally signed and include requests for privileges, you may find it tedious to re-sign a script every time you make a minor change. If you make a change, but do not re-sign the script, Navigator ignores any requests for privileges. To make testing and development of digitally signed scripts easier, you can enable codebase principals. **Codebase principals** recognize the origin of a URL, such as an Internet domain or a local file system, as a principal and recognize the owner of a digital certificate as a principal. This recognition allows JavaScript programs to request privileges without being signed. You should use codebase principals only for testing and development purposes on *your* system. Once you are satisfied with the performance of a program that requests privileges, you must digitally sign it before placing it into service. If you do not sign a script containing privileges, then the privilege requests are ignored—unless users enable codebase principals on their systems.

To enable codebase principals on your system, you would close any instances of Navigator, then locate the JavaScript preferences file, prefs.js, in the Netscape folder on your system. The directory in which the prefs.js file is located depends on your operating system. For Windows 95/98 operating systems, the location of the prefs.js file is usually c:\Program Files\Netscape\Users\default\. You would open prefs.js in a text editor, such as Notepad, and add the following line to the end of the file:

```
user_pref("signed.applets.local_classes_have_30_powers",
    true);
```

Before enabling codebase principals, be sure you understand which line to edit in the Prefs.js file, or you may accidentally cause problems with your installation of Navigator. Also, remember that enabling codebase principals is for testing purposes only—always remember to disable codebase principals once you are finished testing a digitally signed file.

If you added the preceding line to prefs.js, and then saved and closed the file, codebase principals would be enabled the next time you start Navigator. To disable codebase principals, you would reopen Prefs.js and delete the line of code that you had added to the file.

SUMMARY

- The same origin policy restricts how JavaScript code in one window or frame accesses a Web page in another window or frame on a client computer.

- The same origin policy applies not only to the domain name, but also to the server on which a document is located.

- The same origin policy prevents malicious scripts from modifying the content of other windows and frames and prevents the theft of private browser information and information displayed on secure Web pages.

- The domain property of the Document object changes the origin of a document to its root domain name using the statement `document.domain = "domain";`.

- A privilege refers to a restricted feature or information that is not normally available to a JavaScript program. For a JavaScript program to access a privilege, it must make a request to the client, who has the option of granting or denying the request.

- Digital signing clearly identifies the author of a JavaScript program and ensures that a JavaScript program has not been modified from its original format.

- A digital certificate is an electronic identification that the creator of a JavaScript program attaches to a signed script.

- Trusted organizations, known as Certificate Authorities or CAs, issue digital certificates. A Certificate Authority verifies the identity of an owner, or principal, of a digital certificate.

- A principal, or entity, refers to the owner of a digital certificate.

- The Security Info dialog box provides information on digital certificates and other security information for your installation of Navigator.

- Signtool is a Perl program created by Netscape that is necessary for generating signed scripts.

- A target is a category containing related types of privileges. Target names begin with the word *Universal*.

- The enablePrivilege() method uses a dialog box to request a restricted privilege of the client.

- If a privilege is granted, the revertPrivilege() method can be used to revoke the privilege.

- Signing a program creates a separate JAR file that contains the digital signatures of the program's JavaScript code.

- You prepare a JavaScript program for signing using the ARCHIVE and ID attributes of the <SCRIPT> tag.

- Codebase principals recognize the origin of a URL, such as an Internet domain or a local file system, as a principal and recognize the owner of a digital certificate as a principal.

Q U E S T I O N S

1. Which properties of the Window object are restricted by the same origin policy?
    a. the move and resize properties
    b. the open and close properties
    c. the find property
    d. all properties

2. Which property of the Document object changes the origin of a document to its root domain name?
    a. domain
    b. root
    c. server
    d. source

3. How do you prevent JavaScript code from being viewed by users?
    a. Digitally sign the code.
    b. Save it in a JavaScript source file.
    c. Encode it with the encodeURI() method.
    d. You cannot prevent JavaScript code from being viewed by users.

4. How does a JavaScript program gain access to privileges?
    a. by making a request of the client
    b. by residing on the same server where the client browser is located
    c. by using the privilege() method of the Window object
    d. JavaScript programs automatically have access to privileges.

5. Digital signing clearly identifies the author of a JavaScript program and
    _____.
    a. allows JavaScript programs to incorporate DHTML into Web pages
    b. requires a password each time a client opens the JavaScript program's Web page
    c. automatically provides access to secure features of client systems
    d. ensures that a JavaScript program has not been modified from its original format

6. The owner of a digital certificate is called a principal, or _____.
    a. signatory
    b. entity
    c. personage
    d. certificate holder

7. Digital certificates are issued by _____.
    a. InterNIC
    b. the federal government
    c. the Software Publishers Association
    d. Certificate Authorities

8. What is the correct syntax for generating a test certificate with Signtool on a Windows 95/98 system?

```
a. signtool -G dongosselin -d
   "c:\Program Files\Netscape\Users\default\"
b. signtool -g dongosselin -D
   "c:\Program Files\Netscape\Users\default\"
c. signtool -G dongosselin -d
d. signtool -D dongosselin -G
   "c:\Program Files\Netscape\Users\default"
```

9. Information on locally installed certificates is available in the _____ dialog box in Navigator.
   a. Java Console
   b. Security Info
   c. Preferences
   d. Encoding

10. Privilege categories are known as _____.
   a. classes
   b. groupings
   c. vehicles
   d. targets

11. What is the correct syntax for a request for privilege access?

```
a. enablePrivilege("UniversalSendMail");
b. netscape.PrivilegeManager.enablePrivilege("UniversalSendMail");
c. netscape.security.enablePrivilege("UniversalSendMail");
d. netscape.security.PrivilegeManager.enablePrivilege
   ("UniversalSendMail");
```

12. You revoke a privilege using the _____ method.
   a. removePrivilege()
   b. revertPrivilege()
   c. revokePrivilege()
   d. disablePrivilege()

13. What type of file is created in the signing process?
   a. JAR
   b. ZIP
   c. ENC
   d. ARC

14. What is the correct syntax for signing a script with signtool?

```
a. signtool -J certificate_name files_path -d certificates_path
b. signtool -J -k certificate_name d certificates_path
c. signtool -J -k certificate_name files_path
d. signtool -J -k certificate_name files_path -d
   certificates_path
```

15. _____ recognize the origin of a URL, such as an Internet domain or a local file system, as a principal and recognize the owner of a digital certificate as a principal.

a. Domain name principals

b. Unsigned acceptance principals

c. Same origin principals

d. Codebase principals

 **E X E R C I S E S**

Save the solution files for each of the following exercises in their own folders within the Tutorial.09 folder on your Data Disk.

1. Search the Internet for information on digital security for Web pages. Outline the different approaches to Web page security and indicate where you think the technology is headed.

2. Many of the popular Certificate Authorities are located outside the United States. Why you think this is so?

3. Create a signed document that resizes and moves your Web page to your liking, then redirects your browser to your usual home page. You will need to use the UniversalBrowserWrite and UniversalPreferencesRead privileges. Save the document as ResizeWindow.html.

4. Create a signed document that creates a new window with the alwaysRaised parameter of the window.open() method. You will need to use the UniversalBrowserWrite privilege. Save the document as AlwaysOnTop.html.

5. Recall from Tutorial 5 that the History object maintains a history list of all the documents that have been opened during the current Web browser session. More specifically, the history list is stored in an array named history[]. Use the UniversalBrowserRead privilege to create a signed document that opens a new window and displays the current window browsing history by looping through the contents of the history[] array. Save the document as BrowsingHistory.html.

Server-Side JavaScript

case ▶ WebAdventure wants to record the number of times visitors access their Web site and to display a "guest book" containing a list of clients. They would also like Web site visitors to be able to sign the guest book. After researching these features, you discover that you have no way of recording this information using client-side JavaScript, because the only state maintenance method you know stores the information in cookies locally on each user's computer. To be able to maintain the desired information across different user sessions, you must use server-side JavaScript. Before you can use server-side JavaScript, you must know a little about client/server processing, along with the differences among the different flavors of server-side JavaScript.

Previewing the WebAdventure Home Page

In this tutorial you will create a program that can be used as WebAdventure's Web site. The program will store the number of hits the Web site receives and include an area where visitors can sign a guest book. The program you create will not be a complete, robust Web site, because it includes only a hit counter and guest book.

Section A of this tutorial teaches server-side JavaScript with Netscape server-side JavaScript 1.4 (SSJS). Section B teaches server-side JavaScript with Microsoft Active Server Pages (ASP). To preview the WebAdventure home page program, you must have access to an iPlanet or Microsoft Web server. In case you do not have access to an iPlanet or Microsoft Web server, each section contains information on where you can download each company's server software. This preview uses screen captures from Microsoft ASP running in Internet Explorer to demonstrate the program. Note, however, that the program will appear and function the same in Netscape, although the underlying code for the ASP and SSJS versions differs somewhat.

You cannot run the programs from the Tutorial.10 folder on your Data Disk unless the drive containing your Data Disk is under the control of an iPlanet or Microsoft Web server.

To preview the WebAdventure home page:

1. The first page of the ASP WebAdventure program is named Tutorial10_StartPage.asp. Figure 10-1 shows Tutorial10_StartPage.asp running in Internet Explorer.

2. After a user enters his or her first name in the text box and clicks the Continue button, a document named Tutorial10_HomePage.asp opens, as shown in Figure 10-2. Notice that the name entered in Tutorial10_StartPage.asp is used in the first paragraph. The page also includes a hit counter displaying the number of times the page has been accessed, along with buttons that allow you to sign or view a guest book. You will see examples of the documents displayed by each of the buttons later.

3. Now in your text editor or HTML editor, open **Tutorial10_HomePage.asp** from the **Tutorial.10** folder on your Data Disk and examine the JavaScript code. Notice <%...%> tag pairs that contain unfamiliar code syntax. These tags and syntax are the ASP version of server-side JavaScript code. Close the **Tutorial10_HomePage.asp** file.

Figure 10-1: Tutorial10_StartPage.asp in Internet Explorer

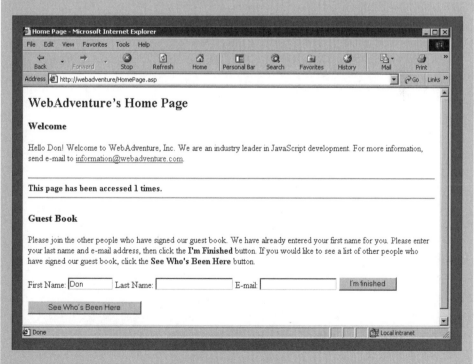

Figure 10-2: Tutorial10_HomePage.asp in Internet Explorer

4 Next in your text editor or HTML editor, open the **Tutorial10_HomePage.html** file from the **Tutorial.10** folder on your Data Disk and examine the JavaScript code. Tutorial10_HomePage.html is the SSJS version of the program. SSJS uses <SERVER>...</SERVER> tag pairs and `characters to designate server-side JavaScript code.

> ASP applications use the file extension .asp, while SSJS applications use the file extension .html.

5 Close your text editor or HTML editor.

In this section you will learn:

■ About client/server architecture

■ About server-side JavaScript development

■ How to create SSJS applications

■ About SSJS core objects

■ How to create a guest book using SSJS

Netscape SSJS

Client/Server Architecture

Your Web browser is a client in the client/server environment of the Web. Up to this point, our focus has been on client-side JavaScript development in Web browsers. For you to develop a full complement of Web development skills, you also need to understand the server side of the Web—how server-side JavaScript fits into Web development. Before getting into server-side JavaScript, let's discuss the fundamentals of client/server architecture, to set the stage.

There are many definitions of a client/server system. In traditional client/server architecture, the server is usually some sort of database from which a client requests information. A server fulfills a request for information by managing the request or "serving" the requested information to the client—hence the term, client/server. A system consisting of a client and a server is known as a **two-tier system**. One of the primary roles of the client, or front end, in a two-tier system is the presentation of an interface to the user. The user interface gathers information from the user, submits it to a server, or back end, then receives, formats, and presents the results returned from the server. The main responsibility of a server is usually data storage and management. Heavy processing, such as calculations, on client/server systems usually takes place on the server. As desktop computers become increasingly powerful, however, many client/server systems place at least some of the processing responsibilities on the client. In a typical client/server system, a client computer may contain a front end that is used for requesting information from a database on a server. The server locates records that meet the client request, performs some sort of processing, such as calculations on the data, then returns the information to the client. The client computer may also perform some processing such as building the queries that are sent to the server or formatting and presenting the returned data. Figure 10-3 illustrates the design of a two-tier client/server system.

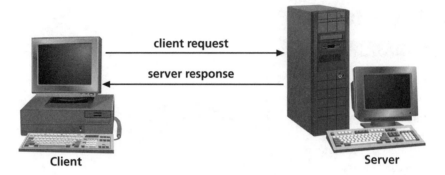

client request

server response

Client   **Server**

Figure 10-3: The design of a two-tier client/server system

tip

The term *distributed application* is used to describe multiple computers sharing the computing responsibility for a single application.

The Web is built on a two-tier client/server system—you have a Web browser
(the client) requesting an HTML document from a Web server. The Web browser is
the client user interface, and the Web server can be viewed as a "database of Web
pages" (in a manner of speaking). Once a Web server returns the requested HTML
document, the Web browser (as the client user interface) is responsible for formatting and presenting the document to the user.

Once you start adding databases and other types of applications to a Web server,
the client/server system evolves into what is known as a three-tier client architecture.
A **three-tier**, or **multitier**, **client/server system** consists of three distinct pieces: the
client tier, the processing tier, and the data storage tier. The client tier, or user interface tier, continues to be the Web browser. However, the database portion of the
two-tier client/server system is split into a processing tier and the data storage tier.
The processing tier, or middle tier, is a "processing bridge" that handles interaction
between the Web browser client and the data storage tier. Essentially, the client tier
makes a request of a database on a Web server. The processing tier performs any necessary processing or calculations based on the request from the client tier, and then reads
information from or writes information to the data storage tier. The processing tier also
handles the return of any information to the client tier. Note that the processing tier is
not the only tier to perform processing. The Web browser (client tier) still renders
HTML documents (which requires processing), while the database or application in
the data storage tier may also perform necessary processing. Client-side JavaScript exists
at the client tier, while server-side JavaScript exists at the processing tier. Figure 10-4
illustrates the design of a three-tier client/server system.

tip

Two-tier client/server architecture is a physical arrangement in which the client and server are
two separate computers. Three-tier client/server architecture is more conceptual than physical,
because the processing tier and data storage tier are often located on the same server.

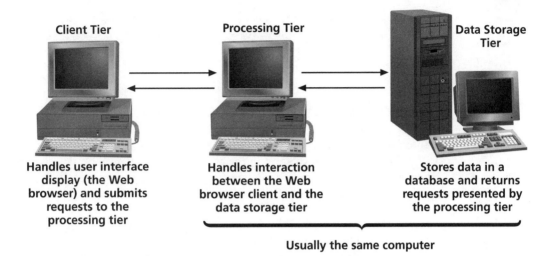

Client Tier   **Processing Tier**   **Data Storage Tier**

Handles user interface display (the Web browser) and submits requests to the processing tier

Handles interaction between the Web browser client and the data storage tier

Stores data in a database and returns requests presented by the processing tier

Usually the same computer

Figure 10-4: The design of a three-tier client/server system

An important aspect in the design of any client/server system is deciding how much processing to place on the client. In the context of Web site development with JavaScript, you must decide whether to use client-side or server-side JavaScript. This decision may sound confusing, because client-side JavaScript and server-side JavaScript share much of the same core language. A general rule of thumb is to allow the client to handle the user interface processing and light processing, such as data validation, but have the server perform intensive calculations and data storage. This division of labor is especially important when dealing with the Web. Unlike with a private network, you do not know the computing capabilities of each client on the Web. You cannot assume that each client (browser) that accesses your client/server application (Web site) has the necessary power to perform the processing required by the application. For this reason, intensive processing should be placed on the server.

Because servers are usually much more powerful than client computers, your first instinct may be to let the server handle *all* processing and only use the client to display a user interface. Although you do not want to overwhelm clients with processing they cannot handle, it is important to perform as much processing as possible on the client for several reasons. First, distributing processing among multiple clients creates applications that are more powerful, because you are not limited to the processing power of a single computer. Client computers become more powerful every day, and advanced capabilities such as JavaScript and DHTML are now available in local Web browsers. It is a logical step for a Web application to harness some of this power and capability. Secondly, local processing on client computers minimizes transfer times across the Internet and creates faster applications. If a client had to wait for all processing to be performed on the server, a Web application could be painfully slow over a busy Internet connection. Finally, performing processing on client computers lightens the processing load on the server. If all processing in a three-tier client/server system is on the server, the server for a popular Web site with heavy traffic could become overwhelmed trying to process requests from numerous clients.

Server-Side JavaScript Development

Tutorial 6 touched on three-tier client/server processing when discussing forms and CGI. You also used JavaScript in the client tier to validate form data before submitting it to a server at the processing tier. At the processing tier, CGI, along with a scripting language, such as Perl, usually prepares and processes the data in some way before submitting it to the data storage tier. Before the development of server-side JavaScript, CGI was one of the most popular methods of developing three-tier client/server applications for the Web. However, CGI is not an actual programming language. Rather, CGI is a protocol that is often used with a scripting language such as Perl to handle the communication between the client tier and the data storage tier.

In comparison, **server-side JavaScript** is a programming language based on client-side JavaScript that has the ability to handle communication between the client tier and the data storage tier. Additionally, server-side JavaScript can interact closely with client-side JavaScript, because they share the same basic programming features. For these reasons, many developers prefer server-side JavaScript for handling the processing tier of a three-tier client/server system.

Server-side JavaScript, however, is not without drawbacks. One of the biggest disadvantages of the language is that it is proprietary and vendor-specific. You must know a slightly different version of server-side JavaScript for each vendor's Web server. *There is no server-side standard similar to ECMAScript.* Because of this lack of standardization, CGI is still a popular technology for use at the processing tier, because virtually every type of server supports it.

Although server-side JavaScript is proprietary and vendor-specific, most implementations use much of the same core language syntax that you have learned for client-side JavaScript. You can write server-side JavaScript programs using many of the skills you have already learned in client-side JavaScript, regardless of the server-side JavaScript version you use.

Web applications created with server-side JavaScript do not necessarily require a data storage tier. For example, you can create a server-side JavaScript program whose only purpose is to dynamically generate a Web page that is presented to a client. Another example of a server-side JavaScript program that does not require a data storage tier is a program that counts the number of hits a Web site receives. Web applications that do not include a data storage tier are not three-tier client/server systems; you refer to these types of applications as **distributed applications**. The server-side JavaScript programs you will create in this tutorial are distributed applications that do not include a data storage tier.

In Tutorial 11, you will continue working with server-side JavaScript and learn how to create three-tier client/server systems using databases.

As mentioned previously, one of the biggest drawbacks of server-side JavaScript is that it is proprietary and vendor-specific. Because this book focuses on Netscape and Microsoft technologies, this tutorial will discuss each of their versions of server-side JavaScript. Section A discusses the Netscape version of server-side JavaScript, which is called SSJS. In Section B, you will learn about the Microsoft version of server-side JavaScript as used in Active Server Pages.

To perform the exercises in this section, you must have access to an iPlanet Web Server. iPlanet is an alliance between Netscape and Sun Microsystems that creates e-commerce software. The examples and figures in this tutorial were created using iPlanet Web Server Enterprise Edition 4.0. You can download iPlanet Web server software from *www.iplanet.com/downloads/download/*. Before you download the server software, be sure you have enough hard drive space. Also, allocate plenty of time for the download process if you have a slow Internet connection, because the iPlanet Web Server software is quite large. The compressed iPlanet Web Server Enterprise Edition 4.0 software ranges from 38 MB to 70 MB, depending on your operating system. In addition, read each server's online data sheet before you download the software to be sure your computer meets the minimum hardware requirements.

help Support of Server-side JavaScript is discontinued in Edition 6 of the iPlanet Web Server Enterprise in favor of other technologies such as Java Servlets and Java Server Pages (JSP). Therefore, in order to complete the exercises in this tutorial and in Tutorial 11, be sure you are using a version of iPlanet Web Server Enterprise earlier than Edition 6.

help Installing a Web server can be an involved process, requiring an in-depth knowledge of networking technology and transmission protocols. Additionally, you must also understand network administration functions to properly maintain a Web server. Because the goal of this book is to teach JavaScript, no time is spent discussing server installation or administration procedures. If you are working on your own, visit the iPlanet and Microsoft Web sites for detailed information on the installation and administration of any of the Web servers mentioned in this tutorial. If you are in a classroom setting, ask your instructor for specific instructions on how to work with the Web server at your institution.

tip This tutorial provides only the briefest overview of SSJS. For more information on server-side JavaScript, visit the Documentation section of the Netscape developer site, DevEdge Online, at *developer.netscape.com/*.

Creating SSJS Applications

Before getting into the specifics of the server-side JavaScript language, you need to understand how to create server-side JavaScript programs. Unlike client-side JavaScript, SSJS programs must be compiled and installed before you can use them. The specific steps for creating server-side JavaScript programs are as follows:

1. Create a server-side script.
2. Compile and deploy the program, using the `jsac` compiler.

3. Install and start the program using the JavaScript Application Manager.

Let us examine each of these steps in detail.

Server-Side Scripts

You create server-side JavaScript in HTML documents or .js source files, the same way you do with client-side JavaScript. In fact, HTML documents can contain both client-side and server-side JavaScript. However, when a client requests an HTML document from a server, the server executes any server-side JavaScript *before* serving the document to the client. Once your Web browser receives the document, it executes the client-side JavaScript.

Server-side JavaScript included in an HTML document is enclosed in a **<SERVER>...</SERVER> tag pair**, and not in a <SCRIPT>...</SCRIPT> tag pair, as is done for client-side JavaScript. The following code contains an example of a <SERVER>...</SERVER> tag pair that includes a single write() method. The server-side JavaScript write() method works much the same way as the client-side write() method, except that instead of designating text to be output to the browser, it designates information to be returned to the client.

```
<SERVER>
write("Hello World");
</SERVER>
```

Notice in the preceding code that the write() method does not include the Document object, as it would in client-side JavaScript. The write() method in server-side JavaScript is a global method not associated with any particular object. In fact, server-side JavaScript does not reference the Document object, Window object, or many of the other browser-specific objects of client-side JavaScript. Instead, server-side JavaScript deals with objects that are part of the processing tier. (You will learn about server-side JavaScript objects later in this section.)

••

See Netscape server-side JavaScript documentation for a listing of global methods.

••

Server-side JavaScript is also placed in source files with a .js extension, the same way that client-side JavaScript source files are. Source files in server-side JavaScript are useful for maintaining libraries of functions that are accessible by all server-side JavaScript code in an application. Unlike client-side JavaScript, you do not reference the name of a server-side source file using the SRC attribute. Instead, you include the name of the .js source file when you compile the application. During the compilation process, the compiler makes the JavaScript code in the .js source file available to HTML documents in the application.

If you need to include server-side JavaScript inside an HTML tag, you enclose the code with backquotes. You represent backquotes using the ` character on the keyboard (usually to the left of the numeral 1 key). For example, the Client object in server-side JavaScript programming is used for creating custom client properties. Let us assume that you have created a custom property, named email, in the Client object and you want to use that property in a link that uses the MAILTO: attribute. To return the custom email property of the server-side JavaScript Client object and use it in the link, you use syntax similar to the following:

```
<A HREF=mailto:`client.email`>
Click here to send an e-mail</A>
```

Before an iPlanet server delivers an HTML document containing server-side JavaScript to a client, it executes the contents of any <SERVER>...</SERVER> tag pairs. If a client were to view the source document after it received the HTML document, it would not see any <SERVER>...</SERVER> tag pairs or the JavaScript code they contain. Instead, the client sees only the results returned by the code. For example, Figure 10-5 shows an HTML document containing client-side JavaScript as well as server-side JavaScript enclosed in <SERVER>...</SERVER> tags and backquotes. Figure 10-6 shows how the document appears once a client receives it. The examples assume that the email property of the Client object contains dongosselin@compuserve.com.

```
<HTML>

<HEAD>

<TITLE>Client and Server-Side JavaScript</TITLE>

<SCRIPT LANGUAGE="JavaScript">

<!-- HIDE FROM INCOMPATIBLE BROWSERS

document.write("<H2>This line is generated by client-side

JavaScript.</H2>");

// STOP HIDING FROM INCOMPATIBLE BROWSERS -->

</SCRIPT>

</HEAD>

<BODY>

<SERVER>

write("<H2>This line is generated by server-side
JavaScript.</H2>");

</SERVER>

<A HREF=mailto:`client.email`>

Click here to send an e-mail to Don Gosselin</A>

</BODY>

</HTML>
```

Figure 10-5: HTML document containing client and server-side JavaScript

```
<HTML>

<HEAD>

<TITLE>Client and Server-Side JavaScript</TITLE>

<SCRIPT LANGUAGE="JavaScript">

<!-- HIDE FROM INCOMPATIBLE BROWSERS

document.write("<H2>This line is generated by client-
side JavaScript. </H2>");

// STOP HIDING FROM INCOMPATIBLE BROWSERS -->

</SCRIPT>

</HEAD>

<BODY>

<H2>This line is generated by server-side JavaScript.</H2>

<A HREF="mailto:dongosselin@compuserve.com">

Click here to send an e-mail to Don Gosselin</A>

</BODY>

</HTML>
```

Figure 10-6: HTML document with client and server-side JavaScript on the client

Next you will create a simple HTML document that will be used as the start page for the WebAdventure home page you saw in the preview.

To create a simple document that will be used as the start page for the WebAdventure home page:

1   Start your text editor or HTML editor and create a new document.

2   Type the opening <HTML>, <HEAD>, <TITLE>, and <BODY> sections of the document, along with a heading tag:

```
<HTML>
<HEAD>
<TITLE>Welcome</TITLE>
</HEAD>
<BODY>
<H2>Welcome to WebAdventure!</H2>
```

3 Enter the following <SERVER>...</SERVER> tag pair, which creates a Date object, then sends the date to the client using the toLocaleString() method:

```
<SERVER>
var curDate = new Date();
write("The current date and time are " +
curDate.toLocaleString());
write("<HR>");
</SERVER>
```

4 Add the following heading tag, a form that contains a text field for the user's first name, and a submit button that calls the main HTML document, HomePage.html. The program uses the submit button to submit the value in the text field to the HomePage.html file.

```
<H3>Please enter your first name and click Continue
to proceed to our home page.</H3>
<FORM METHOD="post" ACTION="HomePage.html">
First Name: <INPUT TYPE="text" NAME="first">
<INPUT TYPE="submit" VALUE=" Continue ">
</FORM>
```

5 Add the following code to close the <BODY> and <HTML> tags:

```
</BODY>
</HTML>
```

6 Save the file as **StartPage.html** in the **Tutorial.10** folder on your Data Disk. You need to compile and install the program before you can execute it as an SSJS application.

help

> If you attempt to open an SSJS document as a local file, or without going through an SSJS-enabled Web server, Netscape 6 will ignore any text that is located between any <SERVER>...</SERVER> tag pairs. However, Internet Explorer and earlier versions of Navigator do not recognize the <SERVER>...</SERVER> tag pair and will render to the screen any statements contained within a <SERVER>...</SERVER> tag pair as if they were standard text.

Compiling and Deploying an Application

After you create your server-side scripts (HTML documents and .js source files), you must compile them. Once you have successfully compiled your application, you must move the resulting .web file to your Web server. You compile SSJS applications using the jsac program. The **jsac program** is a command-line program that compiles server-side scripts into a single file with an extension of .web. The jsac.exe program is installed by default in the C:\Netscape\Server4\bin\https\bin folder on your iPlanet Web Server. iPlanet servers recognize the .web extension as an executable Web application. A collection of related files compiled into a single .web file is referred to as an **SSJS application**. Although the files that make up an SSJS application are stored in a .web extension file, users access them by typing in their Web browser clients the full name of an HTML file, including its .html extension. When an SSJS-enabled Web server receives a request for an HTML document that is part of a SSJS application, it knows to look for the file within the application's .web file. The `jsac` program can be executed with a number of different options. You can view a list of the compiler options by typing `jsac —h` at the command line.

To create an SSJS application containing multiple programs, you append to the `jsac` command the name of each file that is part of the application, separated by spaces. The following code shows an example of how to use the `jsac` program to compile a server-side JavaScript program consisting of two files: homepage.html and functionlibrary.js. Two options are used, –v to display a detailed description of the compilation process, and –o to create the .web file with a name of main.web.

```
jsac -v -o main.web homepage.html functionlibrary.js
```

Next you will compile StartPage.html.

To compile StartPage.html:

1 Go to your system command prompt. Accessing a command prompt differs with each operating system. To access a command prompt from Windows NT, Select **Run** from the **Start** menu and type **cmd**.

2 Change to the **Tutorial.10** folder on your Data Disk.

3 Type the following command to compile your program, and then press **Enter**. Recall that the jsac.exe program is installed by default in the C:\Netscape\Server4\bin\https\bin folder on your iPlanet Web Server. If jsac.exe is installed in a different drive and folder on your system, then replace C:\Netscape\Server4\bin\https\bin with the appropriate path.

```
C:\Netscape\Server4\bin\https\bin\jsac -v -o
WebAdventure.web startpage.html
```

help

> The preceding command includes a line break because of space limitations. Be sure to enter the entire command on a single line before pressing Enter.

4 When the program finishes compiling, close the command prompt window. Before you can run the application, it needs to be installed and started using Application Manager, which will be discussed next.

Installing and Starting an Application

Application Manager installs and manages SSJS applications on a Web server. Once you successfully compile your application, open Application Manager using the URL *server.domain/appmgr/*, substituting the name of your server and domain.

When you start Application Manager for the first time, you may find it useful to add a bookmark in your browser to its URL so you do not need to retype the full URL each time you need to run the program.

Application Manager is a JavaScript application that opens in your browser. The left frame in Application Manager contains a form with a list of installed applications along with a list of links that execute various commands. In the top frame are several command buttons, including an Add Application button that is used for installing and starting SSJS applications. Clicking a link in the left or top frame displays an associated page in the right frame. Figure 10-7 shows an example of the Add Application form of Application Manager after clicking the Add Application button.

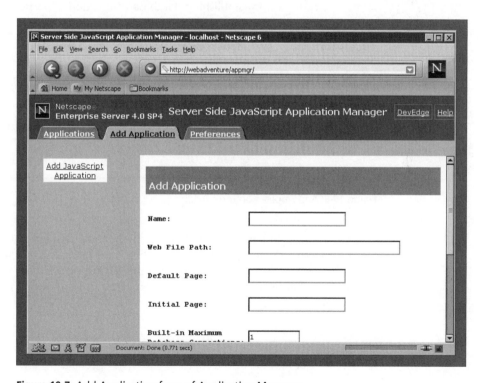

Figure 10-7: Add Application form of Application Manager

The Add Application form is used for adding an application to the Web server. Figure 10-8 describes the purpose of each form field.

Field	Description
Name:	The name of the application. Do not give an application the same name as an existing directory on a Web server, or clients will not be able to access documents in the directory.
Web File Path:	The full pathname to the application .web file created with the `jsac` command.
Default Page:	The default page delivered to a client when they do not request a specific file. This field is optional.
Initial Page:	The first page to execute when you first start the application. This page is used for performing any tasks required at application startup, such as initializing counter values or establishing database connections. This field is optional.
Built-in Maximum Database Connections:	The maximum number of database server connections allowed by a database server license. The default value for this field is zero.
External Libraries:	The pathnames of external libraries to be used with the application. This field is optional.
Client Object Maintenance:	The technique used for maintaining state information. You can select client-cookie, client-URL, server-IP, server-cookie, or server-URL.

Figure 10-8: Add Application form fields

After filling out the required fields in the Add Application form, click the OK button to install the application. Once you add an application, it is automatically started. You can then run the application by selecting it from the list of installed applications and clicking the Run link in the left frame, or by opening its URL in Netscape.

tip

Before you install and run the WebAdventureHome program, take a moment to examine the existing Hangman SSJS sample application that is automatically installed and started when you first install your iPlanet Enterprise Web Server. The Hangman application is an SSJS version of the classic word game that allows you to guess a secret word, letter by letter.

To examine the Hangman SSJS sample application:

1 First locate the file named **hangman.html**, which contains the SSJS code that gives the program its functionality, and open it in your text editor or HTML editor. By default the hangman.html file is installed in the C:\Netscape\Server4\plugins\samples\js\hangman folder. Notice the <SERVER>...</SERVER> tag pair at the top of the file that contains some simple SSJS code. Scrolling farther down in the file, you can see that the program form is submitted to the LiveWire server each time you click the Enter button. The LiveWire server then sends a new HTML page to your Web browser that displays another piece of the hanging man (using one of eight images) if you do not guess correctly. If you scroll farther down in the file, you will find an <IMG> tag that uses backquotes to include SSJS code within an HTML tag.

2 Close **hangman.html**.

3 Start **Application Manager**, then click **Hangman** in the list of applications. Application information for hangman appears in the right frame. Notice that the Status field says *Active*, which means the Hangman application is currently started.

4 Click the **Run** button. A new browser window opens and displays the hangman.html file. Try playing the game by entering letters and clicking the **Enter** button. Figure 10-9 shows the browser window after several guesses. When you are through, close the browser window in which the Hangman game is running.

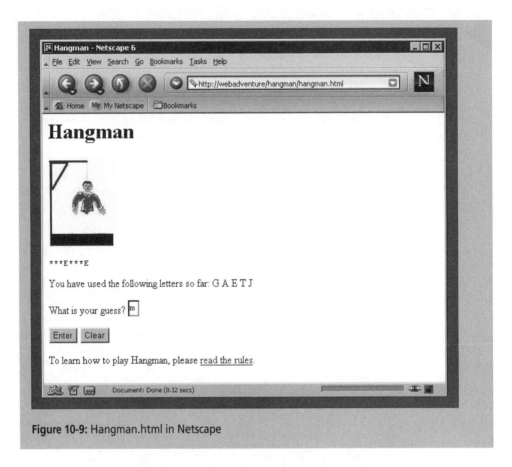

Figure 10-9: Hangman.html in Netscape

Next you will install and run the WebAdventureHome program.

To install and start the WebAdventureHome program:

1   Return to Application Manager, and select the **Add Application** button in the top frame.

2   In the Add Application frame, type **WebAdventureHome** in the Name box. Then in the Web File Path box, type **a:\Tutorial.10\WebAdventure.web**, assuming your Data Disk is in drive a:.

3   Type **StartPage.html** in the Default Page box.

4   Leave the rest of the boxes in the Add Application form set to their default values and select the **OK** button.

5   If necessary, select **WebAdventureHome** from the list of installed applications in the left frame and click **Run** to open the StartPage.html file in your Web browser. Figure 10-10 shows an example of the document in Netscape.

> Once you start an application, you do not necessarily need to run it from within Application Manager. Instead, you can type the URL where the program is installed on your Web server directly into your Web browser address box.

6 After StartPage.html opens in Netscape, select **Page Source** from the **View** menu. In the Page Source window, notice that the document does not contain the server-side JavaScript write() statements. Instead, only the output from the statements is available to the client.

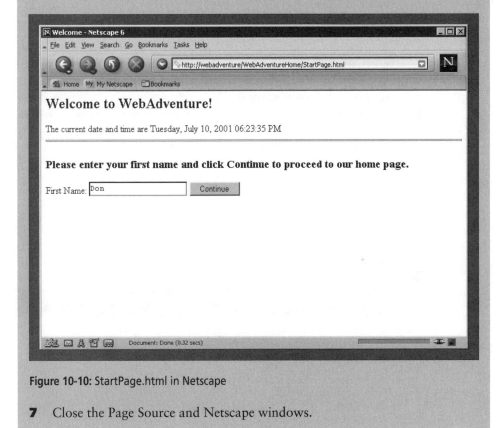

Figure 10-10: StartPage.html in Netscape

7 Close the Page Source and Netscape windows.

SSJS Core Objects

SSJS does not recognize browser Document and Window objects, as client-side JavaScript does. Instead, SSJS recognizes four built-in objects, Request, Client, Project, and Server, that function at the processing tier between the client tier and the data storage tier (if there is one). The Request, Client, Project, and Server objects are called **session management objects** in SSJS. Although the session management objects are built into server-side JavaScript, they each have different lifetimes and availability. You use each of the objects to access specific types of information in the processing tier and for storing state information on the server. Each of these objects will now be discussed in detail.

You can permanently record information stored in the session management objects, using the SSJS File object. See Netscape server-side JavaScript documentation for more information.

Request Object

The **Request object** represents the current URL request from a client. SSJS creates a new Request object each time a client requests a URL. For example, if users request an SSJS application from a Web server, then SSJS creates a Request object. SSJS also creates a Request object when client-side JavaScript uses the document.location or history.go() methods, and when server-side JavaScript uses the built-in redirect() method.

The redirect() method is used for sending a client to a different Web page, in the same manner that you use the href property of the client-side JavaScript Location object.

The Request object has the shortest lifetime of all the session management objects, because it exists only until the current request is fulfilled. In other words, once SSJS serves a Web page to the client, the Request object ceases to exist. The Request object contains a number of predefined properties that return information about the client request. Figure 10-11 lists some of the common predefined properties of the Request object.

Property	Description
agent	The name and version of the client browser
ip	The client IP address
method	The HTTP method of the request
protocol	The HTTP protocol supported by the client browser
imageX	The horizontal position of the insertion point after the user clicks an image map
imageY	The vertical position of the insertion point after the user clicks an image map

Figure 10-11: Request object predefined properties

One important and useful property is the agent property, which returns the name and version of the browser making a URL request. You can use this property to dynamically generate HTML and JavaScript code according to the browser type. For example, if you are using DHTML to add animation to a Web page, you can construct the appropriate code for Netscape or Internet Explorer, then return it to the requestor. This technique is a useful alternative to the cross-browser compatibility techniques you learned about in Tutorial 8.

 tip

You can create your own properties for the Request object by using the syntax request.*property* = *value*;. However, because the property lasts only as long as the Request object exists, it is usually easier to use JavaScript variables.

The Request object is useful for retrieving information about the client. However, one of the most useful features of the Request object is that all of the named elements in a form on the client browser are appended as properties of the Request object. Recall that when you click a form submit button, each field on the form is submitted to the server as a *name=value* pair. Without SSJS, to use the *name=value* pairs, you must use methods of the String object to parse them. In contrast, SSJS creates Request object properties, using each form element NAME attribute, and assigns each property the value contained in the element field. Consider the typical form shown in Figure 10-12.

```
<HTML>

<HEAD>

<TITLE>Customer Information</TITLE>

</HEAD>

<BODY>

<H2>Customer Information</H2>

<FORM METHOD="post" ACTION="ProcessOrder.html"

NAME="customer_information">

Name<BR>

<INPUT TYPE="text" NAME="name" SIZE=50><BR>

Address<BR>

<INPUT TYPE="text" NAME="address" SIZE=50><BR>

City, State, Zip<BR>
```

Figure 10-12: A typical form

```
<INPUT TYPE="text" NAME="city" SIZE=38>

<INPUT TYPE="text" NAME="state" SIZE=2 MAXLENGTH=2>

<INPUT TYPE="text" NAME="zip" SIZE=5 MAXLENGTH=5><BR>

E-Mail<BR>

<P><INPUT TYPE="text" NAME="email" SIZE=50></P>

<INPUT TYPE="reset">

<INPUT TYPE="submit">

</BODY>

</HTML>
```

Figure 10-12: A typical form

After the form in Figure 10-12 has been submitted to an SSJS document named ProcessOrder.html, a Request object is created with properties representing each form element. You refer to each form element in the Request object by using the following Request object properties:

```
request.name
request.address
request.city
request.state
request.zip
request.email
```

Any *name=value* pairs attached to a URL as a query string are also appended as properties of the Request object. The following code appends a query string to a URL. Let us assume that the URL is part of a SSJS application.

```
<A HREF="http://www.URL.com/TargetPage.html?firstName=Don
&lastName=Gosselin&occupation=writer">Link Text</A>
```

After a user clicks the link, you can refer to firstName, lastName, and occupation in SSJS as properties of the Request object as follows:

```
request.firstName
request.lastName
request.occupation
```

Form fields and query string *name=value* pairs are often submitted by a server-side JavaScript program to a database or other type of application at the data-processing tier. You can also use server-side JavaScript to calculate or manipulate the information in some way, then return a result to the client.

Next you will create the main WebAdventure HTML document and include references to the form properties of the Request object.

To create the main WebAdventure HTML document and include references to the Request object:

1 Create a new document in your text editor or HTML editor.

2 Type the opening <HTML>, <HEAD>, <TITLE>, and <BODY> sections of the document:

```
<HTML>
<HEAD>
<TITLE>Home Page</TITLE>
</HEAD>
<BODY>
```

3 Add the following heading tags:

```
<H2>WebAdventure Home Page</H2>
<H3>Welcome</H3>
```

4 Type the following paragraph, which uses the Request object to insert the value of the first name text field from the StartPage.html file:

```
<P>Hello <SERVER>write(request.first);</SERVER>!
Welcome to WebAdventure, Inc. We are an industry
leader in JavaScript development. For more information,
send e-mail to <A HREF="mailto:
information@webadventure.com">
information@webadventure.com</A>.</P>
```

5 Add the following code to close the <BODY> and <HTML> tags:

```
</BODY>
</HTML>
```

6 Save the file as **HomePage.html** in the **Tutorial.10** folder. Recompile the WebAdventureHome program using `jsac`. When you recompile the program, be sure to include both the StartPage.html file and the HomePage.html file on the command line, as follows:

```
C:\Netscape\Server4\bin\https\bin\jsac -v -o
WebAdventure.web startpage.html homepage.html
```

7 Restart the application using Application Manager.

8 Open the **StartPage.html** file in your Web browser from your iPlanet Web Server or, enter the WebAdventure application URL on your Web server, enter your name in the First Name text box, and click the **Continue** button to open HomePage.html. Figure 10-13 shows how HomePage.html appears in Netscape. You can see that the name you typed in StartPage.html has been inserted into HomePage.html.

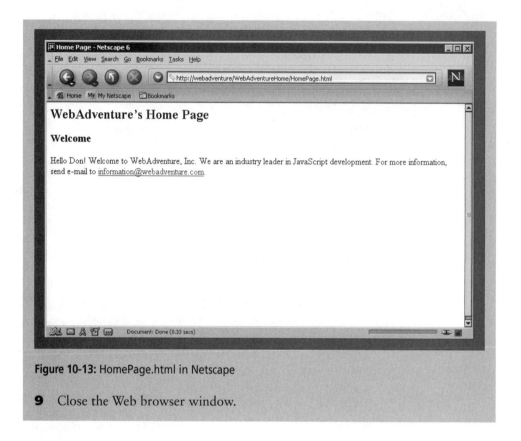

Figure 10-13: HomePage.html in Netscape

9   Close the Web browser window.

Client Object

A new Request object is instantiated each time a client requests an SSJS URL, and then destroyed once the URL is delivered to the client. However, an SSJS application may be composed of multiple documents. This means that you cannot use the same Request object with different pages in an application. To preserve client information across multiple pages in an SSJS application, you must use the Client object. The **Client object** temporarily stores specific client information that is available to all the pages in an SSJS application. A Client object is instantiated the first time a client accesses a URL in a given application.

The Client object does not contain any predefined properties. Instead, you create your own Client object properties to store information about the user on your application. The syntax for creating a new property of the Client object is `client.property = value;`. For example, you may create a property that contains the user's name. You can then use the name property to create a customized greeting for each page of the application that the user accesses. Some other uses of Client object properties include storing shopping cart items for an online store and preserving field values in a multipart form. Let us assume that the following code is the first page in a multipart form. The code shows an example of server-side JavaScript that assigns the values of the form fields as properties of the Client object. You place the code in the HTML document that generates the second page of the multipart form. The code executes when the client requests the second page. In the example, each form element value is retrieved from its associated property in the Request object.

```
<SERVER>
client.name = request.name;
client.address = request.address;
client.city = request.city;
client.state = request.state;
client.zip = request.zip;
client.email = request.email;
</SERVER>
```

SSJS has no way of knowing whether a client is through working with an application. This situation occurs because the Web does not contain any tangible links as a real network does; it relies instead on HTTP to send requests and responses back and forth over the Internet. When users access a Web site, they are only requesting a document. Once an SSJS server returns the requested document, it has no way of knowing whether the client has finished working with an application. The only way a server knows that a client wants to continue working with an application is when the client requests another document. For this reason, the Client object has a default lifespan of 10 minutes. You can change the lifespan of a Client object using the **expiration() method**. The syntax for the expiration() method is `client.expiration(seconds);`. Note that the time is designated in seconds. If you want to increase the lifespan of a Client object to 20 minutes, you use the statement `client.expiration(1200);` because 20 minutes is equal to 1200 seconds.

If you are sure a client is through using an application, you can delete the Client object using the destroy() method. The **destroy() method** deletes a Client object. For example, your SSJS application may include a Complete Sale button that processes a user's order. Once the order has been processed, you can delete the Client object using the statement `client.destroy();`.

There may be a situation in which you do not want to destroy a Client object, only delete the properties it contains and start over. You can delete all information stored in a Client object by setting the expiration() method to zero seconds, using the statement `client.expiration(0);`.

Next you will add a property to the Client object for the WebAdventureHome program.

To add a property to the Client object for the WebAdventureHome program:

1 Open **HomePage.html** in your text editor or HTML editor.

2 Above the </HEAD> tag, type the following server section, which contains a simple `if` statement that uses the logical not (!) operator to check if the sameSession property exists in the Client object. If the sameSession property does not exist, it is created and set to an initial value of true. The sameSession property indicates that a client is working within the same session, regardless of whether it changes to a different page in the application. You will use this value later when creating the page hit counter.

```
<SERVER>
if (!client.sameSession) {
    client.sameSession = "true";
}
</SERVER>
```

3 Save the **HomePage.html** file.

Project Object

A **Project** object is used for storing global application information that can be shared by all clients accessing the application. Each application has its own Project object that is created when you first start the application with the Start button in Application Manager. An application Project object is available until the application is stopped, using the Stop button in Application Manager.

Because each instance of a Project object is intended to contain application-specific information, the Project object does not contain any predefined properties. You create your own properties for an application, using the syntax `project.property = value;`. A common property that is created for the Project object is some type of unique number to identify clients. You can create a Project object property that keeps track of the last assigned number, and then use a function to update the number and assign it to a client. For example, you may have a Web application that takes online orders. Each time a client accesses the application, you want to assign a unique invoice number. The following code checks the value of the lastInvoiceNum property of the Project object and increments it by one. Then, a new invoiceNum property is created in the Client object and assigned the value of the Project object lastInvoiceNum property. You place this code in the first page of the online order application in order to assign an invoice number to a client that accesses the page.

```
<SERVER>
Project.lastInvoiceNum = ++Project.lastInvoiceNum;
Client.invoiceNum = Project.lastInvoiceNum;
</SERVER>
```

Because the properties of the Project object are available to all clients who access the application, there is a possibility that one client may try to access a property before another client is through with it. If this happens, you could experience data integrity problems. For instance, if two clients were able to access the preceding code at the same time, they could be assigned the same invoice number. To prevent one client from accessing a property of the Project object until another client is through with it, you use the Project object lock() and unlock() methods. The **lock() method** prevents other clients from accessing properties of the Project object, and the **unlock() method** cancels the lock() method. You place the `project.lock();` statement before any code that accesses Project properties. You place the `project.unlock();` statement so that it follows the last statement that accesses Project object properties. For example, to prevent data integrity problems with the lastInvoiceNumber code example, you use the lock() and unlock() methods as follows:

```
<SERVER>
project.lock();
project.lastInvoiceNum = ++project.lastInvoiceNum;
client.invoiceNum = project.lastInvoiceNum;
project.unlock();
</SERVER>
```

Because the properties of the Project object are preserved from user to user, you can create a property to count the number of times your site has been visited. Counting the number of times your site has been visited is commonly referred to as having a number-of-hits counter. Next you will add a number-of-hits counter to the HomePage.html file.

To add a number-of-hits counter to the HomePage.html file:

1 Return to **HomePage.html** in your text editor or HTML editor.

2 In the server section, add the following statements above the `client.sameSession = "true";` statement. The first statement locks the project. The `if` statement uses a logical not (!) operator to check if the counter property of the Project object exists. The counter property will hold the number of hits the page receives. If the counter property does not exist, it is created and assigned an initial value of one. If the counter property does exist, its value is assigned to the curNumber variable, which increments it by one. The new value in the curNumber variable is then assigned to the counter property. Finally, the project is unlocked.

```
project.lock();
if (!project.counter)
    project.counter = 1;
else {
    var curNumber = project.counter;
    curNumber = ++curNumber;
```

```
        project.counter = curNumber;
}
project.unlock();
```

3 Next add the following code above the closing </BODY> tag to display the number of times the page has been accessed:

```
<HR>
<B>This page has been accessed
<SERVER>write(project.counter);</SERVER> times.</B>
<HR>
```

4 Restart Netscape to establish a new browser session. This is necessary to ensure that the WebAdventureHome page closes completely before you attempt to recompile and restart it.

5 Save **HomePage.html,** then recompile and restart the WebAdventureHome program. Open **StartPage.html** in Netscape. Type your first name in the First Name text box and press **Continue** to open HomePage.html. The page counter should start at one. Figure 10-14 shows the page after it has been accessed twice.

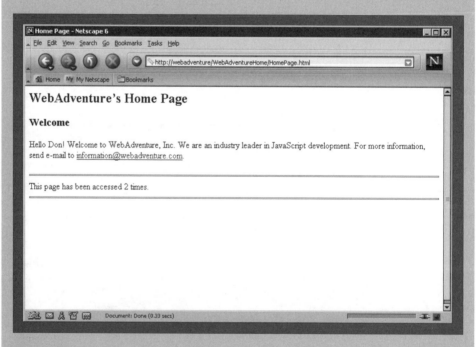

Figure 10-14: HomePage.html with hit counter

6 Close the Web browser window.

Server Object

The **Server object** contains information about the running iPlanet server and comes into existence when the server first starts. Once a server is stopped (by an administrator or if the computer on which the server is running crashes), the Server object is destroyed. If you have more than one server running on the same computer, then each server has its own Server object. The Server object includes several properties that are accessible by all applications on the server. Figure 10-15 lists the Server object properties.

Property	Description
hostname	Full host name
host	Name, subdomain, and domain name
protocol	Communications protocol
port	Port number being used
jsVersion	Version and platform

Figure 10-15: Server object properties

As with other SSJS objects, you can create custom Server object properties. You create Server object properties by using the syntax `server.property = value;`. An example of a custom Server object property is an e-mail address used by different applications to submit status reports or order confirmations.

The Server object includes the same lock() and unlock() methods used with the Project object. If you have multiple applications on a server that change Server object values, be sure to use the lock() and unlock() methods to prevent data integrity problems.

Creating a Guest Book

Next you will add to the WebAdventureHome program a guest book that uses several SSJS objects. You will save guest entries as properties of the Project object. Note that saving guest entries in the Project object is not necessarily the most efficient method of creating a guest book, because the list will be lost if you need to restart your server. A more efficient method is to save the entries to a database. However, the main purpose of this exercise is to understand how to work with core SSJS objects. You will learn how to use SSJS to read and write to databases in Tutorial 11.

First you will add some text and a form to HomePage.html.

To add some text and a form to HomePage.html:

1 Open **HomePage.html** in your text editor or HTML editor.

2 Above the </SERVER> tag, add the following `if` statement, which checks whether the guestCounter property of the Project object exists. The SignGuestBook.html file (which you will create next) will increment the value contained in the guestCounter property each time a new guest signs the guest book. However, if no one has signed the guest book yet, the guestCounter property will have no value assigned to it. The following code ensures that the value *undefined* does not appear in HomePage.html before the first guest signs the guest book.

```
if (!project.guestCounter)
    project.guestCounter = 0;
```

3 Add the following tags and text above the closing </BODY> tag. The text includes the guestCounter property of the Project object, which returns the number of people who have signed the guest book.

```
<H3>Guest Book</H3>
<P>Please join the other
<SERVER>write(project.guestCounter);</SERVER> people
who have signed our guest book. We have already
entered your first name for you. Please enter your
last name and e-mail address, then click the <B>I'm
Finished</B> button. If you would like to see a list
of other people who have signed our guest book, click
the <B>See Who's Been Here</B> button.</P>
```

4 Next add the following form to be used for signing the guest book. The First Name text box uses the Request object to set the value of the first name text field to the value of the text field from StartPage.html. The form ACTION attribute opens a SignGuestBook.html file, which will contain server-side JavaScript code that saves the form values in the guest book.

```
<P><FORM METHOD="post" ACTION="SignGuestBook.html">
First Name: <INPUT TYPE="text" NAME="firstName" SIZE=10
VALUE=`request.first`>
Last Name: <INPUT TYPE="text" NAME="lastName">
E-mail: <INPUT TYPE="text" NAME="email">
<INPUT TYPE="submit" VALUE=" I'm Finished ">
</FORM></P>
```

5 Create another form that will open a file named ShowGuestBook.html. The ShowGuestBook.html file will contain server-side JavaScript code that displays a list of the people who have signed the guest book.

```
<P><FORM METHOD="post" ACTION="ShowGuestBook.html">
<INPUT TYPE="submit" VALUE=" See Who's Been Here ">
</FORM></P>
```

6 Save **HomePage.html**.

Next you will create the SignGuestBook.html file.

To create the SignGuestBook.html file:

1 Create a new document in your text editor or HTML editor.

2 Type the opening <HTML> and <HEAD> sections of the document:

```
<HTML>
<HEAD>
<TITLE>Guest Book</TITLE>
```

3 Add the following server section. The first statement locks the project, then an `if` statement with a logical not (!) operator checks if a guestCounter property has been created in the Project object. The `if` statement creates the property, if it does not exist. The value of the guestCounter property is then assigned to the curGuestNum variable, incremented by one, and then reassigned to the guestCounter property. Another variable, curGuestInfo, is created to hold the first name, last name, and e-mail address of the guest signing the book. The statement `project["guest" + curGuestNum] = curGuestInfo;` creates a new property in the Project object to hold the current guest's information. Note that the property name is built and assigned to the Project object by combining the text *guest* with the curGuestNum variable inside a pair of brackets. The last statement in the server section unlocks the project.

```
<SERVER>
project.lock();
if (!project.guestCounter)
    project.guestCounter = 0;
var curGuestNum = project.guestCounter;
curGuestNum = ++curGuestNum;
project.guestCounter = curGuestNum;
var curGuestInfo = request.firstName + " "
    + request.lastName
    + ", " + request.email;
project["guest" + curGuestNum] = curGuestInfo;
project.unlock();
</SERVER>
```

4 Add the following code to close the head section, and open the body section:

```
</HEAD>
<BODY>
```

5 Type the following heading tag and form, which displays a customized message to the user, using the firstName property of the Request object. The form contains a single button that executes the history.back() method to return to HomePage.html.

```
<H3>Thank you
<SERVER>write(request.firstName);</SERVER>! Your name
and e-mail address have been
added to our guest book.</H3>
<FORM>
<INPUT TYPE="button"
VALUE="Return to WebAdventure's Home Page"
    onClick="history.back();">
</FORM>
```

6 Add the following code to close the <BODY> and <HTML> tags:

```
</BODY>
</HTML>
```

7 Save the file as **SignGuestBook.html** in the **Tutorial.10** folder on your Data Disk.

Finally, you will create the ShowGuestBook.html file.

To create the ShowGuestBook.html file:

1 Create a new document in your text editor or HTML editor.

2 Type the opening <HTML>, <HEAD>, <TITLE>, and <BODY> sections of the document:

```
<HTML>
<HEAD>
<TITLE>Guest Book</TITLE>
</HEAD>
<BODY>
```

3 Add the following information text and tags:

```
<H2>This is the Guest List</H2><HR>
<B>Name, E-Mail</B><BR>
```

4 Type the following server section, which locks and unlocks the project and uses a `for` loop to return the contents of each guest property in the Project object:

```
<SERVER>
project.lock();
var numGuests = project.guestCounter;
for (var count = 1; count <= numGuests; ++count) {
    write(project["guest" + count] + "<BR>");
}
project.unlock();
</SERVER><HR>
```

5 Type the following form, which contains a single button that executes the history.back() method to return to HomePage.html.

```
<FORM>
<INPUT TYPE="button"
VALUE="Return to WebAdventure's Home Page"
    onClick="history.back();">
</FORM>
```

6 Add the following code to close the <BODY> and <HTML> tags:

```
</BODY>
</HTML>
```

7 Save the file as **ShowGuestBook.html** in the **Tutorial.10** folder on your Data Disk.

8 Recompile and restart the **WebAdventureHome** application. Be sure to include all four files when you use the jsac command.

9 Run **StartPage.html** and enter your first name, then click the **Continue** button to open HomePage.html. Fill in your last name and e-mail address, and then click the **I'm Finished** button to sign the guest book. Figure 10-16 shows SignGuestBook.html in Netscape.

Figure 10-16: SignGuestBook.html in Netscape

10 Click the **Return to WebAdventure's Home Page** button to return to HomePage.html, and then click the **See Who's Been Here** button to view a list of people who have signed the guest book. Figure 10-17 displays ShowGuestBook.html after several guests have signed the book.

Figure 10-17: ShowGuestBook.html in Netscape

11 Close the Web browser window and your HTML or text editor.

SUMMARY

- The Netscape version of server-side JavaScript is known as SSJS and is supported by iPlanet Web Server.

- A system consisting of a client and a server is known as a two-tier system.

- A three-tier, or multitier, client/server system consists of three distinct pieces: the client tier, the processing tier, and the data storage tier.

- Server-side JavaScript is a programming language based on client-side JavaScript that has the ability to handle communication between the client tier and the data storage tier.

- Web applications created with server-side JavaScript do not necessarily require a data storage tier.

- Web applications that do not include a data storage tier are not three-tier client/server systems and are referred to as distributed applications.

- SSJS programs must be compiled and installed before you can use them.

- A collection of related files compiled into a single .web file is referred to as an SSJS application.

- <SERVER>...</SERVER> tag pairs are used for designating server-side JavaScript code.

- If you need to include server-side JavaScript inside an HTML tag, you enclose the code with backquotes (`).

- You can compile server-side scripts using the SSJS jsac program.

- Application Manager installs and manages SSJS applications on a Web server.

- SSJS recognizes four built-in objects, Request, Client, Project and Server, that deal with the processing tier. The Request, Client, Project, and Server objects are called session management objects in SSJS.

- The Request object represents the current URL request from a client. SSJS creates a new Request object each time a client requests a URL.

- The Client object temporarily stores specific client information that is available to all the pages in an SSJS application. A Client object is instantiated the first time a client accesses a URL in a given application.

- A Project object is used for storing global application information, which can be shared by all clients accessing the application. Each application has its own Project object that is created when you first start the application with the Start button in Application Manager.

- The lock() method prevents other clients from accessing properties of the Project object or Server object, and the unlock() method cancels the lock() method.

- The Server object contains information about the running iPlanet server and comes into existence when the server first starts.

Q U E S T I O N S

1. A system consisting of a client and a server is known as a _____.
   a. mainframe topology
   b. double-system architecture
   c. two-tier system
   d. wide area network

2. What is usually the primary role of a client?
   a. locating records that match a request
   b. heavy processing, such as calculations
   c. data storage
   d. the presentation of an interface to the user

3. Which of the following functions does the processing tier not handle in a three-tier client/server system?
   a. processing and calculations
   b. reading and writing of information to the data storage tier
   c. the return of any information to the client tier
   d. data storage

4. Which function is safe to allow a client to handle?
   a. data validation
   b. data storage
   c. intensive processing
   d. heavy calculations

5. Prior to the development of server-side JavaScript, what was one of the most popular methods of developing three-tier client/server applications?
   a. CGI
   b. Visual C++
   c. Fortran
   d. Visual Basic

6. You add server-side JavaScript code to an HTML document in SSJS applications, using a _____ tag pair.
   a. <SSJS>...</SSJS>
   b. <SERVER>...</SERVER>
   c. <SERVERSIDE>...</SERVERSIDE>
   d. <SSJSSERVER>...</SSJSSERVER>

7. Which is the correct syntax for including the SSJS write() method inside an HTML tag?
   a. `write("Hello World");`
   b. 'document.write("Hello World");'
   c. ~write("Hello World");~
   d. /document.write("Hello World");/

8. You compile SSJS applications using the _____ command-line program.
   a. jcompile
   b. jsac
   c. ssjscomp
   d. ssjsc

9. Which of the following objects has the shortest lifespan?
   a. Request
   b. Client
   c. Project
   d. Server

10. Which of the following items does not create a Request object?
    a. client-side JavaScript document.location property
    b. client-side JavaScript history.go() method
    c. server-side JavaScript redirect() method
    d. iPlanet Web Server Application Manager

11. How do you refer to a form field named "password," using the Request object?
    a. `request.password`
    b. `request("password")`
    c. `request.form("password")`
    d. `client.request.password`

12. Which method is used for changing a Client object lifespan?
    a. lifespan()
    b. expiration()
    c. persistence()
    d. duration()

12. In which object would you store an incremented invoice number that must be accessible to all users who access the SSJS application?
    a. Request
    b. Client
    c. Project
    d. Server

14. Which method prevents other clients from accessing properties of the Project object or Server object?
    a. session()
    b. frozen()
    c. lock()
    d. preserve()

# EXERCISES

Save your solution files for each of the following exercises in their own folders within the Tutorial.10 folder on your Data Disk.

1. Create a simple program that uses an SSJS write() statement to print *Printed from an SSJS Program* to the screen. Save the HTML document as SimpleOutput.html.

2. Create a document that uses SSJS write() statements to print the names of five technology companies. Place each company name on its own line. Save the HTML document as LineBreaks.html.

3. Create an HTML document that uses SSJS write() statements to display six lines, with each line formatted using one of the six heading-level tags. Start with the largest tag and end with the smallest. Save the HTML document as HeadingTags.html.

4. Create an HTML document that uses SSJS write() statements to print the following text-formatting styles: bold, italic, big, small, strong, emphasized, superscript, and subscript. Save the HTML document as TextFormats.html.

5. Create a document named SimpleForm.html with a simple form containing fields for first name, last name, and profession. The form should include a submit button that posts the form data to an SSJS document named ProcessForm.html. The SSJS document ProcessForm.html should use properties of the Request object to return a response to the user that displays the form information.

6. Replace the value assigned to the myEmail variable in the following code with your personal e-mail address. Then, modify the <A> tag in the HTML section so it references the myEmail variable. After SSJS returns the document to the user, the user should be able to click the <A> tag and send you a message. Save the document as SSJSVariable.html.

```
<HTML>
<HEAD>
<TITLE>SSJS Variable</TITLE>
<SERVER>
var myEmail = "your e-mail address"
</SERVER>
</HEAD>
<BODY>
<H2>SSJS Variable</H2>
<P>Click <A>here</A> to send an e-mail.</P>
</BODY>
</HTML>
```

7. Create a generic redirection page that you can use to send clients to pages other than the one they requested. You can add this page to your library of JavaScript tools. Use the SSJS global redirect() method. Save the document as Redirector.html.

8. Use properties of the Request object to create a client information page that displays information about a client browser and HTTP information. Save the document as BrowserInfo.html.

9. Use properties of the Server object to create a server information page that displays information about your server. Save the document as ServerInfo.html.

10. Refer to the Netscape SSJS documentation for information on the File object, which is used for reading and writing files on the server. Modify the WebAdventure home page you created in this section so that the guest book information is saved to a server file.

11. Read about the Application Manager debugging capabilities in the Netscape SSJS documentation. How do the Application Manager debugging capabilities compare to the Netscape JavaScript Debugger program?

12. SSJS allows you to use five methods to store state information: client-cookie, client-url, server-ip, server-cookie, and server-url. You select a state information maintenance technique in the Client Object Maintenance field in the Application Manager Add Application form. Read about state maintenance in the Netscape SSJS documentation. What are the advantages and disadvantages of each state maintenance technique?

In this section you will learn:

■ About Active Server Pages

■ How to create ASP applications

■ About ASP object collections

■ About ASP core objects

■ How to create a guest book, using ASP

Microsoft Active Server Pages

Introduction to Active Server Pages

The Microsoft version of server-side JavaScript is available in **Active Server Pages (ASP),** which is a built-in feature of Microsoft Web servers. Like SSJS, ASP exists at the processing tier and executes according to client requests. ASP can also be used with or without a data source tier. Although there are differences between SSJS and ASP, as you progress through this section, you will notice many similarities between the two versions of server-side JavaScript, particularly similarities among their core objects.

A significant difference between ASP and SSJS is that ASP allows you to use several different scripting languages for creating server-side programs. SSJS allows you to use only JavaScript. By default, ASP supports JavaScript (JScript in Microsoft terminology) and VBScript. You can also obtain ASP interpreters from third-party developers for the Perl, REX, and Python scripting languages. Additionally, you can mix and match code from different languages within your ASP scripts, which allows you to take advantage of features that may be unique to a specific language. Because our focus is on JavaScript, only ASP features that specifically relate to the JavaScript language will be discussed.

To perform the exercises in this section, you must have access to a computer running one of the Microsoft Web servers on a Windows operating system. Internet Information Server 3.0 and higher running on Windows NT Server 4.0 and Windows 2000, Peer Web Services running on Windows NT Workstation 4.0, and Personal Web Server running on Windows 95/98 all support Active Server Pages. The examples and figures in this section were created using Windows NT Workstation 4.0 running Peer Web Services.

ASP does not include anything similar to the SSJS development environment components. The Active Service Pages components are just the JavaScript and VBScript scripting engines that interpret ASP code. You do not compile ASP applications the way you compile SSJS applications, nor do you need to install, or start and stop, an ASP application. ASP automatically recognizes any changes to an ASP application and recompiles the application the next time a client requests it. Installing an ASP application is as simple as placing the files that make up the application in one of the server's directories. Additionally, an ASP application starts automatically the first time a Web server receives a request for one of the application's pages. Note that whereas the term *SSJS application* refers to a compiled collection of files with a .web extension, the term **ASP application** refers to a collection of related ASP files that exist in the same root directory.

tip

• •

This tutorial provides only a brief overview of ASP and server-side JavaScript. Web site management and administration functions with Microsoft Web servers are not discussed here. For more information on ASP and Microsoft Web servers, visit the Microsoft Developer Network at *msdn.microsoft.com/*.

• •

Creating ASP Applications

Unlike SSJS applications, in which you create server-side JavaScript in HTML documents or .js source files, you create ASP applications in files with an extension of .asp. ASP files are created as text files, the same as HTML files, and can contain both client-side and server-side JavaScript. When a client requests an ASP document, the Web server executes any server-side JavaScript *before* serving the document to the client. Once the client Web browser receives the document, it executes the client-side JavaScript. Be aware that when a client requests an ASP file from a server, the server compiles the file, regardless of whether it contains server-side JavaScript code. Because the compilation process requires extra processing time, you should not use the .asp extension with HTML files that do not contain server-side JavaScript code, because HTML files do not need to be compiled.

Server-Side Scripts

ASP applications do not use <SERVER>...</SERVER> tag pairs to designate server-side JavaScript code, as does SSJS. Instead, ASP uses the script delimiters **<%** and **%>** to designate server-side JavaScript code. A **delimiter** is a character or a sequence of characters used to mark the beginning and end of a code segment. You include within the script delimiters any commands that are valid for the scripting language you are using. The following code contains an example of script delimiters that includes a single Write() method of the Response object.

```
<% Response.Write("Hello World"); %>
```

Notice that the Write() method in the preceding code is appended to the Response object, in the same manner as the write() method in client-side JavaScript is appended to the Document object. Also notice that the Response object and Write() method are written with uppercase first letters. In ASP, server-side specific JavaScript objects and methods are usually written with uppercase first letters. You will learn about the Response object later in this section. The Write() method works the same as the client-side write() method, except that instead of designating text to be output to the browser, it designates information to be returned to the client.

You also use script delimiters if you need to include server-side JavaScript inside an HTML tag. For example, you use the Session object in ASP to create custom client properties, similar to the Client object in SSJS. Let us assume that you have created a custom property, named email, in the Session object, and you want to use that property in a link that uses the MAILTO: attribute. To return the custom email property of the ASP Session object and use it in the link, you use syntax similar to the following:

```
<A HREF="mailto:" + <% Response.Write(
Session.Contents("email")) %>>
Click here to send an e-mail</A>
```

Notice in the preceding code that you refer to the email property of the Session object as an argument of the Contents object. Properties in ASP are stored in data structures known as collections instead of as properties of objects, as they are in SSJS. The Contents object referenced in the preceding code is actually called the Contents collection. You will learn about collections at the end of this section.

If one of your client-side JavaScript functions requires intensive processing that could be too taxing for a client system, you might need to designate a <SCRIPT>...</SCRIPT> tag pair to run on the server. The **RUNAT=SERVER** attribute will force a <SCRIPT>...</SCRIPT> tag pair to run on the server. Within a <SCRIPT>...</SCRIPT> tag pair that includes the RUNAT=SERVER attribute, you can include any server-side JavaScript objects and methods. For example, Figure 10-18 returns a greeting to the client based on the language property of the Request object Form collection. The client never sees the function or code—only a single line written by one of the Response.Write() statements.

```
<SCRIPT LANGUAGE=JScript RUNAT=SERVER>
function returnGreeting() {

    if (Request.Form("language") == "Spain")

        Response.Write("Buenos Dias");

    else if (Request.Form("language") == "Germany")

        Response.Write("Guten Tag");

    else if (Request.Form("language") == "Italy")

        Response.Write("Buon Giorno");

    else if (Request.Form("language") == "France")

        Response.Write("Bonjour");

    else

        Response.Write("I don't speak your language!");

}
</SCRIPT>
```

Figure 10-18: Server-side <SCRIPT>...</SCRIPT> tag pair

Next you will create an ASP version of the WebAdventureHome program. First you will create the start page document. Note that this section duplicates many of the steps you saw in Section A when you created the SSJS version of the program. Instead of retyping the steps, you can copy and modify the documents from the SSJS program. However, be sure to modify the SSJS commands to conform to ASP command syntax, or you will receive an error when you attempt to run the program.

To create the start page document for the WebAdventureHome program:

1 Start your text editor or HTML editor and create a new document.

2 Type the opening <HTML>, <HEAD>, <TITLE>, and <BODY> sections of the document, along with a heading tag:

```
<HTML>
<HEAD>
<TITLE>Welcome</TITLE>
</HEAD>
<BODY>
<H2>Welcome to WebAdventure!</H2>
```

3 Enter the following ASP section, which creates a Date object, then sends the date to the client using the toLocaleString() method:

```
<%
var curDate = new Date();
Response.Write("The current date and time are "
    + curDate.toLocaleString());
Response.Write("<HR>");
%>
```

4 Add the following heading tag, a form that contains a text field for the user's first name, and a submit button that calls the main HTML document, HomePage.asp. You use the submit button to submit the value in the text field to the HomePage.asp file.

```
<H3>Please enter your first name and click Continue to
proceed to our home page.<H3>
<FORM METHOD="post" ACTION="HomePage.asp">
First Name: <INPUT TYPE="text" NAME="first">
<INPUT TYPE="submit" VALUE=" Continue ">
</FORM>
```

5 Add the following code to close the <BODY> and <HTML> tags:

```
</BODY>
</HTML>
```

6 Save the file as **StartPage.asp** in the Tutorial.10 folder on your Data Disk.

ASP Directives

ASP directives are used to designate the scripting language used in an ASP file and to send output to the browser. There are two types of ASP directives: the processing directive and the output directive. The **ASP processing directive** provides a Web server with information on how to process the scripts in an ASP document. ASP processing directives are created using the <%@ ... %> delimiters. You create a processing directive by using attributes that provide information about the script to the Web server. Figure 10-19 lists the processing directive attributes.

Attribute	Description
CODEPAGE	Designates the ASP document character set
ENABLESESSIONSTATE	Determines whether an ASP document maintains state information
LANGUAGE	Sets the document default scripting language
LCID	Sets a script locale identifier
TRANSACTION	Determines whether a script is to be treated as a transaction

Figure 10-19: Processing directive attributes

ASP uses VBScript by default, so you must include the processing directive in order to use JavaScript with your ASP applications. In addition, the processing directive must be placed on the first line of your ASP file, above the <HTML> tag. For example, the following code creates a simple ASP application that designates JScript (JavaScript) as the scripting language and disables state maintenance.

```
<%@ LANGUAGE=JScript ENABLESESSIONSTATE=false %>
<HTML>
HTML tags and script statements
</HTML>
```

The **output directive** sends the result of an expression to a user's Web browser (the client). The syntax for the output directive is <%= *expression* %>. For example, if your script includes a variable named favoriteColor that has been assigned a value of *blue*, then the output directive <%= favoriteColor %> sends the text *blue* to the client Web browser.

The output directive is equivalent to the Response object Write() method.

● ●

You do not need to use the processing directive or the output directive if your SSJS code is enclosed in a <SCRIPT>...</SCRIPT> tag pair that includes the attributes LANGUAGE=JScript and RUNAT=SERVER.

● ●

Figure 10-20 shows examples of both the output directive and the processing directive. The example combines the output directive with the Response object Write() method, and includes the processing directive to designate JavaScript as the default scripting language. The expression in the output directive calculates firstNum and secondNum, then sends the text *The result of 10 minus 2 is 8* to the user's Web browser. Figure 10-21 shows the output.

```
<%@ LANGUAGE=JScript %>

<HTML>

<% var firstNum = 10, secondNum = 2;

Response.Write("The result of " + firstNum + " minus "
      + secondNum + " is "); %>

<%= firstNum - secondNum %>

</HTML>
```

Figure 10-20: ASP directives example

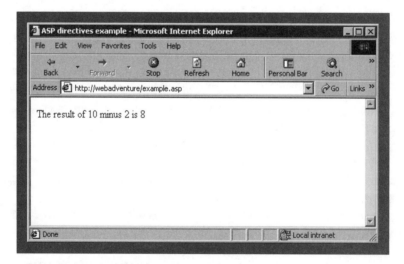

Figure 10-21: ASP directives example in a Web browser

Next you will add a processing directive to the StartPage.asp document.

To add a processing directive to the StartPage.asp document:

1 Return to **StartPage.asp** in your text editor or HTML editor.

2 Add **<%@ LANGUAGE=JScript %>** above the opening <HTML> tag.

3 Save **StartPage.asp**, then copy and upload the file to your ASP server.

4 In the Internet Explorer address box, enter **http://*servername*/StartPage.asp**, replacing *servername* with the name of your server and the directory on the server where you saved StartPage.asp. You cannot open StartPage.asp as a local file using the Open command from Internet Explorer's File menu. You must type the full URL to your server.

> You can configure the server name for your ASP server by using the Personal Web Server program that is installed with Microsoft Web servers.

5 After the document opens, select **Source** from the **View** menu. In the text editor window that opens, notice that the document does not contain the server-side JavaScript Response.Write() statements. Instead, only the output from the statements is available to the client.

6 Close Internet Explorer and the source file windows.

Mixing HTML and Server-Side JavaScript

Before a Microsoft Web server delivers an ASP document containing server-side JavaScript to a client, it executes the contents of any script delimiters. If users were to view the source document after they received the ASP document, they would not see any <%...%> script delimiters or the JavaScript code they contain. Instead, the client shows only the results returned by the code. For example, Figure 10-22 shows an ASP document containing client-side JavaScript as well as server-side JavaScript enclosed in script delimiters. Figure 10-23 shows how the document appears once a client receives it. The examples assume that the email property in the Contents collection of the Session object contains dongosselin@compuserve.com.

```
<%@ LANGUAGE=JScript %>

<HTML>

<HEAD>

<TITLE>Client and Server-Side JavaScript</TITLE>

<SCRIPT LANGUAGE="JavaScript">

<!-- HIDE FROM INCOMPATIBLE BROWSERS

document.write("<H2>This line is generated by client-
side JavaScript.</H2>");

// STOP HIDING FROM INCOMPATIBLE BROWSERS -->

</SCRIPT>

</HEAD>

<BODY>

<% Response.Write("<H2>This line is generated by server-
side JavaScript.</H2>"); %>

<A HREF="mailto:" + <% Session.Contents("email") %>>
Click here to send an e-mail to Don Gosselin</A>

</BODY>

</HTML>
```

Figure 10-22: ASP document with client-side and server-side JavaScript on the server

You can see in Figure 10-22 that HTML tags and text can be interspersed with script delimiters. However, you can go even further and include HTML tags and text as part of a server-side JavaScript decision-making structure, such as an `if...else` statement. For example, in the following code, because each `if` or `else if` statement is enclosed by script delimiters, it is unnecessary to use the Write() method of the Response object to output the correct greeting. Only one greeting is returned, based on the results of the `if...else` construct.

```
<% if (Request.Form("language") == "Spain") %>
    Buenos Dias
<% else if (Request.Form("language") == "Germany") %>
    Guten Tag
<% else if (Request.Form("language") == "Italy") %>
    Buon Giorno
<% else if (Request.Form("language") == "France") %>
    Bonjour
<% else %>
    I don't speak your language!
```

```
<HTML>

<HEAD>

<TITLE>Client and Server-Side JavaScript</TITLE>

<SCRIPT LANGUAGE="JavaScript">

<!-- HIDE FROM INCOMPATIBLE BROWSERS

document.write("<H2>This line is generated by client-
side JavaScript.</H2>");

// STOP HIDING FROM INCOMPATIBLE BROWSERS -->

</SCRIPT>

</HEAD>

<BODY>

<H2>This line is generated by server-side JavaScript.</H2>

<A HREF="mailto:"dongosselin@compuserve.com" + >

Click here to send an e-mail to Don Gosselin</A>

</BODY>

</HTML>
```

Figure 10-23: ASP document with client-side and server-side JavaScript as it appears on the client

You could also write the code within a single pair of script delimiters, as the following code illustrates. However, the greetings are not treated as HTML tags or text, because they are enclosed by the script delimiters. For this reason, each greeting must include a Response.Write() statement to be returned to the client.

```
<%
if (Request.Form("language") == "Spain")
     Response.Write("Buenos Dias");
else if (Request.Form("language") == "Germany")
     Response.Write("Guten Tag");
else if (Request.Form("language") == "Italy")
     Response.Write("Buon Giorno");
else if (Request.Form("language") == "France")
     Response.Write("Bonjour");
else
     Response.Write("I don't speak your language!");
%>
```

Figure 10-24 shows another example of interspersing server-side JavaScript with HTML tags and text to generate a customized Web page. The example shows an HTML document that could be generated in response to a client request for information. Let us assume that the document originating the client request includes a form field named clientName. The example uses the clientName property of the Content collection of the Request object and uses an output directive to intersperse it throughout the text to be returned to the client, creating a customized response. The example also assumes that the company's e-mail address is stored in the email property of the Content collection of the Application object. Figure 10-25 shows the output in a Web browser, assuming that *Don* is the value of the clientName property.

```
<%@ LANGUAGE=JScript %>

<HTML>

<HEAD>

<TITLE>HTML and Server-Side JavaScript</TITLE>

</HEAD>

<BODY>

<P>Dear <%= Request.Form("clientName") %>:</P>

Thank you for your interest in our Web development services.

As you know, it is difficult to keep up with rapidly changing

technology. With WebAdventure's help, you can be confident

that your Web site will be on the cutting edge. Remember,

<%= Request.Form("clientName") %>, WebAdventure is here for

you. For more information, click <A HREF="mailto:" +

<%= Application.Contents("email") %>>here</A> to send us an

e-mail.

</BODY>

</HTML>
```

Figure 10-24: Server-side JavaScript interspersed with HTML

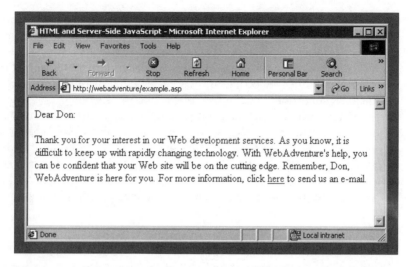

Figure 10-25: Server-side JavaScript interspersed with HTML in a Web browser

Object Collections

Before learning about ASP core objects, you need to understand collections. **Collections** are data structures similar to arrays that store variables in ASP core objects. You can think of collections as similar to the properties stored in SSJS core objects. The syntax for assigning a variable to a collection is *object.collection("variable") = value;*. You then refer to the variable in ASP code by using the syntax *object.collection("variable");*. For instance, the Application object and Session object both contain separate **Contents** collections, which store custom variables. The following code creates a name variable in the Session object Contents collection, assigns it a value of *Don Gosselin*, and then sends the value to the client browser, using a Response.Write() statement:

```
<%
Session.Contents("name") = "Don Gosselin";
Response.Write("Your name is " + Session.Contents("name"));
%>
```

....

Collections are commonly used in Visual Basic programming. Much of ASP non-JavaScript syntax comes from Visual Basic programming because the ASP default scripting language is VBScript, which derives from Visual Basic.

....

If a variable name you assign to a collection is unique throughout all of the collections of an object, then you can eliminate the collection name when referencing the object in code. For example, if the Session object contains only one name variable in all of its collections, then you can refer to the name variable in code by using a statement such as `Response.Write(Session ("name"));`. It is usually safer, however, to include the collection name in order to eliminate any uncertainty as to what collection contains a specific variable. Additionally, eliminating the collection name could cause bugs in your program if you later add the same variable name to another collection in the same object. Therefore, the code in this Tutorial includes collection names when referencing variables.

Each variable in a collection is numbered, similarly to the way element numbers are assigned to arrays. Unlike array element numbers, which begin with zero, collection numbers begin with one. You can refer to collection variables by using numbers instead of variable names. For example, the following code creates three variables, firstName, lastName, and email, in the Contents collection of the Session object, then returns the values to the client, using the collection number of each variable.

```
<%
Session.Contents("firstName") = "Don";
Session.Contents("lastName") = "Gosselin";
Session.Contents("email") = "dongosselin@compuserve.com";
Response.Write(Session.Contents(1));
Response.Write(Session.Contents(2));
Response.Write(Session.Contents(3));
%>
```

Be aware that the number assigned to a variable in a collection can change if you remove items from the collection. You should not assume that a number always represents the same variable in a collection.

▶ **tip**

You can remove items from a collection using the Remove() and RemoveAll() methods of the Contents collection. Both the Application object and Session object contain Contents collections.

ASP collections support a **count** property, which returns the number of variables in a collection. You can use the count property in a looping statement to cycle through the variables in a collection. For example, the following code uses a `for` loop to return the variables in the Contents collection to the client. The `for` loop conditional evaluation compares the curVariable variable to the count property. While curVariable is less than or equal to the count property, the `for` loop continues iterating through the collection.

```
<%
Session.Contents("firstName") = "Don";
Session.Contents("lastName") = "Gosselin";
Session.Contents("email") = "dongosselin@compuserve.com";
for (var curVariable = 1;
curVariable <= Session.Contents.Count;
    ++curVariable) {
    Response.Write(Session.Contents(curVariable));
}
%>
```

ASP Core Objects

Like SSJS, ASP includes several built-in objects that function at the processing tier. The core ASP objects are the Request, Response, Session, Application, and Server objects. You use each of the objects to access specific types of information in the processing tier and to store state information on the server.

●●

Note that many of the examples in this section are identical to the examples you saw in Section A. The same examples are used to demonstrate how to perform the same tasks with the two different versions of server-side JavaScript.

●●

Request Object

The ASP **Request object** represents the current URL request from a client and is equivalent to the SSJS Request object. ASP creates a new Request object each time a client requests a URL. For example, if users click a link or select a new URL in their browser, then ASP creates a Request object. ASP also creates a Request object when client-side JavaScript uses the document.location or history.go() methods. The Request object has the shortest lifetime of all the ASP built-in objects, because it exists only until the current request is fulfilled.

The Request object contains several collections that contain information about the client request. Figure 10-26 lists the Request object collections.

Collection	Contains
ClientCertificate	Field values in the client certificate sent with the request
Cookies	Cookies sent with the request
Form	The value of named form elements in the document displayed in the browser
QueryString	The *name=value* pairs appended to the URL in a query string
ServerVariables	Environment variables

Figure 10-26: Request object collections

●●

The ASP Request object also includes a TotalBytes property, which returns the total number of bytes being sent in the client request, and a BinaryRead method, which retrieves data sent to the server from the client as part of a POST request.

●●

The Form collection of the ASP Request object contains variables representing form elements from the requesting Web page. ASP takes all of the named elements in a form on the user's browser and adds them as variables to the Form collection of the Request object. Recall that when you click a form submit button, each field on the form is submitted to the server as a *name=value* pair. The name portion of the *name=value* pair becomes a variable name in the Form collection, and the value portion is assigned as the value of the variable. Figure 10-27 contains a typical form.

```
<HTML>

<HEAD>

<TITLE>Customer Information</TITLE>

</HEAD>

<BODY>

<H2>Customer Information</H2>

<FORM METHOD="post" ACTION="ProcessOrder.asp"

NAME="customer_information">

Name<BR>

<INPUT TYPE="text" NAME="name" SIZE=50><BR>

Address<BR>

<INPUT TYPE="text" NAME="address" SIZE=50><BR>

City, State, Zip<BR>

<INPUT TYPE="text" NAME="city" SIZE=38>

<INPUT TYPE="text" NAME="state" SIZE=2 MAXLENGTH=2>

<INPUT TYPE="text" NAME="zip" SIZE=5 MAXLENGTH=5><BR>

E-Mail<BR>

<P><INPUT TYPE="text" NAME="email" SIZE=50></P>

<INPUT TYPE="reset">

<INPUT TYPE="submit">

</BODY>

</HTML>
```

Figure 10-27: A typical form

Upon submitting the form in Figure 10-27 to an ASP document named ProcessOrder.asp, the field names and values are assigned as variables to the Request object Form collection. You refer to each form variable in the Request object Form collection by using the following statements:

```
Request.Form("name")
Request.Form("address")
Request.Form("city")
Request.Form("state")
Request.Form("zip")
Request.Form("email")
```

When *name=value* pairs are attached to a URL as a query string, they are assigned as variables to the Request object QueryString collection. Consider the following code, which appends a query string to a URL:

```
<A HREF="http://www.URL.com/TargetPage.asp?firstName=Don
&lastName=Gosselin&occupation=writer">Link Text</A>
```

After users click the link, TargetPage.asp opens. Any ASP code thereafter can refer to firstName, lastName, and occupation as variables in the Request object QueryString collection as follows:

```
Request.QueryString("firstName")
Request.QueryString("lastName")
Request.QueryString("occupation")
```

Now that you understand the basics of the Request object, you will create the main WebAdventure document as an ASP document.

To create the main WebAdventure document as an ASP document:

1 Create a new document in your text editor or HTML editor.

2 Type the opening processing directive and <HTML>, <HEAD>, <TITLE>, and <BODY> sections of the document:

```
<%@ LANGUAGE=JScript %>
<HTML>
<HEAD>
<TITLE>Home Page</TITLE>
</HEAD>
<BODY>
```

3 Add the following heading tags:

```
<H2>WebAdventure Home Page</H2>
<H3>Welcome</H3>
```

4   Type the following paragraph, which uses the Request object with the output directive to insert the value of the first name text field from the StartPage.asp file:

```
<P>Hello <%= Request.Form("first") %>! Welcome to
WebAdventure, Inc. We are an industry leader in
JavaScript development. For more information, send
e-mail to <A HREF="mailto:information@webadventure.com">
information@webadventure.com</A>.</P>
<HR>
```

5   Add the following code to close the <BODY> and <HTML> tags:

```
</BODY>
</HTML>
```

6   Save the file as **HomePage.asp**, then copy and upload the file to your ASP server.

7   Open **StartPage.asp** in your Web browser from your ASP server. Enter your name in the First Name text box and click the **Continue** button to open HomePage.ASP. Figure 10-28 shows how the file appears in Internet Explorer. You can see that the name you typed in StartPage.asp has been inserted into HomePage.asp.

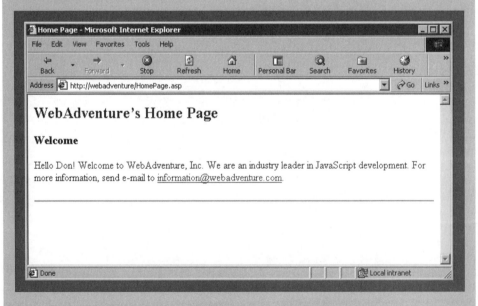

Figure 10-28: HomePage.asp in Internet Explorer

8   Close the Web browser window.

Response Object

The **Response object** sends output and information back to the client. You have used the Response object Write() method to send text back to the client. Although this book discusses only the Write() method, the Response object includes several other methods, as well as properties that are useful in constructing a response to return to the client. For example, the Response object redirect() method sends a client to a different Web page, in the same manner as the href property of the client-side JavaScript Location object.

The Response object is unique to ASP. SSJS uses only the global write() method to send output to the client. Note that many of the Response object methods and properties are equivalent to SSJS global methods.

> **tip**
>
> Visit the Microsoft Developer Network at *msdn.microsoft.com/* for a complete listing of the Response object properties and methods.

> **tip**
>
> The Response object contains a Cookies collection that is used for setting cookies on a client system. The cookies collection is the only collection contained in the Response object.

Session Object

A new Request object is instantiated each time a client requests an ASP URL, and then destroyed once the URL is delivered to the client. Like SSJS, an ASP application may be composed of multiple documents. Because the Request object is destroyed once the URL is delivered to the client, you cannot use the same Request object with different pages in an application. If you want to preserve client information across multiple pages in an ASP application, you must use the Session object. The **Session object** temporarily stores specific client information and makes that information available to all the pages in an ASP application. The ASP Session object is the equivalent of the SSJS Client object. A Session object is instantiated the first time a client accesses a URL in a given application.

You use the Contents collection of the Session object to store information about the user in your application. For example, you may store the values from the Request object Form collection in the Session object Contents collection in order to make the form information available across all the pages in an ASP application. However, you cannot directly assign the values from one collection to another collection using statements similar to `Session.Contents("name") = Request.Form("name");`. If you use the preceding code you will receive a compiler error because ASP will attempt to assign the entire Request.Form("name") *object* to the name variable of the Session object Contents collection. In order to force ASP to assign just the value of a collection variable, you must convert the variable to a string literal using the String() object. The syntax for converting a collection variable to a string literal is `String(object.collection("variable"));`. The following code shows an example of an ASP application that assigns the values of form fields to variables of the Session object Contents collection. The statements use String() objects to convert each variable in the Request object Form collection to string literals.

```
<%
Session.Contents("name")
     = String(Request.Form("name"));
Session.Contents("address")
     = String(Request.Form("address"));
Session.Contents("city")
     = String(Request.Form("city"));
Session.Contents("state")
     = String(Request.Form("state"));
Session.Contents("zip")
     = String(Request.Form("zip"));
Session.Contents("email")
     = String(Request.Form("email"));
%>
```

The Session object also includes a StaticObjects collection that represents objects created with an HTML document <OBJECT> tag.

The Session object includes several built-in properties that are listed in Figure 10-29.

Property	Description
CodePage	The character set used for a given language
LCID	Identifies a user's, region's, or application's preferred human language
SessionID	The user's session identification
Timeout	The lifespan of the Session object

Figure 10-29: Session object properties

One particularly useful property of the Session object is the **Timeout property,** which determines the lifespan of a Session object. The Timeout property is equivalent to the SSJS expiration() method. Like the SSJS Client object, the ASP Session object has a default lifespan of 10 minutes. The syntax for the Timeout property is `Session.Timeout = minutes;`. Note that the time is designated in minutes, not seconds as in the SSJS expiration() method. If you want to increase a Session object lifespan to 20 minutes, you use the statement `Session.Timeout = 20;`.

The Contents collection of the Session object also includes three methods: Abandon(), Remove(), and RemoveAll(). The Abandon() method completely destroys a Session object. The Remove() and RemoveAll() methods remove items from Session object collections.

Next you will add a property to the Session object for the WebAdventureHome program.

To add a property to the Session object for the WebAdventureHome program:

1 Open **HomePage.asp** in your text editor or HTML editor.

2 Above the </HEAD> tag, type the following server section, which contains a simple `if` statement that uses the logical not (!) operator to check if the sameSession variable exists in the Session object. If the sameSession variable does not exist, it is created and set to an initial value of true. The sameSession variable indicates that a client is working within the same session, regardless of whether it changes to a different page in the application. You will use this value later when creating the page hit counter.

```
<%
if (!Session.Contents("sameSession")) {
    Session.Contents("sameSession") = "true";
}
%>
```

3 Save the **HomePage.asp** file.

Application Object

An **Application** object is used for storing global application information that can be shared by all clients accessing the application. The ASP Application object is equivalent to the SSJS Project object. Each application has its own Application object. An ASP application automatically starts the first time a client requests one of the application pages. ASP applications run until the server is shut down.

You create your own variables for the Application object in its Contents collection. A common property that is created for the Application object is some type of unique number to identify clients. You can create a variable in the Application object Contents collection that keeps track of the last assigned number, and then use a function to update the number and assign it to a client. For example, you may have a Web application that takes online orders. Each time a client accesses the application, you want to assign a unique invoice number. The following code assigns to the curInvoiceNum variable the value of the lastInvoiceNum variable of the Application object Contents collection. The curInvoiceNum variable is then incremented by one. Then a new invoiceNum variable is created in the Session object Contents collection and assigned the value of the curInvoiceNum variable. You place this code in the first page of the online order application to assign an invoice number to a client that accesses the page.

```
<%
curInvoiceNum = Application.Contents("lastInvoiceNum");
curInvoiceNum = ++curInvoiceNum;
Application.Contents("lastInvoiceNum") = curInvoiceNum;
Session.Contents("invoiceNum") = curInvoiceNum;
%>
```

The Application object also has access to the Session object StaticObjects collection that represents objects created with HTML document <OBJECT> tags.

You can remove items from an Application object collection using the Remove() and RemoveAll() methods of the Contents collection.

The variables of the ASP Application object are available to all clients that access the application, and there is a possibility that one client may try to access a property before another client is through with it. To prevent one client from accessing a variable of the Application object until another client is through with it, you use the Application object Lock() and Unlock() methods, which perform the same functions as the SSJS lock() and unlock() methods. The **Lock() method** prevents other clients from accessing properties of the Application object, and the **Unlock() method** cancels the Lock() method. You place the `Application.Lock();` statement before any code that accesses Application object properties. You place the `Application.Unlock();` statement so it follows the last statement that accesses Application object properties. For example, to prevent data integrity problems with the lastInvoiceNum code example, you use the Lock() and Unlock() methods as follows:

```
<%
Application.Lock();
curInvoiceNum = Application.Contents("lastInvoiceNum");
curInvoiceNum = ++curInvoiceNum;
Application.Contents("lastInvoiceNum") = curInvoice;
Session.Contents("invoiceNum") = curInvoice;
Application.Unlock();
%>
```

Now that you understand how to preserve variables across multiple user sessions, you will add a number of hits counter to the HomePage.asp file.

To add a number of hits counter to the HomePage.asp file:

1 Return to **HomePage.asp** in your text editor or HTML editor.

2 In the ASP section, add the following statements above the `Session.Contents("sameClient") = "true";` statement. The first statement locks the application. The `if` statement uses a logical not (!) operator to check if the counter variable of the Application object exists. The counter variable will hold the number of hits the page receives. If the counter variable does not exist, it is created and assigned an initial value of one. If the counter variable does exist, its value is assigned to the curNumber variable, which increments it by one. The new value in the curNumber variable is then assigned to the counter variable. Finally, the application is unlocked.

```
Application.Lock();
if (!Application.Contents("counter"))
    Application.Contents("counter") = 1;
else {
    var curNumber = Application.Contents("counter");
    curNumber = ++curNumber;
    Application.Contents("counter") = curNumber;
}
Application.Unlock();
```

3 Next add the following code above the closing </BODY> tag to display the number of times the page has been accessed:

```
<B>This page has been accessed <%= Application.Contents
("counter")
%> times.</B>
<HR>
```

4 Save **HomePage.asp**, and then copy and upload the file to your ASP server.

5 Open **StartPage.asp** in Internet Explorer from your ASP Web server. Type your first name in the First Name text box, and press **Continue** to open HomePage.asp. The page counter should start at one. Figure 10-30 shows the page after it has been accessed twice.

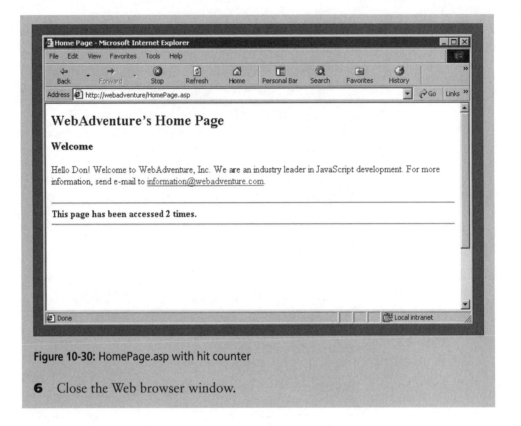

Figure 10-30: HomePage.asp with hit counter

6   Close the Web browser window.

Server Object

The **Server object** provides an ASP application with access to properties and methods that are accessible by all applications on the server. The ASP Server object does not contain any collections, and you cannot add custom variables to it. In contrast to the SSJS Server object, the ASP Server object is used mainly for managing the way an ASP application behaves on the server.

The ASP Server object includes a single property, ScriptTimeout. The **ScriptTimeout property** determines how long an ASP application can run before the server stops it. By default, a server allows an ASP application to run for 90 seconds. If you anticipate that your application will need more time to run, increase its running time, using the syntax `Server.ScriptTimeout = seconds;`. For example, to increase the maximum running time of an application to two minutes, use the statement `Server.ScriptTimeout = 120;`. The Server object also includes the methods listed in Figure 10-31.

Method	Description
CreateObject()	Instantiates a server component
Execute()	Executes an ASP file
GetLastError()	Returns an ASPError object, which describes an error condition that occurred
HTMLEncode()	Encodes a specified string using HTML encoding
MapPath()	Maps a relative or virtual path to the corresponding physical directory on a server
Transfer()	Sends the current ASP application collection variables and objects to another ASP application
URLEncode()	Formats a string with URL encoding

Figure 10-31: Server object methods

You will use several methods of the Server object in Tutorial 11 to access databases.

Creating a Guest Book

Next you will add a guest book to the ASP version of the WebAdventureHome program. You will save guest entries as variables in the Application object Contents collection. As with SSJS, saving guest entries in a core object is not the most efficient method of creating a guest book, because the list will be lost if you need to restart your server. A more efficient method is to save the entries to a database. However, the main purpose of this exercise is to understand how to work with ASP core objects. You will learn how to use ASP to read and write to databases in Tutorial 11.

First you will add some text and a form to HomePage.asp.

To add some text and a form to HomePage.asp:

1 Open **HomePage.asp** in your text editor or HTML editor.

2 Add the following tags and text above the closing </BODY> tag. The text includes a guestCounter variable of the Application object, which returns the number of people who have signed the guest book.

```
<H3>Guest Book</H3>
<P>Please join the other <%= Application.Contents("guest
Counter") %> people who have signed our guest book. We
have already entered your first name for you. Please
enter your last name and e-mail address, then click the
<B>I'm Finished</B> button. If you would like to see a
list of other people who have signed our guest book,
click the <B>See Who's Been Here</B> button.</P>
```

3 Next add the following form to be used for signing the guest book. The First Name text box uses the Request object to set the value of the first name text field to the value of the text field from StartPage.asp. The form ACTION attribute opens a SignGuestBook.asp file that will contain server-side JavaScript code that saves the form values in the guest book.

```
<P><FORM METHOD="post" ACTION="SignGuestBook.asp">
First Name: <INPUT TYPE="text" NAME="firstName" SIZE=10
VALUE=<%= Request.Form("first") %>>
Last Name: <INPUT TYPE="text" NAME="lastName">
E-mail: <INPUT TYPE="text" NAME="email">
<INPUT TYPE="submit" VALUE=" I'm finished ">
</FORM></P>
```

4 Create another form that will open a file named ShowGuestBook.asp. The ShowGuestBook.asp file will contain server-side JavaScript code that displays a list of the people who have signed the guest book.

```
<P><FORM METHOD="post" ACTION="ShowGuestBook.asp">
<INPUT TYPE="submit" VALUE=" See Who's Been Here ">
</FORM></P>
```

5 Save the **HomePage.asp** file, then copy and upload the file to your ASP server.

Next you will create the SignGuestBook.asp file.

To create the SignGuestBook.asp file:

1 Create a new document in your text editor or HTML editor.

2 Type the processing directive and opening <HTML> and <HEAD> sections of the document:

```
<%@ LANGUAGE=JScript %>
<HTML>
<HEAD>
<TITLE>Guest Book</TITLE>
```

3 Add the following ASP section. The first statement locks the application. Then an `if` statement with a logical not (!) operator checks if a guestCounter variable has been created in the Application object. The `if` statement creates the variable if it does not exist. The value of the guestCounter variable is then assigned to the curGuestNum variable, incremented by one, and then reassigned to the guestCounter variable. Another variable, curGuestInfo, is created to hold the first name, last name, and e-mail address of the guest signing the book. The statement `Application.Contents("guest" + curGuestNum) = curGuestInfo;` creates a new property in the Application object Contents collection to hold the current guest's information. The last statement in the server section unlocks the application.

```
<%
Application.Lock();
if (!Application.Contents("guestCounter"))
    Application.Contents("guestCounter") = 0;
var curGuestNum = Application.Contents("guestCounter");
curGuestNum = ++curGuestNum;
Application.Contents("guestCounter") = curGuestNum;
var curGuestInfo = Request.Form("firstName") + " "
    + Request.Form("lastName")
    + ", " + Request.Form("email");
Application.Contents("guest" + curGuestNum) =
curGuestInfo;
Application.Unlock();
%>
```

4 Add the following code to close the head section and open the body section:

```
</HEAD>
<BODY>
```

5 Type the following heading tag and form, which displays a customized message to the user, using the firstName property of the Request object Form collection. The form contains a single button that executes the history.back() method to return to HomePage.asp.

```
<H3>Thank you <%= Request.Form("firstName") %>! Your
name and e-mail address have been added to our guest
book.</H3>
<FORM>
<INPUT TYPE="button" VALUE="Return to WebAdventure's
Home Page"
    onClick="history.back();">
</FORM>
```

6   Add the following code to close the <BODY> and <HTML> tags:

```
</BODY>
</HTML>
```

7   Save the file as **SignGuestBook.asp** in the Tutorial.10 folder on your Data Disk, then copy and upload the file to your ASP server.

Finally, you will create the ShowGuestBook.asp file.

To create the ShowGuestBook.asp file:

1   Create a new document in your text editor or HTML editor.

2   Type the processing directive and opening <HTML>, <HEAD>, <TITLE>, and <BODY> sections of the document:

```
<%@ LANGUAGE=JScript %>
<HTML>
<HEAD>
<TITLE>Guest Book</TITLE>
</HEAD>
<BODY>
```

3   Add the following text and tags:

```
<H2>This is the Guest List</H2><HR>
<B>Name, E-Mail</B><BR>
```

4   Type the following server section, which locks and unlocks the application, and uses a for loop to return the contents of each guest variable in the Application object Contents collection:

```
<% Application.Lock();
var numGuests = Application.Contents("guestCounter");
for (var count = 1; count <= numGuests; ++count) {
    Response.Write(Application.Contents("guest" +
    count) + "<BR>");
}
Application.Unlock();
%><HR>
```

5   Type the following form, which contains a single button that executes the history.back() method to return to HomePage.asp.

```
<FORM>
<INPUT TYPE="button" VALUE="Return to WebAdventure's
Home Page"
    onClick="history.back();">
</FORM>
```

6   Add the following code to close the <BODY> and <HTML> tags:

```
</BODY>
</HTML>
```

7   Save the file as **ShowGuestBook.asp** in the Tutorial.10 folder on your Data Disk, then copy and upload the file to your ASP server.

8   Open **StartPage.asp** in Internet Explorer from your ASP Web server. Enter your first name and click the **Continue** button to open HomePage.asp. Fill in your last name and e-mail address, and then click the **I'm Finished** button to sign the guest book. Figure 10-32 shows SignGuestBook.asp in Internet Explorer.

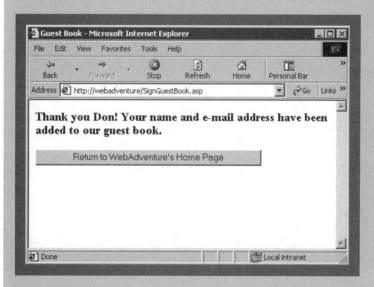

Figure 10-32: SignGuestBook.asp in Internet Explorer

9   Click the **Return to WebAdventure's Home Page** button to return to HomePage.asp, and then click the **See Who's Been Here** button to view a list of people who have signed the guest book. Figure 10-33 displays ShowGuestBook.asp after several guests have signed the book.

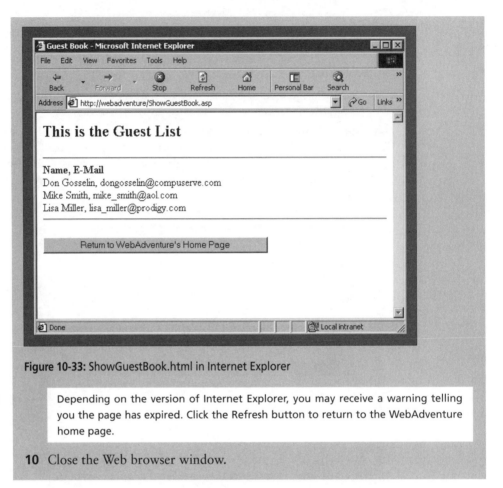

Figure 10-33: ShowGuestBook.html in Internet Explorer

help Depending on the version of Internet Explorer, you may receive a warning telling you the page has expired. Click the Refresh button to return to the WebAdventure home page.

10 Close the Web browser window.

S U M M A R Y

- The Microsoft version of server-side JavaScript is available in Active Server Pages, or ASP, which is a built-in feature of Microsoft Web servers.

- ASP automatically recognizes any changes to an ASP application and recompiles the application the next time a client requests it.

- You create ASP applications in files with an extension of .asp.

- The term ASP application refers to a collection of related ASP files that exist in the same root directory.

- ASP uses the script delimiters <% and %> to designate server-side JavaScript code. A delimiter is a character or a sequence of characters used to mark the beginning and end of a code segment.

- The RUNAT=SERVER attribute forces a <SCRIPT>...</SCRIPT> tag pair to run on the server.

- ASP directives are used for designating the scripting language used in an ASP file and for sending output to the browser.

- The ASP processing directive provides a Web server with information on how to process the scripts in an ASP document.

- The output directive sends the result of an expression to a Web browser.

- You can include HTML tags and text as part of server-side JavaScript decision-making structures such as `if...else` statements.

- Collections are data structures, similar to arrays, that store variables in ASP core objects.

- The Application object and Session object both contain separate Contents collections, which store custom variables.

- The count property returns the number of variables in a collection.

- The core ASP objects are Request, Response, Session, Application, and Server.

- The ASP Request object represents the current URL request from a client and is equivalent to the SSJS Request object. ASP creates a new Request object each time a client requests a URL.

- The Response object sends output and information back to the client.

- The Session object temporarily stores specific client information that is available to all the pages in an ASP application. The ASP Session object is the equivalent of the SSJS Client object. A Session object is instantiated the first time a client accesses a URL in a given application.

- An Application object is used for storing global application information that can be shared by all clients accessing the application. The ASP Application object is equivalent to the SSJS Project object.

- Each application has its own Application object.

- An ASP application starts automatically the first time a client requests one of the application's pages.

- The Lock() method prevents other clients from accessing properties of the Application object, and the Unlock() method cancels the Lock() method.

- The Server object provides an ASP application with access to properties and methods that are accessible by all applications on the server.

QUESTIONS

1. You add server-side JavaScript code to an HTML document in ASP applications using the _____ tags.
   a. <ASP>...</ASP>
   b. <%...%>
   c. <SERVERSCRIPT>...</SERVERSCRIPT>
   d. <ASPSERVER>...</ASPSERVER>

2. The _____ attribute forces a <SCRIPT>...</SCRIPT> tag pair to run on the server.
   a. RUNAT=SERVER
   b. SERVER=TRUE
   c. SERVERSIDE
   d. SERVEREXECUTE

3. Which is the correct syntax for creating a processing directive that sets the default scripting language to JScript?
   a. `<% LANG=JScript %>`
   b. `<%@ DEFAULT=JScript %>`
   c. `<% LANGUAGE=JScript %>`
   d. `<%@ LANGUAGE=JScript %>`

4. Where must you place a processing directive in an HTML file?
   a. in the first ASP scripting section
   b. within the <HEAD>...</HEAD> tag pair
   c. above the <HTML> tag
   d. immediately following the <HTML> tag

5. Which is the correct syntax for including the ASP Write() method inside an HTML tag?
   a. `<% Write("Hello World"); %>`
   b. `<%= Write("Hello World"); %>`
   c. `<% Response.Write("Hello World"); %>`
   d. `<%= Response.Write("Hello World"); %>`

6. How do you compile an ASP application?
   a. using jcompile
   b. using jsac
   c. using aspcomp
   d. by opening a file in the application

7. Which collection is found in both the Application and the Session objects?
   a. Contents
   b. Preferences
   c. Cookies
   d. Properties

8. Which object contains the Form collection?
   a. Request
   b. Response
   c. Session
   d. Application

9. Which of the following objects has the shortest lifespan?
   a. Request
   b. Response
   c. Session
   d. Application

10. How do you refer to a form field named "password," using the Request object?
    a. Request.password
    b. Request.Form.password
    c. Request.Form("password")
    d. Request.Contents("password")

11. Which method is used for changing the lifespan of a Session object?
    a. The timeout() method
    b. The Timeout property
    c. The lifespan property
    d. The Duration() method

12. In which object would you store an incremented invoice number that must be accessible to all users who access the ASP application?
    a. Request
    b. Session
    c. Application
    d. Server

13. Which method prevents other clients from accessing properties of the Application object or Server object?
    a. lock()
    b. Lock()
    c. frozen()
    d. Preserve()

EXERCISES

Save your solution files for each of the following exercises in their own folders within the Tutorial.10 folder on your Data Disk.

1. Modify the following JavaScript program so it runs on the server as an ASP program. Save the HTML document as ServerScript.html.

```
<SCRIPT LANGUAGE="JavaScript">
var sport = "golf";
if (sport == "golf")
  document.write(
    "Golf is played on a golf course.");
else if (sport == "tennis")
  document.write(
    "Tennis is played on a tennis court.");
else if (sport == "baseball")
  document.write(
    "Baseball is played on a baseball diamond.");
else if (sport == "basketball")
  document.write(
    "Basketball is played on a basketball court.");
</SCRIPT>
```

2. Create a simple program that uses an ASP Response.Write() statement to print *Printed from an ASP Program* to the screen. Save the HTML document as SimpleOutput.asp.

3. Create a document that uses ASP Response.Write() statements to print the names of five technology companies. Place each company name on its own line. Save the HTML document as LineBreaks.asp.

4. Create an HTML document that uses ASP Response.Write() statements to display six lines, with each line formatted using one of the six heading-level tags. Start with the largest tag and end with the smallest. Save the HTML document as HeadingTags.asp.

5. Create an HTML document that uses ASP Response.Write() statements to print the following text-formatting styles: bold, italic, big, small, strong, emphasized, superscript, and subscript. Save the HTML document as TextFormats.asp.

6. Create a document named SimpleForm.html with a simple form containing fields for first name, last name, and profession. The form should include a submit button that posts the form data to an SSJS document named ProcessForm.asp. The SSJS document ProcessForm.asp should use properties of the Request object to return a response to the user that displays the form information.

7. Replace the value assigned to the myEmail variable in the following code with your personal e-mail address. Then modify the <A> tag in the HTML section so it references the myEmail variable. After ASP returns the document to the user, the user should be able to click the <A> tag and send you a message. Save the document as ASPVariable.asp.

```
<HTML>
<HEAD>
<TITLE>ASP Variable</TITLE>
<%@ LANGUAGE="JScript" %>
<%
var myEmail = "your e-mail address"
%>
</HEAD>
<BODY>
<H2>ASP Variable </H2>
<P>Click <A>here</A> to send an e-mail.</P>
</BODY>
</HTML>
```

8. Create a generic ASP redirection page that you can use to send clients to pages other than the one they requested. You can add this page to your library of JavaScript tools. Use the ASP Response object redirect() method. Save the document as Redirection.asp.

9. Refer to the MSDN Library for information on the TextStream object, which is used for reading and writing files on the server. Modify the WebAdventure home page you created in this section so that the guest book information is saved to a server file.

10. There is no equivalent to the ECMAScript standard for server-side JavaScript. Search the Internet and read the Netscape SSJS and the Microsoft ASP documentation for information on the topic of a standard for server-side JavaScript. Why is there no sever-side standard? Is a server-side JavaScript standard in the works?

11. What common functionality and objects do client-side and server-side JavaScript support? Write a one-page report using both SSJS and ASP in your analysis.

12. ASP debugging is handled by the Microsoft Script Debugger tool. Read the Script Debugger documentation and write a short paper describing the techniques for debugging an ASP application and the way the techniques differ from debugging client-side JavaScript.

Database Connectivity

case ▶ WebAdventure is starting a training program that will teach various Web development subjects, including client-side JavaScript, SSJS, and Active Server Pages. Your manager at WebAdventure has asked you to create an online registration program that stores student and class enrollment information in a server database. To create the registration program, you need to learn how to use SSJS and Active Server Pages to access databases.

Previewing the Registration Program

In this tutorial, you will use SSJS and ASP to create an online registration program for WebAdventure's computer courses. Note that this Tutorial builds on the SSJS and ASP versions of server-side JavaScript covered in Tutorial 10. Be sure you thoroughly understand basic SSJS and ASP concepts before starting this tutorial.

The registration program works in conjunction with a database. SSJS and ASP have different mechanisms for accessing databases. In Section A, you will learn how to access databases with SSJS; in Section B, you will learn how to access databases with ASP.

You can think of the registration program as a type of online shopping cart that can be modified for use in electronic commerce, or e-commerce, applications. Figure 11-1 shows an example of the first page of the registration program in Netscape.

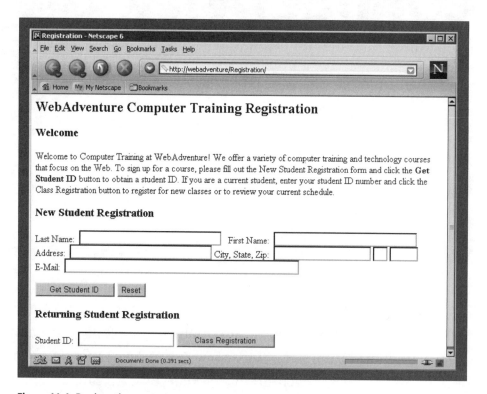

Figure 11-1: Registration program

tip

Actual e-commerce applications that accept credit card payments are set up on secure servers and use many advanced security protocols. The registration program you will create in this tutorial covers only the basics of how to use server-side JavaScript to read from and write to a database. For information on e-commerce security and strategies, look up the word *commerce* or the word *e-commerce* on the Netscape developer site, DevEdge Online, at *developer.netscape.com/* and on the Microsoft Developer Network at *msdn.microsoft.com/*.

In this section you will learn:

- About basic database structure
- About database management systems
- About structured query language
- About the SSJS Database object
- How to execute SQL commands with SSJS
- How to perform transaction processing with SSJS
- How to handle database errors with SSJS

Overview of Databases and Connecting to Databases with SSJS

Understanding Databases

Your goal for this tutorial is to learn how to use server-side JavaScript (SSJS and ASP) to read, write, and modify database information. To accomplish this goal, it helps to understand how databases work. Formally defined, a **database** is an ordered collection of information from which a computer program can quickly access information. You can probably think of many databases in your everyday life. For example, your address book is a database. So is the card file containing recipes in a kitchen. Other examples of databases include a company's employee directory and a file cabinet containing client information. Essentially, any information that can be organized into ordered sets of data and then quickly retrieved, can be considered a database. A collection of hundreds of baseball cards thrown into a shoebox is not a database, since an individual card cannot be quickly or easily retrieved (except by luck). However, if the baseball card collection were organized in binders by team, and further organized according to each player's field position or batting average, then it could be considered a database, since you could fairly quickly locate a specific card.

The information stored in computer databases is actually stored in tables similar to spreadsheets. Each row in a database table is called a record. A **record** in a database contains a single complete set of related information. Each recipe in a recipe database, for instance, is a single database record. The individual pieces of information stored in a record are called **fields**. Examples of fields that may exist in a recipe database include ingredients, cooking time, and cooking temperature.

To summarize, you can think of databases as consisting of tables, which consist of records, which consist of fields. Figure 11-2 shows an example of an employee directory for programmers at WebAdventure, Inc. The database consists of five records, one for each employee. Each record consists of seven fields: Last_Name, First_Name, Address, City, State, Zip, and Extension.

fields

records

Last_Name	First_Name	Address	City	State	Zip	Extension
Blair	Dennis	204 Spruce Lane	Brockfield	MA	01506	x305
Hernandez	Louis	68 Boston Post Road	Spencer	MA	01562	x412
Miller	Erica	271 Baker Hill Road	E. Brookfield	MA	01515	x291
Morinaga	Scott	17 Ashley Road	N. Brookfield	MA	01535	x177
Picard	Raymond	1113 Oakham Road	New Braintree	MA	01531	x213

Figure 11-2: Employee directory database

The database in Figure 11-2 is an example of a flat-file database, one of the simplest types of databases. A **flat-file database** stores information in a single table. For fairly simple collections of information, flat-file databases are usually adequate. With large and complex collections of information, flat-file databases can become unwieldy. A better solution for large and complex databases is a relational database. A **relational database** stores information across multiple related tables. Although you will not actually work with a relational database in this tutorial, understanding how they work is helpful, since relational databases are among the most common in use today.

 tip

Two other types of database systems you may encounter are hierarchical databases and network databases.

Relational databases consist of one or more related tables. In fact, large relational databases can consist of dozens or hundreds of related tables. Although relational databases may consist of many tables, you create relationships within the database by working with two tables at a time. One table in a relationship is always considered to be the primary table, whereas the other table is considered to be the related table. A **primary table** is the main table in a relationship that is referenced by another table. A **related**, or **child table** references a primary table in a relational database. Tables in a relationship are connected using primary and foreign keys. A **primary key** is a field that contains a unique identifier for each record in a primary table. A **foreign key** is a field in a related table that refers to the primary key in a primary table. Primary and foreign keys are what link records across multiple tables in a relational database.

There are three types of relationships within a relational database: one-to-one, one-to-many, and many-to-many. A **one-to-one relationship** exists between two tables when each record in a related table contains exactly one record for each record in the primary table. You create one-to-one relationships when you want to break information into multiple, logical sets. It is important to understand that information in the tables in a one-to-one relationship can also usually be placed within a single table. However, you may want to break the information into multiple tables to better organize the information into logical sets. Another reason for one-to-one relationships is that the information in one of the tables may be confidential and accessible only to certain individuals. For example, you may want to create a personnel table that contains basic information about an employee, similar to the information in the table in Figure 11-2. You may also want to create a payroll table that contains confidential information about each employee's salary, benefits, and other types of compensation, and that can be accessed only by the Human Resources and accounting departments. Figure 11-3 shows two tables, Employees and Payroll, with a one-to-one relationship. The primary table is the employee information table from Figure 11-2. The related table is a payroll table that contains confidential salary and compensation information. Notice that each table contains identical numbers of records; one record in the primary table corresponds to one record in the related table. The relationship is achieved by adding a primary key to the Employees table and a foreign key to the Payroll table.

Employees table

Primary key

ID	Last_Name	First_Name	Address	City	State	Zip	Extension
101	Blair	Dennis	204 Spruce Lane	Brookfield	MA	01506	x305
102	Hernandez	Louis	68 Boston Post Road	Spencer	MA	01562	x412
103	Miller	Erica	271 Baker Hill Road	E. Brookfield	MA	01515	x291
104	Morinaga	Scott	17 Ashley Road	N. Brookfield	MA	01535	x177
105	Picard	Raymond	1113 Oakham Road	New Braintree	MA	01531	x213

Payroll table

Foreign key

ID	Start_Date	Pay_Rate	Health_Coverage	Year_Vested	401K
101	1998	$21.25	No Coverage	NA	No
102	1993	$28.00	Family Plan	1998	Yes
103	1996	$24.50	Individual	NA	Yes
104	1991	$36.00	Family Plan	1996	Yes
105	1992	$31.00	Individual	1997	Yes

Figure 11-3: One-to-one relationship

A **one-to-many relationship** exists in a relational database when one record in a primary table has many related records in a related table. Primary and foreign keys are the only pieces of information in a relational database table that should be duplicated. You create a one-to-many relationship in order to eliminate redundant information in a single table. Breaking tables into multiple related tables in order to reduce redundant and duplicate information is called **normalization**. The elimination of redundant information (normalization) reduces the size of a database and makes the data easier to work with. For example, consider the table in Figure 11-4. The table lists each WebAdventure programmer's primary and other programming languages. Notice that each programmer's name is repeated for each programming language that he or she is familiar with. This repetition is an example of redundant information that can occur in a single table.

ID	Last_Name	First_Name	Programming_Language
101	Blair	Dennis	Client-Side JavaScript
101	Blair	Dennis	Server-Side JavaScript
102	Hernandez	Louis	Client-Side JavaScript
102	Hernandez	Louis	Server-Side JavaScript
102	Hernandez	Louis	CGI
103	Miller	Erica	Client-Side JavaScript
103	Miller	Erica	Server-Side JavaScript
103	Miller	Erica	CGI
103	Miller	Erica	Perl
104	Morinaga	Scott	Client-Side JavaScript
104	Morinaga	Scott	CGI
104	Morinaga	Scott	Perl
105	Picard	Raymond	Client-Side JavaScript
105	Picard	Raymond	CGI

Figure 11-4: Table with redundant information

A one-to-many relationship provides a more efficient and less redundant method of storing this information in a database. Figure 11-5 shows the same information organized into a one-to-many relationship.

"One" side

ID	Last_Name	First_Name
101	Blair	Dennis
102	Hernandez	Louis
103	Miller	Erica
104	Morinaga	Scott
105	Picard	Raymond

"Many" side

ID	Programming_Language
101	Client-Side JavaScript
101	Server-Side JavaScript
102	Client-Side JavaScript
102	Server-Side JavaScript
102	CGI
103	Client-Side JavaScript
103	Server-Side JavaScript
103	CGI
103	Perl
104	Client-Side JavaScript
104	CGI
104	Perl
105	Client-Side JavaScript
105	CGI

Figure 11-5: One-to-many relationship

tip

The "many" side of a one-to-many relationship is sometimes used as the primary table. In these cases, the relationship is often referred to as a many-to-one relationship.

Although Figure 11-5 is an example of a one-to-many relationship, the tables are not normalized, since the Programming_Language field contains duplicate values. Recall that primary and foreign keys are the only pieces of information in a relational database that should be duplicated. To further reduce repetition, you could organize the "many" table in Figure 11-5 into another one-to-many relationship. However, a better choice is to create a many-to-many relationship. A **many-to-many relationship** exists in a relational database when many records in one table are related to many records in another table. Consider the relationship between programmers and programming languages. Each programmer can work with many programming languages, and each programming language can be used by many programmers. To create a many-to-many relationship, you must use a junction table, since most relational database systems cannot work directly with many-to-many relationships. A **junction table** creates a one-to-many relationship for each of the two tables in a many-to-many relationship. A junction table contains foreign keys from the two tables in a many-to-many relationship, along with any other fields that correspond to a many-to-many relationship. Figure 11-6 contains an example of a many-to-many relationship between a Programmers table and a Programming Languages table. The Programmers table contains a primary key named Programmer_ID, and the Programming Languages table contains a primary key named Language_ID. A junction table named Programming Experience contains two foreign keys corresponding to the Programmer_ID primary key in the Programmers table and the Language_ID in the Programming Languages table. The Programming Experience junction table also contains a field named Years_Experience. You add records to the Programming Experience junction table to build a list of the years that each programmer has been working with a particular programming language.

Programmers table

Programmer_ID	Last_Name	First_Name
101	Blair	Dennis
102	Hernandez	Louis
103	Miller	Erica
104	Morinaga	Scott
105	Picard	Raymond

Programming Languages table

Language_ID	Programming_Language
10	Client-Side JavaScript
11	Server-Side JavaScript
12	CGI
13	Perl

Programming Experience junction table

Programmer_ID	Language_ID	Years_Experience
101	10	5
101	11	4
102	10	3
102	11	2
102	12	3
103	10	2
104	12	3
104	13	5
105	11	3

Figure 11-6: Many-to-many relationship

Database Management Systems

With a grasp of basic database design, you can now begin to consider how to create and manipulate databases. An application or collection of applications used to create, access, and manage a database is called a **database management system**, or **DBMS**. Database management systems run on many different platforms, ranging from personal computers, to client-server systems, to mainframes. Different database management systems exist for different types of database formats. A database management system that stores data in a flat-file format is called a **flat-file database management system**. A database management system that stores data in a relational format is called a **relational database management system**, or **RDBMS**. Other types of database management systems include hierarchical and network database management systems. Some of the more popular relational database management systems you may have heard of include Oracle, Sybase, Informix, and DB2 for mainframes, and Access, FoxPro, and Paradox for PCs.

Database management systems perform many of the same functions as other types of applications you may have worked with, such as word-processing and spreadsheet programs. For example, database management systems create new database files and contain interfaces that allow users to enter and manipulate data. One of the most important functions of a database management system is the organization of the database file structure. Additionally, a database management system must ensure that data is stored correctly in the database tables, regardless of the database format (flat-file, relational, hierarchical, or network). For example, in relational databases, the database management system ensures that the appropriate information is entered according to the relationship structure in the database tables. Many DBMS systems also have security features that can be used to restrict user access to specific types of data.

Two other important aspects of database management systems are their querying and reporting capabilities. A **query** is a structured set of instructions and criteria for retrieving, adding, modifying, and deleting database information. A **report** is the formatted, printed output of a database table or the results of a query. Most database management systems use a **data manipulation language**, or **DML**, for creating queries. Different database management systems support different data manipulation languages. However, **structured query language**, or **SQL** (pronounced like the word *sequel*), has become somewhat of a standard data manipulation language among many database management systems.

Many database management systems make it easier for users to create queries by hiding the data manipulation language behind a user interface. Figure 11-7 shows an example of the Access query design screen. Users can create queries by dragging fields from the table objects in the upper portion of the screen to the criteria grid in the bottom portion of the screen. Behind the scenes, Access creates the SQL code shown in Figure 11-8. SQL is the Access data manipulation language.

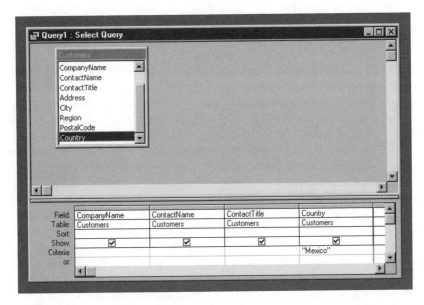

Figure 11-7: Access query design screen

```
SELECT Customers.CompanyName, Customers.ContactName, Customers.ContactTitle
FROM Customers
WHERE (((Customers.Country)="Mexico"));
```

Figure 11-8: Access SQL code

Although working with an interface to design queries is fine for end users, to programmatically manipulate the data in a database, you must learn the database management system data manipulation language. For example, when accessing databases with server-side JavaScript, you must use a data manipulation language. Because SQL is the underlying data manipulation language for many database management systems, you will learn more about SQL later in this section so that you can work with server-side JavaScript and databases.

tip

Many database management systems also utilize a data definition language, or DDL, for creating databases, tables, fields, and other components of a database.

It is important to understand that even though many database management systems support the same database format (flat-file, relational, hierarchical, or network), each database management system is an individual application that creates its own proprietary file types. For example, even though Access and Paradox are both relational database management systems, Access creates its database files in a proprietary format with an extension of .mdb, while Paradox creates its database files in a proprietary format with an extension of .db. Although both Paradox and Access contain filters that allow you to import each other's file formats, the database files are not completely interchangeable between the two programs. This situation occurs for most database management systems: They can *import* each other's file formats, but they cannot directly *read* each other's files. The proprietary nature of database management systems means that to create a JavaScript application to access a particular database management system file format, you must write the application specifically for that database management system.

It is often necessary for an application to access multiple databases created in different database management systems. For example, a company may need a server-side JavaScript application that simultaneously accesses a large legacy database written in dBase and a newer database written in Oracle. Converting the large dBase database to Oracle would be cost prohibitive. On the other hand, the company's needs have grown beyond the older dBase database's capabilities, and it cannot continue using the older database. Still, the company must be able to access the data in both systems. To allow easy access to data in various database formats, Microsoft came up with the open database connectivity standard. **Open database connectivity**, or **ODBC**, allows applications written to comply with the standard to access any data source for which there is an ODBC driver. ODBC uses SQL commands (known as ODBC SQL) to allow an ODBC-compliant application to access a database. Essentially, an ODBC application connects to a database for which there is an ODBC driver and then executes ODBC SQL commands. Then, the ODBC driver translates the SQL commands into a format that the database can understand. SSJS and ASP are both ODBC-compliant applications, allowing you to access any database for which an ODBC driver exists.

In this tutorial you will work with an existing Microsoft Access database named WebAdventureCourses.mdb. Since Access databases are ODBC-compliant, they can be used with both SSJS and ASP. The WebAdventureCourses.mdb database consists of two tables: Students and Registration. The Students table will contain each student's ID and name, along with other personal information. The Registration table will contain a record for each class a student enrolls in. The Students table is the primary table, and the Student_ID field acts as the primary key. The Student_ID field also acts as the foreign key in the Registration table. Since each student can enroll in more than one class, the relationship between the Students table and the Registration table is one-to-many; the Students table is the one side of the relationship, and the Registration table is the many side of the relationship. If you would like to examine the tables in the WebAdventureCourses.mdb database, you can open the database file in Access from the Tutorial.11 folder on your Data Disk.

To make it easier to access ODBC-compliant databases on 32-bit Windows operating systems, such as Windows NT and Windows 98, you create a Data Source Name to locate and identify the database. A **Data Source Name**, or **DSN**, contains configuration information that Windows operating systems use to access a particular ODBC-compliant database. If your iPlanet Web Server is running on a Windows platform, you must set up a DSN to perform the SSJS exercises in this section. You must also set up a DSN to perform the ASP exercises in Section B.

If you are running an iPlanet Web Server on an operating system other than a Windows operating system, refer to the Netscape SSJS documentation at *developer.netscape.com/* for information on connecting to ODBC-compliant databases for your particular platform.

The DSNs to which you can connect in a Windows environment are installed and managed using the ODBC Administrator utility in Control Panel. For SSJS to access data sources in a Windows environment, you must be using ODBC Administrator version 3.5, which includes the latest drivers for ODBC data sources, including Access. You can install ODBC Administrator version 3.5 on your Windows operating system by downloading WX1350.exe from the Microsoft Web site.

There are three types of DSNs: system, user, and file. The system DSN enables all users logged on to a server to access a database. A user DSN restricts database access to authorized users only. A file DSN creates a file-based data source, with an extension of .dsn, that can be shared among users. You will create system DSNs in this tutorial. For the SSJS version of this program, you will create a system DSN named WebAdventureSSJS.

You cannot use a file DSN with SSJS.

To create a system DSN for the SSJS database program:

1   Click the Windows **Start** menu, then select **Control Panel** from the Settings folder.

2   Depending on how your desktop is configured, click or double-click the **ODBC** icon from the Control Panel window. For some Windows operating systems, including Windows 2000, the ODBC icon is located in the Administrative Tools folder.

> Depending on your version of Windows, the ODBC icon in the Control Panel window may have a different caption. For example, in Windows 98, the caption for the ODBC icon reads *ODBC Data Sources (32bit)*. In Windows 2000, the caption for the ODBC icon reads *Data Sources (ODBC)*.

3   In the ODBC Data Source Administrator window, select the **System DSN** tab, then click the **Add** button. In the window that appears, select **Microsoft Access Driver (*.mdb)** and click the **Finish** button.

4 In the ODBC Microsoft Access Setup window, type **WebAdventureSSJS** as the name of the new DSN file, then click the **Select** button. In the Select Database dialog box that appears, select the **WebAdventureCourses.mdb** file from the Tutorial.11 folder on your Data Disk and click **OK**. The Select Database dialog box will close.

5 Click **OK** to close the Microsoft Access Setup dialog box, and then click **OK** to close the ODBC Data Source Administrator window. Finally, close **Control Panel** or Administrative Tools.

Next you will create the main RegistrationSSJS.html document. The RegistrationSSJS.html file is the first Web page students will see when they access the WebAdventure registration Web site. The document contains only HTML text and forms, and does not contain any client-side or server-side JavaScript code. RegistrationSSJS.html will use each form submit button to call SSJS documents that access the database.

To create the main RegistrationSSJS.html document:

1 Start your text editor or HTML editor and create a new document.

2 Type the opening <HTML>, <HEAD>, and <BODY> sections of the document:

```
<HTML>
<HEAD>
<TITLE>Registration</TITLE>
</HEAD>
<BODY>
```

3 Add the following tags, text, and forms that make up the document. The two forms each use submit buttons to call SSJS documents. The first form calls the GetStudentIDSSJS.html SSJS document, which assigns student IDs. The second form calls the CourseListingSSJS.html document, which existing students use to register for new classes or to review their current schedule. Later in this section, you will create the SSJS documents that are called by the submit buttons.

```
<H2>WebAdventure Computer Training Registration</H2>
<H3>Welcome</H3>
<P>Welcome to Computer Training at WebAdventure! We
offer a variety of computer training and technology
courses that focus on the Web. To sign up for a course,
please fill out the New Student Registration form and
click the <B>Get Student ID</B> button to obtain a
student ID. If you are a current student, enter your
student ID number and click the Class Registration
button to register for new classes or to review your
current schedule.</P>
<H3>New Student Registration</H3>
```

```
<FORM NAME="customerInfo" METHOD="post"
      ACTION="GetStudentIDSSJS.html">
<P>Last Name:  <INPUT TYPE="text" NAME="last_name"
            SIZE=30>  
First Name:  <INPUT TYPE="text" NAME="first_name"
            SIZE=30><BR>
Address:  <INPUT TYPE="text" NAME="address" SIZE=30>
      City, State, Zip:  <INPUT TYPE="text"
      NAME="city" SIZE=20>
<INPUT TYPE="text" NAME="state" SIZE=2 MAXLENGTH=2>
<INPUT TYPE="text" NAME="zip" SIZE=5 MAXLENGTH=5><BR>
E-Mail:  <INPUT TYPE="text" NAME="email" SIZE=50></P>
<INPUT TYPE="submit" NAME="submit"
      VALUE=" Get Student ID ">
<P><INPUT TYPE="reset"></P>
</FORM>
<H3>Returning Student Registration</H3>
<FORM METHOD="post" ACTION="CourseListingSSJS.html">
      Student ID:  <INPUT TYPE="text" NAME="id">
<INPUT TYPE="submit" VALUE=" Class Registration ">
</FORM>
```

4 Add the following code to close the <BODY> and <HTML> tags:

```
</BODY>
</HTML>
```

5 Save the file as **RegistrationSSJS.html** in the **Tutorial.11** folder on your Data Disk, and open it in Netscape. Your document should look similar to the document in Netscape shown in Figure 11-9. Later in this section, you will compile RegistrationSSJS.html and the other files that make up the registration program into an SSJS application. You need to create the SSJS documents before you execute the form buttons.

WebAdventure Computer Training Registration

Welcome

Welcome to Computer Training at WebAdventure! We offer a variety of computer training and technology courses that focus on the Web. To sign up for a course, please fill out the New Student Registration form and click the **Get Student ID** button to obtain a student ID. If you are a current student, enter your student ID number and click the Class Registration button to register for new classes or to review your current schedule.

New Student Registration

Last Name: [   ]   First Name: [   ]
Address: [   ]   City, State, Zip: [   ] [ ] [ ]
E-Mail: [   ]

[Submit Query] [Reset]

Returning Student Registration

Student ID: [   ]   [Class Registration]

Document: Done (1.252 secs)

Figure 11-9: RegistrationSSJS.html in Netscape

6   Close the Web browser window.

Structured Query Language

IBM invented SQL in the 1970s as a way of querying databases for specific criteria. Since then SQL has been adopted by numerous database management systems running on mainframes, minicomputers, and PCs. In 1986, the American National Standards Institute, or ANSI, approved an official standard for the SQL language. In 1991, The X/Open and SQL Access Group created a standardized version of SQL known as the Common Applications Environment (CAE) SQL draft specification. Even with two major standards available, however, most database management systems use their own version of the SQL language. ODBC SQL corresponds to the X/Open and SQL Access Group CAE SQL draft specification.

 tip

If you ever work directly with an individual database management system, keep in mind that the ODBC SQL you learn in this tutorial may not correspond directly to that database management system's version of SQL.

SQL uses fairly easy-to-understand statements to execute database commands. SQL statements are composed of keywords that perform actions on a database. Figure 11-10 lists several SQL keywords that are common to most versions of SQL.

Keyword	Description
FROM	Specifies the tables from which to retrieve or delete records
SELECT	Returns information from a database
WHERE	Specifies the conditions that must be met for records to be returned from a query
ORDER BY	Sorts the records returned from a database
INSERT	Inserts a new row into a database table
INTO	Determines the table into which records should be inserted
DELETE	Deletes a row from a database table
UPDATE	Saves changes to fields in a record

Figure 11-10: Common SQL keywords

The simple SQL statement SELECT * FROM Programmers selects all records (using the asterisk * wildcard) from the Programmers table. The following code shows a more complex SQL statement, which selects the Last_Name and First_Name fields from the Programmers table if the record City field is equal to Spencer. The results are then sorted by the Last_Name and First_Name fields, using the ORDER BY keyword.

```
SELECT Last_Name, First_Name FROM Programmers
WHERE City = "Spencer " ORDER BY Last_Name, First_Name
```

When you use ODBC SQL with server-side JavaScript, the SQL statements are created as text strings that are executed as parameters of SSJS and ASP methods. For example, the SSJS database object includes a SQLTable method that executes a SQL string. The preceding code is executed in SSJS, using the following statements. The first statement assigns the SQL string to a variable named SQLString, and the second statement executes the string, using the SQLTable method.

```
var SQLString =
    "SELECT Last_Name, First_Name FROM Programmers
    WHERE City = 'Spencer' ORDER BY Last_Name, First_Name ";
database.SQLTable(SQLString);
```

You will learn how to use several of the basic ODBC SQL keywords in this tutorial. For in-depth information on ODBC SQL, visit the Microsoft Developer Network at *msdn.microsoft.com/*.

Before you learn how to access databases with SSJS, you need to create an HTML document called CourseListingSSJS.html. Students of WebAdventure's computer training division will use the CourseListingSSJS.html file to select courses they want to take and to review their current schedule. CourseListingSSJS.html consists of two forms. The first form allows students to review their current schedule, and the second form allows students to register for new classes. The SSJS documents that are called with each form submit button contain the necessary functionality to read from and write to the registration database.

To create the CourseListingSSJS.html file:

1 Create a new document in your text editor or HTML editor.

2 Type the opening <HTML>, <HEAD>, and <TITLE> tags:

```
<HTML>
<HEAD>
<TITLE>Home Page</TITLE>
```

3 Type the following <SERVER> section. The `if` statement checks if the id property exists in the Request object. If the id property exists, it is assigned to the studentID property of the Client object. The Request object id property contains the value that students enter into the id field of the Registration form. You will use the studentID property throughout the registration program to keep track of users as they navigate through the pages that make up the program.

```
<SERVER>
if (request.id)
        client.studentID = request.id;
</SERVER>
```

help

> The Client object temporarily stores specific client information that is available to all the pages in an SSJS application. The Request object takes all of the named elements in a form on the client browser and appends them as properties of the Request object. You first used the Client and Request objects in Tutorial 10.

4 Add the closing **</HEAD>** tag.

5 Add the following HTML tags, text, and form. The form contains two elements that are used for displaying a student's schedule. The student's ID is printed to the screen inside the form, using <SERVER>...</SERVER> tags.

```
<BODY>
<H3>Course Registration Form</H3>
<FORM METHOD="post" ACTION="ReviewScheduleSSJS.html">
<P><B>Student ID:  <SERVER> write(client.studentID)
```

```
</SERVER></B>
<INPUT TYPE="submit" VALUE=" Review Current Schedule ">
</P>
</FORM>
```

6 Type the next form, which students use to register for classes. The form information is submitted to SSJS in a file named RegisterStudentSSJS.html.

```
<FORM METHOD="post" ACTION="RegisterStudentSSJS.html">
<P><B>Select the course you would like to take:</B><BR>
<INPUT TYPE="radio" NAME="course"
  VALUE="Introduction to Active Server Pages 4.0">
  Introduction to Active Server Pages<BR>
<INPUT TYPE="radio" NAME="course"
  VALUE="Introduction to JavaScript">
  Introduction to JavaScript<BR>
<INPUT TYPE="radio" NAME="course"
  VALUE="Introduction to SSJS">
  Introduction to SSJS<BR>
<INPUT TYPE="radio" NAME="course"
  VALUE="Intermediate Active Server Pages 4.0">
  Intermediate Active Server Pages<BR>
<INPUT TYPE="radio" NAME="course"
  VALUE="Intermediate JavaScript">
  Intermediate JavaScript<BR>
<INPUT TYPE="radio" NAME="course"
  VALUE="Intermediate SSJS 98">
  Intermediate SSJS<BR>
<INPUT TYPE="radio" NAME="course"
  VALUE="Advanced Active Server Pages">
  Advanced Active Server Pages<BR>
<INPUT TYPE="radio" NAME="course"
  VALUE="Advanced JavaScript">
  Advanced JavaScript<BR>
<INPUT TYPE="radio" NAME="course"
  VALUE="Advanced SSJS"> Advanced SSJS<P/>
<P><B>Available Days and Times:</B><BR>
<SELECT NAME="days">
<OPTION SELECTED VALUE="Mondays and Wednesdays">
  Mondays and Wednesdays
<OPTION VALUE="Tuesdays and Thursdays">
  Tuesdays and Thursdays
<OPTION VALUE="Wednesdays and Fridays">
  Wednesdays and Fridays
</SELECT>
  <SELECT NAME="time">
  <OPTION SELECTED VALUE="9 am-11 am">
```

```
      9 am-11 am
<OPTION VALUE="1 pm-3 pm">
   1 pm-3 pm
<OPTION VALUE="6 pm-8 pm">
   6 pm-8 pm
</SELECT></P>
<INPUT TYPE="submit" VALUE=" Register " >
<INPUT TYPE="reset">
</FORM>
```

7 Add the following code to close the <BODY> and <HTML> tags:

```
</BODY>
</HTML>
```

8 Save the file as **CourseListingSSJS.html** in the **Tutorial.11** folder on your Data Disk and then close it. Before you can open the file, you need to write an SSJS script that generates new student IDs.

The LiveWire Database Service

SSJS database access is enabled through a library of objects known as the LiveWire Database Service, or LiveWire. LiveWire is built into iPlanet Web Servers and includes three objects for accessing databases: the DbPool, Connection, and Database objects. The **DbPool** and **Connection** objects are used for creating and managing pools of database connections. The **Database** object is used for creating and managing single connections between a client and a database. This book discusses only single-user database connectivity using the Database object.

See the Netscape LiveWire documentation for information on working with database connection pools.

The Database object does not contain any properties, only various methods for accessing and manipulating databases. Figure 11-11 lists the methods of the Database object.

Method	Description
beginTransaction()	Begins a SQL transaction
commitTransaction()	Saves the current SQL transaction
connect()	Connects to a database
connected()	Returns a value of true if a database connection was successful

Figure 11-11: Database object methods

Method	Description
cursor()	Creates a database cursor for the specified SQL statements
disconnect()	Closes a database connection
execute()	Sends SQL statements to the database management system for processing
majorErrorCode()	Returns a major error code generated by ODBC or the database server
majorErrorMessage()	Returns a major error message generated by ODBC or the database server
minorErrorCode()	Returns a minor error code generated by ODBC or the database server
minorErrorMessage()	Returns a minor error message generated by ODBC or the database server
rollbackTransaction()	Reverses the current SQL transaction
SQLTable()	Executes SQL statements and returns the results as an HTML table

Figure 11-11: Database object methods (*continued*)

The first step in working with a LiveWire database is to create a connection to the database, using the connect() method. The syntax for the connect() method is `database.connect("database type", "server name", "user name", "password", "database name");`. The *database type* argument designates the type of database you are accessing. Valid arguments for the *database type* are DB2, ODBC, ORACLE, INFORMIX, and SYBASE. The *server name* argument indicates the name of the server where the database is located. For ODBC connections on Windows platforms, use the DSN name you defined in Control Panel. The *user name* and *password* arguments indicate a username and password on the server. The *database name* argument is valid for only Informix and Sybase databases. For DB2, ODBC, and Oracle databases, the *database name* argument must be an empty string. Once you are finished working with a database, use the disconnect() method to end the connection. The following statement is an example of how to connect to and disconnect from a Sybase database named Accounting on a server named Server1.

```
database.connect(
"SYBASE", "Server1", "don", "1X347", "Accounting");
additional statements;
database.disconnect();
```

If your database does not support an argument of the connect() method, include an empty string for each unsupported argument. For example, in this tutorial, you are working with the WebAdventureSSJS DSN, which is an ODBC database. With ODBC databases, you do not need to use any connect() method arguments other than *database type* and *server name*. Therefore, to connect to the WebAdventureSSJS DSN, you use the following statement:

```
database.connect("ODBC", "WebAdventureSSJS", "", "", "");
```

It is good practice to make sure you have connected to a database successfully before attempting to read, write, add, or modify records. The connected() method of the Database object returns a boolean value of true if a database connection was successful. The following code adds an **if** statement that checks the connected() method after attempting to connect to a database. If the connection was unsuccessful, then the SSJS write() method returns a message to the client. If the connection is successful, the **else** clause executes necessary statements to perform the desired actions against the database before disconnecting.

```
database.connect(
"SYBASE", "Server1", "don", "1X347", "Accounting");
if (!database.connected())
    write("The database is not available.");
else {
    additional statements;
    database.disconnect();
}
```

Your SSJS application can use LiveWire to access a database using either a standard connection or a serial connection. A **standard connection** allows multiple users to access the database at the same time. A **serial connection** allows only a single user to access a database at one time. How many users can connect to the database at one time is an important consideration, since many database management systems include a license that companies purchase based on the number of concurrent users they anticipate will access a single database. The standard connection usually produces more efficient performance, since multiple users can have their requests processed immediately without having to wait for another user's request to finish. Use the standard connection if you are sure that the maximum number of users will not be reached on your database management system. If you feel that the maximum number of users on your database management system may be exceeded, then use the serial connection. You designate whether a database connection is standard or serial by using the lock() and unlock() methods of the Project object that you learned about in Tutorial 10. If you do not use the lock() and unlock() methods, then a standard connection is established. Using the lock() and unlock() methods establishes a serial connection. For example, the preceding code establishes a standard connection, since it does not include lock() and unlock() methods. The following code shows the same example as a serial connection:

```
project.lock();
database.connect(
```

```
"SYBASE", "Server1", "don", "1X347", "Accounting");
if (!database.connected())
     write("The database is not available.");
else {
     additional statements;
     database.disconnect();
}
project.unlock();
```

Next you will start creating the GetStudentIDSSJS.html file, which generates new student IDs. New student IDs are created by incrementing by one the value contained in the idNum property of the Project object. The new value is then assigned to the studentID property of the Client object. The initial value assigned to the idNum property when the registration program first starts in Application Manager is 100. Note that generating new student IDs from a property in the Project object is not necessarily the best method of generating new student IDs because the value in idNum is reinitialized each time you restart the registration program. (Remember that properties of the Project object are destroyed each time an application is stopped or restarted.) A better solution is to generate new student IDs by using a value stored in the database. However, to focus on the concepts being presented in this tutorial, you will generate new student IDs based on the idNum property in the Project object.

To start creating the GetStudentIDSSJS.html file:

1 Create a new document in your text editor or HTML editor.

2 Type the opening **<SERVER>** tag.

> Since you will not be including any HTML tags in this document, you do not need to create any <HTML> or <BODY> tags.

help

3 Add the following code, which locks the Project object, establishing a serial connection to the database, and generates a new student ID. If the studentID variable does not exist, it is created. If it does exist, the current number is incremented by one.

```
project.lock();
if (!project.idNum) {
     project.idNum = 100;
     client.studentID = project.idNum;
}
else {
     var curID = project.idNum;
     ++curID;
     client.studentID = curID;
     project.idNum = curID;
}
```

4 Type the following section, which will open a database connection to WebAdventureSSJS DSN:

```
database.connect("ODBC",
   "WebAdventureSSJS", "", "", "");
if (!database.connected())
     write("The database is not available.");
```

5 Add the closing **</SERVER>** tag.

6 Save the file as **GetStudentIDSSJS.html** in the **Tutorial.11** folder on your Data Disk.

Executing SQL Commands

Three methods of the Database object, the execute() method, the cursor() method, and the SQLTable() method, are used for executing SQL queries against a database. Each of these methods has different uses, as you will see. Note that for clarity the examples in this text search for records based on an employee's last name. In an actual working environment, you should search for a unique identifier, such as the value assigned to the primary key of a record.

The execute() Method

The **execute() method** sends SQL statements to the database management system for processing. You use the execute() method for updating or modifying a database table. You do not submit ODBC SQL statements with the execute() method. Instead, you submit statements in the native SQL language of the database management system you are accessing. Statements you execute with the execute() method are referred to as **passthrough SQL**, since they are being passed directly to the database management system. The syntax for the execute() method is `database.execute(SQL string);`. When using the execute() method, be sure you understand the SQL syntax for a target database management system, or at least restrict your commands to common SQL keywords such as SELECT, INSERT, and DELETE.

The execute() method does not return query results to SSJS. Therefore, you cannot use the execute() method to retrieve data from a database. Instead, the execute() method is very useful for inserting, updating, or deleting rows in a database. For example, the following code uses the SQL INSERT statement along with the INTO clause to add a new employee record to the Employees database table. The INTO clause in the example is followed by the name of the database table, then by the VALUES statement, followed by parentheses containing the values to insert into each field in the new record. The position of each value in the parentheses corresponds to the field location in the Employees table.

```
var SQLString =
"INSERT INTO Employees VALUES('106', 'Mbuti',
'Pierre', '106 Flagg Road', 'Spencer', 'MA',
'01562', 'x413')";
database.execute(SQLString);
```

The INSERT statement adds a new record to the *end* of a database table. Later in this section you will learn how to use the insertRow() method of the Cursor object to insert a new row into a specific position in a table.

The following code shows another example of the execute() method, which deletes a row from the Employees table. The DELETE statement uses the FROM clause to designate the table from which the row should be deleted.

```
var SQLString = "DELETE FROM Employees
    WHERE Last_Name = 'Miller'";
database.execute(SQLString);
```

The SQL string in the preceding code uses the WHERE clause to look for rows in the table in which the Last_Name field is equal to *Miller*. Note that the preceding statement would actually delete *all* rows in the table in which the Last_Name field is equal to *Miller*. This statement is safe for our purposes because we know that there is only one record in the database that contains *Miller* in the Last_Name field. When using a DELETE statement, be sure you understand exactly what records will be deleted before executing it. Also, be sure to include a WHERE clause when using the DELETE statement or all of the rows in the specified table will be deleted.

Although the execute() method does not return query results, it does return error codes indicating the result of a query operation. See the Netscape SSJS documentation for a list of error codes returned by the execute() method.

Next you will add code to the GetStudentIDSSJS.html file that writes records to the database, using the execute() method. The code will add a new student record to a table in the database named Students. Each record will be created using the studentID property of the Client object, along with form properties of the Request object. The values of the Request object form properties originated in the RegistrationSSJS.html file, which calls the GetStudentIDSSJS.html file.

To add code to the GetStudentIDSSJS.html file that writes records to the registration database, using the execute() method:

1 Return to the **GetStudentIDSSJS.html** file in your text editor or HTML editor window.

2 Above the closing </SERVER> tag, add the following statements that build the SQL string and run the execute() method. The statements are contained in an else structure that executes only if the preceding if statement that checks if the database is connected returns a value of false.

```
else {
    var SQLString = "INSERT INTO Students VALUES('"
        + client.studentID + "', '"
        + request.last_name + "', '"
        + request.first_name + "', '"
        + request.address + "', '"
        + request.city + "', '"
        + request.state + "','"
        + request.zip + "', '"
        + request.email + "')";
    database.execute(SQLString);
    database.disconnect();
```

3 Also above the closing </SERVER> tag, add the following statements that return a response to the client containing the newly created student ID:

```
write("<H2>WebAdventure Computer Training Registration
</H2>");
write("Thanks " + request.first_name
+ "! Your new student ID is <B>" + client.studentID + "
</B>");
write(". Click <A HREF='CourseListingSSJS.html'>
Registration</A>");
write(" to proceed to the course registration page.");
```

4 Finally, add the following code to close the else structure and unlock the project.

```
    }
    project.unlock();
```

5 Save and close **GetStudentIDSSJS.html**.

Next you will compile the registration program.

To compile the registration program:

1   Go to your system command prompt. Accessing a command prompt differs by operating system. To access a command prompt from Windows 95/98, select **Run** from the **Start** menu and type **command**. To access a command prompt from Windows NT, Select **Run** from the **Start** menu and type **cmd**.

2   Change to the **Tutorial.11** folder on your Data Disk.

3   Compile the registration program as **Registration.web**, using the jsac command. When you compile and recompile the program, make sure you include the files named RegistrationSSJS.html, CourseListingSSJS.html, and GetStudentIDSSJS.html, using a statement similar to the following:

```
C:\Netscape\Server4\bin\https\bin\jsac -v -o
Registration.web RegistrationSSJS.html
CourseListingSSJS.html GetStudentIDSSJS.html
```

help

> The preceding command includes line breaks because of space limitations. Be sure to enter the entire command on a single line before pressing Enter.

4   When the program finishes compiling, type **Exit** to close the command prompt window.

Next you will install and run the registration program.

To install and run the registration program:

1   Start Application Manager, and then select the **Add Application** button in the top frame.

2   In the Add Application frame, type **Registration** in the Name box. Then in the Web File Path box, type **a:\Tutorial.11\Registration.web**.

3   Type **RegistrationSSJS.html** in the Default Page box.

4   Leave the rest of the boxes in the Add Application form set to their default values, and select the **OK** button.

5   Select **Registration** from the list of installed applications in the left frame and click **Run** to open the RegistrationSSJS.html file in your Web browser. Fill out the registration information and click the **Get Student ID** button. You should receive a response similar to Figure 11-12.

Figure 11-12: Response returned from GetStudentIDSSJS.html

6 Close the Web browser window.

Next you will create the RegisterStudentSSJS.html file. The RegisterStudentSSJS.html file adds registration information to a Registration table in the registration database, and then returns a response to the student.

 tip

In an actual working environment, you would include code that checks to make sure students do not register for the same class twice or for two classes offered at the same time. For simplicity, the code in RegisterStudentSSJS.html adds new records to the Registration table even if students have already enrolled in that class.

To create the RegisterStudentSSJS.html file:

1 Create a new document in your text editor or HTML editor.

2 Add an opening <SERVER> tag and statements to connect to the DSN file:

```
<SERVER>
project.lock();
database.connect("ODBC", "WebAdventureSSJS", "", "", "");
if (!database.connected())
     write("The database is not available.");
```

3   Next, add the following code to execute the SQL statements, using the execute() method. The statements assign to the SQLString variable a text string containing a SQL statement. The SQL statement uses the INSERT statement with the INTO clause to add the studentID property of the Client object along with the values contained in the form properties of the Request object to the database. The form properties of the Request object contain the values entered into fields in the registration form in the CourseListingSSJS.html file.

```
else {
    var SQLString =
        "INSERT INTO Registration VALUES('"
        + client.studentID + "', '"
        + request.course + "', '"
        + request.days + "', '"
        + request.time + "')";
    database.execute(SQLString);
    database.disconnect();
}
```

4   Add the following statements that return a response to the user:

```
write(
"<H2>WebAdventure Computer Training Registration</H2>");
write("You are registered for " + request.course
+ " on " + request.days + ", " + request.time);
write(". To register for another course, click
<A HREF='CourseListingSSJS.html'>Course Listing</A>.
Or click <A HREF='ReviewScheduleSSJS.html'>
Review Schedule</A>
to review your current schedule.");
```

5   Disconnect the database, unlock the project, and add a closing </SERVER> tag:

```
project.unlock();
</SERVER>
```

6   Save the file as **RegisterStudentSSJS.html** in the **Tutorial.11** folder on your Data Disk.

7   Recompile the registration program, using the jsac command. Be sure to include all four files when you execute jsac, as follows:

```
C:\Netscape\Server4\bin\https\bin\jsac -v -o
Registration.web RegistrationSSJS.html
CourseListingSSJS.html GetStudentIDSSJS.html
RegisterStudentSSJS.html
```

8 Restart and run the application, using Application Manager. On the RegistrationSSJS.html page, enter the student ID you created previously and click the **Class Registration** button to open CourseListingSSJS.html. Figure 11-13 shows how the document appears in Netscape.

Figure 11-13: CourseListingSSJS.html in Netscape

9 Fill out the course registration form and click the **Register** button. Figure 11-14 shows an example of the response returned from RegisterStudentSSJS.html.

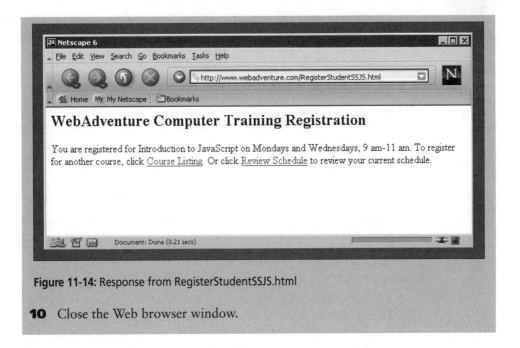

Figure 11-14: Response from RegisterStudentSSJS.html

10 Close the Web browser window.

The Cursor Object

The execute() method allows you to add, delete, and modify records in a table, but does not return results, except for error codes. In addition to adding, deleting, or modifying records, you may want to navigate through the records in a database and make changes or retrieve values when necessary, which you cannot do with the execute() method. To perform these types of functions, you must use the cursor() method of the Database object to create a Cursor object. A **Cursor object** contains the records returned from a SELECT query that was executed with the cursor() method. You can navigate through a Cursor object and retrieve values, or add, delete, and modify records. Any changes you make to the record set in a Cursor object are written to the actual database on the server.

tip

The record set in a Cursor object is sometimes referred to as a virtual table.

You create a Cursor object by using the syntax *variable = database.cursor ("SQL statement", updatable);*. The Cursor object is assigned to a designated variable name. The SQL statement must be a valid SELECT statement written in ODBC SQL. The updatable argument is a Boolean value indicating whether the records in the Cursor object can be modified. A value of *true* indicates that the Cursor object records can be modified; a value of *false* makes the Cursor object read-only. A Cursor object includes several methods for working with record sets, as listed in Figure 11-15.

Method	Description
close()	Closes a Cursor object
columnName(*position*)	Returns the name of a column designated by the position argument
columns()	Returns the number of columns in the record set
deleteRow()	Deletes a row from the record set
insertRow()	Inserts a row into the record set
next()	Moves to the next record in the record set
updateRow()	Saves changes to the current row in the record set

Figure 11-15: Cursor object methods

One Cursor object method you should always use is the close() method. You cannot disconnect a database connection using the disconnect() method of the Database object until all Cursor objects are closed. For example, the following statement creates a read-only Cursor object containing the records from the Employees table, then closes the Cursor object, using the close() method:

```
var employeesTable = database.cursor(
"SELECT * FROM Employees ORDER BY Last_Name, First_Name",
false);
statements;
employeesTable.close();
```

Navigating through a Cursor Your position in a Cursor object record set is called the **cursor**. When you first create a Cursor object using the cursor() method, your cursor is initially placed *before* the first row in the record set. Figure 11-16 shows an example of where your cursor is placed when you first open the Employees table in a Cursor object.

**cursor
position**

100	Blair	Dennis	204 Spruce Lane	Brookfield	MA	01506	x305
101	Hernandez	Louis	68 Boston Post Road	Spencer	MA	01562	x412
102	Miller	Erica	271 Baker Hill Road	E. Brookfield	MA	01515	x291
103	Morinaga	Scott	17 Ashley Road	N. Brookfield	MA	01535	x177
104	Picard	Raymond	1113 Oakham Road	New Braintree	MA	01531	x213

Figure 11-16: Initial cursor position in the Cursor object

 tip

You never actually see the record set in a Cursor object as it is shown in Figure 11-16. The
illustration in Figure 11-16 is for demonstration purposes only.

To navigate through the records in a Cursor object, you use the next() method.
The first time you use the next() method, it places your cursor in the first row of the
record set. For example, the following code creates a new Cursor object, and then
moves the cursor to the first record in the resulting record set:

```
var employeesTable = database.cursor(
"SELECT * FROM Employees WHERE Last_Name = 'Miller'",
false);
employeesTable.next();
statements;
employeesTable.close();
```

When you work with record sets and the next() method, you can never be certain
if there is another record following the current position of the cursor, or even if any
records were returned at all from your SQL SELECT statement. For example, the preceding code assumes that a record with *Miller* in the Last_Name field exists in the
Employees table. However, if someone else has deleted the record, then the Cursor
object will contain no records. To ensure that there is a next record available, the
next() method returns a value of true if it finds a next row in the record set or a value
of false if it does not find a next row in the record set. The following code shows how
to use an if statement to check the value returned by the next() method before moving the cursor. Notice that the next() method is executed as the conditional expression
of the if statement. Also notice that the conditional expression does not include a
comparison operator. The next() method returns a value of true or false automatically
as it is executed, eliminating the need for a comparison operator.

```
var employeesTable = database.cursor(
"SELECT * FROM Employees WHERE Last_Name = 'Miller'",
false);
if (employeesTable.next()) {
    statements;
}
employeesTable.close();
```

The field names in a database table are assigned as properties of an instantiated Cursor object. For example, if you instantiate a Cursor object named employeesTable for the Employees database, then you can refer to the First_Name field by using a statement similar to `employeesTable.First_Name`. Be aware that whenever you use the next() method, the content of each field in a Cursor object property changes to reflect the contents of the record at the current location of the cursor. The following code shows a simple program that returns the name of each programmer in the Employees table to the client, along with the name of the city where each programmer lives. The program uses a `while` statement to move through the records in the table. Figure 11-17 shows the results returned to a client.

```
var employeesTable = database.cursor(
"SELECT * FROM Employees", false);
while(employeesTable.next()) {
     write(employeesTable.First_Name + " "
          + employeesTable.Last_Name + " lives in "
          + employeesTable.City + ", "
          + employeesTable.State + "<BR>");
}
employeesTable.close();
```

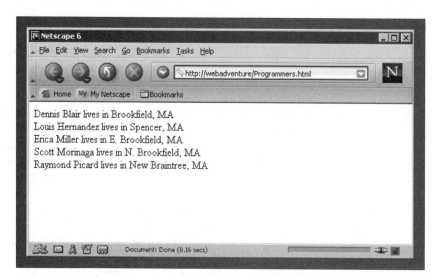

Figure 11-17: Cursor object program results

Next you will create the ReviewScheduleSSJS.html file, which displays the courses a student is registered for.

To create the ReviewScheduleSSJS.html file:

1   Create a new document in your text editor or HTML editor.

2   Add an opening <SERVER> tag and statements to connect to the DSN file:

```
<SERVER>
project.lock();
database.connect("ODBC", "WebAdventureSSJS", "", "", "");
if (!database.connected())
    write("The database is not available.");
```

3   Add an opening **else {** statement to contain the database statements:

4   Type **var rsSchedule = database.cursor("SELECT * FROM Registration WHERE Student_ID = '" + client.studentID + "'", false);** to instantiate the Cursor object. Following the WHERE student_ID = clause, be sure to type a single quotation mark followed by a double quotation mark. Also be sure to type a double quotation mark, followed by a single quotation mark, followed by a double quotation mark after the client.studentID portion of the statement.

5   Add the following section, which returns a response to the student.

```
write("<H2>This is your current schedule</H2>");
while(rsSchedule.next()) {
    write(rsSchedule.Course + ", "
    + rsSchedule.Days + ", "
    + rsSchedule.Time + "<BR>");
}
```

6   Close the Cursor object, disconnect the database, add a closing brace for the `else` statement, unlock the project, and close the server tag.

```
    rsSchedule.close();
    database.disconnect();
}
project.unlock();
</SERVER>
```

7   Save the file as **ReviewScheduleSSJS.html** in the **Tutorial.11** folder on your Data Disk.

8   Recompile the registration program, using the jsac command. Be sure to include all five files when you execute jsac, as follows:

```
C:\Netscape\Server4\bin\https\bin\jsac -v -o
Registration.web RegistrationSSJS.html
CourseListingSSJS.html GetStudentIDSSJS.html
RegisterStudentSSJS.html ReviewScheduleSSJS.html
```

9 Restart and run the application, using Application Manager.

10 Enter an existing student ID in the RegistrationSSJS.html page and click the **Class Registration** button. From the CourseListingSSJS.html document, click the **Review Current Schedule** button. Figure 11-18 shows the output for a student after registering for several classes.

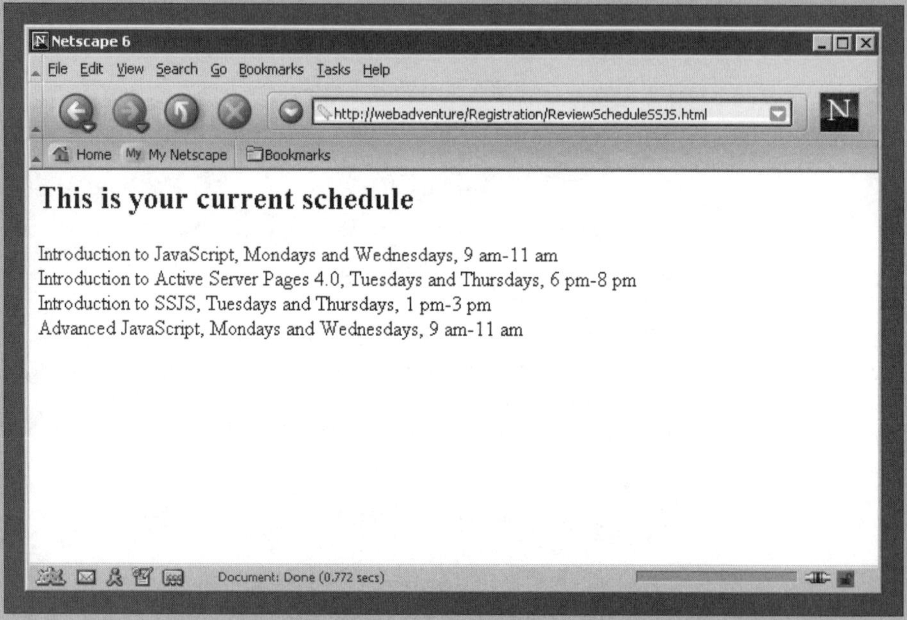

Figure 11-18: ReviewScheduleSSJS.html in Netscape

11 Close the Web browser window.

Updatable Cursors When you use a value of *true* as the *updatable* argument of the cursor() method, you create an updatable cursor. An **updatable cursor** is a Cursor object record set that can be modified. When creating an updatable cursor, you cannot specify multiple tables from a relational database in the SELECT statement. Additionally, you must include the table key values (such as the primary key), and the select statement cannot include a GROUP BY clause, which is used for sorting the results returned from a query. Three Cursor object methods are specific to updatable cursors: the updateRow(), insertRow(),and deleteRow() methods. All three of the methods accept a single string argument containing the name of the table in the database where the row is to be updated, inserted, or deleted. Be sure to include the name of the table in the database and not the name you assigned to the Cursor object.

The updateRow() method saves any changes you make to a row in the record set. You execute updateRow() after changing field values. For example, let us assume that Erica Miller was recently married and is changing her last name to Lee. The following code creates a Cursor object using a SELECT statement with a WHERE clause to retrieve only Erica Miller's record, then uses the next() method to move to the first record in the record set and update the Last_Name field:

```
var employeesTable = database.cursor(
"SELECT * FROM Employees WHERE Last_Name = 'Miller'",
true);
if (employeesTable.next()) {
    if (employeesTable.Last_Name == "Miller") {
        employeesTable.Last_Name = "Lee";
        employeesTable.updateRow("Employees");
}
employeesTable.close();
```

The insertRow() method is similar to the SQL INSERT statement, except that instead of adding a row to the end of a table, it inserts a new row at the location of the cursor in the record set. Before executing the insertRow() method, you assign values to the properties in the Cursor object that represent the field names. The current field values are used if you do not assign new values to any of the fields for the new record. For example, Raymond Picard's wife, Lisa, is joining the WebAdventure programming group. The following code locates Raymond Picard's record by using a while loop, then changes the values of just the Employee_ID, First_Name, and Extension fields. You do not need to change the rest of the field values (the address information), since Raymond and Lisa live together.

```
var employeesTable = database.cursor(
"SELECT * FROM Employees", true);
while(employeesTable.Last_Name != "Picard") {
    employeesTable.next();
}
employeesTable.Employee_ID = "107";
employeesTable.First_Name = "Lisa";
employeesTable.Extension = "x309";
employeesTable.insertRow("Employees");
employeesTable.close();
```

tip

If you execute the insertRow() method before executing the next() method for the first time in a Cursor object, then the new row is inserted at the beginning of the table, and any fields that do not contain a value are assigned a value of null.

The deleteRow() method is similar to the SQL DELETE statement, except that instead of deleting all rows that match the results of the SELECT statement, the deleteRow() method deletes just the record where the cursor is located. For example, if Scott Morinaga leaves WebAdventure, you can delete his employee record by using the following code:

```
var employeesTable = database.cursor(
"SELECT * FROM Employees", true);
while(employeesTable.Last_Name != "Morinaga") {
    employeesTable.next();
}
employeesTable.deleteRow("Employees");
employeesTable.close();
```

tip

••

Like the execute() method, the updateRow(), insertRow(), and deleteRow() methods return error codes indicating the result of the query operation. See the Netscape SSJS documentation for a list of error codes returned by these methods.

••

The SQLTable() Method

The **SQLTable() method** returns the results of a SELECT statement to the client as an HTML table. The SQLTable() method is the quickest way to return database information to the client. The HTML table returned to the client has rows and columns corresponding to database table records and fields, and includes a header row containing the name or caption of each field in the table. Note that you do not have any control over the formatting of the table returned to the client. The following code returns an HTML table from the Employees database table. Figure 11-19 shows the results that are returned to the client.

```
write("<H2>WebAdventure Programmers</H2>");
database.SQLTable(
"SELECT * FROM Employees ORDER BY Last_Name, First_Name");
```

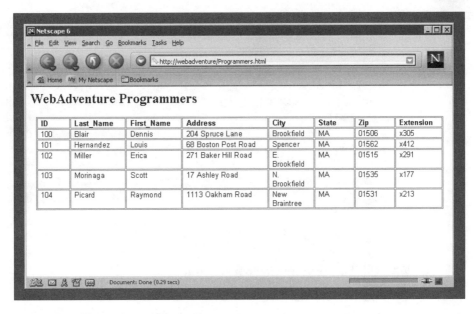

Figure 11-19: Results of the SQLTable() method

Next you will modify the ReviewScheduleSSJS.html file so that it returns a student's schedule, using the SQLTable() method.

To modify the ReviewScheduleSSJS.html file so that it returns a student's schedule, using the SQLTable() method:

1 Return to the **ReviewScheduleSSJS.html** file in your HTML editor or text editor.

2 Delete the following statements:

```
var rsSchedule = database.cursor(
"SELECT * Registration WHERE Student_ID =
'"+client.studentID + "'", FROM false);
write("<H2>This is your current schedule</H2>");
while(rsSchedule.next()) {
     write(rsSchedule.Course + ", "
     + rsSchedule.Days + ", "
     + rsSchedule.Time + "<BR>");
}
rsSchedule.close();
```

3 Type the following statements above the `database.disconnect();` statement:

```
write("<H2>This is your current schedule</H2>");
database.SQLTable(
"SELECT Course, Days, Time FROM Registation
WHERE Student_ID = '"  + client.studentID +"'");
```

4   Save **ReviewScheduleSSJS.html** in the **Tutorial.11** folder on your Data Disk, and then close the file.

5   Recompile the application, and then restart and run it using Application Manager.

6   Enter an existing student ID in the RegistrationSSJS.html page and click the **Class Registration** button. From the CourseListingSSJS.html document, click the **Review Current Schedule** button. Figure 11-20 shows the output from the SQLTable() method.

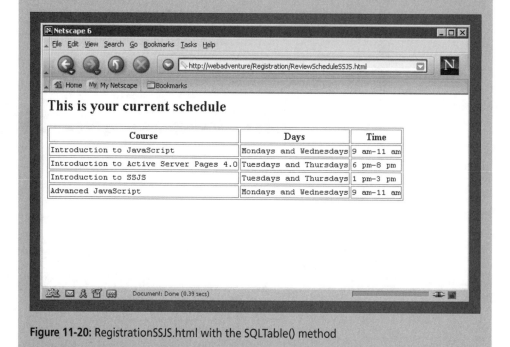

Figure 11-20: RegistrationSSJS.html with the SQLTable() method

7   Close the Web browser window, and close your text editor or HTML editor.

Transaction Processing with LiveWire

When you use an updatable cursor, by default each statement is committed to the database as LiveWire executes it. For example, a statement such as `employeesTable.deleteRow("Employees");` will immediately and permanently delete the row in the database where the cursor is currently located. When you permanently change a database record, you are said to be **committing** the change. Most databases have what is known as an **autocommit** feature, which immediately records a change to a database record or cancels the change if there is an error. You can override a database default autocommit feature by using transactions. A **transaction** commits database statements as a group. You can also cancel, or **roll back**, a transaction if there is some sort of problem with the data you are saving to the database. Without transactions, there is no way for you to undo a change to the database in the event of a problem. It is a good idea to use transactions whenever you add, delete, or modify records in a database. Transactions ensure that all related database changes are made together, or that they fail together.

You begin a transaction by using the beginTransaction() method. All database statements following a beginTransaction() method are called the **current transaction**. Following the database statements that are part of the transaction, you execute the commitTransaction() method to make the changes to the database. At any point following a beginTransaction() method, you can execute the rollBackTransaction() method to cancel all changes that are part of the current transaction. For example, if the current transaction is missing a required field, such as a key field, then you can call rollBackTransaction() to cancel all changes that are part of the current transaction. Note that if you attempt to use commitTransaction() or rollbackTransaction() before you use beginTransaction(), you will receive an error from the database. Also, be aware that the scope of a transaction is limited to the current request. Once a response is returned to a client, you can no longer roll back a transaction. Also, if a response is returned to the client before you execute the commitTransaction() method or rollbackTransaction() method, the transaction statements are automatically committed to the database (provided the *updatable* argument of the cursor() method you used to instantiate the updatable cursor was set to *true*).

▶ **tip**

Informix ANSI databases automatically use transactions, even if you do not use LiveWire's transaction-processing methods.

The following code shows how to use transaction processing to add a new employee record to the Employees table:

```
var employeesTable = database.cursor(
"SELECT * FROM Employees", true);
database.beginTransaction();
while(employeesTable.Last_Name != "Picard") {
    employeesTable.next();
}
employeesTable.Employee_ID = "107";
employeesTable.First_Name = "Lisa";
employeesTable.Extension = "x309";
employeesTable.insertRow("Employees");
database.commitTransaction();
employeesTable.close();
```

The preceding code does not include a rollbackTransaction() method. You will learn how to roll back a transaction in the next section, which is on error handling.

Error Handling with LiveWire

Many methods of the Database object, including the insertRow(), deleteRow(), and updateRow() methods, return error messages in the form of status codes. A return value of 0 indicates that the operation was completed successfully. Any other status code indicates an error. Figure 11-21 lists the LiveWire status codes and their descriptions.

Status Code	Description
0	No error
1	Out of memory
2	Object never initialized
3	Type conversion error
4	Database not registered
5	Error reported by server
6	Message from server
7	Error from vendor's library
8	Lost connection
9	End of fetch
10	Invalid use of object
11	Column does not exist
12	Invalid positioning within object (bounds error)
13	Unsupported feature
14	Null reference parameter
15	Database object not found
16	Required information is missing
17	Object cannot support multiple readers
18	Object cannot support deletions
19	Object cannot support insertions
20, 21	Object cannot support updates

Figure 11-21: LiveWire status codes

Status Code	Description
22	Object cannot support indices
23	Object cannot be dropped
24	Incorrect connection supplied
25	Object cannot support privileges
26	Object cannot support cursors
27	Unable to open

Figure 11-21: LiveWire status codes (*continued*)

When a status code other than 0 is returned, you can find more information about the error by using the majorErrorCode(), majorErrorMessage(), minorErrorCode(), and minorErrorMessage() methods. The majorErrorCode() and majorErrorMessage() methods return the last major error code and message returned from the server. Any secondary error codes and error messages are returned by the minorErrorCode() and minorErrorMessage() methods. For example, to return a major error message to the client you use a statement similar to `write(majorErrorMessage());`.

▶ **tip**

Do not confuse LiveWire status codes with the values returned by the majorErrorCode() and minorErrorCode() methods. The status codes are the errors returned by LiveWire. The values returned by the majorErrorCode() and minorErrorCode() methods are returned by the database server.

You can use the status codes and the error methods with the rollbackTransaction() method to cancel any changes to a database in the event that a problem occurs while performing a transaction. The following code shows an example of a transaction with a rollbackTransaction() method. The code assigns the status code returned by the insertRow() method to a variable named returnedStatus. If the returnedStatus variable is equal to 0, then the commitTransaction() method is called and a message is returned to the client, indicating that the transaction was successful. However, if the returnedStatus variable is not equal to 0, then a message is returned to the client stating that the transaction was unsuccessful, along with the major error code and message.

```
var employeesTable = database.cursor(
"SELECT * FROM Employees", true);
database.beginTransaction();
while(employeesTable.Last_Name != "Picard") {
    employeesTable.next();
}
```

```
employeesTable.Employee_ID = "107";
employeesTable.First_Name = "Lisa";
employeesTable.Extension = "x309";
employeesTable.insertRow("Employees");
if (returnedStatus == 0) {
        database.commitTransaction();
         write("The record was added successfully.");
}
else {
        database.rollbackTransaction();
   write("The record was not successfully added.
The database server returned the following
error code and message:<BR>"
+ "error code: " + database.majorErrorCode()
+ "<BR>" + "error message: "
+ database.majorErrorMessage());
}
employeesTable.close();
```

SUMMARY

- A database is an ordered collection of information from which a computer program can quickly access information.

- A record in a database contains a single complete set of related information.

- The individual pieces of information stored in a record are called fields.

- A flat-file database stores information in a single table.

- A relational database stores information across multiple related tables.

- A one-to-one relationship exists between two tables when each record in a related table contains exactly one record for each record in the primary table.

- A one-to-many relationship exists in a relational database when one record in a primary table has many related records in a related table.

- Breaking tables into multiple related tables in order to reduce redundant and duplicate information is called normalization.

- A many-to-many relationship exists in a relational database when many records in one table are related to many records in another table.

- A junction table contains a one-to-many relationship to each of the two tables in a many-to-many relationship.

- An application or collection of applications used to create, access, and manage a database is called a database management system, or DBMS.

- A query is a structured set of instructions and criteria for retrieving, adding, modifying, and deleting database information.

- A report is the formatted, printed output of a database table or the results of a query.

- Most database management systems utilize a data manipulation language, or DML, for creating queries.

- Structured query language, or SQL (pronounced like the word *sequel*), has become a standard data manipulation language among many database management systems.

- Open database connectivity, or ODBC, allows applications written to comply with the standard to access any data source for which there is an ODBC driver.

- A Data Source Name, or DSN, contains configuration information that Windows operating systems use to access a particular ODBC-compliant database.

- The DbPool and Connection objects are used for creating and managing pools of database connections. The Database object is used for creating and managing single connections between a client and a database.

- A standard connection allows multiple users to access the database at the same time. A serial connection allows only a single user to access a database at one time.

- The execute() method sends SQL statements to the database management system for processing.

- Statements you execute with the execute() method are referred to as passthrough SQL, since they are passed directly to the database management system.

- A Cursor object contains the records returned from a SELECT query that was executed with the cursor() method.

- Your position in a Cursor object record set is called the cursor.

- An updatable cursor is a Cursor object record set that can be modified.

- The SQLTable() method returns the results of a SELECT statement to the client as an HTML table.

- A transaction commits database statements as a group.

- All database statements following a beginTransaction() method are called the current transaction.

- Many methods of the Database object return error messages in the form of status codes. A return value of 0 indicates that the operation was completed successfully. Any other status code indicates an error.

- When a status code other than 0 is returned, you can find out more information about the error using the majorErrorCode(), majorErrorMessage(), minorErrorCode(), and minorErrorMessage() methods.

QUESTIONS

1. What is the correct term for the individual pieces of information that are stored in a database record?
   a. element
   b. field
   c. section
   d. container

2. How many tables does a flat-file database consist of?
   a. 1
   b. 2
   c. any number of tables
   d. A flat-file database does not consist of tables.

3. What is the name of the primary key of one table when it is stored in another table?
   a. key symbol
   b. record link
   c. foreign key
   d. unique identifier

4. Breaking tables into multiple related tables in order to reduce redundant and duplicate information is called _____.
   a. normalization
   b. redundancy design
   c. splitting
   d. simplification

5. A _____ relationship exists between two tables when each record in a related table contains exactly one record for each record in the primary table.
   a. one-to-none
   b. one-to-one
   c. one-to-many
   d. many-to-many

6. A _____ relationship exists in a relational database when one record in a primary table has many related records in a related table.
   a. one-to-none
   b. one-to-one
   c. one-to-many
   d. many-to-many

7. A _____ relationship exists in a relational database when many records in one table are related to many records in another table.
   a. one-to-none
   b. one-to-one
   c. one-to-many
   d. many-to-many

8. A _____ contains a one-to-many relationship to each of the two tables in a many-to-many relationship.
   a. union database
   b. flat-file link
   c. junction table
   d. bridge table

9. An application or collection of applications used to create, access, and manage a database is called _____.
   a. a shell program
   b. a mainframe system
   c. a database management system
   d. three-tier client-server design

10. Most database management systems use a form of _____ for their data manipulation languages.
    a. CGI scripting
    b. C/C++ syntax
    c. structured query language
    d. Java programming

11. A(n) _____ contains configuration information that Windows operating systems use to access a particular ODBC-compliant database.
    a. dynamic-link library
    b. SQL container
    c. ODBC interface unit
    d. Data Source Name

12. What is the correct syntax for connecting to a database in LiveWire?
    a. `database.connect(arguments);`
    b. `Database.connect(arguments);`
    c. `database.Connect(arguments);`
    d. `Database.Connect(arguments);`

13. What should the server name argument be set to when connecting to an ODBC database on Windows platforms?
    a. the name of the table in the database
    b. the name assigned to the Windows NT server
    c. the native database filename
    d. the DSN name

14. Which method returns a value of true if you have successfully connected to a database?
    a. connect()
    b. connected()
    c. success()
    d. dbAvailable()

15. A _____ connection allows multiple users to access a database at the same time.
    a. multiple
    b. serial
    c. standard
    d. parallel

16. A_____ connection allows only a single user to access a database at one time.
     a. multiple
     b. serial
     c. standard
     d. parallel

17. Statements executed with the execute() method are called _____ SQL statements.
     a. passthrough
     b. direct
     c. database
     d. server-side

18. What happens if you do not use a WHERE clause with a SQL DELETE statement?
     a. You will receive an error.
     b. All rows in the target table are deleted.
     c. None of the rows in the target table are deleted.
     d. Nothing happens.

19. A _____ object contains the result of a SELECT query executed with the cursor() method as a record set.
     a. Cursor
     b. Record
     c. Table
     d. Database

20. Which method is used for navigating through a record set?
     a. goto()
     b. moveTo()
     c. record()
     d. next()

21. How do you create an updatable cursor?
     a. by using the cursor() method
     b. by using a value of *true* as the *updatable* argument of the cursor() method
     c. by including the update single string argument with the cursor() method
     d. You cannot create an updatable cursor.

22. Which of the following arguments is not specific to an updatable cursor?
     a. updateRow()
     b. insertRow()
     c. deleteRow()
     d. next()

23. Which method returns the results of a query as an HTML table?
     a. HTMLTable()
     b. SQLTable()
     c. SQLtoTable()
     d. ReturnTable()

24. Which method cancels a transaction?

    a. cancel()

    b. discard()

    c. rollback()

    d. rollbackTransaction()

25. Which error code indicates that a database operation was completed successfully?

    a. OK

    b. SUCCESS

    c. 1

    d. 0

EXERCISES

1. New student IDs in the registration program you created in this tutorial are generated from the idNum property of the Project object. Generating new student IDs from a property in the Project object is not necessarily the best method of generating new student IDs because the value in idNum is reinitialized each time you restart the registration program. Modify the registration program so that new student IDs are generated from the Students table in the database instead of from the idNum property of the Project object. You will need to use the next() method to search through existing records of the Students table to retrieve the last assigned student ID. For this exercise, use the WebAdventureSSJS DSN you used throughout Section A.

2. Database design techniques include the process of being able to identify and design five normalization levels: first normal form, second normal form, third normal form, fourth normal form, and fifth normal form. Search the Internet or visit your local library for information on these techniques. Write a paper describing how to identify and design each normalization level.

3. E-commerce is a hot issue in Web development today because many businesses want to be able to sell their products online. Search the Internet for information on this topic and write a paper describing the current state of e-commerce, including popular database management systems, security issues, and where you feel this technology is headed.

For the following exercises that require databases, use a database management system you have access to, such as Access, Paradox, or SQL Server, to create the database file where you will store the data. Save your solution files for the following exercises in their own folders within the Tutorial.11 folder on your Data Disk.

4. Redesign the following table into a one-to-many relationship. Save the database as Employees and whatever extension is used by your database management system. Use whatever names you like for the database tables.

Employee_ID	Last_Name	First_Name	Hourly_Pay	Department
EMP001	Smith	Lucille	$32.50	Marketing
EMP002	Perez	Frank	$40.00	Legal
EMP003	Okayabashi	Mike	$22.00	Accounting
EMP004	Korso	Anthony	$28.00	Accounting
EMP005	Singh	Tasneem	$37.00	Legal

5. Redesign the following table into a many-to-many relationship. Save the database as Projects, followed by whatever extension is used by your database management system. Use whatever names you like for the database tables.

Employee_ID	Last_Name	First_Name	Project_ID	Project_Name	Hours_On_Project
EMP001	Smith	Lucille	100-002	Ad campaign	14
EMP001	Smith	Lucille	100-003	Marketing brochure	9
EMP002	Perez	Frank	200-056	Vendor contracts	23
EMP005	Singh	Tasneem	200-056	Vendor contracts	17
EMP003	Okayabashi	Mike	300-010	Accounts receivable integration	8
EMP004	Korso	Anthony	300-010	Accounts receivable integration	12
EMP003	Okayabashi	Mike	300-012	Year-end tax returns	56

6. Assume you have an ODBC database with a table named Courses that contains two fields, Course_Name and Student_Name. Write a SQL statement that selects just the Course_Name fields from the Courses table and sorts the records by the Course_Name field. Save the SQL statement in a text file named SQLCourses.txt.

7. Modify the SQL statement you created in Exercise 6 so that the statement selects all of the fields from the Courses table. Also sort the returned records by both the Course_Name and the Student_Name fields. Save the SQL statement in a text file named SQLCoursesAll.txt.

8. Add an `if` statement to the following code that confirms whether the database connection is successful. Save the modified code in a text file named ConfirmConnectSSJS.txt.

```
database.connect("ORACLE", "AppServer", "user1", "rosebud");
// additional statements;
database.disconnect();
```

9. Modify the code from Exercise 8 so that it accesses the database through a serial connection. Save the modified code in a text file named SerialConnectSSJS.txt.

10. Write a SQL statement that inserts the values *SH001*, *Polo Shirt*, *Large*, *Blue*, and *19.95* into a table named Purchases and assign the statement to a variable named purchaseString. Also write a statement that executes the SQL string using passthrough SQL. Assume that the database connection is already established. Save the code in a text file named PassthroughSQLSSJS.txt.

11. Write the code to create a Cursor object named shirtsTable that contains the records returned from the following SQL query: `SELECT * FROM Dress_Shirts WHERE Color = 'blue'`. The records assigned to the shirtsTable Cursor object should be modifiable. Include statements that navigate through the records and modify the Color fields from *blue* to *red*. Be sure to include a statement that closes the Cursor object. Save the code in a text file named CursorObjectSSJS.txt.

12. Write code that returns the records from the following SQL statement as an HTML table: `SELECT * FROM Hospitals ORDER BY Hospital_Name, City`. Save the code in a text file named HTMLTableSSJS.txt.

13. Modify the following statements so that database records are committed using transaction processing and error handling. Save the code in a text file named TransactionsAndErrorsSSJS.txt.

```
var stocksTable = database.cursor("SELECT * FROM Stocks", true);
while(stocksTable.next()) {
   stocksTable.next();
}
stocksTable.Stock_ID = "S367";
stocksTable.Stock_Name = "Oracle":
stocksTable.pricePerShare = 67.5;
stocksTable.numberOfShares = 200;
stocksTable.insertRow("Stocks");
stocksTable.close();
```

14. Create an SSJS program that saves Web site guest book entries to a database.

15. Create a telephone directory application that saves entries to a database. You should include standard telephone directory fields in the database, such as name, address, city, state, zip, and telephone number. Create an HTML document as a main "directory" from which you can select and retrieve records. Also create one HTML document that you can use to add new entries to your database, and another HTML document that you can use to edit entries.

16. Create a shopping cart application for an online bookstore. Use the course registration program you built in this section as a model. Instead of adding course registrations to the database, you add purchase information. Use different pages in the application for different types of books. The shopping cart should build a list of books that users want to purchase and provide a checkout mechanism that writes the information to a database and returns a response to the user.

In this section you will learn:

■ How Active Server Pages connect to databases

■ About the ADO Connection object

■ How to execute SQL commands
with ADO

■ How to perform transaction
processing with ADO

■ How to handle database errors
with ADO

Connecting to Databases with Active Server Pages

Introduction

With Active Server Pages, you use ActiveX Data Objects to access databases. **ActiveX Data Objects**, or **ADO**, is a Microsoft database connectivity technology that allows ASPs and other Web development tools to access ODBC- and OLE-DB-compliant databases. **OLE DB** is a data source connectivity standard promoted by Microsoft as a successor to ODBC. One of the primary differences between OLE DB and ODBC is that ODBC supports access only to relational databases, whereas OLE DB provides access to both relational databases and nonrelational data sources, such as spreadsheet programs. In comparing ASP database connectivity to LiveWire database connectivity, the focus will be on how ADO accesses ODBC databases. Note that many of the examples in this section are identical to the examples you saw in Section A. The same examples are used to demonstrate how to perform the same tasks with the two different versions of server-side JavaScript.

ADO and OLE DB are part of the Microsoft Universal Data Access strategy for providing access to data, regardless of its storage format. The components that make up the Universal Data Access technology are called the Microsoft Data Access Components, or MDAC. MDAC is installed with numerous Microsoft products, including the Windows NT 4.0 option pack, Internet Explorer 4.0, Internet Information Server 4.0, and Microsoft Visual Studio 6.0. Most of these products, including Internet Explorer, install MDAC automatically. However, if you are not sure if MDAC is installed on your system, you can download a program called Component Checker from the Microsoft Universal Data Access site at *www.Microsoft.com/data*. Component Checker helps you determine the components and version of the MDAC installed on your system. You can also download from the Microsoft Universal Data

Access site the latest version of MDAC as well as find out more information on Microsoft data access technologies.

Before diving too deeply into a discussion of ADO objects and collections, you need to create a system-based DSN that will be used with the ASP version of the database program you create in this section. Technically, you can use both the LiveWire and ASP versions of the program to access the DSN. However, to avoid confusion you will create a separate DSN for the ASP version named WebAdventureASP.

To create a system-based DSN for the ASP database program:

1 Click the Windows **Start** menu, then select **Control Panel** from the Settings folder.

2 Depending on how your desktop is configured, click or double-click the **ODBC** icon in the Control Panel window. For some Windows operating systems, including Windows 2000, the ODBC icon is located in the Administrative Tools folder.

3 In the ODBC Data Source Administrator window, select the **System DSN** tab, then click the **Add** button. In the Create New Data Source window that appears, select **Microsoft Access Driver (*.mdb)** and click the **Finish** button.

4 In the ODBC Microsoft Access Setup screen, type **WebAdventureASP** as the name of the new DSN file, then click the **Select** button. In the Select Database dialog box that appears, select the **WebAdventureCourses.mdb** file from the Tutorial.11 folder on your Data Disk and click the **OK** button.

6 Click the **OK** button to close the ODBC Microsoft Access Setup screen.

7 Click **OK** to close the ODBC Data Source Administrator window, and then close the Control Panel.

MDAC installs several files on your system that are necessary in order to use ADO with certain programming languages. The ADO file that is required to access databases with ASP is named adojavas.inc. By default, the ADO files are installed in C:\Program Files\Common Files\System\ado. When you create an ASP application that needs to access a database, you must copy the adojavas.inc file into the directory containing your ASP files and use the #include directive to insert the file into your program. The **#include directive** specifies a file to insert into an ASP file before it is processed by a server. The syntax for including a file in an ASP document is `<!-- #include file ="`*`filename`*`" -->`. You place an #include directive after an ASP file-processing directive, but before any script delimiters. The following code shows how to use the #include directive to insert the adojavas.inc file into an ASP file in order to access a database. The code assumes that the adojavas.inc file is located in the same server directory as the ASP document itself:

```
<%@ LANGUAGE=JScript %>
<!--#include file="adojavas.inc"-->
<%
```

```
ASP statements;
%>
```

Next you will copy the adojavas.inc file to the Tutorial.11 folder on your Data Disk and to your ASP Web server.

To copy the adojavas.inc file to the Tutorial.11 folder:

1   Locate the adojavas.inc file on your computer. The default installation directory is C:\Program Files\Common Files\System\ado.

2   Once you locate adojavas.inc, copy the file into the Tutorial.11 folder on your Data Disk.

3   Finally, copy or upload the adojavas.inc file to your ASP server.

Later versions of Windows operating systems, such as Windows 2000, include an Internet Guest account that is used for configuring the permissions a visitor to a Web server has to the server's local file system. By default, the Internet Guest account does not allow visitors to write to local files through ASP. In order for the ASP version of the Registration program to work, you must give the Internet Guest account write permission to the WebAdventureCourses.mdb file along with the folder where you stored the WebAdventureCourses.mdb file. The name of the Internet Guest account is IUSR_*machine*, where machine is the name of your computer. For example, if your computer is named *server1*, then your computer's Internet Guest account is IUSR_server1.

tip

You can change your computer name using the Network Identification tab in the System Properties dialog box, which can be accessed through the Control Panel.

Next you will give your computer Internet Guest account write permission to the folder where you stored the WebAdventureCourses.mdb file.

To give your computer's Internet Guest account write permission to the WebAdventureCourses.mdb file along with the folder where you stored the WebAdventureCourses.mdb file:

1   Use Windows Explorer or My Computer to locate the Tutorial.11 folder on your Data Disk.

2   Right-click the **Tutorial.11** folder name, and select **Properties** from the shortcut menu. The Properties dialog box opens.

3   Click the **Security** tab in the Properties dialog box. If you see Internet Guest Account in the Name list, then you can skip the remainder of these steps. If you do not see Internet Guest Account in the Name list, click the **Add** button. The Select Users or Groups dialog box appears.

4   In the Select Users or Groups dialog box, locate your Internet Guest account, click it, and then click the **Add** button. (Remember, your Internet Guest account name begins with IUSR_, followed by your computer name.) The Internet Guest account should appear in the list at the bottom of the dialog box.

5   Click the **OK** button to close the Select Users or Groups dialog box.

6   In the Properties dialog box, click **Internet Guest Account** in the Name list, and then click the checkbox under the Allow column for the Write permission.

7   Click the **OK** button to close the Properties dialog box.

Next you will create the main RegistrationASP.html document.

To create the main RegistrationASP.html document:

1   Start your text editor or HTML editor and create a new document.

2   Type the opening <HTML>, <HEAD>, and <BODY> sections of the document:

```
<HTML>
<HEAD>
<TITLE>Registration</TITLE>
</HEAD>
<BODY>
```

3   Add the following tags, text, and forms that make up the document. The two forms each use submit buttons to call ASP documents. Later in this section, you will create the ASP documents that are called by the submit buttons.

```
<H2>WebAdventure Computer Training Registration</H2>
<H3>Welcome</H3>
<P>Welcome to Computer Training at WebAdventure! We
offer a variety of computer training and technology
courses that focus on the Web. To sign up for a course,
please fill out the New Student Registration form and
click the <B>Get Student ID</B> button to obtain a
student ID. If you are a current student, enter your
student ID number and click the Class Registration
button to register for new classes or to review your
current schedule.</P>
```

```
<H3>New Student Registration</H3>
<FORM NAME="customerInfo" METHOD="post"
ACTION="GetStudentIDASP.asp">
<P>Last Name:  <INPUT TYPE="text"
NAME="last_name" SIZE=30>  
First Name:  <INPUT TYPE="text"
NAME="first_name" SIZE=30><BR>
Address:  <INPUT TYPE="text"
NAME="address" SIZE=30>
City, State, Zip:  <INPUT TYPE="text"
NAME="city" SIZE=20>
<INPUT TYPE="text" NAME="state" SIZE=2 MAXLENGTH=2>
<INPUT TYPE="text" NAME="zip" SIZE=5 MAXLENGTH=5><BR>
E-Mail:  <INPUT TYPE="text"
NAME="email" SIZE=50></P>
<INPUT TYPE="submit" NAME="submit"
VALUE=" Get Student ID ">
<INPUT TYPE="reset">
</FORM>
<H3>Returning Student Registration</H3>
<FORM METHOD="post" ACTION="CourseListingASP.asp">
Student ID:  <INPUT TYPE="text" NAME="id">
<INPUT TYPE="submit" VALUE=" Class Registration ">
</FORM>
```

4   Add the following code to close the <BODY> and <HTML> tags:

```
</BODY>
</HTML>
```

5   Save the file as **RegistrationASP.html** in the **Tutorial.11** folder on your Data Disk, close it, and then copy or upload the file to your ASP server. Open the **RegistrationASP.html** file in your Web browser from your ASP server. Figure 11-22 shows how the document appears in Internet Explorer. Before you execute the form buttons, you need to create the ASP documents.

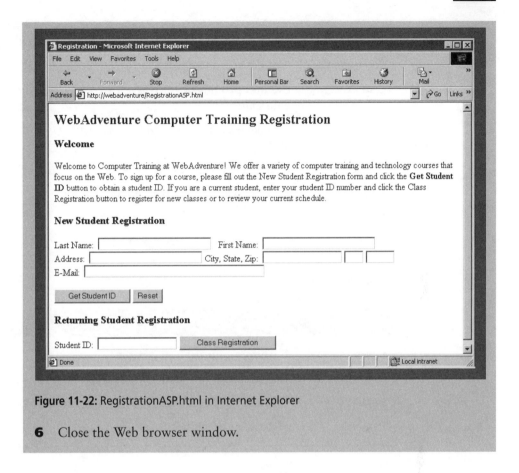

Figure 11-22: RegistrationASP.html in Internet Explorer

6 Close the Web browser window.

ADO Object Model

ADO technology is based on an object model consisting of objects and collections for accessing and manipulating data sources. Figure 11-23 lists the objects in the ADO object model, and Figure 11-24 lists the collections. You will work with several of the ADO objects and collections in this section.

Object	Description
Connection	Provides access to a data source
Command	Executes a command, such as a SQL command, against a data source
Parameter	Provides arguments for commands executed with the Command object
Recordset	Creates a navigable virtual table from the results of a SQL query
Field	Represents Recordset object database fields
Error	Represents errors returned from a database
Property	Represents an ADO object property

Figure 11-23: ADO objects

Collection	Contains
Errors	The errors returned from a database
Parameters	The parameters associated with the Parameter object
Fields	The database fields associated with the Field object
Properties	ADO object properties

Figure 11-24: ADO collections

tip

• •

This tutorial provides only a brief overview of the way to use ASP and ADO to access data-bases. For more information on ASP database access with ADO, visit the Microsoft Developer Network at *msdn.microsoft.com/*.

• •

Before you learn how to access databases with ADO, you need to create the CourseListingASP.asp file that students will use to select the courses they want to take.

To create the CourseListingASP.asp file:

1 Create a new document in your text editor or HTML editor.

2 Type the ASP processing directive, opening <HTML> tag, and an ASP section. The `if` statement checks if the id property exists in the Request object Form collection. If the id property exists, it is assigned to the studentID property of the Session object Contents collection. The id property of the Request object Form collection will contain the value that students enter into the id field of the Registration form. You will use the studentID property throughout the registration program to keep track of users as they navigate through the pages that make up the program.

```
<%@ LANGUAGE=JScript %>
<!-- #include file="adojavas.inc" -->
<HTML>
<%
if (parseInt(Request.Form("id")))
Session.Contents("studentID") = parseInt(Request.Form
("id"));
%>
```

help

> ASP collection variables are saved as text data types. Therefore, you must use a data type conversion function when copying values from an ASP collection variable to a JavaScript variable that you intend to use in an expression. This is one of the few cases, other than with form fields, in which JavaScript does not automatically convert the variable to the appropriate data type.

3 Add the following HTML tags, text, and form. The form contains two elements that are used for displaying a student's schedule. The student's ID is printed to the screen inside the form, using the output directive (<%=).

```
<BODY>
<H3>Course Registration Form</H3>
<FORM METHOD="post" ACTION="ReviewScheduleASP.asp">
<P><B>Student ID:  <%= Session.Contents("studentID")
%></B>
<INPUT TYPE="submit"
VALUE=" Review Current Schedule "></P>
</FORM>
```

4 Type the next form, which students use to register for classes. The form information is submitted to an ASP script named RegisterStudentASP.asp.

```
<FORM METHOD="post" ACTION="RegisterStudentASP.asp">
<P><B>Select the course you would like to take:</B><BR>
<INPUT TYPE="radio" NAME="course"
VALUE="Introduction to Active Server Pages 4.0">
Introduction to Active Server Pages<BR>
<INPUT TYPE="radio" NAME="course"
VALUE="Introduction to JavaScript">
Introduction to JavaScript<BR>
<INPUT TYPE="radio" NAME="course"
VALUE="Introduction to SSJS">
Introduction to SSJS<BR>
<INPUT TYPE="radio" NAME="course"
VALUE="Intermediate Active Server Pages 4.0">
Intermediate Active Server Pages<BR>
<INPUT TYPE="radio" NAME="course"
VALUE="Intermediate JavaScript">
Intermediate JavaScript<BR>
<INPUT TYPE="radio" NAME="course"
VALUE="Intermediate SSJS ">
Intermediate SSJS<BR>
<INPUT TYPE="radio" NAME="course"
VALUE="Advanced Active Server Pages">
Advanced Active Server Pages<BR>
<INPUT TYPE="radio" NAME="course"
VALUE="Advanced JavaScript">
Advanced JavaScript<BR>
<INPUT TYPE="radio" NAME="course"
VALUE="Advanced SSJS">
Advanced SSJS</P>
<P><B>Available Days and Times:</B><BR>
<SELECT NAME="days">
<OPTION SELECTED VALUE="Mondays and Wednesdays">
Mondays and Wednesdays
<OPTION VALUE="Tuesdays and Thursdays">
Tuesdays and Thursdays
<OPTION VALUE="Wednesdays and Fridays">
Wednesdays and Fridays
</SELECT>
<SELECT NAME="time">
<OPTION SELECTED VALUE="9 am-11 am">
```

```
9 am-11 am
<OPTION VALUE="1 pm-3 pm">1 pm-3 pm
<OPTION VALUE="6 pm-8 pm">6 pm-8 pm
</SELECT></P>
<INPUT TYPE="submit" VALUE=" Register ">
<INPUT TYPE="reset">
</FORM>
```

5 Add the following code to close the <BODY> and <HTML> tags:

```
</BODY>
</HTML>
```

6 Save the file as **CourseListingASP.asp** in the **Tutorial.11** folder on your Data Disk, close it, and then copy or upload the file to your ASP server. Before you can open the file, you need to write an ASP script that generates new student IDs.

The ADO Connection Object

The ADO **Connection object** is used for accessing databases in ASP and is similar in functionality to the LiveWire Database object. The Connection object contains various methods and properties for accessing and manipulating databases, as listed in Figures 11-25 and 11-26.

Method	Description
Open()	Opens a data source connection
Close()	Closes a data source connection
Execute()	Executes commands against a data source
BeginTrans()	Begins a transaction
CommitTrans()	Commits a transaction
RollbackTrans()	Rolls back a transaction

Figure 11-25: Connection object methods

Property	Description
ConnectionString	The connection string argument of the Open() method
ConnectionTimeout	The number of seconds to wait until abandoning a connection attempt
CommandTimeout	The number of seconds to wait until abandoning a command attempt
State	The data source connection state: adStateOpen indicates a successful connection and adStateClosed indicates an unsuccessful connection
Provider	The data source used in the connection
Version	The ADO version number
CursorLocation	Returns a value indicating whether the client manages the cursor, the server manages the cursor, or the cursor is not managed

Figure 11-26: Connection object properties

The first step in working with a database in ASP is to create an instance of the Connection object. You create an instance of the Connection object by using the CreateObject() method of the Server object. When you use the CreateObject() method, you pass it through a programmatic identifier, or progID, of a component on your system. The format for a progID is *vendor.component.version*. The progID for connecting to an ADO database is ADODB.Connection, in which *ADODB* is the vendor, and *Connection* is the component to create. The ADODB Connection object does not require a version. The full syntax for using the CreateObject() method to create an instance of the Connection object is var *object* = `Server.CreateObject("ADODB.Connection");`. You use *object* as the variable name to refer to the connection in ASP code.

As with all JavaScript code, the ADODB.Connection progID is case-sensitive.

Once you create an instance of the Connection object, you must use the Open() method to open a specific data source. The Open() method takes a string argument containing a connection string. Depending on how you are connecting to a database, the connection string can be composed of different arguments, including the database source provider, the database filename, a remote provider name, and a remote server path. You can also include other arguments in the Open() method, including a user ID, password, and other options. When working with a system DSN, you simply include a connection string of DSN=*filename*. Once you are finished working with a database, use the Close() method to end the connection. The following statement is an example of how to connect and disconnect to a system-based DSN named Accounting by assigning the connection to a variable named dbConnection.

```
var dbConnection = Server.CreateObject("ADODB.Connection");
dbConnection.Open("DSN=Accounting");
additional statements;
dbConnection.Close();
```

As with LiveWire, it is good practice in ASP to make sure that you have successfully connected to a database before attempting to read, write, add, or modify records. The State property of the Connection object returns a value of adStateOpen if a database connection was successful or a value of adStateClosed if the connection was unsuccessful. The following code adds an `if` statement that checks the State property after attempting to connect to a database. If the connection was unsuccessful, then the ASP Response.Write() method returns a message to the client.

```
var dbConnection = Server.CreateObject("ADODB.Connection");
dbConnection.Open("DSN=Accounting.dsn");
if (dbConnection.State == "adStateClosed")
    Response.Write("The database is not available.");
else {
    additional statements;
    dbConnection.Close();
}
```

In Section A, you learned how to use the LiveWire lock() and unlock() methods to determine whether clients accessed a database by using a standard or serial connection. ASP does not manage standard and serial connections, or any database pooling functions, as does LiveWire. Instead, ASP relies on ODBC drivers to handle database pooling and other connection functions. This means that you cannot include code in ASP to handle multiple requests for access to the same data source. However, you can use the **ConnectionTimeout property** of the Connection object to abandon a client database connection attempt if it has not successfully connected after a specified period of time has elapsed. You may find it necessary to use the ConnectionTimeout property if your site experiences heavy network traffic or server use. You assign an integer to the ConnectionTimeout property representing the number of seconds to wait until dropping a client connection. You place the statement that assigns an integer to the ConnectionTimeout property before the statement that opens the database. Once the number of seconds assigned to the ConnectionTimeout property has elapsed, the connection attempt is abandoned and an error message is returned to the client. By default, ADO waits for 15 seconds before abandoning a connection attempt. The following code shows the preceding example with a ConnectionTimeout property of 30 seconds:

```
var dbConnection = Server.CreateObject("ADODB.Connection");
dbConnection.ConnectionTimeout = 30;
dbConnection.Open("DSN=Accounting");
if (dbConnection.State == "adStateClosed")
```

```
        Response.Write("The database is not available.");
else {
    additional statements;
    dbConnection.Close();
}
```

Next you will start creating the GetStudentIDASP.asp file, which generates new student IDs.

To start creating the GetStudentIDASP.asp file:

1 Create a new document in your text editor or HTML editor.

2 Type the ASP processing directive, along with an opening ASP delimiter:

```
<%@ LANGUAGE=JScript %>
<!-- #include file="adojavas.inc" -->
<%
```

3 Add the following code, which locks and unlocks the Application object and generates a new student ID. If the idNum variable does not exist, it is created. If it does exist, then the current number is incremented by one and assigned to the projectID variable.

```
Application.Lock();
if (!Application.Contents("idNum")) {
    Application.Contents("idNum") = 100;
    var curID = Application.Contents ("idNum");
    Session.Contents("studentID")=curID;
}
else {
    var curID = Application.Contents("idNum");
    ++curID;
    Session.Contents("studentID") = curID;
    Application.Contents("idNum") = curID;
}
Application.Unlock();
```

4 Type the following section, which opens a database connection to WebAdventureASP.dsn. The code adds a ConnectionTimeout of 30 seconds and checks to make sure that the connection was established correctly.

```
var dbConnection =
Server.CreateObject("ADODB.Connection");
dbConnection.ConnectionTimeout = 30;
dbConnection.Open("DSN=WebAdventureASP");
if (dbConnection.State == "adStateClosed")
    Response.Write("The database is not available.");
```

5   Add the closing ASP delimiter **%>**.

6   Save the file as **GetStudentIDASP.asp** in the **Tutorial.11** folder on your Data Disk.

Executing SQL Commands

Three techniques are used for executing SQL queries against a database in ADO: the Connection object Execute() method, the Recordset object, and the Command object. This book discusses the Connection object Execute() method and the Recordset object. The Command object uses more advanced procedures that allow you to compile your query on the data source, and then use different sets of values to repeat the query. See the Microsoft ASP documentation for information about working with the Command object.

The Execute() Method

The Execute() method sends SQL statements to the database management system for processing and is the equivalent of the LiveWire execute() method. You use the Execute() method for updating or modifying a database table. The syntax for the Execute() method is *database.Execute(SQL statements);*. You do not submit ODBC SQL statements with the Execute() method. Instead, you submit SQL passthrough statements in the native SQL language of the database management system you are accessing.

    The ADO Connection object Execute() method returns results from a query to a Recordset object. The Recordset object returned from the Execute() method is a forward-only cursor and is read-only. A **forward-only cursor** is one that allows you to move only forward through the records in a recordset, and not backward or to specific records. If you need more functionality in a Recordset object, then you should construct your own Recordset object. (You will learn about the Recordset object next.) The Execute() method is most useful for quickly inserting, updating, or deleting rows in a database. For example, the following code uses the SQL INSERT statement to add a new employee record to the Employees database table. The SQL code is assigned to the SQLString variable, then executed using the statement `dbConnection.Execute(SQLString);`. If the connection is successful, the `else` clause executes necessary statements to perform the desired actions against the database before disconnecting.

```
var dbConnection = Server.CreateObject("ADODB.Connection");
dbConnection.ConnectionTimeout = 30;
dbConnection.Open("DSN=Accounting");
if (dbConnection.State == "adStateClosed")
    Response.Write("The database is not available.");
else {
    var SQLString =
    "INSERT INTO Employees VALUES ('106', 'Mbuti', 'Pierre',
    '106 Flagg Road', 'Spencer','MA', '01562', 'x413')";
    dbConnection.Execute(SQLString);
    dbConnection.Close();
}
```

The following code shows another example of the Execute() method, which deletes a row from the Employees table.

```
var dbConnection = Server.CreateObject("ADODB.Connection");
dbConnection.ConnectionTimeout = 30;
dbConnection.Open("DSN=Accounting");
if (dbConnection.State == "adStateClosed")
    Response.Write("The database is not available.");
else {
    var SQLString =
        "DELETE FROM Employees WHERE Last_Name = 'Miller'";
    dbConnection.Execute(SQLString);
    dbConnection.Close();
}
```

The SQL string in the preceding code uses the WHERE clause to look for rows in the table where the Last_Name field is equal to *Miller*. Note that the preceding statement would actually delete *all* rows in the table where the Last_Name field is equal to *Miller*. The statement is safe for our purposes, since we know that there is only one record that contains *Miller* in the Last_Name field. However, be sure you understand exactly what records will be deleted before executing the DELETE statement. Also, be sure to include a WHERE clause when using the DELETE statement or all of the rows in the specified table will be deleted.

Next you will add code to the GetStudentIDASP.asp file that writes records to the database, using the Execute() method.

To add code to the GetStudentIDASP.asp file that writes records to the database, using the Execute() method:

1 Return to the **GetStudentIDASP.asp** file in your text editor or HTML editor window.

2 Above the closing ASP delimiter, add the following statements that build the SQL string and run the Execute() method. The statements are contained in an `else` structure that executes only if the preceding `if` statement, which checks if the database is connected, returns a value of adStateOpen.

```
else {
    var SQLString = "INSERT INTO Students VALUES('"
        + curID + "', '"
        + Request.Form("last_name") + "', '"
        + Request.Form("first_name") + "', '"
        + Request.Form("address") + "', '"
        + Request.Form("city") + "', '"
        + Request.Form("state") + "', '"
        + Request.Form("zip") + "', '"
        + Request.Form("email") + "')";
    dbConnection.Execute(SQLString);
```

3 Next add the following statements, which return a response to the client containing the newly created student ID. Be sure not to include any line breaks in the literal strings—they are broken below due to space limitations.

```
Response.Write(
"<H2>WebAdventure Computer Training Registration</H2>");
Response.Write(
"Thanks " + Request.Form("first_name")
    + "! Your new student ID is <B>" + curID + "</B>");
Response.Write(
". Click <A HREF='CourseListingASP.asp'>Registration</A>
to proceed to the course registration page.");
```

4 Close the dbConnection and the `else` structure:

```
    dbConnection.Close();
}
```

5 Save and close **GetStudentIDASP.asp**, then copy or upload the file to your ASP server.

6 Open the **RegistrationASP.html** file in your Web browser from your ASP server. Fill out the registration information, and click the **Get Student ID** button. You should receive a response similar to Figure 11-27. Write down the new Student ID, since you will need it for the next exercise.

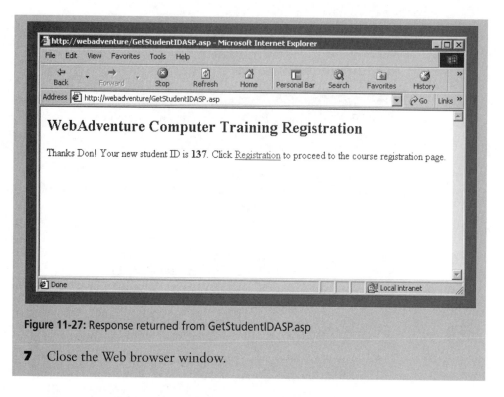

Figure 11-27: Response returned from GetStudentIDASP.asp

7   Close the Web browser window.

Next you will create the RegisterStudentASP.asp file.

To create the RegisterStudentASP.asp file:

1   Create a new document in your text editor or HTML editor.

2   Type the ASP processing directive, along with an opening ASP delimiter:

```
<%@ LANGUAGE=JScript %>
<!-- #include file="adojavas.inc" -->
<%
```

3   Add the following code to open the database connection:

```
var dbConnection =
Server.CreateObject("ADODB.Connection");
dbConnection.ConnectionTimeout = 30;
dbConnection.Open("DSN=WebAdventureASP");
if (dbConnection.State == "adStateClosed")
     Response.Write("The database is not available.");
```

4 Next add the following code to execute the SQL statements, using the Execute() method:

```
else {
    var SQLString =
    "INSERT INTO Registration VALUES('"
        + Session.Contents("studentID") + "', '"
        + Request.Form("course") + "', '"
        + Request.Form("days") + "', '"
        + Request.Form("time") + "')";
    dbConnection.Execute(SQLString);
```

5 Add the following statements, which return a response to the user. Be sure to type the literal string within the parentheses on a single line.

```
Response.Write(
"<H2>WebAdventure Computer Training Registration</H2>");
Response.Write("You are registered for "
    + Request.Form("course") + " on "
    + Request.Form("days") + ", "
    + Request.Form("time"));
Response.Write(
". To register for another course, click
    <A HREF='CourseListingASP.asp'>Course Listing</A>.
Or click <A HREF='ReviewScheduleASP.asp'>
Review Schedule</A> to review your current schedule.");
```

6 Close the dbConnection and the `else` structure, and add the closing ASP directive:

```
    dbConnection.Close();
}
%>
```

7 Save the file as **RegisterStudentASP.asp** in the **Tutorial.11** folder on your Data Disk, close it, and then copy or upload the file to your ASP server. Open **RegistrationASP.html** in your Web browser from your ASP server. Enter the student ID you created previously and click the **Class Registration** button to open CourseListingASP.asp. Figure 11-28 shows how the document appears in Internet Explorer.

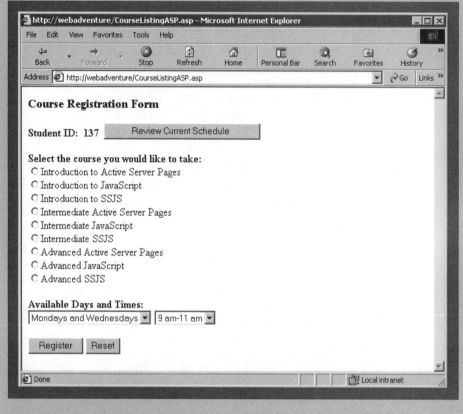

Figure 11-28: CourseListingASP.asp in Internet Explorer

8   Fill out the course form and click the **Register** button. Figure 11-29 shows an example of the response returned from RegisterStudentASP.asp.

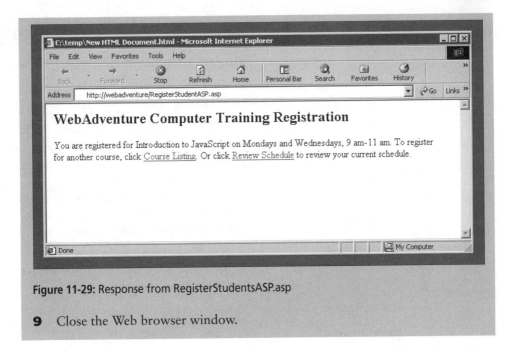

Figure 11-29: Response from RegisterStudentsASP.asp

9　Close the Web browser window.

The Recordset Object

ADO includes a **Recordset object,** which is used for accessing, adding, deleting, and modifying database records. You can think of the Recordset object as being roughly equivalent to the LiveWire Cursor object in that it returns a virtual table of values from a database. Like the LiveWire Cursor object, you can retrieve values, or add, delete, and modify records from the Recordset object virtual table. Any changes you make to the records in the Recordset object virtual table are written to the actual database on the server. You create an instance of the Recordset object the same way you create an instance of the Connection object: by using the CreateObject() method of the Server object. However, you use ADODB.Recordset as the progID instead of ADODB.Connection. The following statement creates a new Recordset object named rsEmployees:

```
var rsEmployees = Server.CreateObject("ADODB.Recordset");
```

Once you create an instance of the Recordset object, you must use the Recordset object **Open() method** to return a specific record set. The syntax for using the Open() method of the Recordset object is *record set variable.Open();*. Before using the open method, you need to assign values to the Recordset object properties to designate connection information, query criteria, and other options that the Recordset object should use when retrieving the record set. Figure 11-30 lists common properties of the Recordset object.

Property	Description
ActiveConnection	The database connection used to open the Recordset object
BOF	Contains a value of true if the cursor is located at the beginning of the file, and false if it is not
EOF	Contains a value of true if the cursor is located at the end of the file, and false if it is not
CursorLocation	Can be set to one of three values that determine where the cursor is managed: adUseNone, adUseClient, or adUseServer; adUseClient indicates that the client manages the cursor; adUseServer indicates that the server manages the cursor; adUseNone indicates that the cursor is not managed
CursorType	The type of cursor used in the record set: adOpenForwardOnly, adOpenKeyset, adOpenDynamic, or adOpenStatic
MaxRecords	The maximum number of records to return from a query
RecordCount	The number of records in the record set
Source	The SQL string used for retrieving the record set

Figure 11-30: Common Recordset object properties

The following example shows how to assign values to the Source and ActiveConnection Recordset object properties before using the Open() method. The ActiveConnection property is used for specifying which database connection the Recordset object should use to access the database records. The example first opens the Programmers database as dbConnection, confirms that the database is available, using the State property of the dbConnection object, and then opens the rsEmployees record set by assigning ADODB.Recordset as the progID of the CreateObject() method. Next, a SQL statement is assigned to the Source property, the dbConnection object is assigned as the ActiveConnection property of the rsEmployees record set, and then the Open() method is called. The SQL statement must be a valid SELECT statement written in ODBC SQL.

```
var dbConnection = Server.CreateObject("ADODB.Connection");
dbConnection.ConnectionTimeout = 30;
dbConnection.Open("DSN=Programmers");
if (dbConnection.State == "adStateClosed")
    Response.Write("The database is not available.");
var rsEmployees = Server.CreateObject("ADODB.Recordset");
rsEmployees.Source =
"SELECT * FROM Employees ORDER BY Last_Name, First_Name";
rsEmployees.ActiveConnection = dbConnection;
```

```
rsEmployees.Open();
additional statements;
dbConnection.Close();
```

Be sure to assign values to the Recordset object connection properties before using the Open() method, or you will receive an error.

In addition to the Open() method, the Recordset object contains a number of other methods and properties. Figure 11-31 lists some of the common methods of the Recordset object.

Method	Description
AddNew()	Creates a new record
CancelUpdate()	Cancels any pending changes to a record
Close()	Closes the Recordset object
Delete()	Deletes the current record
Move()	Moves to a specified record number
MoveFirst()	Moves to the first record
MoveLast()	Moves to the last record
MoveNext()	Moves to the next record
MovePrevious()	Moves to the previous record
Open()	Opens a cursor to a recordset
Requery()	Refreshes the data in a Recordset object by rerunning the query
Resync()	Refreshes the data in a Recordset object without rerunning the query
Save()	Saves the Recordset object data in a file
Seek()	Searches for a record in the Recordset object that matches specified criteria
Supports()	Returns the types of functionality supported by a Recordset object
Update()	Saves any pending changes to a record

Figure 11-31: Common Recordset object methods

One Recordset object method you should always use is the Close() method. You cannot close a database connection using the Close() method of the Connection object until all Recordset objects are closed. The following code shows the preceding example, but with a Close() method for the Recordset object.

```
var dbConnection = Server.CreateObject("ADODB.Connection");
dbConnection.ConnectionTimeout = 30;
dbConnection.Open("DSN=Programmers");
if (dbConnection.State == "adStateClosed")
    Response.Write("The database is not available.");
var rsEmployees = Server.CreateObject("ADODB.Recordset");
rsEmployees.Source =
"SELECT * FROM Employees ORDER BY Last_Name, First_Name";
rsEmployees.ActiveConnection = dbConnection;
rsEmployees.Open();
additional statements;
rsEmployees.Close();
dbConnection.Close();
```

tip

Notice in the preceding code that there are now two Close() methods: one to close the Recordset object and the other to close the Connection object.

Navigating Through a Recordset Object Your position in a Recordset object is called the cursor, the same as when you work with the LiveWire Cursor object. However, when you first create a Recordset object, your cursor is initially placed within the first row of the record set, not *before* the first row in the record set, as occurs with the LiveWire Cursor object. The field names in a database table are assigned as variables in the Fields collection of the Recordset object. For example, if you instantiate a Recordset object named rsEmployees for the Programmers database, then you refer to the First_Name field, using a statement similar to rsEmployees.Fields("First_Name"). To navigate through the records in a Cursor object, you use the MoveNext() method. The following code creates a new Recordset object, and then moves the cursor forward by one row:

```
var rsEmployees = Server.CreateObject("ADODB.Recordset");
rsEmployees.Source =
"SELECT * FROM Employees ORDER BY Last_Name, First_Name";
rsEmployees.ActiveConnection = dbConnection;
rsEmployees.Open();
rsEmployees.MoveNext();
statements;
rsEmployees.Close();
```

tip

The statements that open the database connection are excluded from the preceding code for clarity.

The Recordset object contains more methods for navigating through records than does the LiveWire Cursor object. In addition to the MoveNext() method, ADO includes four other navigation methods: Move(), MoveFirst(), MoveLast(), and MovePrevious(). To use any navigation method other than MoveNext(), you must set the CursorType property before using the Recordset object Open() method. The **CursorType property** designates the type of cursor that will be allowed in the resulting record set. You can designate one of four cursor types as the value for the CursorType property. Figure 11-32 lists the valid cursor type values of the CursorType property.

Cursor Type	Description
adOpenForwardOnly	Forward-only cursor. This cursor allows you to move only forward through a record set, using the MoveNext() method.
adOpenKeyset	Keyset cursor. Allows you to move forward and backward through a record set, but does not allow you to see new records added by other users. You can see any changes made to records by other users, but you cannot access any records deleted by other users.
adOpenDynamic	Dynamic cursor. Allows you to move forward and backward through a record set and see any changes made by other users.
adOpenStatic	Static cursor. Allows you to move forward and backward through a record set, but does not allow you to see any changes made by other users.

Figure 11-32: ADO cursor types

The decision on what type of cursor to use depends on the type of performance you need from your application. Generally, cursors that allow you to see changes made by other users will slow down an application. The fastest cursor is adOpenForwardOnly, since it allows you to move through a record set only once and does not allow you to see any changes made by other users. The adOpenForwardOnly cursor is the default cursor type and the best choice for performance if you need to move through a record set only once. If you want to be able to move forward and backward through a record set, you need to use one of the other cursor types. The following code shows how to set the cursor type to adOpenStatic, which allows you to move forward and backward through a record set, but does not allow you to see changes made by other users. The example uses the MoveNext() method to move to the second record in the record set and print the values in the First_Name and Last_Name fields. Then the MovePrevious() method moves back to the first record and again prints the values in the First_Name and Last_Name fields.

```
var rsEmployees = Server.CreateObject("ADODB.Recordset");
rsEmployees.Source =
"SELECT * FROM Employees ORDER BY Last_Name, First_Name";
rsEmployees.ActiveConnection = dbConnection;
rsEmployees.CursorType = adOpenStatic;
rsEmployees.Open();
rsEmployees.MoveNext();
Response.Write(rsEmployees("First_Name") + " "
    + rsEmployees("Last_Name"));
rsEmployees.MovePrevious();
Response.Write(rsEmployees("First_Name") + " "
    + rsEmployees("Last_Name"));
rsEmployees.Close();
```

When you work with record sets and the navigation methods, you can never be certain if there is another record before or after the current position of the cursor. In addition, you can never be certain if any records were returned at all from your SQL SELECT statement. For example, the preceding code assumes that records exist in the Employees table. However, your SQL query may not have returned any records at all. To ensure that there is a next or previous record available, you use the Recordset object BOF and EOF properties. The **BOF** (beginning of file) **property** returns a value of true if the cursor is located before the first record in a record set and a value of false if the cursor is located on or after the first record. Similarly, the **EOF** (end of file) **property** returns a value of true if the cursor is located after the last record in a record set and a value of false if the cursor is located on or before the last record. The following code shows how to use a `while` loop to check the value of the EOF property before moving the cursor. As long as the EOF property is not equal to true, then the `while` loop continues.

```
var rsEmployees = Server.CreateObject("ADODB.Recordset");
rsEmployees.Source =
"SELECT * FROM Employees ORDER BY Last_Name, First_Name";
rsEmployees.ActiveConnection = dbConnection;
rsEmployees.Open();
while(rsEmployees.EOF != true) {
    Response.Write(rsEmployees.Fields("First_Name") + " "
        + rsEmployees.Fields("Last_Name") + " lives in "
        + rsEmployees.Fields("City") + ", "
        + rsEmployees.Fields("State") + "<BR>");
    rsEmployees.MoveNext();
}
rsEmployees.Close();
```

Next you will create the ReviewScheduleASP.asp file, which displays the courses a student is registered for.

To create the ReviewScheduleASP.asp file:

1 Create a new document in your text editor or HTML editor.

2 Type the ASP processing directive, along with an opening ASP delimiter:

```
<%@ LANGUAGE=JScript %>
<!-- #include file="adojavas.inc" -->
<%
```

3 Add the following code to open the database connection:

```
var dbConnection =
Server.CreateObject("ADODB.Connection");
dbConnection.ConnectionTimeout = 30;
dbConnection.Open("DSN=WebAdventureASP");
if (dbConnection.State == "adStateClosed")
    Response.Write("The database is not available.");
```

4 Add an opening **else {** statement to contain the database statements.

5 Type **var rsSchedule = Server.CreateObject("ADODB.Recordset");** to instantiate the Recordset object.

6 Assign the SQL code to the Source property and dbConnection to the ActiveConnection property. Then run the Open() method. The SQL code restricts the records returned to just those records that match the student ID.

```
rsSchedule.Source =
"SELECT * FROM Registration WHERE Student_ID = '"
  + Session.Contents("studentID") + "'";
rsSchedule.ActiveConnection = dbConnection;
rsSchedule.Open();
```

7 Add the following section, which returns a response to the student and closes the rsSchedule object:

```
Response.Write(
"<H2>This is your current schedule</H2>");
while(rsSchedule.EOF != true) {
    Response.Write(rsSchedule.Fields("Course") + ", "
    + rsSchedule.Fields("Days") + ", "
    + rsSchedule.Fields("Time") + "<BR>");
    rsSchedule.MoveNext();
}
rsSchedule.Close();
```

8 Close the dbConnection object and the `else` statement, and add the closing ASP delimiter:

```
dbConnection.Close();
}
%>
```

9 Save the file as **ReviewScheduleASP.asp** in the **Tutorial.11** folder on your Data Disk, close it, and then copy or upload the file to your ASP server. Open the **RegistrationASP.html** file in your Web browser from your ASP server. Enter an existing student ID, and click the Class Registration button. From the CourseListingASP.asp document, click the **Review Current Schedule** button. Figure 11-33 shows the output for a student who registered for several classes.

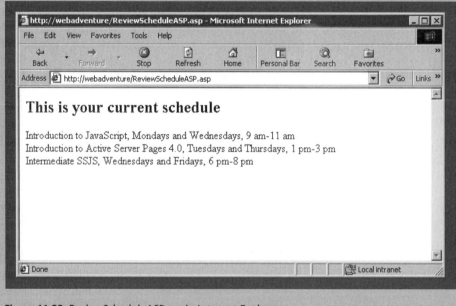

Figure 11-33: ReviewScheduleASP.asp in Internet Explorer

10 Close the Web browser window.

Updatable Cursors You create an updatable cursor in ADO by using the LockType property of the Recordset object before using the Open() method. The value assigned to the LockType property determines whether the cursor is read-only, pessimistic, or optimistic. A read-only cursor prevents users from making any changes to records. An optimistic cursor locks the records only when you execute the Update() method. A pessimistic cursor prevents other users from accessing the record from the time you start editing it until you use the Update() method. You determine whether a cursor is updatable by assigning one of four values to the LockType property. Figure 11-34 lists the valid lock type values of the LockType property.

Lock Type	Description
adLockReadOnly	Read-only
adLockPessimistic	Pessimistic locking, record by record
adLockOptimistic	Optimistic locking, record by record
adLockBatchOptimistic	Optimistic batch updates

Figure 11-34: ADO lock types

The default lock type is adLockReadOnly, which prevents users from making any changes to records. To make changes to records, you must use one of the other three lock types. Use optimistic locking if you do not anticipate that multiple users will simultaneously attempt to edit the same record in your database. However, if there is a possibility that multiple users will simultaneously attempt to edit the same record, then pessimistic locking is safer, since it helps minimize data integrity problems.

Three Recordset object methods are specific to updatable cursors: the Update(), Delete(), and AddNew()methods. The Update() method saves any changes you make to the current row in the record set. You execute the Update() method after you change field values. For example, suppose that Erica Miller was recently married and is changing her last name to Lee. The following code creates a Recordset object, using a SELECT statement with a WHERE clause to retrieve only Erica Miller's records. The LockType property is assigned a lock type of adLockOptimistic so that the record can be edited. Before editing the record, the code makes sure that the EOF property is not equal to true and that the current record is actually Erica Miller's by checking the value of the Last_Name field. Once the record is edited, it is updated using the Update() method.

```
var rsEmployees = Server.CreateObject("ADODB.Recordset");
rsEmployees.Source =
"SELECT * FROM Employees WHERE Last_Name = 'Miller'";
rsEmployees.ActiveConnection = dbConnection;
rsEmployees.LockType = adLockOptimistic;
rsEmployees.Open();
if (rsEmployees.eof != true) {
    if (rsEmployees.Fields("Last_Name") == "Miller") {
        rsEmployees.Fields("Last_Name") = "Lee";
        rsEmployees.Update();
}
rsEmployees.Close();
```

The AddNew() method is similar to the SQL INSERT statement in that it adds a new record to the end of a table. After executing the AddNew() method, the new record becomes the current location of the cursor. You then assign new values to the new record fields and execute the Update() method. The following code shows how to add a record for a new programmer at WebAdventure:

```
var rsEmployees = Server.CreateObject("ADODB.Recordset");
rsEmployees.Source = "SELECT * FROM Employees";
rsEmployees.ActiveConnection = dbConnection;
rsEmployees.LockType = adLockOptimistic;
rsEmployees.Open();
rsEmployees.AddNew();
rsEmployees.Fields("Employee_ID") = "107";
rsEmployees.Fields("Last_Name") = "Picard";
rsEmployees.Fields("First_Name") = "Lisa";
rsEmployees.Fields("Address") = "1113 Oakham Road";
rsEmployees.Fields("City") = "New Braintree";
rsEmployees.Fields("State") = "MA";
rsEmployees.Fields("Zip") = "01531";
rsEmployees.Fields("Extension") = "x309";
rsEmployees.Update();
rsEmployees.Close();
```

 tip

If you call the AddNew() method while editing a record, ADO automatically calls the Update() method for the record you are editing, and then creates the new record.

The deleteRow() method is similar to the SQL DELETE statement except that instead of deleting all rows that match the results of the SELECT statement, the deleteRow() method deletes just the record where the cursor is located. For example, if Scott Morinaga leaves WebAdventure, you can delete his employee record using the following code:

```
var rsEmployees = Server.CreateObject("ADODB.Recordset");
rsEmployees.Source = "SELECT * FROM Employees";
rsEmployees.ActiveConnection = dbConnection;
rsEmployees.LockType = adLockOptimistic;
rsEmployees.Open();
while(rsEmployees.Fields("Last_Name")!= "Morinaga") {
    rsEmployees.MoveNext();
}
rsEmployees.Delete();
rsEmployees.Close();
```

Transaction Processing with ADO

Transaction processing in ASP is handled by the BeginTrans(), CommitTrans(), and RollbackTrans() methods of the Connection object, which are approximately equivalent to LiveWire's beginTransaction(), commitTransaction(), and rollbackTransaction() methods. You begin a transaction using the BeginTrans() method. All database statements following a BeginTrans() method are part of the current transaction. Following the database statements that are part of the current transaction, you execute the CommitTrans() method to make the changes to the database. At any point following a BeginTrans() method, you can execute the RollbackTrans() method to cancel all changes that are part of the current transaction. For example, if the current transaction is missing a required field, such as a key field, then you can call RollbackTrans() to cancel all changes that are part of the current transaction. If you attempt to use CommitTrans() or RollbackTrans() before you use BeginTrans(), you will receive an error from the database. Also, once a response is returned to a client, you can no longer roll back a transaction.

The following code shows how to use transaction processing when adding a new employee record to the Employees table:

```
var rsEmployees = Server.CreateObject("ADODB.Recordset");
rsEmployees.Source = "SELECT * FROM Employees";
rsEmployees.ActiveConnection = dbConnection;
rsEmployees.LockType = adLockOptimistic;
rsEmployees.Open();
dbConnection.BeginTrans();
rsEmployees.AddNew();
rsEmployees.Fields("Employee_ID") = "107";
rsEmployees.Fields("Last_Name") = "Picard";
rsEmployees.Fields("First_Name") = "Lisa";
rsEmployees.Fields("Address") = "1113 Oakham Road";
rsEmployees.Fields("City") = "New Braintree";
rsEmployees.Fields("State") = "MA";
rsEmployees.Fields("Zip") = "01531";
rsEmployees.Fields("Extension") = "x309";
rsEmployees.Update();
dbConnection.CommitTrans();
rsEmployees.Close();
```

The preceding code does not include a RollbackTrans() method. You will learn how to roll back a transaction when error handling is discussed.

Error Handling with the ADO Error Object

All operations involving ADO objects can generate error messages. When an error message is generated in ADO, error objects are added to the Errors collection. The **Errors collection** is a list of error objects returned from the last ADO operation. The Errors collection contains a single property, **Count**, which returns the number of errors added to the Errors collection during the last ADO operation. If the Count property contains a value of zero, then the last ADO operation was completed successfully. When a Count property other than zero is returned, you can find more information about the error, using the properties of each Error object. Error objects include a **Number property**, containing the error number; a **Description property**, containing a description of the error; a **Source property**, identifying the source of the error; and **SQL** and **State properties**, which provide information from the data source.

In the event that a problem occurs while performing a transaction, you can use the Count property and Error object properties with the RollbackTrans() method to cancel any changes to a database. The following code shows the transaction example you saw previously, but this time with a RollbackTrans() method. The code checks the Count property and commits the transaction if it is equal to zero. If the Count property is greater than zero, the transaction is rolled back and a while loop cycles through the contents of the Errors collection, returning each error number and description.

```
var rsEmployees = Server.CreateObject("ADODB.Recordset");
rsEmployees.Source = "SELECT * FROM Employees";
rsEmployees.ActiveConnection = dbConnection;
rsEmployees.LockType = adLockOptimistic;
rsEmployees.Open();
dbConnection.BeginTrans();
rsEmployees.AddNew();
rsEmployees.Fields("Employee_ID") = "107";
rsEmployees.Fields("Last_Name") = "Picard";
rsEmployees.Fields("First_Name") = "Lisa";
rsEmployees.Fields("Address") = "1113 Oakham Road";
rsEmployees.Fields("City") = "New Braintree";
rsEmployees.Fields("State") = "MA";
rsEmployees.Fields("Zip") = "01531";
rsEmployees.Fields("Extension") = "x309";
rsEmployees.Update();
if (dbConnection.Errors.Count == 0) {
    rsEmployees.CommitTrans();
    Response.Write("The record was added successfully.");
}
```

```
else if (dbConnection.Errors.Count > 0) {
    rsEmployees.RollbackTrans();
    Response.Write("The record was not successfully added.
        The database server returned the following error
        number(s) and description(s):<BR>")";
    var curError = 0;
    while(curError < dbConnection.Errors.Count)) {
        Response.Write("Error Number: "
            + dbErrors.Errors.Error(curError.Number);
        Response.Write("Error Description: "
            + dbErrors.Errors.Error(curError.Description);
        ++curError;
    }
}
rsEmployees.Close();
```

SUMMARY

- ActiveX Data Objects, or ADO, is a Microsoft database connectivity technology that allows ASPs and other Web development tools to access ODBC- and OLE-DB-compliant databases.

- OLE DB is a data source connectivity standard promoted by Microsoft as a successor to ODBC.

- When you create an ASP application that needs to access a database, you must copy the adojavas.inc file into the directory containing your ASP files, and use the #include directive to insert the file into your program.

- The #include directive specifies a file to insert into an ASP file before it is processed by the server.

- ADO technology is based on an object model that consists of objects and collections for accessing and manipulating data sources.

- The ADO Connection object is used for accessing databases in ASP and is similar in functionality to LiveWire's Database object.

- The ConnectionTimeout property of the Connection object abandons a client database connection attempt if it has not successfully connected after a specified period of time has elapsed.

- The Execute() method sends SQL statements to the database management system for processing.

- The Execute() method returns results from a query to a Recordset object.

- ADO includes a Recordset object, which is used for accessing, adding, deleting, and modifying database records.

- Once you create an instance of the Recordset object, you must use the Recordset object Open() method to return a specific record set.

- When you first create a Recordset object, your cursor is initially placed within the first row of the record set.

- The CursorType property designates the type of cursor that will be allowed in the resulting record set.

- The BOF (beginning of file) property returns a value of true if the cursor is located before the first record in a record set and a value of false if the cursor is located on or after the first record.

- The EOF (end of file) property returns a value of true if the cursor is located after the last record in a record set, and false if the cursor is located on or before the last record.

- You create an updatable cursor in ADO by using the LockType method of the Recordset object.

- The default lock type is adLockReadOnly, which prevents users from making any changes to records.

- Three Recordset object methods are specific to updatable cursors: the Update(), Delete(), and AddNew()methods.

- Transaction processing in ASP is handled by the BeginTrans(), CommitTrans(), and RollbackTrans() methods of the Connection object.

- The Errors collection is a list of error objects returned from the last ADO operation.

 QUESTIONS

1. What is one of the primary differences between ODBC and OLE DB?
   a. ODBC can be used only on Windows platforms.
   b. OLE DB functions only with relational databases.
   c. OLE DB provides access to both relational databases and nonrelational data sources.
   d. ODBC functions only with nonrelational databases.

2. Which ADO file is required to allow ASP to access data sources?
   a. adojavas.inc
   b. adojavas.dll
   c. adoasp.asp
   d. adodatasource.exe

3. How do you use an external file with Active Server Pages?
   a. by including an SRC attribute with the processing directive
   b. by placing the external file in the ASP program directory
   c. with the #include directive
   d. by including an HREF attribute as part of the <% %> ASP delimiters

4. What is the correct syntax for creating a database object in ASP?
   a. `var dbConnection = Server.CreateObject("ADODB.Connection");`
   b. `var dbConnection = CreateObject("ADODB.Connection"");`
   c. `var dbConnection = new ADODB.Connection;`
   d. `var dbConnection = Server("ADODB.Connection");`

5. Which property of the Connection object abandons a client database connection attempt if it has not successfully connected after a specified period of time has elapsed?
   a. Timeout
   b. Abandon
   c. Cancel
   d. ConnectionTimeout

6. What is the value returned by the State property if you have successfully connected to a database?
   a. adStateClosed
   b. adStateOpen
   c. adStateConnected
   d. adStateReady

7. Which ADO method executes SQL passthrough statements?
   a. dbExecute()
   b. SQL()
   c. Execute()
   d. execute()

8. Which parameter is passed to the CreateObject() method to instantiate a Recordset object?
   a. ADO.Recordset
   b. ADODB.Recordset
   c. ADODB.Record
   d. ADODB.Cursor

9. Which method is used for navigating forward through a record set?
   a. Move()
   b. Next()
   c. MoveNext()
   d. Forward()

10. Which of the following arguments of the CursorType property does not allow you to use the MoveFirst() method?
    a. adOpenForwardOnly
    b. adOpenKeyset
    c. adOpenDynamic
    d. adOpenStatic

11. How do you know when you have reached the last record in a record set?
    a. when the MoveNext() property returns a value of false
    b. when the EOF property returns a value of true
    c. when the BOF property returns a value of true
    d. when both the EOF and BOF properties return values of false

12. How do you create an updatable cursor?

   a. An updatable cursor is created whenever you use the CreateObject() method.

   b. by using a value of *true* as the *updatable* argument of the Open() method

   c. by setting the LockType property of the Recordset object to an updatable value

   d. You cannot create an updatable cursor.

13. Which of the following arguments is not specific to an updatable cursor?

   a. Update()

   b. AddNew()

   c. Delete()

   d. MovePrevious()

14. Which method cancels a transaction?

   a. Cancel()

   b. Discard()

   c. RollbackTrans()

   d. RollbackTransaction()

15. What should the Count property of the Errors object contain to indicate that a database operation was completed successfully?

   a. OK

   b. SUCCESS

   c. 1

   d. 0

 # EXERCISES

Save your solution files for the following exercises in their own folders within the Tutorial.11 folder on your Data Disk.

1. New student IDs in the registration program you created in this tutorial are generated from the idNum property of the Application object Contents collection. Generating new student IDs from a property in the Application object is not necessarily the best method of generating new student IDs because the value in idNum is reinitialized each time you restart the registration program. Modify the ASP version of the registration program so that new student IDs are generated from the Students table in the database instead of from the idNum property of the Application object Contents collection. You will need to use the MoveNext() method to search through existing records of the Students table to retrieve the last assigned student ID. For this exercise, use the WebAdventureASP DSN you used throughout Section A.

2. Visit the Microsoft Universal Data Access site at *www.Microsoft.com/data* and search the Internet for other sources of information on Universal Data Access. What are the competitors of Universal Data Access? How is the industry embracing this evolving technology proposed by Microsoft? Write a paper on your findings.

3. Add an `if` statement to the following code that confirms whether the database connection is successful. Save the modified code in a text file named ConfirmConnectASP.txt.

```
var dbConnection = Server.CreateObject("ADODB.Connection");
dbConnection.Open("DSN=Orders");
dbConnection.Close();
```

4. Modify the code from Exercise 3 so it abandons the database connection attempt if it has not successfully connected after 60 seconds. Save the modified code in a text file named AbandonConnectASP.txt.

5. Write a SQL statement that inserts the values *SH001*, *Polo Shirt*, *Large*, *Blue*, and *19.95* into a table named Purchases and assign the statement to a variable named purchaseString. Also, write a statement that executes the SQL string using passthrough SQL. Assume that a Connection object named dbOrders has already been created and opened. Save the code in a text file named PassthroughSQLASP.txt.

6. Write the code to create a Recordset object named rsShirtsTable that contains the records returned from the following SQL query: `SELECT * FROM Dress_Shirts WHERE Color = 'blue'`. Include all of the necessary statements to open and close the database connection and the Recordset object. Use a DSN named Orders. Also include statements that navigate through the records and modify the Color fields from *blue* to *red*. Be sure to set the appropriate lock type. Save the code in a text file named UpdateShirtsASP.txt.

7. Modify the following statements so that database records are committed using transaction processing and error handling. Save the code in a text file named TransactionsAndErrorsASP.txt.

```
var dbConnection = Server.CreateObject("ADODB.Recordset");
dbConnection.ConnectionTimeout = 30;
dbConnection.Open( "DSN=Stocks");
if (dbConnection.State == "adStateClosed")
  Response.Write("The database is not available.");
else {
  var rsStocks = Server.CreateObject("ADODB.Recordset");
  rsStocks.Source = "SELECT * FROM Stocks";
  rsStocks.ActiveConnection = dbConnection;
  rsStocks.LockType = adLockOptimistic;
  rsStocks.Open();
  rsStocks.AddNew();
  rsStocks.Field("Stock_ID") = "S367";
  rsStocks.Field("Stock_Name") = "Oracle":
  rsStocks.Field("pricePerShare") = 67.5;
  rsStocks.Field("numberOfShares") = 200;
  rsStocks.Update();
  rsStocks.Delete();
  rsStocks.Close();
  dbConnection.Close();
}
```

For the next four exercises, use a database management system you have access to, such as Access, Paradox, or SQL Server, to create the database file where you will store the data.

8. Create an ASP program that saves a Web site hit list counter to a database.

9. Create an ASP program that saves Web site guest book entries to a database.

10. Create a telephone directory application that saves entries to a database. You should include standard telephone directory fields in the database, such as name, address, city, state, zip, and telephone number. Create an HTML document as a main "directory" where you can select and retrieve records. Also create one HTML document that you can use to add new entries to your database and another HTML document that you can use to edit entries.

11. Re-create in ASP the shopping cart application for an online bookstore that you created in the Section A exercises. Use different pages in the application for different types of books. The shopping cart should build a list of books that users want to purchase and provide a checkout mechanism that writes the information to a database and returns a response to the user.

Working with Java Applets and Embedded Data

case ▶ More and more of WebAdventure's clients want to incorporate different types of media into their Web sites, in addition to simple text and images. Some clients want to include programs in the form of Java applets that have greater capabilities than programs created with JavaScript and HTML. Other clients want to include audio capabilities for entertainment and videos for educational and training purposes. To keep up with clients' demands, your manager at WebAdventure has asked you to learn how to include Java applets and embedded data in HTML documents and how to manipulate them with JavaScript.

Previewing the Guessing Game and Embedded Data Programs

In this tutorial, you will create two projects: an HTML document containing a guessing game program that includes a Java applet and an HTML document containing embedded data. You will also learn how to use JavaScript to manipulate Java applets and embedded data.

help

If you are using Netscape, you must have the Java plugin installed in order to perform the exercises in this chapter. You can check your installed plugins, and install new plugins, by selecting the About Plugins command on the Help menu.

To preview the guessing game program:

1 In your Web browser, open the **Tutorial12_RandomNumberGame.html** file from the **Tutorial.12** folder on your Data Disk. The program prompts you to guess a randomly selected number between 0 and 100. Try guessing the random number. Clicking the Reload or Refresh button generates a new random number. Figure 12-1 shows how the document appears in Internet Explorer.

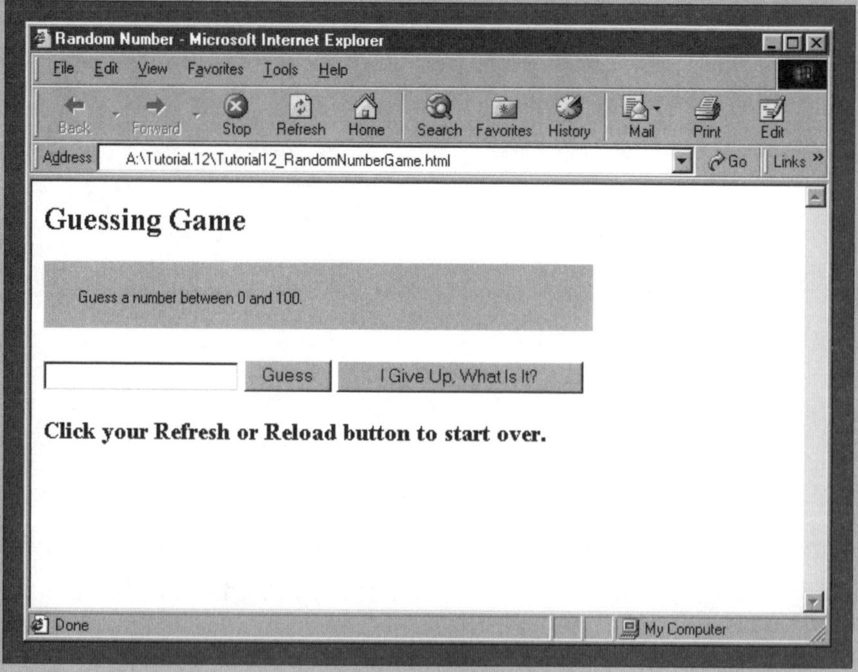

Figure 12-1: Tutorial12_RandomNumberGame.html in Internet Explorer

2 When you are finished playing the game, close your Web browser and open the **Tutorial12_RandomNumberGame.html** file in your text editor or HTML editor. The document includes an <APPLET> tag that loads a Java applet named Tutorial12_RandomNumberGame.class. JavaScript statements in the script section call methods and properties of the applet, using the <APPLET> tag NAME attribute.

3 Next, open the **Tutorial12_RandomNumberGame.java** file in your text editor or HTML editor. This file is the source code that is used to create the Java program. In this section, you will learn how to create the Java program and manipulate it using JavaScript.

4 Close your text editor or HTML editor.

Next you will open the HTML document that contains embedded data controlled by JavaScript. To open the document, you will need to install RealPlayer on your system. **RealPlayer** is a free program that executes multimedia, such as video and audio files. The program installs onto your computer as a standalone program. It also installs plug-in and ActiveX controls that allow multimedia files to be played directly within a Web page. You will need RealPlayer version 8 to run the exercises in this Tutorial. You can download RealPlayer 8 from *www.real.com/player/index.html*.

 tip

ActiveX controls are special objects that act as "miniapplications." You place ActiveX controls inside Web pages and other types of programs. You will learn about ActiveX technology in Section B of this tutorial.

To preview the HTML document containing embedded data controlled by JavaScript:

1 If you use Netscape, in your browser open the document named **Tutorial12_RealPlayerPlugin.html** from the **Tutorial.12** folder on your Data Disk. If you use Internet Explorer, open the document named **Tutorial12_RealPlayerActiveX.html**. Both programs display a video clip that can be started, paused, and executed using form buttons that execute JavaScript code. Try starting, pausing, and stopping the video clip. Figure 12-2 shows how RealPlayerPlug-in.html appears in Netscape.

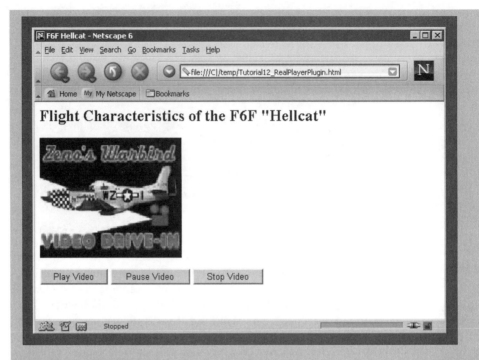

Figure 12-2: Tutorial12_RealPlayerPlug-in.html in Netscape

The video clip displayed by RealPlayer is the first few seconds of a World War II training video for the F6F Hellcat aircraft. This clip was obtained from the Zeno's Warbird Video Drive-In Web site, which contains many RealPlayer videos about vintage military aircraft. If you would like to see the rest of the F6F video, or other vintage military aircraft videos, visit Zeno's Warbird Video Drive-In at *www.zenoswarbirdvideos.com/*. This Web site is an outstanding example of how to incorporate multimedia into HTML documents.

2   When you are finished viewing the video, close your Web browser and open the **Tutorial12_RealPlayerPlugin.html** and **Tutorial12_RealPlayerActiveX.html** files in your text editor or HTML editor. When you view the HTML tags for the Tutorial12RealPlayerPlug-in.html and Tutorial12RealPlayerActiveX.html files, you will see that they use different tags to display the embedded RealPlayer video. The Netscape plug-in file, Tutorial12_RealPlayerPlug-in.html, uses an <EMBED> tag. The Internet Explorer ActiveX file, Tutorial12RealPlayerActiveX.html, uses <OBJECT> and <PARAM> tags. You will learn about plug-ins and ActiveX controls in Section B.

In this section you will learn:
- About applets and embedded data
- About Java classes and methods
- How to compile a Java program
- How to create an applet
- About Java variables and data types
- How to add an applet to an HTML document
- How to control Java applets with JavaScript

A Java Tutorial

Applets and Embedded Data

Web pages can consist of more than just HTML tags, images, and JavaScript code; they can also include applets and embedded data, such as sound and video files. An **applet** is a Java program that runs from within a Web page. **Embedded data** refers to data from one type of application that is stored in another type of application. Netscape displays embedded data using special program extensions called plug-ins, and Internet Explorer displays embedded information using ActiveX controls. To allow JavaScript, Java, and plug-ins to communicate with each other, Netscape uses a technology known as LiveConnect. Internet Explorer uses ActiveX scripting to allow JavaScript to interact with Java and ActiveX controls. This communication between the different elements of a Web page gives a programmer great control over how the page functions and interacts with a user. For example, if a Java applet that calculates mortgage payments is embedded in an HTML document, you can use form fields in the document to assign information to the applet's properties and execute its methods. Similarly, you can include controls within an HTML document to allow the user to start and stop the execution of a plug-in or ActiveX control. Commands that control Java programs and ActiveX components can be, and often are, included as part of an applet, plug-in, or ActiveX control.

This section explains the basic concepts of Java programming and how to manipulate an applet with JavaScript. Although Netscape and Internet Explorer use different technologies to allow JavaScript to manipulate an applet (Netscape uses LiveConnect, and Internet Explorer uses ActiveX), the techniques described in this section can be used interchangeably with both browsers. In Section B, you will learn how to control JavaScript from Java, as well as how to work with Netscape plug-ins and ActiveX scripting with Internet Explorer.

Introduction to Java

Recall that JavaScript and Java are entirely different programming languages. Java is a compiled, object-oriented programming language that was created by Sun Microsystems. It is considerably more difficult to master than JavaScript. Java programs can run as independent, standalone applications or as applets within the context of a Web page. In contrast, JavaScript programs run *only* within a Web page and are used only for controlling Web pages and Web browsers. Java can create essentially the same programs that JavaScript can, and much more, because the language contains many more methods, properties, and programmatic features than does JavaScript. With Java you can create graphics and new types of controls, perform networking functions, and develop complete user interfaces. You can also use a technique called multithreading to create much more powerful animations than can be created with JavaScript.

If Java is so much more powerful, why use JavaScript at all? JavaScript works within the confines of an HTML page. This functionality is limiting because JavaScript cannot be used to develop applications independent of a Web browser. The advantage of JavaScript is that it can be "in touch" with the various elements of an HTML document. You cannot incorporate Java code directly into an HTML document as you can JavaScript code. Instead, you place Java applets on a Web page as encapsulated objects within a bounding box. **Encapsulation** means that all code and required data are self-contained within the object itself. A **bounding box** is the rectangular area on a Web page in which an applet executes.

Java programming is such a popular topic that it would be impossible to list all the Web sites devoted to the subject. You can find numerous Web sites offering professionally developed and free applets, as well as sites devoted to teaching Java programming and sharing Java programming tips and techniques. If you would like to visit one of the many Java Web sites, search for *java* or *applets* in an Internet search engine such as Yahoo! or Google. One of the more popular Java programming Web sites is Gamelan at *www.gamelan.com*.

The JavaScript language was originally called LiveScript. With the release of Navigator 2.0, the name was changed to JavaScript to take advantage of the rising popularity of the Java programming language.

Why is it necessary to control a Java applet using JavaScript when you can create all the necessary functionality using Java? The answer is that you want all of the components of a Web page (JavaScript code, HTML, applets, and plug-ins) to work together as an integrated program. The key to understanding the idea of an integrated program is to gain an understanding of object-oriented programming.

Object-oriented programming (OOP) refers to the creation of reusable software objects that can be easily incorporated into another program. An **object** is programming code and data that can be treated as an individual unit or component. Objects can range from simple controls, such as a button, to entire programs, such as database applications. OOP allows programmers to use programming objects that they have written themselves or that have been written by other programmers. In Java programming, an applet represents an object.

For applets to be programmatic objects, you must be able to incorporate and control them in another programming language. In this case, JavaScript and HTML documents represent the main program into which you will incorporate an applet object. At some times your applet should be a self-contained application, such as a mortgage calculation applet. At other times, you may only want to use an applet to enhance your JavaScript program. For example, you may create a Web page containing a form that gathers financial information that is eventually transmitted to a CGI script. Before it is submitted, you may use a Java applet to perform advanced calculations on the form data, using methods that are not available in the JavaScript language. For this reason, you would need to be able to call the applet's methods and send it the necessary data from the form.

Another aspect of Java that distinguishes it from JavaScript is that it is **architecturally neutral**, which means that it will run on any platform. A **platform** is an operating system and its hardware type. For example, MS-DOS and Windows 95/98/NT/2000/ME for PCs, Mac OS/10 for Macintosh computers, and Solaris for SPARC are different platforms. Before the development of Java, programs were written for a single platform. To use the same program on another platform, you had to redesign the program to work with the new platform. Java eliminates the need to redesign programs for different platforms through a special language interpreter known as the Java Virtual Machine. The **Java Virtual Machine (Java VM)** is the language interpreter for the Java programming language. There is a different Java VM for each platform supported by the Java programming language. To execute a Java program, users need only a copy of the Java VM for their particular platform. When a Java program runs as an applet within a Web page, the Java VM is contained within the Web browser, removing the need for a copy of the Java VM to be distributed with the program.

tip

Think of a Java VM as a universal translator. If the Java VM interpreted languages instead of Java code, it would translate documents from one language to any other language. You could write a letter to anyone in the world in your language. After the Java VM translated the letter, the person to whom you wrote it would be able to read it in his or her native language.

Although JavaScript and Java are not the same language, they still have some similarities. Both languages share much of the same syntax and language structure, because they both derive from the C programming language. As you begin working with Java, you will recognize much of the language syntax and be able to use many of the skills you have already learned in this book. Keep in mind that this section touches on only the most basic aspects of Java so that you can understand how Java and JavaScript can work together.

tip

If you would like to learn more about the Java programming language, refer to Joyce Farrell's *Java Programming***, published by Course Technology.**

To perform the exercises in this section, you will need a copy of the Sun Microsystem Java 2 Platform, Standard Edition, or J2SE. The J2SE includes the **Java Development Kit**, or **JDK**, is the original development environment for creating Java programs, and is available for several platforms including Windows NT/95/98/2000, Solaris, and Linux. Because Java is architecturally neutral, programs created in any JDK implementation will run on any of the other platforms. You can download the J2SE free at *.java.sun.com*. Before you download the J2SE, be sure you have enough hard drive space. Also, allocate plenty of time for the download process if you have a slow Internet connection, because the J2SE software consists of a 34 MB compressed file. Once you download the J2SE, follow the onscreen instructions to install it to your hard drive.

Classes

In object-oriented programming, **classes** are collections of methods, properties, and data. All Java programs begin their lives as classes. Instead of creating functions within a document (as you do with JavaScript), in Java you create methods within classes. A **method** is a structure that contains statements and procedures of a class and is similar to a function. You build Java programs by adding methods, variables, and other classes to a new Java class.

Figure 12-3 shows the beginning of a Java class named HelloWorld. The first line in the HelloWorld class includes the words *public* and *class*. The Java keyword `class` identifies HelloWorld as a class, and the keyword `public` is a class modifier. A **class modifier** determines the type of access that is granted for using a class. Other class modifiers include `abstract` and `final`. In this tutorial, you will work only with the public class modifier. Note that the first line of the class is followed by a pair of opening and closing braces.

```
public class HelloWorld {

}
```

Figure 12-3: Class structure

Java files are created as text files with an extension of .java. When you save a Java file, the name of the file must match the name of the class. For example, the filename for the HelloWorld class in Figure 12-3 must be HelloWorld.java. Like JavaScript, Java is case sensitive, so the case of the HelloWorld class and the HelloWorld.java filename must match exactly.

The methods used to build Java programs are contained in packages of classes. You can compare Java classes to JavaScript objects such as the Window object and the Document object. A **package**, or **class library**, is a collection of related classes. Standard Java packages include java.lang, java.awt, and java.applet, among others. Some packages, such as the java.lang package, which contains many basic types of

Java methods, are automatically imported into every Java program. Other packages and classes must be explicitly imported into the class in which you want to use them. You can either use a reference to the entire class name within a single statement, or import the class or package containing the class into your program. You import a class or package into a program by including an import statement along with the class or package name as the very first line in the program. The syntax for the import statement is `import package or class;`. For example, the java.awt package contains many useful graphical user interface components such as buttons, checkboxes, and menus. One class within the java.awt package is the Label class used for creating text labels. To use the Label class in your program you include the statement `import java.awt.Label;` as the first line of the program. You can also import an entire package by using an asterisk as a wildcard symbol in place of a specific class name. To import the entire java.awt class into a program, you use the statement `import java.awt.*;`. Note that all Java statements *must* end with a semicolon, in contrast to JavaScript statements that *optionally* end with a semicolon. Figure 12-4 shows a modified version of the HelloWorld class importing the java.awt package.

```
import java.awt.*;

public class HelloWorld {

}
```

Figure 12-4: HelloWorld class importing the java.awt package

See the J2SE documentation for a complete listing of packages and classes.

Methods

You place Java program methods within braces of a class. The methods you create in a class depend on whether you are creating a standalone Java program or an applet. To create a standalone Java program, you include a main() method within the braces of a class. The **main()** method is automatically called when you first start a standalone Java program. You can include all of your program code within the main() method, or you can use the main() method to call your own custom methods. The main() method header must be written as `public static void main (String args[])`. The **public** keyword is a method modifier that designates that the method is available outside the class. Like class modifiers, you will work only with public method modifiers in this tutorial. The **static** keyword indicates that only one copy of the method will exist in a computer's memory, regardless of the number of instances of the class. The **void** keyword means that the method does not return a value. Unlike JavaScript methods, Java methods must return a value or include the **void** keyword in the method header.

The (`String args[]`) portion of the method header receives any string arguments passed to the method. Figure 12-5 shows an example of the HelloWorld class with a main() method.

```
public class HelloWorld {

    public static void main (String args[]) {

        // statements go here

    }

}
```

Figure 12-5: HelloWorld class with a main() method

Notice that Figure 12-5 uses the same type of line comments (//) as JavaScript. You can also include block comments by using the syntax /* statements */.

Next you will create a simple Java program that prints several lines of text to the screen. You will use the System.out class, which is imported into Java programs as part of the java.lang package. The System.out class contains two methods, **print()** and **println()**, that are used for printing lines of text to the screen in a command-line environment, such as MS-DOS. The System.out class print() and println() methods are comparable to the JavaScript write() and writeln() methods. Like write() and writeln(), the only difference between the print() and println() methods is that the println() method adds a carriage return after the line of text. The print() and println() methods both accept a single text string or variable as an argument, using the syntax `System.out.print(string or variable);`. For example, to print *Hello world.*, you would use the statement `System.out.print("Hello world.");`.

Unlike the JavaScript writeln() method, the println() method does not require any sort of container element such as a <PRE>...</PRE> tag pair.

To create a simple Java program that prints several lines of text to the screen:

1   Start your text editor and create a new document.

2   Type the following code for the class header and opening brace:

```
public class FirstJavaProgram {
```

3   Add the main() method header and its opening brace:

```
public static void main (String args[]) {
```

4   Next add the following statements that print text to the screen:

```
System.out.println(
        "This is the first line in my Java program.");
System.out.print(
        "This is the second line in my Java program.");
```

5   Add two closing braces, one to close the main() method and another to close the class.

6   Save the file as **FirstJavaProgram.java** in the **Tutorial.12** folder on your Data Disk. If you are using a text editor such as Notepad, be sure to change the default file extension (which is .txt in Notepad) to .java. You will need to compile the program before you can run it.

Compiling a Java Program

After you create a Java program, the .java file must be compiled using the JDK javac program. The **javac program**, also referred to as the Java compiler, is a command-line program that compiles Java code into a file with an extension of .class. When you run the Java compiler, you must type the Java program name using its exact case, along with the extension .java. For example, to compile the HelloWorld.java file, you type `javac HelloWorld.java`. Once a Java program is compiled into a .class file, it is referred to as bytecode. **Bytecode** is the compiled Java program that is executed by a Java VM. When you distribute a Java program, you distribute only the .class file, unless you want users to be able to see your original source code, in which case you also include the .java file. The **java program** in the JDK \bin directory is the Java VM for your platform and is used for executing compiled bytecode. When you run the Java compiler, the path to the JDK bin directory must be in your PATH statement, or you must type the full path to the bin directory. For example, if you installed the JDK in a directory named jdk1.3.1 on the c drive, then you include `c:\jdk1.3.1\bin` in your PATH statement. If you do not add the bin directory to your PATH statement, then to run the Java compiler, you must type the entire path to the bin directory, using a statement similar to `c:\jdk1.3.1\bin\javac HelloWorld.java`.

Next you will compile and run FirstJavaProgram.java.

To compile and run FirstJavaProgram.java:

1 Go to your system command prompt. Accessing a command prompt differs by operating system. To access a command prompt from Windows 95/98, select **Run** from the **Start** menu and type **command**. To access a command prompt from Windows NT or Windows 2000, Select **Run** from the **Start** menu and type **cmd**.

2 Change to the **Tutorial.12** folder on your Data Disk.

3 If the JDK bin directory is part of your path statement, then type `javac FirstJavaProgram.java` and press **Enter** to compile the program. If the JDK bin directory is not part of your path statement, then you need to type the full path to the javac program. Be sure to enter the name of the file in the correct case and include the .java extension. If your file compiles correctly, only a new command prompt appears onscreen. To make sure the file compiled correctly, use the `dir` command at the command prompt to list the files in the Tutorial.12 folder. You should see several files, including the newly compiled FirstJavaProgram.class file.

help

If you receive an error message when compiling, check the code in the Java source file to see if you entered a command using the wrong case. Make sure that all your statements include a semicolon at the end; semicolons are required at the end of Java statements. Also be sure that the case of the name of the class in the class header exactly matches the case you assigned to the name of the .java file. After you correct all errors, be sure to resave and recompile the Java source file.

4 To run the program, type `java FirstJavaProgram`. Do not include the extension of .class. Your screen should be similar to Figure 12-6.

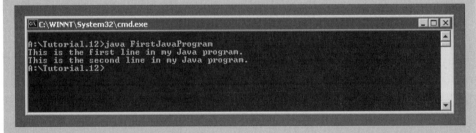

Figure 12-6: Output of FirstJavaProgram

5 Close the command prompt window.

help

On Windows systems you can close the command prompt window by typing exit and pressing Enter.

Creating an Applet

Applets do not use a main() method the way standalone Java applications do. Instead, applets use four methods: init(), start(), stop(), and destroy(). The four applet methods run automatically at different points in an applet's execution. The **init() method** executes when an applet first opens. The **start() method** executes each time an applet becomes active after being inactive. The **stop() method** executes when an applet stops executing. The **destroy() method** executes when the browser containing an applet closes. You write your own versions of each of these methods to handle the execution of an applet. For example, if your applet is an animation sequence, you may use the start() method to restart the animation each time the browser window becomes active again. You are not required to use any of these methods in a Java applet. Instead, you can create your own methods and execute them using Java or JavaScript controls.

To create an applet, you must import the java.applet package into a class. Most applets also import the java.awt package, because it contains many graphical user interface components used to create applets. You must also add the words `extends Applet` to the right of the class name in the class header. The class header syntax for an applet, using the HelloWorld class as an example, is `public class HelloWorld extends Applet`. The **extends** keyword allows you to base a new class on the methods, properties, and other attributes of another class. The init(), start(), stop(), and destroy() methods you use to control an applet's execution are based on, or *inherited* from, the Applet class in the java.applet package.

Another method that is available to every applet is the paint() method. The **paint() method** displays the visual components of an applet in a browser window and runs automatically whenever the browser window is minimized, maximized, or resized. You can also call the paint() method yourself. However, instead of calling the paint() method directly, you call it using the **repaint()** method. The header for the paint() method is `public void paint (Graphics g)`. The argument in parentheses creates an object named *g* from the Graphics class. The Graphics class is used for adding visual elements to an applet's bounding box. A method of the Graphics class that you will use in this tutorial is the drawString() method, which adds a string of text to an applet's bounding box. The syntax for the drawString() method is `g.drawString(text, x-coordinate, y-coordinate);`. The x and y coordinates of the drawString() method place the text in relation to the upper-left corner of an applet's bounding box.

You can use any name you want for a Graphics object, but *g* is commonly used.

Figure 12-7 shows the basic structure of an applet class with all five methods. All of the methods are empty except for the start() method, which calls the repaint() method, and the paint() method, which adds the text *Hello World* to the applet.

```java
import java.applet.*;

import java.awt.*;

public class HelloWorld extends Applet {

    public void init(){

        // statements go here

    }

    public void start(){

        repaint();

    }

    public void stop(){

        // statements go here

    }

    public void destroy(){

        // statements go here

    }

    public void paint(Graphics g){

        g.drawString("Hello World", 30, 30);

    }

}
```

Figure 12-7: Applet class structure

Next you will start creating the Random Number applet.

To start creating the Random Number applet:

1 Create a new document in your text editor.

2 Add the following import statements, which are necessary for the applet:

```
import java.applet.*;
import java.awt.*;
```

3 Next type the class header as follows:

```
public class RandomNumber  extends Applet {
```

4 Type the following code to create a start() method that calls the repaint method:

```
public void start() {
    repaint();
}
```

5 Type the following paint() method, which uses the drawString() method to add a variable named displayText to the applet. The displayText variable displays different messages to users, depending on their answers and the button they click.

```
public void paint(Graphics g) {
    g.drawString(displayText, 30, 30);
}
```

6 Add a closing brace (}) for the class.

7 Save the file as **RandomNumber.java** in the **Tutorial.12** folder on your Data Disk.

Java Variables and Data Types

As you learned in Tutorial 3, many programming languages, such as Java, require that you declare the type of data that a variable contains. Programming languages that require you to declare the data types of variables are called strongly typed programming languages. Programming languages that do not require you to declare the data types of variables are called loosely typed programming languages. JavaScript is a loosely typed programming language. Remember that you are not allowed to declare the data type of variables in JavaScript. Instead, the JavaScript interpreter automatically determines what type of data is stored in a variable and assigns a data type to the variable accordingly. In contrast, Java is a strongly typed programming language. When you declare a variable in Java, you *must* designate a data type. The primitive data types supported by Java are listed in Figure 12-8. Notice that the data types do not precisely match JavaScript data types. For instance, Java has six numeric data types, and JavaScript has only two. Later, you will explore how Java and JavaScript handle each other's data types when you use one programming language to control the other.

Data Type	Description	Example
boolean	A logical value of true or false	True or false
byte	An 8-bit whole number	A value between -128 and 127
char	Any single character contained in single quotation marks or a numeric Unicode character	'A', 'B', 'C', and so on. The letters A, B, and C are represented in Unicode as 65, 66, and 67, respectively.
double	A 64-bit floating-point number	A value between 5e-324 and 1.7976931348623157e+308
float	A 32-bit floating-point number	A value between 1.4e-45f and 3.4028235e+38f
int	A 32-bit whole number	A value between -2,147,483,648 and 2,147,483,647
long	A 64-bit whole number	A value between -9,223,372,036,854,775,808 and 9,223,372,036,854,775,807
short	A 16-bit whole number	A value between -32,768 and 32,767

Figure 12-8: Primitive Java data types

Like JavaScript, the value contained in a Java variable can be assigned at declaration or later in the code. You designate a data type by including the data type name in front of the variable name. You can think of the data type as replacing the var keyword used to declare JavaScript variables. The following code illustrates how to declare several types of variables in Java:

```
int integerVariable = 100;
boolean trueOrFalse = true;
char unicodeVariable = 'A';
```

You may notice that there is no string data type. In Java, text strings are assigned to objects instantiated from the String class, rather than being assigned to a string data type as is done in JavaScript. Java requires that you not only declare data types, but also objects. The syntax for instantiaing a new String object is String *objectName* = new String("*text*");. On the left side of the statement, String is the name of the class on which the variable is based. On the right side of the statement, the new keyword creates the new String object using the String() method of the String class. The String method receives an argument of the text to be contained in the object. The following code shows how to assign the text *Hello World!* to a String object named helloString.

```
String helloString = new String("Hello World!");
```

You can also create a String object using the more simple form `String objectName = "text";`.

You can declare variables at the class level (outside a method) or inside a method. Variables declared inside methods are called local variables, the same as the local variables declared inside JavaScript functions. Variables declared at the class level are called **instance variables** and are comparable to global JavaScript variables that are declared within a <SCRIPT>...</SCRIPT> tag pair, but outside a function. An *instance variable* is the term used in Java to refer to an object property. To use an instance variable outside a class (say from another Java program), it must have an access modifier of `public`. Figure 12-9 shows an example of a String variable that is usable outside a class, because it is declared as an instance variable at the class level () and has an access modifier of `public`.

```java
import java.awt.*;

import java.applet.*;

public class HelloWorld extends Applet{

    public String helloString = new String("Hello World");

    public void paint(Graphics g) {

        g.drawString(helloString, 30, 30);

    }

}
```

Figure 12-9: HelloWorld class with a public instance variable

Next you will add to the Random Number program three instance variables: randomNumber, displayText, and guessCount. The randomNumber variable is an integer and holds the randomly generated number. The displayText variable is a String object and displays different messages to users, depending on their answers and the button they click. The guessCount variable is an integer and holds the number of times the user has tried to guess the random number. The only variable that needs to be public is the randomNumber variable, because you will later access it from JavaScript as a property of the Random Number applet object.

To add to the Random Number program three instance variables to hold the random number, messages to be displayed, and the number of guesses:

1 Return to the **RandomNumber.java** file in your text editor.

2 Above the start() method header, add the following variables:

```
public int randomNumber;
String displayText = new String();
int guessCount = 0;
```

3 Save the **RandomNumber.java** file.

For JavaScript programmers, one of the most confusing aspects of Java programming is that in Java, the data type of a variable cannot change during the course of program execution. If you attempt to assign a different data type to a variable, you generate an error. If you need to use the contents of a variable as a different data type, you must cast the variable to a new data type. **Casting** copies the value contained in a variable of one data type into a variable of another data type. You cast a variable by placing the name of the target data type in parentheses in front of the variable you want to cast and assigning the value to a variable of the target type. The syntax for casting variables is *variable = (new_type) old_variable;*. The following code casts an integer variable named *intNumber* to a float variable named *floatNumber*:

```
int intNumber = 100;
float floatNumber;
floatNumber = (float) intNumber;
```

Next you will add code to the Random Number program that creates a random number and assigns it to the randomNumber instance variable. To create the random number, you will use the random() method of the Math class. The Java Math class contains various numeric properties and methods for performing mathematical operations. For example, the abs() method of the Math class returns the absolute value of a number, and the PI property returns the value of pi (π), which represents the ratio of the circumference of a circle to its diameter. The random() method of the Math class returns a number between 0.0 and 1.0 as a double data type. You use the syntax *variable =* `Math.random();` to generate a random number and assign it to a variable. To convert the random number to a value between 0 and 100, you multiply the random number by 100, and then use the round() method of the Math class to round the number to a whole number. The round() method returns the whole number as a long data type. The syntax for the round() method is *variable =* `Math.round(`*number*`);`. Because the randomNumber instance variable is an int data type, you need to cast the long number returned from the round() method.

tip

JavaScript includes an internal Math object that contains many of the methods and properties found in the Java Math class. See the Appendix for a list of the JavaScript Math object properties and methods.

To add to the Random Number program code that creates a random number:

1 Return to the **RandomNumber.java** file in your text editor.

2 Above the call to the repaint() method in the start() method, add the following statements that generate the random number. The first statement multiplies the result of the random() method by 100 and assigns it to a double variable named doubleNumber. The second statement uses the round() method to round doubleNumber to a whole number, and then assigns the new value to a long variable named longNumber. The third statement casts the longNumber variable to an integer data type and assigns it to the randomNumber instance variable.

```
double doubleNumber = Math.random() * 100;
long longNumber = Math.round(doubleNumber);
randomNumber = (int) longNumber;
```

3 After the statement that casts the longNumber variable to an integer and assigns it to the randomNumber variable, add **displayText = "The random number is " + randomNumber + ".";**. The paint() method displays the displayText variable when the applet first loads.

4 Save the **RandomNumber.java** file and close your text editor or HTML editor. Next go to a command prompt, switch to the **Tutorial.12** folder on your Data Disk, and compile **RandomNumber.java** using the javac program. If you receive any compilation errors, locate and fix the errors, then save the program and recompile it. Next you will learn how to use the applet from an HTML file.

help

> If you are having trouble compiling your program, remember that Java is case sensitive and that all statements must end in a semicolon. Also be sure that the name of the RandomNumber class in the class header statement `public class RandomNumber extends Applet {` is the same case as the name you assigned to the RandomNumber.java file.

Adding an Applet to an HTML Document

Once you have compiled an applet using the Java compiler, you add it to a Web page using an <APPLET>...</APPLET> tag pair. The **<APPLET> tag** designates an applet to include within an HTML document. You use four attributes to create an <APPLET> tag: CODE, WIDTH, HEIGHT, and NAME. The code attribute specifies the applet class file. The width and height tags determine the size of the applet bounding box. The NAME attribute is used to manipulate an applet with JavaScript code. Figure 12-10 contains a simple HTML document that loads the HelloWorld applet from Figure 12-9. Figure 12-11 shows the HTML document and applet as they appear in Netscape. The gray area containing the text *Hello World!* represents the applet bounding box.

```
<HTML>

<HEAD>

<TITLE>Hello World Applet</TITLE>

</HEAD>

<BODY>

<APPLET CODE="HelloWorld.class" NAME="helloApplet"
WIDTH=100 HEIGHT=50>

</APPLET>

</BODY>

</HTML>
```

Figure 12-10: An HTML document containing the HelloWorld applet

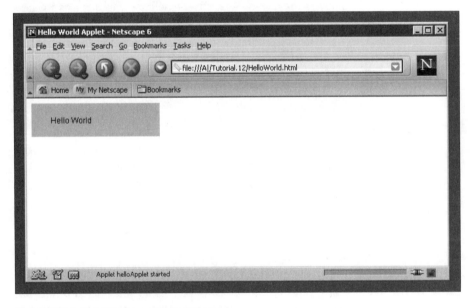

Figure 12-11: HelloWorld applet in Netscape

tip

You can quickly display an HTML document containing an applet using the JDK AppletViewer command. The AppletViewer command is used for quickly displaying an applet without the use of a Web browser. You can find the AppletViewer program file, appletviewer.exe, in the JDK bin directory. AppletViewer is a command-line program. You use AppletViewer by using a command similar to c:\jdk1.3.1\bin\appletviewer HelloWorld.html (assuming that HelloWorld.html is located in the current directory and that the JDK is installed in the jdk1.3.1 folder on drive c). Remember that you do not need to type the entire path if you have added it to your PATH environment variable.

You should be aware that the <APPLET> tag is deprecated (outdated) as of HTML 4.0 in favor of the <OBJECT> tag. The **<OBJECT>...</OBJECT> tag pair** allows you to place applets and other types of objects, such as ActiveX controls, in an HTML document. Internet Explorer allows you to use JavaScript to manipulate applets contained within an <OBJECT> tag in a manner very similar to the way you use JavaScript to manipulate applets contained within an <APPLET> tag. Netscape also supports the <OBJECT> tag. However, Netscape does not allow you to use JavaScript to manipulate an applet contained within an <OBJECT> tag. Therefore, in Netscape, you must continue to use the <APPLET> tag to use JavaScript to manipulate an applet that is embedded in an HTML document. To get around this incompatibility between Internet Explorer and Netscape, you could use one of the cross-browser compatibility techniques you learned in Tutorial 8 to determine which browser is running. After determining the browser type, you could then use JavaScript to add the appropriate tag (<OBJECT> or <APPLET>) as the HTML document is rendered. However, the <APPLET> tag is still widely used and is expected to be supported by the major browsers for a long time to come. If you need to manipulate an applet using JavaScript, for now it is easier to use the <APPLET> tag to embed Java applets in an HTML document.

Next you will create an HTML document to display the Random Number applet.

To create an HTML document to display the Random Number applet:

1   Start your text editor or HTML editor and create a new document.

2   Type the opening <HTML> and <HEAD> sections, along with an opening <BODY> tag:

```
<HTML>
<HEAD>
<TITLE>Random Number</TITLE>
</HEAD>
<BODY>
```

3   Create an <APPLET> tag to contain the Random Number applet by typing `<APPLET CODE="RandomNumber.class" WIDTH=425 HEIGHT=50>`.

4   Type the closing </APPLET>, </BODY>, and </HTML> tags:

```
</APPLET>
</BODY>
</HTML>
```

5   Save the file as **RandomNumber.html** in the **Tutorial.12** folder on your Data Disk. Open the **RandomNumber.html** file in your Web browser. Your screen should be similar to Figure 12-12, although the generated number will probably be different. Clicking your browser Refresh or Reload button changes the random number.

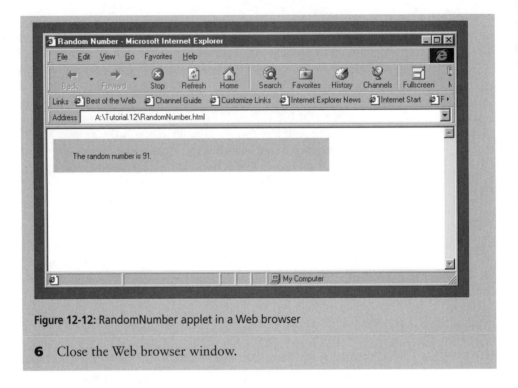

Figure 12-12: RandomNumber applet in a Web browser

6   Close the Web browser window.

Next you will turn the Random Number program into a guessing game.

Controlling Java Applets with JavaScript

To a Web page, Java applets function as objects, similar to JavaScript objects such as the Window object and the Document object. You call an applet's methods and read and write its properties (provided they are public) in the same manner that you call the methods and properties of JavaScript objects. The most difficult task in using JavaScript to control Java applets is finding out which public methods and properties you can control. For applets that you did not write yourself, the only way to discover this information is to read any documentation that came with the applet or ask the applet's developer. In this section, you are writing your own applets and know which methods and properties you can use.

There are two ways you can reference an applet with JavaScript code. You can use the NAME attribute assigned in the <APPLET> tag or its element number in the applets[] array. You append either applet reference to the Document object, along with the method or property you want to use. The **applets[] array** contains a list of applets on a Web page in the order in which they are encountered. The first applet on a page is referenced as applets[0], the second applet on a page is referenced as applets[1], and so on. It is somewhat easier to reference an element's name than to find the order in which it appears on a page, and subtract one to account for an array's starting element number of zero. Therefore, you will reference each applet by its NAME attribute. Figure 12-13 shows a simple HTML document that calls the start() method of an applet named AnimationSequence.class. The document uses an onLoad event handler in the <BODY> tag to call the applet start() method. Notice in the <APPLET> tag that the applet has been assigned a NAME attribute of animationApplet.

```
<HTML>

<HEAD><TITLE>Hello World</TITLE></HEAD>

<BODY onLoad="document.animationSequence.start();">

<APPLET CODE="AnimationApplet.class"
WIDTH=100 HEIGHT=100 NAME="animationApplet"></APPLET>

</BODY>

</HTML>
```

Figure 12-13: HTML document calling the start() method of an applet

Next you will add to the RandomNumber.java file custom methods that give the program its functionality. Later you will call the custom methods from JavaScript as properties of the RandomNumber applet.

To add to the Random Number program code that creates a random number:

1 Return to the **RandomNumber.java** file in your text editor and immediately save it as **RandomNumberGame.java** in the **Tutorial.12** folder on your Data Disk.

2 Change the name of the class in the class header to **RandomNumberGame** so that the header reads `public class RandomNumberGame extends Applet {`.

3 In the start() method, modify the `displayText = "The random number is " + randomNumber + ".";` code so that it reads **displayText = "Guess a number between 0 and 100.";**.

4 After the paint() method and before the class closing brace, add the following tooLow() and tooHigh() methods that will be called from JavaScript if the user guesses wrong. The methods change the displayText variable, increment a guessCount variable by one, and then execute the paint() method by calling the repaint() method.

```
public void tooLow() {
     displayText = "Sorry! You guessed too low.";
     ++guessCount;
     repaint();
}
public void tooHigh() {
     displayText = "Sorry! You guessed too high.";
     ++guessCount;
     repaint();
}
```

5 Next add the following rightNumber() method, which executes if the user guesses correctly. The method changes the displayText variable to include the number of guesses from the guessCount variable and the correct number using the randomNumber variable.

```
public void rightNumber() {
     displayText = "You guessed correctly in " +
guessCount
          + " tries! " + "The number is " +
randomNumber + ".";
     repaint();
}
```

6 Finally, add the last method, giveUp(), which is called when the user clicks an I Give Up, What Is It? button on the Web page.

```
public void giveUp() {
     displayText = "The number is " + randomNumber
          + ". Better luck next time!";
     repaint();
}
```

7 Save and compile the **RandomNumberGame.java** file.

Next you will modify the RandomNumber.html file so that it contains JavaScript code that controls the methods and properties of the RandomNumberGame applet.

To modify the RandomNumber.html file so that it contains JavaScript code that controls the methods and properties of the RandomNumberGame applet:

1 Return to the **RandomNumber.html** file in your text editor or HTML editor and immediately save it as **RandomNumberGame.html** in the **Tutorial.12** folder on your Data Disk.

2 Change the NAME attribute of the <APPLET> tag to the **RandomNumberGame.class** file. Also create a name for the RandomNumber applet by adding **NAME="RandomNumberGame"** just before the closing bracket of the <APPLET> tag.

3 After the opening <BODY> tag, add **<H2>Guessing Game</H2>**.

4 Add the opening tags for a <SCRIPT> section just before the closing </HEAD> tag:

```
<SCRIPT LANGUAGE="JavaScript">
<!-- HIDE FROM INCOMPATIBLE BROWSERS
```

5 Press **Enter** and type the opening header for a JavaScript function named checkGuess() that receives a single argument named guess: **function checkGuess(guess) {**. You will execute the checkGuess() function using a form button.

6 Press **Enter** and type the following code, which creates a variable named answer and assigns to it the randomNumber property of the RandomNumberGame object appended to the Document object:

```
var answer = document.RandomNumberGame.randomNumber;
```

7 After the declaration of the answer variable, add the following if...else construct that calls different methods of the RandomNumber applet, depending on the result returned after comparing the guess variable to the answer variable.

```
if (guess > answer)
    document.RandomNumberGame.tooHigh();
else if (guess < answer)
    document.RandomNumberGame.tooLow();
else
    document.RandomNumberGame.rightNumber();
```

8 Type a closing brace for the checkGuess() function along with the closing <SCRIPT> tags:

```
}
// STOP HIDING FROM INCOMPATIBLE BROWSERS -->
</SCRIPT>
```

9 Finally, add the following form and <H3> tag just before the closing </BODY> tag. In the form, the Guess button calls the checkGuess() function from the <SCRIPT> section. Notice that the onClick event handler for the I Give Up, What Is It? button directly calls the giveUp() method of the RandomNumberGame applet.

```
<FORM NAME="guessForm">
<P><INPUT TYPE="text" NAME="guessField">
<INPUT TYPE="button" VALUE=" Guess " onClick=
     "checkGuess(document.guessForm.guessField.value);">
<INPUT TYPE="button" VALUE=" I Give Up, What Is It? "
     onClick="document.RandomNumberGame.giveUp();">
</FORM></P>
<H3>Click your Refresh or Reload button to start
over.</H3>
```

10 Save the file, then open it in your Web browser. Test the program by entering some guesses. Figure 12-14 shows an example of how the program appears in Netscape when it is first opened.

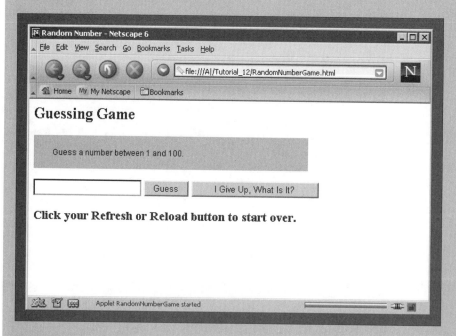

Figure 12-14: RandomNumberGame.html in Netscape

11 Close the Web browser window.

S U M M A R Y

- An applet is a Java program that runs from within a Web page.

- Netscape displays embedded data using special program extensions called plug-ins, and Internet Explorer displays embedded information using ActiveX controls.

- To allow JavaScript, Java, and plug-ins to communicate with each other, Netscape uses a technology known as LiveConnect. Internet Explorer uses ActiveX scripting to allow JavaScript to interact with Java and ActiveX controls.

- Encapsulation means that all code and required data are self-contained within the object itself.

- A bounding box is the rectangular area on a Web page in which an applet executes.

- Object-oriented programming (OOP) refers to the creation of reusable software objects that can be easily incorporated into another program.

- An object is programming code and data that can be treated as an individual unit or component.

- Java is architecturally neutral, which means that it will run on any platform. A platform is an operating system and its hardware type.

- The Java Virtual Machine (Java VM) is the language interpreter for the Java programming language. There is a different Java VM for each platform supported by the Java programming language.

- JavaScript and Java share much of the same syntax and language structure, because they both derive from the C programming language.

- The Java Development Kit (JDK) is the original development environment for creating Java programs and is available for several platforms, including Windows NT/95/98/2000, Solaris, and Macintosh.

- In object-oriented programming, classes are collections of methods, properties, and other attributes.

- Object-oriented programming languages, such as Java, create objects from classes.

- A method is a structure similar to a function that contains the statements and procedures of a class.

- You build Java programs by adding methods, properties, and other classes to a new Java class.

- A public class modifier determines the type of access that is granted for using a class.

- A package, or class library, is a collection of related classes.

- The main() method is automatically called when you first start a standalone Java program.

- The `public` keyword is a method modifier that designates the method as available outside the class.

- The **static** keyword indicates that only one copy of the method will exist in computer memory, regardless of the number of instances of the class.

- The **void** keyword means the method does not return a value. Unlike JavaScript methods, Java methods must return a value or include the **void** keyword in the method header.

- The javac program is a command-line program that compiles a Java program into a file with an extension of .class.

- Bytecode is the compiled Java format that is executed by a Java VM.

- The java program in the JDK \bin directory is the Java VM for your platform and is used for executing compiled bytecode.

- Applets use four methods: init(), start(), stop(), and destroy(), which run automatically at different points in an applet's execution.

- The **extends** keyword allows you to base a new class on the methods, properties, and other attributes of another class.

- The paint() method displays the visual components of an applet in a browser window and runs automatically whenever the browser window is minimized, maximized, or resized.

- The paint() method is called using the repaint() method.

- When you declare a variable in Java, you must designate a data type.

- Variables declared at the class level are called instance variables. *Instance variable* is also the term used in Java to refer to an object property.

- Casting copies the value in a variable of one data type into a variable of another data type.

- The <APPLET> tag designates an applet to include within an HTML document. You use four attributes to create an <APPLET> tag: CODE, WIDTH, HEIGHT, and NAME.

- The <OBJECT>...</OBJECT> tag pair allows you to place applets, ActiveX controls, and other types of objects in an HTML document.

- The applets[] array contains a list of applets on a Web page in the order in which they are encountered.

QUESTIONS

1. A Java program that runs from within a Web page is called a(n) _____.
   a. plug-in
   b. ActiveX control
   c. applet
   d. scriplet

2. _____ means that all code and required data are self-contained within the object itself.
   a. Polymorphism
   b. Encapsulation
   c. Blind implementation
   d. Code concealment

3. A(n) _____ is the rectangular area on a Web page in which an applet executes.
   a. bounding box
   b. subdocument
   c. applet container
   d. applet frame

4. _____ refers to the creation of reusable software objects that can be easily incorporated into another program.
   a. Procedural programming
   b. Object-oriented programming
   c. Code reusability
   d. Open architecture

5. Java code runs on any platform because _____.
   a. programmers are required to create a different program for every platform
   b. different versions of a Java program are automatically created when the program is compiled
   c. Microsoft designed it to work with all operating systems
   d. it is architecturally neutral

6. The _____ is the language interpreter for the Java programming language.
   a. Java RealPlayer
   b. Sun Virtual Machine
   c. Java Virtual Machine
   d. Universal Java Compiler

7. _____ is the original development environment for creating Java programs.
   a. The Java Development Kit
   b. The Microsoft Applet Tool
   c. Borland Cafe
   d. ActiveX Control Pad

8. A _____ is a structure similar to a function, which contains the statements and procedures of a class.
   a. procedure
   b. class container
   c. method
   d. function source file

9. What is the correct syntax of the class header for a Java file named PayrollApplet?
   a. `public class PayrollApplet {`
   b. `public PayrollApplet {`
   c. `public class (PayrollApplet) {`
   d. `public class Header {`

10. Collections of related classes are called packages or _____.
  a. class containers
  b. source objects
  c. class structures
  d. class libraries

11. The _____ keyword makes a method available outside its class.
  a. `static`
  b. `open`
  c. `public`
  d. `final`

12. Which Java methods are similar to the JavaScript write() and writeln() methods?
  a. screen() and screenln()
  b. print() and println()
  c. output() and outputln()
  d. writeTo() and writeToln()

13. Which program compiles Java code into a file with an extension of .class?
  a. java
  b. javac
  c. javah
  d. compile

14. The compiled Java code executed by the Java interpreter is called _____.
  a. bytecode
  b. machine code
  c. source code
  d. class code

15. The method that acts as the entry point for a standalone Java program is the
  _____ method.
  a. start()
  b. entry()
  c. begin()
  d. main()

16. Which of the following is *not* one of the four applet methods that run automatically at different points in an applet's execution?
  a. load()
  b. start()
  c. stop()
  d. destroy()

17. Which of the following is the correct class header for an applet saved in a file named AccountingApplet.java?
  a. `public class AccountingApplet{`
  b. `public class AccountingApplet extends Applet {`
  c. `public class Applet AccountingApplet{`
  d. `public class Applet extended AccountingApplet{`

18. The _____ method displays the visual components of an applet in a browser window and runs automatically whenever the browser window is minimized, maximized, or resized.

    a. paint()

    b. draw()

    c. display()

    d. view()

19. Which of the following statements declares a string variable in Java?

    a. `var String textString = "This is my text string";`

    b. `String textString = new String("This is my text string");`

    c. `var textString = new String("This is my text string");`

    d. `textString = new String("This is my text string");`

20. For an instance variable to be available outside a class, it must have an access modifier of _____.

    a. static

    b. final

    c. open

    d. public

21. The random() method of the Math class returns a number between _____.

    a. 0.0 and 1.0

    b. 0.0 and 10.0

    c. 1.0 and 10.0

    d. 1.0 and 100.0

22. You add an applet to an HTML document using the _____ tag.

    a. <CLASS>

    b. <JAVA>

    c. <OBJECT>

    d. <APPLET>

EXERCISES

Save your solutions for the following exercises in the Tutorial.12 folder on your Data Disk.

1. Create a Java program named PersonalInfo.java. In the program's main() method, use print() and println() methods to print your name, address, and date of birth to the screen.

2. Create a Java program that contains variables to hold your hourly pay rate and the number of hours worked. Display your gross pay, tax withholding (which is 15 percent of your gross pay), and your net pay. Save the program as Paycheck.java.

3.   Create a Java applet that declares variables to represent the length and width of a room in feet. Use an appropriate data type for the variables. Assign values to the variables, compute the floor space of the room in square feet, and save the result in another variable. Save the program as RoomSize.java. Next create an HTML document that retrieves the values in the RoomSize.java file variables. In the HTML document, display the room size and floor space using explanatory text and the variables. For example, "The room is 10 feet by 12 feet." Save the HTML document as RoomSize.html.

4.   Create a Java program named FavoriteMovies.java. The program should contain five methods: the start() method, the paint() method, one method that assigns the names of your three favorite comedies to instance variables, another method that assigns the names of your three favorite dramas to instance variables, and a final method that assigns the name of your absolutely favorite movie to an instance variable. Each method should call the repaint() method to display the contents of the variables it controls in the applet's bounding box. Next create an HTML document containing three buttons, Favorite Comedies, Favorite Dramas, and Favorite Movie. Each button should call the appropriate method from the Java program. Save the HTML document as FavoriteMovies.html.

5.   Create an applet containing five instance variables: employee, employer, jobTitle, startingSalary, and age. Create the startingSalary variable as a long data type, the age variable as an int data type, and the rest of the variables as String objects. Use a Graphics object with the paint() method to display the variables in an applet bounding box. Save the program as JobInfo.java. Use an HTML form to gather the information, then use a form button to send the information as arguments to a method in the applet named reassignValues(). Before sending the numeric values from the form text fields to the Java applet be sure to use a type conversion function (parseInt() or parseFloat()) to convert the string literals to numeric data types. Save the HTML document as JobInfo.html. To create arguments in a Java method header, you must declare the data type of each argument, the same as for variables. Note that for String arguments, you do not need to use the entire String object declaration syntax of `String variable = new String();`. Instead, simply declare the argument of the String data type. For example, to create a method named myMethod() with a String argument, a long argument, and a double argument, you write a header similar to `public void myMethod(String stringArgument,long numberArgument, double floatArgument){`.

6.   Create a Java applet version of a temperature conversion calculator that converts Fahrenheit to Celsius and Celsius to Fahrenheit. Save the program as ConvertTemperature.java. To convert Fahrenheit to Celsius, subtract 32 from the Fahrenheit temperature, then multiply the difference by .55. To convert Celsius to Fahrenheit, multiply the Celsius temperature by 1.8, then add 32. Gather the numbers to convert in an HTML form and send them to the Java applet. Use float data types for the arguments and variables in the Java applet. Be sure to use the parseFloat() function to convert the string literals from the form fields to floating point numbers. Display the converted temperature in the applet bounding box. Save the HTML document as ConvertTemperature.html.

In this section you will learn:

- About Java packages and LiveConnect
- About data conversion between Java and Netscape JavaScript
- How to control Netscape JavaScript with Java
- How to directly access Java classes from Netscape JavaScript
- How to manipulate embedded data (plug-ins and ActiveX controls)

LiveConnect, Plug-Ins, and ActiveX

Overview

Section A introduced Java programming and how to control Java applets with JavaScript. This section demonstrates how to use Java and LiveConnect to manipulate JavaScript programs in Netscape. You will also learn how LiveConnect allows JavaScript programs in Netscape to directly access Java classes and communicate with plug-ins. The majority of this section does not apply to Internet Explorer, because it does not support LiveConnect or plug-ins, nor does it allow Java programs to manipulate JavaScript. In contrast to Netscape, Internet Explorer uses ActiveX technology to display and manipulate embedded data. Using ActiveX technology to work with embedded data will be demonstrated at the end of the section.

LiveConnect is available in Navigator 4.7 and earlier versions. Netscape 6 does not support LiveConnect, although the technology is expected to be added to future releases of the browser. For this reason, the LiveConnect exercises and examples in this section are created using Navigator version 4.7. Once the LiveConnect technology has been added to future versions of Netscape, you can expect most of the LiveConnect techniques presented in this chapter to be applicable to those versions.

Java Packages and LiveConnect

The packages and classes used by Java are arranged in a series of folders. The top-level Java folder contains other folders for each Java package. Each package folder contains class files with an extension of .class for each class contained within the package. Java packages and their class structures are contained in compressed JAR files located within the JDK directory. Various JAR files exist for different features of the Java language. The JAR file you will work with most often is named rt.jar (*rt* is short for *runtime*), and is located within the jre\lib folder in the JDK folder. The rt.jar file contains the most commonly used Java packages, including the java.lang and java.awt packages.

Whenever you compile a Java program, the Java compiler opens the rt.jar file (and any other JAR files required by your program), and extracts the packages and classes required by your program. Figure 12-15 shows a partial listing of the folders contained in rt.jar, along with some of the classes contained in the java.lang package.

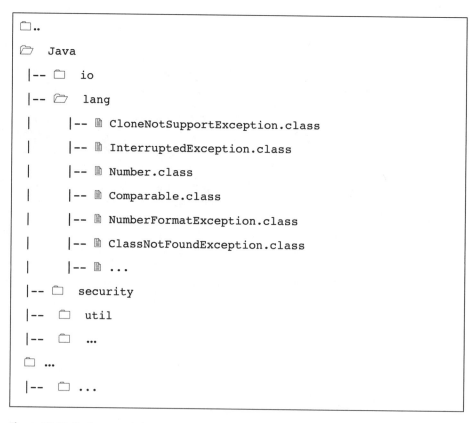

Figure 12-15: Package and class structure

In Navigator, LiveConnect packages enable JavaScript and Java to communicate with each other. **LiveConnect packages** provide Navigator with access to core Java functionality and contain classes necessary for Java programs to control JavaScript. Java knows by design to look in the \lib directory for the classes.zip file. However, Java does not automatically know where to find the LiveConnect packages required for Java-to-JavaScript communication. The LiveConnect packages are contained in the compressed java40.jar file located somewhere in the Netscape folder on your computer.

▶ **tip**

A .jar file is a type of compressed file, similar to a ZIP file.

▶ **tip**

To use LiveConnect in Navigator, you must have the Enable Java and Enable JavaScript options selected in the Advanced category of the Preferences dialog box.

The location of the java40.jar file depends on the platform you use and whether you are using Communicator or Navigator. For Java to be able to locate the LiveConnect packages, you must locate the java40.jar file and set a CLASS-PATH environment variable to it as well as to the JDK /bin directory. The **CLASSPATH environment variable** tells the Java VM and JDK applications in the /bin directory where to search for classes required by Java applications. The procedure for setting the CLASSPATH environment variable differs by platform. On Windows NT/2000, you can set an environment variable using the System icon in Control Panel. In the System Properties dialog box, click the Environment Variables button on the Advanced tab and add an environment variable similar to the following. The paths you enter will depend on where the JDK is installed and on the location of the java40.jar file on your system.

```
CLASSPATH=C:\Program Files\Netscape\Navigator\Program\Java\
Classes\java40.jar
```

▶ **tip**

Navigator is the original name of the Netscape Web-browsing product (which is now simply called *Netscape*), whereas Communicator is the Netscape full suite of Internet tools, which includes Navigator, Messenger, Calendar, Composer, and AOL Instant Messenger.

If you are working with Windows 95/98, then you will need to add a SET statement to your autoexec.bat file to create the CLASSPATH environment variable. For example, you would add to your autoexec.bat file a statement similar to the following, to create a CLASSPATH environment variable on a Windows 95/98 system. Again, the exact path you enter will depend on where the JDK is installed and on the location of the java40.jar file on your system.

```
SET CLASSPATH=C:\Program Files\Netscape\Navigator\Program\
Java\Classes\java40.jar
```

Be sure that you enter the SET statement on one continuous line, not on separate lines as in the preceding example. After editing your autoexec.bat file, you will need to reboot your system for the CLASSPATH environment variable to be available.

tip

••

If you are using a platform other than Windows, see your operating system documentation for information on setting the CLASSPATH environment variable. Additionally, if you are using a Java development program other than the Sun JDK, consult the software documentation for information on setting the CLASSPATH environment variable.

••

Data Conversion Between Java and JavaScript

When using JavaScript to control a Java program, or Java to control a JavaScript program, it is common to pass data in the form of variables back and forth between the programming languages. Passing variables back and forth between the two languages can cause problems, because Java and JavaScript do not have the same data types. For example, JavaScript has only two numeric data types, integers and floating-point numbers. Java has six. Additionally, because Java is a strongly typed programming language, you must pass the correct data type from JavaScript to a Java variable or an error will occur. You cannot, for instance, pass a JavaScript string variable to a Java integer variable. Passing the correct data type can be confusing for JavaScript programmers, because the data type of a JavaScript variable can change during program execution. Remember, Java data types cannot change during execution. To make JavaScript and Java programs work together, you need to know how data types are converted between the two languages. Figure 12-16 lists how data types are converted between JavaScript and Java.

JavaScript Data Types	Java Data Types
array	Array object
boolean	Boolean
floating-point or integer number	byte, char, short, int, long, float, and double
null	Null
undefined	Void
all other JavaScript objects	JSObject wrapper
JavaObject wrapper	all other Java objects

Figure 12-16: Data type conversion between JavaScript and Java

Passing data from JavaScript to Java can be tricky, especially when you are dealing with numeric data types. Number variables passed from JavaScript to Java convert to the closet matching numeric data type. However, if your Java program is expecting a float variable and the variable passed from JavaScript converts to an integer, an error will occur. You handle this situation by casting the passed variable to the correct data type. You learned about casting earlier, in Section A.

Passing data from Java to JavaScript is not as complex an issue, because JavaScript is loosely typed. If JavaScript receives any of the six numeric data type variables from Java, the variable is converted either to a floating-point or integer data type.

Complex objects passed from JavaScript to Java are wrapped in the JSObject wrapper, and complex objects passed from Java to JavaScript are wrapped in the JavaObject wrapper. A **wrapper** is a class or object that contains, or wraps around, something else. Because complex objects (such as the JavaScript History object) passed between JavaScript and Java cannot be converted into an equivalent object in the other language, they are wrapped in an object that the other language can understand. The other language can then manipulate the wrapper object and extract information from it. Simple objects, such as number and Boolean variables, are also wrapped in the JSObject class, but can be cast into a corresponding Java data type. You will work with the JSObject class later in this section.

Controlling JavaScript with Java

Just as you can control Java with JavaScript, you can control JavaScript with Java. However, it is important to understand that if you design an applet to control JavaScript, you are severely limiting its portability, because your applet will need to look for specifically named JavaScript functions and variables on a Web page. You may have some very good reasons for creating this type of applet. To use an earlier example, suppose that you create a Web page containing a form that gathers financial information that will be transmitted to a CGI script. Because the form consists of several pages, you find it easier to create it in HTML and submit it using CGI, rather than to develop an entire Java application. However, you want to use some calculation methods in Java that are not available in JavaScript. To use Java calculation methods, you use a Java applet to gather data from the form, perform calculations on the data using methods that are not available in the JavaScript language, and return the results of the calculations to the form. You also use the applet to execute the form submit event. In this scenario, there is no need for the applet to be portable, because it is so tightly coupled to the Web page.

To allow a Java applet to control JavaScript you must:

- Import the JSObject and JSException classes into your applet.
- Use methods of the JSObject class to access the browser window containing the applet and to access functions and variables in JavaScript.
- Add the MAYSCRIPT attribute to the <APPLET> tag.

To learn about each of these steps, you will modify the RandomNumberGame applet you created in Section A so that it controls the HTML document and accesses JavaScript objects, variables, and methods. In the original program, a

JavaScript function evaluated the user's guess and called methods in the applet that wrote text to the applet bounding box, depending on the user's guess. In the new version, the applet will evaluate the user's guess by reading the value from the form text field (named guessField). Then the applet will call the JavaScript alert() method to display an alert dialog box telling users whether they guessed correctly. The main purpose of the exercises in the following sections is to show how an applet can read JavaScript objects and variables as well as execute JavaScript methods.

Importing the JSObject and JSException Classes

To use an applet to control JavaScript, you must first import two classes contained in the LiveConnect packages: JSObject and JSException. The **JSObject class** contains methods that allow Java and JavaScript to interact and acts as a wrapper for JavaScript objects. The **JSException class** passes JavaScript errors back to a Java class. Both classes are contained in the LiveConnect netscape.javascript package. To import both classes into an applet, you include the statement `import netscape.javascript.*;` at the beginning of your program. Note that some systems experience compile errors when using this statement. If you receive a compile error when importing the netscape.javascript package, try importing the JSObject and JSException classes individually, as follows:

```
import netscape.javascript.JSObject;
import netscape.javascript.JSException;
```

Next you will import the LiveConnect packages into the RandomNumberGame applet. Remember that for the next few exercises, you will need to use Navigator 4.7 or earlier.

To import the LiveConnect packages into the RandomNumberGame applet:

1 Open the **RandomNumberGame.java** file in your text editor or HTML editor and immediately save it as **RandomNumberGame2.java** in the **Tutorial.12** folder on your Data Disk.

2 Above the statement that imports the java.applet class, add `import netscape.javascript.*;`.

3 Change the name of the class in the class header to **RandomNumberGame2** so that the header reads `public class RandomNumberGame2 extends Applet {`.

4 Save and compile the file.

help

If your file does not compile correctly, try replacing the single statement that imports the LiveConnect packages with the two separate statements to import each class individually: `import netscape.javascript.JSObject;` and `import netscape javascript. JSException;`. Also, be sure your CLASSPATH environment variable correctly points to the location of the java40.jar file on your system.

Using the JSObject Class Methods

The JSObject class contains methods used for accessing and manipulating JavaScript. Figure 12-17 lists JSObject class methods.

Method	Description
call(String *functionName*, Object args[])	Executes a JavaScript method or function
eval(String *expression*)	Executes a JavaScript string expression
getMember(String *propertyName*)	Returns the value of a JavaScript object property
getSlot(int *index*)	Returns an array element in a JavaScript object
getWindow(applet)	Obtains a handle to the window containing the applet
removeMember(String *propertyName*)	Deletes a property in a JavaScript object
setMember(String propertyName, Object *value*)	Sets a property in a JavaScript object
setSlot(int index, Object *value*)	Sets an array element in a JavaScript object
toString()	Returns the string value in a JavaScript object

Figure 12-17: JSObject class methods

To use the JSObject methods to gain access to a JavaScript program, you must first use the getWindow() method to access the browser window, using a handle. A **handle** identifies an operating system resource. In this case, the resource is a browser window. You can think of a window handle as being equivalent to the window or self object references in JavaScript. The syntax for obtaining a handle is `JSObject variableName = JSObject.getWindow(this);`. The `this` keyword refers to the current window containing the applet. The following statement creates a handle named jsWindow:

```
JSObject jsWindow = JSObject.getWindow(this);
```

After creating a handle, you append the getMember() method to the handle name to return references to other objects in a JavaScript program. Each reference to an object in a JavaScript program must be cast to the JSObject type. You include the name of the object in quotation marks as an argument to the getMember() method. For example, to return a reference to the Document object and cast it to the JSObject type, you use the statement JSObject javaScriptDoc = (JSObject) jsWindow. getMember("document"); (assuming that you have already created a handle named jsWindow). The following code creates a handle to a browser window, then uses three instances of the getMember() method to gain access to a text field on a form. Notice that each statement appends the getMember() method to the previous object in the object hierarchy.

```
JSObject jsWindow =
          JSObject.getWindow(this);
JSObject jsDoc =
          (JSObject) jsWindow.getMember("document");
JSObject jsForm =
          (JSObject) jsDoc.getMember("ProductInfo");
JSObject jsElement =
          (JSObject) jsForm.getMember("CustomerName");
```

Notice in the preceding example that each object is cast to the JSObject type. Casting each object to the JSObject type creates a JSObject wrapper around each object name. At this point, the objects are still "wrapped" in JavaScript. To use the property of an object in Java, you must cast the value to a Java variable. When you cast a value to a JSObject wrapper, the data conversion rules come into play. For example, the jsElement object from the preceding example is a JavaScript text field on a form. To cast the value of the field into a Java variable named javaCustomerName, you use a statement that returns the value using the getMember() method, and then casts the value to a String object. In the following code, the argument being sent to the getMember() method is the value property of the form element in quotation marks.

```
String javaCustomerName =
          (String) jsElement.getMember("value");
```

Next you will start adding to the RandomNumberGame2.java file a checkGuess() method that is similar to the checkGuess() function you originally created with JavaScript code. Within the checkGuess() method, you will create object references to the JavaScript Document object, guessForm form, and guessField text field.

To start adding to the RandomNumberGame2.java file a checkGuess() method:

1   Return to the **RandomNumberGame2.java** file in your text editor or HTML editor.

2   Add the method header for the checkGuess() method above the start() method: `public void checkGuess() {`.

3   Following the checkGuess() method header, add the following statements to create object references to the Document object, guessForm form, and guessField text field:

```
JSObject gameWindow = JSObject.getWindow(this);
JSObject gameDoc = (JSObject)
     gameWindow.getMember("document");
JSObject gameForm = (JSObject)
     gameDoc.getMember("guessForm");
JSObject gameElement = (JSObject)
     gameForm.getMember("guessField");
String guessString = (String)
     gameElement.getMember("value");
```

4   The value returned from the guessField text field on the form is cast to a String variable named guessString. To compare the number contained in guessString to the randomNumber variable, you need to cast the String variable to an integer, because that is the data type of randomNumber. To cast a string to an integer, you must pass the String variable to the parseInt() method of the Integer class and assign the result to a new integer variable as follows:

```
int guess = Integer.parseInt(guessString);
```

5   Add a closing brace } for the checkGuess() method.

6   Save the file.

Another method of the JSObject class you will use is the eval() method, which executes JavaScript statements in Java. You append the eval() method to a handle and pass a text string containing the statement to be evaluated. For example, if you have a handle named jsWindow, then the following Java code executes an alert dialog box that displays the text *Hello World*. Notice that the text argument passed to the alert() method is contained within single quotation marks.

```
jsWindow.eval("alert('Hello World');");
```

 tip

•••

The Java eval() method performs the same function as the JavaScript eval() method that you used in Tutorial 3 to evaluate text strings in the calculator program.

•••

Next you will add to the RandomNumberGame2.java file an `if...else` structure that compares the guess variable to the randomNumber variable and displays a JavaScript alert dialog box with an appropriate message.

To add to the RandomNumberGame2.java file an `if...else` structure that compares the guess variable to the randomNumber variable and displays a JavaScript alert dialog box with an appropriate message:

1 Return to the **RandomNumberGame2.java** file in your text editor or HTML editor.

2 Before the closing brace for the the checkGuess() method, add the following `if...else` structure that compares the guess variable to the randomNumber variable and displays an alert dialog box based on the evaluation. If the guess is too low or too high, the guessCount variable is incremented by one.

```
if (guess > randomNumber) {
    gameWindow.eval(
    "alert('Sorry! You guessed too high.')");
    ++guessCount;
}
else if (guess < randomNumber) {
    gameWindow.eval(
    "alert('Sorry! You guessed too low.')");
    ++guessCount;
}
else {
    String rightGuess = new String();
    rightGuess = "alert('You guessed correctly in "
        + guessCount + " tries!"
        + " The number is " + randomNumber + ".')";
    gameWindow.eval(rightGuess);
}
```

3 Finally, delete the **tooLow()**, **tooHigh()**, and **rightNumber()** methods. You no longer need these methods, because their functionality is being handled by the checkGuess() method.

4 Save and compile the file. Before you can test the program, you must make some modifications to the HTML document that contains it.

The MAYSCRIPT Attribute

The last step necessary to allow a Java applet to control JavaScript is to add the MAYSCRIPT attribute to the <APPLET> tag containing the applet. The **MAYSCRIPT attribute** gives an applet permission to manipulate JavaScript code on a Web page. For example, to allow a Java applet named MyApplet.class to control JavaScript, you use a statement similar to <APPLET CODE="MyApplet.class" MAYSCRIPT>.

Next you will modify the RandomNumberGame.html file to work with the new RandomNumberGame2 applet.

To modify the RandomNumberGame.html file to work with the new RandomNumberGame2 applet:

1 Open the **RandomNumberGame.html** file in your text editor or HTML editor and immediately save it as **RandomNumberGame2.html** in the **Tutorial.12** folder on your Data Disk.

2 Delete the **<SCRIPT>** section from the head of the document. You no longer need the JavaScript code it contains, because the program functionality is now being handled by the Java applet.

3 Change the CODE attribute in the <APPLET> tag to **RandomNumberGame2.class**.

4 Add the **MAYSCRIPT** attribute before the closing bracket for the <APPLET> tag.

5 Change the value executed by the Guess button onClick event handler to **document.RandomNumberGame.checkGuess();**, which calls the checkGuess() method in the Java applet instead of the old checkGuess() function from the deleted <SCRIPT> section.

6 Save the file, and then open it in Navigator 4.7 or earlier. Test the program by entering some guesses. Figure 12-18 shows an example of how the program appears in Navigator.

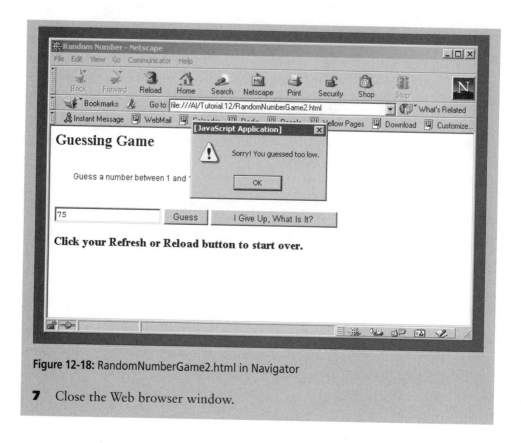

Figure 12-18: RandomNumberGame2.html in Navigator

7   Close the Web browser window.

Directly Accessing Java Classes from JavaScript

Java packages and classes in the LiveConnect packages are part of the JavaScript Packages object. The **Packages object** provides JavaScript with access to the Java packages, classes, and methods in LiveConnect. With direct access to Java classes, you can enhance your JavaScript programs without the need to create applets. As a simple example, the getProperty() method of the java.lang.System class returns information about your system. Although much of the information that the getProperty() method returns can be obtained using methods of the JavaScript Navigator object, some of the information cannot be obtained with JavaScript. Using the getProperty() method, you can learn the operating system architecture and version number of a client computer, two pieces of information that the Navigator object does not have access to.

The getProperty() method is a minor example of what you can do with Java packages in JavaScript. You can also perform more complex tasks such as using the java.awt package to build user interfaces or create new design elements. Although it may be easier to perform these types of tasks with a true Java applet, they are available to you in JavaScript. Before you decide to use Java code in your JavaScript programs, remember that most of the common methods you need are already available in the

JavaScript language. For example, although Java includes more methods for manipulating strings, the relatively few JavaScript string methods are the ones you will use most often.

▶ **tip**

There are limits to what you can do with Java classes in JavaScript. For example, you cannot create new classes, and Java code is bound by the same security restrictions as JavaScript code.

You use an uppercase P when referring to the Packages object to distinguish it from the JavaScript keyword `packages`. However, you are not required to explicitly reference the Packages object when calling a Java method contained in the Java, Sun, and Netscape packages. The following two calls to the getProperty() method of the java.lang.System class that return the operating system architecture are equivalent:

```
Packages.java.lang.System.getProperty("os.arch");
java.lang.System.getProperty("os.arch");
```

▶ **tip**

The `package` keyword is reserved in JavaScript for the possible incorporation of package capabilities in future versions of JavaScript.

Next you will modify the RandomNumberGame.html file you created in Section A so that it accesses Java classes directly.

To modify the RandomNumberGame.html file so that it accesses Java classes directly:

1 Open the **RandomNumberGame.html** file from the **Tutorial.12** folder on your Data Disk in your text editor or HTML editor and immediately save it as **RandomNumberGameDirect.html**.

2 Add the following three statements above the checkGuess() function header. The first statement returns a number from the Java Math.random() method, multiplies it by 100, then assigns the result to the answer variable. The second statement uses the Java Math.round() method to round the answer variable to a whole number. The third statement declares a global variable named guessCount to keep track of how many times a user tries to guess the random number.

```
var answer = Packages.java.lang.Math.random() * 100;
answer = Packages.java.lang.Math.round(answer);
var guessCount = 0;
```

3 Delete the statement `var answer = document.RandomNumberGame.randomNumber;` from the checkGuess() function.

4 Replace the `if...else` structure in the checkGuess() function with the following `if...else` structure, which is similar to the one you added to the RandomNumberGame2.java file:

```
if (guess > answer) {
    alert("Sorry! You guessed too high.");
    ++guessCount;
}
else if (guess < answer) {
    alert("Sorry! You guessed too low.");
    ++guessCount;
}
else {
    alert("You guessed correctly in " + guessCount
        + " tries!" + " The number is "
        + answer + ".");
}
```

5 Delete the **<APPLET>...</APPLET>** tag pair.

6 Modify the onClick event handler for the I Give Up, What Is It? button so that it reads `onClick="alert('The number is ' + answer + '. Better luck next time!');"`.

7 Save the file and open it in Navigator. The file should function the same way as the other two versions of the Random Number Game program you created in this tutorial.

8 Close the Web browser window.

Embedded Data

For the rest of this tutorial, the goal is understanding how to manipulate embedded data, using JavaScript. LiveConnect provides the ability for JavaScript to manipulate plug-ins in Navigator. Internet Explorer provides support for plug-ins, but uses ActiveX as its underlying technology instead of LiveConnect.

To learn how to manipulate plug-ins and ActiveX controls with JavaScript, you will use RealPlayer and the hellcat.rpm file in the Tutorial.12 folder on your Data Disk. If you have not already done so, download RealPlayer from *www.real.com/player/index.html* and install it. Running the RealPlayer install program creates a standalone program and installs both a plug-in and an ActiveX control.

Plug-Ins

Web browsers display two basic types of media: text contained within HTML documents and graphic images, such as .jpg and .gif files, which are referenced by an HTML document's <IMG> tags. As the Web grew in popularity, so did the demand to include other types of media in Web documents. Many different types of media are available today, ranging from word-processing documents and other static information, to audio, video, and animation. Each of these types of media is contained in different file formats. Additionally, new types of file formats are constantly being developed. Given the range of media and the constant development of new file formats, Web browsers cannot possibly support every conceivable type of file format.

Navigator solves this problem by allowing helper applications to open file types not supported in Navigator. **Helper applications** are external programs that Navigator opens to display unsupported file types. For example, you can configure Navigator to use Word as a helper application to open files with an extension of .doc.

A disadvantage of helper applications is that media are not displayed as part of a Web page, but are opened in a separate window. Opening media in a separate window is fine for certain types of information, such as word-processing documents or spreadsheets, but Web designers prefer to include other types of information, such as video clips, as part of a Web page. To be able to display and execute additional types of media within a Web page, Navigator introduced plug-ins. **Plug-ins** are software components created by third-party developers that allow the display and execution of different types of information inside a Navigator window. Plug-in technology allows Navigator to support newly developed file types, without having to continually update the browser.

The RealPlayer program you are using in this tutorial can be used as both a helper application and a plug-in. If you visit Zeno's Warbird Video Drive-In at *www.zenoswarbirdvideos.com*, the video links open in a separate RealPlayer program window. However, the RealPlayer examples you create in this tutorial will execute as plug-ins inside an HTML document.

Netscape maintains a Web page that contains descriptions and links to many popular plug-ins that can be used with Navigator. Netscape's plug-in Web page is located at *home.netscape.com/plugins/index.html*.

Plug-ins are platform specific—you can only use a plug-in if a version of it exists for your platform.

MIME Types and File Extensions Recall that MIME is a standard method of exchanging files over the Internet. When you access a Web page from a server, Navigator starts a plug-in or helper application to open the page in a specific media format according to its MIME type. When a plug-in is first installed, it automatically registers with Navigator the MIME types and file extensions it opens. Occassionally, a plug-in will register a MIME type or file extension that you want opened with a different plug-in or helper application. For example, you may download a plug-in that automatically configures Navigator to open video files with an extension of .avi. However, you may prefer to use the Navigator LiveVideo plug-in to open video files. You can manage the way your installation of Navigator handles MIME types and file extensions by using the Helper Applications option in the Navigator category of the Preferences dialog box. Figure 12-19 shows an example of the Helper Applications option in the Preferences dialog box in Navigator.

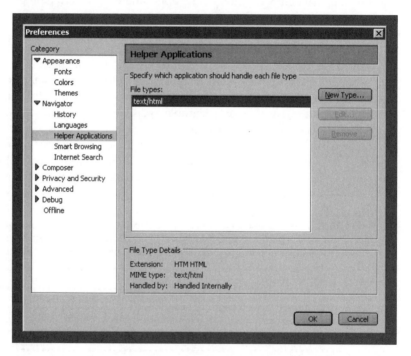

Figure 12-19: Helper Applications options in the Navigator Preferences dialog box

The <EMBED> tag Once you have installed a plug-in or helper application, you add embedded data to a Web page by using an <EMBED> tag, which is similar to the <APPLET>...</APPLET> tag pair. The <EMBED> tag creates a rectangular area on a Web page, known as the plug-in area, which is similar to an applet bounding box. Figure 12-20 lists <EMBED> tag attributes that are available to both Navigator and Internet Explorer.

Attribute	Description
HEIGHT	The height of the plug-in area
HIDDEN	Plug-in visible or hidden specification. The default value is visible.
NAME	A name to associate with the <EMBED> object
PALETTE	The plug-in color palette
SRC	The document to be displayed as embedded data
UNITS	The type of units associated with the HEIGHT and WIDTH attributes. The default is pixels.
WIDTH	The width of the plug-in area

Figure 12-20: <EMBED> tag attributes available to Navigator and Internet Explorer

Unlike most HTML tags, the <EMBED> tag can include custom attributes specific to a given plug-in. For example, the Navigator 4.7 LiveAudio plug-in includes an AUTOSTART="true" attribute that automatically plays a sound file when the Web page first loads.

See your plug-in documentation for information on its custom attributes.

Figure 12-21 shows an example of an HTML document containing an embedded sound file with a .wav extension. The <EMBED> tag includes an AUTOSTART attribute along with a HIDDEN attribute that hides the <EMBED> tag, because it does not need to be visible to execute a sound file.

```
<HTML>

<HEAD><TITLE>LiveAudio Demo</TITLE></HEAD>

<BODY>

<EMBED SRC="sound_file.wav" NAME="audio" AUTOSTART="true"
       HIDDEN="true">

</BODY>

</HTML>
```

Figure 12-21: <EMBED> tag playing a sound file

Next you will create an HTML document that uses the RealPlayer plug-in to display the F6F "Hellcat" aircraft video you saw in the preview. You will use several custom RealPlayer attributes to configure the <EMBED> tag. Custom RealPlayer <EMBED> attributes are listed in Figure 12-22.

Attribute	Description
CONTROLS	Selects the RealPlayer components to display. Values include ALL, ControlPanel, InfoVolumePanel, ImageWindow, InfoPanel, StatusBar, PlayButton, StopButton, VolumeSlider, PositionSlider, PositionField, and StatusField.
CONSOLE	Designates a name that can be used for managing multiple instances of RealPlayer.
AUTOSTART	When set to true, automatically executes a RealPlayer plug-in when the Web page first loads. Valid values are true or false.
NOLABELS	Turns off the Title, Author, and Copyright label text in the controls window, but displays each field's text strings.

Figure 12-22: RealPlayer <EMBED> attributes

To create an HTML document that displays the F6F "Hellcat" aircraft video, using the RealPlayer plug-in:

1 Start your text editor or HTML editor and create a new document.

2 Type the opening <HTML>, <HEAD>, and <BODY> sections of the document:

```
<HTML>
<HEAD>
<TITLE>F6F Hellcat</TITLE>
</HEAD>
<BODY>
```

3 Next add **<H2>Flight Characteristics of the F6F "Hellcat"**
</H2> as a heading for the document.

4 Type the following <EMBED> tag, which executes the RealPlayer plug-in. The tag includes a NAME attribute of *hellcat*, which you will use later in JavaScript code. The tag also includes the AUTOSTART=`"true"` attribute so that the plug-in executes automatically when the Web page loads. A value of ImageWindow is assigned to the CONTROLS attribute, which creates a single video window with no visible controls.

```
<P><EMBED NAME="hellcat" SRC="hellcat.rpm" AUTOSTART=
"true"
      WIDTH=220 HEIGHT=180 CONTROLS="ImageWindow"></P>
```

5 Add the following code to close the <BODY> and <HTML> tags:

```
</BODY>
</HTML>
```

6 Save the file as **RealPlayerPlugin.html** in the **Tutorial.12** folder on your Data Disk. Open the **RealPlayerPlugin.html** file in your Web browser. The video should execute as soon as the page loads. Figure 12-23 shows the page in Navigator.

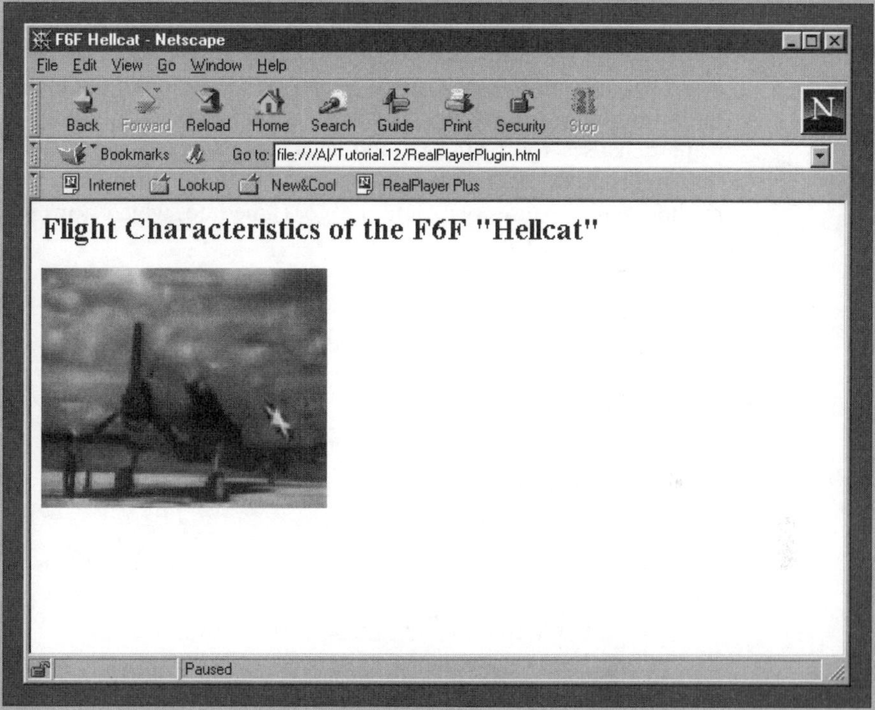

Figure 12-23: RealPlayerPlugin.html in Navigator

7 Close the Web browser window.

Next you will learn how to start and stop the plug-in, using JavaScript.

Manipulating Plug-Ins with JavaScript You can refer to embedded data with JavaScript code by using the NAME attribute assigned in the <EMBED> tag or by using its element number in the embeds[] array. The **embeds[] array** contains a list of the embedded data on a Web page in the order in which it is encountered. The first embedded data on a page is referred to as embeds[0], the second embedded data on a page is referred to as embeds[1], and so on. You append either the embedded data array number or the embedded data's NAME attribute to the Document object, along with the method or property you want to use. You may notice that referring to embedded data is very similar to referring to applets. As you did with applets, you will reference embedded data by using the NAME attribute, because it is easier to remember.

You control a plug-in by accessing its methods and properties, the same way you control an applet. You append the plug-in NAME attribute to the Document object, along with a method or property name. To control a plug-in with JavaScript, you must first find out what the methods and properties of the plug-in are. You must consult the developer of the plug-in to learn about the methods and properties of a plug-in. Most good plug-in developers have Web pages containing detailed technical information for manipulating their plug-ins using JavaScript as well as other languages, such as Java and VBScript. For example, the Navigator LiveAudio plug-in includes various methods for controlling the execution of an audio file. Figure 12-24 contains an HTML document that uses form buttons and JavaScript onClick event handlers to call several LiveAudio methods, including the start() method, which executes the file; the pause() method, which pauses play; and the stop() method, which stops playing the file.

```
<HTML>

<HEAD><TITLE>LiveAudio Demo</TITLE></HEAD>

<BODY>

<P><EMBED SRC="sound_file.wav" NAME="audio"
     AUTOSTART="true" HIDDEN="true"></P>

<H2>LiveAudio Demo</H2>

<FORM>

<INPUT TYPE="button" VALUE=" Play Audio File "
     onClick="document.audio.play();">

<INPUT TYPE="button" VALUE=" Pause Audio File "
     onClick="document.audio.pause();">

<INPUT TYPE="button" VALUE=" Stop Audio File "
     onClick="document.audio.stop();">

</FORM>

</BODY>

</HTML>
```

Figure 12-24: JavaScript controlling the LiveAudio plug-in

RealPlayer plug-ins include a number of methods for controlling file execution. You will use three of these methods: DoPlay (), DoPause(), and DoStop(), to control the execution of the RealPlayerPlugin.html file. The DoPlay() method plays the video, the DoPause() method pauses the video, and the DoStop() method stops execution.

Developer information for RealPlayer can be found at *www.realnetworks.com/devzone*.

Next you will add to the RealPlayerPlug-in.html file controls that handle the execution of the video clip.

To add to the RealPlayerPlugin.html file controls that handle the execution of the video clip:

1   Return to the **RealPlayerPlugin.html** file in your text editor or HTML editor.

2   Add the following form after the <EMBED> tag. The form includes three buttons: one button that plays the video, using the DoPlay() method; one button that pauses the video, using the DoPause() method; and another button that stops the video, using the DoStop() method.

```
<FORM>
<INPUT TYPE="button" VALUE=" Play Video "
    onClick="document.hellcat.DoPlay();">
<INPUT TYPE="button" VALUE=" Pause Video "
    onClick="document.hellcat.DoPause();">
<INPUT TYPE="button" VALUE=" Stop Video "
    onClick="document.hellcat.DoStop();">
</FORM>
```

3   Save the file and open it in your Web browser. Try starting, pausing, and stopping the video to see if the buttons function correctly. Figure 12-25 shows the file in Navigator.

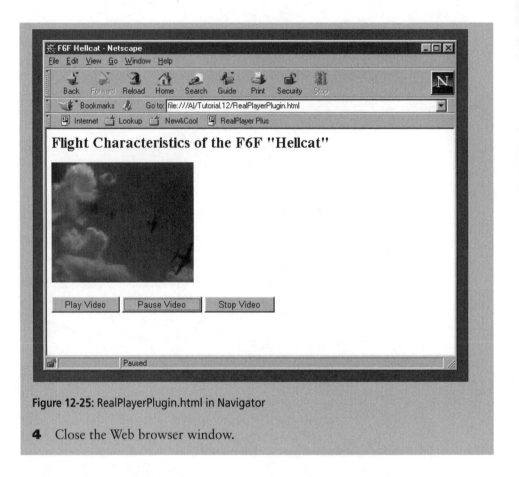

Figure 12-25: RealPlayerPlugin.html in Navigator

4   Close the Web browser window.

ActiveX Controls

ActiveX is a technology that allows programming objects to be easily reused with any programming language that supports the Microsoft Component Object Model. The **Component Object Model**, or **COM**, is an architecture for cross-platform development of client/server applications. **ActiveX controls** are objects that are placed in Web pages or inside programs created in COM-enabled programming languages. Using a scripting language, such as JavaScript or VBScript, to control ActiveX controls in a Web page is known as **ActiveX scripting**. You can compare ActiveX controls to a combination of plug-ins and Java; they can be used to display embedded information and to execute miniapplications such as applets. ActiveX controls are very popular in Windows programming—you can literally find thousands of types of ActiveX controls in various places on the Web. Their popularity is one of the reasons Microsoft added support for them in Internet Explorer.

Many ActiveX controls are licensed products that must be purchased from their developers. However, on the Internet you can find many free ActiveX controls that you can include in your Web pages. If you would like to find listings of professionally developed, as well as free, ActiveX controls, visit the Microsoft COM Resources Web site at *www.microsoft.com/com/resources/websites.asp*. The COM Resources Web site also lists technical information and training resources, so you can develop your own ActiveX controls.

You may wonder why ActiveX controls are necessary, because Internet Explorer supports plug-ins. For instance, the RealPlayerPlugin.html file works as well with Internet Explorer as it does with Navigator. Unlike RealPlayer, many types of ActiveX controls do not exist as plug-ins. If you want to use the functionality of an ActiveX control that does not have a corresponding plug-in, you must add the ActiveX control directly to your Web page. You can greatly enhance your Web pages by including ActiveX controls, given the large number that are available. If you use ActiveX controls in your Web pages, remember they will currently run only on Windows operating systems.

ActiveX controls were formerly known as OLE controls.

You can use the <OBJECT>...</OBJECT> tag pair to place ActiveX controls in an HTML document. Four important attributes of the <OBJECT> tag are ID, CLASS ID, HEIGHT, and WIDTH. The **ID attribute** assigns a unique identifier that can be used to manipulate the object with JavaScript, similar to the <EMBED> tag NAME attribute. The **CLASSID attribute** is a unique identifier for an object embedded with an <OBJECT> tag. All ActiveX controls are marked with a unique identifier, which you can usually find in the ActiveX control documentation. The syntax for specifying an ActiveX control in the CLASSID attribute is CLASSID="clsid:*unique id*". For example, the unique identifier for RealPlayer is CFCDAA03-8BE4-11cf-B84B-0020AFBBCCFA. To designate an <OBJECT> tag to run RealPlayer, you include the attribute CLASSID="clsid:CFCDAA03-8BE4-11cf-B84B-0020AFBBCCFA". The HEIGHT and WIDTH attributes of the <OBJECT> tag create a rectangular area on a Web page for an ActiveX control, similar to an applet bounding box.

To specify additional attributes for an ActiveX control, you place <PARAM> tags inside an <OBJECT>...</OBJECT> tag pair. Each **<PARAM> tag** specifies a single parameter for the control, includes a NAME attribute containing the parameter name, and includes a VALUE attribute for the parameter. The <PARAM> tags are comparable to the custom attributes that a plug-in developer can create for the <EMBED> tag. You can obtain the necessary <PARAM> tags for a specific ActiveX control from its developer.

Next you will create an ActiveX version of the RealPlayerPlugin.html file.

To create an ActiveX version of the RealPlayerPlugin.html file:

1 Return to the **RealPlayerPlugin.html** file in your text editor or HTML editor and immediately save it as **RealPlayerActiveX.html** in the **Tutorial.12** folder on your Data Disk.

2 Replace the <EMBED> tag with the following <OBJECT>...</OBJECT> tag pair. A value of hellcat is assigned to the <OBJECT> tag ID property, and the RealPlayer ActiveX control unique identifier is assigned to the CLASSID attribute. Two parameters are included in the <OBJECT>...</OBJECT> tag pair: one parameter that designates an SRC value of hellcat.rpm and another that designates a CONTROLS value of ImageWindow.

```
<OBJECT ID="hellcat"
CLASSID="clsid:CFCDAA03-8BE4-11cf-B84B-0020AFBBCCFA"
     AUTOSTART="true" WIDTH=220 HEIGHT=180>
<PARAM NAME="SRC" VALUE="hellcat.rpm">
<PARAM NAME="CONTROLS" VALUE="ImageWindow">
</OBJECT>
```

3 Save the file and open it in Internet Explorer.

4 Close the Web browser window.

SUMMARY

- LiveConnect packages provide Navigator versions earlier than 4.7 with access to core Java functionality and contain classes necessary for Java programs to control JavaScript.

- The CLASSPATH environment variable tells the Java VM and JDK applications in the /bin directory where to search for classes required by Java applications. On Windows 95/98 systems, the CLASSPATH environment variable needs to be set in the autoexec.bat file.

- You must be sure to pass the correct data type from JavaScript to a Java variable, because Java is a strongly typed programming language.

- Complex objects passed from JavaScript to Java are wrapped in the JSObject class, and complex objects passed from Java to JavaScript are wrapped in the JavaObject class.

- A wrapper is a class or object that contains, or is wrapped around, something else.

- The JSObject class contains methods that allow Java and JavaScript to interact, and acts as a wrapper for JavaScript objects.

- The JSException class passes JavaScript errors back to a Java class.

- The JSObject class and the JSException class are contained in the LiveConnect netscape.javascript package.

■ To use the JSObject methods to gain access to a JavaScript program, you must first use the getWindow() method to create a handle. A handle identifies an operating system resource; in this case, the resource is a browser window.

■ After creating a handle, you append the getMember() method to the handle name to return references to other objects in a JavaScript program.

■ The MAYSCRIPT tag gives an applet permission to manipulate JavaScript code on a Web page.

■ The Packages object provides JavaScript with access to the Java packages, classes, and methods in LiveConnect.

■ LiveConnect provides JavaScript with the ability to manipulate plug-ins in Navigator.

■ Internet Explorer provides support for plug-ins, but uses ActiveX as its underlying technology instead of LiveConnect.

■ Helper applications are external programs that Navigator uses to display unsupported file types.

■ Plug-ins are software components created by third-party developers that allow the display and execution of embedded data within a Navigator window.

■ When you access a Web page from a server, Navigator starts a plug-in or helper application to open a specific media format according to its MIME type. Local files are opened with the correct plug-in or helper application according to their file extension.

■ Once you have installed a plug-in or helper application, you add embedded data to a Web page by using an <EMBED> tag.

■ You can reference embedded data with JavaScript code by using the NAME attribute assigned in the <EMBED> tag or its element number in the embeds[] array.

■ ActiveX is a technology that allows programming objects to be easily reused with any programming language that supports the Microsoft Component Object Model.

■ ActiveX controls are objects that are placed in Web pages or inside programs created in COM-enabled programming languages.

■ Using a scripting language, such as JavaScript or VBScript, to control ActiveX controls in a Web page is known as ActiveX scripting.

■ The ID attribute of the <OBJECT> tag assigns a unique identifier that can be used to manipulate an object with JavaScript, similar to the <EMBED> tag NAME attribute.

■ The CLASSID attribute is a unique identifier for an object embedded with an <OBJECT> tag.

■ You place <PARAM> tags inside an <OBJECT>...</OBJECT> tag pair to specify additional attributes for an ActiveX control.

QUESTIONS

1. Java packages and their directory structure are contained in a compressed ZIP file named _____.
   a. java.zip
   b. java.jar
   c. classes.jar
   d. classes.zip

2. The LiveConnect packages for Navigator are contained in the _____ compressed file.
   a. java40.jar
   b. nav40.jar
   c. java40.zip
   d. nav40.zip

3. The _____ environment variable tells the Java VM and JDK applications in the /bin directory where to search for classes required by Java applications.
   a. JDKPATH
   b. JAVACLASS
   c. CLASSPATH
   d. JAVAPATH

4. The _____ class contains methods that allow Java and JavaScript to interact, and acts as a wrapper for JavaScript objects.
   a. JSObject
   b. JavaToJavaScript
   c. JavaScriptObjects
   d. JavaScriptJava

5. Which of the following statements imports the LiveConnect packages into a Java program?
   a. `netscape.javascript.*;`
   b. `netscape.*;`
   c. `netscape.packages.*;`
   d. `netscape.liveconnect.*;`

6. Which of the following is the correct syntax for obtaining a handle to a window?
   a. `windowVar = JSObject.getWindow(this);`
   b. `JSObject windowVar = getWindow(this);`
   c. `windowVar JSObject = JSObject.getWindow(this);`
   d. `JSObject windowVar = JSObject.getWindow(this);`

7. Which of the following returns a reference to the window Document object, assuming that you have already declared a handle named windowVar?
   a. `JSObject windowVar = (JSObject)`
      `jsWindow.getMember("document");`
   b. `windowVar = (JSObject) jsWindow.getMember("document");`
   c. `JSObject windowVar = jsWindow.getMember("document");`
   d. `JSObject windowVar = getMember(jsWindow.Document);`

8. How do you assign the value of a JavaScript form element to a Java string variable, assuming that you have already created a reference to a text box named textField?

 a. `String javaStringVar = textField.getMember("value");`

 b. `String javaStringVar = (String) textField.getMember.value;`

 c. `String javaStringVar = textField (getMember.value);`

 d. `String javaStringVar = (String)`
 `   textField.getMember("value");`

9. What is the correct syntax for executing a JavaScript alert dialog box from a Java program, assuming that you have already declared a handle named windowVar?

 a. `windowVar.eval(alert("Text String"););`

 b. `windowVar.eval.alert("Text String");`

 c. `windowVar.eval("alert('Text String');");`

 d. `windowVar.alert("Text String").eval;`

10. Which attribute gives Java programs access to HTML document elements and JavaScript?

 a. SCRIPT="true"

 b. MAYSCRIPT

 c. JAVA="true"

 d. SCRIPTALLOWED

11. Which of the following statements gives JavaScript programs in Navigator access to the round() method of the Java java.lang.Math class?

 a. `Packages.java.lang.Math.round();`

 b. `Java.java.lang.Math.round();`

 c. `Packages.Math.round();`

 d. `Packages.java.Math.round();`

12. Plug-ins are software components created by _____ that allow the display and execution of embedded data inside a Navigator window.

 a. Microsoft

 b. Navigator

 c. Sun Microsystems

 d. third-party developers

13. Embedded data is associated with a particular plug-in by its MIME type or _____.

 a. the HTTP protocol specified in the SRC attribute

 b. the value assigned to its NAME attribute

 c. directory location

 d. file extension

14. Embedded data is added to a Web page by using the _____ tag.

 a. <LINK>

 b. <OBJECT>

 c. <PLUG-IN>

 d. <EMBED>

15. You refer to embedded data in JavaScript by using its NAME attribute or by

    _____.

    a. directly accessing its methods and properties
    b. appending its SRC attribute value to the java.Objects class
    c. referring to its element number in the embeds[] array
    d. You cannot refer to embedded data in JavaScript.

16. On which of the following platforms can you use ActiveX controls?

    a. Windows
    b. Macintosh
    c. Windows and Macintosh
    d. UNIX

17. ActiveX controls are added to a Web page by using the _____ tag.

    a. <LINK>
    b. <OBJECT>
    c. <PLUG-IN>
    d. <EMBED>

18. You refer to an embedded ActiveX control in JavaScript by using its

    _____.

    a. ID attribute
    b. NAME attribute
    c. element number in the objects[] array
    d. class name

19. The unique identifier required by the system to locate a specific ActiveX control is called a _____.

    a. DATAID
    b. CONTROLID
    c. ACTIVEXID
    d. CLASSID

20. Values are passed to an ActiveX control _____.

    a. through various attributes
    b. through <PARAM> tags
    c. by appending a text string to the SRC attribute
    d. You cannot pass values to an ActiveX control.

E X E R C I S E S

Save your solutions for the following exercises in the Tutorial.12 folder on your Data Disk.

1. Create an HTML document with a form containing sections for each of your last three jobs. Include fields listing the employer's name, salary, and the number of years you worked there. Next, write a Java applet that reads the salary and number of years from the forms and uses the Java Math.max() method to calculate your highest salary and the longest amount of time you worked for any of the three employers. Also use the Java Math.min() method to calculate your lowest salary and the shortest amount of time you worked for any one of the three employers. After you calculate the new information, display it in the applet bounding box. Save the files as WorkHistory.html and WorkHistory.java. If you haven't worked for three employers, use fictitious names and salaries.

2. Use direct Java calls from Navigator to create a more advanced version of the calculator you created in Tutorial 3. Refer to the JDK documentation on the methods available in the Math class that you can use in your calculator, including the exp() (exponential value) method and the sqrt() (square root) method. Remember that only Navigator supports direct Java calls. If you do not have Navigator 4.7 or earlier, create the calculator portion of the program as a Java applet and use an HTML form to enter values and select operations.

3. Search the Internet for information on how to create plug-ins and write a short paper on the topic.

4. The Microsoft Web site contains many articles and much information on creating ActiveX controls. Using information from the Microsoft Web site, write a short paper describing the history and development of COM and ActiveX.

5. Write a paper that discusses the different types of programming languages that can be used to create ActiveX controls. Specifically focus on how you can integrate ActiveX controls with Java programming.

APPENDIX
A

JavaScript Reference

Comment Types

Line Comments

```
<SCRIPT LANGUAGE="JavaScript">
// Line comments are preceded by two slashes.
</SCRIPT>
```

Block Comments

```
<SCRIPT LANGUAGE="JavaScript">
/*
This line is part of the block comment.
This line is also part of the block comment.
*/
/* This is another way of creating a block comment. */
</SCRIPT>
```

Javascript Reserved Words

abstract	delete	function	null	throw
boolean	do	goto	package	throws
break	double	if	private	transient
byte	else	implements	protected	true
case	enum	import	public	try
catch	export	in	return	typeof
char	extends	instanceof	short	var
class	false	int	static	void
const	final	interface	super	volatile
continue	finally	long	switch	while
debugger	float	native	synchronized	with
default	for	new	this	

Identifiers

Legal Identifiers

```
my_identifier
$my_identifier
_my_identifier
my_identifier_example
myIdentifierExample
```

Illegal Identifiers

```
%my_identifier
1my_identifier
#my_identifier
@my_identifier
~my_identifier
+my_identifier
```

Built-In JavaScript Functions

Function	Description
eval()	Evaluates expressions contained within strings
isFinite()	Determines whether a number is finite
isNaN()	Determines whether a value is the special value NaN (Not a Number)
parseInt()	Converts string literals to integers
parseFloat()	Converts string literals to floating-point numbers
encodeURI()	Encodes a text string into a valid URI
encodeURIComponent()	Encodes a text string into a valid URI component
decodeURI()	Decodes text strings encoded with encodeURI()
decodeURIComponent()	Decodes text strings encoded with encodeURIComponent()

Built-In JavaScript Objects

Object	Description
Array	Creates new array objects
Boolean	Creates new Boolean objects
Date	Retrieves and manipulates dates and times
Error	Returns run-time error information
Function	Creates new function objects
Global	Represents the JavaScript built-in methods
Math	Contains methods and properties for performing mathematical calculations
Number	Contains methods and properties for manipulating numbers
Object	Provides common functionality to all built-in JavaScript objects
RegExp	Contains properties for finding and replacing in text strings
String	Contains methods and properties for manipulating text strings

Events

JavaScript Events

Event	Triggered When
Abort	The loading of an image is interrupted
Blur	An element, such as a radio button, becomes inactive
Click	An element is clicked once
Change	The value of an element changes
Error	There is an error when loading a document or image
Focus	An element becomes active
Load	A document or image loads
MouseOut	The mouse moves off an element
MouseOver	The mouse moves over an element
Reset	A form is reset
Select	A user selects a field in a form
Submit	A user submits a form
Unload	A document unloads

HTML Elements and Associated JavaScript Events

Element	Description	Event
<A>...</A>	Link	Click MouseOver MouseOut
<IMG>	Image	Abort Error Load
<AREA>	Area	MouseOver MouseOut

HTML Elements and Associated JavaScript Events (continued)

Element	Description	Event
<BODY>...</BODY>	Document body	Blur Error Focus Load Unload
<FRAMESET>...</FRAMESET>	Frame set	Blur Error Focus Load Unload
<FRAME>...</FRAME>	Frame	Blur Focus
<FORM>...</FORM>	Form	Submit Reset
<INPUT TYPE="text">	Text field	Blur Focus Change Select
<TEXTAREA>...</TEXTAREA>	Text area	Blur Focus Change Select
<INPUT TYPE="submit">	Submit	Click
<INPUT TYPE="reset">	Reset	Click
<INPUT TYPE="radio">	Radio button	Click
<INPUT TYPE="checkbox">	Check box	Click
<SELECT>...</SELECT>	Selection	Blur Focus Change

Primitive Data Types

Data Type	Description
Integers	Positive or negative numbers with no decimal places
Floating-point numbers	Positive or negative numbers with decimal places, or numbers written using exponential notation
Boolean	A logical value of true or false
String	Text, such as "Hello World"
Undefined	A variable that has never had a value assigned to it, has not been declared, or does not exist
Null	An empty value

JavaScript Escape Sequences

Escape Sequence	Character
\b	Backspace
\f	Form feed
\n	New line
\r	Carriage return
\t	Horizontal tab
\'	Single quotation mark
\"	Double quotation mark
\\	Backslash

Data Type Conversion Functions and Methods

Function or Method	Description	Syntax
parseFloat() function	Converts string literals to floating-point numbers	parseFloat(*variable*);
parseInt() function	Converts string literals to integers	parseInt(*variable*);

Data Type Conversion Functions and Methods (continued)

Element	Description	Event
toString() method	Converts object values or number literals to string literals	*variable*.toString();
valueOf() method	Returns the primitive value of an object	*object*.valueOf();

Operators

JavaScript Operator Types

Operator Type	Description
Arithmetic	Used for performing mathematical calculations
Assignment	Assigns values to variables
Comparison	Compares operands and returns a Boolean value
Logical	Used for performing Boolean operations on Boolean operands
String	Performs operations on strings
Special	Used for various purposes, and includes the conditional, instanceof, in, delete, void, new, this, typeof, and comma operators

Arithmetic Binary Operators

Operator	Description
+ (addition)	Adds two operands
− (subtraction)	Subtracts one operand from another operand
* (multiplication)	Multiplies one operand by another operand
/ (division)	Divides one operand by another operand
% (modulus)	Divides two operands and returns the remainder

Arithmetic Unary Operators

Operator	Description
++ (increment)	Increases an operand by a value of one
– – (decrement)	Decreases an operand by a value of one
– (negation)	Returns the opposite value (negative or positive) of an operand

Assignment Operators

Operator	Description
=	Assigns the value of the right operand to the left operand
+=	Combines the value of the right operand with the value of the left operand, or adds the value of the right operand to the value of the left operand and assigns the new value to the left operand
–=	Subtracts the value of the right operand from the value of the left operand and assigns the new value to the left operand
*=	Multiplies the value of the right operand by the value of the left operand and assigns the new value to the left operand
/=	Divides the value of the left operand by the value of the right operand and assigns the new value to the left operand
%=	Modulus—divides the value of the left operand by the value of the right operand and assigns the remainder to the left operand

Comparison Operators

Operator	Description
== (equal)	Returns true if the operands are equal
=== (strict equal)	Returns true if the operands are equal and of the same type

Comparison Operators (continued)

Operator	Description
!= (not equal)	Returns true if the operands are not equal
!== (strict not equal)	Returns true if the operands are not equal or not of the same type
> (greater than)	Returns true if the left operand is greater than the right operand
< (less than)	Returns true if the left operand is less than the right operand
>= (greater than or equal to)	Returns true if the left operand is greater than or equal to the right operand
<= (less than or equal to)	Returns true if the left operand is less than or equal to the right operand

Logical Operators

Operator	Description
&& (and)	Returns true if the both the left operand and the right operand return a value of true, otherwise it returns a value of false
|| (or)	Returns true if either the left operand or right operand returns a value of true. If neither operand returns a value of true, then the expression containing the || (or) operator returns a value of false
! (not)	Returns true if an expression is false and returns false if an expression is true

Operator Precedence

- Parentheses (() [] .) *highest precedence*
- Negation/increment (! -- ++ - typeof void)
- Multiply/divide/modulus (* / %)
- Addition/subtraction (+ -)
- Comparison (< <= > >=)
- Equality (== !=)
- Logical and (&&)
- Logical or (||)
- Assignment operators (= += -= *= /= %=) *lowest precedence*

Control Structures and Statements

```
if (conditional expression) {
    statement(s);
}

if (conditional expression) {
    statement(s);
}
else {
    statement(s);
}
switch (expression) {
    case label :
        statement(s);
        break;
    case label :
        statement(s);
        break;
    ...
    default :
        statement(s);
}

while (conditional expression) {
    statement(s);
}

do {
    statement(s);
} while (conditional expression);

for (initialization expression; condition; update statement) {
    statement(s);
}

for (variable in object) {
    statement(s);
}

with (object) {
    statement(s);
}
```

   break A break statement is used to exit switch statements and other program control statements such as the while, do...while, for, and for...in
looping statements. To end a switch statement once it performs its required task,
you should include a break statement within each case label.

Continue The `continue` statement halts a looping statement and restarts the loop with a new iteration. You use the `continue` statement when you want to stop the loop for the current iteration, but want the loop to continue with a new iteration.

Objects

This section lists the properties, methods, and events of the major JavaScript objects. Only properties, methods, and events compatible with both Internet Explorer and Navigator are listed.

Array Object

Method	Description
concat()	Combines two arrays into a single array
join()	Combines all elements of an array into a string
pop()	Removes and returns the last element from an array
push()	Adds and returns a new array element
reverse()	Transposes elements of an array
shift()	Removes and returns the first element from an array
slice()	Creates a new array from a section of an existing array
splice()	Adds or removes array elements
sort()	Sorts elements of an array
unshift()	Adds new elements to the start of an array and returns the new array length

Property	Description
length	The number of elements in an array

Date Object

Method	Description
getDate()	Returns the date of a Date object
getDay()	Returns the day of a Date object
getFullYear()	Returns the year of a Date object in four-digit format
getHours()	Returns the hour of a Date object
getMilliseconds()	Returns the milliseconds of a Date object
getMinutes()	Returns the minutes of a Date object
getMonth()	Returns the month of a Date object
getSeconds()	Returns the seconds of a Date object
getTime()	Returns the time of a Date object
getTimezoneOffset()	Returns the local timezone offset in minutes from the current date and GMT
getUTCDate()	Returns the date of a Date object in universal time
getUTCFullYear()	Returns the four-digit year of a Date object in universal time
getUTCHours()	Returns the hours of a Date object in universal time
getUTCMilliseconds()	Returns the milliseconds of a Date object in universal time
getUTCMinutes()	Returns the minutes of a Date object in universal time
getUTCMonth()	Returns the month of a Date object in universal time
getUTCSeconds()	Returns the seconds of a Date object in universal time
setDate()	Sets the date of a Date object
setFullYear()	Sets the four-digit year of a Date object
setHours()	Sets the hours of a Date object
setMilliseconds()	Sets the milliseconds of a Date object
setMinutes()	Sets the minutes of a Date object
setMonth()	Sets the month of a Date object
setSeconds()	Sets the seconds of a Date object

Date Object (continued)

Method	Description
setTime()	Sets the time of a Date object
setUTCDate()	Sets the date of a Date object in universal time
setUTCFullYear()	Sets the four-digit year of a Date object in universal time
setUTCHours()	Sets the hours of a Date object in universal time
setUTCMilliseconds()	Sets the milliseconds of a Date object in universal time
setUTCMinutes()	Sets the minutes of a Date object in universal time
setUTCMonth()	Sets the month of a Date object in universal time
setUTCSeconds()	Sets the seconds of a Date object in universal time
toGMTString()	Converts a Date object to a string in the GMT time zone format
toLocaleString()	Converts a Date object to a string in the current time zone format
toString()	Converts a Date object to a string
toUTCString()	Converts a Date object to a string in universal time format
valueOf()	Converts a Date object to a millisecond format

Document Object

Property	Description
anchors[]	An array referring to document anchors
applets[]	An array referring to document applets
body	The element that contains the content for the document
cookie	The current document cookie string
domain	The domain name of the server where the current document is located
forms[]	An array referring to document forms
images[]	An array referring to document images
lastModified	The date the document was last modified

Document Object (continued)

Property	Description
links[]	An array referring to document links
referrer	The URL of the document that provided a link to the current document
title	The title of the document as specified by the <TITLE>...</TITLE> tag pair in the document <HEAD> section
URL	The URL of the current document

Method	Description
close()	Notifies the Web browser that you are finished writing to the window or frame and that the document should be displayed
getElementById()	Returns the HTML element represented by an ID
getElementsByName()	Returns an array of HTML elements represented by a tag name
open()	Opens a window or frame, other than the current window or frame, and is used to update its contents with the write() and writeln() methods
write()	Creates new text on a Web page
writeln()	Creates new text on a Web page followed by a line break

Event	Triggered When
onBlur	When a document loses focus
onError	When a document generates an error
onFocus	When a document receives focus
onLoad	When a document loads
onUnload	When a document unloads

Form Object

Property	Description
action	The URL to which form data will be submitted
method	The method in which form data will be submitted: GET or POST
encoding	The form MIME encoding as specified with the ENCTYPE attribute
enctype	The format of the data being submitted
target	The window in which any results returned from the server are displayed
name	The name of the form
elements[]	An array representing form elements
length	The number of elements on a form

Method	Description
reset()	Clears any data entered into a form
submit()	Submits a form to a Web server

Event	Triggered When
onReset	A reset button is pressed or the reset() method is called
onSubmit	A submit button is pressed or the submit() method is called

History Object

Property	Description
length	Contains the specific number of documents that have been opened during the current browser session

Method	Description
back()	The equivalent of clicking a Web browser's Back button
forward()	The equivalent of clicking a Web browser's Forward button
go()	Opens a specific document in the history list

Image Object

Property	Description
border	A read-only property containing the border width, in pixels, as specified by the BORDER attribute of the <IMG> tag
complete	A Boolean value that returns true when an image is completely loaded
height	A read-only property containing the height of the image, as specified by the HEIGHT attribute of the <IMG> tag
hspace	A read-only property containing the amount of horizontal space, in pixels, to the left and right of the image, as specified by the HSPACE attribute of the <IMG> tag
lowsrc	The URL of an alternate image to display at low resolution
name	A name assigned to the tag
src	The URL of the displayed image
vspace	A read-only property containing the amount of vertical space, in pixels, above and below the image, as specified by the VSPACE attribute of the <IMG> tag
width	A read-only property containing the width of the image, as specified by the WIDTH attribute of the <IMG> tag

Event	Triggered When
onLoad	An image finishes loading
onAbort	The user cancels the loading of an image, usually by clicking the Stop button
onError	An error occurs while loading an image

Location Object

Property	Description
hash	A URL's anchor
host	A combination of the URL's hostname and port sections
hostname	A URL's hostname
href	The full URL address
pathname	The URL's path
port	The URL's port
protocol	The URL's protocol
search	A URL's search or query portion

Method	Description
reload()	Causes the page currently displayed in the Web browser to open again
replace()	Replaces the currently loaded URL with a different one

Math Object

Property	Description
E	Euler's constant e, which is the base of a natural logarithm
LN10	The natural logarithm of 10
LN2	The natural logarithm of 2
LOG2E	The base-2 logarithm of e
LOG10E	The base-10 logarithm of e
PI	A constant representing the ratio of the circumference of a circle to its diameter
SQRT1_2	1 divided by the square root of 2
SQRT2	The square root of 2

Method	Description
abs(x)	Returns the absolute value of x
acos(x)	Returns the arc cosine of x
asin(x)	Returns the arc sine of x
atan(x)	Returns the arc tangent of x
atan2(x,y)	Returns the angle from the x-axis
ceil(x)	Returns the value of x rounded to the next highest integer
cos(x)	Returns the cosine of x
exp(x)	Returns the exponent of x
floor(x)	Returns the value of x rounded to the next lowest integer
log(x)	Returns the natural logarithm of x
max(x,y)	Returns the larger of two numbers
min(x,y)	Returns the smaller of two numbers
pow(x,y)	Returns the value of x raised to the y power
random()	Returns a random number
round(x)	Returns the value of x rounded to the nearest integer
sin(x)	Returns the sine of x
sqrt(x)	Returns the square root of x
tan(x)	Returns the tangent of x

Navigator Object

Property	Description
appCodeName	The Web browser code name
appName	The Web browser name
appVersion	The Web browser version
platform	The operating system in use
userAgent	The user agent

Method	Description
javaEnabled()	Determines whether Java is enabled in the current browser

Number Object

Method	Description
toString()	Converts a number to a string

Property	Description
MAX_VALUE	The largest representable number
MIN_VALUE	The smallest representable number
NaN	The value "Not a Number," which is returned when an arithmetic expression returns a value that is not a number
NEGATIVE_INFINITY	A value that is more negative than the largest negative number
POSITIVE_INFINITY	A value that is larger than the largest positive number

String Object

Methods

Method	Description
anchor(anchor name)	Adds an <ANCHOR>...</ANCHOR> tag pair to a text string
big()	Adds a <BIG>...</BIG> tag pair to a text string
blink()	Adds a <BLINK>...</BLINK> tag pair to a text string
bold()	Adds a <B>...</B> tag pair to a text string

String Object Methods (continued)

Method	Description
charAt(*index*)	Returns the character at the specified position in a text string. Returns nothing if the specified position is greater than the length of the string
fixed()	Adds a <TT>...</TT> tag pair to a text string
fontcolor(*color*)	Adds a <FONT COLOR=*color*>...</FONT> tag pair to a text string
fontsize(*size*)	Adds a <FONT SIZE=*size*>...</FONT> tag pair to a text string
indexOf(*text, index*)	Returns the position number in a string of the first character in the *text* argument. If the *index* argument is included, then the indexOf() method starts searching at that position within the string. Returns -1 if the text is not found
italics()	Adds a <I>...</I> tag pair to a text string
lastIndexOf(*text, index*)	Returns the position number in a string of the last instance of the first character in the *text* argument. If the *index* argument is included, then the lastIndexOf() method starts searching at that position within the string. Returns -1 if the character or string is not found
link(*href*)	Adds an <A HREF=*URL*>...</A> tag pair to a text string
small()	Adds a <SMALL>...</SMALL> tag pair to a text string
split(*separator*)	Divides a text string into an array of substrings, based on the specified separator
strike()	Adds a <STRIKE>...</STRIKE> tag pair to a text string
sub()	Adds a _{...} tag pair to a text string
substring(*starting index, ending index*)	Extracts text from a string starting with the position number in the string of the *starting index* argument and ending with the position number of the *ending index* argument
sup()	Adds a ^{...} tag pair to a text string
toLowerCase()	Converts the specified text string to lowercase
toUpperCase()	Converts the specified text string to uppercase

Properties

Property	Description
length	Returns the number of characters in a string

Window Object

Property	Description
defaultStatus	Default text that is written to the status bar
document	A reference to the Document object
frames[]	An array listing the frame objects in a window
history	A reference to the History object
location	A reference to the Location object
name	The name of a window
opener	The Window object that opens another window
parent	The parent frame that contains the current frame
self	A self-reference to the Window object—identical to the window property
status	Temporary text that is written to the status bar
top	The topmost Window object that contains the current frame
window	A self-reference to the Window object—identical to the self property

Method	Description
alert()	Displays a simple message dialog box with an OK button
blur()	Removes focus from a window
clearInterval()	Cancels an interval that was set with setInterval()
clearTimeout()	Cancels a timeout that was set with setTimeout()
close()	Closes a window

Window Object (continued)

Method	Description
confirm()	Displays a confirmation dialog box with OK and Cancel buttons
focus()	Makes a Window object the active window
open()	Opens a new window
prompt()	Displays a dialog box prompting a user to enter information
setInterval()	Repeatedly executes a function after a specified number of milliseconds have elapsed
setTimeout()	Executes a function once after a specified number of milliseconds have elapsed

Event	Triggered When
onBlur	The window becomes inactive
onError	An error occurs when the window loads
onFocus	The window becomes active
onLoad	A document is completely loaded in the window
onResize	The window is resized
onUnload	The current document in the window is unloaded

Index